CRIMINALITY AND
ECONOMIC CONDITIONS

THE MODERN CRIMINAL SCIENCE SERIES

Published under the Auspices of

THE AMERICAN INSTITUTE OF CRIMINAL LAW AND CRIMINOLOGY

Criminality

AND

Economic Conditions

BY

WILLIAM ADRIAN BONGER

of Amsterdam, Netherlands

TRANSLATED BY

HENRY P. HORTON

of Ithaca, New York

WITH AN EDITORIAL PREFACE BY

EDWARD LINDSEY

of the Warren, Pa., Bar

AND WITH AN INTRODUCTION BY

FRANK H. NORCROSS

Justice of the Supreme Court of Nevada
*Vice-President of The American Institute of Criminal Law
and Criminology*

AGATHON PRESS, INC.

New York, N.Y.

1967

Reprinted 1967, with permission, by
AGATHON PRESS, INC.
150 Fifth Avenue
New York, N.Y. 10011

Library of Congress Catalog Card Number: 67-20715

Printed in U.S.A. by
NOBLE OFFSET PRINTERS, INC.
NEW YORK 3, N. Y.

CONTENTS

PART ONE

CRITICAL EXPOSITION OF THE LITERATURE DEALING WITH
THE RELATION BETWEEN CRIMINALITY AND ECONOMIC
CONDITIONS

CHAPTER I

THE PRECURSORS

AUTHORS WHO TREATED THE SUBJECT BEFORE THE BIRTH OF MODERN
CRIMINAL SCIENCE

CHAPTER II

THE STATISTICIANS

CHAPTER III

THE ITALIAN SCHOOL

CHAPTER IV

THE FRENCH SCHOOL (THE SCHOOL OF THE ENVIRONMENT)

CHAPTER V

THE BIO–SOCIALISTS

CHAPTER VI

THE SPIRITUALISTS

CHAPTER VII

THE THIRD SCHOOL AND THE SOCIALISTS

CHAPTER VIII

PART TWO

Book I

THE PRESENT ECONOMIC SYSTEM AND ITS CONSEQUENCES

CHAPTER I

CHAPTER II

SOCIAL CONDITION OF THE DIFFERENT CLASSES

CHAPTER III

THE RELATION OF THE SEXES AND OF THE FAMILY

CHAPTER IV

CHAPTER V

Book II

CRIMINALITY

CHAPTER I

GENERAL CONSIDERATIONS

CHAPTER II
ECONOMIC CRIMES

CHAPTER III
SEXUAL CRIMES

CHAPTER IV
CRIMES FROM VENGEANCE AND OTHER MOTIVES

CHAPTER V

CHAPTER VI

CHAPTER VII

GENERAL INTRODUCTION TO THE MODERN CRIMINAL SCIENCE SERIES.

AT the National Conference of Criminal Law and Criminology, held in Chicago, at Northwestern University, in June, 1909, the American Institute of Criminal Law and Criminology was organized; and, as a part of its work, the following resolution was passed:

"*Whereas*, it is exceedingly desirable that important treatises on criminology in foreign languages be made readily accessible in the English language, *Resolved*, that the president appoint a committee of five with power to select such treatises as in their judgment should be translated, and to arrange for their publication."

The Committee appointed under this Resolution has made careful investigation of the literature of the subject, and has consulted by frequent correspondence. It has selected several works from among the mass of material. It has arranged with publisher, with authors, and with translators, for the immediate undertaking and rapid progress of the task. It realizes the necessity of educating the professions and the public by the wide diffusion of information on this subject. It desires here to explain the considerations which have moved it in seeking to select the treatises best adapted to the purpose.

For the community at large, it is important to recognize that criminal science is a larger thing than criminal law. The legal profession in particular has a duty to familiarize itself with the principles of that science, as the sole means for intelligent and systematic improvement of the criminal law.

Two centuries ago, while modern medical science was still young, medical practitioners proceeded upon two general assumptions: one as to the cause of disease, the other as to its treatment. As to the cause of disease, — disease was sent by the inscrutable will of God. No man could fathom that will, nor its arbitrary operation. As to the treatment of disease, there were believed to be a few remedial agents of universal efficacy. Calomel and blood-letting, for example, were two of the principal ones. A larger or smaller dose of calomel, a greater or less quantity of bloodletting, — this blindly indiscriminate mode of treatment was regarded as orthodox for all common varieties of ailment. And so his calomel pill and his bloodletting lancet were carried everywhere with him by the doctor.

Nowadays, all this is past, in medical science. As to the causes of disease, we know that they are facts of nature, — various, but distinguishable by diagnosis and research, and more or less capable of prevention or control or counter-action. As to the treatment, we now know that there are various specific modes of treatment for specific causes or symptoms, and that the treatment must be adapted to the cause. In short, the individualization of disease, in cause and in treatment, is the dominant truth of modern medical science.

The same truth is now known about crime; but the understanding and the application of it are just opening upon us. The old and still dominant thought is, as to cause, that a crime is caused by the inscrutable moral free will of the human being, doing or not doing the crime, just as it pleases; absolutely free in advance, at any moment of time, to choose or not to choose the criminal act, and therefore in itself the sole and ultimate cause of crime. As to treatment, there still are just two traditional measures, used in varying doses for all kinds of crime and all kinds of persons, — jail, or a fine (for death is now employed in rare cases only). But modern science, here as in medicine, recognizes that crime also (like disease) has natural causes. It need not be asserted for one moment that crime is a disease. But it does have natural causes, — that is, circumstances which work to produce it in a given case. And as to treatment, modern science recognizes that penal or remedial treatment cannot possibly be indiscriminate and machine-like, but must be adapted to the causes, and to the man as affected by those causes. Common sense and logic alike require, inevitably, that the moment we predicate a specific cause for an undesirable effect, the remedial treatment must be specifically adapted to that cause.

Thus the great truth of the present and the future, for criminal science, is the individualization of penal treatment, — for that man, and for the cause of that man's crime.

Now this truth opens up a vast field for re-examination. It means that we must study all the possible data that can be causes of crime, — the man's heredity, the man's physical and moral make-up, his emotional temperament, the surroundings of his youth, his present home, and other conditions, — all the influencing circumstances. And it means that the effect of different methods of treatment, old or new, for different kinds of men and of causes, must be studied, experimented, and compared. Only in this way can accurate knowledge be reached, and new efficient measures be adopted.

All this has been going on in Europe for forty years past, and in limited fields in this country. All the branches of science that can help have been working, — anthropology, medicine, psychology, economics, sociology, philanthropy, penology. The law alone has abstained. The science of law is the one to be served by all this. But the public in general and the legal profession in particular have remained either ignorant of the entire subject or indifferent to the entire scientific movement. And this ignorance or indifference has blocked the way to progress in administration.

The Institute therefore takes upon itself, as one of its aims, to inculcate the study of modern criminal science, as a pressing duty for the legal profession and for the thoughtful community at large. One of its principal modes of stimulating and aiding this study is to make available in the English language the most useful treatises now extant in the Continental languages. Our country has started late. There is much to catch up with, in the results reached elsewhere. We shall, to be sure, profit by the long period of argument and theorizing and experimentation which European thinkers and workers have passed through. But to reap that profit, the results of their experience must be made accessible in the English language.

The effort, in selecting this series of translations, has been to choose those works which best represent the various schools of thought in criminal science, the general results reached, the points of contact or of controversy, and the contrasts of method — having always in view that class of works which have a more than local value and could best be serviceable to criminal science in our country. As the science has various aspects and emphases — the anthropological, psychological, sociological, legal, statistical, economic, pathological — due regard was paid, in the selection, to a representation of all these aspects. And as the several Continental countries have contributed in different ways to these various aspects, — France, Germany, Italy, most abundantly, but the others each its share, — the effort was made also to recognize the different contributions as far as feasible.

The selection made by the Committee, then, represents its judgment of the works that are most useful and most instructive for the purpose of translation. It is its conviction that this Series, when completed, will furnish the American student of criminal science a systematic and sufficient acquaintance with the controlling doctrines and methods that now hold the stage of thought in Continental Europe. Which of the various principles and methods will prove best adapted to help our problems can only be told after our students and workers have tested them in our own experience. But it is certain that we must first acquaint ourselves with these results of a generation of European thought.

In closing, the Committee thinks it desirable to refer the members of the Institute, for purposes of further investigation of the literature, to the " Preliminary Bibliography of Modern Criminal Law and Criminology " (Bulletin No. 1 of the Gary Library of Law of Northwestern University), already issued to members of the Conference. The Committee believes that some of the Anglo-American works listed therein will be found useful.

COMMITTEE ON TRANSLATIONS.

Chairman, JOHN H. WIGMORE,
   Professor of Law in Northwestern University, Chicago.
ERNST FREUND,
   Professor of Law in the University of Chicago.
MAURICE PARMELEE,
   Professor of Sociology in the State University of Missouri.
ROSCOE POUND,
   Professor of Law in Harvard University.
EDWARD LINDSAY,
   Of the Warren, Pa., Bar.
WM. W. SMITHERS,
   Secretary of the Comparative Law Bureau of the American Bar Association, Philadelphia, Pa.

EDITORIAL PREFACE TO THE PRESENT VOLUME.

By Edward Lindsey.

ANY adequate study of the phenomena of crime and of the criminal must take into account the economic phase — must consider the subject matter of the study from the economic standpoint; for while few will follow the socialist theorists in the controlling importance they assign to the economic factors of social life it is nevertheless manifest that these factors are powerful elements in the totality of social conditions and must be given due consideration in the survey of all societal phenomena, including that of crime. The work selected to represent this viewpoint in the Modern Criminal Science Series is that of one of the younger criminalists — an able and thorough study of the effect of economic conditions on crime and distinguished by the extensive and critical use made of a wide range of statistical data.

WILLIAM ADRIAN BONGER, the author of the work here translated, of Amsterdam, Holland, is a Dutch Publicist, a pupil of Professor Van Hamel, well known as one of the founders of the International Union of Penal Law and the most eminent of Dutch students of criminology. He was born at Amsterdam, September 16, 1876, and received the degree of Doctor in Law from the University of Amsterdam in June, 1905. The first part of the present work, which consists of a survey, with copious extracts and critical comments, of the previous literature upon the subject of the relation of crime to economic conditions is a revision of a thesis originally presented at the University.

Dr. Bonger is also the author of "Religion and Crime: A Criminological Study"; Leiden, 1913, and numerous articles in Dutch and German periodicals. Among these are the following in "Nieuwe Tÿd" (The New Age), a well-known Dutch socialist review: "An Apology for War", a critical review of "Die Philosophie des Krieges"

by Professor Steinmetz (1908); "Capital and Income in the Netherlands" (1910); "Marxism and Revisionism" (1910); "Crime and
Socialism: A Contribution to the Study of Criminality in the Netherlands" (1911); and "Religion and Irreligion in the Netherlands"
(1911). Two noteworthy contributions to "Neue Zeit" are "Cesare
Lombroso" in Vol. XXVIII, number one (1910), and "Verbrechen
und Sozialismus: Zugleich ein Beitrag zum Studium der Kriminalität
im Deutschland" in Vol. XXX, number two (1912). In 1912 also
appeared "The Social Factors of Crime and their Significance in
Comparison with the Individual Causes" in Vol. XXIII of the
"Tÿdschrift voor Strafrecht", the only Dutch journal of criminal law.

In the first part of this work, instead of stating in his own language
the views expressed in the previous literature on the subject Dr.
Bonger has by extracts from the various authors given us their
opinions in their own language, adding brief critical comments of his
own. The second part contains Dr. Bonger's own discussion of
the phenomena of crime based upon an unusually thorough collection
of statistical data and the elaboration of his views. In the selection
of authors from whom he quotes Dr. Bonger shows his sympathy
with the social philosophy of socialism which appears as well in the
exposition of his own explanation of criminality; but the facts which
he collects together with the evidence on which they rest are so ex-
plicitly set forth and his own conclusions so carefully distinguished
that the value of the study is not diminished even for those who are
not disposed to accept his social philosophy.

Dr. Bonger sees clearly that the concept of crime is a social and not
a biological one. It is the social value or harmfulness of acts or conduct that is involved in the concept and if we use terms that have
a predominantly biological connotation such as "normal" or "abnormal", we must be careful to distinguish that use as referring to a
social standard or we will be in danger of a confusion of thought.
That some of the acts which society has classed as crimes may be
deemed pathological is incidental; it is not on this account that they
are termed crimes but because they are socially detrimental. That
some of the individuals who have committed crimes may be called
"abnormal" is incidental; it is not because of this that they are classified as criminals. That the economic factor has a large influence in
connection with that kind of conduct the social significance of which
stamps it as criminal the author abundantly shows. The extent to
which this is the case and the extent to which the economic conditions involved are inherent in our present social organization are

matters on which there will be difference of opinion with the author. Dr. Bonger's expressed belief that his main positions will be received without sympathy in this country we venture to think will not prove to be well founded.   On the contrary so clearly has he set them forth and so well has he supported them that they can hardly fail of appreciation.   If this work serves to some extent as a corrective to a too prevalent tendency toward a confusion of thought between biological and social concepts and standards in the study of human conduct — and especially that kind of conduct which we have deemed so socially detrimental as to brand as crime — its inclusion in this series will be amply justified.

WARREN, PA.
February 26, 1916.

INTRODUCTION TO THIS VOLUME.

By Frank H. Norcross.[1]

Dr. Bonger's work — "Criminality and Economic Conditions" — will arrest the attention of students of criminology, sociology and kindred subjects. In it, also, the political economist may delve with profit.

The eminent scholar and author in his preface to the American edition expresses the conviction that his "ideas about the etiology of crime will not be shared by a great many readers of the American edition," and, also, "that the book is sure to meet with many disapproving critics on this side of the ocean." The distinguished author may be agreeably disappointed in the number of American readers who will agree in a large measure with his conclusions as to the causes of crime generally. I am inclined to think that the remedy which Dr. Bonger proposes is more apt to elicit controversy than the correctness of his diagnosis. The great value of Dr. Bonger's work to Americans, however, will be independent of the number of readers who concede the force of his reasoning or accept the logic of his conclusions. Disagree with the author's conclusions as the reader may and its value to the reader will not be impaired. One cannot take issue with the conclusions of a scholar based on study and research, without an exercise of processes of the mind valuable to the reader, and probably so to others. From the right quantity and quality of criticism comes the truth. One of the most valuable portions of Dr. Bonger's work will be found in his own criticisms of the writings of other European authors, particularly those comprising the so-called Italian and French schools.

"Criminality and Economic Conditions" is the nearest approach to an exhaustive treatment of the question of the agencies productive of crime which has thus far been published in this country. The

[1] Chief Justice of the Supreme Court of Nevada; Vice-President of the American Institute of Criminal Law and Criminology.

work is a result of great study and research, and little existing data
can have been overlooked.   Agree or not with the conclusions of the
author, doubt the force of his reasoning if one will, nevertheless, such
reasoning and conclusions have their basis in statistics and data furnished, from which other reasoning or conclusions may be formed
if the reader thinks the author's conclusions are not supported by the
facts.

Whether existing economic conditions are fundamentally wrong,
and crime is but the natural concomitant of a false economic basis
upon which society is organized, is a controversial question which is
so forcefully presented by the author that the reader must concede
that his views have been presented by a master.

Dr. Bonger's thesis, doubtless, will have the effect of increasing
the number of Americans who regard environment as the greatest
contributory cause of crime and who place heredity or innate criminality in a subordinate position, though many may continue to regard
these matters as of greater importance than the author attributes to
them.   The author does not hesitate to express his contempt for the
theory recently espoused by some Americans that "sterilization"
may be an effective method of reducing the "army of criminals."
"One should be inclined to ask," he says, "if the advocates of 'sterilization' have never heard of Australia, where a considerable number
of inhabitants have descended from the worst of criminals and where
yet the rate of criminality is low."   The Australian might reply that
this is not a fair test, for at the time England was transporting so
many of her criminals to Australia, the English criminal code was so
drastic that "the worst of criminals" constituted but a small per cent
of those who became its victims.   But this observation does not mili-
tate against the correctness of the Doctor's observation that "sterilization" is "as useful as the efforts to stop with a bottle a brook in its
course."   If the advocates of "sterilization" are wrong in their theory,
it is only illustrative of the fact that we Americans have been so
busy developing a new country that, until very recent years, we gave no
thought to the immense problem of the causes of crime, or attempted
to apply to the subject any sort of intelligent, to say nothing of
scientific, consideration.   When at last it dawned upon a few of the
American people that the cost in dollars and cents of dealing with
our crime problem, to say nothing of the incidental economic waste,
exceeded a billion dollars annually, or, as Professor Münsterberg in
one of his books forcibly puts it: "that this country spends annually
five hundred millions of dollars more on fighting the existing crime

than on all its works of charity, education, and religion ", — it began
to be considered worth while to study this tremendous social problem
with a view, if possible, of improving conditions. Those who investigated the subject found little in the way of statistics or reliable data
upon which to base a study of conditions with a view of applying
remedies. Some few had written upon various phases of the subject.
It was not, however, until the organization of the American Institute
of Criminal Law and Criminology in 1909 that intelligent direction
along practical lines was given to a study by Americans of this great
social and economic problem. The Journal of the Institute was the
first periodical of its kind published in the English language. In
Continental Europe a number of such journals were being published
and many students of the problem had contributed valuable works
upon different phases of the subject. The American Institute has
deemed the quickest way for Americans to become abreast of the best
modern thought on criminal law and criminology, is to make available for American readers the best scientific thought of European
writers, hence, "The Modern Criminal Science Series," of which Dr.
Bonger's work becomes one of the most valuable volumes.

Until very recent years, most American judges and prosecuting
attorneys gave little thought to the underlying causes of crime. It
was the general assumption that courts and court officers had performed their full functions when the guilt or innocence of a defendant
had been determined and he was discharged or committed to some
penal institution. Here again little thought was given to the one
incarcerated other than to hold and generally to exploit him until
by law he was entitled to be discharged. Those whose province it
was to get men into prison and those whose duty it was to keep them
in custody gave little attention to the question whether the convict
was a better or a worse unit of society when he came out than when he
entered upon a prison term. Even less thought was given to the more
important question — why so many commit crime at all. If normal
human beings under normal conditions do not commit crime, then
crime is evidence of the abnormal, either in the person or in the condition. If this is a correct hypothesis, then the administration of
criminal law must to a greater degree in the future than in the past
be predicated upon a comprehension and due consideration of this
fact.

If, in order to materially reduce the quantum of crime, it is necessary to change the economic basis upon which modern society rests
and reorganize it "based upon the community of the means of pro-

duction ", then the outlook for an early diminution in the volume of crime may not be overly encouraging.   Such a change in the economic basis of society is hardly to be expected otherwise than as the result of the slow process of social evolution.   Progress in this respect has not been perceptibly rapid since Moses gave to the world the Book of Deuteronomy.   Many abuses of our present economic system, however, may be modified or abolished without waiting for or conceding the necessity of the change which the eminent scholar holds is fundamental.

Again, in conclusion, let me reiterate that the value of Dr. Bonger's work does not depend upon an agreement with all the views of the author.   The book will bring to the American reader a depth and breadth of view most valuable to the administrators of criminal law and to those interested in the wider field of general social progress.

CARSON CITY, NEVADA,
  February 18, 1916.

TRANSLATOR'S NOTE.

THIS translation is based upon the Amsterdam edition of 1905, but the translator has been furnished by the author not only with special notes for the American edition, but also with the latest corrections to the French text. Dr. Bonger has also furnished a revised bibliography, and kindly wrote the American preface in English. In the translation some slight condensation of the work has been made, with the approval of the committee, by the omission of a few passages of a parenthetical nature, in quotations and notes. The very valuable bibliographical notes have been retained intact. Grateful acknowledgment is due to the Editorial Committee for suggestions as to some difficult legal terms, and to Mr. Georgio de Grassi for assistance in the translation of Italian passages.

HENRY P. HORTON.

ITHACA, N.Y.,
September, 1914.

CRIMINALITY AND
ECONOMIC CONDITIONS

PREFACE TO THE AMERICAN EDITION.

THE resolution of the "Committee on Translations of the American Institute of Criminal Law and Criminology" to include my book "Criminalité et conditions économiques" among the European works, that were assigned for translation was welcomed by me with gladness. The fact that the difference of language is an obstacle for many to become acquainted with a book, is for its author very disagreeable. This was also the reason which obliged me to publish my work not in my own but in the French language.

I am fully convinced that my ideas about the etiology of crime will not be shared by a great many readers of the American edition. As far as I can see, in the English-speaking countries the causes of criminality are sought in man himself rather than in his surroundings. Heredity, too, is considered there of great importance. Hence the attempts to reduce the army of criminals by so-called "sterilization." Against this point of view my book is in sharp opposition; I consider it one of the most fatal errors. There was a time in Europe when it was thought with Lombroso that crime was rooted in man himself; the progress of sociology has shown more and more clearly that the roots are found outside man, in society. There is nothing more variable than man! That heredity plays a great part on the scene of criminality has never been proved. Have the advocates of "sterilization", one should be inclined to ask, never heard of Australia, where a considerable number of the inhabitants are descended from the worst of criminals, and where yet the rate of criminality is low? The army of prostitution has been for a great many centuries by far more "sterile" than the army of criminals can ever be made, and yet prostitution is not decreased; the increase and decrease of this phenomena is ruled by social factors. In short, the effect of "sterilization" seems to me as useful as the efforts to stop with a bottle a brook in its course, as Manouvrier once called it. On the other hand I beg the adherents of the individualistic theory of crime to take into consideration that in some European countries the beginning of the rise of the lower classes, who form the greatest contingent of criminals, has been sufficient to arrest the increase of crime, even in many cases to occasion a decrease.

My book will thus be sure to meet with many disapproving critics on the other side of the ocean. I fear them not. If only facts are opposed to facts, truth will come to light. " Du choc des opinions jaillit la vérité ! "

According to my undertaking I have stated in notes the principal literature of the latest years. In concert with the desire of the Committee I have shortened the text as much as possible. The whole passage about "race and crime" I have omitted because — maintaining in general what I had written about it — I now have much more to say on the subject, but the space therefor was not at my disposition. For the same reason I left the passage on "Physical Environment and Crime" as it was. The treatment in detail of both these questions will take place in due time elsewhere.

I will not close this preface without assuring the Committee on Translations how highly I value their broad view and large-minded resolution to give a hearing to one whose opinions differ so much from the usual. To my translator, my hearty thanks for the good care bestowed on my book.

W. A. BONGER.

AMSTERDAM,
    June, 1914.

THE AUTHOR'S PREFACE TO THE ORIGINAL EDITION.

HONORABLE mention has been given to the first part of this work, which was written upon a subject proposed by the juridical faculty of the University of Amsterdam, and entitled "A Systematic and Critical Exposition of the Literature Dealing with the Relation between Criminality and Economic Conditions." To this exposition I have added the opinions of some additional authors, and have treated some others more fully than in the original; but on the whole this part of the work has been little changed. The second part, on the other hand, is almost entirely new; though it is true that in my thesis I had already marked out a line of investigation which, in my opinion, required a profound study of the relation between criminality and economic conditions. The period of one year fixed by the faculty was too limited a time in which to give more than a brief survey of the question. I have left the exposition as it was without restating it in the second part (now the more important division of the work), although I am aware that objections might be made, especially as to the form. However, I have not felt that these are of sufficient importance to demand a complete recasting of the work.

I take advantage of this opportunity to express my sincere thanks to those who have expressed their good will by lending me their aid; especially to my highly esteemed colleague, Professor G. A. van Hamel, and my friends Dr. A. Aletrino and N. W. Posthumus.

AMSTERDAM,
  February, 1905.

I have taken great pains neither to deride human actions, nor to deplore them, nor to detest them, but to understand them.

— Spinoza.

INTRODUCTION.

In systematizing the literature of my subject I have pursued the following method: I begin with some significant extracts from authors who wrote before the birth of modern criminal science. After these I take up the statisticians, that is to say, those who, without belonging to any special school of criminologists, have treated the subject principally by the aid of statistics. Next I give an exposition of the school which insists especially upon the individual factors in crime, and ascribes only a secondary place to economic factors (the Italian school); following this I treat of the school which considers the rôle played by environment as very important (the French school); and afterwards that of the bio-sociological doctrine which forms the synthesis of the two schools. Then follow the "spiritualists", that is to say the religious authors who have been more or less influenced by modern criminal science; and finally, the authors who belong to the "terza scuola", and the socialists who consider the influence of economic conditions as being very important or even decisive. The authors coming under the same heading have been treated in chronological order.

Like every classification this is more or less arbitrary. Several authors might have been placed under two different headings. We may add that as time goes on the differences between the Italian and French schools are becoming less and less marked, so that their opinions and those of the bio-sociologists no longer show any great divergences as far as our subject is concerned.

PART ONE.

CRITICAL EXPOSITION OF THE LITERATURE DEALING WITH THE RELATION BETWEEN CRIMINALITY AND ECONOMIC CONDITIONS.

CHAPTER I.

THE PRECURSORS.

AUTHORS WHO TREATED THE SUBJECT BEFORE THE BIRTH OF MODERN CRIMINAL SCIENCE.

I.

THOMAS MORE.[1]

IN the first part of his "Utopia" More severely criticises the economic conditions of his time in England, and adds some observations upon the criminality of that period.

Raphael Hythloday, whom More makes the speaker in his work, and through whom he expresses his own opinions, says:

"It chanced on a certain day, when I sat at the Cardinal's table, there was also a certain lay man cunning in the laws of your realm. Who, I cannot tell whereof taking occasion, began diligently and earnestly to praise that strait and rigorous justice, which at that time was there executed upon felons, who, as he said, were for the most part twenty hanged together upon one gallows. And, seeing so few escaped punishment, he said he could not choose but greatly wonder and marvel, how and by what evil luck it should so come to pass, that thieves nevertheless were in every place so rife and so rank.

---

[1] [NOTE TO THE AMERICAN EDITION: In my opinion, More is the first author who has noted in a scientific way the relation between criminality and economic conditions. Before him there were other authors, to whom this relationship did not remain totally unperceived; but they treated the subject by chance, as it were, and in a very superficial way. *Cf. J. van Kan,* "Les Causes économique de la Criminalité", pp. 15 *ff.*]

"Nay, Sir, quod I (for I durst boldly speak my mind before the Cardinal) marvel nothing hereat; for this punishment of thieves passeth the limits of justice, and is also very hurtful to the public weal.   For it is too extreme and cruel a punishment for theft, and yet not sufficient to refrain and withhold men from theft.   For simple theft is not so great an offense, that it ought to be punished with death.   Neither is there any punishment so horrible, that it can keep them from stealing, which have no other craft whereby to get their living.   Therefore in this point, not you only, but also the most part of the world, be like evil schoolmasters, which be readier to beat, than to teach their scholars.   For great and horrible punishments be appointed for thieves, whereas much rather provision should have been made, that there were some means, whereby they might get their living, so that no man should be driven to this extreme necessity, first to steal, and then to die.

"Yes (quod he) this matter is well enough provided for already. There be handicrafts, there is husbandry to get their living by, if they would not willingly be nought.   Nay, quod I, you shall not scape so; for first of all, I will speak nothing of them that come home out of the wars, maimed and lame, as not long ago, out of Blackheath field, and a little before that, out of the wars in France; such, I say, as put their lives in jeopardy for public weal's or the king's sake, and by reason of weakness or lameness be not able to occupy their old crafts, and be too aged to learn new; of them I will speak nothing, forasmuch as wars have their ordinary recourse.   But let us consider those things that chance daily before our eyes.   First there is a great number of gentlemen, which can not be content to live idle themselves, like drones, of that which others have labored for; their tenants, I mean, whom they poll and shave to the quick, by raising their rents (for this only point of frugality do they use, men else through their lavish and prodigal spending, able to bring themselves to very beggary) these gentlemen, I say, do not only live in idleness themselves, but also carry about with them at their tails a great flock or train of idle and loitering serving men, which never learn any craft whereby to get their livings.   These men as soon as their master is dead, or be sick themselves, be incontinent thrust out of doors.   For gentlemen had rather keep idle persons, than sick men, and many times the dead man's heir is not able to maintain so great a house, and keep so many serving men as his father did.   Then in the mean season they that be thus destitute of service, either starve for hunger, or manfully play the thieves.   For what would you have them do?

When they have wandered abroad so long, until they have worn threadbare their apparel, and also impaired their health, then gentlemen because of their pale and sickly faces, and patched coats, will not take them into service. And husbandmen dare not set them a work, knowing well enough that he is nothing meet to do true and faithful service to a poor man with a spade and a mattock for small wages and hard fare, which being daintily and tenderly pampered up in idleness and pleasure, was wont with a sword and buckler by his side to jet through the street with a bragging look, and to think himself to be as good as any man's mate.

"Nay, by Saint Mary, sir (quod the lawyer), not so. For this kind of man must we make the most of. For in them as men of stouter stomachs, bolder spirits, and manlier courages than handicrafts men and plowmen be, doth consist the whole power, strength, and puissance of our army, when we must fight in battle. Forsooth, sir, as well you might say (quod I) that for war's sake we must cherish thieves. For surely you shall never lack thieves while you have them. No, nor thieves be not the most false and fainthearted soldiers, nor soldiers be not the cowardliest thieves; so well these two crafts agree together. But this fault, though it be much used among you, yet is not peculiar to you only, but common also almost to all nations. Yet France besides this is troubled and infected with a much sorer plague. The whole realm is filled and besieged with hired soldiers in peace time (if that be peace) which be brought in under the same color and pretense, that hath persuaded you to keep these idle serving men. For these wise fools and very archdolts thought the wealth of the country herein to consist, if there were ever in readiness a strong and sure garrison, specially of old practised soldiers, for they put no trust at all in men unexercised. And therefore they must be forced to seek for war, to the end that they may have practised soldiers and cunning manslayers, lest that (as it is prettily said by Sallust) their hands and their minds through idleness and lack of exercise, should wax dull. But how pernicious and pestilent a thing it is to maintain such beasts, the Frenchmen by their own harms have learned, and the examples of the Romans, Carthaginians, Syrians, and of many other countries do manifestly declare. For not only the empire, but also the fields and cities of all these, by divers occasions have been overrunned and destroyed by their own armies beforehand had in a readiness. Now how unnecessary a thing this is, hereby it may appear, that the French soldiers, which from their youth have been practised and inured in feats of arms, do not crack nor advance themselves to have very often gotten the upper hand and mastery of your new made and unpractised soldiers. But in this point I will not use many words, lest perchance I may seem to flatter you.

"No, nor those same handicraftmen of yours in cities, nor yet the rude and uplandish plowmen of the country, are not supposed to be greatly afraid of your gentlemen's idle serving men, unless it be such as be not of body or stature correspondent to their strength and courage, or else whose bold stomachs be discouraged through poverty. Thus you may see, that it is not to be feared lest they should be effeminated, if they were brought up in good crafts and laborsome works, whereby to get their livings, whose stout and sturdy bodies (for gentlemen vouchsafe to corrupt and spill none but picked and chosen men) now either by reason of rest and idleness be brought to weakness or else by easy and womanly exercises be made feeble and unable to endure hardness. Truly howsoever the case standeth, this methinketh is nothing available to the public weal, for war's sake, which you never have, but when you will yourselves, to keep and maintain an innumerable flock of that sort of men, that be so troublesome and noyous in peace, whereof you ought to have a thousand times more regard than of war.

" But yet this is not the only necessary cause of stealing. There is another, which, as I suppose, is proper and peculiar to you Englishmen alone. What is that? quod the Cardinal. Forsooth my Lord (quod I) your sheep that were wont to be so meek and tame, and so small eaters, now as I hear say, be become so great devourers and so wild, that they eat up, and swallow down the very men themselves. They consume, destroy, and devour whole fields, houses, and cities. For look in what parts of the realm doth grow the finest and therefore dearest wool, there noblemen and gentlemen, yea and certain abbots, holy men no doubt, not contenting themselves with the yearly revenues and profits, that were wont to grow to their forefathers and predecessors of their lands, nor being content that they live in rest and pleasure nothing profiting, yea much noying the public weal, leave no ground for tillage, they inclose all into pastures; they throw down houses; they pluck down towns, and leave nothing standing, but only the church to be made a sheephouse. And as though you lost no land by forests, chases, lands, and parks; those good holy men turn all dwelling places and all glebeland into desolation and wilderness. Therefore that one covetous and unsatiable cormorant and very plague of his native country may compass about and enclose many thousand acres of ground together within one pale or hedge, the husbandmen be thrust out of their own, or else either by fraud, or by violent oppression they be put besides it, or by wrongs and injuries they be so wearied, that they be compelled to sell all. By one means therefore or by other, either by hook or crook they must needs depart away, poor, silly, wretched souls, men, women, husbands, wives, fatherless children, widows, woeful mothers, with their young babes, and their whole household small in substance and much in number, as husbandry requireth many hands. Away they trudge, I say, out of their known and accustomed houses, finding no place to rest in. All their household stuff, which is very little worth, though it might well abide the sale; yet being suddenly thrust out, they be constrained to sell it for a thing of nought. And when they have wandered abroad till that be spent, what can they do but steal and then justly pardy be hanged, or else go about begging. Yet then they also be cast into prison as vagabonds, because they go about and work not, whom no man will set to work, though they never so willingly profer themselves thereto. For one shepherd or herdman is enough to eat up that ground with cattle, to the occupying whereof about husbandry many hands were requisite.

"And this is also the cause why victuals be now in many places dearer. Yea, besides this the price of wool is so risen, that poor folks which were wont to work it, and make cloth thereof, be now able to buy none at all. And by this means very many be forced to forsake work, and to give themselves to idleness. For after that so much ground was inclosed for pasture, an infinite multitude of sheep died of the rot, such vengeance God took of their inordinate and insatiable covetousness, sending among the sheep that pestiferous murrain, which much more justly should have fallen of the sheep-masters' own heads. And though the number of sheep increase never so fast, yet the price falleth not one mite, because there be so few sellers. For they be almost all comen into a few rich men's hands, whom no need forceth to sell before they lust, and they lust not before they may sell as dear as they lust.

"Now the same cause bringeth in like dearth of the other kinds of cattle, yea and that so much the more, because that after the farms plucked down and husbandry decayed, there is no man that careth about the breeding of young stock. For these rich men bring not up the young ones of great cattle as they do lambs. But first they buy them abroad very cheap and afterward, when they be fatted in their pastures, they sell them again exceeding dear. And therefore (as I suppose) the whole incommodity hereof is not yet felt. For yet they make dearth only in those places where they sell. But when they fetch them away from thence where they be bred faster than they can be brought up; then shall there also be felt great dearth, stock beginning there to fail where the ware is bought. Thus the unreasonable covetousness of a few hath turned that thing to the utter undoing of your island, in the which thing the chief felicity of your realm did consist. For this great dearth of victuals causeth men to keep as little houses and as small hospitality as they possibly may, and to put away their servants, whither, I pray you, but abegging or else (which these gentle bloods and stout stomachs will sooner set their minds unto) astealing?

"Now to amend the matter, to this wretched beggary and miserable poverty is joined great wantonness, importunate superfluity and excessive riot. For not only gentlemen's servants, but also handicraftman, yea and almost the plowmen of the country, with all other sorts of people, use much strange and proud newfangledness in their apparel, and too much prodigal riot and sumptuous fare at their table. Now bawds, queans, whores, harlots, strumpets, brothelhouses, stews, and yet another stews, winetaverns, alehouses and tippling houses, with so many naughty, lewd, and unlawful games, as dice, cards, tables, tennis, bowls, quoits, do not all these send the haunters of them straight astealing when their money is gone?

" Cast out these pernicious abominations, make a law that they, which plucked down farms and towns of husbandry, shall reëdify them, or else yield and uprender the possession thereof to such as will go to the cost of building them anew. Suffer not these rich men to buy up all, to engross and forestall, and with their monopoly to keep the market alone as please them. Let not so many be brought up in idleness, let husbandry and tillage be restored, let clothworking be renewed, that there may be honest labors for this idle sort to pass their time profitably, which hitherto either poverty has caused to be thieves, or else now to be vagabonds, or idle serving men, and shortly will be thieves. Doubtless unless you find a remedy for these enormities, you shall in vain advance yourselves of executing justice upon felons. For this justice is more beautiful in appearance, and more flourishing to the show, than either just or profitable. For by suffering your youth wantonly and viciously to be brought up, and to be infected, even from their tender age, by little and little with vice, then in God's name to be punished, when they commit the same faults after being come to man's state, which from their youth they were ever like to do; in this point, I pray you, what other thing do you, than make thieves and then punish them?"[1]

II.

JEAN MESLIER.[2]

In speaking of the faults which cling to society Meslier, among other things, says the following about crime:

"Another abuse, and one that is almost universally accepted and authorized in the world, is the appropriation of the wealth of the soil by individuals, in place of which all ought to possess it equally in common and enjoy it equally in common. I mean all those of the same district or territory, so that they as well as those who inhabit the same city, town, village, or parish should compose but one great family. They should all regard themselves as being brothers and sisters one to another and all children of the same fathers and mothers, who, for this reason ought to love one another as brothers and sisters and, in consequence, live peaceably together, having all things common. All should have the same or similar food, should be equally well lodged, clothed and shod, but should also apply themselves equally to their business, that is to say, to work or to some other honest and useful employment, each following his or her profession, or whatever is most necessary and fitting to be done according to the time or season or the things especially needed. And all this should be done, not under the direction of those who would like to dominate over others tyrannically and imperiously, but only under the direction of the wisest and best intentioned, for the maintenance and advancement of the public weal. All cities and other communities should also on their own account take great pains to make alliances with their neighbors and keep inviolable the peace and union between them, in order to aid and succor one another in time of need; for without this the public well-being cannot be maintained, and the greater part of mankind must be wretched and unhappy.

"For first, what results from this individual appropriation of the wealth of the soil for each to enjoy it severally apart from the others, as it seems good to him? It results that each is eager to get as much as he can, in all sorts of ways, good and bad. For cupidity, which is insatiable and, as we know, the root of all evils, looking through an open door, so to speak, toward the accomplishment of its desires, does not fail to take advantage of the opportunity, and makes all

---

[1] Pp. 28-36. [2] "Le testament de J. Meslier."

men do whatever they can in order to have an abundance of goods and riches, and to be so protected from indigence as to have the pleasure and contentment of enjoying whatever they wish. From this it happens that those who are the strongest, the most crafty, the most skilful, and often even the most wicked and unworthy, have the largest share in the wealth of the soil and are best provided with all the good things of life." [1]

"This is not all, but it also results from this abuse of which I have been speaking, namely that wealth is so badly distributed among men, some having everything, or at least much more than their true share, and others having nothing, or lacking a part of what is useful and necessary . . . it results from this, I say, that hatred and envy first of all arise. From these spring in turn murmurings, complainings, commotions, insurrections, and wars, which cause an infinity of evils among men. From these again proceed thousands and millions of mischievous lawsuits which the private owners are obliged to have among themselves to defend their property and to maintain what they consider their rights. These suits cause thousands of pains to the body, and tens of thousands of disquietudes to the mind, and often enough cause the entire ruin of both parties. From this it also happens that those who have nothing, or who have not all that they need, are constrained and obliged to employ evil means to get subsistence. From this come the frauds, deceptions, rascalities, injustices, extortions, robberies, thefts, murders, assassinations, and brigandages which cause such an infinity of evils among men." [2]

III.

J. J. ROUSSEAU.

I believe that the following observation, which I find in the "Discourse upon the Origin and Foundations of Inequality among Men ", is worth quoting.

"The first man who, having enclosed a piece of ground, took it into his head to say, 'This is mine', and found people simple enough to believe him, was the true founder of civil society. What crimes, wars, and murders, what miseries and horrors would the human race have been spared if some one had torn up the stakes, or filled the ditch, and cried to his comrades; 'Beware of heeding this impostor. You are lost if you forget that the fruits of the ground belong to all, and the ground itself to no one.'" [3]

[1] Pp. 210–212.   [2] Pp. 214, 215.   [3] P. 67.

IV.

MORELLY.

In his "Code de la nature" this author seeks to show that the harmony in which men lived in primitive society (when common property existed) has been destroyed by the institution of private property, which, coming in little by little, has changed common interests into contrary interests. He expresses himself on this point as follows:

"Every division of goods, whether equal or unequal, and all individual appropriation of the portions so formed are what Horace calls 'Summi materiam mali.' All political or moral phenomena are the effects of this pernicious cause. It is by this that we can explain all theorems and problems with regard to the origin, development, connection, and affinity of virtues or vices, disorders, and crimes; also with regard to the true motives of good or bad actions, the determinations and perplexities of the human will, the depravity of the passions, the inefficacy of precepts and laws to restrain them; and, finally, with regard to the monstrous creations resulting from the aberrations of the mind and the heart. The reason, I say, for all these things can be ascribed to the general obstinacy of legislators about breaking or letting any one else break the cord with which sociability was first bound by those who usurped to their own use soil that ought to belong indivisibly to all humanity." [1]

Farther along he defines the same idea more exactly when he says: "Take away property, I repeat without ceasing, and you destroy forever a thousand factors which lead men to desperate extremities. I say that, delivered from this tyrant, it is totally impossible that man should give himself to crimes, that he should be a thief, an assassin, or a conqueror. The laws which authorize property punish him, it is true, for these crimes. Even his own remorse and fears, sprung from the prejudices of the moral system in which he has been raised, punish him still more. But the most severe chastisement of the offender is the primitive and innate feeling of benevolence. This inner voice of Nature, though commonly confined to the indifferent admonition not to injure, has still force enough to make the criminal feel keenly." [2]

[1] Pp. 79, 80.
[2] Pp. 144, 145. See also pp. 38 ff., and pp. 150 ff.

V.

C. BECCARIA.

The following passage taken from the introduction to Beccaria's "Des délits et des peines" is not without importance for our subject:

"The advantages of society ought to be equally divided among all its members. However, when men are gathered together we note a constant tendency to collect privileges, power, and happiness in the hands of a small minority, and to leave for the multitude only poverty and weakness. It is only by good laws that this tendency can be checked. But ordinarily men leave the regulation of the most important matters to temporary laws and to the caution of the moment, or even entrust them to the discretion of those whose interests are opposed to the best institutions and the wisest laws." [1]

"If we turn to history we shall see that laws, which ought to be agreements freely made between free men, have oftenest been only the instrument of the passions of the minority or the result of the chance of the moment, never the work of a wise observer of human nature who has known how to direct all the actions of the multitude to this single end: *The greatest good of the greatest number*." [2]

In Section 35 ("On Theft") we read, among other things, as follows:

"A theft committed without violence ought to be punished merely by a fine. It is just that he who takes the property of another should be deprived of his own. But if theft is ordinarily the crime of poverty and despair, if this offense is committed only by that class of unfortunate men to whom the right of property (a terrible right and perhaps not a necessary one) has left no possession but mere existence, the imposition of a fine will contribute only to multiply thefts, by increasing the number of the indigent, and robbing an innocent family of bread to give it to a rich man who is perhaps himself a criminal." [3]

VI.

S. N. H. LINGUET.

In his "Theorie des lois civiles", directed principally against Montesquieu's "L'esprit des lois", in which Linguet seeks to defend the thesis, "The spirit of the laws is Property", there are some in-

---

[1] P. 9.　　　　　[2] P. 10.　　　　　[3] P. 167.

teresting passages. After having shown that private property has been founded upon violence, he treats of the origin of the laws and, at the same time, of the causes of crime, and says:

"Among men all equal, all robust, passionate, sanguinary, and accustomed to arms, dangerous disputes would continually arise. It would be impossible but that chance and intelligence should produce great inequality of fortune. He who believed that he had been injured would wish to get justice for himself. The association formed to secure the booty would be troubled by the difficulty of enjoying it. These inconveniences occurred to the clearest thinkers and they sought to find a remedy. It was a totally new art that they created. But as it is almost always science that misleads, and as truth is never so easy to discover as at a distance from the Doctors, they looked about to see what route they should take.

"They thought that a primary act of violence was incontestably necessary. They could not disavow it, since it was the sole basis of their rights. But they also saw that it was necessary to prevent any further violence, since this would fall upon themselves. They conceived that the primitive usurpation ought to be regarded as a sacred title; but they perceived no less clearly that it was necessary to proscribe any new usurpation, which would contradict the ancient one and destroy it. In order to succeed in this they proposed to authorize only those brigandages which were carried on in common, and to punish severely those persons who dared to commit individual acts of spoliation. In response to their suggestions it was decreed that society should have the right to take everything, but that the members of society, as individuals, should be deprived of this right. They agreed that each should have peaceful possession of the part allotted to him, and that whoever tried to take it from him should be declared a public enemy and prosecuted as such.

"Here, then, in a few words is the source of all human laws. From it spring laws of every kind except the divine law, the source of which is as pure as its author. Upon this basis are founded all imaginable constitutions. This it is which sanctions the law of nations and the civil law, of which the one legitimates conquests, and the other proscribes robbery, only punishing, however, the thefts not committed by a large company. Finally this same principle has directed the steps of all politicians and of all founders of governments and empires.

"They have come by different ways, the details of which it is useless to discuss here, to change the original social anarchy, in which these principles were discovered, into administrations more or less imperfect. Violence thus formed the foundation of their rights, but all wished to keep with justice what they got possession of very unjustly. They took precautions to prevent those who assisted them in their wholesale conquest from imitating them in detail. After making sure of the general domain they did not wish any one to be able to dispute the particular distribution of it. They confirmed by regulations all their accomplices in the possession of what they had had the address or the good fortune to seize. They decreed that any one who, seeing these possessions stolen by force, should attempt to secure restitution by the same method, should be punished as guilty of an offense against society." [1]

In the chapter "Good and Evils which Laws Produce" Linguet pronounces the following trenchant and satirical judgment:

"The aim [of justice and law], as we have said, is to give society a fixed position. There results from them an invariable order which keeps each member in his place. It is by their means that the multitude who do not know them, even while they respect them, submit without repugnance to the small number who are armed by them. In this sense there is nothing so admirable as the law. It is the most sublime invention that ever presented itself to the human mind. It offers to any reflective individual the most satisfying, the most beautiful of spectacles. To restrain force and violence by pacific means; to subjugate the liveliest passions; to assure to painful virtues the preference over easy and delusive vices; to direct the eyes, the hands, and the hearts of men; to subdue them without preventing them from believing themselves free; to prescribe duties capable of securing the repose of docile souls who performed them, and of protecting them against rebellious spirits, who wish to be exempt from them; all this the laws do or ought to do. It would be difficult to join together so much greatness with so many benefits.

"But as the theory of the laws is honorable to the humanity which has been able to grasp it, so the practical application of the laws has been most distressing, when, after the observance of them has been recommended, it is necessary to pass on to the punishments decreed for the offenses which violate them. The passions which self-interest unceasingly incites often necessitate this grievous extremity. Then we see men authorized by general consent to exercise an inflexible rigor upon their fellows. We hear justice pronounce sentences which would pass for cruel if they were not indispensable. It makes use of prisons, executioners, gallows. Liberty and even life become pledges

[1] Pp. 284–288.

of which justice deprives men at pleasure when they abuse them. To make good the losses which the state suffers from the crimes that disturb it, it comes back upon the criminals, and consequently suffers almost equally from the crime and from the punishment." [1]

VII.

P. H. D. d'HOLBACH.

In the third section of his "Système social", under the heading, "The Influence of Government upon Morals", Holbach, in treating of the causes of crime says among other things:

"In China they punish the mandarin in the department in which a great crime has been committed. A bad government has its own negligence or its own injustice to blame for the great number of malefactors who are found in a state. The multiplicity of criminals proclaims an administration as tyrannical and careless. The severity of taxes, the vexations and hardships inflicted by the rich and great multiply the number of the unfortunate, whom poverty often reduces to despair and who avail themselves of crime as the promptest means of escape from their condition. If wealth is the mother of vices, poverty is the mother of crimes. When a state is badly governed and wealth is too unequally divided, so that millions of men lack the necessaries of life, while a small number of citizens are surfeited with luxuries, there we commonly see a great number of criminals, whose number punishments do not diminish. If a government punishes the unfortunate it leaves undisturbed the vices that are leading the state to its ruin; it erects gibbets for the poor, whereas by bringing men to poverty it has itself made thieves, assassins, and criminals of every kind; it punishes crime, while it continually invites men to commit crime." [2]

"The man who has no share in the wealth of the state is not held to society by any bond. How can we expect a crowd of unfortunates to whom we have given neither principles nor morals to remain quiet spectators of the abundance, the luxury, the unjustly acquired riches of so many corrupt individuals, who seem to insult the general poverty, and are only rarely disposed to relieve it? By what right can society punish the thieving servant who has been a witness of the unpunished robberies and extortions of his master, or has seen public thieves strutting along, enjoying the consideration of their

---

[1] Pp. 186–189. See also pp. 199, 200, and 207–209.   [2] Pp. 33, 34.

fellow citizens, and shamelessly displaying the fruits of their extortions under the very eyes of the heads of the state? How can we make the poor respect the property of others when they themselves have been the victims of the rapacity of the rich, or have seen the property of their fellow citizens snatched away by violence or fraud with impunity? Finally how can we successfully preach submission to men to whom everything proves that the laws, armed against themselves alone, are indulgent toward the great and happy, and are inexorable only for the unhappy and poor? 'A man dies but once' and the imagination of the criminal familiarizes itself little by little with the idea of the most cruel punishments. He ends by regarding them as a 'mauvais quart d'heure', and would as soon perish by the hand of the executioner as die of hunger, or even work all his life without reward." [1]

VIII.

G. B. DE MABLY.

This author's opinion of crime is best expressed by the following quotation taken from his "De la legislation ou principes des lois":

"The more I reflect upon it the more I am convinced that inequality of fortune and condition disorders man and alters the natural sentiments of his heart, for the habit of luxury gives him a desire for things that are useless for his true happiness and fills his mind with the most unjust and absurd prejudices and errors. I believe that equality, while satisfying modest requirements, keeps those requirements modest, and preserves in the soul a peace which is opposed to the birth and progress of the passions. By what strange folly should we have cultivated a studied elegance and refinement in our needs if inequality of fortune had not accustomed us to regard this ridiculous fastidiousness as a proof of superiority, and attained thereby a certain consideration? Why should I consider as below me a man who is perhaps my superior in merit; why should I pretend to have authority over him and so open the door to tyranny, to servitude, and all the vices most fatal to society, if the inequality of conditions had not exposed my soul to ambition, as the inequality of fortune has exposed it to avarice? It is inequality alone that has taught men to prefer many useless and harmful things to virtue. I believe that it has been demonstrated that in a state of equality nothing would be easier than to prevent abuses and maintain the law.

[1] Pp. 36, 37.

Equality is certain to produce all good, because it unites men, elevates their souls, and prepares them for mutual feelings of benevolence and amity. Inequality, on the other hand, produces all evil, because it degrades men, humiliates them, and sows division and hatred among them." [1]

IX.

J. P. Brissot de Warville.

In his "Théorie des loix criminelles" we find among others the following passages that are of interest in connection with the subject which occupies our attention:

"A man is not born an enemy to society. It is circumstances which give him that title, such as poverty or misfortune. He does not disturb the general tranquillity until he has lost his own. He ceases to be a good citizen only when the name becomes meaningless in his case; and it is when poverty has destroyed his own privileges that he dares to attack those of his fellows. To make all citizens happy is, then, to prevent the inception of crime; and the rarity of crime is in direct ratio to the goodness of the administration. This simple principle, however unknown to administrators even to the present day, is no less solid on that account, no less luminous, and ought no less to serve as the basis for government. If it has been neglected, it is because it has appeared easier to rulers to punish the unfortunate being who demands the rights that nature gave him, than to satisfy his just demand; to stifle the cries of anguish, than to change them to shouts of applause. The penal code of every nation is much like the bull of Phalaris; its imposing garb of juridical forms, like the timbrels and other instruments surrounding the brazen monster, prevent the cries of the victims from reaching the ear. Tyrants cry out to the credulous spectators that blood is necessary to the public safety; good legislators are greedy of it.

"The first and most efficacious means of preventing crimes consists, then, in a wise administration that procures the general happiness. When the rays of the beneficent star that rules extend their influence even to the lowest ranks of society, they are rarely sullied by punishments; each, concentrating itself upon the spot where heaven has thrown it, makes the day that it lightens joyous and blessed (and crime is so near to the man who is forced to curse his fate!) If the taxes are light and not severely felt, if subsistence is

[1] Pp. 47, 48. See also pp. 72 *ff.*

easy, the number of marriages increases, they are happy, and the population multiplies. The people then do not regret their labors, since they are interspersed with pleasures. They are attached to the fatherland, which offers them good fortune, and to life, which gives them the means of enjoying it. A man does not disturb the public peace, because his own prosperity is the fruit of it. A property-holder himself, he takes good care not to do any violence to the right of property, and even where he would not naturally have a horror of bloodshed, his days are too precious to him for him to dare to cut short those of his fellow-citizens." [1]

" . . . What sovereign, I say, cannot easily see that he has in his hand the true means of restraining crime, namely to secure the public well-being by means of civil legislation. Yes, the more perfect civil legislation becomes the less need there will be for criminal legislation. And this need will disappear entirely when the twofold basis upon which civil legislation ought to rest becomes fixed and invariable; when the property and the liberty of subjects are respected by the monarch; when the unfortunate man who has been born without property (though with the same needs as others) can, by working, correct the injustice of fate, and destroy the inequality of the distribution of wealth; when, finally, the fruit of his labor will not be the prey of the greedy tax-gatherer. The rich man can then enjoy his wealth in safety, because despair will no longer expose him to the knife of the poor man whom his proud opulence insults. We posit here as the foundation of good legislation the security of real and personal property, but a masterpiece of statesmanship would be, to make them useless, if it were possible, by abolishing them altogether. This would be to tear up crime by the roots. It was thus that Lycurgus, whose laws have been so calumniated because to narrow minds they seemed impossible of imitation, cleverly dried up the source of all crime. To avoid attacks upon property he abolished it; to prevent adultery he had all women held in common; to make the Spartan a hero he made him the slave of his harsh legislation; finally to prevent the sad effects of the passions he permitted none but the passion for the public weal. This is why crimes were so rare in Sparta as long as these laws were faithfully observed. But when Lysander brought back from the fatal conquest of Athens treasures, the taste for art and the rage for luxury, all the vices were rapidly introduced. Then crimes broke out; ambition made men commit perjuries, assassinations, treasons; then the virtuous Agis, who wanted to revive

[1] Pp. 37–39.

morality, perished under the perfidious knife of the royal servitude; then men like Nabis and Machanidas appeared; and finally a penal code was introduced, and Sparta was reduced to the status of an ordinary city." [1]

"Ought we to be astonished that the attacks upon the social laws are so multiplied to-day, and that there are always so many thieves and assassins, when to the causes of crime which we have developed it is necessary to add that horrible malady of European states, mendicity? When the water destined by nature to quench the thirst of all men is artificially diverted into particular channels for the exclusive use of certain individuals, the unfortunate man, tormented by need, falls into despair, and in a rage breaks these fatal channels, making the fragments fall upon the heads of his enemies. Exclusive possession of property has everywhere produced poverty in the most numerous class, and poverty has given birth to mendicity, which, robbing with one hand to satisfy hunger, with the other plunges a dagger into the bosom of the rich to stop their cries. Here we have in two words the origin of theft and murder. To destroy the roots of these it would be necessary to restore among men the equality of condition so praised by modern philosophers, but not at all included in the programs of modern governments. It would be necessary to distribute wealth equally among all citizens, to eradicate from their hearts the corrosive desire of ambition, and to blunt the spur of their personal interest." [2]

In his "Recherches philosophiques sur la propriété et sur le vol" Brissot gives an exposition of natural property, and of property as established by society. He says of crime: "Civil property is very different from natural property, as we have shown. It is not based upon the same title, and has not the same aim or the same bounds. Need is the limit of natural property. Civil property goes further and includes superfluities. In nature each man has a right to everything; in society the man to whom his parents have left no property has a right to nothing. In nature he would be guilty if he did not satisfy his needs; he is guilty in society when he satisfies them if he has no property. Society has, then, upset all the ideas of property given by nature. It has destroyed the equilibrium between human beings which nature established. Equality banished there appear the odious distinctions of rich and poor. Society has been divided into two classes, the first consisting of citizens with property, living in idleness; the second and more numerous class composed of the

[1] Pp. 43–45.　　　　[2] Pp. 74, 75.

mass of the people, to whom the right to exist has been sold dear, and who are degraded and condemned to perpetual toil. To confirm this new right of property the most cruel punishments have been pronounced upon all those who disturb or attack it. The breach of this right is called theft; and see how far we are from nature! The thief in the state of nature is the rich man, the man who has a superfluity; in society the thief is he who robs this rich man. What a complete transposition of ideas!" [1]

"If man retains, even in society, the inalienable right of property which nature has given him, nothing can take it from him, nothing can prevent his exercising it. If the other members of society concentrate in their own persons the possession of all the soil; if those who are robbed by this spoliation and forced to have recourse to labor cannot by this means secure their whole subsistence, then they have the right to exact from the others, who hold property, the means of satisfying their needs. They have a claim upon the wealth of others in proportion to their own necessity, and force used to resist this claim is violence. The rich man is the only thief; he alone ought to hang from those infamous gallows which are raised only to punish the man born in poverty for being needy; only to force him to stifle the voice of nature, the cry of liberty; only to compel him to subject himself to a harsh servitude in order to avoid an ignominious death." [2]

X.

W. GODWIN.

In the third chapter of the First Book of his "Enquiry Concerning Political Justice", Godwin treats of two important kinds of crime, theft and fraud.

Of these he says: "Two of the greatest abuses relative to the interior policy of nations which at this time prevail in the world, consist in the irregular transfer of property, either first by violence, or secondly by fraud. If among the inhabitants of a country there existed no desire in one individual to possess himself of the substance of another, or no desire so vehement and restless as to prompt him to acquire it by means inconsistent with order and justice, undoubtedly in that country guilt could scarcely be known but by report. If every man could with perfect facility obtain the necessities of life, and, obtaining them, feel no uneasy craving after its super-

[1] Pp. 331–333.   [2] Pp. 333, 334.

fluities, temptation would lose its power. Private interest would visibly accord with public good; and civil society become what poetry has feigned of the golden age. Let us inquire into the principles to which these evils are indebted for their existence." [1]

According to him these crimes are the consequence:

First, Of poverty, which has reached enormous dimensions (in England one person out of every seven has at some time received public aid). The situation has become such that for the poor man the state of society is a state of war. He considers society not as a body whose object is to maintain personal rights and to procure to each individual the means of providing for his own support, but as a body that protects the advantageous position of one class of persons, while holding others in a state of poverty and dependence.

Second, Of the ostentation of the rich, who make the poor man feel all the more what he is deprived of.

Third, Of the tyranny of the rich, made permanent by legislation, by the administration of the laws, and by the distribution of wealth.

In his Eighth Book ("Of Property"), Godwin elaborates the ideas given above. Speaking of the moral improvement that would result from the abolition of private property, he says: "And here it is obvious that the great occasions for crime would be cut off forever. All men love justice. All men are conscious that man is a being of one common nature, and feel the propriety of the treatment they receive from one another being measured by one common standard. Every man is desirous of assisting another; whether we should choose to ascribe this to an instinct implanted in his nature which renders this a source of personal gratification, or to his perception of the reasonableness of such assistance. So necessary a part is this of the constitution of mind, that it may be doubted whether any man perpetrates any action, however criminal, without having first invented some sophistry, some palliation, by which he proves to himself that it is best to be done. Hence it appears, that offense, the invasion by one man upon the security of another, is a thought alien to the human mind, and which nothing could have reconciled us to but the sharp sting of necessity. To consider merely the present order of society, it is evident that the first offense must have been his who began a monopoly, and took advantage of the weakness of his neighbors to secure certain exclusive privileges to himself. The man on the other hand who determined to put an end to this monopoly, and who peremptorily demanded what was superfluous to the

---

[1] Pp. 15, 16.

possessor and would be of extreme benefit to himself, appeared to his own mind to be merely avenging the offended laws of justice. Were it not for the plausibleness of this apology, it is to be presumed that there would be no such thing as crime in the world.

"The fruitful source of crimes consists in this circumstance, one man's possessing in abundance that of which another man is destitute. We must change the nature of mind before we can prevent it from being powerfully influenced by this circumstance, when brought strongly home to its perceptions by the nature of its situation.   Man must cease to have senses, the pleasures of appetite and vanity must cease to gratify, before he can look on tamely at the monopoly of these pleasures.   He must cease to have a sense of justice before he can clearly and fully approve this mixed scene of superfluity and want.   It is true that the proper method of curing this inequality is by reason and not by violence.   But the immediate tendency of the established administration is to persuade that reason is impotent. The injustice of which they complain is upheld by force, and they are too easily induced, by force to attempt its correction.   All they endeavor is the partial correction of an injustice, which education tells them is necessary, but more powerful reason affirms to be tyrannical.

"Force grew out of monopoly.   It might accidentally have occurred among savages whose appetites exceeded their supply, or whose passions were inflamed by the presence of the object of their desire; but it would gradually have died away, as reason and civilization advanced.   Accumulated property has fixed its empire; and henceforth all is an open contention of the strength and cunning of the one party against the strength and cunning of the other.   In this case the violent and premature struggles of the necessitous are undoubtedly an evil.   They tend to defeat the very cause in the success of which they are most deeply interested; they tend to procrastinate the triumph of truth.   But the true crime in every instance is in the selfish and partial propensities of men, thinking only of themselves, and despising the emolument of others; and of these the rich have their share.

"The spirit of oppression, the spirit of servility, and the spirit of fraud, these are the ultimate growth of the established administration of property.   They are alike hostile to intellectual and moral improvement.   The other vices of envy, malice, and revenge are their inseparable companions.   In a state of society where men lived in the midst of plenty, and where all shared alike the bounties of nature, these sentiments would inevitably expire. The narrow principle of selfishness would vanish. No man would be obliged to guard his little store, or provide with anxiety and pain for his restless wants, each would lose his individual existence in the thought of the general good. No man would be an enemy to his neighbor, for they would have no subject of contention; and of consequence philanthropy would resume the empire which reason assigns her; mind would be delivered from her perpetual anxiety about corporal support, and free to expatiate in the field of thought which is congenial to her. Each would assist the inquiries of all." [1]

XI.

R. OWEN. [2]

The author in several works has given us his ideas upon the relation between crime and the social environment, and especially economic conditions. It is in "The Book of the New Moral World", which appeared in 1844, that his views are best expressed. [3]

They may be summed up as follows: It is not the man himself, it is his circumstances that form his character; an unfavorable environment produces a bad man, a favorable one a good man. The organization of the society of today is such that it awakens in a man all evil qualities. The greater part of mankind live in conditions of the greatest poverty, and become physically, intellectually, and morally inferior. The working classes are housed in unsanitary dwellings, work too hard and too long, and are insufficiently clothed and nourished.

Improper production and distribution of wealth are the causes of the prevalence of disorder and anarchy. The means of production, the raw materials and the productive forces, are sufficient to provide

[1] Pp. 455–458.
[2] See also the work entitled: "An Inquiry into the Principles of the Distribution of Wealth" (Chapters II and III), by *W. Thompson*, a disciple of Owen. On page 17 he says: "The unrestrained tendency of the distribution of wealth, being so much toward equality, excessive wealth and excessive poverty being removed, almost all the temptations, all the motives, which now urge to the commission of crime, would be also removed." In general, the English socialists from the commencement of the nineteenth century (*e.g.* Charles Hall, Thomas Hodgskin, Charles Bray, and others) have had a notion, more or less clear, of the relation between the nascent industrial capitalism and criminality. Upon these authors *cf. Quack*, "De Socialisten" (Tome Supplementaire), and *Beer*, "Geschichte des Sozialismus in England", I.
[3] See his "Essays on the Formation of Character"; and "Reports of the Proceedings at the Several Public Meetings held in Dublin."

amply for the needs of all. But competition by devouring wealth prevents this, and brings it about that while some have a super-fluity, the majority have not even the necessaries of life (a fact which is one great cause of criminality). The process of distribution adds enormously to the waste because of the great number of intermediaries.

Education and instruction are neglected to the last degree. The children of the lower classes are almost entirely deprived of instruction, not to say education; their parents, never having been taught themselves, are incapable of imparting instruction, nor have they the leisure for it. However, the children of all classes are made egotistical and anti-social; they have impressed upon them the maxim "Each one for himself", in place of being taught that the love of one's neighbor is the principle upon which society ought to be based.

Owen finds the cause of crime, then, in the organization of society upon the basis of private property. The following is a characteristic passage from Volume VI, "General Constitution of Government and Universal Code of Law" :

"Private property has been, and is at this day, the cause of endless crime and misery to man, and he should hail the period when the progress of science, and the knowledge of the means to form a superior character for all the individuals of the human race, render its continuance not only unnecessary, but most injurious to all; injurious to an incalculable extent to the lower, middle, and upper classes. The possession of private property tends to make the possessor ignorantly selfish; and selfish, very generally, in proportion to the extent of the property held by its claimant. . . .

"Private property also deteriorates the character of its possessor in various ways; it is calculated to produce in him pride, vanity, injustice, and oppression, with a total disregard of the natural and inalienable rights of his fellow men. It limits his ideas within the little narrow circle of self, prevents the mind from expanding to receive the extended views beneficial for the human race, and understand great general interests that could be made most essentially to improve the character and condition of all. . . .

"Private property alienates mind from mind, is a perpetual cause of repulsive action throughout society, a never-failing source of deception and fraud between man and man, and a strong stimulus to prostitution among women. It has caused war throughout all the past ages of the world's known history, and has been a stimulant to innumerable private murders.

"It is now the sole cause of poverty and its endless crimes and miseries over the world, and in principle it is as unjust as it is unwise in practice.

"In a rational-made society it will never exist. Whatever may have been its necessity or utility, before the introduction of the supremacy of machinery and chemistry, it is now most unnecessary and an unmixed evil; for every one, from the highest to the lowest, may be ensured through life much more of all that is really beneficial for humanity, and the permanent happiness of the individual, through public scientific arrangements, than it is possible to obtain through the scramble and contest for procuring and maintaining private property.

"Private property also continually interferes with or obstructs public measures which would greatly benefit all, and frequently to merely please the whim or caprice of an ill-trained individual. . . .

"With a well arranged scientific system of public property, equal education and condition, there will be no mercenary or unequal marriages; no spoiled children; and none of the evils which proceed from these errors in the present system, if crudities which pervade all the departments of life, and are thoroughly inconsistent, can be called a system of society.

"In fact, as soon as individuals shall be educated and placed — and it is for the best and permanent interest of society that all should be educated and placed — the saving of time, labour, and capital, between public and private property, will be beyond any estimate the mind of man can form in favour of public property. . . .

"Therefore the twelfth law [1] will be, that —

"'Under the Rational System of society — after the children shall have been trained to acquire new habits and new feelings, derived from a knowledge of the laws of human nature — there shall be no useless private property.'

"The old system of the world has been created and governed on the assumed principle of man's responsibility to *man*, and by *man's* rewards and punishments.

"And this principle has been assumed upon the original supposition, that man was born with power to form himself into any character he liked; to believe or disbelieve whatever he pleased; and that he could love, hate, or be indifferent as to all persons and things, according to an independent will which enabled him to do as he liked in all these respects.

[1] One of the laws which, according to Owen, should produce the change from modern society to the society of the future.

"The present system is, therefore, essentially a system supported and governed by laws of punishment and reward of man's creating, in opposition to nature's laws of punishing and rewarding. The former system is artificial, and always produces crime and misery, continually increasing, and therefore requiring new laws to correct the evils necessarily forced upon society by the old laws; thus laws are multiplied without limit by man to counteract nature's laws, and ever without success. While nature's beautiful and benevolent laws, if consistently acted upon in a system made throughout in accordance with them, would produce knowledge, goodness, and happiness, continually increasing, to the human race.

"By man's laws being forced upon the population of all countries, in continual opposition to nature's laws; with law added to law, in the vain attempt to remedy endless previous laws, the world had been made and kept criminal, with crimes multiplying as human laws increased.

"The laws of man are made to support injustice, and give additional power to the oppressor and to the man devoid of truth and honesty over the innocent and just. And such must be the result, as long as human laws, lawyers, and law paraphernalia shall be sanctioned by society. . . .

"Nature's laws carry with them the only just rewards and punishments that man should experience; and they are, in every case, efficient for nature's purposes, and to ensure the happiness of man in all countries and climes; and, differing from man's puny, short-sighted laws, they are always adequate to the end intended to be accomplished. And this end is evidently to increase human knowledge and happiness. It is through these laws of nature, that man has attained the knowledge which he has acquired. He has been continually urged onward to make discoveries, and to invent, through pain experienced, or pleasure enjoyed or anticipated.

"But man has been trained to have his character formed, and to be governed by laws of his own making; his habits, manners, ideas, and associations of ideas have emanated, directly or indirectly, from his artificial and injurious source; and, in consequence, the mind, language, and practice of all individuals have become a chaos of confusion. And this chaos in the character and conduct of individuals has made a yet greater chaos in all the proceedings of society: and, in consequence, man is now opposing man, and nation opposing nation, all over the earth. Yet all nature declares, that it shall be by union of man with man, and nation with nation, that the human race can ever attain a high degree of permanent prosperity and happiness, or become rational.

"Nevertheless, while this irrational individual and general character shall remain, those men and women who have been made to receive this character, and to be so injured, must continue for a time to be governed by these most injurious laws. The laws of nature being alone applicable to a society, whose laws are in accordance with the laws of nature.

"When this rational society shall be formed, and men, individually and generally, shall be trained to act in accordance with it, then shall human punishments and rewards cease, and cease for ever.

"The thirteenth law will therefore be, that —

"'As soon as the members of these scientific associations shall have been educated, from infancy, in a knowledge of the laws of their nature, trained to act in obedience to them, and surrounded by circumstances all in unison with them, there shall be no individual reward or punishment.'

"The Rational System of society is one and indivisible in its principles and practices; each part is essential to its formation. It is one unvarying consistent system for forming the character of all individuals, and for governing their affairs; and it is essentially a system to prevent evil, and render individual punishment and reward as unnecessary, as they are unjust and injurious to all. . . .

"Individual punishments and rewards, ignorance, the inferior feelings and passions, with all crimes and miseries, will go together when the irrational system shall be abolished. *When the cause of evil shall be removed, then will the evil cease, and not before.*" [1]

XII.

E. CABET.

In the second part of his "Voyage en Icarie" the author treats of the relation between crime and economic conditions. In his opinion

---

[1] Pp. 40–45. It is well known that Owen put his theories into practice when he founded the village of New Lanark. The disastrous consequences of industrial capitalism, such as excessive hours of labor, insufficient nourishment, unsanitary housing, the lack of education for children, etc., were diminished there or altogether avoided. Among the population of the colony, though originally alcoholized and demoralized by capitalism, little by little the favorable environment made itself felt, so that for nineteen years there was no judicial prosecution, and drunkenness and illegitimate births disappeared. (See *Denis*, "Le socialisme et les causes économiques et sociales du crime", p. 283, and *Quack*, "De Socialisten", II, pp. 279 *ff.*)

money and inequality of fortune and of property are the causes of all crimes. The following quotation explains his views. (The work speaks of present day society as in the past, and supposes the existence of a state with common property.)

"Wealth and superfluity being, by their nature, as I have already said, injustice and usurpation, the poor often thought only of robbing the rich; and theft, under all its forms (swindling, pocket-picking, bankruptcy, breach of trust, fraud, cheating, etc.), was the almost universal occupation of the poor as well as of the rich. And the poor robbed not only the rich, they robbed even the poor themselves, so that all, rich and poor, were both robbers and robbed.

"It would be impossible to enumerate all the kinds of theft and classes of thieves. It was in vain that the rich had terrible laws made against theft; it was in vain that the prisons and galleys were kept filled with poor thieves, and that their blood was often poured out upon the scaffold. Buoyed up by the hope of not being discovered, the poor robbed in the fields, or in houses, or upon the highroads, or even in the streets at night. The skilful pick-pocket stole even in open day. The audacious swindler robbed by means of trickery and deceit, sometimes by selling things of no value, sometimes by taking advantage of credulity or even of beneficence.

"Shall I speak of the counterfeiters of every description? Shall I also speak of the usurers, the great thieves, the wolves of the bourse and the bank, the contractors and monopolists? Shall I speak of those who enriched themselves by means of public calamities, who desired or provoked invasions or wars in order to make their fortunes, and famines in order to amass money in the midst of corpses? Shall I speak of the thieves who risked the public health by adulterating the food and drink that they sold, and of those other great robbers, the heads of the army, who pillaged foreign peoples while exposing their own country to terrible reprisals? Finally shall I speak of the innumerable means of amassing money at the expense of others, and of the innumerable individuals in almost all classes who daily practiced them?

"Not all these acts were classed as thefts by the law. The most inexcusable, the most harmful, those which were only practiced by the rich, even enjoyed legal impunity. But all of them were, nevertheless, in reality according to the rules of a sound morality, thefts. Each class presented, without doubt, many exceptions. There were some rich men as honest as possible, and many workers and poor men were persons of probity; but it may be said that by force of circumstances, and as an irresistible consequence of the inequality of fortune, all men, rich and poor, were generally induced to commit actions which were in reality only a kind of theft.

"And often theft led to all kinds of cruelty, to murder, and even to the most barbarous tortures in order to make owners reveal where they had hidden their gold. How many poisonings and parricides did the thirst for gold or inheritance excite! Thieves kidnapped children in order to prostitute them. They even stole and murdered young people in order to sell the flesh of their corpses!

"In a word, neither confidence nor security was possible. Each individual saw enemies in almost all the others; and society seemed, as it were, but a haunt of cut-throats in the midst of a forest! And all these horrors, which you will find more or less everywhere, were with us, and are still elsewhere — I cannot repeat it too often — the inevitable result of the unrestricted right of property." [1]

XIII.

F. ENGELS.

Among the disastrous consequences which industrial capitalism draws in its train the author ranks the tremendous increase of criminality. In his "Condition of the Working Class in England" he says: "The failings of the workers in general may be traced to an unbridled thirst for pleasure, to want of providence, and of flexibility in fitting into the social order, to the general inability to sacrifice the pleasure of the moment to a remoter advantage. But is that to be wondered at? When a class can purchase only a few and only the most sensual pleasures by its wearying toil, must it not give itself over blindly and madly to those pleasures? A class about whose education no one troubles himself, which is a playball to a thousand chances, knows no security in life — what incentives has such a class to providence, to 'respectability', to sacrifice the pleasure of the moment for a remoter enjoyment, most uncertain precisely by reason of the perpetually varying, shifting conditions under which the proletariat lives? A class which bears all the disadvantages of the social order without enjoying its advantages, one to which the social system appears in purely hostile aspects — who can demand that such a class respect this social order? Verily that is asking much! But the working-man cannot escape the present arrangement of society so long as it exists, and when the individual worker resists it, the greatest injury falls upon himself.

[1] Pp. 315–317.

"Thus the social order makes family life almost impossible for the worker. In a comfortless, filthy house, hardly good enough for mere nightly shelter, ill-furnished, often neither rain-tight nor warm, a foul atmosphere filling rooms overcrowded with human beings, no domestic comfort is possible. The husband works the whole day through, perhaps the wife also and the elder children, all in different places; they meet night and morning only, all under perpetual temptation to drink; what family life is possible under such conditions? Yet the working-man cannot escape from the family, must live in the family, and the consequence is a perpetual succession of family troubles, domestic quarrels, most demoralizing for parents and children alike. Neglect of all domestic duties, neglect of the children, especially, is only too common among the English working-people, and only too vigorously fostered by the existing institutions of society. And children growing up in this savage way, amidst these demoralizing influences, are expected to turn out goody-goody and moral in the end! Verily the requirements are naïve, which the self-satisfied bourgeois makes upon the working-man!

"The contempt for the existing order is most conspicuous in its extreme form — that of offenses against the law. If the influences demoralizing to the working-man act more powerfully, more concentratedly than usual, he becomes an offender as certainly as water abandons the fluid for the vaporous state at 80 degrees, Reaumur. Under the brutal and brutalizing treatment of the bourgeoisie, the working-man becomes precisely as much without volition as water, and is subject to the laws of nature with precisely the same necessity; at a certain point all freedom ceases. Hence with the extension of the proletariat, crime has increased in England, and the British nation has become the most criminal in the world. From the annual criminal tables of the Home Secretary, it is evident that the increase of crime in England has proceeded with incomprehensible rapidity. The number of arrests for *criminal* offenses reached in years: 1805, 4,605; 1810, 5,146; 1815, 7,898; 1820, 13,710; 1825, 14,437; 1830, 18,107; 1835, 20,731; 1840, 27,187; 1841, 27,760; 1842, 31,309 in England and Wales alone. That is to say, they increased seven-fold in thirty-seven years. Of these arrests, in 1842, 4,497 were made in Lancashire alone, or more than 14 per cent. of the whole; and 4,094 in Middlesex, including London, or more than 13 per cent. So that two districts which include great cities with proletarian populations, produced one fourth of the total amount of crime, though their population is far from forming one fourth of the whole. Moreover, the criminal tables prove directly that nearly all crime arises within the proletariat; for in 1842, taking the average, out of 100 criminals, 32.35 could neither read nor write; 58.32 read and wrote imperfectly; 6.77 could read and write well; 0.22 had enjoyed a higher education, while the degree of education of 2.34 could not be ascertained. In Scotland, crime has increased yet more rapidly. There were but 89 arrests for criminal offenses in 1819, and as early as 1837 the number had risen to 3,176, and in 1842 to 4,189. In Lanarkshire, where Sheriff Alison himself made out the criminal report, the population has doubled in thirty years, and crime in five and a half, or six times more rapidly than the population. The offenses, as in all civilized countries, are, in the great majority of cases, against property. The proportion of offenses to the population, which in the Netherlands is as 1 : 7,140, and in France as 1 : 1,804, was in England, when Gaskell wrote, as 1 : 799. The proportion of offenses against persons to the population in the Netherlands, 1 : 28,904; in France, 1 : 17,537; in England, 1 : 23,395; that of crimes in general to the population in the agricultural districts, as 1 : 1,043; in the manufacturing districts as 1 : 840. ('Manufacturing Population of England', chap. 10.) In the whole of England today the proportion is 1 : 660; though it is scarcely ten years since Gaskell's book appeared!" [1]

[1] Pp. 128–131. See also: *F. Engels*, "Umrisse zu einer Kritik der Nationalökonomie", pp. 449 and 459; *F. Engels* and *K. Marx*, "Die heilige Familie oder Kritik der kritischen Kritik", pp. 239–241. See also, the following: *Plato*, "The Republic", I. 5.; *C. A. Helvetius*, "De l'homme", X. p. 49; *J. P. Marat*, "Plan de la législation criminelle", pp. 18 *ff.*; *J. Bentham*, "Traités de la legislation civile et pénale", III ch. V, pp. 45 *ff.*; *Ch. Fourier*, "Theorie des quatre Mouvements", III; "Theorie de l'unité universelle" ("Traité de l'association domestique-agricole"), Introduction. 2. p. 51; "Le nouveau monde industrial et sociétaire", Sect. VI; *B. P. Enfantin*, "Les enseignments", pp. 92, 93; *W. Weitling*, "Die Menschheit wie sie ist, und wie sie sein sollte", p. 47; "Garantien der Harmonie und Freiheit", pp. 53, 54, and 104, 105; "Das Evangelium eines armen Sünders", p. 102; *V. Considérant*, "Theorie du droit de propriété et du droit au travail", p. 33; *L. Blanc*, "Organisation du travail", pp. 57 *ff.*; *C. Pequeur*, "Des améliorations matérielles", pp. 86–88, 232–234, 239–241; *J. A. van Royen*, "Wetgering en armalde beschouwd in betrekking tot het misdrijf", pp. 9 *ff.*; *C. J. A. den Tex*, "De causis criminum", pp. 84 *ff.*; *Chaillou des Barres*, "L'influence du bien-être matériel sur la moralité d'un peuple" ("Journal des Economistes", 1846); *E. Mercier*, "Influence du bien-être matériel sur la criminalité"; *P. J. Proudhon*, "De la justice dans la révolution et dans l'église", pp. 533–534.

[NOTE TO THE AMERICAN EDITION: For the opinions of the scientific world of Holland at the end of the eighteenth century and the beginning of the nineteenth : *J. A. v. Hamel*, "Strafrechtspolitik van voor honderd jaar" (Gids, 1909, II).

See for the same period in England : *L. von Thôt*, "Die positive Strafrechtsschule in einigen europäischen Ländern", pp. 407 *ff.* (" Monatschr. f. Kriminal-Psychologie u. Strafrechts-reform ", VIII).]

CHAPTER II.

THE STATISTICIANS.

I.

A. M. GUERRY.

In his "Essai sur la statistique morale de la France", the author has made a study of the influence of age, sex, season, education, etc., upon criminality. But there is scarcely to be found an exposition of the influence of economic conditions upon the subject which we are considering. The following passages, however, are not devoid of interest.

"Wealth, (as determined by the amount of taxes on personal and real property) more often than density of population, coincides with crimes against property, of which it thus appears to be an indirect cause. We shall observe, however, that while the maximum of wealth falls in the departments of the North, where the greatest number of crimes against property are found; and the minimum in the center where these crimes are most rare; yet in the South the average is almost as high as in the North. Now if in the North is wealth which indirectly produces the crimes against property, why is it that the same is not true of the South? It would be unsafe to conclude from the fact that the poorest departments are those where the fewest crimes against property are committed, that poverty is not the principal cause of these crimes. In order to justify this conclusion, which in other regards we are far from rejecting, more direct proofs would be necessary. As a matter of fact, it is possible that the departments where there is the least wealth are not those where there are the greatest number of the very poor; and that the departments where the largest fortunes are to be found are just those where the poverty of a part of the population is greatest.

"The question of the effect of wealth or poverty upon morality presents more difficulty than one would suspect at first glance. To study it it would be necessary to determine the ratio of the indigent and pauper class in each department. Some documents upon the subject have been published, it is true, but they have no authentic character, and do not appear to merit enough confidence for us to give the analysis of them here." [1]

Further along Guerry shows that the departments where commerce and manufacturing are most highly developed furnish also the greatest number of crimes against property. But the author has not investigated the connection between these two symptoms. Although not rejecting, then, entirely the hypothesis that poverty is not the principal cause of crimes against property, Guerry recognizes nevertheless that a causal connection between poverty and crime is possible, that is to say he perceives that the department where the greatest poverty prevails is not necessarily that which is the poorest, nor that the richest is the one that has the fewest of the very poor.

II.

AD. QUETELET.

An exposition of the whole system of this author would lead us too far. But the following quotations from his "Physique sociale" will suffice to show the breadth of his views and the vastness of his conception of society.

"Thus, to make our manner of procedure plain by an example, anyone who examines too closely a small portion of a very great circumference traced upon a plane, will see in this portion only a certain number of physical points, assembled in a more or less accidental way. . . . From a greater distance his eye will take in a greater number of points, which will already appear regularly distributed in an arc of a certain extent; soon, if the observer continues to recede, he loses sight of the individual points . . . grasps the law that has presided over their general arrangement, and recognizes the nature of the curve traced. . . .

"It is in this way that we shall study the laws that concern the human race; for when we examine them from too near at hand it becomes impossible to grasp them; we are struck only with individual peculiarities, which are infinite." [2]

"In all that relates to crimes, the same figures are reproduced with

[1] Pp. 42, 43. [2] P. 94, I.

such constancy that it is impossible to misconstrue them, even in the case of those crimes which, it would seem, should be most likely to escape human prevision, such as homicides, since these are in general committed as a consequence of quarrels arising without motive, and under apparently fortuitous circumstances. Experience, however, proves that not only is the annual number of homicides nearly constant, but that even the weapons employed are used in the same proportions. What can be said then of crimes that are the result of reflection?

"This constancy with which the same crimes reappear annually in the same order, and lead to the same penalties in the same proportions, is one of the most curious of the facts that we learn from court statistics. . . . A budget which we pay with frightful regularity is that of the jails, the penitentiaries, and the gallows. . . . We can enumerate in advance how many individuals will stain their hands with the blood of their fellows, how many will be forgers, how many poisoners; almost as we can predict the births and deaths. . . .

"Society contains within itself the germs of all the crimes that are about to be committed. It is society, in a way, which prepares them, and the criminal is only the instrument that executes them.

"Every social state supposes, then, a certain number and certain order of crimes as a necessary consequence of its organization. This remark, which might appear discouraging at first sight, becomes consoling, on the contrary, when we consider it more closely, since it shows the possibility of the improvement of men, by the modification of their institutions and habits and whatever, in general, influences their manner of being. At bottom this is only the extension of the well known law . . . that so far as the same causes are present we must expect the repetition of the same effects. What has produced the belief that this did not apply to moral phenomena is the too great influence commonly ascribed to man in matters relating to his actions." [1]

In the second volume of the "Physique sociale", Quetelet studies the influence of climate, age, and sex upon the tendency to crime. Although he merely touches upon our subject and treats it only indirectly, the following passages are worth the trouble of quoting:

"Poverty also is very generally regarded as leading to evil; however the department of the Creuse, one of the poorest in France, is that which shows in every respect, the highest morality. In the same way in the Netherlands, the most moral province is Luxemburg,

[1] Pp. 95–97, I.

where there is most poverty reigning. We must, however, be clear about the word *poverty*, which is here employed with a significance to which exception may be taken. A province is not really poor for having less extreme wealth than another, if the inhabitants, as in Luxemburg, are sober and industrious; if, by their labor, they succeed in providing in a dependable way for their needs, and in satisfying tastes that are so much the more modest, as the inequality of fortune is less felt, and causes less temptation; it may be said with more justice that this province enjoys a modest competence. Poverty makes itself felt in the provinces where great wealth is piled up, as in Flanders, Holland, the department of the Seine, etc., and especially in manufacturing countries, where the slightest political disturbance, the slightest obstruction in the channels of trade, will suddenly reduce thousands from a state of well-being to one of distress. It is these sudden changes from one state to another that give birth to crime, especially if those who suffer from them are surrounded by temptations, and are irritated by the continual sight of luxury and an inequality of fortune that makes them desperate." [1]

In speaking of the three races that make up the population of France, Quetelet says:

"The most remarkable anomaly that the Celtic race seems to present is found in the departments that belong to the valley of the Seine, especially below Paris. Several causes contribute to bring this about. We shall note first that these departments are those which, by reason of their extent, contain most persons and things, and consequently offer most opportunities to commit crimes; it is there that there is most movement and that most vagrants flow in from all districts. . . . Finally, it is here also that we find most industrial establishments and these establishments support a congested population whose means of support are more precarious than in other vocations. . . . The commercial and industrial provinces of the Netherlands are likewise those in which most offenses are committed." [2]

III.

Edw. Ducpetiaux.

One of the parts of his "Paupérisme dans les Flandres" treats of the criminality in the two provinces of that name. We quote the following from it:

[1] Pp 278, 279.　　　　　　　　[2] P. 281.

"Criminality is the inseparable companion of poverty. As the number of indigent persons increases, we see the number of crimes also increase. Hunger is a bad counselor. In the midst of crushing destitution, a man gradually loses the notion of justice and injustice, of good and bad; beset by needs that he cannot satisfy, he disregards the laws, and ends by recoiling from no attempt that appears capable of bettering his condition. Visiting a prison is enough to convince one of the influence of this cause upon the number and the nature of the offenses, and before even questioning the statistics that attest the progress of criminality in Flanders, we could be assured that this progress had coincided with that of pauperism. It is not then a demonstration (which we judge quite unnecessary) that we are about to offer here, it is only a series of facts that may serve to make the reader appreciate the greatness of the evil and the urgent necessity of attacking its source.

"The first of these facts is the high figure for convicts belonging to East and West Flanders, when compared with the total number of convicts in the central prisons. . . . In the ten years between 1858 and 1847, 23,075 convicts were received in the central prisons of the kingdom; 10,308 belonged to the two Flanders and 12,767 to the other provinces; the proportion, to 1000 convicts, was 447 for the first two provinces, and 553 for the seven others. Now this proportion is considerably in excess of that of the respective populations of the two divisions, since, to the thousand inhabitants, there are only 331 in Flanders and 669 in the rest of the kingdom. In other words, during the decennial period in question, one prisoner was received to 139 inhabitants in Flanders, and to 227 in the seven other provinces.

"The second fact is the increase in the number of persons arraigned and convicted in the Flemish provinces during the last few of these years, and particularly since the food shortage of 1845. In a space of seven years, the number of those arraigned in the two Flanders increased about in the ratio of 7 to 17; that of those condemned to imprisonment grew, during the same period from 35 to 123, or nearly quadrupled.

"These data are confirmed by an abstract of the numbers received into the jails and prisons of the two provinces, as well as by the average population of these establishments, during the period from 1839 to 1848:

YEARS.	PERSONS RECEIVED INTO THE JAILS AND PRISONS OF				TOTALS.	AVERAGE POPULATION OF THE PRISONS.
	WEST FLANDERS.					
	Bruges.	Courtrai.	Ypres.	Furnes.		
1839	1,578	592	572	169	2,911	233
1840	1,502	643	821	196	3,162	238
1841	1,377	795	599	175	2,946	311
1842	1,489	863	836	271	3,459	346
1843	1,478	922	790	298	3,488	374
1844	1,502	941	696	270	3,409	379
1845	1,876	935	600	254	3,665	376
1846	2,378	1,108	935	601	5,022	574
1847	3,751	2,012	1,238	909	7,910	820
1848	2,859	1,960	1,070	690	6,579	694
	EAST FLANDERS.					
	Ghent.	Audenarde.	Termonde.			
1839	2,094	842	754		3,690	289
1840	2,311	919	852		4,082	357
1841	2,163	771	852		3,786	351
1842	2,171	844	905		3,920	333
1843	3,610	991	870		5,471	408
1844	2,548	760	718		4,026	345
1845	2,579	1,061	1,461		5,101	360
1846	5,499	2,732	2,092		10,323	619
1847	7,491	6,943	3,240		17,674	972
1848	6,309	4,462	2,829		13,600	698

"The increase in the numbers received into the jails and prisons of the two provinces took place especially in the years 1845, 1846, and 1847; in 1848 we note quite a pronounced decrease, which continues in 1849. Of all the signs to prove the existence and progress of pauperism, this is perhaps the most certain. During the disastrous years that had just elapsed, the prisons became in a sense annexes of the hospitals and almshouses; a great number of offenses were committed with the sole object of finding asylum. . . .

"As to the children, we shall understand the imminence of the danger when we realize that in the short space of three years, from 1845 to 1847, 26,247 children and young persons of both sexes under 18, were incarcerated in prison or were inmates of workhouses. Most of these children belonged to the two provinces of Flanders, and a great number were arrested outside the limits of their province. Here is the increase in the number of those received into the prisons of Ghent and Bruges, and the jails of Audenarde, Termonde, Courtrai, Ypres, and Furnes:

CITIES.	YOUNG PRISONERS (UNDER 18) RECEIVED IN			TOTAL DURING THE 3 YRS.		
	1845.	1846.	1847.	Boys.	Girls.	General Total.
PRISONS OF E. FLANDERS.						
Ghent	350	1,345	1,898	2,671	922	3,593
Audenarde . . .	207	315	674	929	267	1,196
Termonde . . .	123	235	406	616	148	764
PRISONS OF W. FLANDERS.						
Bruges	459	299	550	1,110	198	1,308
Courtrai	116	170	331	560	57	617
Ypres	70	184	250	414	90	504
Furnes	43	139	57	151	88	239
Totals . . .	1,368	2,687	4,166	6,451	1,770	8,221

" This deplorable fact of the increase of criminality among the young is explained by the statistics of indigence. We see in fact that, among the indigent persons aided in East Flanders, in 1847, there were:

	IN THE CITIES.	IN THE COUNTRY.	TOTAL.
Indigent persons under 6 yrs. . . .	6,693	34,637	41,530
" " " 12 "	8,327	37,437	45,764
" " " 18 "	5,597	20,060	25,653
General total			112,947

"Supposing that West Flanders, which has more dependents in proportion than East Flanders, has the same proportion of children, we arrive at a total for the two provinces, of 225,894 indigent persons whose age is not above 18. In this number there are 174,588 who have not passed their twelfth year! And there are thousands of orphans!

"Notwithstanding the improvement that begins to make itself felt, thanks to the resumption of work and the low price of provisions, many of these young unfortunates continue to give themselves up to begging and vagrancy. But lately driven from their homes by cold and hunger, they form a wandering population, incessantly buffeted from almshouse to almshouse, from prison to prison.

"In Brussels at this present moment (July, 1849) there are still to be found in the annex of the prison, about 250 mendicants, among whom are 97 children below the age of 17. In the prisons of Ghent and Bruges their number is equally great." [1]

"It is an established fact, then, that the increase of criminality in Flanders has gone hand in hand with the extension of poverty. The latter brings about the abandonment of homes; . . . from this come mendicity, vagrancy, marauding, and theft. The incarceration of so great a number of unfortunates brings the most disastrous consequences. The germs of corruption, brutality, and crime are continually injected into a large fraction of the population. The habit of working is lost, energy is relaxed, idleness becomes incurable. When we think especially of the mass of children who, during the last few years, have passed through the prisons and almshouses, we cannot picture without pity, mingled with fear, the future of this generation, initiated at an early age into the existence of criminals, and condemned to the dangers and evils inseparable from the abandonment and degradation to which they are a prey." [2]

IV.

L. M. MOREAU-CHRISTOPHE.[3]

In speaking of England, after having sketched how industrialism, as it spread more and more, drew after it an increase of pauperism, the author says of the connection between criminality and economic conditions:

"Parallel with the ascending figure for pauperism, rises the growing figure for criminality. The number of persons arraigned at the assizes of England and Wales has increased as follows:

YEARS.	TOTALS.	ANNUAL AVERAGE.
1814 to 1820	78,762	11,252
1821 to 1827	99,842	14,263
1828 to 1834	134,062	19,152
1834 to 1840	162,502	23,214
1841 to 1847	193,445	27,760

[1] Pp. 39–46. [2] P. 47.
[3] "Du Problème de la Misère et de la solution chez les peuples anciens et modernes", III ("Peuples modernes"). See also by the same: "Le monde des coquins."

"Thus in a space of thirty-four years the number of crimes has more than doubled in England, while, in the same interval, the increase of the population has hardly passed 40%.

"The parallelism between the growing pauperism and growing criminality is even more striking when the comparison is applied to the delinquents under the summary jurisdiction of the justices of the peace.　Up to the time of the establishment of the workhouses in 1834 the number of poor persons assisted increased progressively from year to year.　Well, the number of persons arrested by the metropolitan police followed the same progression.　This number was 72,824 in 1831, and 77,543 in 1832.　In 1833 the new poor law with its terrible workhouses was approaching; consequently the number of arrests was no more than 69,959.　In 1834 the law was promulgated, and up to 1838 was executed with great rigor; as a result the number of arrests fell to 64,269 in 1834, to 63,674 in 1835, and to 63,584 in 1836. In 1837 the severity began to relax; consequently the number of arrests increased to 64,416.　In 1839 the laxity continued, and the number of arrests increased to 70,717.　Laxity reached its height in 1842, and the number of arrests rose to 76,545; this was an arrest to each 25 of the population.

"In Newcastle in 1837 the magistrates sentenced 1 person to 24 of the whole population.　In Leeds during a period of six years, from 1833 to 1838, there was one person arrested to 32 of the population. In Manchester in 1841 . . . the ratio of persons arrested, to the population, was as 1 to 21. . . .　In 1831, ten years earlier, the proportion was still only 1 to 78.　It almost quadrupled, then, in the interval.　In Liverpool in 1840 there was one arrest to 12 inhabitants." [1]

V.

G. MAYR.

The statistical data that form the basis of Dr. Mayr's "Statistik der gerichtlichen Politzei im Königreiche Bayern und in einigen anderen Ländern" are different from those used in similar works.　For, while generally only the number of crimes whose authors have been convicted, or that of delinquents punished, are considered, Dr. Mayr is of the opinion that to obtain a true picture of the morality of a people, it is necessary to take into account the number of crimes known to the police.　"If we wish really to form an exact picture of

[1] Pp. 222–224.

the moral condition of a people, we must first of all ask ourselves the question, how great is the number of the cases of crimes of different kinds that are of common notoriety, before we ask how great is the number of the individuals who are convicted of these crimes. The immorality of a people is determined not by the number of individuals convicted, but by the number of crimes committed; else that people would be most moral in which no offender ever let himself be caught, even if more crimes were committed there than elsewhere." [1]

Bavaria.

The results of Dr. Mayr's researches in regard to crime in this country are shown by him in a number of charts.[2]

Cis-Rhenal Territory. A comparison of the curves for crimes against property and those for crimes against persons shows us that the first descends as the other ascends, and vice versa. In seeking for the causes we find that in general the motives for the latter class of crime are, among others, coarseness, passion, and dissoluteness, while that of the first kind of crime is the desire to secure objects for direct use. The more difficult it is to gain a livelihood in a lawful manner, the more this tendency will develop.

According to the author, the fluctuation in the price of grain is one of the most important factors bearing upon criminality. And indeed, in examining his nine statistical charts the connection between the high or the low cost of grain, and the great or the small number of offenses against property comes out clearly. The curve for offenses against persons, on the other hand, falls when the price of grain rises, and vice versa. The improvement of living conditions, both subjectively (through having the means to purchase the necessaries) and objectively (through a fall in prices) must consequently exercise a considerable influence upon criminality. This is seen very well in the last years of the period 1835–61, when the price of grain was low, and wages very generally increased. Hence, from 1857 on, there was an increase in the crimes against persons, and a decrease in the crimes against property.

It ought to be remarked here that however just in itself Dr. Mayr's

---

[1] P. 2.
[2] [The charts being unnecessarily detailed for the purposes of this work, and the results being sufficiently summed up in the paragraphs which follow, they are omitted in this translation, though given by Dr. Bonger. — TRANSL.]

observation may be, we must beware of drawing the erroneous conclusion that those who feel most strongly the influence of the fall of
prices and the rise in wages must necessarily, according to a law of
nature, commit crimes against persons.   This is true only for gross
and uncultivated individuals who do not know how to occupy their
leisure.   But the degree of civilization of an individual depends
above all upon the economic conditions under which he was placed
by his birth.   There are, then, economic causes for both kinds of
crime.

Upper Bavaria.   This district shows a higher figure for crime than
any other province in Bavaria.   It is especially the great increase
since 1857–1858 that is most striking, and which is explained at least
partially by the application of another system of examining offenses.
The increase in the number of crimes against the person is the consequence of prosperous years, while the high figure for crimes against
property is explained by the great influx of individuals from neighboring districts, who, from an economic standpoint, were not independent.   In the period from 1837 to 1864 the population increased
49,128 by birth, and 66,299 by immigration.

Lower Bavaria.   The connection between crimes against property and the price of grain is weaker in this province than in any of
the others, because of its great production of cereals, which, for the
most part, are destined for home consumption.

The upper Palatinate, Upper, Central, and Lower Franconia, and
Swabia, all give convincing proofs of Dr. Mayr's thesis, though in
Franconia the truth is less apparent through the fact that bad years
brought increased emigration, which cut down the normal increase
in the number of crimes.

Where he treats of the different forms of crime, we read the following remarks, which are of interest in connection with our subject:
"As we have just seen, crimes against persons increase when the
price of grain goes up.   We must except from this rule, however,
two kinds of crime: infanticide and abortion."   The first of these
crimes reached its maximum in the critical years 1854–55, and the
second in 1853–1854.

As a proof of the coincidence of the fluctuations of crimes against
property with those of the price of grain in the period preceding
that which he studied especially, Dr. Mayr gives the following
table:

| Years. | Number of Crimes against Property to 100,000 of Population. | | Price of Rye in Munich. |
	District of the Isar.	District of the Lower Danube.	
1818/19	—	138	8 fl. 15 kr.
19/20	—	148	6 31
20/21	233	157	7 28
21/22	297	200	7 58
22/23	267	195	7 57
23/24	276	—	6 2
24/25	295	166	6 59
25/26	317	157	6 18
26/27	315	144	6 55
27/28	463	241	11 11
28/29	416	234	11 6
29/30	401	216	10 48
30/31	427	264	11 12
31/32	530	302	12 35
32/33	493	313	8 21
33/34	—	318	8 42
34/35	487	318	7 47

In chapter **IV** ("Zahl und Bewegung der Polizeiübertretungen im Gebiete diesseits des Rheins") Dr. Mayr gives some interesting information with regard to thefts of wood. The following table gives the figures for these crimes in this district compared with the others:

Above the Average (Cis-Rhenal Territory).		Below the Average (Cis-Rhenal Territory).	
The Upper Palatinate	18 %	Central Franconia	1 %
Upper Franconia	80 "	Swabia	63 "
Lower Franconia	178 "	Upper Bavaria	99.2 "
		Lower Bavaria	99.5 "

The great difference between these figures is explained by the fact that in Lower Franconia only a quarter of the woods are privately owned (the rest belonging to corporations, etc.). In Upper Bavaria the private forests are 92%, and in Lower Bavaria 96½% of the whole. Besides, the price of wood is very high in Lower Franconia. Once more, then, economic conditions are the cause of crime.

Upon the movement of the figures for mendicity Dr. Mayr remarks that they are strongly influenced by the cost of the primary necessities. "The parallel movement of the food-price and mendicity offers little to astonish us if we learn from the statistics of crimes that the objective difficulty or ease of getting food resulting from the fluctuations in price, exercises a direct influence upon increase and decrease of serious crimes against property. It is explicable that only a small portion of individuals who become economically dependent proceed to serious crime, while the majority fall into the minor misdemeanors involved in a living obtained through begging and vagrancy. The same force that appears in the increase and decrease of attacks upon property, must consequently appear much more intensively in the fluctuations of mendicity and vagrancy."

Bavaria.[1]

YEARS.	PRICE OF RYE (BAVARIAN BUSHEL).				NUMBER OF MENDICANTS AND VAGRANTS ARRESTED TO 100,000 OF THE POPULATION.								
	Cis-Rhenal Territory.		Palatinate.		Upper Bavaria.	Lower Bavaria.	Palatinate.	Upper Palatinate.	Upper Franconia.	Central Franconia.	Lower Franconia.	Swabia.	The Kingdom.
	fl.	kr.	fl.	kr.									
1835/36	6	53	8	17	2696	1558	1542	1952	2165	1348	665	1456	1685
1836/37	7	31	10	26	2100	1839	2075	2277	2421	1229	711	1262	1727
1837/38	10	18	12	21	2065	2483	2472	2233	2255	1438	639	1306	1842
1838/39	11	30	13	40	2232	1989	2056	2076	2195	1435	519	1640	1771
1839/40	10	35	12	6	2032	1805	2238	2111	2584	1233	515	1829	1781
1840/41	8	49	10	4	1887	1608	1845	1711	1810	1006	410	1531	1467
1841/42	9	14	12	39	1777	1318	1878	1625	1814	1008	434	1599	1433
1842/43	14	10	15	19	1810	1757	2479	2365	2679	1450	615	2177	1893
1843/44	14	1	10	28	1905	1690	1970	2286	2264	1475	475	2151	1758
1844/45	15	15	13	30	1857	1698	2411	2364	1412	1119	423	1722	1622
1845/46	19	53	21	45	2182	1836	3528	2856	1447	1475	535	2332	2033
1846/47	21	36	22	44	2902	2166	4276	3757	1904	1850	949	2586	2584
1847/48	10	12	10	22	1916	1635	2704	2290	1348	1364	548	1985	1746
1848/49	7	34	8	46	2269	1439	2555	1360	1015	1270	586	1545	1563
1849/50	7	57	8	57	2346	1528	2801	1782	991	1351	716	1893	1686
1850/51	12	20	13	10	2213	1790	3269	1734	1096	1294	1002	2023	1845
1851/52	17	53	15	57	2927	2243	4562	3030	1637	2274	2236	2969	2705
1852/53	17	39	17	46	2572	1918	5010	2289	2017	1795	2165	2535	2592
1853/54	23	38	24	13	2932	2097	5854	2983	2127	2282	2894	2671	3027
1854/55	23	19	23	38	2964	2591	5026	3326	2470	2215	2831	2804	3229
1855/56	17	45	22	2	2423	1817	4637	2367	2050	1595	2515	1939	2443
1856/57	15	26	18	5	2157	1724	3265	2059	1176	1412	1931	1435	1922
1857/58	12	31	12	58	1956	1237	2595	1537	588	974	1621	1203	1505
1858/59	10	28	12	13	1949	1170	2309	1334	462	497	940	1029	1255
1859/60	11	45	15	15	2084	1219	2622	1538	525	890	994	1105	1419
1860/61	14	8	16	19	2055	1304	2580	1318	484	720	750	1069	1336
Average	13	35	14	44	2234	1741	3083	2155	1649	1388	1120	1842	1920

[1] Pp. 136, 137.

England.

In speaking of the influence of economic conditions upon mendicity Dr. Mayr gives the following table:

England and Wales.

Years.	Price of Wheat (Quarter).		Number of Vagrants.
	sh.	d.	
1858	44	2	22,559
1859	43	10	23,353
1860	53	3	22,666
1861	55	4	24,001
1862	55	5½	29,504
1863	44	9	33,182
1864	40	2	31,932

However, in this case the increase of mendicity does not rest upon the high prices alone, but also upon the crisis which, owing to the depression of the cotton industry from 1860 on, lowered the plane of living of hundreds of thousands of workers, or drove them into the street.

England and Wales.

Number and Kind of Cases Tried by Jury.

Years.	Offenses against Persons.	Offenses against Property with Violence.	Offenses against Property without Violence.	Forgery and Counter-feiting.	Violent Attacks against Property.	Other Offenses.	Total.
1858	14	29	233	13	2.5	4.5	296
1859	13	22	209	11	3	5	263
1860	11	20	207	8.5	2.5	4	253
1861	12	25	200	8.5	2.5	4	252
1862	12.5	28	203	9.5	3	6	262
1863	14.5	26	194	9	3.5	7	254
1864	15	24	190	6.5	3.5	7	246
Average	13	25	205	9	3	5	260

Here the influence of the fall of prices is distinctly seen; offenses against property have decreased, those against persons, on the contrary, have increased.

England and Wales.

Total Offenses Tried by Jury, and Offenses not Specified.

Years.	Assaults upon Persons to 100,000 of the Population.	Attacks upon Property without Violence to 100,000 of the Population.
1858	439	439
1859	438	399
1860	399	392
1861	383	415
1862	403	433
1863	436	392
1864	469	365
Average	426	405

The great fall in the price of grain in 1863–1864 is once more accompanied by a diminution of the offenses against property, and an increase in those against persons.

We might conclude from this table that the remark concerning crimes against property and those against persons is not applicable, since in 1858 the number of crimes against property was very high, notwithstanding the reduced price of grain. Here is Dr. Mayr's explanation of it:

"The reason must be the following: The occasion for high spirits to be found in improved living conditions follows immediately upon any such improvement, and disappears at once when times grow worse. For this reason the fluctuation in attacks upon persons harmonizes exactly with the fluctuation in the price of food. The effects of hard times are only partially such as lead to punishable offenses; in most cases economic ruin occurs first, which leads only after an interval to attacks upon property. For this reason the effects of hard times continue to manifest themselves at a time when the hard times themselves are already practically over. This is the explanation both of the great number of attacks upon property in the year 1857, when the effects of the immediately preceding hard times were making themselves felt, as well as the gradual increase in the number of attacks against property in the years 1860–1862." [1]

[1] Pp. 160, 161.

*Number of Persons against whom
Action was Brought for Abandonment.*

YEARS.	To 100,000 OF THE POPULATION.
1858	20
1859	18
1860	17
1861	21
1862	21
1863	19
1864	18
Average	19

The fall in the price of grain in 1863–1864 was accompanied by a diminution in the number of crimes of this kind.

Violations of the Vagrant Act to 100,000 of the Population.

YEARS.	PROSTITUTES.	MENDICANTS.	WITHOUT MEANS OF EXISTENCE.	FURNISHED WITH BURGLAR'S TOOLS.	PRESENCE IN A CLOSED BUILDING WITH CRIMINAL INTENT.	PRESENCE IN PUBLIC PLACES WITH CRIMINAL INTENT.	INCORRIGIBLE VAGABONDS.	OTHER OFFENSES AGAINST THE VAGRANT ACT.	TOTAL.
1858	51.4	50.2	18.9	0.3	14.2	18.0	2.0	13.0	168
1859	37.1	39.2	15.9	0.3	12.2	12.7	1.6	12.0	131
1860	33.6	37.9	15.2	0.2	11.5	10.1	1.2	9.4	119
1861	35.4	41.3	17.7	0.4	12.5	11.7	1.2	10.7	131
1862	41.4	55.4	20.1	0.4	14.0	14.5	2.1	12.8	161
1863	39.2	52.9	18.6	0.2	13.3	15.3	2.5	15.5	157
1864	35.8	46.0	18.0	0.2	13.3	14.8	2.2	12.7	143
Average	39.7	46.1	17.7	0.3	13.0	13.9	1.8	12.3	144

The maximum number of infractions of the Vagrant Act took place in 1858, when the harmful consequences of the rise in the price of grain, which took place immediately before, were still making themselves felt. The increase in 1861–1862 was the result of the high price of wheat, and of the crisis in the cotton industry.

France.

Years.	Arrests in the Department of the Seine to 100,000 of the Population.	Average Price of Grain per Hectolitre.
1855	1222	fr. 29.37
1856	1170	30.22
1857	1169	23.83
1858	1154	16.44
1859	1008	16.69
1860	1074	20.41
1861	1128	24.25
1862	1250	23.24
1863	1133	19.78
1864	1158	17.58

Here also the influence of price makes itself felt.

The following table gives the number of persons arrested in the department of the Seine, grouped according to the alleged crimes, and compared with the price of wheat. Group I contains offenses against the public order; Group II, offenses against persons; Group III, offenses against morals; group IV, offenses against property; Group V, miscellaneous. Taking 100 as the average figure for the price of grain as well as for crimes in the economically favorable years 1858–59, the proportion is as follows:

Years.	Price of Wheat.	I.			II.		III.	IV.		V.	
		Total.	For Vagabondage.	For Mendicity.	Total.	For Assault.[1]		Total.	Simple Theft.		Total.
1855	178	128	122	148	76	72	100	102	116	106	113
1856	182	117	118	114	81	80	104	106	121	92	108
1857	144	119	127	117	82	81	98	101	114	100	108
1860	123	96	90	134	103	106	100	110	123	80	99
1861	146	95	99	105	95	96	131	116	124	103	104
1862	140	120	128	147	94	98	108	116	131	108	116
1863	119	112	119	186	90	94	92	101	114	97	105
1864	106	115	124	176	84	87	85	111	123	84	107

[1] [To avoid awkwardness of expression the term *assault* will be used for assaults other than those peculiarly against women, the original being about equivalent to our "assault and battery."—Transl.]

Here it is to be observed:

a. that the movement of mendicity and vagrancy is not in direct correlation with that of the price of grain.

b. that Group IV shows only a slight correlation with the price of grain, since there are included in it many crimes whose causes are not of an economic nature.

c. that during the last years of this period the increase of crimes against property was greater than the figures for the price of grain would lead one to suppose; a fact which is explained, according to Dr. Mayr, by the lack of work resulting from the war of secession.

The law that crimes against persons increase with the fall of prices is confirmed by these statistics.

VI.

A. CORNE.[1]

According to this author the laws regulating moral phenomena are at present hidden by thick clouds.

"We may await with confidence the dissipation of these clouds, when some great principle, about which our observations of detail will group themselves, will appear to us in a flood of light. Everything seems to indicate to me that this master principle is no other than the principle of activity. In fact, the first rudiments of social science have as yet been given us only by political economy, and its sole foundation is the affirmation of human activity. On the other hand, since giving myself up without any preconceptions to this special study of criminality I have been little by little led by a close examination of the facts, to find the general cause of crimes in the absence of this principle of activity.

"When we reflect upon this, it appears quite in the natural order of things that the development of criminality, that is to say of the spirit of destruction and dissolution, should manifest itself at the time of the weakening or disappearance of the generative principle of all production and of all society. There is here, then, if I am not deceived, more than a mere coincidence. There is a relationship which deserves to be noted so much the more since it is from the principle of activity that all physical laws also are derived today." [2]

Let us accompany the author to the domain of facts. After having given an exposition of the movement of criminality in France in

[1] " Essai sur la criminalité " (" Journal des Economistes ", 1868).
[2] P. 64.

comparison with that of other countries, he finally takes up the question of etiology. For the crowd, says the author, the criminal is a kind of monster in the midst of society, a monster predestined to crime because of his innate tendencies. Looked at in this way criminality is an individual evil. Corne, on the contrary, believes it to be a social evil. For, however much society may be developed in all respects, it is nevertheless always imperfect, since the ignorance and corruption of morals are great. The author lays stress upon two facts, namely, the corruption of morals in the upper classes, and militarism. Not only does militarism draw after it the ruin of peoples, and develop man's violent instincts, but it has still other very serious moral consequences, by forcing celibacy upon young men at the passionate age.

The author admits that there are facts which might seem to give the lie to his opinion — the influence, for example, of the price of grain upon the decrease and increase of criminality.

Years.	Average Price of a Hectolitre of Wheat.		Number of Persons Arraigned.
	fr.	c.	
1850	14	32	147,757
1851	14	48	146,368
1852	16	75	159,791
1853	22	39	171,351
1854	28	82	170,940
1855	29	32	163,748
1856	30	75	162,049
1857	24	37	161,556
1858	16	75	157,815
1859	16	75	150,948
1860	20	24	144,301
1861	24	55	151,112
1862	23	24	152,332
1863	19	78	144,072
1864	17	58	146,230

Although, according to Corne, the high price of grain may be only an accidental fact, there must yet be some importance attached to it in view of the disastrous consequences which may result from it to families that have in any case a hard time to make both ends meet. But the figures given above do not prove the influence to be very great. For prices rise sometimes although the other figures fall, and vice versa. And then the sudden increase of [detected] crime from 1849 to 1853 must be attributed to a better organization of the police.

Then the author gives the following table:

Years.	Price of a Hectolitre of Grain.		Number of Persons Convicted of Attacks upon Property (to 1000 of Population).
	fr.	c.	
1850	14	32	14.058
1851	14	48	14.678
1852	16	75	16.217
1853	22	39	16.652
1854	28	82	20.442
1855	29	32	19.223
1856	30	75	18.222
1857	24	37	17.218
1858	16	75	15.437
1859	16	75	14.655
1860	20	24	15.707
1861	24	55	16.518
1862	23	24	16.742
1863	19	78	15.309

We see that the coincidence of the figures is here naturally greater than in the first table.

"The situation of criminals may be summed up in a word: *isolation*. Most of them hardly know what a family is. They are miserable, they have no home, no fixed occupation which attaches them little by little to men and things. They are immersed in the gloom of ignorance. Aside from what affects their immediate physical wants the rest of the world is for them as if it did not exist." [1] They are alone, isolated from birth. For among juvenile prisoners there are reckoned not only many illegitimate and orphaned children, but also many who have been deserted. Out of 8006 young criminals in prison December 31st, 1864, 60% were illegitimate, orphaned, or deserted.

The author then depicts the environment in which the children of the proletariat ordinarily grow up — bad hygienic conditions, demoralizing surroundings, etc. — and points out the harmful effect of labor in factories upon the young. Corne also considers celibacy to be one of the causes of crime, since the individual has no one to care for him or be interested in his fate. Crime is developed much more in the great cities than in the country, for the reason, the author thinks, that men are much more isolated, much more left to themselves in the city than in rural neighborhoods.

[1] P. 82.

— Here I would remark that it is for economic reasons that men are prevented from marrying, and that the great criminality of cities is best explained by the marked difference in economic situation, and by the more frequent opportunities for wrong-doing found there. —

According to Corne one of the best preventives of crimes is property, since it engenders a feeling of responsibility. The property owner exerts himself to increase his wealth, and hence property has a moral influence.[1]

"Criminality comes from a lack of vitality. It is an anemia. In order to prevent it we must excite a desire for activity." It is in this that the usefulness of education appears. The man who knows how to read and write, has in his hands an instrument which can multiply his means of action indefinitely.[2]

— As regards education, it has been proved that Corne and many others have exaggerated its importance for the etiology of crime. When education extends beyond the art of reading and writing, it has a civilizing influence, and causes a diminution of violent crimes, but it does not result in a decrease of criminality in general, since the economic causes of crime remain. Education changes, indeed, the nature of criminality, but not its extent.[3] —

The author concludes by saying "The man who has a family, who has property, who is educated, who is known by his fellow citizens and has his share of influence upon them, can not be the individual whom we have seen to be criminal, because of weakness and isolation . . . he has energy, determination, and can control his passions because he is surrounded and sustained, because a thousand bonds of interest and affection attach him to society, order, and property." [4]

VII.

H. Von Valentini.

The work "Das Verbrecherthum im Preussischen Staat", published in 1869 by Prison-director von Valentini, treats especially of the results obtained by the penal system then in force in Prussia, and of the means of improving it.

[1] See Part II of this work, where I have shown that in my opinion the influence of property upon morality is much more complex than Corne has suggested, and quite different.
[2] Pp. 89, 90.
[3] See *Guerry*, "Essai de la statistique morale de la France," p. 51, and L. del Baere, "De invloed van opvoeding en onderwijs."
[4] P. 93.

Von Valentini sees in crime primarily the consequence of social conditions, at least he considers that the best means of combating it is for society to prevent the criminal tendency from manifesting itself, and make efforts to raise the moral level of the people. For, according to our author, 90% of the criminals are "purely material and entirely neglected" and ought to "undergo a spiritual regeneration." [1]

After these general observations he proceeds to more particular observations upon the criminals themselves in society. He examines statistically the proportion of criminals in the population. Obtaining different proportions for different districts of Prussia he investigates the causes. For this purpose he classifies crimes as: first, crimes from personal interest, and second, crimes from passion. Finding then that the provinces of the East give 9 % of crimes from personal interest more than the others, he thinks he has found the cause in "an existing destitution both material and intellectual, and in the arrangement of the prisons." [2]

Chapter Three, upon the "Dimensionen des Nothstandes" contains detailed tables for each province, the great cities, and the rich and poor countries. He obtains, then, the following result for the eight provinces:

PROVINCES.	PAUPERISM NUMBER OF INDIGENT PERSONS IN THE POOREST DISTRICTS.	To 100 OF THE POPULATION.	PERCENTAGE OF CRIMES AGAINST PROPERTY TO 100,000 OF THE POPULATION.	RATIO OF THE PERCENTAGE OF THE CRIMES AGAINST PROPERTY TO THAT OF PAUPERISM.
Posen	536,495	36.1	32.89	0.91 : 1
Prussia	792,948	27.6	24.69	0.89 : 1
Pomerania	314,383	22.6	20.57	0.91 : 1
Silesia	517,528	15.2	36.94	2.43 : 1
Total of Eastern group	2,161,354	23.6	115.09	4.91 : 1
Rhenish provinces . . .	397,350	12.0	5.59	0.46 : 1
Brandenburg	84,011	3.4	26.27	7.72 : 1
Westphalia	45,849	2.8	9.21	3.29 : 1
Saxony	259,901	1.3	18.33	14.10 : 1
Total of Western group	553,111	5.9	59.40	25.57 : 1

Another thing that strikes him is the influence of the small landed proprietor. "The possession of even a small piece of property in land . . . is no slight preventative of crime against property." [3] The author gives the following statistical summary.

[1] P. 10.   [2] P. 24.   [3] P. 58.

He ranks in the class of small land holdings estates of 30 acres [1] and below.   The total amounts to 10,655,460 acres to 1,716,535 estates, with an average of 6 acres.

There were in the following provinces:

Posen . . . .   57,519 of these estates, or 1 to 25 inhabitants.
Prussia   93,793   "   "   "   30   "
Pomerania   61,752   "   "   "   22   "
Silesia   230,710   "   "   "   14   "
Total of the Eastern group . .   443,774   "   "   "   18   "

Rhenish provinces   788,473   "   "   "   4   "
Brandenburg   112,532   "   "   "   22   "
Westphalia   197,383   "   "   "   8   "
Saxony   174,373   "   "   "   11   "
Total of Western group . . .   1,272,761   "   "   "   8   "

"The Rhenish provinces alone, then, have nearly twice as many as the four Eastern provinces together!   This explains the figure, 5.59, for this district given in the table above, taken in connection with the noteworthy care given to the poor.   Can the connection between the ratios given above and those of the occurrence of crimes against property be denied?" [2]

In this connection he treats of housing conditions, for which he gives the following figures.

Dwellings to 1 league:

Posen   258   Rhenish Provinces   901
Prussia   230   Brandenburg   304
Pomerania   218   Westphalia   579
Silesia   546   Saxony   529
Total   1252   Total   2313

A more detailed summary of the number of inhabitants shows us that there were:

	POSEN.	PRUSSIA.	POME-RANIA.	SILESIA.	RHENISH PROV.	BRANDEN-BURG.	WEST-PHALIA.	SAXONY.
	Inhab.	Inhab.	Inhab.	Inhab.	Inhab.	Inhab.	Inhab.	Inhab.
In each dwelling	9.8	9.8	10.1	7.9	6.9	10.0	7.2	7.5
In the cities	11.2	13.2	11.6	13.3	10.4	14.0	8.7	9.8
In the hamlets	8.8	10.6	10.0	8.1	6.1	9.6	7.0	6.8
In the villages	9.3	8.4	9.3	7.0	5.7	7.7	6.7	6.5

In these figures von Valentini sees a parallelism with those for small holdings, and draws the conclusion that this isolation of households is one of the best preventives of crimes against property.

[1] ["Arpents de Magdebourg." — TRANSL.]   [2] P. 57.

VIII.

A. Von Oettingen.[1]

In chapter IV ("Die ungeordnete Geschlechtsgemeinschaft und die Prostitution"), the author treats of the influence of the fluctuations of price in certain important articles of food upon crimes against property, against morals, against persons, and incendiary crimes (Prussia).[2]

Percentage.

Year.	Offenses against Morals.	Arson.	Offenses against Property.	Offenses against Persons.	Combined Price per Bushel of Wheat, Rye, and Potatoes in Groschen.
1854	2.26	0.43	88.41	8.90	218.1
1855	2.57	0.46	88.93	8.04	252.3
1856	2.65	0.43	87.60	9.32	203.3
1857	4.14	0.53	81.52	13.81	156.3
1858	4.45	0.60	77.92	17.03	149.3
1859	4.68	0.52	78.17	16.63	150.6
Average . .	3.34	0.48	84.42	11.76	188.2

This table shows then : first, that crimes against property diminish as prices fall; second, that under these same conditions crimes against morals and against persons increase.

— We must be on our guard, however, against drawing false conclusions from this second fact. The relationship in question is observed only during a certain period and in certain countries, and is not to be regarded as a law of nature, *i.e.*, it must not be understood that an improvement in economic conditions invariably causes an increase in sexual and violent crimes. If this were the case, the well-to-do classes, who are always in a position to provide for all their needs, would furnish most of the criminals of this description. The facts show just the contrary to occur everywhere. (See Part Two, where I treat this subject fully.) —

In the chapter, "Die social ethische Lebensbethätigung in der bürgerlichaen Rechtsphäre," the author treats our subject more fully. Reasoning from different data taken from other authors, he points out the connection between economic conditions on the one hand and vagabondage and mendicity on the other. Having shown a con-

[1] "Die Moralstatistik in ihrer Bedeutung für eine Socialethik."
[2] P. 239.

siderable increase in these offenses in the revolutionary period of
1848, he attributes this increase to the lack of social discipline, for
the price of provisions was then low.   We pass all this part of von
Oettingen's book in silence, his data being taken for the most part
from other authors.   We would merely point out his error in ranking
the year 1848 among those economically favorable because of the fall
in the price of food.   As a matter of fact there was a terrible economic
crisis in Europe at the time.

We take the following data from the section entitled "Getreide-
preis und Criminalität."

To 100 complaints there were (in Prussia) :

| YEARS. | CRIMES AGAINST | | PRICE OF RYE PER BUSHEL. |
	Property.	Persons.	
	%	%	Sgr. Pf.
1862	44.3	15.8	63.10
1863	41.6	17.0	54.3
1864	41.6	18.4	45.6
1865	38.5	17.7	49.11
1866	44.4	14.5	58.5
1867	50.2	13.1	79.0
1868	52.3	13.8	78.8
1869	45.7	14.3	64.7

We find here this rule, that a rise in the price of food is accompanied
by an increase in the crimes against property and a decrease in crimes
against persons, and vice versa.   This table also shows that, if a very
pronounced rise in prices has caused a great increase in criminality,
the later fall in prices does not make itself felt in the number of crimes
until some time after its commencement.   (See 1867–1868.)

This phenomenon is very distinctly shown by the following table :

YEARS.	CASES TRIED.	TOTAL PRICE OF A BUSHEL OF WHEAT, OF RYE, AND OF POTATOES IN GROSCHEN.
1854	644,483	221.6
1855	686,207	241.4
1856	766,628	228.4
1857	705,291	161.1

It was only in 1857, then, that the fall in prices, beginning in 1856,
commenced to produce its effect.

In conclusion we call attention to the following tables :

Saxony.

YEARS.	CRIMES AGAINST		PRICE OF WHEAT, OF RYE, AND OF POTATOES PER BUSHEL.
	Property.	Persons.	
1860	37.25	35.04	Gr. 170
1861	40.28	33.10	181
1862	38.78	34.65	173
1863	36.56	35.09	147

Bavaria.

YEARS.	OFFENSES AGAINST		PRICE OF RYE.
	Property.	Persons.	
1862/63	38.38	33.16	Fl. Kr. 14, 48
1863/64	36.16	37.72	12, 16
1864/65	36.55	39.79	11, 53
1865/66	33.42	41.18	10, ʻ57

Here is another proof of the rule, then, that crimes against property decrease and those against persons increase as prices fall.

IX.

H. STURSBERG.

In the first part of a brochure edited in 1878 and entitled, "Die Zunahme der Vergehen und Verbrechen und ihre Ursache," the author attempts, with the aid of statistics, to discover in what measure criminality increased or decreased in Germany during the years 1871–1877. As a result of these researches he finds a considerable increase in all Germany.[1]

As regards the causes of this increase, Stursberg, though not rejecting entirely the opinion of Quetelet that society prepares the crime and that the criminal is only the instrument that executes it, is nevertheless of the opinion that it is very necessary to take into account the personal factor, *i.e.* the presence or absence of religious and moral sentiments.

[1] On p. 442 of his "Moralstatistik," *von Oettingen* criticises Stursberg for basing his comparison upon the year 1871 in which the figures were very low as a consequence of the war, and for not having taken into account that in the year 1876 the new penal code was put into effect.

There are those, says the author, who seek the cause in the consequences of the war against France. Although believing also that the war has had unfavorable effects upon criminality, it is impossible, in his opinion that this war should be the cause of the increase of criminality, since crime decreased after the wars of 1864 and 1866. He considers that one of the causes is the great mildness of the penalties imposed by the new penal code of the empire. But according to him, this is not important, for since 1871 there has been rather a diminution than an increase of recidivism. Nor can bad economic conditions be the cause, says Stursberg; for criminality had already begun to increase before the bad years, and it is not theft that has increased the most. Nevertheless, Stursberg recognizes that prolonged poverty weakens the moral sentiments, which shows that criminality and poverty are closely connected.

But there are, in his opinion, more serious causes. There follows a description of the impetus taken by industry in Germany during the early seventies, a description not easily surpassed in pointlessness, and in the naïve ignorance that it evinces. Without comprehending the significance of the really important events that are happening about him, the author fulminates against certain consequences of modern capitalism.

— This appears to him as the consequence of a suddenly awakened desire for riches. But why should this desire arise at this time? The author does not tell us. But notwithstanding this he has unquestionably discovered here one of the principal causes, since the prodigious increase of industry, shortly followed by the inevitable crisis, has infallibly caused an increase in criminality. Since Stursberg treats this question rather as a moralist than as a man of science, we have no interest in spending longer time upon it. —

In the first few pages of his brochure Stursberg speaks of the disastrous consequences of alcoholism, after the enactment of the law of 1869, which increased the number of spirit shops. Armed with quotations without number he combats in turn the cafés-chantants, immoral literature, etc., etc.; after which he introduces all at once the matter of professional liberty. He speaks of the "influence, impossible to estimate, which honest and pious masters exercised for centuries upon the journeymen and apprentices, who were like members of the family." "The freedom of the trades came in and loosed the bonds of piety and discipline which had retained the journeyman and apprentices in the home of their master."

— As far as we can see, the ideas of the author are rather those of a writer of the Middle Ages, than of a contemporary of modern capitalism. It cannot be denied that there is truth at the bottom of this reasoning. For it is incontestable that in the time of the guilds the position of the journeymen was in general more favorable than that of the proletariat today. But it does not follow that the religion of the master was the cause of this. And a demonstration in which professional liberty is represented as being in fact a legislative error, and not the logical and inevitable consequence of the birth of modern capitalism, is so unscientific that it has no place in an investigation into the causes of the increase of criminality. —

Then he preaches more particularly against the greater and greater extension of the study of the natural sciences, against social democracy, the lack of respect for constituted authorities, etc., etc., without, however, alleging the slightest proof of the connection of all this with the increase of crime. But at the end he says, "the fundamental cause of the increase of crime is the rapid growth of irreligion, and the weakening of Christian sentiment in church and school." [1]

X.

L. Fuld.

Before entering upon his special investigation, the author of "Der Einflusz der Lebensmittelpreise auf die Bewegung der strafbaren Handlungen" makes the following observation: Everywhere it is noted that assaults upon morals with acts of violence increase when the price of provisions falls. Adhering to the opinion of von Oettingen that "as the consequence of an increase of prosperity, the tendency to crime shows itself more by crimes against morals than by those against property", Fuld also mentions the opinion of Valentini, that "in this case the people become audacious and commit these crimes more easily."

Here are other salient facts; that the number of young criminals increases, and that the city produces more criminals than the country, although the sexual morality especially is far from ideal in the country. Finally in speaking of the influence of profession, Fuld mentions that the increase in the number of criminals which accompanies a rise in prices is greater for the first offenders than for recidivists. The following table which he gives to prove this point, however, plainly fails to do so:

[1] P. 58.

England.

Years.	Good Character Hitherto.	Character Unknown.	Price of Wheat.	
			Sh.	d.
1858	153,576	138,388	43	11
1859	153,369	150,084	43	8
1860	137,574	144,485	52	9
1864	167,038	165,808	40	2

The author explains that the crimes against property are one of the consequences of the struggle for existence, a fact which accounts in part for the high figures for criminality in the great cities, where competition is most intense.   The author treats of theft, and begins by saying that the connection between the price of provisions and theft is very close.

France.

Years.	Thefts.	Price of Cereals.
		fr.
1856	18,222	16.75
1857	17,218	"
1858	15,537	"
1859	14,755	"
1860	15,707	20.24

During the following years the prices fell.   Nevertheless the number of thefts increased.   According to Fuld we can draw the conclusion that the influence of price is only relative! — This table proves little. For, while in 1856 criminality attained its highest point, prices were lower than in 1860; and, while the figures for theft diminished greatly, prices remained constant. —

England.

Years.	Thefts.		Price of Cereals.	
	With Violence.	Without Violence.		
			Sh.	d.
1857	6471	43,397	42	10
1858	5723	45,618	43	11
1859	4433	41,370	43	8
1860	4065	41,151	52	9
1861	5062	40,242	55	4
1862	5746	40,191	55	5
1863	5433	39,801	44	9
1864	5022	39,481	40	2
1865	5160	40,383	41	10
1866	5088	39,731	43	10
1867	6355	46,502	49	10

Here there is some agreement between the number of thefts and prices. But it is not as great as Fuld would make out. For example, notwithstanding the sudden rise on prices in 1860, criminality diminished, while the year following there was a still further fall in the thefts without violence.

Prussia.

YEARS.	THEFTS OF WOOD.	PRICE OF RYE.
		Sgr. Pf.
1862	387,000	63.10
1863	354,276	54.3
1864	366,667	45.6
1865	426,336	49.11
1866	425,551	58.5
1867	412,165	79.0
1868	419,158	78.8
1869	406,662	64.7
1870	389,746	62.3
1871	439,288	66.0
1872	401,280	82.0
1873	337,112	93.0
1874	356,859	108.0

We can indeed find here some agreement between the two columns, but that is all that can be said.

Then the author says that differences in price are not as great as formerly, on account of the development of international commerce. He gives a table of comparative prices from 1870 to 1879 which shows that five staples show no consistent movement in price. But during the same period theft was continually on the increase. The number of male delinquents from 18 to 50 alone varies with prices; the figures for delinquents between 50 and 60 follow the course of prices but slightly. Other economic crimes show little conformity.

The final conclusion of Fuld upon crimes against property is: "The influence of the price of provisions upon these offenses is quite important." Although not giving my opinion upon the correctness of this judgment at this time, I may say that the statistics furnished by Fuld give almost no proof of it.

The following part treats of crimes against life. It is evident that we are not concerned with crimes of passion. The only ones that enter into consideration are those that have an economic object. But since criminal statistics do not make this distinction, the results of the author's investigation can be but small. He is indeed convinced that the influence of the price of provisions is very perceptible, but he does not prove it. The same may be said with regard to sexual crimes.

XI.

B. WEISZ.[1]

"The wants that man must satisfy are numerous, but there is none which makes itself felt so much as hunger. If he cannot satisfy his wants in a lawful fashion, necessity drives him to other means."

To prove what he says Dr. Weisz produces the following table:

France.

YEARS.	ACCUSATIONS OF CRIME.	PRICE OF WHEAT.
1845	5054	19.75
1846	5077	24.05
1847	5857	29.01
1848	4632	16.65
1849	4910	15.37
1850	5320	14.32
1851	5287	14.48
1852	5340	17.23
1853	5440	22.39
1854	5525	28.82
1855	4798	29.32
1856	4535	30.75
1857	4399	24.37
1858	4302	16.75
1859	3918	16.74
1860	3621	20.24
1861	3842	24.55
1862	3906	23.24
1863	3614	19.78
1864	3447	17.58

With but seven exceptions criminality here follows prices. When the figures for crimes against property are substituted for those for general criminality in the table, the agreement becomes greater:

[1] "Ueber einige wirthschaftliche und moralische Wirkungen hoher Getreidepreise."

Years.	Crimes against Property.	Price of Wheat.
1847	4537	29.01
1848	3020	16.65
1849	2895	15.37
1850	3174	14.32
1851	3126	14.48
1852	3327	17.23
1853	3519	22.39
1854	3761	28.82
1855	3133	29.32
1856	2766	30.75
1857	2689	24.37
1858	2315	16.75
1859	2019	16.74
1861	2146	24.55
1862	2144	23.24
1863	1941	19.78
1864	1744	17.58

Belgium.

Years.	Price of Wheat.	General Criminality.	Offenses against Property.
1841	20.02	444	332
1842	22.17	468	361
1843	19.41	434	346
1844	17.75	455	336
1845	20.06	387	275
1846	24.53	616	498
1847	25.20	579	496
1848	17.37	529	427
1849	17.15	451	338
1850	16.15	270	168
1851	16.71	247	132
1852	20.16	290	140
1853	25.13	264	191
1854	31.48	336	238
1855	32.92	299	212
1856	30.73	332	268
1857	22.96	309	197
1858	23.55	278	167
1859	24.00	314	187
1860	31.15	254	161

It is to be noted here that in the years 1850–1860 the penal law was changed. The correlation is not constant but appears in many cases. The years of the crisis, 1846–1847, are especially interesting.

YEARS.	INFANTICIDE.	YEARS.	INFANTICIDE.
1845	5	1853	13
1846	17	1854	12
1852	7	1855	14

England.

YEARS.	PRICE OF WHEAT.	NUMBER OF CRIMINAL OFFENDERS.
1816	78.6	9,091
1817	96.11	13,932
1846	54.8	20,072
1847	69.9	22,451
1852	40.9	24,443
1853	53.3	27,187
1854	72.5	27,760
1855	74.8	31,309
1856	69.2	29,591
1857	56.4	26,542
1858	44.2	24,303

— The value of Dr. Weisz's information would be greater if he had given us the relation of the figures for criminality to those for population. —

XII.

W. STARKE.[1]

The first chapter that interests us is Chapter V ("Die Umgestaltung des Volkslebens, ihre Einwirkung auf die Kriminalität," etc.) Sec. 3 ("die Sorge für die nothwendigsten Lebensbedürfnisse und die Lebensmittelpreise").

Just as the influence of the price of food makes itself felt in the number of marriages and births, it is also visible in the figures for criminality. So, when the temperature of the winter is very low (*e.g.* 1855, '56, '65, and '71), since men have greater wants than ordinary, criminality rises. Thefts of wood increase during these years,

---

[1] "Verbrechen und Verbrecher in Preussen 1854–1878." This book (especially the statistical material) has been severely criticised by *Mittelstadt* ("Zeitschrift für die ges. Strafrechtswissenschaft", 1884), *Aschrott* ("Jahrbuch für Gesetzgebung etc." *von Schmoller*, 1884), and *Illing* ("Zeitschrift des Königlich Preussischen statistischen Bureaus", 1885). *Körner* has refuted their views ("Jahrbücher für d. Nat. Oek. u. Stat. Neue Folge", Vol. XIII).

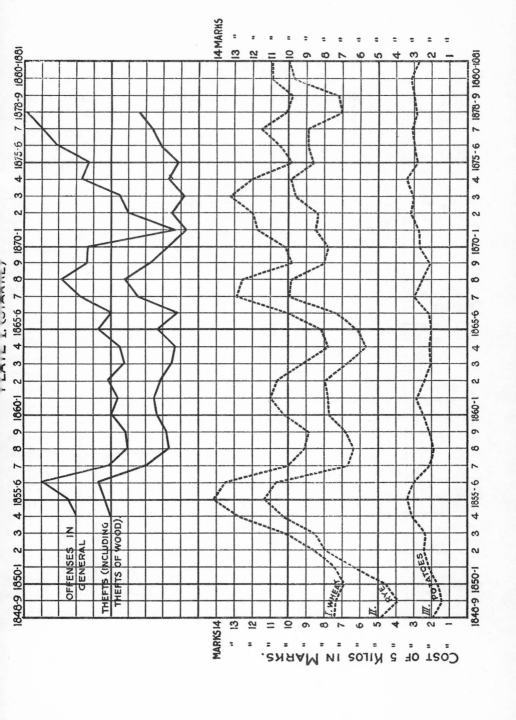

OFFENSES IN GENERAL

THEFTS (INCLUDING THEFTS OF WOOD).

I. WHEAT

II. RYE

III. POTATOES

MARKS 14

COST OF 5 KILOS IN MARKS.

14 MARKS

Cost of 5 Kilos in Marks.

PLATE II. (STARKE)

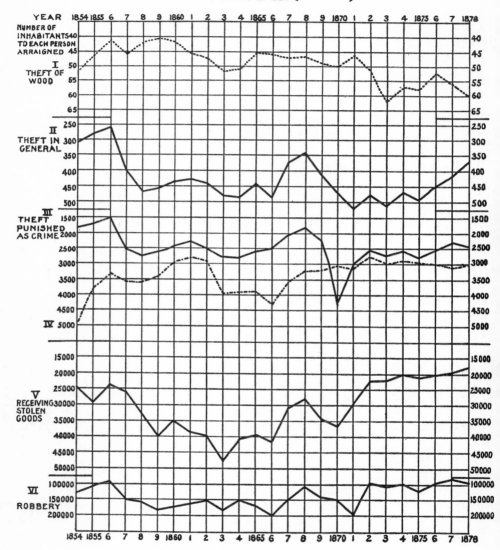

for example. But it is in only one part of the year that the cold makes itself felt, while the high price of food lasts the whole year. Hence the latter has much more influence on criminality.

In the first of the plates which the author gives (see Plates I–VI), the effect of the rise in prices is distinctly seen in the period 1849–1855. The fall that follows is also accompanied by a diminution in the number of crimes. When, at the close of 1858, the price of rye and potatoes begins to rise again, criminality also increases, though not so much. We do not see this agreement during the years 1861–1865. While prices rise in 1866, criminality declines as a consequence of the war with Austria, and of economic events.

The years 1870–1871, during which prices rose, show a fall in the figures for crime, a second exception to the rule therefore, since 1866. At the close of 1875 criminality increased greatly, although prices rose but little, and when, in 1877, prices begin to come down, the curve for criminality goes on rising. As for the years 1870–1871, the explanation is to be found in the war, which strengthened the feeling of solidarity (as in a less degree in 1866). Further, the development of manufacturing had already begun by the end of the war, and the war itself withdrew from ordinary life many persons who, without it, might have committed crime. The author mentions also the great diminution of crime in France during these years.

We note, however, that the French statisticians (Lafargue, for example) consider these years as of little importance in the study of criminality, since the police and the courts were then much less active than at ordinary times. The same causes may be supposed to have been active in Prussia also, though in a less degree than in France.

At the close of the middle of this century manufacturing was but slightly developed in Prussia. But after the war its development assumed gigantic proportions. Wealth increased, but was not evenly distributed, as the following table from the income tax returns shows :

	PERSONS.	PERCENTAGE.
I. Having an income of 1000 thalers . . .	139,556	1.2
II. " " " " 400–1000 " . . .	643,628	5.6
III. " " " " 140–400 " . . .	4,207,163	36.4
Not liable to the income tax		
IV. (Average income, 120 Th.)	6,582,066	56.8
Total	11,572,413	100

Total number of those having an income of 400 thalers or under, 93.2 %.

Education (Men and Boys over 10).

CLASSES.	PERSONS.	PERCENTAGE.
I. Higher education	93,000	1.023
II. Intermediate education	193,000	2.122
III. Elementary education	7,885,423	86.703
IV. Illiterate	923,274	10.152
Total	9,094,757	100.00

There were 96% of the population, then, with no education or only an elementary one.

Little by little manufacturing so forged ahead of agriculture that the necessary food was no longer produced in the country. From this time dates the importation of large quantities of grain.

The year 1873 saw the beginning of the terrible reaction that made itself felt in all strata of the population. The number of marriages diminished as well as the number of births, and criminality increased. (See Plate I.)

At first the curves for theft and criminality in general run parallel in their rising and falling. But with 1854 they begin to diverge, and this divergence is especially plain from 1871 on. Consequently something else must have had an influence upon criminality. And this other thing, according to Starke, is the modification of the political position of the people. According to him the participation of the mass of the people in politics, made possible by the right of suffrage, has been one of the causes of the increase of the number of crimes against the authority of the state, as the socialistic movement has been a second cause.[1]

— Without doubt the participation of all classes in the political life will lead to crimes, especially when in the strife of classes the propertied class makes use of violent means. The assertion that the socialistic movement causes many crimes has only a semblance of truth. It is rather because of the manner in which the socialists are treated, than because of their doctrine that they are driven to acts of

---

[1] It is not possible for me to treat this question at length here. The reader is referred to my studies: "Misdaad en socialisme. Te gelijk eene bijdrage tot de studie der criminaliteit in Nederland" ("Nieuwe Tijd", XVI), and "Verbrechen und Sozialismus. Zugleich ein Beitrag zum Studium der Kriminalität in Deutschland" ("Neue Zeit", XXX, 2), where I have proved in a decisive manner, as it seems to me, that the socialistic movement is not productive of crime, but the contrary.

PLATE III (STARKE)

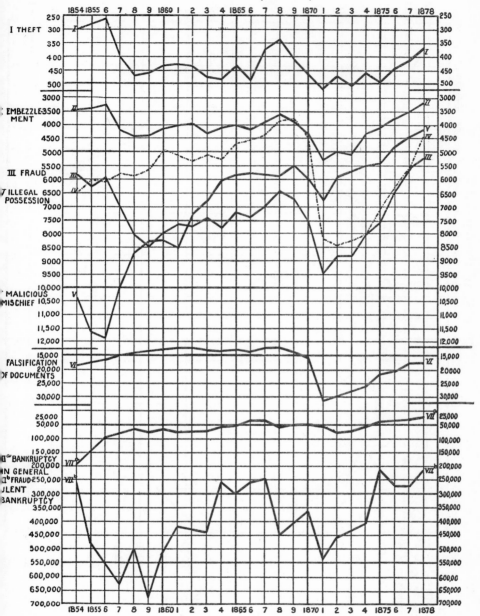

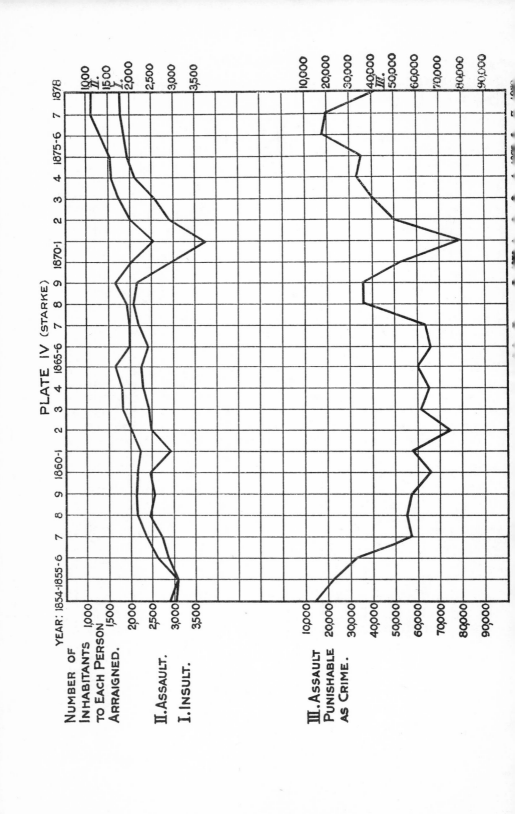

PLATE IV (STARKE)

violence. For the socialists wish to attain their end by pacific and legal, political and economic means, and it is only when they are opposed by force that they are incited to the use of violent means. —

Starke finally draws the following conclusion as to the causes in the movement in criminality: "Hardly ever in the short space of a generation have so many mighty factors of different kinds influenced the life of our people, as in the years from 1848 to 1878; a complete metamorphosis of the courts and the police; so extraordinary an increase in the numbers and density of the population that the soil could no longer produce enough to feed such numbers; connected with this a great development of manufacturing with repeated crises, brought on by the high price of the necessaries of life, and by epidemics; the development of intercourse and commerce world-wide in extent; bloody wars, which, through the system of universal military service, disturb the whole population of every class; a politico-economic crisis so severe that there has been none like it hitherto; and in addition to and at the same time with all these factors, the entrance of the people into the exercise of political rights; and finally, dependent upon these, a deep-seated socialistic agitation.

"All these factors have their part in the moulding of the life of the people in good as well as bad directions and accordingly influence the movement of criminality. In the first rank stand the effects upon the physical life of the lack of warmth and nourishment. The great significance of the coldness of the winter upon the increase and decrease of the theft of wood has been noted. Much greater is the effect of the anxiety about daily bread, which finds expression in the movement of the price of provisions. . . . Parallel with the curve of food-prices runs that of thefts and the movement of the latter is again impressed upon the curve of crimes and misdemeanors in general." [1] Let us consider now some of the important kinds of crime.

Offenses and contraventions against property.

"It is egoism which chiefly governs man, shows itself positively in the desire to acquire as much as possible, and negatively in the desire to lose as little as possible, and which reduces activity to insatiability, and economy to avarice." [2] Now, cupidity leads to most of the crimes against property, while hatred, vengeance, etc. drive men to malicious mischief.

Examining now Plates II and III, the influence of the years of high prices (1856 and 1867), of the years of war (1866 and 1870–1871), and

[1] P. 88.   [2] P. 94.

of the years of crisis shows itself very plainly.   It is to be noted that the curve of crimes of "malicious mischief" takes a course totally different from that of crimes against property committed from other motives.   Plate III shows the great influence of economic events upon fraudulent bankruptcies (1857 and 1873 having been years of crisis).

Offenses against persons.

We see that the curves of these crimes shown upon Plates IV and V have a course quite different from that of the curves of the crimes against property.   It is only in 1870 that both fall together.   Starke deduces the rule, confirmed by many statisticians, that an improvement in economic conditions is accompanied by an increase in assaults, etc., and vice versa.   The facts confirm this rule during the first part of the period that Starke has studied, but not later.   (Compare Plates I and IV.)

In studying the curve of infanticide we note that it reaches the highest point in the bad years, 1857, 1863, 1866, 1867 (Eastern Prussia), and 1868.   In 1857 the first commercial crisis took place, and in 1864 and 1866 the cholera raged and war was declared; a number of fathers of illegitimate children died, leaving the mothers unable to support the children.

A comparison between the curve of crimes of arson, with those of the crimes against property in Plate III, committed with the same end, shows a great resemblance; the increase in this crime also shows itself in bad years.

XIII.

RETTICH.[1]

The part of this author's work dealing with crimes and misdemeanors against property contains some observations which are of importance for our subject.

I cannot show the views of the author better than by quoting the following: "That the number of offenses against property must be related to the prevailing economic conditions, seems to need no proof.   For the man who lives in the possession of abundance, the motive for appropriating the property of others is lacking, even though the inclination to commit all possible crimes slumbers within him.   It is a favorite expression of the Social-democrats, that the abolition of private property would cause all crimes against property to disappear.   They forget, while maintaining this, the probability

---

[1] "Die Würtembergische Kriminalität."

PLATF V. (STARKE)

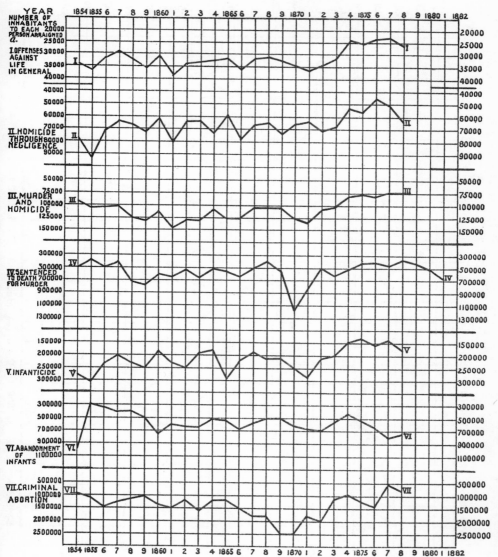

a Under IV the figures are for those *sentenced*.

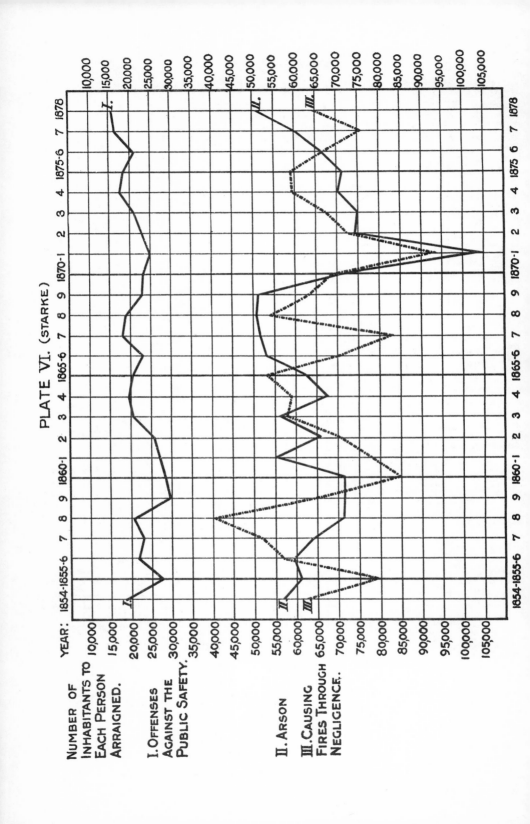

PLATE VI. (STARKE)

NUMBER OF
INHABITANTS TO
EACH PERSON
ARRAIGNED.

I. OFFENSES
AGAINST THE
PUBLIC SAFETY.

II. ARSON

III. CAUSING
FIRES THROUGH
NEGLIGENCE.

YEAR: 1854-1855-6 7 8 9 1860-1 2 3 4 1865-6 7 8 9 1870-1 2 3 4 1875-6 7 1878

that just as earlier private individuals were robbed, so under the new order the state would be, by people of the same kind — those who today, without living in want, still are not content with their lawful gains, and reach out after unlawful ones. The apostles of state-ownership, in order to make their contention credible, must at least offer proof that the offenses against property which are now punished, are *entirely* due to hunger and need on the part of those convicted. They cannot however, offer such proof. This is not because the government statistics . . . give no data with regard to the economic condition of the convicts, but because, as a matter of fact, the worst offenses against property are not committed by the hungry. The merchant who goes into a fraudulent bankruptcy, the banker who embezzles deposits, the worldling who forges drafts, have all taken the step into crime from a life, if not of abundance, at least of a competence. People of this kind will not disappear from the socialistic state. In their case the lack is not in the social system, but in their individual make-up." [1]

— We have given this quotation simply to furnish a typical example of the incorrect way in which many authors represent the socialistic opinion with regard to the genesis of crime. What nonsense, to assert that according to the theory of socialism all crimes against property find their causes in hunger and misery! See the second part of this work, where the reader will find that socialists hold an entirely different opinion, and that they have facts to prove the truth of their theories. —

With regard to the relation between the movement of the price of certain important cereals and a great part of the crime against property, the author gives the following table:

YEARS.	AVERAGE PRICE PER 200 KILOGR. IN MARKS.			ARRESTS FOR THEFT TO 10,000 PERSONS.
	Wheat.	Grain.	Rye.	
1882	22.57	23.63	18.81	26.0
1883	19.04	19.29	16.30	25.2
1884	18.44	18.75	17.17	22.7
1885	17.92	18.11	16.17	21.5
1886	17.68	17.94	14.69	20.7
1887	18.88	18.95	15.26	20.5
1888	20.23	20.64	16.19	20.3
1889	20.03	20.52	16.50	21.4
1890	21.43	21.71	17.97	21.2
1891	22.48	22.92	19.26	19.3

[1] P. 360.

There is at first a certain correlation between the figures in the different columns, but there is none in the later years. It is very probable that the diminution in crimes against property is due, during these years, to a combination of favorable economic circumstances at that time.

XIV.

A. MEYER.

The second section of the second chapter of the work, "Die Verbrechen in ihrem Zusammenhang mit dem wirthschaftlichen und sozialen Verhältnissen im Kanton Zürich",[1] treats of the influence of the price of provisions and crop-returns (see Plate I).

The author first calls attention to the years 1853–1861. We see that the curves of the price of cereals and of offenses against property are then quite closely parallel. However, the curve of the price of cereals was lowest in 1858, and that of offenses in 1859. It is a well-known fact that economic phenomena make their influence upon criminality felt only after some time. Further, it is only by the following year that a part of the offenses are counted in the criminal statistics. Crimes against persons increase when prices fall, and vice versa. The less the price of food is influenced by bad industrial conditions, the more its influence upon criminality will strike the eye.

The section following is entitled: "Schuldbetreibungs- und Konkurs-statistik als Ausdruck der wirtschaftlichen Lage der Bevölkerung und Kriminalität." When we examine Plate II for the period 1832–1852, we see that the curves of bankruptcy and of offenses against property are parallel. From Plate III (1852–1892) we note that offenses against property are influenced by failures as well as by the price of grain. At times the two forces act in the same direction and reënforce one another, and at times their direction is opposite, and they more or less neutralize each other. It must be remarked that in 1867 an epidemic of cholera raged in the canton, and that the relief fund which was then given out kept the figure for criminality below what the economic situation would have produced.

Dr. Meyer's conclusion from what has been said is this: "The result of the researches proves that in the course of years the number of crimes against property is strictly bound up with material conditions; the greater the difficulty of getting a living, the more numerous

---

[1] See upon this book the criticism of Professor *F. Tönnies* in "Archiv für soziale Gesetzgebung und Statistik", 1896.

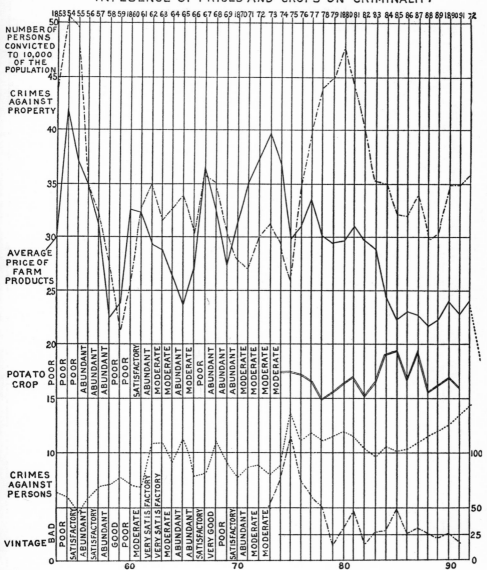

PLATE I (MEYER)

INFLUENCE OF PRICES AND CROPS ON CRIMINALITY

PLATE II (MEYER)

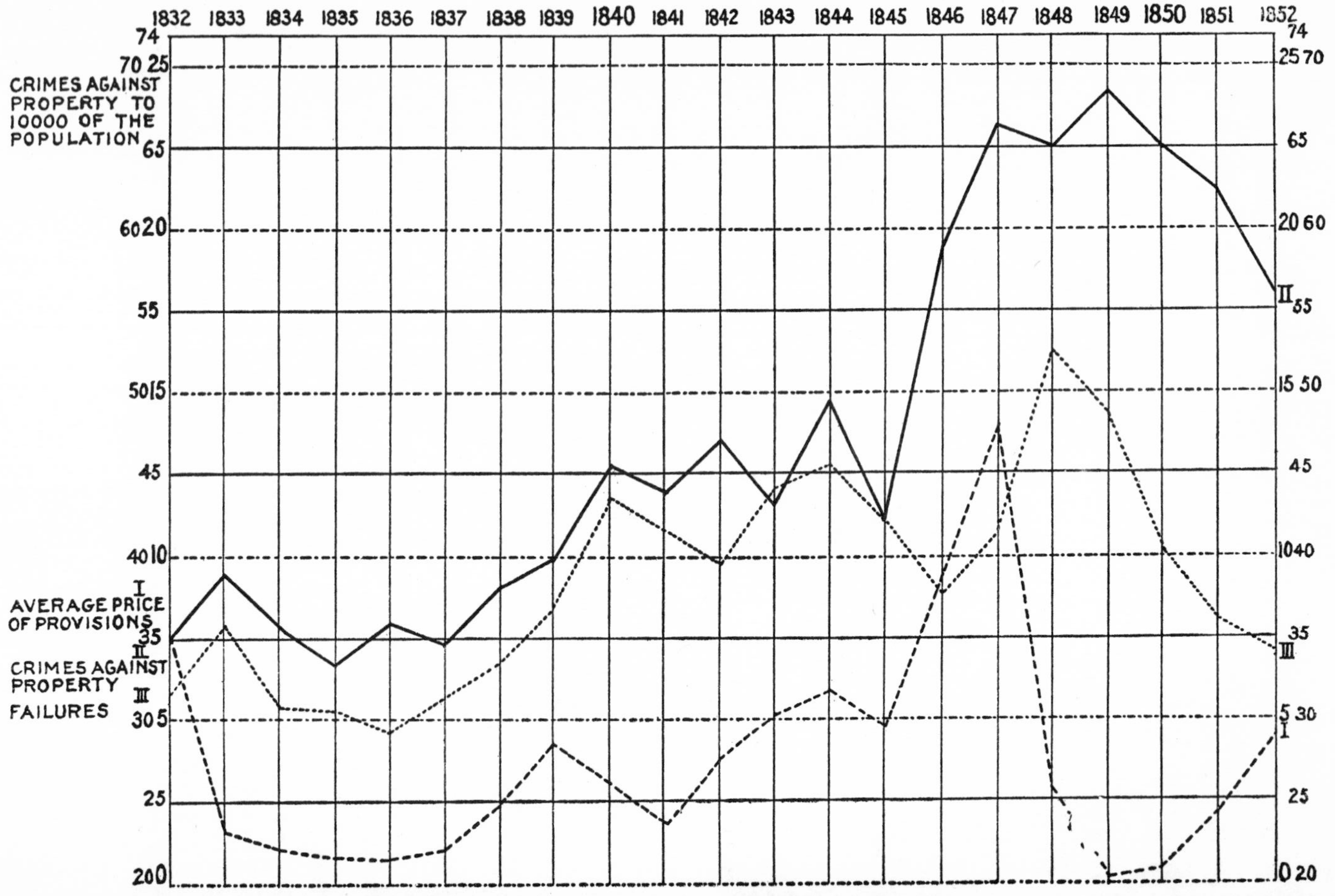

the crimes against property. The statistics of crimes against property show at the same time the degrees of the prosperity of the country, as the statistics of failures, for example, prove." [1]

Plate IV gives a comparison of crimes against persons with economic conditions, and shows that these crimes increase when economic conditions improve, and that vintages more or less abundant are not without importance.

On page 44, the author commences his examination of the criminality in the different districts of the canton of Zürich, investigating its distribution, both as to where the crimes are committed, and where the criminals come from.

According to the first distribution the districts of Zürich, of Dielsdorf, and of Horgan have the highest figures; those of Hinweill, of Meilen, and of Pfäffikon the lowest. According to the second distribution it is again the districts of Dielsdorf and of Horgan that have the highest figures, while Hinweill, Meilen, and Pfäffikon take the last place here also. Zürich and Winterthür, which in the first distribution held the first place, in the second have the eighth and tenth. We see from this that, however great the number of crimes the last two districts produce, the authors of the crimes are outsiders.

Dr. Meyer then compares the districts of Hinweill and Pfäffikon, which have the lowest figures, with the districts of Horgen and Dielsdorf, which have the highest. He concludes that the two former districts are the poorest, and the two latter the most well-to-do, a conclusion which he bases upon different facts, among others upon the appropriations which the public charities of the different districts receive from the state. And according to him it follows that in this case the connection between criminality and economic conditions is not direct.

The author then explains the indirect connection as follows: "In Hinweill as in Pfäffikon, there exists a general impoverishment, caused by the unfavorable state of the soil and of the population, heavy mortgages, bad cultivation by the small farmers, the diminution of industry, the lack of education, etc, — an impoverishment that threatens the ruin of entire communities." [2] Then, an increase of crime is not to be feared in countries where poverty strikes the whole population, for the thief has nothing to steal. Since in the well-to-do districts the differences of possessions are more marked, the opportunity for wrong-doing is greater, and it is this which makes criminality greater also.

[1] P. 41.   [2] P. 57.

The conclusion of Dr. Meyer upon what has gone before is this: "Criminality is an historical product, and economic conditions are only one, though a significant, factor. Under like economic conditions . . . the number of crimes against property need not necessarily be like. It depends upon how the population has accommodated itself to the economic situation, whether it makes higher or lower demands upon life, what views it holds as to the end of human existence, etc." [1]

As to the occupations of those convicted the data of Dr. Meyer are incomplete. The conclusion drawn from them is that the agricultural population is less criminal than the industrial proletariat. Here is the reason, according to Dr. Meyer: "An explanation of this phenomena that agrees fully with our investigations has already been given by von Valentini when he says : 'Small holdings make direct and exhausting demands upon the labor of the whole family, while, on the other hand, they provide sufficiently for the immediate and indispensable needs of the household, so that idleness as well as anxiety about sustenance are generally both excluded from such a family.'" [2]

"It is otherwise in manufacturing. The greater independence of the industrial worker, his receiving his wages in money exclusively, the dependence of industry upon the conjunctures of the market, give instead of the stability of existence, enjoyed by agriculture, a life fluctuating and insecure. Abundance as well as want visits industrial workers, and each of the two begets in him a corresponding kind of crime." [3]

— The expression "abundance" as describing the state in which the proletariat live, is a strange one. A man who is not indigent and has a few sous does not on that account live in abundance. The author adds a quotation from Garofalo to point out how the proletariat spend a great part of their "abundance" in the wine-shops. The reader is, however, referred to Part II of this work, where I have pointed out the social and economic causes of alcoholism. —

Dr. Meyer concludes his work by saying that he does not believe that an improvement of economic conditions will inevitably lead to an increase of crimes against persons, but that the causes of them are rather to be found in frivolity, grossness, and dissipation consequent upon an improvement of conditions.

But — youth does not possess wisdom! It is only by advancing

[1] P. 61.   [2] P. 66.   [3] P. 67.

PLATE III. (MEYER)

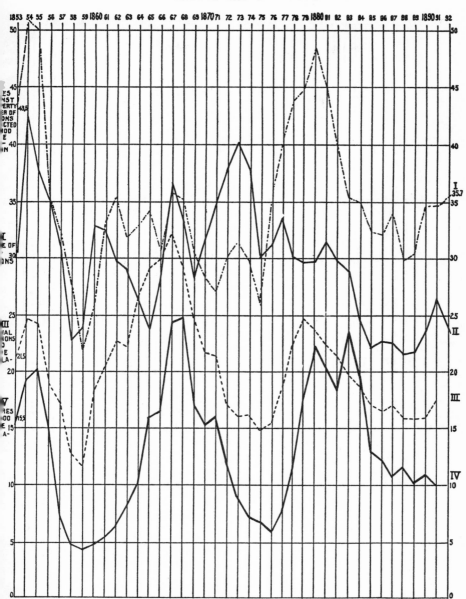

PLATE IV. (MEYER)

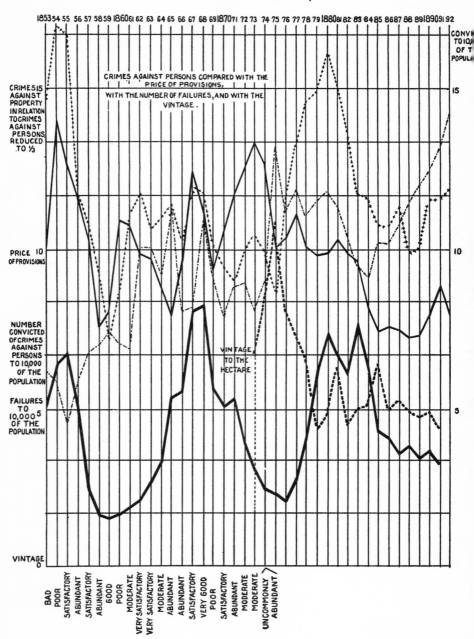

1853 54 55 56 57 58 59 1860 61 62 63 64 65 66 67 68 69 1870 71 72 73 74 75 76 77 78 79 1880 81 82 83 84 85 86 87 88 89 1890 91 92

CONV—
TO 10,0—
OF T—
POPUL—

CRIMES AGAINST PERSONS COMPARED WITH THE
PRICE OF PROVISIONS,
WITH THE NUMBER OF FAILURES, AND WITH THE
VINTAGE.

CRIMES 15
AGAINST
PROPERTY
IN RELATION
TO CRIMES
AGAINST
PERSONS
REDUCED
TO ⅓

15

PRICE 10
OF PROVISIONS

10

NUMBER
CONVICTED
OF CRIMES
AGAINST
PERSONS
TO 10,000
OF THE
POPULATION

VINTAGE
TO THE
HECTARE

FAILURES
TO
10,000 5
OF THE
POPULATION

5

VINTAGE
0

BAD
POOR
SATISFACTORY
ABUNDANT
SATISFACTORY
ABUNDANT
GOOD
POOR
MODERATE
VERY SATISFACTORY
VERY SATISFACTORY
MODERATE
ABUNDANT
ABUNDANT
SATISFACTORY
VERY GOOD
POOR
SATISFACTORY
ABUNDANT
MODERATE
MODERATE
UNCOMMONLY ⟩
ABUNDANT ⟩

in age that rash, rough youth becomes wise and gentle. Now, in the same way society will lose, one by one, the faults of its youth!

XV.

M. Tugan-Baranowsky.

"Die sozialen Wirkungen der Handelskrisen in England ",[1] by this author, aims to prove that the commercial crises in England in the years 1823–1850 had a much more violent character than those of the years 1871–1896, which occurred less suddenly, and made themselves felt for a long time afterwards. Since criminality is one of the social phenomena pointed out as caused by these crises, it is worth while giving a résumé of the work in question.

Dr. Tugan-Baranowsky has examined the influence that commercial crises have exercised, first, upon the agricultural counties, Cambridge, Essex, Norfolk, Oxford, Lincoln, Suffolk and Wilts (Diagrams 1 and 4); second, upon the industrial counties of Lancaster and Chester (Diagrams 2 and 5); third, upon all England (Diagrams 3 and 6).

Let us study the first three diagrams. The first shows that the commercial crisis of 1825 had a very slight effect upon criminality. It was the high price of grain in 1829 that made crime increase. The same effect was produced by the famous law of 1834 (by which not only was the aid given to poor working people very much limited, but which prescribed the placing in work-houses of those who were without means of support) and by the crisis of 1836. In 1844–1845, years of good harvests, criminality declined, after which the bad crops of 1847 brought about a contrary effect.

We note from Diagrams 2 and 3 that the effect of commercial crises was much greater in the manufacturing than in the agricultural counties (more plainly seen in 2 than in 3). The crisis of 1825 made the curve of criminality rise considerably; the favorable years 1833–1836 made it descend from 1834 on; while the crisis of 1836 caused a considerable increase in the number of crimes in 1837. The bad years 1840–1843 caused a formidable increase in the criminal population, which must also be attributed, at least in part, to the Chartist movement. The favorable period that followed had the contrary effect. It is interesting to compare the curves (in Diagram 3) of exports and crime, which cross continually.

---

[1] *Cf.* by the same: "Studien zur Theorie und Geschichte der Handelskrisen in England ", II, Chap. I, where still more explicit data are given.

Let us consider now the last three diagrams. Dr. Tugan-Baranowsky attributes the descent of the curve of criminality in Diagram 4 to the improved condition of the agricultural population. Further, the number of crimes was greatly diminished by the alteration in the criminal procedure in 1879, and it goes without saying that this influence must also be taken into account in studying the last two diagrams. By Diagrams 5 and 6 we see that the influence of criminality is much less marked. Thus, for example, the diminution of criminality was not prevented by the crisis at the beginning of the period 1890–1896.

The final conclusion of Dr. Tugan-Baranowsky is this: "The first three diagrams give a picture of the life of the English people in the second quarter of this century [the nineteenth]. We see abrupt periodical changes of important phenomena in the life of the people, which are plainly connected with the changes in the industrial situation. Especially sudden are the variations in the life of the industrial population. Each crisis has a devastating effect upon the ranks of the working-classes, the workhouses are swamped with the unemployed, the prisons fill up as well, mortality mounts enormously, the mass of people out of work readily take up with any political agitation, and the years of crisis are likewise years of revolutionary movements.

"At the same time the manufacturing and commerce of the country increase rapidly. The enormous growth of exportation in England, the curve of which mounts continually, is in sharp contrast with the deterioration of the living-conditions of the working-class.

"The last three diagrams show us an entirely different picture. English exports no longer increase. In place of a steady rise of the curve with a sharp depression in the critical years, there are regular, wave-like variations in the same plane. The industrial development of the country proceeds at a slackening pace.

"And at the same time in the life of the people there are signs to be noticed of increasing well-being. Mortality, criminality, and pauperism fall quickly. Crises no longer have their former influence upon the condition of the people. Even in manufacturing districts business stagnation no longer has its former disastrous effect upon the working-class; crime and the death-rate no longer increase, and even the increase in the number of paupers is hardly noticeable. Organized labor supports even the unemployed. Wages are only a little lower in years of industrial depression than they are in a time of prosperity!"

DIAGRAM No. 1. (TUGAN-BARANOWSKY)
AGRICULTURAL COUNTIES

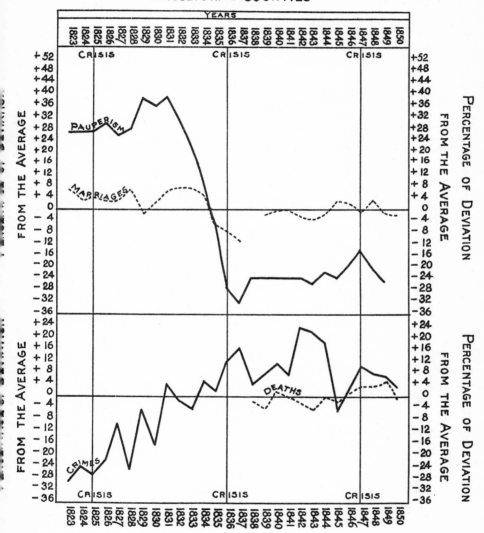

DIAGRAM No. 2. (TUGAN-BARANOWSKY)

INDUSTRIAL COUNTIES

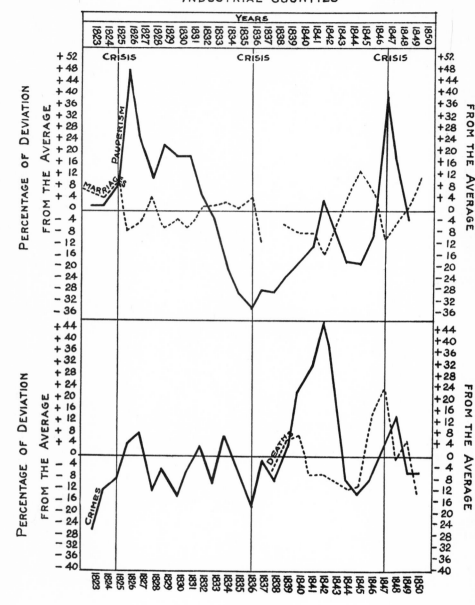

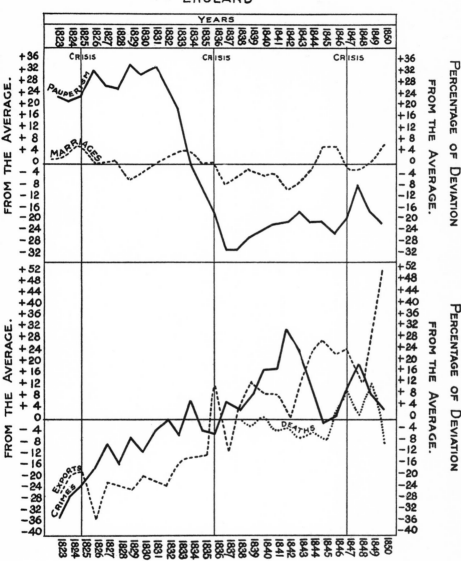

DIAGRAM No. 3. (TUGAN-BARANOWSKY)

ENGLAND

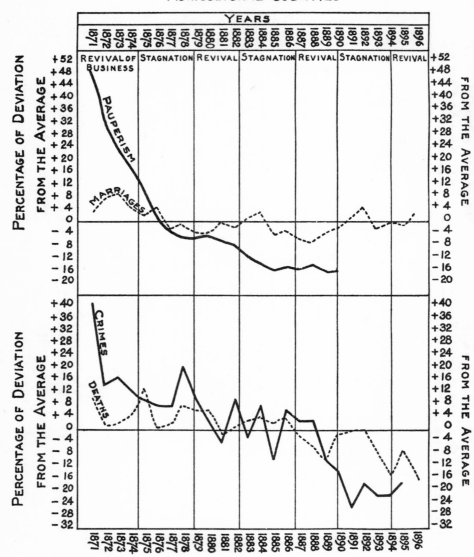

DIAGRAM No 4. (TUGAN-BARANOWSKY)
AGRICULTURAL COUNTIES

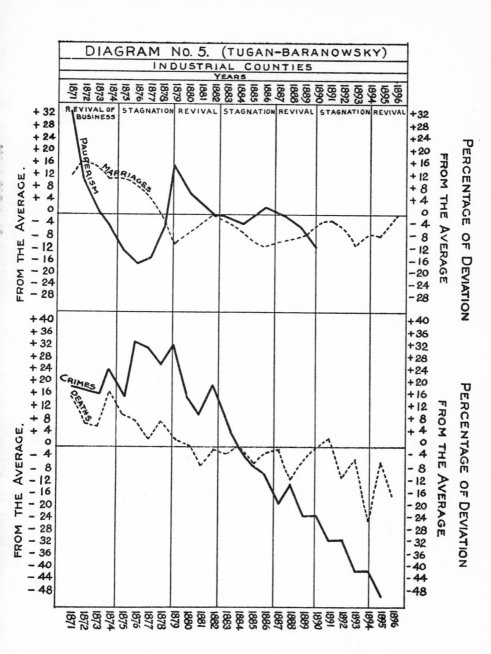

DIAGRAM No. 5. (TUGAN-BARANOWSKY)

INDUSTRIAL COUNTIES

YEARS

DIAGRAM No. 6. (TUGAN-BARANOWSKY)

ENGLAND

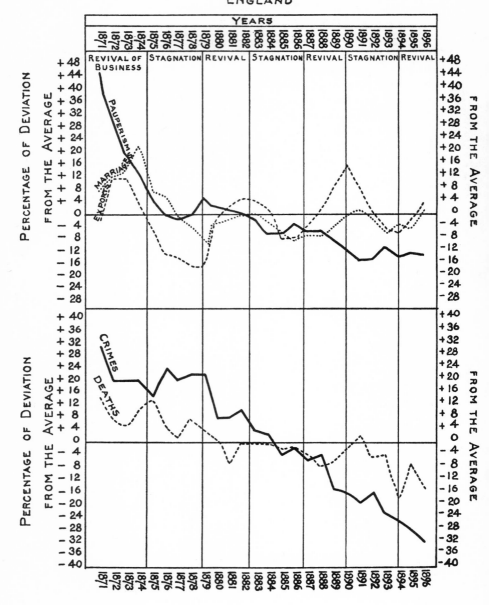

XVI.

E. TARNOWSKI.[1]

At the end of his study the author gives the following table, which contains some data upon the relation between the price of grain and abundance of the crops, on the one hand, and criminality on the other. The figures in the second column have to do with the different kinds of theft.   The law of May 18th, 1882, having considerably modified the penal code, the figures for the years 1882 and 1883 cannot be compared with those of preceding years.   This is why they have been suppressed.

YEARS.	NEW CASES TO 100,000 OF THE POPULATION.	PRICE OF A "PUD" OF RYE IN KOPECKS.	RATIO OF CEREAL CROP TO AVERAGE OF 25 YEARS (=100).
1874	76	75	105
1875	77	73	90
1876	78	76	95
1877	86	80	103
1878	95	76	106
1879	90	86	93
1880	104	99	87
1881	103	129	105
average **1874–81**	**89**	**87**	—
1884	45	90	108
1885	46	77	90
1886	44	74	100
1887	45	67	114
1888	43	65	108
1889	43	70	83
1890	46	68	97
1891	52	129	73
1892	52	89	87
1893	50	61	104
1894	50	50	121
average **1884–94**	**47**	**76**	—

According to the author it may be doubted whether the years of poor harvests could cause an increase in the number of thefts in Russia. For the agricultural population is benefited by the high price of grain.

[1] " La delinquenza e la vita sociale in Russia."   Another publication by the same author is entitled: "Upon the relations between criminality and the price of cereals" (published in Russian).   *Cf.* also: "Le mouvement de la criminalité en Russie, 1874–1894" ("Archives d'anthr. crim.", XIII.), and "Répartition géographique de la criminalité en Russie" ("Arch. d'anthr. crim.", XVI).

However, it is proved by the figures given above that these years have an unfavorable effect upon criminality, which can be understood if we take into account the fact that most of the Russian peasants only raise grain for their own consumption, and that bad crops accordingly affect them seriously.

XVII.

H. Müller.

In the introduction to his work, "Untersuchungen über die Bewegung der Criminalität in ihrem Zusammenhang mit dem wirthschaftlichen Verhältnisses", Dr. Müller describes the result of his researches as follows : "In the course of our discussion it will appear that with time the state of industry, the greater or less chance to get work, the activity or depression of the general economic life, have gradually become of far more significance for the increase or decrease of crime, than a rise or fall in the price of provisions, and that at present these factors have reduced the economic meaning of the price of provisions to a minimum." [1]

The period examined (1854–1895) is divided into two parts, because the criminal statistics of the empire, which are to be had from 1882 on, give the number of crimes and criminals, while the Prussian statistics give the number of new cases brought before the examining magistrate.

The figures for these years are as follows :

Prussia, 1854–1878.   New Cases to 100,000 of the Population.

YEARS.	AGAINST PROPERTY.	AGAINST PERSONS.	AGAINST THE STATE, PUBLIC ORDER, AND RELIGION.
1854	416	78	—
1855	436	78	41
1856	472	81	47
1857	324	95	55
1858	288	103	54
1859	295	103	51
1860	310	102	56
1861	314	93	52
1862	313	105	54
1863	288	111	53
1864	290	115	56
1865	325	121	58
1866	314	109	55

[1] P. 4.

Prussia, 1854–1878 — Continued

YEARS.	AGAINST PROPERTY.	AGAINST PERSONS.	AGAINST THE STATE, PUBLIC ORDER, AND RELIGION.
1867	360	112	51
1868	392	117	52
1869	338	126	53
1870	296	99	46
1871	254	75	41
1872	281	94	56
1873	266	106	64
1874	295	125	81
1875	284	135	84
1876	315	142	89
1877	341	160	87
1878	370	164	103

Prussia, 1882–1895. Persons Convicted to 100,000 Inhabitants over 12 Years.

YEARS.	AGAINST PROPERTY.	AGAINST PERSONS.	AGAINST THE STATE, PUBLIC ORDER, AND RELIGION.
1882	545	328	180
1883	520	343	174
1884	527	382	188
1885	492	385	185
1886	488	402	196
1887	475	421	203
1888	466	404	200
1889	503	423	197
1890	496	449	199
1891	520	443	190
1892	575	458	199
1882–91	510	404	194
1894	528	527	219

Now, the causes that make crime increase when there is an economic depression are, according to the author, the following: "The instinct of self-preservation, which in its harmonious development is the motive for the lawful and moral struggle of men for existence, and in more restricted form is the principal ground for industrial activity, in its degeneration . . . demands a certain, often high, percentage of victims, who fall into crime, especially theft, fraud, embezzlement, and other offenses against property.   And experience shows that the greater the care to maintain existence, or often simply to procure daily bread, the greater is the number of offenses against property.   When need appears, at the same time comes the instinct impelling a man to seize the property of another, better situated than himself.   Infractions of property are in part to be ascribed to other motives.   There is nothing to show, however, that these motives (greed and covetousness, for example) are stronger in one year and weaker in another throughout a whole people.   We must rather ascribe to them a certain uniformity in their influence upon criminal activity.   The determining factor in the increase and decrease of crimes remains the general well-being of a people, in earlier times the price of the necessities of life, at the present the opportunity for employment." [1]

Let us study in the first place crimes and misdemeanors against property :

I.   *Offenses, against Property.*

PRUSSIA, 1854–1878.   NEW CASES TO 100,000 OF THE POPULATION.

YEARS.	THEFT.	EMBEZZLE-MENT.	ROBBERY AND BLACKMAIL.	RECEIVING STOLEN GOODS, ETC.	PERJURY, ETC.	FORGERY.	MALICIOUS MISCHIEF.
1854	334	28	1.0	40	17	5.4	10
1855	354	29	1.1	34	16	5.7	8
1856	386	31	1.1	43	17	6.0	8
1857	246	23	1.0	38	15	7.0	10
1858	213	22	0.8	30	12	7.3	11
1859	219	22	0.8	25	12	7.5	12
1860	229	24	0.8	30	13	7.7	12
1861	232	24	0.8	26	13	8.1	12
1862	229	24	0.9	25	13	8.2	14
1863	206	23	0.8	21	14	7.5	15
1864	206	24	1.0	25	13	7.4	17
1865	227	24	0.8	25	14	7.6	17
1866	222	23	0.8	24	14	7.2	17
1867	265	25	0.9	32	15	8.1	17
1868	293	27	1.2	36	16	8.0	17
1869	241	25	1.0	30	15	7.1	18
1870	211	22	0.9	27	14	6.4	17
1871	190	18	0.8	33	10	3.2	14
1872	209	20	1.4	46	11	3.4	17
1873	196	19	1.4	46	11	3.5	18
1874	216	22	1.7	50	13	3.7	19
1875	209	23	1.7	49	13	4.2	19
1876	223	25	1.9	50	16	4.9	21
1877	238	28	2.4	51	18	5.5	22
1878	257	30	2.4	55	20	5.6	24

---

[1] Pp. 24, 25.

PRUSSIA, 1882–1896. PERSONS CONVICTED TO 100,000 INHABITANTS OVER 12 YEARS.

YEARS.	THEFT.	EMBEZZLE-MENT.	ROBBERY AND BLACKMAIL.	RECEIVING STOLEN GOODS, ETC.	PERJURY, ETC.	FORGERY.	MALICIOUS MISCHIEF.
1882	337	44	1.5	30	29	8.0	38
1883	323	42	1.4	27	29	7.7	37
1884	322	44	1.7	27	31	8.4	41
1885	289	44	1.4	25	30	8.0	41
1886	282	43	1.5	24	32	8.3	41
1887	267	42	1.4	24	35	8.6	43
1888	262	43	1.2	23	36	8.6	38
1889	289	46	1.4	25	41	10.0	40
1890	278	46	1.5	25	41	10.0	42
1891	292	47	1.6	25	44	10.9	41
1892	329	52	1.6	30	48	11.7	42
1893	298	45	1.5	26	36	9.0	41
1894	276	51	1.4	25	51	12.9	47
1895	271	53	—	24	52	13.2	—
1896	259	50	—	22	50	12.8	—

The following table gives the prices of certain important foods (per 50 Kilogr.) :

YEARS.	WHEAT.	RYE.	POTATOES.
1848	7.49	4.82	1.84
1849	7.29	3.87	1.45
1850	6.91	4.55	1.55
1851	7.47	6.26	2.08
1852	8.59	7.72	2.48
1853	10.25	8.50	2.47
1854	12.90	10.40	3.17
1855	14.21	11.45	3.37
1856	13.51	10.64	3.13
1857	10.18	6.87	2.18
1858	9.08	6.38	1.91
1859	8.93	6.79	1.98
1860	10.48	7.65	2.41
1861	11.04	7.71	2.79
1862	10.68	7.79	2.47
1863	9.18	6.78	2.04
1864	7.95	5.69	2.10
1865	8.13	6.24	2.03
1866	9.80	7.30	2.05
1867	12.89	9.87	2.95
1868	12.48	9.84	2.62
1869	9.70	8.08	2.16

YEARS.	WHEAT.	RYE.	POTATOES.
1870	10.14	7.78	2.58
1871	11.70	8.60	3.05
1872	12.10	8.40	2.95
1873	13.20	9.60	3.00
1874	12.00	9.90	3.35
1875	9.80	8.60	2.75
1876	10.50	8.70	2.82
1877	11.50	8.85	3.18
1878	10.10	7.15	2.82
1879	9.80	7.20	3.08
1880	10.95	9.65	3.25
1881	11.00	10.10	2.85

A comparison of these figures with those of crime will show that the crimes against property increase in the years of high prices up to 1855. In 1857 prices fell and crime decreased.

In the figures for foreign countries we see this relation much less clearly. Dr. Weisz has indeed succeeded in establishing a similar relation in France, but in Belgium it is much slighter. In England it is not possible to show that there is any parallelism between the curves of criminality and of the price of grain. In the years 1831–1840 and 1841–1850 the curve of crime even goes down, while provisions were then very dear. There must therefore be some other cause, and this is probably that England had a great industrial development long before any other country.

After an extremely rapid development up to 1847, manufacturing had to pass through a formidable crisis. While the average annual number of persons convicted in England and Wales was 20,455, and this figure fell to 18,100 and 17,400 in the prosperous years, 1845–1846, it rose during the years of crisis, 1847–1848, to 21,500 and 22,900, falling again to 21,000 in 1849, when business had resumed its normal course.

In the years following, industry received an enormous impetus, in consequence of the discovery of gold in California, the repeal of the Corn Laws, and many other causes. In 1857 came the panic, which affected all industrial countries, especially England. In 1856–1860 there was an annual average of 13,565 convictions; in 1857 it was 15,307, an increase of 12%. That the consequences of this crisis are not to be observed in the figures for crime in Prussia, is to be attributed to the fact that in that country manufacturing was little developed.

After the very dear years 1852–1856 the price of grain remained fairly constant in Prussia. It was only in 1860–1862 that it rose a little and caused an increase in the cases of fraud and theft. 1867–1868 were years which were marked by an extraordinarily high price for grain, which had some influence upon crime, without equalling that of such years as 1852–1856.

Crime decreased in the years of war, 1866 and 1870–1871, due as Dr. Müller thinks, to two facts; first, that a great part of the population capable of committing crimes were then out of the country; and second, that the feeling of solidarity is stronger in time of war.

Notwithstanding the rise in the price of grain in 1871–1874, crime decreased greatly after the war of 1870. A modification of the penal law could not be the cause of it; its origin was deeper. Since 1871 Germany has seen its industries develop prodigiously. The period of prosperity was of short duration, for in the summer of 1873 came the crisis, which lasted till 1878. Now it is during these years that the crimes against property were much increased.

When we study this period in other countries, in Austria and England, for example, we see a great industrial development, accompanied by a decrease in crime. The average number of criminals in Austria for the years 1860–1870 was 32,800, and 26,900 for the years 1871–1875. In England the figures for the same period were 14,100 and 11,200 respectively. France alone was an exception, for in this country manufacturing did not begin to develop immediately after the war.[1] But in Austria and England the effects of the crisis upon crime were felt just as in Prussia. In Austria, for example, criminality increased 10%. From 1878 on, business improved in Prussia and in other countries also, and little by little the number of crimes against property decreased (between 1885 and 1890 7% in France, 9% in Austria, and 20% in England).

In 1889 there was another great disturbance in the economic field, which was prolonged till 1892. During these years there was a new increase of crime; in Austria, for example, the average number of convictions was 29,483 in 1890–1894, as against 28,834 for the five years preceding. In England we see the same phenomenon, and in Prussia as well.

Dr. Müller calls attention to the marked fall in the price of grain in 1892, and sees in it a proof that prices have no longer any great

[1] See *Lafargue*, "Die Kriminalität in Frankreich, 1840–86." In France the development of manufacturing did not receive an impetus till 1874, from which year the decrease in crime dates.

influence.   Since 1892 there has been a new period of prosperity, and at the same time a constant diminution of crimes against property.

Dr. Müller reminds us that preceding moralistic statisticians have brought out the fact that crimes against persons increase when the price of grain falls, and vice versa, as is distinctly seen in the tables for the years 1854–1860.   But there is a change during the ten years following.   In 1867–1868 the price of grain was high, but crimes against persons and the public order rose also.   Crimes against persons decreased in the years of war, 1866 and 1870, just as crimes against property did.   Since 1871 crimes against persons have in general diminished, principally because of favorable economic conditions.   (The diminution of crimes against morals is chiefly due to a modification of the law, which prescribed that a case could not be

II.   *Crimes against Persons.*

a. 1854–1878.   New Cases to 100,000 Inhabitants.

Years.	Offenses against Morals.	Insult.	Murder and Homicide.	Assault in General.	Bodily Injuries Punished as Crime.	Offenses against Personal Liberty.
1854	8.7	32	1.1	34	6.7	0.9
1855	10.2	32	0.9	32	4.5	0.7
1856	10.8	34	0.9	37	3.0	0.8
1857	12.6	36	0.9	42	1.8	1.0
1858	12.5	40	0.8	46	1.8	1.1
1859	13.1	39	0.8	47	1.8	1.0
1860	12.4	40	0.9	46	1.5	0.8
1861	11.6	33	0.7	44	1.7	1.0
1862	12.9	39	0.8	49	1.4	1.4
1863	14.2	40	0.7	53	1.6	1.2
1864	14.0	43	0.9	54	1.6	1.4
1865	14.9	44	0.8	58	1.7	1.3
1866	13.4	40	0.8	50	1.5	1.3
1867	14.0	44	0.9	50	1.6	1.0
1868	14.8	47	0.9	52	2.8	1.0
1869	14.9	45	1.0	58	2.8	1.3
1870	12.3	39	0.8	49	1.9	1.1
1871	5.3	26	0.7	39	1.2	1.2
1872	6.2	34	0.8	50	2.0	1.8
1873	6.7	38	0.9	56	2.4	2.8
1874	7.8	47	1.1	64	3.0	3.3
1875	8.2	50	1.2	65	2.9	3.6
1876	9.3	51	1.2	73	5.5	4.1
1877	11.1	54	1.3	86	5.0	4.7
1878	12.3	54	1.4	89	2.5	5.5

b. 1882–1895. Persons Convicted to 100,000 Inhabitants over 12 Years.

Years.	Offenses against Morals.	Insult.	Murder and Homicide.	Assault in General.	Bodily Injuries Punished as Crime.	Offenses against Personal Liberty.
1882	7.8	117	1.0	60	111	10
1883	7.6	119	1.0	63	121	11
1884	7.6	127	0.8	68	142	15
1885	7.6	119	0.9	65	151	17
1886	8.9	124	0.8	68	153	19
1887	8.8	133	0.8	68	163	19
1888	9.1	130	0.6	64	156	18
1889	8.4	131	0.6	68	166	21
1890	8.8	138	0.6	74	175	23
1891	8.5	133	0.6	74	173	24
1892	9.0	137	0.9	76	177	26
1882–91	8.3	129	0.8	68	153	18
1894	10.5	156	0.7	87	208	29
1895	10.9	161	0.7	—	220	—
1896	11.1	158	0.6	—	220	—

prosecuted except upon complaint. The increase after 1876 was caused by a revocation of this requirement.) The crimes in question increased anew considerably after the crisis of 1874. Here is an important exception, then, to the rule that the earlier statisticians laid down, namely that crimes against persons decrease when economic conditions grow worse.

"The great economic crisis beginning in 1873 was accompanied by the characteristic phenomenon that dissatisfaction with the existing economic, social, and political conditions affected wider circles than heretofore, that this embittered people's minds, and brought about sharp oppositions and struggles of the industrial classes against each other, especially the struggle of labor against capital. The need of an economic reform was more and more felt, which is to be attained, in the opinion of the powerful, by force, and in that of the thoughtful, by social legislation. All public life since the seventies has been dominated by this idea." [1]

Here also economic conditions are causes of crime, and show themselves principally in resistance to officials, etc. The tables show also an increase in the cases of perjury, bodily injuries, and other crimes that are the consequences of grossness. The increase is due, according to Dr. Müller, to bad economic conditions. For as a consequence of these the number of civil cases rose from 60,000 (the average for

[1] P. 56.

III. *Crimes against the Public Order.*

a. 1854–1878. NEW CASES.

YEARS.	REBELLION.	OFFENSES AGAINST PUBLIC ORDER.	PERJURY.	COUNTERFEIT-ING.	LEZE-MAJESTY.
1854	18.6	—	3.0	0.83	0.63
1855	18.2	16.7	2.6	0.64	0.71
1856	18.0	23.2	2.7	0.71	0.40
1857	19.5	29.8	2.9	0.49	0.34
1858	19.7	28.7	2.7	0.50	0.53
1859	18.6	26.9	2.9	0.48	0.68
1860	19.7	30.2	3.0	0.39	0.51
1861	17.2	29.6	3.0	0.42	0.38
1862	19.9	29.0	3.0	0.50	0.47
1863	20.8	26.9	3.2	0.38	1.16
1864	23.1	26.6	3.2	0.40	1.00
1865	23.8	28.1	3.4	0.28	0.64
1866	23.4	24.2	3.1	0.39	1.94
1867	23.1	21.0	3.0	0.49	0.91
1868	22.5	22.8	3.4	0.57	0.54
1869	23.5	23.6	3.6	0.48	0.38
1870	19.0	21.7	3.1	0.36	0.66
1871	19.4	17.9	2.4	0.45	0.96
1872	23.6	26.4	3.2	0.38	0.67
1873	24.7	31.8	3.2	0.41	0.73
1874	28.6	43.7	3.7	0.45	1.23
1875	32.2	41.3	3.8	0.87	1.26
1876	32.7	47.0	4.2	1.21	0.86
1877	33.8	43.4	4.8	1.45	0.93
1878	33.7	49.6	5.5	2.24	9.93

b. 1882–1896. PERSONS CONVICTED.

YEARS.	VIOLENCE TO OFFICIALS.	VIOLATION OF DOMICILE.	PERJURY.	EMBEZZLEMENT IN MILITARY SERVICE.
1882	40	56	3.1	49
1883	39	52	2.7	54
1884	42	60	3.0	55
1885	40	57	3.0	57
1886	42	61	2.5	61
1887	43	58	8.8	66
1888	39	53	8.5	72
1889	39	58	8.6	61
1890	40	59	8.7	61
1891	40	57	8.5	56
1892	41	59	8.5	58
1882–91	41	58	8.8	60
1894	47	62	8.3	51
1895	47	65	—	—
1896	47	63	—	—

1871–1873) to 120,000 and 135,000 (1876–1877) and it is by these cases that perjury becomes possible. It is necessary to attribute to the same causes the great increase in the number of cases of crimes against personal liberty (also, since 1876, to the abolition of the requirement of a complaint for prosecution).

"The chief reasons why this crime (against personal liberty), like most crimes against persons, has constantly increased up to the present, in addition to the growing discontent with the present economic situation, are two; first, the effect of the spread of great manufactories in breaking up the family life, with concomitant lack of moral and religious education, and the too early necessity for self-supporting labor . . . ; and second, the present inordinate desire for pleasure, whose results are seen not least in the harmful effects of the immoderate consumption of alcohol; for that this is a prolific source of the multiplication of crime can hardly be doubted." [1]

Dr. Müller's final conclusion is as follows: "We may regard it as an established truth that, in the last analysis, the cause for the increase and decrease of crime as a whole is to be found in the presence or absence of a chance for employment and gain, in the condition of individual lines of industry, and in the greater or less degree in which the population as a whole in consequence of this, are in a position to consume." [2]

— Recently it has been proved that the conclusion of Dr. Müller with regard to the slight influence of the price of grain upon criminality was not entirely correct. Notwithstanding the growing influence of the industrial situation upon criminality, the price of grain has retained a certain influence.[3] —

---

[1] Pp. 60, 61. [2] Pp. 65, 66.

[3] *Cf. H. Berg*, "Getreidepreise und Kriminalität in Deutschland seit 1882", and my study already cited, "Verbrechen und Socialismus", pp. 805, 806.

See also: *Whitworth Russell*, "Abstract of the Statistics of Crime in England and Wales, from 1839 to 1843"; *J. Fletcher*, "Moral and Educational Statistics of England and Wales"; *G. R. Porter*, "The Influence of Education Shown by Facts Recorded in the Criminal Tables for 1845 and 1846"; *L. Faucher*, "Mémoire sur le caractère et sur le mouvement de la criminalité en Angleterre"; *J. Clay*, "On the Effect of Good or Bad Times on Committals to Prison"; *R. Everest*, "On the Influence of Social Degradation in Producing Pauperism and Crime, as Exemplified in the Free Coloured Citizens and Foreigners in the United States"; "Criminality Promoted by Distress" ("The Economist", 1856); *R. H. Walsh*, "A Deduction from the Statistics of Crime for the Last Ten Years"; *W. Westgarth*, "Statistics of Crime in Australia"; *Bernard*, "De la criminalité en France depuis 1826 et de la repression pénale au point de vue de l'amendement des prisonniers"; *J. H. Elliot*, "The Increase of Material Prosperity and of Moral Agents Compared with the State of Crime and Pauperism"; *E. Levasseur*, "La population française", II pp. 442–444; *Prof. Dr. B. Földes*, "Einige Ergebnisse der neueren Kriminalstatistik", pp. 544 *ff.*; *G. F. Kolb*, "Handbuch

XVIII.

CRITICISM.

The authors treated of in this chapter, and many others whom I have had to put under other headings as belonging to some special school, all have this point in common, that they try to find the causes of crime by means of statistics.   The first question that arises is this : do criminal statistics give a real and complete picture of criminality ? The answer is categorically, No.   To give only a few reasons, there are a great many crimes, naturally insignificant, which remain unknown even to the person injured; there are others of which justice never takes cognizance, because the injured party has filed no complaint, either because he has pardoned the offender, or fears the trouble of a criminal trial, etc.

In general, not all the cases known to justice are included in the criminal statistics but only those in which sentence is pronounced. An exception is found in Mayr's book (§ VI of this chapter), in which all the crimes known to justice appear.   In the first place the public officer dismisses many cases because of their insignificance (Germany is an exception — there the officer must prosecute); and in the second place there are a number of crimes whose authors remain unknown.   Finally, only a part of those arraigned are convicted. Criminal statistics, therefore, cover only a part of the crime that exists.[1]

The enemies of statistics have drawn from the preceding fact the conclusion that criminal statistics are useless for the study of the etiology of crime.   This is an absolutely false conclusion, as false as

der vergleichenden Statistik ", pp. 516, 517; *M. A. de Malarce*, "Moralité comparée des diverses parties de la France d'après la criminalité"; *J. E. Wappäus*, "Allgemeine Bevölkerungstatistik", II, pp. 429, 430; *Mayhew* and *Binny*, "The Criminal Prisons of London", pp. 450, 451; *E. Bertrand*, "Essai sur la moralité comparative des diverses classes de la population et principalement des classes ouvrières"; *G. Lindenberg*, "Ergebnisse der deutschen Kriminalstatistik", 1882–1892, pp. 718 *ff*.

[NOTE TO THE AMERICAN EDITION: See the following recent statistical studies: For Germany: *H. Berg*, "Getreidepreise und Kriminalität in Deutschland seit 1882"; *R. Wassermann*, "Beruf, Konfession, und Verbrechen"; *G. Schnapper-Arndt*, "Sozialstatistik", pp. 624 *ff*.; *P. Alterthum*, "Das Problem der Arbeitslosigkeit und die Kapitalistische Wirtschaftsentwicklung", pp. 47 *ff*.; *W. A. Bonger*, "Verbrechen und Sozialismus." For Austria: *H. Herr*, "Verbrechen und Verbrechertum in Oesterreich." For the Balkan States: *A. Wadler*, "Die Verbrechensbewegung im östlichen Europa", I.   For Belgium: *C. Jacquart*, "La criminalité Belge, 1868–1909." For the Netherlands: *J. R. B. de Roos*, "Inleiding tot de beoefening der crimineele aetiologie"; *W. A. Bonger*, "Misdaad en Socialisme, etc."; *C. A. Verrijn Stuart*, "Inleiding tot de beoefening der statistik", II, pp. 223 *ff*.]   [1] See *Wulffen*, "Psychologie des Verbrechers ", I, p. 369.

it would be to claim that doctors cannot find the cause of a disease, because besides the thousands of cases known to them, there are at least as many that remain unknown. The only question that arises is the following : is the number known sufficient? is there a sufficiently large body of facts in hand for inductive studies? As far as criminality is concerned the answer can be perfectly positive. The number of offenses that do not appear in the criminal statistics is certainly large ; they are, however, chiefly insignificant misdemeanors, such as insults, trifling assaults, petty thefts, etc. These would have little value in determining the etiology of crime, even if the statistics included them all. Serious crimes, on the other hand, in the majority of cases, without any doubt appear in the statistics. The great reason why criminal statistics suffice for etiological investigations is *that the ratio of known crime to unknown remains relatively constant.* The proofs of this are to be found in the criminal and judicial statistics themselves. The ratio between cases dismissed and those prosecuted, between convictions and acquittals, etc., etc., remains practically the same from one year to another. Further, every statistician of any experience is convinced that the law of averages rules more absolutely than any despot.

Finally it must be noted that the fact that there are a number of *offenses* which do not appear in the criminal statistics, does not mean that there are many *criminals* of whom the same can be said. It is the Italian school in particular that has maintained the proposition that in the struggle between the criminal and society it is the criminal that has the upper hand. This is a mistake; the criminal generally loses, and in the great majority of cases very quickly. Certainly the criminals are not punished for *each* crime, but the cases in which they *remain* unpunished are very rare. In the world of criminals itself there is no other opinion on this point.[1]

Although the value of statistics in studying the etiology of crime is certain, it must not be thought that they tell us everything.[2] I pass over here numerous things which most statistics still lack, for example, a classification by motive rather than according to the technical distinctions of the penal laws,[3] — and will simply call attention to the

---

[1] See (with regard to the social factors of crime and their importance in comparison with individual causes) my study : "Over de maatschappelijke faktoren van de misdaad en hunne beteekenis in vergelikjing met de individueele oorzaken" ("Tijdschrift v. Strafrecht", XXIII, pp. 413 *ff.*).

[2] See further *H. v. Schul*, "Kriminalstatistik" ("Handwörterbuch der Staatswissenschafte", VI, p. 246).

[3] See *v. Liszt*, "Kriminalpolitische Aufgaben" ("Zeitschr. f. d. ges. Strafrw.", IX).

difficulty of making international comparisons.   The difference merely
in the penal laws makes the comparison very difficult, and in many
cases even impossible.   Further, the dissimilarity of procedure, the
differences in the organization of the police, etc., increase this
difficulty.[1]   In general, we can say that international comparisons
give results where the nature of the crime (as homicide, for example)
minimizes the difference between the codes, and where the figures
show considerable differences.   We can truly say that for the etiology
of crime statics are much less important than dynamics.   When we
apply the dynamic method to a fairly long period, we have also to
allow for the changes that have taken place in the penal codes and in
the police organization, etc.

   The statistical method certainly contains many sources of error.
It goes without saying that this is not a reason for not using it at all,
but simply for being careful.   We must guard against conclusions
too hastily drawn.   If statistics show less criminality among the
Jews — as is generally the case — it is not safe to say, therefore, that
the innate morality of the Jew is greater than that of other men.   If
crime increases during a certain period together with irreligion, we
have no right to conclude that there is a causal connection between
the two.   The connection between the movement of the price of
grain and that of crimes against property has been proved many
times, as we have seen ; if this parallelism of the two curves no longer
occurs, we cannot say on that account that economic conditions no
longer play a part in the etiology of these crimes ; we have seen that
in manufacturing countries the industrial situation in general dominates the course of economic criminality.   Similar examples could
easily be multiplied.

   The statistical method is one of the most effective for discovering
the etiology of crime, and my readers will see that I use it much of
the time.   Nevertheless, it must not be forgotten that this method,
however important, is only one among several.   It is chiefly valuable
in finding the direct causes of crime ; as to indirect causes it gives us
much less information.   I would call attention to the following example : several authors have proved that there is an inverse connection between economic conditions and crimes against persons, *i.e.*

---

[1] See *Levasseur*, "La population française", p. 445; also *v. Oettingen*,
"Moralstatistik", p. 445; Dr. *E. Würzburger*, "Ueber die Vergleichbarkeit
kriminalstatistischer Daten" ("Jahrb. f. Nationaloekonomie u. Statistik",
1887); *Tarde*, "Penal Philosophy", pp. 72, 73 (The Modern Criminal
Science Series, Little, Brown, & Co., 1912); *Földes*, "Einige Ergebnisse der
neueren Kriminalstatistik" ("Zeitschr. f. d. ges. Strafrw.", XI, pp. 517–518);
de Roos, op. cit., pp. 192 *ff*.

that these crimes increase in times of prosperity (this does not apply to recent times, however). The conclusion has often been drawn from these facts that an improvement in the lot of the working-class would lead, as a law of nature, to an increase in crimes of violence. This is a typical example of the insufficiency of the statistical method alone. When we seek for the cause of this phenomenon in another way, in the structure of society, we discover that it is to be found in the low moral and intellectual condition of the working-classes. There can be no law of nature at the root of the matter, else the well-to-do classes would be the violent criminals "par excellence." It goes without saying that just the contrary is the case.

To sum up, I conclude that statistics furnish a powerful means of discovering the causes of crime, provided they are used critically and carefully. The statistical method is not the only one; to be a good criminologist, it is necessary to be a statistician, but it is necessary to be a sociologist also.

[NOTE TO THE AMERICAN EDITION: Upon the relation between sociology and statistics see also *Zizek*, "Soziologie und Statistik."

In recent years there has been a violent controversy over the statistical method. It was opened by *Hoegel* in his "Die Grenzen des Kriminalstatistik" and "Kriminalstatistik und Kriminalaetiologie"; then came *Wassermann* with his "Begriff und Grenzen der Kriminalstatistik", and "Georg v. Mayr als Kriminalstatistiker und Kriminalsociologe und die moderne Methodenlehre", which goes farther and denies almost all value to the statistical method. On the other side, we find *v. Mayr* in his "Statistik und Gesellschaftslehre", II, p. 441, "Forschungsgebiet und Forschungsziel des Kriminalstatistik", "Kriminalstatistik und Kriminalaetiologie", and *Wadler* in his "Erkenntnistheorie und Kriminalstatistik."]

CHAPTER III.

THE ITALIAN SCHOOL.[1]

I.

C. LOMBROSO.

IN "Crime, Its Causes and Remedies",[2] one of his last works, Professor Lombroso treats, among other things, of the influence of economic conditions upon criminality.

Chapter VI, bearing the title, "Subsistence (famine, price of bread)", is the first in which we find any observations especially interesting to us. By the aid of data from von Oettingen, Starke, Corre, and Fornasari di Verce, which we treat separately, the author calls attention to the fact that the course of criminality is very little influenced by the price of provisions. He closes by drawing the following conclusion:

"But, admitting the action of scarcity of food upon the increase of thefts and of abundance upon the increase of homicides, assaults, and debauchery, it is easy to understand its slight influence upon the variation of criminality in general, if one group of crimes increases with a given state of the market, and another group decreases under the same conditions, and vice versa. Even when the price of food moves in a constant direction it does not modify essentially the proportion of certain crimes. For example, in Italy the effect of the rise in price of food upon aggravated thefts is very marked; yet the greatest difference is between 184 and 105, that is to say, a variation of 79 to the 100,000. Likewise, when the sexual crimes increase on account

---

[1] The opinions of partisans of the Italian school with regard to the correlation between criminality and economic conditions are very different. Garofalo and Ferri especially are not in agreement upon this point. Nevertheless, I have thought that I ought to class them together, because of the uniformity of their point of view with regard to criminality in general.

[2] The Modern Criminal Science Series. Translated by *Horton*. Boston, Little, Brown, & Co., 1911.

of the low price of food, the greatest difference is 2.14 to the 100,000, — a fact easy to understand when one thinks of the greater influence of heredity, climate, and race." [1]

The circumstance that the thefts of food represent hardly 1% of the total cases of theft (according to Guerry), that in London bread occupies only the 43d place among 43 categories of articles stolen, and that Joly has shown that the cases of theft of money are much more numerous than those of meal, domestic animals, etc. — all of this leads the author to the conclusion that the proportion of crimes caused by lack of food and real misery is not so great as has been supposed.

— I will not make any criticism of the preceding at this point, but wait until I analyze the works themselves. The exposition of the work of Dr. G. Mayr, for example, shows how superficial the observations made by Professor Lombroso are. (See also the analysis of the work of Dr. Müller, in which it is shown that now the industrial situation plays a preponderating part in causing crime.) I would only call attention to the naïve error involved in Professor Lombroso's last remark, that there are only a few articles stolen that could immediately provide for pressing needs, and that this proves that poverty is not an important factor in criminality. If society were not based upon exchange this might be true, but the assertion has no basis in the present state of things, when anything may be bought for money. The reason that more money than food is stolen is to be found, in part, in the facts; first, that money is less bulky, and consequently can be more easily taken and concealed; and second, that money has more value than the same quantity of provisions, so that more can be procured with the same effort. But this proves nothing with regard to the influence of poverty upon crime.[2] —

In the second part of the chapter Professor Lombroso tries to show that the effect of hunger upon revolts is not very great. He cites a number of cases where there were no revolts although prices were high and work scarce. Thus, for example, in Strasburg from 1451 to 1500 and from 1601 to 1625, the price of beef rose 134% and that of pork 92%, and during many years wages fell 10%; and yet there was no insurrection.

— I must vigorously protest against any such argument, which, in my opinion, has no value. I will leave out of consideration the last example, which proves but little, since during these periods the price of bread may have been very low, neutralizing the effect of low wages

---

[1] P. 81.   [2] See *Battaglia*, "La dinamica del delitto", pp. 227, 228.

(it is quite problematical whether the poorer classes of the population were great consumers of beef and pork !).   But it is inaccurate to conclude from the fact "that prices were high and there was no insurrection" an absence of influence of the economic conditions.   There may have been a number of factors working in the opposite direction, which prevented the manifestation of the economic factor. To cite but one example, it may be that during those times an excessively severe penal law was in force, threatening the least attempt at insurrection with cruel death. —

We shall next sum up Chapter IX, "Influence of Economic Conditions — Wealth."   After saying that it is difficult to estimate the wealth of a country at all accurately, the author produces the following data in the first section of the chapter.   He divides the provinces of Italy into three groups according to the total wealth (estimated from taxes on consumption, direct taxes, and taxes on business), and compares the figures thus gained with some of the principal kinds of crimes, reaching the following results :

	WEALTH, 1885–86.			WEALTH, 1890–93 (BODIO).		
	Maximum.	Mean.	Minimum.	Maximum.	Mean.	Minimum.
Fraud	70.6	66.0	43.0	55.13	39.45	37.39
Sexual crimes . .	15.6	13.4	19.4	16.15	15.28	21.49
Thefts	206.0	143.0	148.0	361.28	329.51	419.05 [1]
Homicides . . .	11.3	17.0	23.0	8.34	13.39	15.40

Professor Lombroso draws the conclusion, "that fraudulent crimes increase positively with the increase of wealth, and the same is true of thefts, but if we add rural thefts we get the maximum where wealth is least ; and this last is always true of homicides." [2]

"The results for sexual crimes are more unexpected.   They show their minimum in Italy where wealth is moderate, and their maximum where there is the minimum of wealth.   Italy thus presents an exception, as the usual course of sexual crimes is to increase with the increase of wealth." [3]

Another way of estimating the wealth of a country is by means of the inheritance tax.   For different Italian provinces the following results are thus obtained :

[1] Bodio includes rural thefts.   [2] P. 121.   [3] P. 122.

(Indictments.   Average to 100,000 Population, 1887–89.)

	AVERAGE WEALTH.	THEFTS.	FRAUDS.	HIGHWAY ROBBERIES.	HOMICIDES.	ASSAULTS.
Latium . . .	3333	639	116	18	25	513
Piedmont ⎫ Liguria ⎭ . .	2746	267	44	7	7	164
Lombardi . .	2400	227	44	3	3	124
Tuscany . .	2164	211	34	6	7	165
Venice . . .	1935	389	43	3	4	98
Reggio . . .	1870	320	49	7	13	287
Emilia . . .	1762	250	38	6	6	130
Sicily . . .	1471	346	65	16	26	410
Naples . . .	1333	435	47	6	21	531
Marches ⎫ Umbria ⎭ . .	1227	222	33	3	10	239
Sardinia . . .	—	670	113	14	20	277

This table gives very little information as to the influence of wealth upon criminality, since we can draw from it the most contradictory conclusions.   Note, for example, that the highest figures for theft are to be found in the regions of Latium and Sardinia, *i.e.* in the richest and the poorest provinces, etc., etc.

— I have more than once had occasion to show that the value of such researches is fictitious.   It is not the total amount of wealth but its distribution that bears upon criminality.   (See, for example, Quetelet and Colajanni) —

In the 3d section the author treats of the effect of involuntary unemployment.   Wright tells us that in Massachusetts of every 220 persons convicted, 147 are without regular work, and that 68% of criminals have no occupation.   According to Professor Lombroso this is easily explained by the fact that criminals do not like to work. According to Bosco there were only 18% of murderers in the United States without work (— the proportion not being given for noncriminals, these figures have little value —).   Finally, Professor Lombroso mentions the opinion of Coghlan, who says that unemployment has no influence upon criminality in New South Wales (— upon what he bases his opinion, we do not know —).

— Such data as these (to a subject of such high importance as this the author gives but thirty lines) suffice for the conclusion that the phenomenon in question has little significance for criminality.   I have only to recall the extensive studies of Mayr, Denis, Müller,

NUMBER OF PERSONS (TO THE 100,000 INHABITANTS) CONVICTED FOR:

DAYS OF WORK EQUIVALENT TO A YEAR'S FOOD		Homicide		Assault		Sexual Offenses		Theft	
1		2		3		4		5	
England and Wales	⎱ 127	Scotland	0.51	England and Wales	2.67	Spain	1.03	Spain	59.63
Scotland	⎰	England and Wales	0.56	Ireland	6.24	Ireland	0.85	Belgium	110.44
Ireland	130	Ireland	1.06	Scotland	11.59	Scotland	1.41	France	110.95
Belgium	132	Germany	1.11	Spain	43.17	England and Wales	1.66	Italy	165.89
France	148	Belgium	1.44	France	63.40	Italy	4.01	Ireland	65.81
Germany	152	France	1.53	Germany	126.40	Austria	9.33	England and Wales	165.63
Austria	153	Austria	2.43	Italy	155.35	France	10.26	Scotland	268.39
Italy	154	Spain	8.25	Belgium	175.39	Belgium	13.83	Germany	226.02
Spain		Italy	9.53	Austria	230.45	Germany	14.87		

NOTE.—Column 1 is taken from Mulhall's Dictionary of Statistics (quoted by Coghlan, *op. cit.*); and columns 2–5 are figured from the data published by the Director of Italian Statistics ("Movimento dena Domquenza secondo de Statistiche degli Anni 1873–83", Rome, 1886).

Lafargue, and others, upon this subject, to prove the inaccuracy of this idea. —

In the table on the preceding page the figures for criminality of different countries are compared with the number of days' wages equivalent to the annual cost of food for one individual. These figures give us a composite picture of the price of food and the wage-scale.

This table shows; first, that excessive labor with a low wage, *i.e.* with a lack of proper nutrition, has a certain correspondence with homicide; second, there is also a certain correspondence with assaults (Spain and Belgium furnishing exceptions); third, sexual crimes are most common where we find the fewest days' work and vice versa (Great Britain and some other countries being exceptions); fourth, that theft shows no correspondence.[1]

In another way Lombroso attempts to compare the economic conditions of different countries and their criminality, namely, by means of the number of savings-bank books. For Europe the figures are as follows (taken from Coghlan):

	Persons to Each Savings-bank Book.	Crimes to 100,000 Inhabitants.	
		Homicide.	Theft.
Switzerland	4.5	16	114
Denmark	5	13	114
Sweden	7	13	—
England	10	5.6	163
Prussia	10	5.7	246
France	12	18	103
Austria	14	25	103
Italy	25	96	150

These figures show how homicides move in inverse ratio to the number of savings-bank books, while the contrary is the case with thefts. The author forgets to point out that there are five exceptions to this rule.

In Italy the greatest number of accounts corresponds to the smallest number of homicides, as the following table shows:

[1] As the author himself observes, the conclusions drawn from this table must be taken with reserve, because of the great difference in the penal laws of these countries.

AVERAGE NUMBER OF CRIMES IN 20 PROVINCES IN WHICH THE WEALTH (ACCORDING TO THE NUMBER OF SAVINGS-BANK BOOKS) IS:

	Maximum.	Intermediate.	Minimum.
Fraudulent crimes . . .	57	45	45
Sexual crimes	11	12.6	20
Thefts	132	133	160
Homicides	10	12.6	27.4

There are several exceptions to this rule; for example, the richest, like Palermo, Rome, Naples, and Leghorn, give very high figures for homicides. According to Professor Lombroso the explanation in the case of Palermo and Naples is to be found in the geographical situation; in the case of Palermo, in race and the abuse of alcohol; and in the case of Rome, in race, the abuse of alcohol, and in the political situation.

For France we get the following results:

IN DEPARTMENTS WHERE THE DEGREE OF WEALTH IS:	AVERAGE NUMBER OF:		
	Homicides.	Thefts.	Rapes.
Minimum	64	83	17
Medium	86	99	26
Maximum	89	186	29

Here is just the opposite of what we get in Italy. The author explains this in the following manner: first, the richest districts are those that are industrial, where the influx of immigrants is greatest (these latter committing four times as many crimes as the French); second, because of ethnic and climatic factors; third, because of the greater wealth of France, which is four times as rich as Italy; and fourth, because of the demoralizing influence of quickly acquired wealth.[1]

The industrial activity of a country causes a considerable increase of criminality, especially when it displaces agriculture. Of 42 agricultural departments only 11, or 26%, go beyond the average number of assassinations in France; while the average is exceeded by

[1] My exposition would be too long if I should examine this explanation (which seems insufficient to me) at length. For the chief explanation of the great number of murders in countries that are intellectually backward, see "L'homicide en Italie", by *Colajanni* ("Revue socialiste", 1901).

10 out of the 26 departments of mixed industry, or 38%, and by 7 out of 17 manufacturing departments, or 41%. Rapes upon adults and crimes against persons show similar results.[1]

Percentage of departments exceeding the average of all France in:

	RAPES.	CRIMES AGAINST PERSONS.
Agricultural Departments (42)	33 %	48 %
Mixed (26)	39 %	39 %
Manufacturing (17)	52 %	59 %

Not only poverty, but often wealth as well may cause crime. This is why some very wealthy districts show a figure for criminality as high as do the very poor. "The cause of all this is only too clear. On the one side poverty and the lack of absolute necessities impel toward the theft of indispensable things for the satisfaction of the individuals' own needs. This is the first cord binding poverty and assaults upon property. On the other hand, poverty makes men impulsive through the cortical irritation following the abuse of wine and alcohol, that terrible poison to which so many of the poor resort to still the pangs of hunger. Account must be taken also of the degeneration produced by scurvy, scrofula, anemia, and alcoholism in the parents, which often transforms itself into epilepsy and moral insanity. Poverty also drives men to commit brutal eliminations of individuals who are an unwelcome burden upon the family, . . . Poverty is indirectly a cause of sexual crimes, on account of the difficulty which the poor have of obtaining satisfaction through prostitution; on account of precocious promiscuity in factories and mines; etc., . . . On the other hand, when a slight temptation toward evil is presented to an individual in comfortable circumstances, he is rendered physically and morally stronger by sufficient nutrition and a sounder moral training, and is less pressed by need, so that while he feels the impulsion to do evil, he can more easily resist it.

"But wealth, in its turn, is a source of degeneration from other causes, such as syphilis, exhaustion, etc. It drives men to crime through vanity, in order to surpass others, and from a fatal ambition to cut a figure in the world." [2] It may be asked why it happens then that the inmates of prisons are almost always poor and rarely rich. The answer, according to the author, is that because of the influence

[1] P. 131.   [2] Pp. 133, 134.

of his fortune, family, etc., the rich man can more easily extricate himself from the clutches of the law than the poor man, who knows no one, cannot employ a famous lawyer, etc. etc.

Professor Lombroso sums up his opinion as follows : " The economic factor has a great influence upon crime, not, however, that poverty is the principal cause of it, for excessive wealth, or money too quickly acquired, plays a large part as well; and poverty and wealth are frequently neutralized by the effect of race and climate." [1]

II.

R. GAROFALO.

In Chapter III of his "Criminologie", and more especially in the first part, bearing the title "la Misère", this author treats of the influence of economic conditions upon criminality.[2]   The question which must be answered with regard to this subject, according to Garofalo, is the following : "Whether the so-called 'economic iniquity', a condition by which all citizens are either proprietors or proletarians, is the chief cause or, at least, one of the most important causes, of criminality." [3]

It may be that a workman, i.e. a person who can only provide for his own needs and those of his family by selling his labor, can find no work, and for that reason falls into theft; but the author is of the opinion that in our days this almost never happens (leaving aside periods of crisis), and that if it happens the worker will generally find some one ready to help him, and that crime is therefore not a necessity. There is, indeed, absolute poverty, but it is almost always the result of a lack of courage and energy, and not due to a lack of work.   It is not hunger, but a desire to procure the same pleasures as those enjoyed by the favored of fortune, that impels the working-man to commit crime.   But this is not only the case with the working class but with other classes as well.   For this desire belongs to every man ; the millionaire envies the multimillionaire, etc.   In order that this desire should lead to crime, it is not necessary that there should be a particular economic situation, but only a particular psychic condition

---

[1] P. 137.
[2] American edition, "Criminology" (The Modern Criminal Science Series; Little, Brown, & Co., 1913), from which quotations are made. See by the same author, "La superstition socialiste", and "Le Crime comme phénomène social" ("Annales de l'Inst. intern. de Sociologie", II).
    [NOTE TO THE AMERICAN EDITION: See also his report to the Congress of Cologne, "L'influence des prèdispositions et du milieu dans la criminalité."]
[3] Pp. 144, 145.

— the individual must have his sense of honesty weakened or wanting. Desire will cease to lead to crime only when there is no longer any advantage to be gained by it, and since this is inconceivable, crime will always exist. This explains why the number of crimes committed by the proletariat is very great, but at the same time why the cases of forgery, bankruptcy, etc. are very numerous among the other classes. In 1880 the figure for crimes against property (and analogous crimes) committed in Italy by proletarians, compared with those committed by property-owners, was as 88 to 12, while the ratio of the number of proletarians to that of property-owners was as 90 to 10. These proportions are nearly the same, which proves that as regards these crimes the proletarian class is no more criminal than the others.

Some authors are of the opinion that crimes against persons are equally caused in large measure by bad economic conditions, since bad education, lack of discretion, etc. are consequences of these conditions. In Garofalo's opinion this idea is inaccurate, since the bad conditions in which the proletariat live lead indeed to roughness, *i.e.* make them insensible to the suffering of others, but it does not follow that the proletarians are totally deprived of moral sentiments. The criminal statistics of Italy show that 16% of the correctional criminality was committed by property-owners, though they form but 10% to 11% of the population. Garofalo attempts to prove the truth of his thesis also by a classification of criminals by trades. The agricultural class in Italy, the poorest and most ignorant, form 25.39% of those brought before the correctional tribunals, while those engaged in manufacturing, commerce, the army, etc., those with some education, therefore, who are much less numerous in the population, form 13.58%. In 1881 the Italian population included 67.25% of illiterates, and in 1880 68.09% of those correctionally convicted were illiterate. Further it has been proved many times that an improvement in economic conditions is accompanied by an increase of crime. In France, for example, wages have risen, the consumption of cereals, like that of meat, has increased, and the number of children enjoying the advantages of a primary education is more extensive and yet criminality has grown greatly in the same period. To the possible objection "that many authors, like Mayr, have proved that the rise in the price of grain is accompanied by an increase of crimes against property, and vice versa, and that economic conditions are consequently an important cause of crime", Garofalo responds that crimes against persons increase with the fall in the price of grain, and that consequently, by the changes in the economic life there has been brought about a change in the kind, but not in the extent, of criminality. Exceptional occurrences, such as famines, commercial crises, etc., increase crime only in appearance. If the question is probed to the bottom (the author appears not to have done so himself, at least he does not record any results) it is probable that it will be discovered that what happens is only that the form of crime becomes more serious, that the vagrant, for example, becomes a highwayman, etc.

The conclusions that the author draws are the following:

"First. The present economic order, that is to say, the distribution of wealth as it exists today, is not a cause of criminality in general.

"Second. The fluctuations which are wont to occur in the economic order may bring about an increase in one form of criminality, but this increase is compensated for by the diminution of another form. These fluctuations are, therefore, possible causes of specific *criminality*." [1]

— My criticism of what has gone before will be limited to some principal points only.

First. The author dodges the question when he includes under economic conditions poverty only, and this in the very limited sense of the lack of the absolute necessities. He who writes upon the connection between crime and economic conditions must analyze the whole present economic system, and not stop with one of the consequences of that system, the poverty in which the proletarians find themselves. Consequently Garofalo's whole argument, tending to show that the bourgeoisie have a great part in the crimes against property, is beside the mark, for capitalism results in great uncertainty of existence for the bourgeoisie also. It is then quite comprehensible that this class should be guilty of crimes of this kind. According to Fornasari di Verce, however, the Italian statistics show that the well-to-do class take less part in crime than the poor   According to him 13% of all those convicted in 1887 were well-to-do, a class which, roughly speaking, forms 40% of the whole population. (See also Colajanni, "La Sociologia Criminale", II, pp. 536, *ff*.)

In consequence of this arbitrary restriction of the subject the author's remarks are of little value. But aside from this there are still serious charges to be made against his manner of treating the subject.

Second. The assertion of Garofalo that in general in our present society he who wishes to work can find work, is not worth combating in a serious book. To say that machinery does not every day make

[1] P. 164.

some workers unnecessary, that there are no industrial crises causing an enormous amount of involuntary unemployment, is conclusive proof that one does not know the present mode of production. The existence of a group of the population, the so-called lower proletariat ("bas-proletariat", "Lumpen-proletariat") cannot be a natural phenomenon, since it has not been always and everywhere present; it is strictly bound up with certain modes of production.

Third. As I have had occasion to show already in more than one place, the increase of crimes against persons during periods of prosperity has a very great, though indirect, connection with economic conditions.

Fourth. That poverty in the strict sense of the word is not the sole cause of economic criminality, that cupidity plays also an important rôle, I do not wish to deny. Only, this cupidity is not an innate quality of man, present everywhere and always, but is awakened only under certain economic conditions. This is especially the case in our present society.

Fifth. According to the author there are certain circumstances which may lead to the commission of a crime, but the true cause of crime is to be found in the absence or weakness of the instinct of honesty. That there exists such an "instinct of honesty" is one of numerous assertions made by Garofalo for which he produces no proof, and, in accordance with the general opinion of sociologists, I class it among the most profound errors. A moral disposition is innate in man, and varies greatly with individuals, but moral concepts — for example, that it is forbidden to steal — are certainly not innate. The very way in which Garofalo puts the question is wrong; we must not set the circumstances that have influenced a man at a certain moment over against an innate quality of honesty (fictitious besides) but must examine all the conditions which have influenced his innate moral disposition through the whole of his life, as well as his environment at a given moment.

To say that the influence of environment cannot be great, because persons well brought up sometimes commit crimes, is very superficial. Upon this point there is something deeper and more important to be said. —

III.

E. FERRI.

In order to present Professor Ferri's views, I shall analyze "Socialismo e criminalità" and a passage connected with our subject, taken

from "Sociologia criminelle." [1]   This analysis will be more detailed
than that of most of the other authors, since in reality the opinion
of Professor Ferri is the synthesis of the opinions of many other
authorities.   For this reason and others it is of the highest importance.

"Socialismo e criminalità" is a polemic work directed in part
against "Il delitto e la questione sociale" of Turati, and in part as Professor Ferri himself says in "Socialismo e scienza positiva", against
socialism as far as that involves the revolutionary method and the
concomitant "nebulous romanticism."

In his "Preliminari" the author gives some definitions of socialism;
combats socialism of every kind, declares it to be unscientific, and
sets in opposition to it sociology, which is entirely scientific.[2]   We
pass over this part of the work in silence, since it has little importance
for our subject, and turn our attention to the end of the "Preliminari",
where the author gives an exposition of the ideas which the socialists,
according to him, have about crime:

"I. The origin of the phenomenon of crime is to be found in society
as at present constituted.

"II. More especially, the economic disorder of the population
caused by the unjust inequality of individuals and classes, is the cause
of every other disorder, moral or intellectual, and therefore of crime
also.

"III. When the social transformation or revolution which the
socialists desire has taken place, the social atmosphere will be most
favorable.

"IV. In the socialistic order the individual also will be much superior to the man corrupted or demoralized by present conditions.

"V. And then crime, like poverty, ignorance, prostitution, and
immorality in general, will have ended its unhappy tyranny over the
human race."

— It is not certain that an adherent of scientific socialism would
agree that these theses are entirely accurate; for example, the second,
that the bad economic condition of the population is the cause of
crime — for the expression "economic condition" has here too limited
a meaning, namely that of poverty, misery, etc.   In place of this he

[1] See also "Studi sulla Criminalità in Francia (1826–1876)."

[2] Although I do not wish to attack the proposition that socialism in Italy
at that period (preceding 1880) was unscientific, I cannot conceal my astonishment that Professor Ferri should fulminate against socialism in general
"because of its lack of the scientific spirit", apparently quite ignorant of the
scientific socialism of Marx and Engels, which had existed since the middle
of the century!

would rather make use of the expression, "mode of production." It is this which, in the last analysis, rules the whole social life, according to the Marxists. —

The first chapter of Professor Ferri's work, bearing the title of "la genesi sociale e individuale del delitto", begins by remarking that the socialists blame society as the cause of all evils, including poverty and crime. On the one hand, they do this because of their "strategy of propaganda", on the other hand it is a reaction against the extreme individualism which sprang from the French Revolution. They generally pay no attention to individual factors, or perhaps recognize them in part, but attribute their origin to society also. Between these two extremes is to be found criminal sociology, which says that the causes of crime are manifold.

According to the author there are three groups of the factors of crime: the *anthropological* or *individual* factors, the *cosmic* or *physical* factors, and the *social* factors. Since many authors, wholly or partially, share this view, which constitutes an attack against the very foundation of the idea of the social origin of crime, we will examine it here fully.

We take from "Sociologie criminelle", where this doctrine is best set forth, the following statement of it. "Every crime is the resultant of individual, physical, and social conditions." [1] The individual factor is, according to the author, the most important, the primordial factor, so to speak, for he says: "The social environment gives form to the crime; but this has its origin in an anti-social biological constitution (organic or psychic)." [2] The factors pointed out are the following:

"The anthropological factors, inherent in the person of the criminal, are the first condition of crime, and divide themselves into three subclasses, according as the person of the criminal is looked at from an organic, psychic, or social point of view.

" *The organic constitution of the criminal* constitutes the first subclass of anthropological factors and includes all the anomalies of the skull, brain, viscera, sensibility, reflex activity, and all bodily characteristics in general, such as physiognomy, tattooing, etc.

" *The psychical constitution of the criminal* includes anomalies of intelligence and feeling, especially of the moral sense and the peculiarities of the criminal dialect and literature.

" *The personal characteristics of the criminal* include the purely

[1] "Sociologie criminelle", p. 161.   [2] P. 43.

biological features of his condition, such as race, age, sex; and the bio-social features, such as civil status, profession, residence, social class, and education, which have been up to this time the almost exclusive subject of criminal statistics.

" *The physical factors of crime* are the climate, nature of the soil, length of nights and days, the seasons, the annual temperature, meteorological conditions, and agricultural production.

" *The social factors* include the density of population; public opinion, morals, religion; condition of the family; the educational system; industrial production; alcoholism; economic and political conditions; public administration, the courts, the police; and in general the legislative, civil, and penal organization : — that is to say, a medley of latent causes, which interlace and combine in all parts of the social organism, and almost always escape the attention of . . . criminologists and legislators." [1]

ANTHROPOLOGICAL FACTORS.

Let us consider first the "personal characteristics of the criminal." Professor Ferri draws the following conclusions with regard to the existence of anthropological factors in general : "In fact, if crime were the product of the social environment exclusively, how could the fact be explained, that in the same social environment and in like circumstances of poverty, abandonment, and lack of education, out of 100 individuals, 60 commit no crime, and of the 40 that remain, 5 prefer suicide to crime, 5 become insane, 5 become beggars or non-dangerous vagrants, and only the 25 others become real criminals? And why is it that among these, while some limit themselves to theft without violence, others commit robberies, and even, before the victim resists, or threatens, or calls for help, commit a murder with the sole aim of theft?" [2]

— It seems to me that there are many objections to be made to this rather carelessly drawn conclusion. In the first place, Professor Ferri is of the opinion that it may be assumed that it will be easy to find groups of persons only a quarter of whom become criminal, though they all live in the same bad environment. Leaving out of account the individuals who, because of their physical condition are incapable of crime, I do not believe that there are, for example, 60% who have never been convicted. However, even admitting that this assertion is accurate, then, that out of 100 persons living in the same environment, only one part will fall into crime, I believe that it

---

[1] Pp. 150, 151.   [2] "Soc. crim.", p. 157.

is impossible to find even *two* persons who live, and have lived, in an environment *exactly* similar, and whose parents also have always lived in the same surroundings. In this way only can the question be clearly put. It is not only present conditions that influence a man; all past conditions have their part in the motives of present acts. It cannot be denied that the present includes the past. Nor ought the conditions which have influenced the parents to be excluded. Let us put the following case: A, B, and C live in the same very bad surroundings. A commits suicide, B becomes crazy, C commits a crime. The parents of A were well-to-do, gave their child a good education, and accustomed him to consider many things as necessities. Fallen into poverty, then weakened and become incapable of good work, A believes that it is impossible for him to restore himself. His moral ideas, acquired in his youth, are opposed to his engaging in crime. And then the few francs that he would be able to steal would not be sufficient to maintain him in the life to which he has been accustomed. Consequently he commits suicide. B is the child of a father who became an alcoholic from actual poverty. Inferior on this account, B cannot keep up the struggle for existence and becomes insane. The parents of C were indigent. He received no education; moral ideas are totally unknown to him; he has never lived in anything but poverty, and commits a theft when the opportunity presents itself without any hesitation. In these three cases, which occur daily, circumstances are the only factor that enters into consideration.

I have said above that there are no two persons who live in *exactly* the same circumstances. This word "exactly" is not used by Professor Ferri, and in this, in my opinion, he is wrong. In ordinary life we speak of great and small causes. But in treating of scientific questions this is surely forbidden. For no one is ignorant that what is apparently the least important occurrence may have the most extensive consequences.

May I here be permitted to make a quotation from an interesting page of Professor Manouvrier upon this question: "That the effect of environment is generally understood in too limited a way, we see proved every day in the appreciation expressed, of the causes that have determined certain differences of productive power or moral conduct. It is a question, perhaps, of two brothers. It is said that they have been brought up *exactly* in the same manner, that they have received exactly the same education, and that the question of environment is thus settled. Immediately the doctors begin to call in

atavism, to feel the bumps of the head, to study facial asymmetry, etc.
Anatomy must be appealed to, since the influence of environment has
been eliminated.   It can be put down to bad luck if some bump,
some depression, some asymmetry is not found that will serve, whether
or no, to account for a solution of the question.   There remains
always, further, the resource of invoking invisible, hypothetical
vices of the internal constitution.   The phrenologists were in a relatively difficult situation; they had to find a fixed anatomical character, a bump for a function specified in advance, or they were obliged to
imagine a conflict of bump with bump.   The present method is less
exacting; it is enough to find no matter what deviation from morphological perfection, without its being necessary to show the connection between this deviation and the physiological inferiority to be
explained.   But what am I saying?   The question is often of an
inferiority of a sociological order, and trouble is not even taken to
make sure, to begin with, that this corresponds to a psychological
inferiority.   Yet however indispensable this may be as a preliminary,
it is not enough; it must be ascertained that this inferiority implies a
functional trouble before calling in pathological anatomy at all hazards.

"The statement is made that the two brothers have been subjected to the same environmental influences merely because they have
been brought up in the same house, taught in the same school, fed
and clothed alike.   Yet the mere fact of having been born first or
second is not without importance.   To have been reared with an
older or with a younger brother constitutes a difference of environment that may contribute powerfully to differentiate character.
Add to this the differences of environment proceeding from nurses,
servants, diseases, games, etc., and you will have opened headings
under which may be classed differences innumerable.   There are no
small things in such a matter.   Biographies as now written are no
more than outlines when one thinks of what truly psychological biographies ought to be.   To have been taught in the same college in the
case of two brothers is a similarity that may, and certainly does,
conceal the greatest differences.   They have not had the same teachers,
the same fellow-pupils, nor, above all, the same comrades.   Between
the education given, and that actually received, the difference may
be great. . . .

"The influences that act upon the child outside of the curriculum
have the more chance to be effective, since the curriculum is carried
out in the less agreeable manner." [1]

[1] "Les aptitudes et les actes", pp. 328, 329.

In consequence of what has been said, I believe that the conclusion of Professor Ferri that there are anthropological factors of crime, is too hasty. But there are still other objections to be urged to it.

Let us suppose that two persons who live, and have lived, in the same circumstances are in a position to commit a very advantageous crime, and their morality does not prevent. At the moment when the time comes to act, one commits the crime and the other does not — he lacks the courage. Courage, then, is a factor of crime, and the lack of it a factor of virtue ! *Not so, that depends upon circumstances.* In another case, he who commits a crime is stupid, and does not consider the risk, and he who does not commit it is a crafty man. Stupidity, then, is a factor of crime, and craft of virtue ! *Not so, that depends upon circumstances.* The reverse is also true, probably more true still. Thousands of great criminals so far from being stupid have had something of the genius in them.

The famous individual factors are only ordinary human qualities, like courage, strength, needs, intelligence, etc. etc.,[1] which men possess in differing degrees, and which in like circumstances lead the one rather than the other to commit a crime. *These qualities in themselves, however, have nothing to do with crime.* Professor Manouvrier expresses my thought on this subject in the following: "There are, however, certain individuals more moved to crime than others, in circumstances otherwise equal. Certainly, as man is more given to crime than woman, as a robust and bold man is more given to crimes of violence than one who is miserable and timid, etc., yet each type of character finds some kind of crime practicable, if only arson. The athlete will be more inclined to strike, the smooth talker to play the confidence man, but we do not for that reason indict muscular strength, nor ready speech, nor boldness, nor agility, nor address. No more do we indict violence or trickery, qualities defined from the vicious use made of qualities valuable for honest purposes." [2]

The reasoning of Professor Ferri, that there is in every crime, besides others, an anthropological factor, is only the statement of the fact, known long before the rise of modern criminology, that the predisposition to crime is not the same with all men. This predisposition, as we have seen, considered by itself, has nothing to do with crime as such. So much the more is the conclusion of Professor Ferri and the Italian school in general absolutely false, when they deduce from the undeniable fact that the predisposition is not the

[1] Upon crime and sex see Pt. II, Ch. II, § I, C., d.
[2] "Genèse normale du crime", p. 451.

same for all, the notion that this predisposition is by nature pathological.

Thus we have finally come to two other groups of anthropological
factors: *the organic constitution of the criminal*, as, for example, the
anomalies of the skull, brain, etc. and *the psychical constitution of the
criminal*, as, for example, the anomalies of intelligence and feeling.[1]
This is the special territory of the Italian school: the criminal is a
being apart — "genus homo criminalis" — with special stigmata
peculiar to him; there is a criminal type, anatomically recognizable;
most criminals are born-criminals, etc. The explanation of this
special character is to be found in atavism, an hypothesis later
replaced by that of epilepsy; finally it has been claimed that the
character of the criminal is in general of a pathological nature.

In our purely sociological work, though it combats in an indirect
way the hypothesis of the Italian school, we do not have to concern
ourselves with the conflict between the different anthropological
schools, with regard to the origin of crime. We demonstrate merely,
what no one who judges fairly will attempt to deny, that the hypothesis of the Italian school is erroneous. The anthropological
authorities like Manouvrier, Baer, Naecke, and others, have broken
this doctrine down.[2] There are no stigmata belonging to criminals
only, nor is there any criminal type; the atavistic hypothesis is one
of the profoundest errors.

Although the doctrine of Lombroso and his school is in general
abandoned by anthropologists, it still persists in the acceptance of one
fact, to which it is its immortal merit to have called attention, namely
that there are a number of criminals (though a very limited number)
who show a truly pathological nature, and whose criminal character
can only be explained by this pathological nature. For example,
when someone in an epileptic condition commits a murder, without
any motive; or the case in which a well-to-do individual steals
continually useless articles, of little value, etc., etc. Even in most
of these instances, which are a small minority in the colossal mass of
criminality, the social environment plays its part; but it must be
recognized without reserve that here we have to do with true individual factors, peculiar to certain individuals. The hypothesis of the

[1] Among the anthropological factors Professor Ferri includes also education, profession, civil status, etc., called all together the bio-social conditions.
I am of the opinion that these factors ought not to be classed as anthropological, but as social.

[2] [NOTE TO THE AMERICAN EDITION: Among the recent works against the
Italian school must be named that of Dr. *S. Ettinger*, "Das Verbrecherproblem".]

Italian school is, then, accurate for the exception, but false as a rule. —

PHYSICAL FACTORS

It is evident that the nature of the soil, the climate, the physical environment in a word, must have an important influence upon the mode of production, and consequently upon society.[1]

It is easily understood why those who inhabit the regions of Siberia covered with snow have not become agriculturists; and why Holland, without mines of iron and coal has not become a great manufacturing country, but instead, situated upon the sea and traversed by great rivers, has become commercial. But these physical factors have remained constant or nearly constant during historical periods, while the organization of society has undergone changes that have great effects. We cannot explain these changes by a constant factor.

Plechenow formulates this very well in his "Beiträge der Geschichte des Materialismus." He says: "The character of man's natural environment determines the character of his productive activity, of his means of production. The means of production, however, determines the reciprocal relationships of men in the process of production as inevitably as the equipment of an army determines its entire organization, and all the relationships of the individuals of which it is made up. Now the reciprocal relations of men in the social process of production determine the entire structure of society. The influence of the natural environment upon this structure is therefore incontestable. *The character of the natural environment determines that of the social environment.* For example: 'The necessity of computing the time of the rising of the Nile, created Egyptian astronomy and with it the domination of the priestly caste as guides in agriculture.'

"But this is only one side of the matter. Another side must also be considered if one is not to draw entirely false conclusions. The circumstances of production are the *result*, the productive forces are the cause. But the effect becomes a cause in its turn; the circumstances of production become a new source of the development of the productive forces. This leads to a double result.

"1. The mutual influence of the circumstances of production and the productive forces causes a social movement, which has its own logic and a law of its own, independent of the natural environment.

[1] It is not correct, in my opinion, to class agricultural production among the physical factors as Professor Ferri does. It is rather one of the social factors.

For example : Private property in the primitive phase of its development is always the fruit of the labor of the property-holder himself, as may be very well observed in the Russian villages.   There necessarily comes a time, however, when it becomes the reverse of what it was before : it supposes the work of another, and becomes capitalistic private property, as we can likewise see any day in the Russian villages.   This phenomenon is the effect of the immanent law of the evolution of private property.   All that the natural environment can accomplish in this case consists in accelerating this movement through favoring the development of the productive forces.

"2.   Since the social evolution has its own logic, independent of any direct influence from the natural environment, it may happen that a people, though inhabiting the same land and retaining almost the same physical peculiarities, may have at different epochs of its history social and political institutions which are very little similar, or even totally different one from another." [1]

Crime being a social phenomenon, and society being influenced, as we have seen, by the physical environment, one might say that this environment is a factor in criminality.   He who reasons thus would have to grant that the physical environment is only an indirect factor, and therefore a very remote cause.   It would be as fair to say that the invention of gunpowder was one of the causes of all murders committed with fire-arms.   However, in reasoning thus I believe we forget that crime is an *historic* phenomenon, modifying itself according to the condition of society, and consequently regulated by laws that are independent of the physical environment.   In other words, the environment is the reason why a people provides for its needs by working the material that nature has furnished ; but the manner in which this work is done is independent of this environment. And it is upon this manner of working that criminality depends.   An example taken from practice will make clear what I have been saying.

From the nature of the soil of Sicily it is possible to work sulphur mines there.   The criminality of Sicily is very great, especially in the parts where the mines are found, and many murders particularly are committed there.   We might be disposed to believe that here the physical factors came into play.   Now it is true that the nature of the soil is the cause of the exploiting of the mines, but the criminality is dependent entirely upon the way in which the exploiting is done, and this has nothing to do with the physical environment.   To particularize : these mines are exploited in the capitalistic fashion, *i.e.*,

[1] Pp. 199–201.

with the aim of getting as much profit as possible, which brings it about that the workers are untaught, demoralized and made degenerate by ill-paid labor, excessively severe, and carried on in an unwholesome atmosphere. Hence come the higher figures for criminality.[1]

Most authors who have concerned themselves with the influence of these physical factors, have only observed their direct influence upon man. Many of them have paid no attention to the importance that these factors may have for the character of society, and they have taken no account of the fact that society develops according to laws independent of the physical environment. Phenomena have been ascribed to the direct influence of the physical environment, which have no such relationship. It is a fact pretty generally recognized, for example, that the number of violent crimes is greater in the South than in the North. The cause frequently given is the obvious one that it is the difference of climate. But this overlooks the fact that the phase of social development reached in the southern countries is totally different from that in the northern countries, and this difference explains that of the criminality against persons. Upon this subject Professor Tarde says: "Statistics compiled in epochs when, civilization not having passed from the South to the North, the North was more barbarous, would certainly have shown that crimes of blood were more numerous in the northern climates, where now they are more rare, and would have induced the Quetelets of that day to formulate a law precisely the reverse of the one now stated. For example, if we divide Italy into three zones, Lombardy, Central, and Southern Italy, we shall find that at present there are in the first 3 homicides to the 100,000 inhabitants annually, in the second nearly 10, and in the third more than 16. But shall we estimate that in the palmy days of Grecia Major, when Crotona and Sybaris flourished in the south of a peninsula which, in the North, was totally peopled with brigands and barbarians, except for the Etruscans, the proportion of bloody crimes would not have been reversed? At present there are in Italy, in proportion to the population, sixteen times as many homicides as in England, nine times as many as in Belgium, and five times as many as in France. But we could swear that under the Roman Empire it was quite otherwise, and that the savage Britons, and even the Belgians and the Gauls surpassed the effeminate Romans in habitual ferocity of manners, in vindictive fury and bravery.

[1] See *Niceforo;* "Criminalità e condizioni economiche in Sicilia" ("Rivista scientifica del diretto", 1897), and *Colajanni,* "L'homicide en Italie" ("Revue Socialiste", July, 1901).

According to Maine the Scandinavian literature shows that homicide during the period of barbarism was a 'daily accident' with these peoples of the North, at present the mildest and most inoffensive in Europe." [1]

It is plain from what has gone before that I have not wished to deny the *direct* influence of the physical environment upon man. Indeed, it is a fact which the whole world has observed. According to many persons, then — and a number of scientific researches have proved it — a high degree of criminality against persons proceeds from a hot temperature, while a low temperature, on the other hand, leads to many crimes against property. This implies not only that the kind of crime is different in hot countries from that in cold, but also that the change of the seasons with their variations in temperature have the corresponding effects.

I will not fatigue the reader by citing an unlimited number of examples to prove that the exceptions to this rule are very numerous. We cannot find a greater number of crimes against persons and a smaller number of crimes against property with each degree nearer the equator. If this were the case dishonesty would be unknown at the equator, and everyone there would be very violent. There are countries which, though in the same latitude, are very different as to crime, as there are others, much alike as to crime though situated far from each other, etc., etc.[2] The adherents of the theory of the "physical environment" explain these exceptions by saying that they are caused by the "social environment." By so doing they recognize that the latter may entirely alter and even annihilate the influence of the former. Let us concern ourselves rather with the different kinds of crime, and investigate the influence which the physical environment exercises upon it.

In the first place, as to the assertion that cold increases the number of crimes against property it is unnecessary to speak at length, for nearly all authors are agreed that not physical but economic causes come into play here. Cold increases men's needs; they must have warmer clothing and a well heated dwelling. But it is clear that all this is no motive for stealing. For the person of means gets what he wants with his own money. It is the present social organization that,

---

[1] "Criminalité comparée", p. 153.

[2] It is *Colajanni* in particular who, in his "Sociologia criminale", II, has cited a great number of examples of this kind. See Chs. VII, VIII, IX. See also his "Oscillations thermométriques et delits contre les personnes" ("Archives d'anthr. crim.", 1886). See also *Földes*, "Einige Ergebnisse der Neueren Kriminalstatistik" ("Zeitschr. f. d. ges. Strafrw.", XI, p. 544).

during the severe weather, does not permit people to provide for the needs that are more numerous then, for the opportunity to work is more often lacking in winter than in summer.

As to crimes against persons Professor Ferri is of the opinion that the direct influence of temperature is as follows: "The increase of acts of violence to persons, which is observed in connection with higher temperatures, must be chiefly dependent upon the direct physiological effect of heat upon the human organism. For by the greater warmth the consumption of material for the production of animal heat is cut down, and hence a surplus of force is stored up capable of being used for other purposes. But this, in union with the heightened irritability of temper, may easily degenerate into that criminal activity which shows itself in acts of violence to persons. With this psychological effect of the heat, it is true, there is coupled, in the case of the poorer classes who form the majority of the population, the effect of more easily obtained and more plentiful food, but this social cause in this connection is of less importance than the direct biological influence." [1]

The first explanation of Professor Ferri is astonishing because everyone feels that the heat has a different effect upon himself than the one given. The fact that during hot weather the consumption of bodily fuel is not so great as in cold weather cannot be considered as the most important point in treating of the question of crime. Heat enervates men, weakens their organism, and is the cause of men's doing as little as possible. It has, then, just the opposite effect to that ascribed to it.[2]

More than once I have had occasion to point out that it is unjust to say that the improved food of the poorer classes in summer can be the cause of the greater criminality during that season. If this were the case the persons who are well nourished at all times would furnish the greatest number of violent criminals. Now we know that just the contrary is the case. In my opinion the explanation is to be sought in the fact that in summer people come into contact with one another more, and consequently there is more opportunity for evil doing.[3] But this in itself cannot naturally explain the increase of crimes. Watering-places, where the bourgeoisie attempt to escape from the effects of the heat, are not places where crimes against per-

---

[1] "Das Verbrechen in seiner Abhängigkeit von dem jährlichen Temperaturwechsel" ("Zeitschr. f. d. ges. Strafrw.", II, p. 13).

[2] See *Colajanni*, "Soc. crim.", II, pp. 427 *ff*.

[3] See: *Tarde*, "Penal Philosophy", p. 303; *Quetelet*, "Physique sociale", II, p. 288; *Colajanni*, "Soc. Crim.", II, pp. 431 *ff*.

sons occur in great numbers.   Yet the concentration of many people
in a limited space is there very great.   The degree of cultivation of
the people determines the greater or less ease with which quarrels
arise.   And what proves that this degree need not be very high is the
fact that acts of violence are very rare among the bourgeois, the
greater number of whom have only a superficial culture.

The most convincing proof that the increase of violent crimes in
spring has no direct connection with the heat, is found in the fact
that this increase is already very great in the months in which in the
North of Europe there is absolutely no question of heat properly so
called (*i.e.* in March and April) ; and in the second place the course of
crimes during the week must be noted, with the maximum on Sunday,
when naturally the heat is no greater than on other days ; and in the
third place, the maximum is not to be found at the hottest time of the
day.[1]

The increase of sexual crimes in hot seasons is in part only apparent,
because those who commit these crimes then operate more out of
doors, and a greater number of arrests results.   For the rest, it must
be conceded that the sexual instinct in general is quickened a little
during the spring and summer, and as a consequence sexual acts
increase.   But this does not mean that these acts are therefore criminal.   The principal reason why sexual crimes increase during the hot
weather is to be found in opportunity, which occurs much more frequently than in cold weather.   The proverb says : "opportunity
makes the thief ", and this is still more applicable to sexual criminals.[2]

I am therefore of the opinion that the social factors must not be
included in the etiology of crime.   They have their influence upon the
structure of society, they have also their influence upon man, but it
depends upon social conditions whether this influence takes a criminal
direction or not.[3]

[1] See "Introduction to the Criminal Statistics of England and Wales,
1905 ", p. 53.
[2] Besides the authors cited, see also, as regards the influence of physical
factors, *Mischler*, "Hauptergebnisse in moralischer Hinsicht" ("Handbuch
des Gefängniswesens", II, p. 485) ; *Fr. von Liszt*, "Die sozialpolitische Auffassung des Verbrechens" ("Sozial-politisches Centralblatt", 1892).
[3] [NOTE TO THE AMERICAN EDITION : Upon the relation between criminality
and the physical environment see also the recent works : *Aschaffenburg*,
"Das Verbrechen und seine Bekämpfung", pp. 13 *ff.*; *de Roos*, "Quelques
recherches sur les causes de l'augmentation des vols pendant l'hiver et des
coups et blessures pendant l'été" ("Comptes rendu du VIe Congres internat.
d'anthrop. crim."); *Wulffen*, "Psychologie des Verbrechers", I, pp. 381 *ff.*;
P. Gaedeken, "Contribution statistique à la réaction de l'organisme sous
l'influence physico-chimique des agents météorologiques" ("Archives d'anthr.
crim.", XXIV); *Verrijn-Stuart, op. cit.*, pp. 176 *ff.*; *v. Mayr*, "Statistik u.
Gesellschaftslehre", pp. 605 *ff.*]

Before taking up our analysis of "Socialismo e criminalità", I would remark that this division of the factors into three groups has to do exclusively with the individual criminal, and thus loses sight of the question why such an action in any place whatever, at any time whatever, is regarded as criminal? Such a query brings out the fact that we are here concerned with social factors only.

Let us take up now the exposition of Chapter I of "Socialismo e criminalità." Turati, in his "Il delitto e la questione sociale" has made the following objections to Professor Ferri's theses. Professor Ferri distinguishes five categories of criminals: insane criminals, incorrigible born-criminals, habitual criminals, criminals from passion, and occasional criminals. In the first two categories individual factors play a very important rôle; however, according to Professor Ferri's investigations these two groups include but 20% to 25% of the whole number of criminals, and deducting the insane, only 10% remain. Since criminals form only the minority of the population, and physical factors have only a slight influence, it follows that these factors influence rather the form than the cause of the crime. The three factors work nearly all the time. It is clear, therefore, that the two other factors alone will not be strong enough to produce crime at a time when the social factor is eliminated, as has been proved by the socialistic colony at New Lanark, which preserved an exemplary morality for four years. Then, without taking account of the crimes that are the consequence of viciousness of life or of the abnormal economic condition, the authors of great crimes (except technical and professional ones) are less numerous among the well-to-do than among the lower classes, where the anthropological elements are nearly the same. And if the different classes show anthropological differences, this is not because these differences are innate in individuals on account of being born in the lower classes, but because they are produced and brought about by poverty, bad education, etc. The true causes of crime are consequently social conditions, and in the last analysis economic conditions.

Professor Ferri's argument against what has just been said may be summed up as follows: Will there be no social atmosphere in a socialistic state? Or rather, will this atmosphere be so perfect that the germ of the smallest social factor of crime will be absent? Do we suppose that when poverty is suppressed, jealousy will disappear at the same time? If legal marriage is abolished will that prevent an ugly man from violating or killing a beautiful woman who refuses to accept him? It may be objected that in this case the man is not an habitual or an occasional criminal, but a born-criminal, or an insane criminal, or a criminal from passion. Well and good, but then in this future state we shall still be far removed from an earthly paradise.

Turati commits the following errors in his reasoning: First, he sets aside the insane criminals; wrongly, according to Professor Ferri, for, although insane, they are criminals. Second, 20%, the figure to which born and insane criminals count up, is a very large number out of 60,000 prisoners. Third, Professor Ferri claims that it is incorrect to say that the other causes are reduced to zero the moment the social factors of crime are suppressed. For even with occasional criminals, where the environment plays a very important part, an individual factor must make its effect felt, or the individual would not become criminal.

Professor Ferri asks, on the other hand: How does it happen that out of a hundred working-men living in the same environment, only a very few fall into crime? This can be explained only by admitting individual and physical causes. When socialists say that these individual differences are innate simply in consequence of the poverty in which ancestors of the persons in question have lived for thousands of years, the author admits this reasoning in great part, but thinks nevertheless that he is right in maintaining that these qualities are *innate* in certain individuals at the present time.

With regard to the fact that a very high morality was maintained in New Lanark, the author says: first, that he would very much like to convince himself with his own eyes, especially since he has read that in this colony the habit of celebrating Christmas eve with excessive drinking was kept up; second, that he knows that crimes were committed in a communistic colony of that time; further we are not to forget that difficulties are increased in a great city.

The following chapter is entitled: "Benessere e criminalità." To the unproved assertion of the socialists that bad economic conditions are the principal if not the only cause of crime, the author opposes some facts to prove that this statement is largely incorrect. To this end he divides crimes into three groups: first, crimes against property, second, crimes against persons or crimes of blood, and third, crimes against morals. Besides these three categories there are many crimes which have neither directly nor indirectly any connection with bad economic conditions; for example, crimes against honor, insults, or abuse of power.

First, then, the crimes against property. The author recognizes that most of these crimes are caused by bad economic conditions. But it is an exaggeration, he says, to say that all these crimes result from such conditions. This is to overlook crimes against property committed out of revenge. However, in a communistic society there would necessarily be cases of theft still, without taking into account kleptomania, etc. For the articles of consumption would still remain private property; and why should one not rob his fellow-citizen from jealousy? Or is it not probable that someone would prefer to take from his neighbor the thing he needs rather than make a trip of some miles to get it from a central store? But if we admit that the bad economic conditions of the time are the cause of the crimes against property, it remains to find the causes of the crimes of the other groups. Though he recognizes that economic conditions occupy a place in the etiology of these last crimes, as, for example, murder from cupidity, the author does not believe that this can be made a general rule. When socialists object that the man of the future will be morally improved, Professor Ferri is of the opinion that at the present moment we have to do with the men of today and not with the men of the future.

The study of criminality in France during the years 1825–80 has shown an extraordinary increase in crimes against persons and against morals during the years 1848–52. A minute examination shows the author that it was due to the great increase in the consumption of meat and wine, both very cheap at this time, and also to a rise in wages. The result of the betterment in economic conditions was, therefore, an increase in the crimes mentioned.

Professor Ferri finds another proof in the following table:

Number of Persons Arraigned to 100,000 of Each Class (France).

CRIMES.	AGRI-CULTURAL CLASS.	MANU-FACTURING CLASS.	ARTS AND TRADES.	OTHER PROFES-SIONS.	WITHOUT OCCUPATION, VAGRANTS, ETC.
Thefts	6.6	12.9	18.1	11.1	136.3
Forgery	0.7	1.3	2.1	3.4	8.3
Arson	0.4	0.4	0.5	0.3	5.2
Infanticide	0.4	0.3	0.4	0.4	4.1
Serious assaults	1.0	1.2	1.8	0.8	2.7
Homicide	0.5	0.4	0.6	0.5	2.4
Murder	0.9	0.7	1.1	0.9	5.8
Sexual crimes with violence .	0.4	0.7	1.0	0.4	1.9
" " against children	0.7	1.4	2.1	1.1	5.5
Average of all crimes . .	13.9	23.0	32.5	22.4	193.0

It follows from this table that the farming class, which, if you except vagabonds, is the class with the least means, shows the figure relatively lowest, and that the assertion of the socialists, that those who are brought to the bar of justice are almost all from the proletariat, is inaccurate.

— I shall not discuss the question, whether the proletariat furnishes a disproportionately large contingent of criminals. The arguments of Professor Ferri do not seem very strong to me. "Agricultural class", for example, is too vague a distinction. What an enormous distinction between the rich farmer and the poor day-laborer, who earns only a few francs a week! Yet both are included in the first group. —

When we examine the course of crime in France during the period 1826–80, we see a considerable increase in the crimes against property, morals, and persons, while the economic conditions have improved during these years even for the proletariat. To what cause is this increase to be ascribed? It is impossible to attribute it to a relaxation of the strictness of the police and the courts, for the activity of these has become greater. Further, where it is evident that there are such strong causes of crime, it would be madness to think that a greater severity of penalties leads to a diminution of criminality. It is for this reason that the school to which the author belongs insists not upon the increase of penalties, but rather upon the elimination of causes. Hence the doctrine of "penal substitutes."

The true cause is the following: The more abundantly a man is nourished, the more his organic forces are developed; there is, therefore, a greater activity which may express itself in more acts of honest labor, but may also express itself in an increased number of unlawful acts. And then we must not lose sight, especially with regard to sexual crimes, of the existence of a biological and of a sociological law, namely, first, that the generative force of animals and of man increases in proportion to the abundance and ease of nutrition ; second, that by a continual development of foresight, the nations which follow the advice of Malthus are more and more giving the lie to the law that he formulated, since with them population shows a tendency to increase less rapidly than the means of existence, and almost in inverse proportion to wealth. This is why criminality is increasing in France, where the system of foresight is greatly developed, and where the population enjoys better nutrition than formerly.

Professor Ferri is of the opinion that we can derive from the observed facts the following rules: first, criminality increases in extent but diminishes in violence; second, scarcity makes crimes against property increase, and decreases those against persons, while abundance has the opposite effect; third, civilization decreases the number of homicides, but increases that of suicides; fourth, a development of foresight with regard to births prevents an excessive increase of the population, and consequently an excessive increase of pauperism, but increases the figures for sexual crimes.

Turati makes the following objections to these statements: In the first place, in civilized countries, crimes against persons are much less numerous than crimes against property, and just in proportion to the degree of civilization. Why is it not likely that in the end the criminogenous influence of nutrition will disappear in consequence of the law in accordance with which crimes increase in number, but decrease in grossness and intensity? Further, it is doubtful whether this influence is so strong. The true cause is not good nutrition but the Malthusian check, and it is this last which leads to crime, precisely in the proletariat, since in this class prostitution cannot act as a safety valve; and bad economic conditions are the cause of the "moral restraint."

Professor Ferri recognizes that there is a partial truth in this reasoning, but makes the following objections: that crimes of blood are more numerous than crimes against morals and yet have no relation to the Malthusian check; that, as regards crimes against morals, it is not correct to say that the proletariat are driven to them by economic causes; that it is the proletariano that multiply the fastest, and the well-to-do classes, who do not wish to have many children; and that the individual and biological factors would always remain, and lead to crimes against persons, even if the aforesaid cause of sexual crimes were to disappear. In the following chapters the author treats of the assertion of Turati that an improvement in education and the new "social atmosphere" will bring about a change.

— The criticism of the chapter of which I have just been speaking may be summed up as follows: Like so many other authors, Professor Ferri understands the expression, "economic conditions", in a very limited sense. He includes only direct influences, and in this way it is very easy to prove that they explain only a part of criminality. But this interpretation is very incomplete, since all social life is influenced by economic conditions. In proving, therefore, like many other authors, that while an improvement in the economic condition of the working-class is accompanied by a decrease in crimes against property, it is also accompanied by an increase of sexual crimes and crimes against persons, Professor Ferri forgets not only that the lack of education leads to crimes of violence, but also that in our present society the possibility of satisfying the sexual appetites depends upon the social position of the individual. The argument, in opposition to Turati, "that Malthusianism is applied chiefly by persons of some means" is not a happy one for one who wants to prove that economic conditions have not a considerable influence. For the reason of this is just the difficulty of procuring a good position for many children, and, in the case of landholders, the desire to avoid a too great division of the land. These are purely economic causes. —

"Educazione e criminalità" is the title of the third chapter. The human brain is an organic mechanism, similar (but with numerous exceptions) to an inorganic mechanism in this, that it is subject to the great law of the conservation of energy, which manifests itself, among other ways, in inertia. From which it comes that man at all times has had an irresistible tendency to make use of a general principle as a basis for his logical structures. Without this he would always be forced to build each new structure from the ground up, which would involve the waste of too much cerebral energy. Opposed to this law is another which teaches us that life is impossible in a state of absolute repose, but that it requires a perpetual changing of the organic and physio-psychic materials. Hence it comes that eternal and absolute truths change at different epochs, and that they seem stable only when compared with the secondary truths, which are subject to the fashions of the time.

According to the author, then, there are truths that are more general and nearly inalterable, but there are others which, though general also, are more secondary, only retain their force during several generations, and end by being changed. Such, for example, are the views concerning human life, formulated by the great thinkers, then accepted by the majority, and finally supplanted by other truths. This is why science makes progress by dogmas. It is modern science that has made the great step in recognizing that these dogmas are relative and alterable.

Against this reasoning two objections can be alleged. First, that Spencer has given the name "hypothesis" to his doctrine of evolution, while Professor Ferri calls it a dogma. The author on the other hand thinks that his opinions and those of Spencer are exactly alike, for he calls the doctrine in question a relative and alterable dogma, and Spencer says of it : what I have given is an hypothesis ; but so long as there is nothing better, that will explain a greater number of facts, I have a right to consider it as the image of the knowable truth, until the contrary is proved. In the second place, it may be asked : "Does man always oscillate between truth and error; will he never know an absolute and eternal truth?" According to Professor Ferri the answer to this question is not difficult. The origin as well as the aim of faith is the effort to give to men a relatively stable support, which they cannot find elsewhere. All discussion with the adherents of a theological opinion is excluded; and as for the others, ought they not to recognize that the life of human thought is just the constant proof of the continual modification of the so-called eternal verities?

After this introduction the author enters upon the subject itself. At the beginning of the 19th century the dogma was dominant, that instruction was the panacea for all crimes. Later many of the publicists, including the socialists, advanced the opinion that the true remedy for criminality was education. Just as the first theory was incorrect, Professor Ferri would show that the second is equally so.

The question is, can education lead man to good or to evil; and if it can, how far can it lead him? The scientific pedagogues have not treated this question, as far as the author knows. Without furnishing proofs the socialists admit that education can modify man in many respects. Owen, for example, says : "every child may be brought up to have in his later life only good habits, or bad, or a mixture of the two, according to his education."

It is necessary to distinguish three kinds of education — physical, intellectual, and moral. First, a general observation applicable to all kinds of education. In his physical, intellectual, and moral make-up, each individual is the product of a countless number of ancestors, to whom he is bound by unchangeable laws of heredity. From this it is clear that the power of education, which acts only during a limited number of years, is small compared to that of the influences to which a man's ancestors have been subjected for thousands of years. The question becomes, then : "what are the limits of such modification?" Further it is necessary to determine just how far this modification is due to education, and how far to environment. For education, properly so called, *i.e.* the direct and methodical influence of the educator upon his pupil, differs in many respects from that of the physical and social environment. This is why the author treats this latter in a special chapter, and limits himself now to education alone.   The question is therefore reduced to this : "how far can a man (the educator) modify the constitution of another man (the pupil) ? "

One more observation should precede the study of the question, namely that a force, or a complexus of forces, can be influenced only by other *homogeneous* forces.   Now when we examine how far physical or biological education can make its influence felt, we see that this influence may be very great, though naturally limited, in proportion to the knowledge we have of the structure and functioning of the organs which it is attempted to modify.   As to intellectual education, the results are much less, since the knowledge of the organs involved is much smaller.   As to moral education, the following question is one to which pedagogues have given little attention : "how far do morality or immorality, good or bad character, depend upon the education received at home and in school?"

Spencer lays down the fundamental rule that the *moral* conduct of man can be studied scientifically only on condition of being considered as forming part of the conduct in general, and also of the activity in general, of all living beings.   Sergi is of the same opinion.   And this is correct, Professor Ferri thinks, if, as these two authors do, one studies the conduct and character of man in their constituent elements, in their genesis and development, without taking into consideration the variability of the character, and consequently of the conduct, of man because of his education.   In our case, in studying the constituent elements, the genesis, the development, and the variability of the moral part of the character and conduct of man, it is necessary to separate these parts, and to limit ourselves to a special study of one of them.

All psychologists are agreed that the moral conduct of a man (including criminal conduct) although having naturally a certain relationship with his muscular and intellectual condition, depends directly and intimately upon the condition of his feelings, emotions, and passions in their moral aspect.   Hence it is clear that the problem is : "how far can these feelings be modified by education?"

Let us first of all note that the expression, "a man of good (or bad) birth", does not imply that there are persons who are totally good or totally bad, for these two qualities always appear in combination. It only indicates whether the good or the bad qualities predominate.

It is certain that some persons have become criminals from lack of moral education, added to bad surroundings.   In this case this lack of education has favored the greater development of the bad germs, which, however, gives us no right to conclude that the converse would be true : that education can improve the moral character, strengthening the good germs to such a point that they have the mastery over the bad. For we must not lose sight of two things : first, that the bad germs that show themselves in our present society are the anti-social instincts, opposed to the sociability and sympathy upon which life is based, while the good germs are the social instincts ; second, that, since individuals reproduce morphologically and physiologically during life the different phases that man and animal have gone through, it is in the lowest strata of his character that man preserves the savage and anti-social feelings that are the consequences of the condition in which the race has lived heretofore, while the germs of the modern social ideas are to be found in the higher and more recent parts. Hence it follows that the anti-social instincts, being of a more ancient date than the social instincts, are stronger than they and are not stifled by them. And then, the environment, the present civilization, is also partly the cause. This is why the author agrees with Sergi that in our present society there are individuals who are constantly driven to crime by their organic and psychical constitution, made up in great part of the deeper, anti-social strata (the born-criminals and incorrigibles), and that there are others whose constitution is formed primarily of the more recent, social strata, and who become criminal only under extraordinary impulses, in consequence of a volcanic eruption, as it were, from the deeper, anti-social strata (criminals from passion). While Sergi is of the opinion that the anti-social instincts will little by little become latent, lose their force, and cease to act, Professor Ferri thinks that this will be the case only with the minority of men.

Now in order to weaken the anti-social tendencies, it is, according to the author, necessary to know, first, their seat ; second, their composition. Up to the present, psychology has made no study of the human passions, emotions, and feelings, and consequently cannot give us this information. It must therefore be considered as impossible that education should so stifle the existing bad germs and strengthen the good ones that these last should finally have the upper hand.

Moral education consists only of a series of auditory and visual sensations, impressed upon the individual by means of advice and example, which brings it about that it is more especially a moral *instruction*, which makes its mark in the intellect, but leaves intact the seat of the passions and feelings, which are the true motive forces

of the moral conduct.   Moral education becomes little by little more
systematic, bases itself more than formerly upon the biological principle that each organ and function is developed by exercise, and consequently is improving.   The author believes that we must nevertheless not deceive ourselves into fancying that too much has been
accomplished, so long as the origin and condition of the moral and
immoral germs are unknown.   Further, he is of the opinion that the
product of centuries is not to be destroyed in a few years.

In order to prove what has just been said the author cites the following example, which, according to him, is not uncommon.   A
family includes four or five children ; all are reared with the greatest
care, each in a different manner according to his character.   The result is that three or four of them become more or less good and industrious citizens, while one becomes an incorrigible vagabond.   This
difference does not depend upon education.

Now it will be asked : is education, then, always and altogether
useless ? Here a distinction must be made.   There is one small
category of persons who are good and honorable and remain so under
all circumstances, and this exclusively from their organic condition.
Opposed to this is another group who are always bad and show anti-
social instincts.   These last are such from an innate organic and psychic anomaly.   Between these two is to be found the very numerous
class of individuals in whom the good and bad qualities are combined.
For this last class education may be of some importance, but environment is still more so.   Hence, in order to lower the number of occasional criminals, criminal sociology demands "penal substitutes."
For it is from this intermediate class that criminals are recruited.
However, environment and education are of less importance for this
category than heredity.

The conclusions drawn by the author are, then : first, that a development of the physiology and psychology of the human passions is
very desirable, in order to improve the means at the disposal of education ; and second, that the opinion of Owen, that education can
make a bad man good, is incorrect.

— In my criticism I shall limit myself to the principal questions.
In the first place I believe that the argument of Professor Ferri,
based on the supposition that scientific socialists believe that "education is the omnipotent fact", is futile.   For scientific socialists do
not hold this opinion.   Owen (who belongs to the Utopists) might
be thought to hold it, though he does not use the word education in

the narrow sense given by Professor Ferri, but it will be very difficult to find such an opinion in Marx, or Engels, or any of their followers. Although holding that circumstances have a very great influence upon the individual, they do not attribute this to the systematic, conscious influence of one individual upon another, which is what is commonly meant by education. For the purposes of Professor Ferri's argument it may be very useful to make a nice distinction between education and atmosphere, but this distinction is not therefore justified. The impressions gained by a child whether from the atmosphere in which he lives or deliberately impressed upon him by his teacher, are hardly distinguishable. Just out of class he plays with his comrades, and this easily makes him forget the moral lessons he has just received. A mother forbids her child to do a certain thing, and a little later he sees an older member of the family do with impunity what has been forbidden in his own case. It is because of this over-nice distinction that the argument of the author loses much of its value.

In the second place, as the author himself partly admits, the influence that education *may* exert cannot be exactly fixed, no matter what progress pedagogical science may make, for the following reasons. It is only in school that the scientific pedagogical method is applied, and plainly in an incomplete and imperfect manner. In order that children shall be taught and developed they must be well fed and well clothed. Without this the results will be very small, but pupils insufficiently fed and clothed are to be counted by thousands. It is also necessary that a class include as few pupils as possible, in order that the instructor may not have to divide his attention too much. Yet how many cases are there where this is found? For these reasons, to which might be added others, all of an exclusively economic nature, the school does not contribute as much as it might to moral education. The advantage of the education given in school over that furnished by the parents consists in its practical application, at least in part, according to pedagogical rules. The parents who set themselves to bring up their children on scientific principles are so few as to be easily counted. Almost all are novices in this very difficult trade; little attention is paid to whether parents are ignorant or educated, good or bad, patient or irascible, capable or incapable, in short, of bringing up their children. The present organization of society is based upon the fiction that the person who gives life to a child is also fitted to bring it up. Further, existing social conditions put many parents, however capable they might otherwise be, in a position where they cannot give their children any care, on account of the long working-day, the labor of married women, etc.   These remarks, it seems to me, are in themselves enough to show that we cannot just now come to a definite conclusion, that the influence of education may extend to such and such a point, but no further.

In the third place, it remains to make valid objections to the principal thesis that forms the foundation of the chapter.   Here it is in brief.   There was a time when men lived in anti-social conditions; all were enemies one of another.   This situation lasted for ages until the social sentiments grew up and civilization developed.   But these anti-social germs having lasted for ages, while the social germs are only of recent date, it follows that the former are generally much stronger than the latter.   This is why the tendency to evil has predominated in man, and why crime has such enormous dimensions.

I am of the opinion that this argument is based upon an error.   In Part II of this work I shall attempt to show that the opinion of Professor Ferri (and other authors), that in the early ages all men were enemies and animated by anti-social feelings, is false.   I shall endeavor also to show that the present constitution of society does not give rise to social feelings, but anti-social.   Finally it is very problematical whether the hypothesis the author uses, namely that acquired characteristics may be inherited, is defensible; the contrary is coming more and more to be believed.   But we cannot in any case admit the transmission of morality itself by heredity, as Professor Ferri does, when he speaks of men who remain good under all circumstances, and consequently of men who must have been born with innate moral prescriptions.   A child is never born with *positive knowledge;* he is born with a brain more or less fitted for the reception and development of knowledge.   There was never a child who, from his birth, knew the rules "thou shalt not steal", "thou shalt not kill", etc.   But the organs destined to become the seat of morality differ with each individual like other organs.   When the author says, then, that there are men who remain good under all circumstances, he says, in effect, that there are men whose moral organs are very susceptible, and who consequently remain better than men whose organs are less susceptible.   Therefore the accumulation of anti-social feelings in man of the present day, through heredity, is imaginary.   Finally, Professor Ferri neglects to note the difference in nature and intensity between the needs of different men.   For this is the cause of the great inequality of results obtained from the same education given to persons of equal capacity for receiving moral impressions. If a man has great needs it takes a much more intense moral effort to keep him from satisfying them in an immoral manner, than is the case with a man whose needs are slight. —

The following chapter, "Ambiente e criminalità", begins with the assertion of Professor Ferri that the thesis of the socialists concerning the influence of the social atmosphere upon all the manifestations of human activity, and consequently upon criminality, is in great measure correct. The difference between the views of socialism and of sociology, therefore, is here only a question of limits.

According to the author here is the thesis in question : as soon as the social revolution or transformation which the socialists desire has taken place, the social atmosphere will become excellent, and man will then be morally higher than he is at present. He then examines the parts of this statement one by one.

First, Professor Ferri gives the classic formula of historic materialism, set forth by Marx in his "Zur Kritik der politischen Oekonomie", taken by the author, however, from Loria's criticism of the work of Puviani in the "Rivista critica delle scienze giuridiche e sociali." "In the memorable preface to the *Kritik der politischen Oekonomie*, published in 1859, Marx sets forth for the first time the daring theory that all the manifestations of mankind, in the juridic order as well as in the religious, philosophical, artistic, criminal, etc., are *exclusively* determined by economic relations, so that to each phase of these there corresponds a different form of human manifestations, as its necessary product."

Just as in biology the phenomena of nutrition are related to the other vital phenomena, so is the economic aspect of human activity related to the other aspects. Economic conditions have, then, a great influence on the social life, but the author believes it an exaggeration to say that economic conditions fix it *exclusively*. Further, in this statement no attention is paid to the fact that the other phenomena react in their turn upon the economic conditions, and therefore become determining factors.

Then it is said that man will be morally better when he finds himself in a purified atmosphere. This the author admits in part — how far he admits it will be easily understood by one who knows his opinion with regard to the physical, individual, and social factors of crime, and his ideas about education.

Like most of the statements of the socialists, this has, according to Professor Ferri, the fault of being too simple and consequently too absolute. Human life is already so complicated (and social life still more so) that only very little can be explained by simple formulae. It is easy to say, "Abolish private property and all the cases of theft will disappear"; "abolish legal marriage, and adultery, uxoricide, infanticide, and the other crimes against morality will disappear." But it is not therefore true. For, even in a communistic society a born-vagabond, who has a constitutional aversion to work, will commit thefts just the same. To all this it may be objected that these cases are pathological, and that these persons should be shut up in an insane asylum — but in reasoning thus one admits at the same time that such a society would not yet be an earthly paradise. Further it is pure metaphysics to believe that social institutions like property and the family are the consequences of a caprice of man or of a dominant class, and can therefore be abolished by a stroke of the pen. Everything that exists, in nature as in society, is the result of causes that are only the links in an infinite chain. Hence it is impossible to modify society at a stroke, in accordance with a plan drawn up by a theorist. This does not mean that *every* modification of society is excluded; but the situation predicted by the socialists is so much more beautiful than the present that it would not be a step, but a leap, forward. And by their prediction they deny evolution, for they constantly preach to the proletariat that the whole will be realized in the very near future.

We come now to the major premise of the socialistic thesis, namely the social revolution or transformation. The question which Professor Ferri puts to the socialists in regard to the matter is this: how long will it take you to realize your projects? There are two answers to be given according as one believes this realization possible by revolution or by evolution.

First, that by revolution. Leaving out of consideration the fact that a revolution could not take place without cruel acts being committed, with a consequent upsetting of the moral feelings, it must first of all be asked whether it is easy to bring about a revolution. The author is of the opinion that Laveleye is perfectly right when he says: "that a revolution has become an easy thing; that a social evolution is inevitable; but that a social revolution is impossible, since one cannot change by force in a single day the economic constitution of society."

Neither the word nor the fact of revolution inspires the author with fear. He recognizes that it may be in the line of evolution, although it remains an exception and is in fact a pathological manifestation of evolution. Nevertheless the question arises, what does the revolution of a day, a month, or even a year signify in comparison with the evolution that goes on during thousands of years? Does not a revolution always lead to a reaction? Suppose, however, that this reaction does not happen; will the whole people have become more moral at a single shock? What did the great French Revolution accomplish? Much, in appearance; in reality, little. It follows from what has gone before that we can modify the environment in a way and with a rapidity that will seem great to one generation but not at all great to the whole of humanity.

Now the solution by evolution. As we have already remarked, Professor Ferri recognizes that criminality will be diminished by an improvement of the environment. However, since it is impossible to make all at once general and substantial changes, it is necessary to make every effort to obtain partial improvements. This is why the positive penal school defends the doctrine of "penal substitutes." In his "Il delitto, etc.", Turati calls them palliatives; he says that it is impossible to find a specific remedy for each crime; that there is only one universal remedy: the equal distribution of wealth, education, and the happiness coming from love and knowledge, in so far as this will be socially possible. Professor Ferri thinks that Turati's objections are not based upon good reasons, because, first, the theory of penal substitutes is not limited to the designation of special means of treating special crimes, but it gives also universal means for all kinds of crimes; second, the improvements suggested by the author and his adherents have the great advantage of having been drawn up according to scientific researches, and of being immediately practicable. How could the desired transformation ever be reached if the whole system of penal substitutes were only a useless palliative?

There are only two roads leading to success; that of a violent revolution — which Turati rejects — and that of successive improvements. But it is just this which the positive penal school desires, and this is why the difference between this school and the scientific socialists has entirely disappeared. However, the error of the socialists is always that they want to get everything at one blow, and they attach too little value to what is within reach. There are many socialists who fear that the bourgeoisie will never give up their privileges without force, and who consequently have still much sympathy with revolution. However, this fear is not well founded. For most social improvements have been made by the dominant class without being compelled by revolutionary force.

Professor Ferri draws the conclusion that the social environment is circumscribed by economic conditions for the most part, and that these have a very great influence upon criminality. The socialists and the evolutionary sociologists differ, then, in this, that the first believe they can make themselves useful by protesting and prophesying, while the others think that it is more practical and more scientific to apply themselves to partial improvements.

— One cannot read this chapter without being astonished at the decided tone with which the author declares himself against a theory which he only knows from what he has heard said about it. The classic formula of historic materialism is quoted at second hand from a criticism of Professor Loria upon a work of Puviani, who says that the economic evolution is in its turn determined by the constant increase of the population (a theory entirely opposed to that of Marx).

And how the idea of this theory is treated! Let the reader judge for himself. In the original we read: "In the social production of their life men enter into fixed, necessary relationships in production, independent of their will, relationships which correspond to a definite stage in the development of their material powers of production. The sum total of these relationships forms the economic structure of society, the real basis upon which the juristic and political superstructure is erected, and to which definite forms of social consciousness correspond. The form of production of the material life conditions the social, political, and intellectual life-process in general. It is not the consciousness of mankind that determines their being, but their social being that determines their consciousness."[1]

It is unnecessary for us to linger over this point. Professor Loria has stated the theory inaccurately, and Professor Ferri, who has depended upon Loria, combats something that Marx never said, and thinks that he has discovered the further error that account is not taken of the fact that each cause is in its turn an effect, and vice versa. This too it is an injustice to impute to the founders of historic materialism. Engels says upon this subject: ". . . according to the materialistic conception of history, production and reproduction

---

[1] "Zur Kritik der politischen Oekonomie", Preface, p. xi.

of the material life are, in the last analysis, the determining factors in history. Marx and I have never claimed more. When the proposition is distorted thus: the economic factor is the *sole* determinant, the proposition is transformed into one devoid of sense, abstract, absurd. The economic situation is the basis, but the different factors of the superstructure — political forms of the struggle of the classes and its results — constitutions imposed by the victorious class after the battle has been won, etc. — juridical forms, and also the reflections of all these actual conflicts in the minds of those who have taken part in them, political, juridical, and philosophical theories, religious conceptions, and their ulterior development into systems of dogmas, have also their influence upon the march of the historic struggles, and especially in many cases determine the *form* of it. All these factors act the one upon the other, and finally the economic movement ends necessarily by dominating over the infinite crowd of chances. . . . Without this the application of the theory to any historic period would be easier than the solution of a simple equation of the second degree." [1]

Among the reproaches that Professor Ferri throws at the head of the socialists there is also that they wrongly believe it possible to change society at a single stroke. The author adds here some observations upon revolution and evolution. It is necessary to take up this question, since again Professor Ferri does not correctly represent the opinions of the Marxists. There is no question that Marx and his adherents do not suppose that they can change society at a stroke. Although evolutionists, Marx and his followers call themselves revolutionists. Many of their adversaries consider this a contradiction. I think that they are wrong, and that on the contrary the opposite is true, that every evolutionist in social matters who is not a revolutionist, has not the courage to support the consequences of his doctrine. For he who believes that society constantly undergoes *quantitative* changes ought to recognize that these must lead in the long run to a *qualitative* difference, in which case a *revolution* has taken place. The Marxists are consequently at once evolutionists and revolutionists, since, recognizing that there are continual quantitative changes, they strive for the total overturning of society as based upon the capitalistic system, and consequently for the foundation of the socialistic order. All this relates, then, only to an economic and social revolution. It follows, then, logically from what has

---

[1] "La conception materialiste de l'histoire", pp. 229, 230 ("Devenir Social", 1897).

gone before that the scientific socialists do not aspire primarily to a
political revolution; on the contrary they wish to attain their ends
as far as possible by legal means; *as far as possible*, which means, if
the ruling classes *do not prevent them* from obtaining by legal means
what they want.   But in the contrary case they do not dread undertaking even a political revolution as soon as the proletariat shall be
sufficiently prepared and organized.   Professor Ferri is further of the
opinion that there is no longer any difference between the socialists
who are at the same time evolutionists, and the sociologists, since all
reach out toward quantitative changes.   However, Professor Ferri
forgets to say that the abolition of the private ownership of the
means of production is not one of his "penal substitutes", and that
there is consequently a fundamental difference, since socialists advocate only the modifications which accord with the tendencies of
collectivism.

Finally, Professor Ferri is of the opinion that the bourgeoisie will
voluntarily relinquish their privileges, as the ruling classes have often
already done.   For this tremendous assertion he does not give any
proofs, and would find it difficult to do so. —

The title of the fifth chapter is: "L'avvenire morale dell' umanità."
The socialists — so the author begins — believe that there is a great
difference between them and the positivist sociologists, in that the
latter consider crime as an inevitable social evil, while the socialists
see in it only a passing phenomenon.   Professor Ferri, on the contrary, claims that crime, that is, the act which endangers the conditions of existence, as well as the penalty, the corresponding reaction,
defensive or preventive, both have their roots in the animal kingdom,
and are consequently phenomena more or less inseparable from humanity.   However, this sociological induction is not to be taken in
an absolute, but in this relative sense: first, that in criminality it is
necessary to distinguish two divisions, of which the one is determined
by the normal saturation, and the second by the abnormal super-
saturation; second, that the author and his adherents do not understand by the "absolute necessity" of crime that crime will always
exist, but only that it will exist in the immediate future (19th and
20th centuries), and that they retain this expression because they
regard it as useless and impossible to make predictions concerning
times more remote than this.

With regard to future morality Professor **Ferri** considers in this
chapter the two following socialistic theses:

I. The struggle for existence which has hitherto reigned among men, will find no place in the socialistic society.

II. In the socialistic society, egoism, which has been the basis of the moral and social life, will have to give place to altruism.

First, then, the question of the permanence of the struggle for existence. Professor Ferri cites here the opinions of Labusquière ("Rivista internazionale del socialismo," 1880) and of Professor Loria ("Discorso sur Carlo Darwin," 1882). Abridged, Labusquière says as follows: Is the struggle for existence, an integral part of the evolution of animals, also a "conditio sine qua non" of the development of humanity? No, since it prevents the total development by putting the majority of men in a most precarious situation. We cannot picture man as living all alone. He has always lived and will always live in a society. This demands a certain solidarity, without which a society is not imaginable. We cannot admit, then, the necessity of a continual struggle — at least we cannot admit the necessity, on the part of some, of receiving the fruits of the labor of others. The struggle for existence is necessary among animals, since they are not able to produce, and consequently must live upon such fruits as nature gives. But man can produce, and the productive forces increase just as men support one another more.

The opinion of Professor Loria is summed up as follows: the thesis that the Darwinian theory is entirely applicable to political economy is false. It is said that it justifies social inequality; nature being aristocratic, in society also the aristocracy occupies the place that belongs to it. According to Professor Loria this argument is as without sense as the argument that, since nature is a murderess, murder is justifiable. The view in question is not a legitimate conclusion from the theory as advanced by Darwin, but is simply a false interpretation made by some of his followers. There are no reasons why this struggle should always exist, but we are quite justified in supposing that it will disappear, having been but a transitory stage. For as long as egoism was the sole human motive, the struggle for existence was a necessary condition of initiative and progress. But altruism is more and more developing, and it is not Utopian to believe that some day man will reach out after physical and moral perfection, not with the aim of conquering his less-favored fellows, but with the higher aim of self-development. We forget too much how different is the struggle for existence among animals and among men. While in nature it is the strongest, hardiest, and most skillful who come out of the contest victorious, and consequently survive, in the present contest it is not the best (the workers and the capitalists who introduce improved methods of work), but those who are enriched by the labor of others, who are the conquerors. In the social struggle we perceive three phenomena which do not appear in the struggle in nature: *military selection* (which is an obstacle to the perfection of the human race); *sexual selection* (in which not strength and beauty, but money and class-prejudice determine the choice); and the economic system (which by the accumulation of capital in the hands of a few, forces the workers to lead a life that exhausts them, and is the reason why the ill-nourished classes form the majority). This is why the results of the struggle for existence are so different for man from those of the combat in nature.

Professor Ferri makes the following objections to what has been said above: In treating questions like these it is necessary not to confuse two theories, that of Spencer and that of Darwin. For the latter is connected with the former as a part with the whole. Darwinism is expressed in the law of natural selection, while the theory of Spencer is that of evolution, a law which rules not only the animal and human world, but also the whole knowable universe.

After this introductory observation he attacks the theses that Labusquière and Loria have developed. The great error committed by Labusquière and by most of the socialists is their failing to grasp the idea of the continuity and naturalness of social phenomena. There results in such cases an erroneous distinction between societies of man and those of animals; hence they do not see that the combat, proved as always existing in the case of animals and men as well, is a *natural* law. And then Labusquière and his followers forget that while the sociologists explain this combat, that is not at all saying that they justify it. In any case the assertion of the socialists that it will be possible to make this combat cease at once, after only a very brief delay, is false. As to the question of knowing whether it will ever cease, this will be examined later.

Then Professor Ferri remarks that we must not confuse the principle of a natural law with its manifestations. In the case in question this would be saying that in recognizing that the struggle for existence is a law which rules in the animal kingdom and among men, it is necessary also to think that the *forms* of the combat have been, and remain, the same. The author believes, for example, that it would be desirable to mitigate the present economic combat and to carry it to a higher plane, without therefore being an adherent of the maxim, "each one according to his needs", the application of which would ruin the human race entirely.

In criticising the law of the struggle for existence, we very often forget that it does not stand alone, but that there is another beside it, which in the long run levels all the inequalities produced by this conflict. We see thus that individuals, families, and races raise themselves above the general plane, reach the maximum of power, wealth, and intelligence, to fall again below the average.

We cannot admit that the struggle for existence, which is a principle of life, and the cause of human and animal evolution, will disappear some day because men, animated by humanitarian ideas, ardently desire it. The opinion that in the course of time this struggle is becoming and will become less and less violent and brutal, is scientifically more correct and humanitarian as well. It may be that after centuries and centuries a day will come when every individual will have his *material* existence assured. But the struggle for *moral* existence will not yet disappear on that account. For every need satisfied causes in its turn new needs to spring up, and rekindles the conflict. The socialists evince great one-sidedness in understanding by the struggle for existence only the struggle for food, forgetting that there is a struggle in every sphere.

It is claimed that there is a great difference between the struggle for existence among men and that among animals, and that consequently the results differ; that in the animal kingdom it is the strongest who remain victorious, while among men it is only a small minority of the weaker and less industrious who rule over the majority making up the ill-nourished classes. According to Professor Ferri this opinion also is incorrect; otherwise the consequences of the conflict would have a result entirely contrary to that in the animal kingdom; the human race would deteriorate instead of advancing. And the facts prove that the human race has made progress, organic, mental, social, and economic. The survival of the weaker, the less industrious, is only partial and apparent. Malon says that in our present society it is not those who are individually superior who conquer, but those who have the exclusive disposition of the social forces. But how have these forces fallen into the hands of these few? Only because *in this phase of human evolution*, they were the stronger, the best fitted. It is forgotten that there is not only a struggle between classes, but also between individuals, and that, by the greater and greater increase of altruism it is also the more altruistic workmen and employers who conquer. For an altruistic workman, who works with zeal and has his employer's interests at heart, and an altruistic employer who treats his employes well, will be more able to maintain themselves than those who act differently. It is only in appearance, then, that the less strong and industrious property-owners are the victors; if this were the case it would soon cease to be so.

The conclusion of the author, then, is that the struggle for existence, which is a normal aspect of honorable activity, and an abnormal aspect in criminal activity, is the supreme law of the human race in the past and in the present, and consequently in the future; but this struggle will be carried on by means less and less rude and bloody.

The second part of the chapter treats of egoism and altruism. The individual, considered as such, is only egoistic; but considered as a member of a community he is also altruistic. We must therefore interpret the subject in the following manner : that a gradual evolution is taking place from egoism to altruism, between which, accordingly, is found ego-altruism.

There are now two questions that must be answered, first, will man ever come to be purely altruistic? second, if so, how long will it take to bring it about?

According to the author every evolutionist must answer affirmatively to the first question (at least if we exclude the absolute form in which it is put by many socialists, namely that egoism will disappear entirely), for the slow and continual evolution of morality teaches us that egoism is always decreasing and altruism increasing. But how much time is needed to realize this moral paradise? The answers made to this question by the socialists and by the sociologists differ greatly. The former are of the opinion that this will be possible almost immediately, or at least in a little while, while the latter think that it is impossible that it should take place so quickly. Since the author has busied himself in the preceding chapters with the influence of education upon morality he limits himself now to treating the question, *how much time is needed for this moral progress?*

According to Professor Ferri we do not properly grasp this question if we do not recognize that the evolution of morals has progressed but very slowly during the past centuries. Doubtless much has been accomplished, but not enough to justify the prediction of the socialists. Soury is quite right when he says : "we deceive ourselves greatly if we think that the man of the present day differs much from the man of antiquity, from the barbarian, and the savage." When we examine the period of barbarism we see that homicide, cannibalism, and theft form the greater part of the criminality, while the first two are not often punished by the tribe, or are even obligatory. Impetuosity of the passions, ferocity, insensibility to pain in self or others, disloyalty, implacable revenge, improvidence, and superstition form the principal part of the moral life. All these traits still exist, though less strongly than formerly, in the man of the present, and especially in the individual born in the lower classes. Except in pathological cases cannibalism no longer appears in the civilized world, but this does not make it impossible that it would reappear in time of great famine. However, the high moral qualities which present-day man can show, are also to be found among savages, only with gradual differences.[1] The number of honorable and moral persons has increased relatively, which makes it certain that in the future morality will rise higher than at present, but this will not take place quickly, but very slowly, like all the other changes that have taken place.

It is therefore impossible that the predictions of the socialists should come true in a short time, and that crime, poverty, ignorance, and immorality should disappear as soon as society is transformed and revolutionized. It will only be the sublime end toward which the human race must always aspire.

— In order to avoid repetitions I will make no criticism of this chapter, since I should have to refute almost all the theses here laid down, but will treat of the questions of the struggle for existence, and egoism and altruism, in Part II of this work. —

In his "Conclusione"[2] Professor Ferri compares society to a sick person at whose bedside there meet three friends of his, who all wish him well. The first declares confidently that the soul dominates the body and that consequently material remedies are of no avail. The second says, on the contrary, that it is only a total change of the environment in which he is living that can cure the invalid. The third also believes that modifications are necessary, but he contents him-

---

[1] See the examples given by Professor *Ferri*, pp. 197–201.
[2] I will not speak of Ch. VI, which is only a repetition of a theme treated of several times, "how much more scientific the sociologists are than the socialists."

self with partial improvements, though the second friend calls them only palliatives.   The first is the spiritualist,[1] the second the socialist, and the third the sociologist.

— Having given my opinion after each chapter, a general criticism of "Socialismo e Criminalità" is superfluous.   The impression that the book makes is strange.   The author attacks the socialists as "excessively anti-scientific and sentimental", while he vaunts the "great scientific character of the sociologists."   Yet these last, notwithstanding their great scientific character, combat a doctrine which they know only in part or not at all.   Scientific socialism is left out of the discussion.

The best proof of the weakness of his attack against socialism is to be found in the fact that the author has for several years ranked himself among the socialists, of whom he has become one of the most fervent and intelligent chiefs.

As regards his opinion on the criminal question Professor Ferri has made no change, or almost none.[2] —

IV.

H. KURELLA.

This author gives some pages of his "Naturgeschichte des Verbrechers" to the subject we have in hand.   What he says may be summed up as follows.

The attempts to draw parallels between the fluctuations of the price of grain and those of the figures for criminality, according to the author, prove nothing, inasmuch as it is impossible to compare them with the statistics of wages and of forced unemployment.   In fact any one who tries to show in this way the correlation between criminality and economic conditions, begs the question, that poverty is the principal cause of crime.   Further, the hypothesis that the regularity with which human acts occur is fixed by the condition of the society in which they take place, is little by little giving

---

[1] [See the author's explanation of his use of this word, in the preface. — TRANSL.]

[2] See "Le crime comme phénomène social" ("Annales de l'institut international de Sociologie", 1896, p. 414), and "Kriminelle Anthropologie und Sozialismus" ("Neue Zeit", 1895–96, II).

[NOTE TO THE AMERICAN EDITION: *Cf.* the recent work of *C. Manes* (a disciple of Ferri), "Capitalismo e criminalità."]

way. From personal examinations, and from the information given by Ferri and von Oettingen (this proves that the literature of our subject is little known to the author) Dr. Kurella thinks he can draw the conclusion that insufficient food, caused by scarcity or low wages, does not cause the commission of crimes. Malnutrition may perhaps influence criminality indirectly; that is it may cause degeneration after some successive generations, which in its turn predisposes to crime.

A priori it is incontestable that we cannot picture to ourselves a society, if established by the socialists,[1] in which cupidity, hatred, and the instinct of the oppressor, the principal motives of crime, will have been annihilated or deprived of their influence because of social institutions. Nevertheless it is of importance that Morrison, Garofalo, and Ferri [2] have, according to the author, shown that poverty is not a factor of crime. At the International Congress of Criminal Anthropology at Brussels, the attempt was made to defend the contrary, but, according to Dr. Kurella, without success. (According to him it can only be in case of being suddenly thrown out of work that a person hitherto honest commits a crime from indigence.)

The necessity of the moment being consequently only rarely a cause of criminality, not only do the present social anomalies produce an increase of degeneracy, as has been said above, but also there are a number of persons who live in badly built and unsanitary dwellings, so that the family life is injured, and the development of feelings of honesty, modesty, etc., is interfered with. And it is also the social anomalies that strongly influence alcoholism, which is one of the important factors of crime.

The author draws the following conclusion: "As little as a change of environmental conditions can change an individual of one kind immediately into an individual of another kind, as little as we ever, under however modified circumstances, see a chimpanzee change himself into a gorilla, so little do social factors change a normally endowed man into a criminal. In isolated cases it may appear as if passion or opportunity had caused a crime; social forces do indeed have their effect upon the individual, but they do not essentially change his fundamental attributes — which include his character;

[1] P. 217. The author insinuates, without bringing the slightest proof, that persons with criminal dispositions have often contributed to the formation of the socialistic theories.

[2] See my criticisms upon these authors. It is not clear why Ferri is cited as an adherent of the opinion expressed by Dr. Kurella; for he gives an important place in the etiology of crime to economic factors.

the slight modifications through environment that individuals experience, must constantly recur, heap themselves up in the course of generations, until a socially significant change of type has arisen. Accordingly it is the permanent social distresses, the chronic evils of society which influence criminality, because by unnoticeable influences they go on for generations gnawing at the inmost kernel of man; misery and intellectual and moral neglect must be as long continued as in the Papal States, in the Kingdom of Naples, in Ireland, and among the Poles, drained by the territorial nobility for centuries, before an entire people becomes innoculated with the 'penchant for crime.'" [1]

— I will refrain from making any criticism. One does not argue with a man who gives convincing proofs that even the meaning of criminal sociology is unknown to him. Assertions, for example, that the character of man is invariable, that the distance between the honest man and the dishonest man is as great as that between the chimpanzee and the gorilla, are only absurdities. What author will deny at this time that the differences between men are, in the last analysis, only quantitative?

In general, Dr. Kurella still shares the opinions of the Italian school (*cf.*, for example, "Anthropologie und Strafrecht", which appeared in 1912); nevertheless he should have recognized, when he wrote "die Naturgeschichte des Verbrechens", that he was not familiar with the social factors of crime. He has written the following remarkable words, which do him honor. "I do not hesitate to confess that deeper socio-political studies, which became possible to me only after the publication of that work ["Naturgeschichte des Verbrechens"] show me today the social factors of crime more plainly and sharply, than I was able to recognize them ten years ago" (Vorrede, "Zurechnungsfähigkeit, Kriminalanthropologie"). —

V.

E. FORNASARI DI VERCE. [2]

In the first chapter (on poverty and criminality in Italy) the author calls attention to the following facts. According to the statis-

[1] P. 179.

[2] "La criminalità e le vicende economiche d'Italia dal 1873 al 1890 e osservazioni sommarie per il Regno Unito della Gran Bretagna e Irlanda (1840–1890) e per la Nova Galles del Sud (1882–1891)."

tics of 1881 there were in Italy to the thousand (of both sexes over nine years of age) 390.66 persons who were rich, well-to-do, moderately well-off, or with enough to live on, and 609.34 who had scarcely the necessities of life. Out of 100 persons convicted there were:

1887	1888	1889	
56.34	57.45	56.00	Necessitous
22.99	30.77	32.15	Having only the bare necessities
11.54	9.98	10.13	Moderately well-off
2.13	1.80	1.72	Well-to-do or rich

Here the favorable influence of means comes out distinctly. For 40 % of the population had some means and 60 % were in need; but among those convicted there were 13 % with means and nearly 87 % who were poor.

Then the author gives a sketch of the influence of poverty in causing degeneracy among the proletariat and predisposing them to crime, for poverty is very destructive to men's mental faculties. He cites in support of this many authors of weight.

By comparing the different Italian districts, grouped about the average figure for wealth per capita, with the number of prisoners to the 100,000 of the population, grouped according to the place from which they came, the following result is obtained.

WEALTH.		PRISONERS ACCORDING TO THE PLACE FROM WHICH THEY CAME.	
(3.333) Latium.	VII	—	
—	VI	—	
—	V	—	
(2.746) Piedmont-Liguria.	IV	—	
(2.400) Lombardy.	III	Lombardy (43) Piedmont-Liguria (51) Venice (53)	
—	II	Tuscany (76)	
(2.164) Tuscany.	I	Emilia (95)	
(1.935) Venice, (1.876) Kingdom. (1.762) Emilia.	Average.	Kingdom (118)	
—	1st	Marches-Umbria (137)	
(1.471) Sicily. (1.333) Naples	2d	Sardinia (167)	
(1.227) Marches-Umbria	3d	Naples (173)	
(?) Sardinia	4th	—	
	5th	Sicily (212)	
	6th	—	
	7th	Latium (250)	

According to the author this table shows that wealth and criminality present a certain symmetry, to this extent, that the wealthy regions have in general a lower criminality than the poor ones. It is only Latium that forms an exception, which is explained, according to Dr. Fornasari di Verce, first, by the circumstance that the capital is situated in that district, second, by the climate, and third, chiefly by the fact that the absolute wealth of a country gives no indication of the distribution of wealth. We can properly expect to find that where great wealth is heaped up there will also be considerable pauperism.

Not only does poverty predispose to crime, but it also furnishes the motives for it. Leading to alcoholism it is the cause of violent crimes; it drives persons who cannot find work to vagrancy and mendicity, which in their turn are the preparatory school for greater crimes; it puts the great number of those who cannot provide honestly for their needs to the necessity of stealing. And when these factors act upon a man already predisposed, they even lead as far as homicide.

In the following table the different Italian districts, as well as the crimes committed, have been grouped about their average figures.

WEALTH.		CRIMES.
(3.333) Latium	VII	—
—	VI	—
—	V	—
(2.747) Piedmont-Liguria	IV	—
(2.400) Lombardy	III	—
—	II	—
(2.164) Tuscany	I	Lombardy (649)
		Tuscany (710)
		Piedmont-Liguria (732)
		Emilia (749)
		Marches-Umbria (774)
(1.935) Venice		Venice (857)
(1.876) Kingdom	Average.	Kingdom (926)
(1.762) Emilia		Sicily (1021)
—	1st	Naples (1150)
(1.471) Sicily	2d	Sardinia (1440)
(1.333) Naples		
(1.227) Marches-Umbria	3d	—
Sardinia.	4th	Latium (1797)

According to the author it appears from this table that, with the exception of Latium, the districts with wealth above the average have a number of crimes below the average. Nevertheless the regions with a figure for wealth above the average, i.e. Piedmont-Liguria, Lombardy, and Latium, show a greater number of crimes than one would expect, while Sicily, Naples, Marches-Umbria, and Sardinia show lower figures for crime than would be supposed. This contradiction is only apparent, according to the author, and is to be explained as follows: first, because where there is wealth there is also poverty and frequent opportunities to steal; second, because dangerous individuals migrate less to districts where there is less wealth; third, because, as John Stuart Mill says, it results from the social conditions of our day that the education of the poor is nil and that of the rich bad.

The second chapter, having as its title, "Il fattore economico e la delinquenza. — Dinamica", contains some data upon the trend of criminality in the period in question. Criminality in general is increasing; serious crimes remain nearly stationary, while less serious crimes increase. As Ferri observes, criminality is decreasing, even in Italy, as to its intensity and violence, but increasing as to its extent.

Finally, the author considers the influence of emigration. It is chiefly the crimes against property that feel the favorable effects of it, as murder does among crimes against persons. The cause of this favorable influence is easily explained. Emigration removes a number of persons who, not having the means of existence, would easily become criminals.

The consequences of *agricultural vicissitudes* are as follows: the years of abundant harvests show a decrease in criminality, bad years, on the contrary, an increase; good vintages, however, lead to the same result. It is chiefly crimes against property (especially rural thefts) that yield to the influence of the degree of the abundance of the harvest; while among crimes against persons it is principally assaults that show the effect of the character of the crops. It is plain that the agricultural class is that which especially shows the effect of a bad harvest. During the years 1887–1889 the proportion of the farming class among those convicted rose from 35.3 % to 37.8 % and 38.2 %.

The effect of *the fluctuation of the price of food* is the following: criminality in general shows the influence of it greatly. When prices fall crime diminishes, and vice versa. This is more clearly to be seen in crimes against property. Crimes against persons increase especially when the price of wine is low, and vice versa. When a fall in the price of food coincides with a fall in the price of wine, the increase of crimes against persons is great.

According to Dr. Fornasari di Verce the cause of the increase of crimes against persons in the case of low food prices is not to be found

in the improved nutrition that results, but in the greater consumption
of alcohol.   The other crimes feel the effect of the fluctuations in
the price of provisions less.

The author then takes up *manufacturing*.   (As a consequence of
the defectiveness of the official statistics the data are incomplete.)
During the period of which the author speaks, manufacturing increased enormously, and crime in general increased also.   The serious forms, however, decreased while the less serious ones increased.
Industrial crises bring an increase chiefly of crimes against persons.

The condition of the working-people.   According to the author it
would be of the highest importance to establish for each year the number of industrial workers.   For this has a greater importance for
criminality than the price of food or the rate of wages.   In default
of official data such an investigation cannot take place, and he has
to limit himself to an examination of wages.   With some few exceptions these wages increased about 35 % during the period 1873–1889.
However, to obtain a clearer picture of the condition of the working-
class, the author has combined the fluctuation of wages with those
of the price of grain; that is, he has made a calculation of the
number of hours each man has had to work to get 100 kilograms
of grain.

After having called attention to the fact that the average wage of
the Italian workman is lower than in other industrial countries, the
author gives the following results of his researches: the influence of
the fluctuation of wages upon crime in general is less than, and almost
always subordinated to, that of the fluctuation of food-prices.   However, it must not be forgotten here that wages do not always represent exactly the condition of the majority of the proletariat.   With
some few exceptions, all crimes against property decrease when wages
rise (in combination with the price of grain).   This influence is not
noted in commercial crimes and counterfeiting.   Crimes against persons increase a little when wages rise; but when this rise coincides
with a low price of wine, they increase considerably.

The influence of *strikes* is exclusively limited to the crime of rebellion.

From the investigation into criminality and *commercial occurrences*
we learn that fraudulent bankruptcy, and also forgery in great measure, are almost entirely independent of economic occurrences; and
the fluctuations of the number of commercial crimes, in so far as they
are not influenced by other economic facts, are explained in great
part by commercial occurrences.

Financial occurrences (credit and deposits) do not make themselves felt in criminality in general, but in crimes against property and commercial crimes.

The author concludes finally from the increase shown by *private fortunes* and the rise in wages, that there is a correlation of these phenomena with a decrease of certain serious forms of crime.

The results of the study are summarized in the following table:

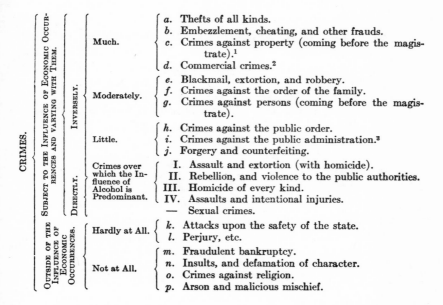

		Much.	*a.* Thefts of all kinds. *b.* Embezzlement, cheating, and other frauds. *c.* Crimes against property (coming before the magistrate).[1] *d.* Commercial crimes.[2]
	INVERSELY.	Moderately.	*e.* Blackmail, extortion, and robbery. *f.* Crimes against the order of the family. *g.* Crimes against persons (coming before the magistrate).
SUBJECT TO THE INFLUENCE OF ECONOMIC OCCURRENCES AND VARYING WITH THEM.		Little.	*h.* Crimes against the public order. *i.* Crimes against the public administration.[3] *j.* Forgery and counterfeiting.
	DIRECTLY.	Crimes over which the Influence of Alcohol is Predominant.	I. Assault and extortion (with homicide). II. Rebellion, and violence to the public authorities. III. Homicide of every kind. IV. Assaults and intentional injuries. — Sexual crimes.
OUTSIDE OF THE INFLUENCE OF ECONOMIC OCCURRENCES.		Hardly at All.	*k.* Attacks upon the safety of the state. *l.* Perjury, etc.
		Not at All.	*m.* Fraudulent bankruptcy. *n.* Insults, and defamation of character. *o.* Crimes against religion. *p.* Arson and malicious mischief.

According to the author it follows from his investigation, that the economic factors fill a very important place in the etiology of crime, but that all crime is not to be explained by that means. He is of the opinion that if we are to combat crime effectively we must make use of the "penal substitutes" recommended by Professor Ferri.

The author treats the influence of economic occurrences upon criminality in Great Britain and Ireland in the same way. Here are his results:

[1] Excepting rural thefts, included under *a.*
[2] Excepting fraudulent bankruptcy.
[3] Excepting rebellion and violence to public authorities.

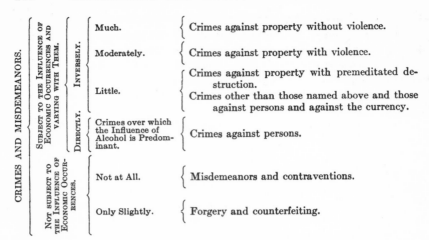

CRIMES AND MISDEMEANORS.	SUBJECT TO THE INFLUENCE OF ECONOMIC OCCURRENCES AND VARYING WITH THEM.	INVERSELY.	Much.	Crimes against property without violence.
			Moderately.	Crimes against property with violence.
			Little.	Crimes against property with premeditated destruction. / Crimes other than those named above and those against persons and against the currency.
		DIRECTLY.	Crimes over which the Influence of Alcohol is Predominant.	Crimes against persons.
	NOT SUBJECT TO THE INFLUENCE OF ECONOMIC OCCURRENCES.		Not at All.	Misdemeanors and contraventions.
			Only Slightly.	Forgery and counterfeiting.

His investigation gives the following results for New South Wales:

CRIMES AND MISDEMEANORS.	SUBJECT TO THE INFLUENCE OF ECONOMIC OCCURRENCES AND VARYING WITH THEM.	INVERSELY.	Much.	1. Theft and receiving stolen goods. / 2. Petty larceny. / 3. Horse-stealing.
			Moderately.	4. Minor offenses against property. / 5. Domiciliary thefts. / 6. Sheep-stealing. / 7. Forgery.
			Little.	8. Cattle-stealing.
		DIRECTLY.	Crimes and Misdemeanors over which the Influence of Alcohol is Predominant.	9. Murder. / 10. Arson. / 11. Homicide. / 12. Assaults. / 13. Extortion. / 14. Robbery. / 15. Other minor offenses. / I. Offenses against public decency. / II. Offenses against morals (homosexuality). / III. Offenses against morals. / IV. Minor offenses against persons.
	Not subject to the Influence of Economic Occurrences.			A. Blackmail and cheating. / B. Perjury.

— It is incontestable that the researches of Dr. Fornasari di Verce
must be placed in the front rank of the works that show the correctness of the thesis that the economic factors are the most important
factors of criminality. An objection may be made, however, that the
question has been conceived in too mechanical a fashion, in consequence of the exclusive use of the statistical method. He seeks the
correlation between criminality and each economic phenomenon
separately, in place of that of the *ensemble* of these phenomena. For

the economic life does not exist in reality as separated and isolated parts, but forms a great whole, a compact mass, of which the parts fit in together. When an important economic occurrence takes place, in case the expected effect upon crime is not observed, we must not be too quick to say that it has no importance for criminality, for it may be that it is neutralized by something else.

With this remark is connected a final objection. The author has not proved the truth of his conclusion that criminality cannot be explained exclusively by means of economic conditions. For, although his researches include very important economic factors, the author leaves out many economic factors and, with one exception (the degenerating influence of poverty), the numerous consequences of economic conditions, which are of the highest importance for the question in hand. In other words the author has not called attention to the fact that we live under an economic system of a comparatively recent date, having peculiar characteristics that are of great significance for criminality. He has indicated some very important consequences of the system, but he has not analyzed the system itself.

I am of the opinion that the work that I have been treating, and which has a great value for the subject, shows that economic conditions are of great importance for criminality. However, it does not prove that this influence is not greater than is shown by statistics. —

VI.

A. NICEFORO.

In the first part of his study, "Criminalità e condizioni economiche in Sicilia", the author calls attention to the fact that Sicily is one of the Italian districts where crime is greatest and is increasing most rapidly. One could draw upon the map lines enclosing a definite criminal zone, taking in the provinces of Caltanissetta, Girgenti, and Catania. This zone might, in its turn, be divided into two others, one of which would give a high figure for robberies and homicides, and the other chiefly for crimes against property and against morals.

The author divides the economic causes into direct and indirect. In speaking of *direct factors* he treats successively:

a. *Large real-estate holdings.* The landed proprietor rents his lands to the "gabelletto", who in turn sublets them to the laborers. This system exhausts the latter. The proprietor rids himself of all expense by charging it to the "gabelletto", and makes his profit; the "gabelletto" does the same by the laborer and makes *his* profit. The latter is always the person that suffers.   Then the "gabelletto" advances the necessary provisions to the laborer until the harvest comes in ; but since he does so at a high rate, the laborer is bowed down by the burden of his debts. In consequence of this system the agricultural population is ill-nourished and degenerate.   The consequences of this system as it affects criminality are apparent.   In the province of Caltanissetta, where large land-holdings are the rule, crimes against property, and especially rural thefts, cattle-stealing, vagrancy, etc., are the most numerous.

b. *Small holdings.*   However, it is not only the agricultural population dependent upon great property-holders that lives in poverty, for the small farmers also have a hard life.   They raise chiefly grapes and citrous fruits.   The price of citrous fruits has fallen greatly through overproduction and foreign competition.   Wine also has gone down in price, and the cultivators have had enormous losses from phylloxera besides.   Consequently the small farmers are crushed with debts; failures are the order of the day; their situation, then, is most unfortunate.   But that of the non-property-holders is still worse if possible.   For the small holder also often rents his land to others, and from this follows a kind of "sweating-system."

At the end of these observations the author gives, in the following table, the movement of some prices in relation to criminality :

Years.	Price of Wheat per 1000 Kilos.	Price of Wine per Hectolitre. (Sicily.)	Price of Meat per Kilo. (Sicily.)	Homicides Prosecuted.	Robberies, Extortion, Blackmail.
1875	27.42	13.00	3.09	—	658
1876	28.78	21.62	2.91	—	1,039
1877	33.66	30.38	2.98	—	777
1878	31.43	29.04	2.89	—	1,110
1879	31.35	19.03	2.80	—	1,138
1880	32.27	29.65	2.74	1,063	829
1881	26.36	30.92	2.74	1,001	708
1882	20.42	28.35	2.80	938	560
1883	23.11	22.11	2.75	943	419
1884	21.52	17.95	2.77	949	340
1885	21.24	31.84	2.76	822	330
1886	21.28	35.63	2.42	859	418
1887	21.48	15.66	2.44	863	446
1888	21.50	11.85	2.46	899	485
1889	22.83	15.06	2.40	865	478
1890	22.63	22.07	2.46	869	547
1891	24.60	16.92	2.77	966	710
1892	24.32	14.32	2.87	1,117	677
1893	21.08	15.76	2.95	1,066	902
1894	18.77	18.38	2.98	—	—
1895	20.30	18.42	2.75	—	—

c. *The mining zone.* The production of sulphur, formerly of great importance, when Sicily was the principal source of supply for Europe and America, has decreased greatly now that sulphur is manufactured from chemical products. The condition of the miners is pitiful. The mines are often exploited by middle-men, which makes the condition of the laborers worse. Degeneracy has consequently taken on enormous proportions. When we compare the change in wages with the number of thefts, we see that thefts decrease when wages rise, and vice versa, and that the price of grain also influences criminality. It is the provinces of Sicily where the sulphur mines are found that give the highest figures for criminality in general, and homicide in particular.

d. *The class-conflict.* The property owners, whose economic position is already very influential, also control the political forces, and consequently the case of those who have nothing is made much worse. Taxes, indirect for the most part, weigh most heavily upon the poor; public property is exploited for the benefit of the rich, etc., etc. Hence it follows that in the districts where the non-possessors are unconsciously struggling against the possessors, this strife of classes engenders class-hatred, and consequent crimes.

In the last part of his study the author speaks of *indirect economic factors,* among which he includes:

a. *The increasing decline in the altruistic feelings.* The miner and the laborer, both ill-nourished, humiliated, and despised, dwelling in miserable hovels, are pariahs far removed from any feeling for their fellow men.

b. *Organic degeneracy.* As a consequence of the economic conditions named, degeneracy is always increasing more and more among the poor, especially among the miners. This degeneracy becomes in its turn a factor of criminality, since it predisposes individuals to crime.

See also: *Virgilio Rossi:* "Influence de la temperature et de l'alimentation sur la criminalité in Italie, de 1875 à 1883" ("Rapport 1er Congrès d'Anthropologie Criminelle. Actes", pp. 295 *ff.*); *N. Pinsero:* "Miseria e Delitto" ("Scuola Positiva", 1898).

CHAPTER IV.

THE FRENCH SCHOOL (THE SCHOOL OF THE ENVIRONMENT).

I.

A. LACASSAGNE.

WHILE the Italian school reigned supreme at the first congress of criminal anthropology at Rome, Professor Lacassagne opposed it with his so-called "hypothesis of the environment" in the following terms: "The important thing is the social environment. Allow me to make a comparison borrowed from a modern theory. The social environment is the bouillon for the culture of criminality; the microbe, that is the criminal, is an element which is only of importance when it has found a medium in which it can grow.

"The criminal with anthropometric and other characteristics seems to us to have only a moderate importance. All these characteristics may be found elsewhere among honest men.

"But you should look at the different social consequences of these two points of view. On the one hand is the fatalism which flows inevitably from the anthropometric theory; and on the other, social initiative. If the social environment is everything, and if it is so defective as to favor the growth of vicious or criminal natures, it is to this environment and its conditions of functioning that our reforms must be directed.

". . . This phrase . . . sums up my whole thought, and is, so to speak, the conclusion of what I have been saying; *societies have the criminals they deserve.*" [1]

In his "Marche de la criminalité en France, 1825–1880", the author points out, among other things, the connection between criminality and economic conditions. An examination of the move-

[1] Pp. 166, 167.

ment of crimes against property shows that the great fluctuations to be observed there are intimately connected with economic conditions. The number of crimes against property corresponds almost exactly with the fluctuation in the price of wheat; and all the economic crises make their influence felt.

During the years 1828, 1835–1837, 1847, 1848–1854, 1865–1868, and 1872–1876, in which the price of wheat was high, there were also a great number of crimes against property. The year 1855 was the sole exception, for then crimes against property did not increase, although the price of grain was very high. This is to be explained by the fact that the government then took measures to lessen the consequences of this calamity. Further, other provisions were then very cheap. From 1860 on the number of crimes against property decreases, which, according to the author, is to be explained by the importation of grain, which increased greatly at this time.

The influence of the production and consumption of alcohol is strongly felt in crimes against persons, especially in assaults.

I would further call attention to the report made by Professor Lacassagne to the Fourth Congress of Criminal Anthropology at Geneva, entitled, "Les vols à l'étalage et dans les grands magasins", in which he shows how the display of goods on the counters in the great bazaars, which are meant to fascinate visitors, and force them to buy, so to speak, leads to crime in individuals predisposed to kleptomania.

Professor Lacassagne has always remained faithful to the judgment that he pronounced at Rome; at the Congress at Brussels,[1] and at Amsterdam as well [2], he repeated: "Societies have the criminals they deserve."

II.

G. TARDE.

This author considers criminality as being preëminently a social phenomenon, which, like all social phenomena, is to be explained by imitation.

"All the important acts of the social life are performed under the sway of example. One begets, or one does not beget, through imitation; the statistics of births have shown us that. One kills, or one does not kill, through imitation; should we have the idea today

---

[1] "Actes", p. 240.   [2] "Compte rendu", p. 232.
    [NOTE TO THE AMERICAN EDITION: See also Professor *Lacassagne's* preface to *Laurent's* "Le criminel."]

of fighting a duel, or declaring war, if we did not know that this is always done in the country where we live? One kills himself, or he does not kill himself, through imitation; it is recognized that suicide is an imitative phenomenon in the highest degree . . . . How can we doubt, then, that a man steals or does not steal, murders or does not murder, through imitation?" [1]

Imitation, says the author, is governed by two laws, namely, that men imitate one another more the more closely they come together, and that imitation of the high by the low is what most often takes place (that the customs of the nobility are imitated by the people, etc.). If we test these rules in their application to crime, we shall find that they hold good there also. The author gives the following examples, among others, in support of this:

"Vagrancy, under its thousand actual forms, is an offense essentially plebeian; but if we go back into the past it will not be difficult to connect our tramps and street singers with the noble pilgrims and minstrels of the Middle Ages. Poaching, another nursery of criminals, which in the past, together with smuggling, has played a part comparable with vagrancy in the present, is still more directly connected with the life of the lord of the manor." [2] "Arson, a crime of the lowest classes today, was once the prerogative of the feudal nobility. Was not the Margrave of Brandenburg heard to boast one day that he had burned in his life 170 villages? Counterfeiting takes refuge at present in mountain caverns, or subcellars in the city, but we know that coining was long a royal monopoly.

"Finally, theft, so degrading in our day, has had a brilliant past. Montaigne tells us, without being very indignant at it, that many young gentlemen of his acquaintance, whose fathers did not give them enough money, procured more by stealing." [3]

There was a time, then, when criminality extended itself from the higher classes to the lower; at present new forms of crime take their rise in the great cities and spread out into the country. The increase of crime in the cities is very considerable, and it is very probable that, in accordance with the law cited, criminality will at length increase in the country as greatly. It is especially the crimes of assassination, sexual crimes against minors, abortion, and infanticide, that have increased. So the opinion of several Italian criminologists, "that crimes against persons decrease where crimes against property increase, and vice versa", is wrong, according to Professor Tarde, since both kinds of crime increase in the great cities.

[1] "Penal Philosophy", p. 322.   [2] *Op. cit.*, p. 332.   [3] *Op. cit.*, p. 334.

"To sum up, the prolonged action of the great cities upon criminality is manifest, it seems to us, in the gradual substitution, not exactly of trickery for violence, but of covetous, crafty, and voluptuous violence, for vindictive and brutal violence." [1]

Nevertheless, civilization improves men, and the growing criminality is in opposition to the greater and greater increase of civilization. This contradiction is explained by the author by means of another law of imitation; the law of insertion, *i.e.* the alternate passage from fashion to custom.

"All industry is thus fed by a stream of improvements, innovations today, traditions tomorrow; every science, every art, every language, every religion obeys this law of the passage from custom to fashion and of the return from fashion to custom, but to an enlarged custom.

"For at each of these steps in advance the territorial domain of imitation increases; the field of social assimilation, of human brotherhood, extends itself, and this is not, as we know, the least salutary effect of imitative action from the moral point of view." [2]

After having mentioned how these different currents of imitation meet, the author applies the idea set forth above to the influence of education upon criminality. He shows that instruction, by itself, is not a remedy for crime, since it may furnish new means for committing crimes, and hence may only change the character of criminality. Finally the author points out the influence of labor upon criminality, combating the theory of Poletti, who says that it is necessary to take into account the economic development (for example, if during the period 1826–78 criminality in France increased in the ratio of 100 to 254, and productive activity was quadrupled, criminality did not increase, but really diminished). The fundamental error in Poletti's argument, according to Professor Tarde is, that he considers crime as a regular, permanent, and inevitable effect of industrialism.

"Only, there is labor and labor; and if in a more laborious class the work is badly divided, excessive for some, whom it enervates and disorders, insufficient for others, who become dissipated, or if it is badly directed, turned toward deleterious compositions and reading which excite the senses . . . — in this case it will probably happen that progress in labor is accompanied by a growing lack of discipline and by academic vices of different kinds. An analogous phenomenon takes place in our cities, where the mad chase for luxury outruns the rise of wages, and where sexual crimes are sextupled or septupled

[1] *Op. cit.*, p. 359.　　　　　　　　[2] *Op. cit.*, pp. 362, 363.

while wealth is tripled and quadrupled. The socialists, then, are right in imputing, in part, to unjust distribution and to the objectionable direction of the productive activity, the moral evil that has grown with it, and which, further, does not decrease when productive activity becomes weaker. For since the period when Poletti made his observations upon the prosperity of France, this has ceased to grow, and has even decreased rapidly, as we know only too well, but crime has continued its onward march with a more marked impetus.

" In short, there remains nothing of the law laid down by this distinguished writer, and all the statistics contradict him. Delinquency, as Garofalo remarks, is so little proportional to commercial activity that England, where crime is on the decrease, is the nation most remarkable for the increase of its commerce, and that Spain and Italy, where the criminality is greater than that of the other principal states of Europe, are far behind them in business development. We may add that in France the most hard-working class is without any doubt the peasant class, and this shows the smallest proportionate number of delinquents, notwithstanding unfavorable conditions. We may conclude that work is in itself the adversary of crime, that if it favors it it is by indirect, not necessary action, and that its relation to crime is like that between two antagonistic forms of work." [1]

In the following section the author treats the influence of wealth and of poverty upon the criminal. He mentions the different opinions of Turati and of Colajanni on the one hand, and of Ferri and Garofalo on the other. The former tried to prove that poverty is often a cause of a poor man's becoming a criminal. Garofalo tries to disprove it by calling attention, among other things, to the fact that, according to the criminal statistics of Italy for 1880, property owners committed as many crimes in proportion as the proletariat did.

In opposition to this Professor Tarde points out that the French criminal statistics in 1887 show that there were, out of 100,000 of each class of the population, the following number of persons arraigned : 20 out of the class of domestics, one of the poorest classes ; 12 from the liberal professions including persons of independent income ; 139 from the class of vagrants and persons without occupation (the most necessitous class, therefore) ; 21 from commerce ; 26 from manufacturing (a very high figure considering the profits of that year) ; and 14 from the farming class (a very low figure considering their relative poverty).

[1] *Op. cit.*, pp. 383, 384.

The author explains these contradictions as follows: "Let us not forget that, the desire for wealth being the ordinary motive and more and more the preponderating motive of crime as it is the only motive of industrial labor, the possession of wealth must keep the most dishonest man from crime as it does the most laborious man from industrial labor — for it is impossible to desire what one has — at least if the satisfaction of this desire has not meant the over-exciting of it. . . . Now in business circles, where on account of men's throwing one another into a fever, a constant gaining of wealth, rather than wealth itself, is the end pursued, a fortune is like those peppered liqueurs which arouse thirst more than they quench it. Hence it comes, doubtless, as well as from the excitement prevailing in these circles, that criminality there is as great as among domestic servants. In the same way, in the licentious environments, in the great cities, where there are masses of working people, sexual crimes are as much more numerous as the pleasures of the senses are there more easily come by. But we can lay it down as a principle that where wealth is an obstacle to activity it is also an obstacle to crime, very much as political power ceases to be dangerous at the moment when it ceases to be ambitious. This is the situation among the rural proprietors, small and great, among stockholders, and even in the majority of the liberal professions . . . ; content with his relative well-being, man indulges in an intellectual half-labor, artistic rather than mechanical, honorable rather than mercenary, and abstains from flagitious means of obtaining an increase of income which he desires moderately. The French peasant, in general, partakes of this moderation of desires, and, rich from his sobriety, his stoicism, his frugality, his plot of ground at last acquired, he is happier than the feverish millionaire, financier, or politician, driven by his very millions to sow the seed of his rotten speculations, rascalities, and extortions upon a vast scale. Further the well-to-do agriculturists are in general the most honest people. Let us not speak of wealth and poverty, to tell the truth, not even of well-being and the reverse, but rather of happiness and unhappiness, and be careful how we deny this truth, as old as the world, that the wicked man's excuse is often to be found in his being unhappy. Children of this century . . . let us confess that under its brilliant exterior our society is not happy, and if we had no other assurances of its great evils than its numerous crimes, without giving a thought to its suicides, and its increasing cases of insanity, without lending an ear to the cries of envy, of suffering, and of hatred . . . we should not be able to call its woes in question.

"From what does it suffer? From its internal trouble, from its illogical and unstable condition, from intestine contradictions, stirred up by the success even of its unheard-of discoveries and inventions, piling one on top of the other, the material for contrary theories, the source of unbridled, egoistic, and antagonistic desires. Upon this obscure gestation, a great Credo, a great common end awaits; it is creation before the Fiat Lux. Science multiplies its notions, it elaborates a high conception of the universe; . . . but where is the high conception of life, of human life, that it is ready to make prevalent? Industry multiplies its products, but where is the collective work that it brings to birth? The preëstablished harmony of interests was a dream of Bastiat, the shadow of a dream of Leibnitz. The citizens of a state exchange information, scientific and otherwise, through books, newspapers, or conversation, but to the profit of their contradictory beliefs; they exchange services, but to the profit of their rival interests; the more they assist one another, therefore, the more they nourish their essential contradictions, which may have been as profound at other times, but were never so conscious, never so painful, and consequently never so dangerous." [1]

Suppose, asks the author, there was no more foreign war, how could we avoid civil war? There have, indeed been historic periods when there existed a common aim uniting individuals, as the faith did in the Middle Ages. In our days this aim can be nothing but "art, philosophy, the higher cultivation of the mind and imagination, the æsthetic life."

In order to be able to answer the question whether civilization (the collective name for education, religion, science, arts, manufacturing, wealth, public order, etc.) causes a diminution of criminality, it is necessary to discriminate between two stages of civilization. In the first there is an afflux of inventions; this is the stage at which Europe is at the present time. In the second this afflux decreases and it forms itself into a coherent whole. A civilization may be very rich, then, and but little coherent, or very coherent and not very rich, like that of the commune in the Middle Ages.

"But is it by its wealth or by its cohesion that civilization makes crime recede? By its cohesion without any doubt. This cohesion of religion, of science, of all forms of work and of power, of all kinds of different innovations, mutually confirming one another, in reality or in appearance, is a true implicit coalition against crime, and even when each of these fruitful branches of the social tree combats but

[1] *Op. cit.*, pp. 389–391.

feebly the gourmand branch, their agreement will suffice to divert all the sap from it." [1]

— This is not the place to criticise the theory of imitation in general, with which Professor Tarde thinks that we can explain every social phenomenon.   In my opinion, this theory, in so far as it is new is not correct, and in so far as it is correct is not new.   It is true as explaining how a social phenomenon, having taken its rise in a locality, has been rapidly propagated, or why it still persists when the original causes have ceased to operate.

However, it is plain that by means of imitation one can give but a partial explanation of the phenomena mentioned.   Other factors must be pointed out to explain, for example, why something spreads everywhere in consequence of imitation, at a certain moment, while before it passed unperceived, etc.

I agree, then, that the significance of imitation and tradition is very important in explaining social phenomena, but I am of the opinion that imitation and tradition represent the *conservative* element, and give us no information with regard to the birth of *new* social phenomena.[2]

In the domain of criminality also imitation plays a great part. Children brought up in a vicious environment, easily contract bad habits by imitation; the harmful influence of prison is proverbial; a sensational crime often leads to analogous crimes.   It is also by imitation that we can explain, in part at least, the existence of the Mafia and the Camorra, of which Professor Lombroso says, among other things: "The long persistence and obstinacy of such associations as the Mafia, the Camorra, and brigandage, seem to proceed in the first place from the antiquity of their existence, for the long repetition of the same acts transforms them into a habit, and consequently into a law.   History teaches us that ethnic phenomena of long duration are not to be eradicated easily at a stroke."[3]

Since the phenomena named remain permanent, there must be other important social factors which have nothing to do with imitation.   Thus, for example, faith, whose prevalence is based to a great extent upon tradition, would have disappeared long since, notwith-

[1] Pp. 392, 393.
[2] On this subject see *Kautsky*, "Die materialistische Geschichtsauffassung und der psychologische Antrieb", p. 655 ("Neue Zeit", 1895–1896, II). See the criticism of the imitation theory by Professor *Ferri*, in the "Devinir Social", 1895, entitled "La théorie sociologique de M. Tarde."
[3] "Crime", p. 212.

standing tradition, if there had been no factors in the present society to make it persist.

Admitting what has gone before, there is no reason to see in most of the examples cited by the author in support of his theory, anything else than his great knowledge of historic details of little or no importance for the question of criminality. Where, for example, is the connection between the minstrels of the Middle Ages and the vagrants of our own days? There is certainly none but this, that both went from place to place. But even if there had never been wandering minstrels, the social phenomenon called "vagrancy" would have existed all the same. It has nothing to do with imitation, but on the contrary has everything to do with the existing social organization. It could thus be proved by many examples that Professor Tarde exaggerates the extent of the influence of imitation. We must not lose sight of the fact that imitation teaches us nothing of the essential causes of a social phenomenon. When we seek the causes of a disease that some one has, we frequently see that it is the result of a contagion; we know, then, that the disease is contagious, and this knowledge will point out precautions to be taken to limit or prevent the spread of the disease; but as to the causes of the disease itself we still know nothing.

It is the same way with regard to crime. It is certain that immoral ideas and customs are easily contracted by children. The removal of children from a harmful environment is therefore a preventive of the extension of crime. But we are still ignorant of everything that concerns the rise of these immoral ideas and customs, which is, however, the essential thing.

With regard to the remarks of the author upon the influence of labor, wealth, poverty, and civilization, I simply observe that these very important and very complicated questions occupy but a few pages in his work. It will be, then, quite superfluous to note in detail how the whole has been treated in a very incomplete manner, although very true remarks are found there (for example, those upon the bad distribution of labor, upon the desire for wealth as a cause of crime, etc.). —

Beside an article that appeared in the "Revue Philosophique" (1890), entitled "Misère et criminalité", Professor Tarde has taken up his subject again in a report: "La criminalité et les phénomènes économiques" (Fifth Congress of Criminal Anthropology at Amsterdam). Of this report we give a synopsis.

According to Professor Tarde, since it has been recognized that the social factors of criminality are the most important, there has been a manifest tendency to exaggerate the importance of economic factors. Their high importance, which is incontestable, does not at all justify our forgetting the stronger and more decisive action of the beliefs and feelings in the aberrations of the will. Which of the two sources of criminality is the more important, the economic or the religious (or intellectual)? That cannot be decided. But it is much more important to know in what phases, from what sides the economic life is criminogenous.

Each economic phase, as, for example, domestic economy or urban economy, has its special form of criminality. But political and religious changes, whether they correspond or not to the transformations in the mode of production, have, perhaps, a much greater part in criminality than have the economic transformations. The domestic economy, for example, gives rise to different crimes in which no economic factor comes into play; as uxoricide, for example.

Neither poverty alone nor wealth alone is an obstacle to honesty. Poor peoples or classes, accustomed to poverty, are often very honest, nor is there any more need that great differences of wealth should lead to crime. But it is the abrupt passing from wealth to poverty and from poverty to wealth that is dangerous to morality.

"In short, criminality and morality are less dependent upon the economic *state* of a country, than upon its economic *transformations*. It is not capitalism as such that is demoralizing, it is the moral crisis that accompanies the passage from artisan production to capitalistic production, or from some particular mode of the latter to some other mode.

"Economic phenomena may be regarded from three points of view: first, from the point of view of their repetition, which has to do chiefly with the propagation of habits of consumption, called *needs*, and of the corresponding habits of labor; second, from the point of view of their opposition, which includes principally the contests of producers among themselves by acute or chronic competition, during strikes, or crises of overproduction, — or contests of consumers among themselves, through sumptuary laws, aristocratic or democratic, or monopolies of consumption over which they dispute in a thousand ways, in time of famine, or scarcity, or any form of *underproduction*, — or contests of producers with consumers, through their attempts to exploit one another, monopolize prices, or laws regulating the maximum price, municipal tariffs, or protectionist rights, etc.;

third, finally from the point of view of their adaptation, always being renewed and always incomplete, which embraces the series of successful inventions, fortunate associations of ideas from which proceed all fruitful associations of men, from the division of labor and of commerce, an association spontaneous and implicit, to industrial, commercial, financial, and syndical societies, etc." [1]

It is through the second aspect that the economic life can give a direct explanation of crime; that which is given by the other two is only an indirect explanation. That is to say, each invention gives rise to a contest among producers, and the progress of manufacturing creates the possibility of satisfying needs, but at the same time makes those who for want of the means cannot satisfy them, feel their needs all the more strongly.

Every individual must satisfy a certain number of needs which have their marked recurrences. A peaceful and honest society will be one in which the great majority of the persons who compose it have, in measure, the means of satisfying these needs. "Regular habits of consumption and production form the first condition for good moral health whether individual or collective, just as regular digestion is the foundation of good physical health. Those who are irregular become easily the 'déclassés.' Nothing is more contagious than disorder." [2]

Hence, then, comes the importance for criminality of social crises, since during these production and consumption are deranged.

According to Professor Tarde, the *social contradictions*, which are the *chronic crises* of societies, can be the sole causes of criminality. If a society succeeds in avoiding every internal contradiction there can hardly be any further question of crime.

Our opinions can always harmonize with those of the people around us, while we are foreign to them in desire and feeling. "The criminal is he who, undergoing conformity to the ideas of the community in which he lives, yet escapes from conforming to the feelings and acts of the community. He acts contrary to his own principles, which are those of society." "It is, then, not to a social crisis that we must mount, but to a psychological crisis that we must descend, to explain crime." [3]

Social crises are of two kinds: politico-religious, and economic. In opposition to divers statisticians, who are of the opinion that the former class cause a diminution in criminality, the author thinks that this diminution is only apparent, and that in reality the number

---

[1] "Compte Rendu", p. 199.   [2] *Ibid.*, p. 200.   [3] P. 204.

of crimes increases at these times; which is shown, for example, for France by the addition of cases not prosecuted to those prosecuted.

As to the effect of economic crises, statisticians, Professor Tarde claims, have not yet examined it. It seems to him that there is no parallelism between economic crises and criminality.

The struggle of classes, which springs up and grows during the periods of crisis, is a great danger to public morals, since it gives rise to a class spirit, and consequently increases the contempt for the rights of individuals of another class. However, the class struggle does not increase the number of individual crimes, but only the number of collective crimes.

To sum up, Professor Tarde is of the opinion, then, that social crises in general, and economic crises in particular, are not the only source nor a continual source of crime. The question of what is the cause of economic crises remains unexplained. To solve this we must call in all political economy. The causes of these economic crises are in brief: first, unlimited competition; second, unforeseen disasters. "We may add that these acute conflicts lead to suicide more than to crime; they are a factor of crime much less important than the sullen conflicts, the low but continuous fevers of troubled epochs in quest of a stable state. And these are then less the conflicts of production with itself, or of production with consumption, than the conflicts of consumption with itself, *i.e.* the conflicts of needs that have grown but cannot be satisfied at the time, within the limits of the always insufficient wages or profits, a fertile source of criminal suggestions. When labor no longer suffices to satisfy the legitimate needs in accordance with the prevailing standards, the desire of gain without labor invades the heart and becomes general. The only remedy for this danger would be the advancement of manufacturing and its reorganization upon a vaster and better conceived plan than the present one, if, at the same time that any industrial progress gave more wealth for less labor, it did not give rise to still more new wants. The individual organization of wants, their *hierarchization*, by virtue of a certain unanimity of fundamental principles, must precede the social organization of labor, if we wish this latter really to make for peace and morals." [1]

— Professor Tarde's report is characterized by many very true observations (as, for example, that every economic phase has its own form of criminality; that sudden transitions from wealth to poverty, and

[1] Pp. 203, 204.

vice versa, are morally more dangerous than slow changes; etc., etc.),
but at the same time is still more marked by a certain elasticity and
lack of close reasoning.   Hence it is almost impossible to frame a
criticism of the report that will follow it step by step.

However there are some things to be noted.   According to the
author there are two sources of criminality, the one economic, the
other intellectual.   I consider that this distinction is not correct.
Every crime has an intellectual source, in this sense, that it is an act
conceived by the intellect.   It is impossible, therefore, to see beside
this source an economic cause.   But the intellect considered by itself
is empty; it is from the environment that it must draw the material
which it will transform into ideas.   Consequently the question
becomes this: how far is the economic environment the cause of the
formation of criminal thoughts.   Intellect and economic conditions
do not stand side by side but the one follows upon the other.   It is
only making use of a commonplace to say that crime has an intellectual source; that explains nothing.

In reading the first pages of the report one expects, after the historical exposition which says that every economic phase has its own
form of criminality, to find an exposition of the present economic
system, and an inquiry into how far the criminality of our own day
is bound up with it.   This would have been, I think, most important,
and would have advanced the subject.   The most serious criticism
that I have to make is that nothing of the kind is attempted.   What
follows is only a series of isolated remarks, which are correct only in
part, and in which the whole question is reduced to a matter of economic *crises*, although the title speaks of economic *conditions*.

It is incorrect to say that the statisticians have not investigated the
influence of economic crises, as the second chapter of this work proves.
In it I have analyzed the works of the different authors who have
especially treated of this subject.   Finally, I would call attention to
the fact that he furnishes no proof of his assertion that the class struggle takes its rise in times of crisis — and would find it difficult to do so.

What Professor Tarde means in speaking of "the advancement of
manufacturing and its reorganization upon a vaster and better conceived plan", is not clear.   But it is certain that the final observation
that there must be "an individual organization of wants", is purely
Utopian.   For it is one of the characteristic phenomena of our present
society that it has strongly excited the cupidity of men, and that
this will disappear only when its cause has ceased to exist.

All Professor Tarde's works upon criminality convince us of the

great knowledge of their author. The report of which I have been
speaking contains also ideas that are often very original, but this
does not prevent the necessity of confessing that it does not contribute
much to the solution of the problem that it treats. —

III.

A. CORRE.

In the third book of his "Crime et Suicide" the author treats of the
influence of economic conditions upon criminality, beginning with
"labor, wages, and needs."

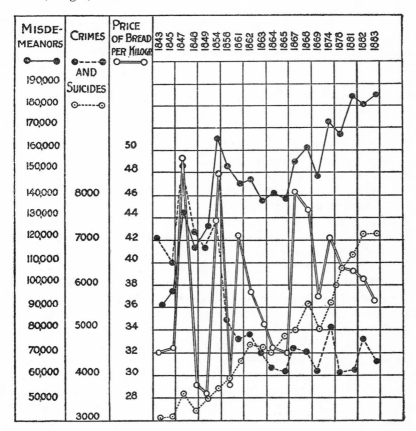

Dr. Corre notes first the true condition of the free workman. No
one is obliged to give him work or bread, and it is forbidden to beg

or even to be idle. "There is no opinion more monstrous, more revolting, and more cowardly. It is a social crime as well as the most dangerous of follies. For it is necessary to be logical. If you oblige a man under all circumstances to live by his own means, in the midst of a limited circle, where the places are distributed in advance, the land divided to the smallest fragments, if you refuse him the right to alms after having refused him work . . . you drive him to suicide or crime." [1] We must give work to everyone who wants to work, in order that he may support himself and his family, and help must be given to those to whom work cannot be given, as in the case of workmen not longer able to work because of sickness or old age. On the other hand idleness must be punished as well as professional crime. Wages must be so high that they are sufficient not only for the strict necessities, but for others as well; for example, for a progressive education, without, however, arousing in the laboring class the desire for luxury that always corrupts morals. Though naming a single exception, Dr. Corre is of the opinion that wages are in general very insufficient, especially if we take into account the fact that there are times of unemployment, sickness, etc., during which nothing is earned. The question of wages is one of great importance, then, for the etiology of criminality. Nevertheless all the improvement of the material condition of the working class will accomplish nothing unless there is at the same time a moral improvement.

As other authors have already proved, the price of bread also has an influence upon the course of criminality.

Under the heading "economic conditions", he calls attention, in the second place to "assistance, savings, property." When we study the effect of charity upon criminality in the departments of France, we see that mendicity and vagrancy decrease, and that crimes are only of moderate frequency, in places where the official assistance given is the smallest, while criminality is pretty prevalent and even on the increase where the greatest amount of official assistance is given. "Thus very limited assistance will do less harm than if it were more extensive. Such is the interpretation the mind gathers from a comparison of the economic and judicial statistics. Excess in alms-giving, with difficulty separable from a bad distribution of wealth, will therefore have a demoralizing influence; it enervates and sterilizes, and its fruits would appear more bitter if it were possible to unveil the little secrets of assistance under the thousand forms that it wears." [2]

"Saving enlarges the field of the needs of the laborer, gives him

[1] P. 142.   [2] P. 430.

security for the future, strengthens his independence with regard to the state, and his dignity in his relations with other citizens; it permits him to surround his family with a greater degree of comfort, and through education to raise his children into the professional hierarchy. It is therefore useful, and has a moralizing influence."[1]

However, exaggerated saving is very prejudicial to morality for it degenerates into avarice and thus becomes the cause of crime. We often find the average number of depositors in savings-banks in the departments that gave the lowest figure for crime. The departments with a number of depositors above or below this average are apt to have high figures for crime.

"It is possible to criticise academically the famous saying of Proudhon, 'property is theft.' To refute it will be at times difficult. I do not mean to say that all property is theft, but I maintain that property in a measure that can be fixed is nothing else. As it is organized with use, it is often immoral and one of the most active factors in anti-social crime, latent or actual."[2] According to the author, one who owns property is a supporter of the state. For this reason the number of small proprietors ought to be increased, even if this is possible only by dividing great estates, which, however, have almost always been gotten together by immoral means, by pillaging, by paying very small wages in manufacturing, by gambling, etc. "They are all, in the first instance, the fruit of a skill and a want of scruple which would never obtain the sanction of a really equitable society; at their blaze, which scorns poverty, the passion for gain is kindled, and dull rage begins to develop the germ of reprisals. How shall we make men who have nothing, and exhaust themselves to gain the bare necessaries of life, satisfied that the persons who do no work and only amuse themselves possess everything? You may talk of legal limitations as much as you like, but conscience will revolt against a doctrine that makes stolen property sacred after a certain period of impunity, and leads to the cynical conclusion that any article or piece of land, acquired by crime, is the legitimate possession of the bandit if during 5, 10, 20, 30 years he succeeds in warding off the attacks of the law."[3] Not only has property often been acquired in an illegal manner, but the transmission of it is also immoral. For it is by this means that persons have acquired great fortunes which they would never have earned by their labor. It would be preferable to make private fortunes accrue to the state, after provision had been made for the widow and children "to provide for the needs of persons who

[1] P. 431. [2] Pp. 434, 435. [3] P. 436.

are useful but made unproductive by poverty, and to reënforce the
collective labor." In this way a general prosperity would replace
great fortunes; this would increase the feeling of solidarity, while
great fortunes only awaken cupidity and lead to the commission of
crimes. The richest departments give the highest figures for criminality. By the suppression or limitation of inheritance we should
suppress also the numerous crimes against life resulting from it.

In the sixth chapter, in which Dr. Corre examines the relative
importance of the principal sociological factors, he sums up his
opinion as to the influence of economic conditions upon criminality.
Too great wealth and too great poverty are both causes of crime.
"The first corrupts and the second degrades; both lead to crime
through lessening the resistance to temptation that promises the
satisfaction of wants fictitious or real, and when they both appear in
the same environment, they give more energy to bad impulses, more
violence to conflicts." [1] This is why the agricultural class, in which
moderate prosperity prevails, is the least criminal. The means by
which this condition of things is to be improved is complex: "it is
not altogether to be found in the solution of the question of wages;
it is chiefly to be found in a better system for making the masses
moral, in the reduction of the influences which tempt them to improvidence and idleness, lead them to drunkenness and alcoholism." [2]

— The second part of this work will show sufficiently why, in my
opinion, the treatment of Dr. Corre is confused and incomplete, notwithstanding the truth of some observations made by him with
regard to the subject which concerns us. The criticism of the author
upon the organization of society at present is that of the petty
bourgeoisie; he expects salvation only from the multiplication of small
holdings, and hopes that this will make mankind happier. However,
the development of large industries makes me believe that this hope
will never be realized. —

IV.

L. MANOUVRIER.

Of all the adherents of the "hypothesis of the environment,"
Professor Manouvrier is undoubtedly the one who has set forth this
doctrine in the clearest manner. Being an anthropologist it is evident
that he has not given his attention more especially to economic condi-

[1] P. 561.   [2] P. 568.

tions. But it seems to me that what he says in opposition to the theory of Professor Lombroso, and in support of that of the environment, is of the greatest importance. I will give a résumé, therefore, of his "Genèse normale du crime",[1] and in doing so will quote his own words as far as possible, in order to give their full value. Although there is no connection between the doctrine of Professor Lombroso and his adherents, and this work, I shall be forced to follow his whole demonstration, because of the interlacing of the theories of the Italian school and the detailed exposition of the doctrine of the "environment."

The doctrine of the innate character of crime and the phrenology of Gall and Spurzheim are closely connected. Gall thought that he had discovered in the brain the organs of homicide and theft, without, however, denying the importance of surroundings, so that he explained a case of theft by means of circumstances when the bump of theft was wanting in the thief.

This doctrine has been entirely supplanted by the theories of Lamarck and Darwin. "In the place of attributing to the environment the rôle of a simple player of a hand-organ, Lamarck sees in it a true musician playing upon his instrument any airs suited to its complexity and qualities. Further, the quality and characteristics of the instrument can be modified, transformed under the influence of this marvelous musician and that of the music executed. This was the ruin of craniomancy. The diagnostics of phrenology found themselves limited at once and for always to the faculties, the elementary dispositions that Gall and Spurzheim had tried in vain to discover, and which are consistent with the execution of acts indefinitely variable.

"The phrenologists are right in connecting the 'properties of the soul and mind' with organization, but they are wrong in connecting such acts as theft and homicide with organic causes, as if these acts had the value of real, irreducible functions." [2]

Notwithstanding the bond between phrenology and the positivist school, this school does not rely upon the theory in question, but upon the transformist theory, i.e. upon the theory that gives its attention to environment. The cause of this is that the fundamental error that forms the point of departure is still universally prevalent. "This error consists in believing that acts sociologically defined, like crimes,

[1] See also by the same author: "Les crânes des suppliciés", "Les aptitudes et les actes", "L'atavisme et le crime", and his reports to the Congress of Criminal Anthropology at Paris and at Brussels.
[2] Pp. 408, 409.

can be connected with the anatomical conformation, without being first referred by a psychological analysis to their psychological elements, the only ones, whether normal or pathological, that depend directly upon anatomy. The same error consists in confusing the combinations of aptitudes formed under the influence of environment, with the elementary aptitudes resulting from the native organization or its successive modifications. It also leads to a misunderstanding of the primary fact that two individuals similarly constituted can be led, in consequence of the influence of dissimilar environments to which they have been subjected since their birth, to conduct themselves in different, and even quite opposite, ways, without their acts ceasing to be, on that account, conformed to their anatomical constitution." [1]

It is a fact well known to biologists that in all living beings qualities often occur that did not appear in their immediate forebears but in more remote generations. This reappearance of qualities is called atavism. Its importance has been too much exaggerated, however, and it has been made into a magic word with which, it has been thought, everything could be explained, including crime. The line of reasoning has been as follows: crime is one of the ordinary phenomena among savage peoples, and must therefore have been so among the ancestors of the civilized peoples. It is observed that among the criminals of our day there are more of the anatomical stigmata indicating atavism than among non-criminals; consequently crime is a phenomenon of atavism! There are numerous errors in this reasoning. "Since we are treating the question of crime, we must first of all know what is understood by crime, must give a definition of it indicating what crime corresponds to physiologically, and to what order of anatomical characteristics the physiological tendency to crime corresponds. Considered in themselves, these acts suppose only the existence of a conformation permitting, and of needs demanding, their accomplishment. If such a conformation and such needs no longer exist in the normal state among civilized peoples, where nevertheless the acts are frequent, it would be proper to examine the authors of them for abnormal characteristics; not merely *any* abnormal characteristics, but characteristics, anatomical or physiological, that it would be possible to connect with these aptitudes and needs that have become abnormal." [2]

Among the anatomical stigmata observed in criminals in prison there are several which, considered by themselves, have nothing

[1] Pp. 409, 410.   [2] Pp. 414, 415.

abnormal about them; none of them would serve to characterize criminals. We often find, for example, that murderers have relatively large jaws, which are ordinarily thus an index of a conformation disposed to brutality; "but this brutality is absolutely of the same order as that of men compared with women; it is a masculine characteristic, and the masculine conformation is indubitably favorable to crimes of violence much more than the feminine; but happily it happens that most men, in civilized countries, live under conditions in which their natural brutality does not prevent their being very peaceable citizens, though it would be imprudent to molest them. Very vigorous men are ordinarily endowed with square and very solid jaws; they are men for attack or defense, who may be very useful to society or very harmful, as the case may be. Given to acting vigorously and brutally, this they may be, but inclined to crime they are not, any more than the men with small jaws, whose mildness is often the effect of muscular weakness, and who, though little given to striking and breaking down doors, nevertheless know how to be brutal and violent in their own way." [1]

However, it might be thought that these anatomical characteristics, though not dangerous in themselves, are nevertheless an indication of a tendency on their part to act like savages. But this is not the case; these characteristics " are morphological accidents that are purely local and are compatible with the most fortunate conformation." But this is not saying that every peculiarity must remain unutilized. Thus, for example, there are persons who are able to move their ears. "If murder and theft were acts as little complicated, and of as little importance as moving the ears, and if these acts, having become criminal, did not suppose very complex anatomical and psychological coördinations; if there were, in other words, as Gall supposed, cerebral organs specially and innately fitted for murder and theft, we could believe that the mere atavistic presence of these organs would constitute a tendency to commit these crimes; but neither anatomo-physiological analysis, nor psychology will justify today so simple a conception." [2]

And then it has not been proved that murder and theft were habitual with our ancestors; they had recourse to them only under stress of circumstances, quite like any normal man of today. Considered from an anatomical point of view our means of injuring our fellows have decreased; on the other hand we have now other means at our disposal (firearms, etc.). "As to the need of pleasure and of

[1] Pp. 416, 417.   [2] Pp. 418, 419.

life, this can only have increased, and never can cupidity have been more aroused than in our civilized society.   Never have the temptations to appropriate the goods of others been stronger and more frequent.   Civilization tends to develop wants and appetites, whence there comes this colossal extension of the means of repression and of coercion employed to make criminal attempts dangerous, in order that crime may not be too easy a means of acquiring fortune.   Except for purely pathological cases, the criminal is moved by his wants, by wants that have nothing extraordinary about them; when a man has an interest, or thinks he has an interest in committing a crime, he brings into play muscular and cerebral aptitudes which every normal man possesses, the same elementary aptitudes as those he might have made use of, under other circumstances, to pursue and punish a criminal." [1]

Some biological facts are to be explained by atavism; their explanation nevertheless remains mysterious.   But atavism loses all its importance as a means of explanation as soon as we know how to explain a fact by actually existing causes, as is the case with crime. "We should understand that it would be a question of atavistic tendencies if assassins killed for the sole pleasure of killing, if thieves stole for the pleasure of stealing.   Now we know well that theft and murder are only means, and that their use is called 'work' by professional criminals.   If they prefer this kind of work it is because it is quicker and less painful than regular work." [2]

It might be objected here that the horror of blood being natural to most men it would be necessary just the same to have recourse to atavism to explain murder.   This horror of blood is assuredly found in most men, but only so far as their interest requires.   Not a single surgeon or butcher pursues his bloody trade through atavism, but only because forced to it by his interests.   More than one born-bourgeois thinks that he would never eat meat rather than have to kill cattle himself, but this is only pure illusion or an unconscious hypocrisy.   For he would do it without any doubt if he could not gain his livelihood in any other way.   Do not the bourgeoisie shoot their inoffensive fellow citizens who revolt against a social condition that no one would dare to call ideal?   Do they not mow down savages with machine guns in order to divide up their country?   Or do they not make war against other states in order to protect their own commercial interests?   It will be objected that these things are not crimes; this is a question of definition, but assuredly they are similar to crime.

[1] P. 419.   [2] P. 429.

"It is not only in the prisons that we find born-criminals; but we are all such, if we understand by this abusive expression the possession of hereditary tendencies to enjoy things ourselves, in case of need, to the detriment of our fellows.   The human crimes to which I have just alluded indicate chiefly the cruelty and ferocity of the species, and of ethnic collectivities, social or otherwise.   As to the individual equivalents of crime, I will recall further that they are not difficult to discover in the conduct of honest men, most of whom do not trouble themselves to make use of means as harmful and immoral as those which criminals do.   The equivalents of crime among honest men present, it is true, the great advantage of remaining more or less unperceived by the penal code, by the police at least, and the psychologists of the New School; but they are nevertheless recognized as immoral and harmful by those who have recourse to them, and they suffice to show in what way honest men would conduct themselves if the conditions in which they live and have lived had not driven them away from crime, legally so-called, with as much force as the opposite environmental conditions have driven others to it." [1]

Having made fuller remarks to the effect that the cruel and repugnant professions referred to above are not practiced because of atavistic tendencies, but solely from necessity, the author ends this part of his article as follows: "There nevertheless remains a tremendous difference between the killing of an animal and the killing of a man, from a moral point of view, of course, but also from the point of view of the motives generally fitted to prevent the killing.   But it must be remarked that these motives are connected with environmental influences which are exceedingly variable, and which, for too many persons, are considerably diminished and at the same time replaced by influences of the opposite environment.   Most assassins have received a certain *culture* appropriate to the conception of murder and to its realization, and this is simply facilitated by their conformation, which is in no wise exceptional.   If we had only to twirl our thumb to get rid of an enemy we should have to put forth all our efforts to harm no one.   Already too many respectable men can order murders that they would not be courageous enough to execute.   Let us congratulate ourselves that self-interest more often deters men from murder than drives them to it, for every normal man possesses the cerebral and muscular qualities necessary to conceive, prepare, and execute the crime.   It is not necessary to call in the return to animal instincts through atavism.   The continuity of man and the animals is much

[1] Pp. 431, 432.

more perfect than the atavistic school pretends.   Man is always an animal; the most dangerous of all because he is the most intelligent and because he can utilize his faculties in all sorts of ways, harmful or useful to his fellows according to his own interest.   The formula to be applied is to arrange things so that every man will find more advantage in being useful to his fellows than in injuring them.   Progress in this regard would be more rapid without this unfortunate predilection for occult causes, which leads so many excellent minds to seek in the clouds for explanations that lie under their noses, but which have to be found just where they are.

"Those ferocious instincts which seem the return of another world, in brawls or in times of revolution, are not returning at all, because they have never disappeared.   During a certain time they do not manifest themselves in the individual or the family, because there is no need that they should; or possibly they manifest themselves in ways less dangerous, in connection with ordinary circumstances and relatively favorable to tranquillity.   But let there arise any need, no matter what, of a "mobilization of the offensive and defensive forces", then the mobilization takes place, and the most civilized man appears under the form of the dangerous animal he has never ceased to be, happily for himself and his species.   This man whom you take for an atavistic throw-back, appears such to you only because you have failed to recognize in their mild form, in yourself and in others, the fundamental brutality and egoism of the human species.   Notwithstanding the civilizing influences in the midst of which you have lived, notwithstanding the peaceable habits that you have contracted, and all the horror with which you are inspired by the contrary habits of which you fear to fall the victim, it is enough that you should be worked upon rather strongly by a combination of annoying circumstances, that even you should become a dangerous individual. When we wish to study crime as anthropologists or as psychologists, we must not be afraid to look the truth in the face, and it is important to clear our minds beforehand, as far as possible, of the illusions of self-love, and of deceptive conventions." [1]

Then Professor Manouvrier criticises in a manner as just as it is witty, the hypothesis of the "delinquent man." He demonstrates that, according to the method of the New School, a work could be written upon the "hunting man" also, full of scientific observations upon his argot, his boasting, etc., etc., upon all sorts of signs, in short, which go to show that a taste for hunting is an atavistic phenomenon.

[1] Pp. 434–436.

The explanation of crime by atavism is no more true than this other, for both can be explained by the environment.

If we hold absolutely to the expression : "born-criminal", every man is one, just as every dog is a born-swimmer. Every dog knows how to swim very well, but this does not prevent a number of dogs from never swimming, since ordinarily there are more convenient ways of crossing the water. In the same way every man is a born-criminal, but most men refrain from becoming actual criminals, since that course is more advantageous to them than the other.

"No one is ignorant that the educational influences to which one is subjected during his whole life and especially during infancy, and the solicitations of self-interest, are exceedingly variable under different circumstances and for different individuals; and that the educational influences and the solicitations of self-interest unite very generally to furnish the motive for criminal conduct and for honest conduct as well. And it is this that governs every man's manner of acting in his relations with others; and it must not be forgotten in treating of anthropology, whether anatomical, physio-psychological, or sociological. It is never forgotten in practical life.

"We all know that, whatever our fundamental character may be and the honest habits that we have been able to form, our manner of conducting ourselves may vary considerably under the influence of changes in our environment, and in proportion to those changes. It is a temptation to which the most austere man would greatly dread to be exposed, and to which he would never voluntarily expose himself, because he knows that the tendencies imputed to criminals (said to be atavistic, but all simply human) are not lacking in himself. These tendencies, when they have found abundant and honorable means of satisfaction during long years, become so much the more to be dreaded on this account, and run great danger of becoming criminal as soon the legal means of satisfaction disappear. The man who comes to lack these means finds himself in a much more dangerous situation as far as the likelihood of his becoming a criminal is concerned, than one who had become accustomed to privations." [1]

Professor Manouvrier begins the last section of his study by asking what is the significance of the anatomical peculiarities observed in the so-called born-criminals. "The truth probably is that we do find in a number of criminals in prison more of the lower or abnormal characteristics than in a like number of persons chosen at random. But this is no wise proves that those among the criminals who have such

[1] Pp. 445, 446.

characteristics, have been predestined to crime from their physical make-up.   Those among them who are not so constituted are nevertheless criminals, and honest men who bear the criminal marks have nevertheless remained honest.

"The truth is that the 'new school' consider as criminals only the refuse of this class, the prisoners; just as, when they wanted to depict prostitutes, they took poor syphilitic girls who had been at least three years in brothels, that is to say, the refuse of refuse.   Under what family and social conditions these criminals and prostitutes lived during childhood and afterward, it is easy for anyone to imagine who has caught but a glimpse of the slums of manufacturing towns.   In order to escape crime and prostitution or mendicity when one has grown up in such an environment, it is necessary to have virtues that are extremely rare among respectable people, so much the more so since, to the temptations that come from poverty in the midst of luxury, is ordinarily added the effect of example, and even of education of the particular kind that is called criminal education.   All this may be resisted for some time, but it is only the first step that costs. The good qualities themselves that one possesses become the causes of crime.   It may even be maintained that physical excellencies themselves drive men to crime more strongly than defects, when once the external conditions become favorable for crime." [1]

The fact that we generally find more inferior individuals among the criminals imprisoned than among other men must be attributed to the two following circumstances: first, that criminals who have not been arrested, owe their liberty generally to the fact that they are better endowed; and second, that in all social classes a selection goes on by which those best constituted are always in possession of the most desirable and least painful means of existence, while to those less privileged fall the lowest professions, and they "end sooner or later by falling into the ditch where the influences that drive men to crime reach their maximum frequency and power, while the contrary motives are proportionately weak."   Those who have known better days sometimes prefer suicide to crime; but those who are born in the ditch, know no other life, and are consequently led into crime.

What is much more astonishing than crime is the fact that workmen labor courageously and patiently for ten or twelve hours a day, and notwithstanding this lead only a miserable life.   The reason is that they have known nothing but labor since infancy and have always

[1] Pp. 449, 450.

had to be content with very simple amusements. It goes without saying that one man is more moved to commit crimes than another, although the conditions under which they are living are the same, just as an athlete will use violence quicker than a weakling. But this is no reason to declare strength a factor of crime, since it serves for useful acts as well. Acts which are contrary to the proper working of society are, therefore, called abnormal and those are called normal that are in harmony with it. But it is not therefore permissible to transfer this distinction to the field of biology, and call the criminal abnormal. "Aptitudes that are very normal physiologically, may be employed for acts that are equally normal physiologically, but which, from a social point of view are classed as abnormal, because contrary to the social prosperity. Yet this is an abuse of the word 'abnormal', because society as at present constituted is, in its normal functioning, consistent with innumerable causes of conflict between its own interests and those of individuals. And just as the annoying consequences of our mistakes often make us recognize the truth, so crimes very often serve to indicate to societies the reforms they ought to bring about in order to perfect themselves.

"Every individual has wants to satisfy, wants primordial or secondary, that may become infinitely complicated and clothed in forms as much more various as the environment becomes more complex. Now it happens in every society, and especially in very civilized societies, that the different individuals do not find the same facilities, and further, do not possess the same means of action. There is an evident disproportion between the existing needs and the milder means of satisfying them; whence the struggle for existence and well-being.

"In our estimating the intrinsic worth of criminals, we must not fail to take account of this fact, that most honest men do not deprive themselves of any of the pleasures which are the aim of criminals, and that most criminals, in order to escape crime would have had to have rare virtue. Among the legal means of satisfaction offered by society there are those that are easy and agreeable, among others that of drawing the income from capital amassed by one's parents. There are also difficult and painful ones, which are the lot of those whom pecuniary heredity has not secured against the so-called criminal heredity. In order to share legally in the pleasures of which they are witnesses, those whom we may call disinherited by fortune, must make efforts of which those born to wealth have no idea. This is why, if the disinherited seek a short-cut, we must ask ourselves, before we consider them as monstrous beings, whether under the same circumstances we should be able to keep to the legal path.

"The struggle for existence and well-being is regulated by social laws. If these were perfect, each individual could satisfy his wants in an equitable measure, that is to say in the measure of his faculties, his labor, and the service he renders to the community. Crimes would then be diminished in an enormous proportion, but they would not be suppressed, for there would still be inevitable competitions, and the time will probably never come when, on the one hand, each individual will have just the wants that his social worth will permit him to satisfy legally, and, on the other, will have sufficient virtue to renounce the satisfaction of wants, even factitious ones, which he has once contracted without being able to comply with the conditions which the most just law imposes for this satisfaction." [1]

The penal law is one of the means the object of which is combating the illegal satisfaction of wants. Everyone knows, however, that this means does not always attain the end sought. The penal law will, in fact, produce a diminution of criminality only when it shall have brought about profound penal changes, — when punishment shall be no more than the *useful and necessary reaction* against acts that are harmful to the well-being of the community and to the development of society.

It is to be proved that there is, besides the normal, or ordinary, origin of crime, a pathological, or extraordinary, origin. "It is quite superfluous to bring in tendencies atavistically recalled by pathological degeneracy, in order to explain the harmful effects of this degeneracy, and of mental diseases, upon the way in which the degenerate and mentally diseased act. The least functional trouble is enough to alter our sensations, our judgment, our imagination, our deliberations, and consequently, to make us act wrongly." [2]

The theory of the innate character of crime through atavism is consequently quite erroneous. "It would be unseemly on my part to refer it, through atavism, to *original sin* or to the *call of the blood* of the ancient melodramas. I will not even say that it is derived through tradition, which is an environmental influence, from the old phrenological doctrine, although that is an error of the same kind. Errors, in fact, are like crimes; they have no need of atavism nor of immediate heredity, nor even of tradition, in order to repeat themselves. Causes of error or causes of crime, the springs are far from being dried up. They always flow abundantly. It is necessary in

[1] Pp. 452, 453.   [2] P. 455.

science to react against errors, and in society to react against crimes. But it must never be forgotten that every man is normally exposed to commit both errors and crimes." [1]

— I shall make only a few observations upon Professor Manouvrier's study, a work which, in my opinion, is one of the best, not to say *the* best, upon the origin of crime, and in about fifty pages says more than many a bulky volume.

In the first place Professor Manouvrier shows that in our days wants have increased greatly, and he believes that civilization is the cause of it. I am of the opinion that this last assertion is not correct and that civilization has nothing to do with it. Many writers commit this error of confusing civilization and the present mode of production, and it is just for this reason that it is useful and necessary to correct it. All the evils that have been brought upon the peoples of Africa and of China, war, alcohol, etc., etc., have been called by the collective name of "civilization." In reality it is those who have brought all these calamities upon these countries, and have tried to destroy a veritable, age-long civilization like that of China, who are the barbarians. It is not a civilizing instinct that has driven European states to a policy of expansion, but rather cupidity, eagerness for gain on the part of the owning class, who are seeking a new outlet for their merchandise; in short, it is the present mode of production, capitalism.

The same is true with regard to the constant increase of wants; it is the present system which *creates* wants. New methods of procuring profit are invented, and it is only with this in view that many inventions are made, most of them useless, often even harmful. And on the other hand there is a class of persons who grasp at any means, even the most absurd, of passing the time, and have the money to procure these means. And these wants spring up in other persons also, and the impossibility of satisfying them makes men the more eager. Consequently it is not civilization, but capitalism, which must be designated as the cause of this phenomenon.

In the second place, Professor Manouvrier thinks that criminality would diminish enormously, but without disappearing entirely, if the social laws were perfected so that each individual could satisfy his wants according to his capacities, his labor, and his services to the community. This is, in my opinion, entirely correct; but the maxim of Saint-Simon, "to every man according to his capacities, to each

[1] P. 456.

capacity according to its works", which, in Professor Manouvrier's opinion, is perfect, by many others is not thought to be so, though superior to the present distribution of commodities. We can set over against this the rule, "that each shall work according to his faculties and his strength, and receive according to his needs." If this were realized, crime would become almost unimaginable. Many persons are of the opinion that such a thing could never be realized. But they forget that it is exclusively from the environment that the enormous differences in wants arise (the wife of the millionaire has perhaps a thousand times as many needs as the wife of the proletarian). If these two persons had been born and brought up in the same environment, the wants of the one would have been to those of the other perhaps as 1 to 3, or even less, but certainly not more. And then those who believe in a future distribution according to needs, are of the opinion (and think they can prove it) that, if in the present organization of society egoism is omnipotent, the feeling of solidarity will be so strengthened in the future social organization, that the man endowed with great abilities and much energy, will not begrudge his fellow less highly endowed, the satisfaction of all his wants.

I would, at the same time, make a remark concerning the environmental school in general, a remark not to be considered as a criticism, for I agree perfectly that it is the environment that makes the criminal. It is this: it is not enough for the treatment of the question of criminality, to furnish proof of the assertion that the cause of crime is not inherent in man; it is also necessary to show in what respects the environment is criminogenous, and in what way it can be improved. Now the French School has given but little attention to this. —

V.

A. BAER.

The work of Dr. Baer, "Der Verbrecher in anthropologischer Beziehung", has only an indirect importance for our subject, as the title indicates. Since his medical and anthropological studies lead him to the conclusion that the social atmosphere is the fundamental cause of crime, it is worth while to note his opinion. For this it will be sufficient to quote the following: "For us crime is, as Prins excellently expresses it, not an individual phenomenon, but a social one. 'Criminality is made up of the elements of human society itself, it is not transcendent but immanent. We can see in it a kind of degeneration of the social organism. . . . The criminal and the honest man are each dependent upon their environment. There are social conditions that are favorable to moral health, where there is no tendency, no inclination toward crime; there is a social environment where the atmosphere is corrupt, where unwholesome elements have accumulated, where crime settles as soot does in a flue, where the tendency toward crime bears fruit.' Though Ferri has recently advocated the opinion that the criminal is the result of three factors, operative at the same time, and that these three causes are individual (*i.e.* anthropological), physical,[1] and social; in our opinion, on the other hand, these three causes are actually to be reduced to a single one, if, as he himself points out, we take into consideration the fact that the first two are both dependent upon social conditions. The anthropological and physical stigmata of criminals are, as we have endeavored to show above, in most cases wholly conditioned by the influences and circumstances of their environment.

"Crime, we will close this work by saying, is not the consequence of a special organization of the criminal, an organization which is peculiar to the criminal alone, and which forces him to the commission of criminal acts. The criminal, such by habit and apparently born as such, bears many marks of bodily and mental deformity, which have, however, neither in their totality nor singly, so marked and peculiar a character as to differentiate the criminal from his fellows as a distinct type. The criminal bears the traces of degeneracy that are to be found in abundance among the lower classes from which he mostly takes his rise. These traces, acquired through social conditions and transmitted, in his case at times emerge in stronger form. Whoever would do away with crime must do away with the social wrongs in which crime takes root and grows, and, in establishing and applying forms of punishment, must give more weight to the individuality of the criminal than to the category under which the crime falls." [2]

[1] ["Somatisch." Though capable of being translated thus, this word is plainly not "physical" in the sense in which that is used for one of Ferri's three causes. — TRANSL.]

[2] Pp. 410, 411.

See also: Dr. *A. Bournet*, "De la criminalité en France et en Italie"; *G. Richard*, "Les crises sociales et la criminalité" ("L'année sociologique", 1898–99); *L. Gumplowicz*, "Das Verbrechen als soziale Erscheinung" ("Soziologische Essays").

[NOTE TO THE AMERICAN EDITION: Compare further the recent works of the French school: *E. Laurent*, "Le criminel"; *J. L. de Lanessan*, "La lutte contra le crime"; *J. Maxwell*, "Le crime et la société."]

CHAPTER V.

THE BIO–SOCIOLOGISTS.

I.

AD. PRINS.

I CANNOT better give Professor Prins's opinion upon the subject of my work than by quoting what he says in his book, "Criminalité et répression", and especially in his first chapter entitled "De la criminalité en général. Des classes criminelles. Des délinquants d'accident et des délinquants de profession." There we read: "There exists no abstract type of a moral man, nor of a guilty man; crime is not an individual phenomenon, but a social phenomenon. Criminality proceeds from the very elements of humanity itself; it is not transcendent, but immanent; we can see in it a sort of degeneration of the social organism." [1]

There is an environment favorable to moral health, where the tendency to crime is almost wholly lacking; there is a social environment where the atmosphere is corrupt, where unwholesome elements are heaped up, where the most vigorous perish, where criminality spreads like the mould in the dunghill; the tendency toward crime there is formidable, and we can say in this sense that it is a social fact with a social cause, and that it is in intimate connection with a given social organization.

Let us consider our own epoch for a moment. A century of progress and refinement is a century of vices; the increasing complexity of our mechanism creates, with new temptations, new occasions of falling. The car of civilization, like that of Juggernaut, destroys many of those who throw themselves under its wheels. The world has enormous appetites that it cannot satisfy: sensuality, greed of gain, a taste for and facility in speculation; the contrast between

[1] P. 13.

great wealth and extreme poverty; the brutal necessities of the struggle for existence in the face of the concentration of property and of capital; the defects of the industrial organization, which abandons the proletariat to chance, keeps no watch over apprenticeship, and leaves the child of the working-man to the excitations of the streets and the promiscuity of the workshop, and finally sharpens everywhere the obscure instincts of animalism; all this recoils upon criminality with deplorable certainty. How far wrong we should be in such an environment simply to contrast the delinquent with the honest man! It is two social states that are contrasted; the one is based upon comfortable means, sociability, mutual protection, useful work, and thrift; the other upon poverty, isolation, egoism, and unproductive labor. And in the great urban agglomerations, pauperism, mendicity and vagrancy, idleness, the spirit of adventure, prostitution, the dissipation of strength, everything, in short, naturally concurs in developing social anemia.

"Take any district whatsoever, however poor, uncivilized, and wild, and you will always find in the great cities, London or Paris, New York or San Francisco, a worse environment and greater depravity. It is here, in the lowest slums, where never a glimmer of physical or moral well-being penetrates, that the disinherited live. They get a glimpse of the splendor of luxury only to hate it; they respect neither property nor life, because neither property nor life has any real value for them; they are born, grow pale, struggle, and die, without suspecting that for certain persons existence is good fortune, property a right, virtue a habit, and calm a constant state. Such is the natural and fatal home of criminality.

"In a quarter subjected to detestable hygiene, built upon marshy soil, devoid of drainage and potable water, furrowed with narrow and filthy streets, covered with hovels without life or air, where an atrophied population vegetates, epidemics are inevitable and propagate themselves with great intensity. In the same way, crime finds an easy and certain prey in the environment of the poor of a great city. The illegitimate and abandoned children, the children of convicts and prostitutes, the vagrants, etc. are so many designated recruits. Without family, without traditions, without fixed home or settled occupation, without relations with the ruling classes, what wonder that they have no other motive than complete egoism, no other activity than selfish and transitory efforts for the immediate satisfaction of their material appetites? The emigration from the country to the city still further increases this army and multiplies the chances of crime.   When the sons of peasants leave the plow for the workshop and come to seek fortune in the furnace of great cities, they follow the spirit of adventure; they must have, at any price, a means of subsistence, and as competition is great and temptations arise at every step, the prisons profit by this overplus that the country gives to the city.   Another consequence of the immigration from the country is that the population becomes excessive, places are lacking, and wages fall below the living expenses.   Ducpetiaux showed, in 1856, that the budget of the working-man in the great cities is lower than the sum representing the budget of the working-man in prison.   This situation has not changed, and the laboring class, badly lodged, badly nourished, vegetate at the mercy of economic crises.   The working-man is always on the verge of vagrancy, the vagrant always on the verge of crime.   The whole proletariat is thus exposed in the front rank, and whether it is a question of sickness or crime, it is the first to fall." [1]

"Such are the conditions of the development of the criminal classes, that is to say of the classes where we meet the tendency to crime. And it is of importance to remark that we can determine their legal character; they are the vagrants and delinquents by profession. They are clearly differentiated from the vagabonds and delinquents by accident.   This distinction, which modern statistics has brought into relief, is now the basis of penal science, and the judge can no longer overlook it.

"The occasional delinquents constitute the minority, their life is regular, their instincts are right; a sudden passion, an unpremeditated outburst, a passing depression of the will, leads them into crime; a sort of fever dominates them and, the fit once past, their normal life takes up its course again.

"On the other hand, the professional delinquents, who make up the largest part of the population of the prisons, are really the criminal class.   They are the hardened, the incorrigible, the recidivists.   They form, by the side of regular society, the great rebel tribe, where gather and mingle poverty, ignorance, vice, idleness, and prostitution. The soldiers of this army obey, not a momentary desire, but a permanent tendency.   They do not always commit crime for crime's sake, but the most trivial incident drives them to it; they profit by every opportunity, and we can say that, as in certain circles virtue is a reflex act, so crime is a reflex act with them.   Further, they have, quite like the civilized world, a public opinion which supports them,

[1] Pp. 13–18.

arouses them, gives them their own kind of popularity, and constitutes, in a word, an incentive for the heroes of vice, just as the other public opinion encourages the soldiers of duty.

"What is true of criminal society as a whole, is equally true of the individual as such. In each infraction of the law, besides the accidental factor, *i.e.* age, character, temperament, in a word, the personal disposition, there is the collective or social factor, *i.e.* the environment, the permanent conditions, the general laws. With the occasional delinquent the individual factor predominates, it is especially the man that appears. With the habitual delinquent, it is the social factor, the collectivity that comes upon the scene.

"In the well-to-do, polished, educated classes, who have lacked nothing and have had the benefit of civilizing influences from the cradle, the fault is chiefly personal, and, it is the exception. In the lower strata, where everything is lacking, where, to combat evil, men have neither in the present, social protection, nor in the past, the generations of ancestors who have enjoyed power, wealth, and education, it is chiefly collective. In this sense, then, the collective forces have a dominant action in criminality; in order to combat it these must be attacked, and the legislator finds in the law only a blunted weapon if he does not understand this supreme truth, the social character of criminality." [1]

II.

W. D. MORRISON.

The preface to "Crime and its Causes" contains an abridgment of the opinion of the author upon the influence of economic conditions. He says there:

"Economic prosperity, however widely diffused, will not extinguish crime. Many people imagine that all the evils afflicting society spring from want, but this is only partially true. A small number of crimes are probably due to sheer lack of food, but it has to be borne in mind that crime would still remain an evil of enormous magnitude even if there were no such calamities as destitution and distress. As a matter of fact easy circumstances have less influence on conduct than is generally believed; prosperity generates criminal inclinations as well as adversity, and on the whole the rich are just as much addicted to crime as the poor." [2]

The chapter "Climate and Crime" contains some observations that

---

[1] Pp. 19–22.　　　　　　　　　　　　　　[2] P. 6.

are of interest in connection with our subject.   In speaking of the
great number of crimes against persons in Italy, the author says:

"Nor can it be said to be entirely due to economic distress.   A condition of social misery has undoubtedly something to do with the
production of crime.   In countries where there is much wealth side
by side with much misery, as in France and England, adverse social
circumstances drive a certain portion of the community into criminal
courses.   But where this great inequality of social conditions does not
exist — where all are poor as in Ireland or Italy — poverty alone is
not a weighty factor in ordinary crime.   In Ireland, for example,
there is almost as much poverty as exists in Italy, and if the amount of
crime were determined by economic circumstances alone, Ireland
ought to have as black a record as her southern sister.   Instead of
that she is on the whole as free from crime as the most prosperous
countries of Europe." [1]

— This quotation is one of the best samples of Morrison's logic and
knowledge of facts !   Italy is poor;   Ireland is poor;   the former has
many crimes, the latter few.   Hence, economic conditions are not an
important factor.   To say nothing of the care necessary in comparing
two countries where the penal law, police, courts, etc. are very different, there is an error of logic in the quotation.   For poverty may be
in one of these countries a determinant that leads to a certain phenomenon, while in another country it does not lead to it, because neutralized by a counter-determinant.   And then, the knowledge of facts
that Morrison gives evidence of here, is not great.   It is not at all
true that in Italy every one is poor.   On the contrary, there is plenty
of wealth in that country, while Ireland, on the other hand, is drained
by landlords who *live elsewhere*. [2] —

The chapter that interests us next is that entitled "Destitution
and Crime."   " A ' destitute person ' is a person who is without house
or home, who has no work, who is able and willing to work but can
get none, and has nothing but starvation staring him in the face." [3]

According to Morrison there are two kinds of crime of which a
destitute person may be guilty, namely theft and mendicity.   Two
questions must be answered, then, first, what percentage is there of
these crimes ?   second, how far can one attribute theft and mendicity
to destitution ?

During the years 1887–1888 the number of cases tried in England

[1] P. 37.
[2] *Cf. Colajanni*, "Sociologia criminale ", II., p. 558.
[3] Pp. 82, 83.

and Wales was 726,698, of which 8% were crimes against property
and 7% offenses against the "Vagrancy Acts." Consequently 15%
of all the crimes might have been committed because of destitution.
From investigations made by himself, half the thieves had work and
were earning something at the time they committed their crimes.

Now we still have to explain the other half of the cases of theft.
Those who committed these thefts were without work, then; but
there were among them habitual criminals, and these could probably
have found work, but did not want to work. Therefore they were
not "destitute persons." This leaves still 25% of the thieves.
Among these destitution is now truly the direct cause. However
lack of work is not the sole cause, but the fact that children of proletarians are left to themselves when their parents are sick or dead,
enters in. And then many aged working-men become criminals
because they are too old to work and no one supports them. Drunkards also at times come to commit crimes because of poverty, since
they find it difficult to work. The estimate is, then, as follows:

Proportion of criminals earning at the time of arrest				4 %
"	"	"	habitual thieves	2 %
"	"	"	adults without shelter and old men	1 %
"	"	drunkards, vagrants		1 %
"	"	crimes against property compared with total		
			number of crimes	8 %

Then come the infractions of the "Vagrancy Acts." The offenses
that are punished under these laws are chiefly prostitution, presence
in public places with criminal intentions, presence in a particular house
with criminal intentions, and carrying burglars' implements. Prostitution aside, destitution ought not to be considered as the cause of these
infractions, according to the author, because the guilty persons are
those who ordinarily will not work and would not change their lot for
anyone else's. The class of vagrants is no more unhappy than any
other; it has even its own philosophy. (— Who could be unhappy,
then? This statement of the case gives one a great desire to ask the
author how it happens that no people of means have adopted this
enviable career. —) The same reasoning applies to most of the
mendicants (45% of those who break the vagrancy laws), they do not
want to work. Another fraction is made up of those who cannot find
work; their number is difficult to determine; according to Morrison's
opinion it is not very high (he estimates it at 2% for mendicants).
It is especially aged persons who belong to this class. There are
two principal reasons for this.

First, the increasing use of machines, which throw workmen out of employment, while increasing the possibility of utilizing the labor of women and children.

— However true this observation, it is nevertheless very incomplete. It is not the machine that is the cause, but the system of free labor, which throws everyone on his own resources when he can work no longer, whether this is from lack of work or from the disability of the worker. —

A second cause of vagrancy and mendicity is to be found in the Trades Unions. For these Unions have been able to obtain a uniform wage, and aged workmen must, in accordance with their rules, earn as much as the young ones although not able to do as much work. The employers, not being able to afford to give them the whole amount, discharge them.

The circumstance that there are more male than female beggars is a proof to the author that economic conditions are not the cause of mendicity, etc., for women ordinarily live under worse conditions than men.

" The only possible explanation of this state of thing is that vagrancy is, to a very large extent, entirely unconnected with economic conditions; the position of trade either for good or evil is a very secondary factor in producing this disease in the body politic; its extirpation would not be effected by the advent of an economic millennium; its roots are, as a rule, in the disposition of the individual and not to any serious degree in the industrial constitution of society." [1]

After having stated that, in his opinion, prostitution also has little to do with economic conditions, Morrison arrives at the conclusion that 14% of the delinquents under the Vagrancy Acts have been made so by destitution; as such delinquents constitute 7% of the total of the criminal population, these destitute persons form 2% of the whole.[2] Adding these 2% to the 2% of destitute persons among the thieves, we get a total of 4%. Further, the author estimates the destitute persons among the other criminals (those not punished for theft or infractions of the Vagrancy Acts) at 1%. Of all criminals, then, 5% have become such from destitution, according to Morrison.

— I shall not insist upon proving that these calculations have little value. In the first place all the figures are only estimates,

[1] Pp. 106, 107.
[2] [14% of 7% is about 1%, of course. The mistake is Morrison's. — TRANSL.]

without any indication of what they are based on. In the second place Morrison has only proved, supposing his estimates are correct, that 5% of the criminals belong to a category defined by the author himself. All this gives him absolutely no right to conclude that economic conditions are not a powerful factor in crime. Just where the writer believes that the question has been solved the difficulties properly commence. If we wish to treat the question of vagrancy in a scientific manner we must ask : how does it happen that with the present mode of production there are found persons who prefer vagrancy to work ? This is one of the questions that must be answered, yet for Morrison it does not exist. The causes of professional theft, alcoholism, etc. seem, according to the author, to have nothing to do with economic conditions. I shall show in the second part of this work how far wrong he is. —

The following chapter treats of "poverty and crime." To prove the slightness of the causal connection between the two, Morrison gives the following table :

Italy	1880–84	New cases of theft per an. to 100,000 inh.	221
France	1879–83	" " " " " " " " "	121
Belgium	1876–80	" " " " " " " " "	143
Germany	1882–83	" " " " " " " " "	262
England	1880–84	" " " " " " " " "	228
Scotland	1880–84	" " " " " " " " "	289
Ireland	1880–84	" " " " " " " " "	101
Hungary	1876–80	" " " " " " " " "	82
Spain	1883–84	" " " " " " " " "	74

England is six times as rich as Italy, and the figure for theft is greater; hence, economic conditions are not causes, etc. etc.[1]

— It has been some years since Quetelet pointed out (see Chap. II, Sec. II, of this work) that *absolute* wealth throws no light on the criminal question, because the total wealth of a country gives no idea of its distribution. Yet Morrison thinks that the preceding table proves the correctness of his statement ! —

The author sees a second proof in support of his reasoning in the fact that during the prosperous period of 1870–74 criminality in England was greater than during the period of economic depression from 1884 to 1888. (— See our summaries of the works of Tugan-Baranowsky and of Müller, where it is shown that the economic conditions

[1] In his article, "The Interpretation of Criminal Statistics" ("Journal of the Royal Statistical Society"), 1897 *Morrison* says : "I am inclined to agree . . . that the attempt to institute . . . comparisons (of international character) is at present impracticable" (p. 15). It would have been well if he had not forgotten this opinion when he wrote "Crime and its Causes."

of that period do have a relation to criminality. There is perhaps
no country where the connection between crime and the course of
economic events is so close as in England; and it is surprising that
there are authors like Morrison who are so little in touch with the
situation, and who yet express themselves so decidedly. —)

In America the immigrants commit fewer crimes on the average
than those who are born in the country; the position of these last
being better, economic conditions are not causes of crime. (— As if
assertions as vague as this: "the American has a better position
than the immigrant", could have any value! —)

Morrison sees another proof in the fact that the criminality in
the English colony of Victoria, where prosperity is fairly general,
differs little from that of other countries where the prosperity is less.
(— See A. Sutherland, "Resultats de la déportation en Australie",
Compte Rendu du Ve Congr. d'Anthr. Crim., p. 270, where it is
shown that criminality in Australia on account of the deportation
of English criminals is great, but has fallen continually since 1850,
and now is not so high as in Italy, Sweden, Saxony, and Prussia.
So this proof given by the author is not convincing. —)

Then the author draws attention to the fact that, according to
him, the number of criminals in the different classes of society in
England is proportional to the respective numbers of individuals
in each of these classes. Finally he also thinks that his thesis is supported by the fact that during the summer months the prisons in
England are more populated than in winter.

— The author deceives himself, for to find out that more crimes
are committed in winter than in summer one has only to consult,
not the statistics of the prisons, but those of the courts; the former
give no information as to the time when the offense was committed;
it is even probable that a part of the prisoners incarcerated in summer committed their offenses in winter. Many writers who have
not fallen into this error have come to the conclusion that crimes
and misdemeanors against property, which are those chiefly in question, increase in winter and decrease in summer.

If one wished to make a complete criticism of Morrison's work it
would be necessary to write a whole book, so great is the number of
his errors and omissions, which is why I refer to the second part of
my work.

The fundamental error of the author is that he believes that the
question of how far economic conditions lead to crime is exhausted
when the effect of poverty has been investigated. This is only

a part (though an important one) of the question, which though apparently simple is in reality very complicated.

Finally, I must protest against the unmerited reproach that the English Trades Unions are the cause of criminality among aged working-men. We live in a society in which a great proportion of the men wear themselves out for a small wage in order to enrich others, and where aged working-men who can now do little or no work are tossed aside like oranges from which the juice has been squeezed. When they commit crimes, therefore, it is society that is the cause of it, and not the unions, which, after years of struggle, have succeeded in getting higher wages for their members than those of non-union labor.[1] —

III.

F. Von Liszt.

The following quotation, taken from "Die gesellschaftlichen Ursachen des Verbrechens",[2] gives the opinion of this author in a few words:

"Crime is the necessary result of the joint action of two groups of conditions. The first group is due, partly to the innate, partly to the acquired character of the agent; the other to the environment surrounding him. The microbe of crime flourishes only in the culture medium of society. This sentence, which has gradually become a commonplace, indicates the significance of social conditions for the origination and development of criminality."[3]

"It is obvious that a diminution in the number of certain crimes may be brought about by an improvement in the social order. The impulse toward crime is undoubtedly quickly strengthened by social conditions, and also quickly made weaker. Political and religious offenses become so much the more numerous, the more definitely and relentlessly the dominant opinion takes its stand against diverse persuasions. If today a certain tendency in art were to attain state recognition and the protection of the criminal law, tomorrow the aesthetic heretic would be persecuted as the religious heretics were persecuted in earlier centuries. The sexual instinct will constantly long for satisfaction and take it where it finds it. If you prohibit the possibility of such satisfaction within the bounds of legality, the

---

[1] See, by the same author: "Juvenile Offenders" (chaps. VII and VIII).
[2] See, by the same author, "Das Verbrechen als sozialpathologische Erscheinung."　　　[3] P. 59.

instinct will break the bonds and lead to crime.   And whoever finds
neither bread nor work will, in the great majority of cases, be able
to discover ways and means of securing the one without the other at
the expense of society. . . .   'The beast in man' is in all circles, in
all strata of our society. . . .   But the beast, with all its wild passions, with rage and hate, with covetousness and envy, with thirst
for blood and insatiable vanity, is it not derived from father or mother,
who have drained the pleasures of life or the woes of life to the dregs,
who were corrupted in blood through their own fault, or without their
own fault, before they gave life to the germ to which they imparted
the curse of their forefathers as a heritage?

"A reorganization of our social order will materially lessen the
impulsion to crime in the men who are living today, but infinitely
more important and infinitely more permanent will be its effect upon
coming generations.   While diminishing the number of those tainted
by heredity it will tame the beast in man.   This is no Utopia.   It
will be easier, perhaps, to underestimate the effect of such a transformation, than to appreciate its full value.

"But *which* transformation?   That is the question that we must
answer, if we are not to be pushed aside as harmless visionaries.

"Our entire education, in school as in life, rests upon suggestion.
What keeps us from crime is the inhibitory ideas, which are instilled
into us until they permeate our flesh and blood and control our actions, without our being conscious of it.   'Thou shalt', 'thou shalt
not', these general prescriptions of right and morality, of religion
and philanthropy, or whatever you choose to call it, must determine
our conduct, unless we stop to consider, hesitate, and delay. . . .

"The inhibitory ideas, however, retain their force only if we live
in the community of our fellows, the enclosed circle held together
by like views and a community of interests.   Put upon his own
resources, the true man makes himself known.   But the men who
can do this are rare.   The great majority of us need outside support.
Who has not seen in his own experience how the judgment and prejudice, the beliefs and superstitions of his associates have a determining effect upon him; how he supports others and is supported by
them?   Break up the enclosed circle and you weaken or annihilate
the inhibitory ideas; shatter society to atoms, so that each stands
by himself in the war of all against all, and you set loose whatever
evil instincts have their roots in us; 'declass' man and you have
driven him into the arms of crime.

"And this declassing has been most abundantly provided for by our present economic system. It has unshackled egoism without setting any bounds to it. It reaps what it sows. In the proletariat it has created the very medium in which the microbe of crime flourishes. Next to the wealth of individuals lies the misery of the masses. Do we still wonder, then, that the criminal-statistician laments an increasing number of cases. Every society has the criminals that it deserves." [1]

— The opinion of Professor von Liszt and of other bio-sociologists with regard to crime is a union of the doctrine of the Italian and French schools. Having already given a criticism of these schools I will limit myself to a few remarks.

The formula, "every crime is the product of an individual factor on the one side, and of social factors on the other", is of little value for the question, being applicable to every act, even the most laudable, and explains very little of what is peculiar to crime. A more special examination of the so-called individual factor of crime shows that it is formed, for example, of great needs, of highly developed muscular strength — in short, of things which do not belong to crime alone; or it may be a lack of moral conceptions (the result of an unfavorable environment, of bad education, etc.). A veritable individual factor is to be found only in some special cases, where crime is the result of a predisposition, resulting from a morbid mental condition, combined with unfavorable circumstances. At times, then, crime is the resultant of an individual factor with a social factor; in most cases this is not so. In maintaining that it is always these two together which give birth to crime, one makes use of a commonplace, since by individual factors are understood conditions necessary to every act; or else the statement is quite inaccurate.

Finally it may be said also that most of the bio-sociologists, while recognizing the great influence exercised by environment do not give any description of this environment. It is not enough to name social imperfections existing in our days, and to demand their reform, one after another; we must first of all find out whether these imperfections are connected with the present economic system, and can be removed without attacking the system itself. [2] —

[1] Pp. 59, 60.

[2] [NOTE TO THE AMERICAN EDITION: I am glad to be able to call the reader's attention to the fact that Professor von Liszt has changed his opinion with regard to the bio-sociological hypothesis of crime, and must now be ranked with the partisans of the environmental school. (See "Die gesellschaftlichen Faktoren der Kriminalität", pp. 438–439, "Strafrechtliche Aufsätze und Vorträge", II.)

Chiefly on account of Professor von Liszt's initiative, there has appeared

IV.

P. Näcke.[1]

In his work, "Verbrechen und Wahnsinn beim Weibe", Dr. Näcke treats the criminal question from the medico-anthropological point of view. However, his remarks upon the connection which exists between economic conditions and crime are very important. In the fifth chapter, entitled, "Die anthropologisch-biologischen Beziehungen zum Verbrechen und Wahnsinn beim Weibe", he puts the question: can one fix the idea of "crime" anatomically?

According to him the answer must be an absolute negative. "Semal is right when he says: 'The moral sense is a slow and gradual acquisition of the ages . . . The conscience of peoples like that of the individual, calls every act moral that is useful to the agent himself or to others . . . ' Every people, then, fixes the concept 'crime' according to the moral code prevailing among them at the time; it is consequently not rooted in man physiologically, but is as Manouvrier brilliantly demonstrates, purely sociological. It is therefore really nonsense to seek for anthropological stigmata for a sociological concept.

"But another consideration also leads us to the same result. The stability of a people demands the establishing of certain boundaries, called 'laws', the transgression of which might disturb the social order, and therefore must be punished. But the laws form only single boundary marks, not a tight enclosure, so that between them many, consciously or not, pass through without being caught or

in Germany a series of monographs upon the criminality of a province, of a district, etc. (criminal topography). Here are the titles in chronological order: *K. Böhmert*, "Die sächsische Kriminalstatistik mit besonderer Rücksicht auf die Jahre 1882–1887" ("Zeitschr. d. K. Sächsische Statistischen Bureaus", XXXV; *Damme*, "Die Kriminalität in ihre Zusammenhänge in der Provinz Schleswig-Holstein vom Januar 1882 bis dahin 1890" ("Zeitschr. f. d. ges. Strafrrechtsw.", XII.); *W. Weidemann*, "Die Ursachen der Kriminalität im Herzogtum Sachsen-Meiningen"; *B. Blau*, "Kriminalstatistische Untersuchung der Kreise Marienwerder und Thorn"; *P. Frauenstädt*, "Kriminalistische Heimatkunde" ("Zeitschr. f. Socialwissenschaft", VI.); *E. Peterselie*, "Untersuchungen über die Kriminalität in der Provinz Sachsen"; *F. Dochow*, "Die Kriminalität im Ambtsbezirk Heidelberg"; *F. Galle*, "Untersuchung über die Kriminalität in der Provinz Schlesien" ("Gerichtssaal" LXXI, LXXII); *W. Stöwesand*, "Die Kriminalität in der Provinz Posen und ihre Ursachen"; *A. Sauer*, "Frauenkriminalität in Amtsbezirk Mannheim".]

[1] To my great satisfaction Dr. Näcke says, in a criticism of my book, that through reading it, from a bio-sociologist he has almost become an out-and-out follower of the environmental theory (of the French school) ("Archiv F. Krim.-anthr. u. Kriminalstatistik," XXI, p. 188).

punished. Besides, the laws of a higher morality do not always correspond with the prevailing legal system, so that many things are offenses in the eyes of the moral code that are not such in the eyes of the law, a fact which, as is well known, the conscienceless take advantage of. It is plain, therefore, that there are innumerable transgressions that are not punished, innumerable criminals who pass as honest men, so that we cannot really speak of criminals and honest men, but simply of the punished and the unpunished.

"Punishment is, however, as we have already seen, a poor criterion. Habitual criminals are often not nearly so depraved as many persons of good reputation, especially in certain districts whose moral concepts are of a very elastic kind; or as others who have, to be sure, been punished but once, but who, in all their actions, have always been crafty criminals." [1]

"As there is to be found no such thing as absolute bodily and mental soundness, so there is no such thing as an absolutely 'honest' man. 'We are altogether sinners', say the Scriptures with entire truth — and not in thought only — none of us is proof against becoming a criminal, and under certain circumstances, even a great one." [2]

"There is an unbroken gradation from the purest to the worst man. When we speak simply of 'criminals' we mean only those standing on the farthest step, who are not always, however, the worst. It is a question, then, of the refuse of the world, and not of real crime. In every environment there are always individuals who become evil-doers exclusively or chiefly through circumstances — this possibility no mortal can escape — and on the other hand there are those who owe this in part (seldom, however, exclusively) to their inferior psychic personality, which allows them to run counter to the prevailing morality and drives them to breach of the law; these last constitute the criminals in the narrow sense." [3]

In chapter VI, "Zusammenhang von Verbrechen und Wahnsinn", the author explains that in case an individual factor exists, it is not ordinarily this alone that leads to crime, but it must be coupled with a social factor.

This is what Dr. Näcke says of the causes of this individual factor: "Indeed it is even probable that in the last analysis the individual factor is dependent upon the environment, since this so influenced the parents, grandparents, etc. that the germ of the next generation must have been injured directly or later through corrupted blood

[1] Pp. 96, 97.   [2] P. 98.   [3] Pp. 98, 99.

or narrow pelvis on the part of the mother (both again dependent upon the environment)." [1]

Further along he makes this idea more specific, when he is examining the different causes of crime. Among these causes the author cites the following:

1. Lesion of the germ (favored especially by the marriage of degenerates).
2. Alcoholism.
3. Syphilis.
4. Malnutrition and unhealthy mode of life.
5. Excessive labor of women and children.
6. Bad domestic life.
7. Desertion in which children under age are left.

The author sums up in the following terms: "In what has gone before we have attempted to pick out and follow up some threads of the complex social fabric, in the firm persuasion that only an improvement of the environment in its thousand-fold ramifications will be able effectively to combat crime, and gradually to exert a favorable influence upon the individual factors, which are certainly not to be undervalued.

"If we survey the whole matter, everything comes in the end to the stomach-question; only so long as this is not solved — and perhaps it never can be satisfactorily solved — must we keep the point of view given above practically before us, which, upon the solution of the matter, becomes in large measure no longer necessary." [2]

V.

HAVELOCK ELLIS.[3]

The work of Dr. Havelock Ellis, entitled "The Criminal", contains only one passage which is of importance for the question of

---

[1] P. 177.   [2] P. 208.

See also, by the same author: "Die neuern Erscheinung auf kriminal-anthropologischen Gebiete und ihre Bedeutung" ("Zeitschrift f. d. ges. Strafrw.", XIV.).

[NOTE TO THE AMERICAN EDITION: See also Näcke's "Die Ueberbleibsel der Lombrososchen kriminalanthropologischen Theorien" ("Archiv f. Krim.-anthr. u. Kriminalität", L. (1912), pp. 326 ff.)]

[3] In his introduction this author distinguishes three groups of factors the cosmic, the biological, and the social. Consequently he can be ranked in the same category with Professor Ferri. However, I have thought that he ought rather to be classed among the bio-sociologists, because he gives a preponderating importance to the social factors. As he himself says (p. vii of the introduction), his work is one of the proofs that the divergences of opinions of the schools of criminologists is not great.

criminality considered from the economic point of view. Like most bio-sociologists he considers the social factors as the most important. This is the passage in question :

"The problem of criminality is not an isolated one that can be dealt with by fixing our attention on that and that alone. It is a problem that on closer view is found to merge itself very largely into all those problems of our social life that are now pressing for solution, and in settling them we shall to a great extent settle it. The rising flood of criminality is not an argument for pessimism or despair. It is merely an additional spur to that great task of social organization to which during the coming century we are called.

"It is useless, or worse than useless, to occupy ourselves with methods for improving the treatment of criminals, so long as the conditions of life render the prison a welcome and desired shelter. So long as we foster the growth of reckless classes we foster the growth of criminality. So long as there are a large body of women in the East of London, and in other large centers, who are prepared to say, 'It's Jack the Ripper or the bridge with me. What's the odds?' there will be a still larger number of persons who will willingly accept the risks of prison. 'What's the odds?' Liberty is dear to every man who is fed and clothed and housed, and he will not usually enter a career of crime unless he has carefully calculated the risks of losing his liberty, and found them small; but food and shelter are even more precious than liberty, and these may be secured in prison. As things are, the asylum and the workhouse, against which there is a deep prejudice, ingrained and irrational, would have a greater deterring effect than the prison. There are every morning in Paris 50,000 persons who do not know how they will eat or where they will sleep. It is the same in every great city; for such the prison can be nothing but a home. It is well known that the life of the convict, miserable as it is, with its dull routine and perpetual surveillance, is yet easier, less laborious, and far more healthy than that to which thousands of honest working-men are condemned throughout Great Britain." [1]

VI.

CARROLL D. WRIGHT.

The author of the brochure, "The Relation of Economic Conditions to the Causes of Crime", begins by declaring that there are two kinds

[1] Pp. 371, 372.

of criminals; persons who have become such from their psycho-
physical constitution, and others who have become such from circumstances.

"I believe the criminal is an undeveloped man in all his elements,
whether you think of him as a worker or as a moral and intellectual
being.   His faculties are all undeveloped, not only those which enable
him to labor honestly and faithfully for the care and support of himself and his family, but also all his moral and intellectual faculties.
He is not a fallen being: he is an undeveloped individual." [1]

The author then continues by saying that since there is a relation
more or less close between all the important social questions and the
labor question, it is necessary to take that up also in studying the
criminal question.

We know that there are three great systems of labor : the system
resting upon slavery, the feudal system, and the system now in force,
i.e. that of free labor.   In the first two, which intrinsically do not
differ much, crime had a totally different character from what it
has under the last.   Under the feudal system the peasants lived in
the most deplorable condition, without hope of betterment.   In
many countries conditions were so bad that great bands of thieves
and brigands overran them.   During the reign of Henry VIII, which
lasted 38 years, 72,000 criminals were executed.   "Pauperism, therefore, did not attract legislation, and crime, the offspring of pauperism and idleness, was brutally treated ; and these conditions, betoken-
ing an unsound social condition, existed until progress made pauperism, and crime as well, the disgrace of the nation, and it was then that
pauperism began to be recognized as a condition that might be relieved
through legislation." [2]

In the end the feudal system was overthrown and that of free labor,
the present system, became general.   Since then the differences between poverty and wealth have appeared more distinctly.

"Carry industry to a country not given to mechanical production
or to any systematic form of labor, employ three-fourths of its inhabitants, give them a taste of education, of civilization, make them
feel the power of moral forces even in a slight degree, and the misery
of the other fourth can be gauged by the progress of the three-fourths,
and a class of paupers and resultant criminals will be observed.   We
have in our own day a most emphatic illustration of this in the emancipation of slaves in this country (America).   Under the old system the negro slave was physically comfortable, as a rule.   He was

cared for, he was nursed in sickness, fed and clothed, and in old age his physical comforts were continued. He had no responsibility, and, indeed, exercised no skill beyond what was taught him. To eat, to work and to sleep were all that was expected of him, and, unless, he had a cruel master, he lived the life that belongs to the animal. Since his emancipation and his endowment with citizenship he has been obliged to support himself and his family, and to contend with all obstacles belonging to a person in a state of freedom. Under the system of villeinage in the old country it could not be said that there were any general poor, for the master and the lord of the manor took care of the laborers their whole lives; and in our Southern towns, during slavery, this was true, so that in the South there were few, if any, poorhouses, and few, if any, inmates of penal institutions. The South today knows what pauperism is, as England learned when the system of villeinage departed. Southern prisons have become active, and all that belongs to the defective, the dependent, and the delinquent classes has come to be familiar to the South. . . ." "But so far as the modern industrial order superinduces idleness or unemployment, in so far it must be considered as having a direct relation to the causes of crime." [1]

After having tried to show, by the aid of some historical examples, that the conditions in the system which preceded ours were of a nature much more serious than those of our own day, he continues as follows:

"In the study of economic conditions, and whatever bearing they may have upon crime, I can do no better than to repeat, as a general idea, a statement made some years ago by Mr. Ira Steward, of Massachusetts, one of the leading labor reformers in that state in his day. He said: 'Starting in the labor problem from whatever point we may, we reach, as the ultimate cause of our industrial, social, moral, and material difficulties, the terrible fact of poverty. By poverty we mean something more than pauperism. The latter is a condition of entire dependence upon charity, while the former is a condition of want, of lack, of being without, though not necessarily a condition of complete dependence.'

"It is in this view that the proper understanding of the subject given me, in its comprehensiveness and the development of the principles which underlie it, means the consideration of the abolition of pauperism and the eradication of crime; and the definitions given by Mr. Steward carry with them all the elements of those great

[1] Pp. 100, 101.

special inquiries embodied in the very existence of our vast charitable, penal, and reformatory institutions, 'How shall poverty
be abolished, and crime be eradicated?'" [1]

Let the circumstances be favorable or unfavorable, let the governments be liberal or despotic, let the religion and commercial systems
be what they may, crime has always existed. This is why it would
exist even if there were no longer any unemployment, if everyone
had received an education, if the efforts of temperance societies and
social reformers had been realized, and Christianity were universal.
But all these good influences together would certainly reduce crime
to the minimum.

Criminality will decrease but little if the improvements have to
do simply with the physical condition and not at the same time with
moral and intellectual conditions. It is, on the other hand, not to
be disputed, according to the author, that a development of these
last qualities will have a favorable influence upon criminality. For
the man who has received an education will betake himself to crime
less quickly than the ignorant man, while on account of his education he will generally be able to find work to protect him against
poverty and crime. The lack of work is an important cause of crime;
for example, among the convicts of Massachusetts there were 68%
who had been without work, and in the whole United States in 1890,
74% of the murderers had been without work. This lack of employment may have been because of an antipathy to work or of a lack of
opportunity. And it is this last case especially that occurs only too
often in the present social organization.

Great improvements are urgently demanded; living conditions
must become better and more sanitary, and work must be better
paid. The fundamental complaint of the writer against political
economy is that it has not considered moral forces as one of its elements. As soon as it shall have considered them as such it will have
entered upon the way that leads to real improvements.

After having indicated what these improvements ought to be, the
author goes on in these terms: "In a state in which labor had all
its rights there would be, of course, little pauperism and little crime.
On the other hand, the undue subjection of the laboring man must
tend to make paupers and criminals, and entail a financial burden
upon wealth which it would have been easier to prevent than to
endure; and this prevention must come in a large degree through
educated labor.

[1] Pp. 103, 104.

"Do not understand me as desiring to give the impression that I believe crime to be a necessary accompaniment of our industrial system. I have labored in other places and at other times to prove the reverse, and I believe the reverse to be true. Our sober, industrious working men and women are as free from vicious and criminal courses as any other class. What I am contending for, relates entirely to conditions affecting the few. The great volume of crime is found outside the real ranks of industry." [1]

It might still be asked whether civilization favors crime. The answer would have to be at once affirmative and negative. Affirmative in exceptional times, otherwise negative. The more civilization advances, the better the condition of the working people will become, the more equitable will be the division of profits, and the more crime will diminish. The attempts of Robert Owen and many others prove the truth of this.

The author closes his study with these words : " Trade instruction, technical education, manual training — all these are efficient elements in the reduction of crime, because they all help to better and truer economic conditions. I think, from what I have said, the elements of solution are clearly discernible. Justice to labor, equitable distribution of profits under some system which I feel sure will supersede the present, and without resorting to socialism, instruction in trades by which a man can earn his living outside a penal institution, the practical application of the great moral law in all business relations — all these elements, with the more enlightened treatment of the criminal when apprehended, will lead to a reduction in the volume of crime, but not to the millennium; for 'human experience from time immemorial tells us that the earth neither was, nor is, nor ever will be, a heaven, nor yet a hell', (Dr. A. Schäffle) but the endeavor of right-minded men and women, the endeavor of every government, should be to make it less a hell and more a heaven." [2]

— The study of Carroll D. Wright contains some very true observations upon the relation between crime and economic conditions (for example, upon the difference between the slave and the free laborer, whose liberty consists chiefly in this, that he can die of hunger if he cannot find work or is no longer able to work). But in general the work gives the impression of vagueness and hesitation proper to the school of economists and sociologists to which the writer belongs. They condemn certain manifestations of capitalism, but

[1] P. 113.　　　　　　　　　　[2] Pp. 115, 116.

wish to maintain the "causa causarum", the system itself. This is not the place to speak of this more fully and I will confine myself to pointing out some historical errors of the author.

In the first place, a classification of economic systems into only three is incomplete. It is very surprising that this error should have been made by an American. For the North American Indians neither lived under the feudal system nor under that of free labor, and for the most part never knew slavery; the author has forgotten to mention the primitive-communistic mode of production.

In the second place, it is incorrect to call all those who lived under the feudal system "poor."

In the third place it was not to the feudal system that the famous executions under Henry VIII belong, but rather to incipient capitalism which, by dispossessing a great number of peasants, made them poor. (Compare More, "Utopia", and Marx, "Capital.") —

Among the partisans of the bio-sociological doctrine, I think that certain other authors should also be classed, for example : *L. Gordon Rylands*, "Crime, Its Causes and Remedy"; *Dallemagne* (see p. 224 of the "Actes du IIIme Congrès d'Anthrop. Crimin."); *Drill* (see "Des principes fondamentaux de l'école d'anthropologie criminelle" and "Les fondements et le but de la responsabilité pénale"); *Kovalewsky*, "La psychologie criminelle"; *Orchanski*, "Les criminels russes." With regard to Russian criminologists see *Frassati*, "Die neue positive Schule des Strafrechts in Ruszland."

The Dutch criminologists must be reckoned as among the bio-sociologists. *G. A. v. Hamel*, "De tegenwoordige beweging op het gebied van het strafrecht", and "L'anarchisme et le combat contre l'anarchisme au point de vue de l'anthropologie criminelle"; *G. Jelgersma*, "De geborenmisdadiger"; *A. Aletrino*, "Twee opstellen over crimineele anthropologie", and "Handleiding bij de studie der crimineele anthropologie"; *S. R. Steinmetz*, "De ziekten der maatschappij." *Dr. C. Winkler* inclines, as it seems to me, rather toward the opinion of the Italian criminologists. See: "Iets over crimineele anthropologie."

[NOTE TO THE AMERICAN EDITION : Of the recent literature there should be mentioned : in Germany, especially *Aschaffenburg*, "Das Verbrechen und seine Bekämpfung", and *Wulffen*, "Psychologie des Verbrechens." In Holland the authors already named, van Kan, and de Roos are to be classed among the bio-sociologists. For Russia there should be added *von Bechterew*, "Das Verbrechertum im Lichte der objektiven Psychologie." In America it seems to me more reliance is placed upon the Italian theory than in Europe; see, for example, *Henderson*, "Introduction into the Study of the Dependent, Defective, and Delinquent Classes." Upon the recent development of criminology in Holland, England, Sweden, Denmark, Russia, Greece, and Servia see the study already cited of *von Thót*, "Die positive Strafrechtsschule in einigen europischen Ländern."]

CHAPTER VI.

THE SPIRITUALISTS.[1]

I.

H. JOLY.

It is in the second chapter of his "France criminelle", bearing the title of "Richesse et misère", that the author gives his opinion of the connection between criminality and economic conditions.[2]

According to Joly, the opinion expressed by many persons that poverty is the great factor in criminality, appears to be true, at least at first sight; for the problem, is, in fact, very complex and difficult.

In the first place a distinction must be made between voluntary and involuntary poverty. "With vagrants by profession, beggars from choice and speculation, drunkards, those who have made up their minds to live no matter how, gamblers who have systematically used up their capital and that of their family, workmen who have given up work only from rebellion against society, yes, with all these poverty leads to crime."[3] The second kind of poverty springs from disease, accidents, etc., *i.e.* from causes independent of the will of man.

"There are, then, evidently innocent poor people; and there are others so much the more pardonable as the consequences have been aggravated by the fault of others. Is it then in the intermediate region that we must seek for the influences that lead to evil? It may be. This region is not unknown to us. Let us seek here, without taking sides in any way, and examine the facts as well as we can."[4]

In opposition to the continual increase of criminality the author shows that the national wealth has increased, although — and this should not be forgotten — real property, with the exception of small

---

[1] [See the author's explanation of his use of this term in the preface. — TRANSL.]

[2] See also Chaps. II and IV.　　　[3] P. 346.　　　[4] Pp. 348, 349.

holdings, has decreased; the condition of the rural workers, on the contrary, has improved.

In the second place Joly calls attention to the condition of working-men in the cities. According to him the question of whether it has grown worse must be answered in the negative, for the emigration from the country to the city always keeps up. Notwithstanding their higher wages men are no better off there, since they spend upon amusements their additional earnings. If criminality increases among them it is not, then, in involuntary poverty that the cause is to be found.

At the same time with the increase of wages the price of food must be noted. In most of the departments of France these prices have risen in the same proportion as wages. Consequently the working-man has not become better off. He has new needs, but when he has met these he has not enough left for the primary necessities. It is not economic factors, but moral factors, that come into play here.

The proportional increase of wages and the price of food, of which mention has been made above, in the different departments of France, is not met with in the departments of Morbihan, Vendée, Bouches-du-Rhone, and Hérault. In the first two, prices have risen much more than wages, while the contrary appears in the last two. As regards criminality, the first two take their place among those that show the lowest figures, the last two among those that show the highest. Joly draws from this the conclusion that social life is too complicated for us to be able to learn the morality of persons merely from the rise or fall of wages. In any case it is certain, according to him, that the increase of criminality that has been shown is not due to poverty, and that consequently we have not the right to say that poverty in general is one of the primary causes of crime.

However, it must not be lost sight of that in speaking of the increase of wealth and the rise in wages, we are speaking only of average figures, and that there are many individuals whose wages remain below this average. "Now, where do we see the greatest differences, and where are they most felt? Exactly in wealthy epochs and in wealthy surroundings. So it is in the poor departments that crimes against property develop the least. There are two reasons for this, psychological and social. What any man feels the most is not being or having absolutely; it is being or having more or less than those who surround him. What must drive men to crime chiefly, then, is the comparison of wealth with poverty." [1]

[1] P. 355.

Joly thinks he can produce further data upon the connection between crime and poverty by checking up the kind of articles that are
most frequently stolen. Out of 1000 cases of theft (assizes, 1830–
1860) there were 395 cases of theft of money, next came thefts of
personal property, then clothing, etc., then successively, different
kinds of merchandise, jewelry and table-ware, food, grain, etc., and
living domestic animals. This information does not teach us much
about the relationship in question. For the articles stolen can be
sold, which prevents our discovering the motives of the crime.

The analysis of the value of the objects stolen also gives us little
information. During a period of 25 years the cases of theft of 10 to 50
francs were the most numerous (about 30%), next those of 100 to 1000
francs, then those of less than 10 francs. Ten years later the most
numerous were those of 100 to 1000 frances (33%).

However, on the strength of the statements of an old police officer,
Joly thinks he can draw the conclusion that poverty enters only to a
small extent into the etiology of crime. Nevertheless the established
fact that a rise in the price of grain is associated with an increase of
criminality, contradicts this. But according to Joly the contradiction
is only apparent. "Famines are exceptional; theft is constant and
while famines are always decreasing, theft is always increasing.
Suppose that in ordinary years people did not steal or stole very
little; the difficult moments would find them more patient, more
resolute to have recourse to legal and permissible means; we should
not see them so prompt to extricate themselves from their difficulties
by simply taking the property of others. But what resistance can
we count on from those who have long had the habit of stealing from
fancy, cupidity, or a desire to gormandize? What resistance can be
hoped for, especially when the habit has begun in youth? Now, we
have seen that a third of the thefts are committed by minor children."[1]

The weakness of the influence of economic conditions upon criminality is, according to Joly, further proved by the fact that times of prosperity are not accompanied by a decrease in the number but by a
change in the kind of crime committed (as Prins and Garafalo have
shown). Cheap wine makes most crimes against persons increase.
But the low price of grain has the same effect, since the working-man,
when his condition has improved even a little, spends his additional
earnings in all kinds of amusements, which, in their turn, may be the
source of crime. This is proved, for example, by the fact that in
Marseilles suicides are most numerous on Sunday and Monday, and

[1] Pp. 358, 359.

fewest on Friday and Saturday, a fact explained by the pay-days of the working people.   This is also applicable to crimes against persons.

To prove his thesis the author reminds us of the fact that domestics, although not subject to privations, furnish a large percentage of the thefts; that the percentage of thefts committed by unmarried persons continually increases; and finally, that the investigation (of 107 cases tried in 10 years before the assizes at Rheims), made by a magistrate (Ch. Vuébat), has proved that economic factors have little importance for criminality, and moral factors much.   "To sum up, it is not the increase of poverty that is the cause of the increase of crime; it is not property in general that leads to crime against property.   This is not saying that poverty, and innocent poverty, does not exist, nor that it is not a bad counselor, nor that it is not the duty of the upper classes and of the government to concern themselves with the lot of the poor.   It does mean that a man is less led into evil-doing by the faults of others or by the fault of destiny than by his personal faults." [1]

— If one considers the study of the question by Joly from a critical point of view, the thing that most strikes the attention is this; that he puts economic causes *by the side of* the moral causes of criminality. As I have already more than once remarked, this is not sound.   Every crime finds its origin in moral causes, or better, in the lack of moral ideas dominant at a certain period.   But one of the principal questions to be answered is this; how far do these moral ideas find their origin in definite economic conditions?   Joly, being a spiritualist, has not succeeded in formulating this problem well, still less in solving it.

His entire treatment of the relation between criminality and economic conditions is characterized by a striking narrowness.   He speaks of poverty and wealth as if they were the most natural things in the world, and had no need to be explained.   Then he makes a distinction between voluntary and involuntary poverty, and excludes the former from the discussion as having nothing to do with the problem in question.   This manner of reasoning has rather the air of a penitential sermon than of a scientific investigation.   "Voluntary poverty" [2]

---

[1] P. 365.
[2] ["Misère." The word *may* mean misery, of course, as the author has interpreted it in proving a contradiction of terms, but Joly seems to use it, as it is generally used, to describe an external condition rather than a mental state.   In any case, all that Joly seems to mean is that there are those who deliberately prefer effortless indigence to a competence acquired by toil, being *willing* to put up with the indigence for the sake of the *wished for* escape from effort. — TRANSL.]

is a contradiction in terms. For a man tries as far as possible to spare himself suffering and to gain happiness. There can never be any such thing then as voluntary poverty.

Though his terms are unhappily chosen, Joly only wishes to point out that poverty may originate in circumstances or in the person himself. But in treating this problem he should not have been silent on a very important, and very difficult point, namely how far these individual causes of poverty are based upon the present economic system.

If the question treated by Joly is incomplete, what he says neither has any great value, nor does it prove at all his statement that the influence of economic conditions is small. He gives but a few pages to the very difficult question of whether the standard of living of the working class has been raised. He brings out the universally observed fact that the wants of all classes have increased, but he seems not to have noted that this is intimately bound up with the present mode of production. He cites the testimony of an old police officer, and the investigations of a magistrate (investigations, it may be said in passing, that reached the colossal number of 107 cases) in order to prove that most crimes are not committed as a consequence of immediate privations — as if this were enough to solve the question of how far economic conditions enter into the causes of crime. —[1]

II.

L. PROAL.[2]

In his ninth chapter, entitled "Le crime et la misère," this author gives some pages to our subject. It is incontestable, according to him, that poverty exerts an influence upon criminality. The number of crimes increases in the years of poor crops, or when there is a lack of work owing to industrial or agricultural crises. Thus, criminality reached high figures in 1840, 1847, and 1854, when the price of grain was high.

In consequence of this and of his personal experience (the author is a magistrate) he thinks the opinion of Garofalo is incorrect, that poverty only gives crime its form and is not a cause of it. For indigence not only puts morality in danger by depriving some persons of the bare necessities, but it also causes the children of the poor in the great cities to be brought up in a pitiable manner.

---

[1] [NOTE TO THE AMERICAN EDITION: Cf. "La Belgique criminelle", by the same author.] [2] "Le crime et la peine."

Although the author is of this opinion, however, he does not subscribe to the view that "the poor man is dedicated to crime." On the contrary, a great proportion of the poor are as honest as possible, and have honorable toil as their only means of support. Judicial statistics show that the rich are as guilty of crime as the poor.

"We see, then, that even if all the citizens had means and education, there would always be criminals; the number of them would be a little less, but not much. There would always be traders practising deception with regard to the quantity and quality of their goods, merchants adulterating food, employes abusing the confidence of their employers, notaries embezzling the funds entrusted to them; there would always be wives poisoning their husbands, and husbands killing their wives, and teachers of lay and denominational schools committing sexual crimes." [1]

Most crimes are not committed to escape from want, but rather to procure luxury and pleasure. Hence the rich as well as the poor commit them. "To sum up, I do not believe that the rich are less tempted to take the property of others than the poor. The more wealth one has the more he wants; further, the more wealth increases, the more factitious wants increase, and if one's wealth becomes insufficient to satisfy these wants, the thought of increasing it by any means is not slow in coming. Admitting that some day all men may be rich and educated, though that seems to me to be an impossible dream, cupidity will always make thieves, rogues, and forgers; hatred and revenge will always inspire homicide, murder, and arson; debauchery will always lead to sexual crimes. Material and intellectual progress will never suppress the passions and will not free men from the struggle that must be maintained against them. It will always be necessary to repress anger and sensuality, to put a bridle upon cupidity, and, in a word, to set the soul free from its passions. The increase of well-being and education will never make the police and the penal code unnecessary." [2]

— It will be superfluous to give a criticism of this discussion. We have already met several authors who took this point of view. Proal is like the others who do not even know how to put the question of the influence of economic conditions clearly, who do not comprehend that poverty and riches are both the inevitable consequences of the same system. —

---

[1] Pp. 204, 205.   [2] P. 207.

III.

M. DE BAETS.[1]

"It is an incontestable fact that the influence of poverty upon criminality is immense." It is thus that the author expresses himself in the introduction to his work. I shall set forth his manner of defending this thesis in the following lines.

The most disastrous consequence of poverty is the temptation to procure illicitly what is needed for one's well-being. We can see this in the crimes of crowds as well as in individual crimes. At the 3d Congress of Criminal Anthropology, Professor H. Denis gave certain facts with regard to the correlation between crime and the economic status.[2] During the years from 1845 to 1849 the curve of criminality coincides exactly with that of the price of wheat. But at the close of 1850 the two curves diverge, when the curve of wheat is replaced by that of staple foods in general. If we follow the trend of wages attentively we shall note that they also are higher in the last years. The increase of criminality is no longer to be explained, therefore, by this rise. To what, then, is it due?

In the author's opinion we must note, first, that forced unemployment is increasing; second, that poverty and wealth have force only by comparison.

The well-being of the working man has increased, but that of men in general much more so. This explains only a part of the phenomena given above. The rest of his explanation is as follows: "There are, in fact, other elements, which may neutralize the influence of the environment. To all the solicitations of vice and crime man can offer resistance, finding his refuge and support in moral force.

"Now, go to the poor and unhappy, and ask them what prevents them from quickly slipping downhill into crime, and you will find in their mouths the expression, naïve, but strong, of the idea of duty; and this idea of duty you will find precisely and clearly only in that of submission to an absolute, incontestable, unconditioned authority, that of God. A man whom no one would suspect of any extraordinary good-will toward religion, M. Jules Simon, said a few months ago, 'The peoples must be brought to God if we want justice and order to reign.'

"Must not even those who do not themselves believe, recognize in

[1] "Les influences de la misère sur la criminalité." See also "L'école d'anthropologie criminel", by the same author.
[2] See the following chapter.

this idea of duty, of law imposed by a God, the creator, an 'idée-force,' a source in itself of energy and activity against evil and for good?

"It is in the diminution of this energy, in the efforts that have been made to tear out of the hearts of the poor this root, whose flower is hope, and whose fruit is virtue, that I am inclined to see one of the causes of the frightful increase of crime, which all concede, some with surprise and all with dismay." [1]

In the second part of his discussion the author brings up the degenerating influence of poverty. Although a man has a free will at his disposal, it is necessary that he should also have an organism capable of putting the will into action. Hence it is that degeneracy makes its effect felt upon man.

"Now, misery is just the totality of the most imperious desires remaining unsatisfied; it is the love of life, the love of well-being left without gratification; it is the suffering of the wife one would like to see happy, the hunger of the children to whom one would like to give bread. And if crime can give this bread that one cannot find, if crime can satisfy all these appetites, all these desires, it will present itself with the most powerful attractions, with the charm of fascination. Will the unfortunate man have the supreme energy to prefer duty to enjoyment?" [2]

Poverty is a bad preparatory school for this contest; a weakened organism will succumb more easily to temptation. And generally this is accompanied by a lack of education and of the development of the higher faculties.

In following the course of life of a proletarian we see that the child of the proletariat carries, often from his birth, the signs of degeneracy, since his mother was forced to work hard during her pregnancy. From his childhood he is ill nourished, and grows up in an unhealthful environment. There can hardly be any question of education, for his father and mother work in the shop, which prevents any family life. The child is not attached to the dwelling of his parents and wanders in the street, where he picks up bad habits. Arrived at adolescence, he enters the factory to pass the greater part of his time in monotonous occupations. And once full grown, life for him consists only in routine labor, monotonous and without end. "However, this man has a soul, he has a mind! But it slumbers in a perpetual inertia. Nothing in his life has awakened what is grand, noble, and divine in this reasonable being. How can we hope to have the moral energy and the sublime ambition for good survive in him?" [3]

[1] Pp. 18–20.   [2] Pp. 22, 23.   [3] Pp. 31, 32.

However unhappy this manner of life may be, there is still lacking the greatest misfortune that can befall the proletarian; forced inaction. This is one of the chief causes that can drive him to commit crime! And then there is another scourge of the working class, alcoholism. "Source of poverty without any doubt, but fruit of poverty incontestably." Finally, of all the proletarians the most unhappy are the women. Low wages and the monotony of tiresome work too often make prostitutes of them.

To all these criminogenous causes the Christian must oppose the moral sentiments which are drawn from his religion. His motto must be, "rather death than dishonor." But for that he must have heroic courage, which most people lack. Perhaps before God these sinners will find grace.

But all this cannot be a reason for society to allow to exist these scandalous conditions, which, in a few words, are as follows: "Insufficiency of the means of subsistence; work too long continued, as measured by the exhaustion resulting from it; work demanded of mothers of families; excessive and unsuitable labor expected of children; improper conditions in certain industries." [1]

This must be changed, and it is possible to do so. Not, however, with the aid of the state, for then industry would lose the elasticity so necessary to it. But the change must be brought about by association of the proletarians. "In the forced individualism of the laborers is to be found the cause of their ruin; the salvation must be found in association." The author closes by referring to the encyclical, "Rerum novarum", in which it is said that Christian workmen must band together, and by encouraging the rich to help their less privileged brothers. [2]

IV.

CRITICISM.

The authors of whom I have just been speaking, together with others, like von Oettingen and Stursberg, of whom I have spoken in Chap. II, have this idea in common, that the continually growing irreligion is a cause of the increase in criminality; in other words, that

---

[1] P. 43.
[2] [NOTE TO THE AMERICAN EDITION: *Cf.* also the following authors: Dr. *G. von Rohden*, "Von den sozialen Motiven des Verbrechens" and "Verbrechensbekämpfung und Verbrechensvorbeugung" ("Zeitschr. f. Socialwissenschaft", VII and IX), and *F. A. K. Krauss*, "Der Kampf gegen die Verbrechensursachen."]

irreligion is a powerful factor of crime and that the irreligious are predisposed to crime.

What proofs have been given by these authors in support of their thesis, their very serious accusation against those who are no longer religious? Most of them have not even tried to prove it. It is a dogma, with which, therefore, we have nothing to do. An increase of irreligion had been shown, also an increase in criminality, *therefore* there is a causal connection. Protest must be made against any such methods of reasoning. If there is a parallelism upon the chart between two curves that do not undulate, we must be very careful about drawing the conclusion that there is a connection, much more a causal one. That irreligion has increased is certain; is the same thing true of criminality? Certainly not. The trend of criminality *as a whole* is very rarely uniform, there is almost always a divergence; for example, economic criminality and violent criminality very rarely keep pace with each other. If we wish to give a general idea of the trend of criminality, we can only say that it is decreasing rather than increasing. The spiritualist authors often cite Germany in support of their thesis. This is no longer possible, for, after an increase in the total figures up to the end of the nineteenth century, there is now a fluctuating decrease.

In the Netherlands we can estimate the increase of irreligion; [1] according to the censuses of 1879 and 1909, the percentage of those who are not members of any church has increased enormously, from 0.31 to 4.97, an increase of 1500% in 30 years! What an increase of crime must we look for! The reality is very different. The curve of crime has fallen without any doubt.[2] The facts and the thesis do not agree.

Another way of examining the question is to be found in "criminal geography." Since irreligion shows enormous differences in the different parts of a country, we ought to find considerable criminality in the provinces where the lack of religion is most in evidence. For the Netherlands, in my study already referred to, I have given detailed tables with the result that there is no connection between the phenomena in question. In general we have even the right to say that the provinces with the lowest figures for irreligion show a high criminality, and vice versa!

---

[1] [Throughout this section the author uses "religion" as meaning a professed connection with a cult and "irreligion" as the repudiation of any such connection. This is not the use we commonly make of these terms in English, but I know of no others that more accurately express Dr. Bonger's meaning. — TRANSL.]

[2] See *Bonger*, "Geloof en misdaad" (Religion and crime), p. 6.

The best means of settling the question is by a direct statistical study. I have made calculations, based upon the criminal statistics, of more than 126,000 individuals sentenced during the period from 1901 to 1909, in the Netherlands. Here are the results:

Netherlands, 1901–1909.

OFFENSES.	NUMBER SENTENCED TO 100,000 OF THE POPULATION OVER 10 YEARS OLD.				
	Prot-estant.	Catholic.	Jew.	Not Members of Any Religion.	Total Popula-tion.
All offenses	308.6	**416.5**	212.7	84.2	337.3
Theft	40.0	**54.8**	25.5	9.6	43.9
Aggravated theft	19.9	**24.0**	12.7	5.2	20.7
Receiving stolen goods	2.6	3.5	**9.2**	0.7	3.0
Embezzlement	8.6	9.3	**13.1**	1.9	8.7
Fraud	2.4	2.5	**3.9**	0.4	2.4
Offenses against public decency	1.9	**3.4**	2.0	0.5	2.4
Minor sexual offenses	1.2	1.0	0.3	0.2	1.0
Rape	1.5	**2.2**	1.5	0.7	1.8
Sexual crimes with persons under 16	**0.3**	**0.3**	0.1	0.0	0.3
All sexual crimes	5.1	**7.1**	4.1	1.6	5.7
Rebellion	25.9	**37.0**	13.2	12.2	29.0
Assaults	74.4	**98.2**	43.2	20.1	80.1
Serious assaults	8.5	**11.0**	3.9	1.9	9.1
Homicide and murder	0.4	**0.6**	0.5	0.1	0.5

The results are the following, then: the first place is almost always occupied by the Catholics, the second by the Protestants, and then come the Jews (except in cases of receiving stolen goods, embezzlement, and fraud), and the minimum of criminality (in all crimes without exception) is shown by the irreligious!

Here we have not the task of explaining this fact, we only bring it out; and we have the right to declare that the thesis: "irreligion leads to crime", is not correct.

CHAPTER VII.

THE THIRD SCHOOL[1] AND THE SOCIALISTS.

I.

F. TURATI.

IN the first chapter of his "Il delitto e la questione sociale", the author shows that among the numerous misfortunes from which the proletariat suffers, this must be reckoned, that it is almost exclusively from its ranks that criminals are recruited. "The criminal tribute is the almost exclusive privilege of one social class. And as the bourgeoisie has so far thought out no better plan than to oppose the degradation of crime with another degradation called punishment, it has come about that to the monopoly of the criminal tribute is added, for the poor, the monopoly of the penal tribute." [2]

---

[1] See also, as members of the "Terza Scuola": *Vaccaro*, "Genesi e funzione delle leggi penali"; *Carnevale*, "Una terza scuola di diritto penale"; *Alimena*, "Naturalismo critico e diritto penale." In the "Mitteilungen der internationalen kriminalistischen Vereinigung", Vol. IV, is found an article by Dr. *E. Rosenfeld*, entitled "Die dritte Schule", in which the doctrine of this school is fully treated.

In a discourse more distinguished by hatred of Marxism than by a knowledge of that doctrine, Professor Benedikt said at the Congress of Criminal Anthropology held in Brussels: "The partisans of the 'Terza Scuola' are in reality only Marxists." Among those considered as belonging to the Third School, there is only one Marxist as far as I know. Professor Benedikt may have been led into his error by the fact that Dr. Colajanni, one of the principal partisans of the Third School, and also one of the few criminologists of this school who has written upon the affinity between criminality and economic conditions, is in agreement with the Marxists in this, that he finds the causes of crime, in the last analysis, in economic conditions. This is why I speak of Dr. Colajanni, as representing the Third School, and of the socialists in the same chapter. Although Colajanni calls himself a republican in political matters, he is nevertheless a partisan of an eclectic socialism. (See "Il Socialismo.") It is for this reason also that it is well to name him in this chapter. Other partisans of the Third School are also, as it appears, more or less of this opinion (see p. 18 of "Die dritte Schule", where Dr. Rosenfeld treats of Professor Carnevale). However, it is evident from the manner in which Dr. Colajanni treats the question, that he is not a Marxist.

[2] P. 42.

After having spoken, in the following chapter, of "free will", Dr. Turati gives his attention to an opinion of Dr. Lelorrain, who says that we must modify man if we wish to make criminality disappear or decrease.   Dr. Turati objects that it is exceedingly difficult to change man, and that there is an easier and more effective way, namely to change society.   In a society where everything is bad, where the exploitation of one by the other is the rule, where the enjoyment of some goes on at the detriment of others, and this under the protection of the law — in such a society there is a perpetual incitement to crime.   It is the ideal of socialism to create a society in which crime shall be neither necessary nor advantageous.   However short its duration, the colony of New Lanark founded by Owen, is one of the best proofs of the correctness of this idea.   In a society formed in accordance with this socialistic ideal, crime would appear only exceptionally, by atavism, for example, and would cease to be a general and always threatening danger.

"The social penal question is a question above all of social transformation."   Many objections have been made to this statement. The school of Lombroso and Ferri sets up in opposition its theory of the triplex character of the factors of crime; cosmic, individual, and social.   When society is so modified that the interests of the individual are identical with those of the community, it would be only one part of crime that would disappear; one could not, for example, prevent an extraordinary heat from causing crimes against morals.

According to Dr. Turati it is not impossible to refute this objection, though it may be difficult to do so.   In the first place Ferri recognizes the social causes as more important than the other two put together.   He estimates that the number of persons driven to crime by social reasons (passion and occasion) is more than 60 %; the others (insane or half-insane criminals, born-incorrigibles, and habituals) form a minority, then.   But among these there are many criminals by habit, who were not born as such, but have become such from force of circumstances.   Dr. Turati estimates that from 70 % to 75 % of criminals have come to commit their crimes from social causes. When we take account further of the fact that about 18 % of the prisoners are insane, the number of real criminals who have become such from other than social causes is reduced to 10 % at the most.

According to Dr. Turati the physical and anthropological factors exert an influence upon the form, but not upon the nature, of the crime.   Further, these three causes are present in every crime, but

almost no crime would be committed without the social cause. It is
this last that is always the predominant factor. When it is removed,
then, the other two are reduced to zero. The facts have proved this.
Owen's colony was not made up of peculiar material, and the physical
surroundings were neither better nor "more honest" than any other.
Nevertheless, crime was unknown there. But the author furnishes still
further proofs in support of his thesis that physical and anthropological causes amount to nothing in comparison with social causes, which
in turn are dependent upon economic conditions. With the exception of crimes committed by the propertied class, which are in general
the result of excessive cupidity, or a commercial uneasiness, and which
will "ipso facto" disappear without any doubt when once society is
otherwise organized, the greatest contingent of criminals is furnished
by the class of non-possessors. Now all the physical influences, such
as climate, act upon the two classes in the same way, nor are there
anthropological differences between the two classes, yet the difference
between them as regards criminal tendencies is great. It is the social
factors, then, that explain the difference.

However, another observation must be made here. Ferri cites in a
mass, as social factors, the increase of population, emigration, public
opinion, customs, etc. But when we examine and classify these
factors minutely, it becomes clear that in reality they are based
upon economic conditions alone.

However, this observation is not applicable to "criminals by passion", since in their case the influence of the environment appears to
be but weak. Lombroso estimates that they form 5 % of all criminals,
and Ferri is of the opinion that it is only 5 % of those who commit
crimes against persons who are criminals by passion.

One of the anthropological causes of crime is "man", and one of the
cosmic causes is "the universe." But neither has anything to do
with crime as such. Otherwise the air we breathe and the food that
we eat would be causes of crime. On the contrary, it is the organization of society that is the cause of crime, and physical and anthropological influences are only conditions. (Speaking scientifically we do
not separate causes and conditions, but this is the common usage.)
If the causes ceased to exist the conditions would have no further
importance.

Next, Dr. Turati treats of certain kinds of crime. First, *crimes
against property*. As almost every criminologist will admit, these
crimes are intimately connected with the unequal division of property. "But," an opponent will object, "it is not possible, by means

of social institutions, to change cosmic influences, such as a low temperature, or the failure of the crops, both of which cause an increase of the crimes against property." Those who are of this opinion forget, however, that a man does not become criminal because he is cold, but he who is cold becomes criminal only if society neglects to provide for the needs born of the cold.

The influence of society is not seen so distinctly when *crimes against persons* are in question. Nevertheless it is very great; the economic conditions of our day work in two ways, through poverty on the one side, and injustice on the other. Poverty injures not only the physique but also the morals of a man, since it leaves him in ignorance and grossness, and does not develop his moral sentiments. And then it is harder to bear the evils caused by society than those caused by nature. In the second place, economic inequality stifles the sense of justice in man, since it accustoms him to this inequality. "The law is equal for all", is only a phrase, for all are not socially equal.

One of the most wide-spread objections to the proposition that crimes spring from social conditions is that if an improvement in these conditions leads to a decrease of the crimes against property, the crimes against persons increase. This is urged by Ferri, among others, as one of the most effective arguments against Turati and his partisans. But against this may be urged another fact brought out by Ferri, namely that while crime is increasing, it is becoming less intense and less brutal. We see clearly, then, that it is possible to have a powerful counter-determinant to the tendency to commit crimes against persons, *i.e.* education.

As to *sexual crimes*, they increase when the food supply increases. This is the cause: sexual needs have a direct relation to nutrition. An increase of the sexual needs, however, has nothing to do with criminality. It is only the social organization that changes these needs that have become more intense, into crimes, by subordinating the satisfaction of them to economic considerations. There are, besides, other social causes, like bad housing etc., that lead the proletariat to commit the crimes in question.

The author then points out the enormous influence of the abuse of alcohol upon criminality, the causes of this abuse being also found in the social organization.

Another argument of Ferri's must be refuted, *i.e.* that Turati and his followers attach too much weight to education. *Notwithstanding* the equality in the education of two brothers, says Ferri, one becomes a scamp and the other a hero. To which the author replies that we can say with just as good right, *thanks to* education the brother of a scamp becomes a hero.

But in speaking of education Ferri has in mind that of the bourgeoisie, which is in opposition to morality, and can consequently have but little influence. From the day when the state of society shall have become sound, and the interests of all taken to heart, morality can be in harmony with reality.

"The true, all-inclusive penal substitute is the equal diffusion, so far as is socially possible, of well-being and education, of the joys of love and thought."

II.

B. BATTAGLIA.

Before speaking of the influence of economic factors upon criminality, I feel obliged to point out, by the following quotation, what the author of "La dinamica del delitto" understands by crime: "Primarily it must be noted that crime is not, in itself, a phenomenon that assumes the criminal character from its own nature; but the criminal character is affirmed or denied according to certain purely accessory circumstances that accompany the act; and in all cases the crime is such with reference to social relations." [1]

"From the human point of view a crime represents the satisfaction of a need of the criminal, like the satisfaction of any other need, and comes under the law of the struggle for existence. In fact, a need not satisfied constitutes a pain, and pain, whatever its nature be, first excites and then depresses and exhausts the functional power of the organism. The organism, under the influence of pain, loses a quantity of phosphates proportional to the intensity of the pain; the physiological equilibrium is broken, and some functions important for the internal economy are neutralized. The organism, because of the law of conservation, is called upon to relieve the pain. Often it can do this without injury to others; at other times it comes into collision with social interests, and in such a case falls into crime." [2]

After having spoken of the anatomical and physiological characteristics that have been observed in criminals, Dr. Battaglia comes to the investigation into the causes that produce crime. In examining the factors of crime we see, according to the author, that they consist of two great groups, first, *criminogenous factors*, and second, *occasional factors*. These last are important only when they are

[1] P. 201.   [2] P. 202.

present with the first. Among the occasional factors are to be classed in the first place, age, meteorological occurrences, etc., in short, the influences to which the whole population are subjected. In the second place, sex, economic conditions, education, etc. *i.e.* influences which have a less universal sphere. However, none of the occasional factors can, by itself, cause a crime to arise. Otherwise a whole population would be criminal in the same way, since some factors, climate for instance, exercise their influence upon the whole population. In order to lead to crime these factors must exert their influence upon intellectual faculties especially disposed toward crime.

The factors really criminogenous, are those which create certain physico-psychical conditions, from the complexus of which results the personal capacity for crime, such as the diseases and defects of development and nutrition, cranial and intracranial; improper education; psychical heredity; and atavistic reversions.

"When these factors have prepared the mental condition, by making it different from that of all others, any opportunity whatever is a sufficient psychical factor, and a crime is committed. Therefore the criminogenous factors are those that have the real social importance, because they prepare inevitably for delinquency.

"It is true, on the other hand, that any of the occasional factors, acting in a certain way, and with a certain intensity and persistency, can produce criminogenous factors, like education or alimentation." [1]

The author then treats some of the so-called "occasional factors", such as age, sex, and religion. I shall speak only of what Dr. Battaglia says upon the influence of alcoholism and poverty upon criminality, since this is pertinent to my work.

Alcoholism is a cause of crime in two ways, first, direct, *i.e.* when crimes are committed under the actual influence of intoxication; second, indirect, since chronic alcoholism causes demoralization and degeneracy. As evidence in support of this the author cites the opinions of Baer, Virgilio, and others.

As to poverty, Dr. Battaglia remarks that the opinion of Professor Lombroso on this subject cannot be correct. The latter believes that the importance of the fact that crimes against property decrease when prices fall, is weakened by the circumstance that, according to Guerry, the theft of food holds only the hundredth place in the table of articles stolen. According to Dr. Battaglia this has no weight in a critical examination of the influence of poverty. For anyone who is driven to crime by hunger tries by preference to seize articles that

[1] Pp. 235–238.

are of great value and little volume, since he can at once exchange them for other articles that are directly consumable. Further it must not be forgotten that alcoholism and bad education are intimately connected with poverty, and lead in their turn to crime. Not only does acute hunger incite to theft indirectly, it may lead to it directly, for it may (according to Professor Follet) bring on a delirium. Chronic hunger and malnutrition may cause pellagra, rachitis, tuberculosis, scrofula, etc., or predispose to these diseases, which may cause crime in their turn.

In the second part of "La dinamica del delitto" the author makes an examination of what he has called the "criminogenous factors." Crime is a phenomenon that develops itself in society in accordance with certain constant laws. Consequently the criminogenous factors must be found in society. To discover them, then, it is necessary to examine the different social institutions.

The family. In nature and in primitive society there rules a natural selection by which the weak and sickly are prevented from reproducing themselves, or from reproducing themselves as freely as those who are stronger. But at present this selection is no longer felt; even the most wretched, the most diseased can procreate, since it happens constantly that marriages take place with a secondary object. Hence transmission of degeneracy may go on from one generation to another, and consequently, the indirect propagation of crime.

The social position of woman. The inferior position in which woman finds herself in general (the cause of this is in social conditions, since the position of woman varies among different people) occasions crimes in different ways. First, since woman takes no part in the public life, she is circumscribed in intellect, and consequently, vain, egoistic, and ignorant. It follows that her influence upon her children is often very bad. Then, because of her inferior position she easily becomes the victim of unscrupulous men, who seduce her, so that she is often driven to prostitution. In consequence of her ignorance she often marries a man who has asked for her in marriage with an interested motive. Further, her manner of living (lack of healthful work, etc.) may bring on neuroses that are transmissible to her children.

Human reproduction. As an animal, man must satisfy two predominant necessities, that of feeding himself, and that of procreating. Though this last is not as strong as the other, it must nevertheless be satisfied, and without this the human organism would experience very painful consequences. Celibacy is very harmful to morality; it leads to prostitution (with its consequences, like syphilis), to misconduct, and hence to the abuse of alcohol, etc. — in short, it favors the birth of anti-social sentiments.

The present laws governing the relations between man and woman are also harmful to morality. The author here refers to the indissolubility of marriage. When the motive for a marriage has ceased to exist, namely when mutual love no longer exists, the marriage ought to be dissolved. The harmful consequences of this indissolubility are numerous. Adultery and many homicides flow from it; the education of children suffers from it enormously; and finally if the mother expects a child, the vexation consequent upon discord may exercise an unfavorable influence upon the newly born.

Education. The development of the intellect and especially of the feelings is of the highest importance to morality. For example, where a disagreement will be settled in an amicable manner among persons who are well brought up, the same disagreement among persons ill-trained will often lead to brawls. Education is a very complex and difficult task, requiring much tact and knowledge. It is not astonishing that as practised it leaves much to be desired. And the consequences of this absence of a good education are exceedingly favorable to the development of criminality. However, it must not be forgotten that some persons, in consequence of qualities transmitted by heredity, become immoral despite the best imaginable education. The answer to the question "should education be left to the parents, *i.e.* to private persons, who can consequently corrupt their pupils entirely, and not be under public control?" must, according to Dr. Battaglia, be absolutely negative. In order that education may be effective in the family it must be supplemented by the moral influence of the environment, which also plays an important part in the education of the child. The great congestion of persons in the cities, for example, should disappear, because of its bad influence.

Instruction. The double end of instruction is in the first place to strengthen the intellect by exercising it, from which it will result that it will have a greater power over the feelings; and in the second place to furnish a certain amount of positive knowledge, by which the individual is put into a position to adapt himself to his environment and to foresee the consequences of his acts. From this it follows that instruction is of great importance in dealing with criminality. Those who deny this mean by the "instructed man" one who has learned to read and write; but it is evident that such instruction is not enough to exercise an influence of any real importance. It is undeniable that persons well reared may also become criminals, but in every case their crimes have a less ferocious character than those of persons without education.

Religion and State. Religion is opposed to progress, to the development of the faculties, and to the general dissemination of knowledge that improves men and increases solidarity; and it incites to intolerance. Further, the confessional instruction is harmful to the intellectual faculties of children. The state puts obstacles in the way of the free movements of individuals; maintains civil marriage; prevents free discussion, one of the primary requirements for progress; it sets up compulsory education, but does not prevent the population's being brought up in error; by drafting great armies, it withdraws the best forces from agriculture and manufacturing, so that the vigorous individuals marry late, and prostitution is thereby encouraged; it tolerates stock exchanges and lotteries; it favors crowding into great cities, something that is very favorable, directly and indirectly, to crime (bad housing conditions, alcoholism, etc.).

In the chapter that follows, Professor Battaglia reduces the factors that he has just named "criminogenous", to economic elements. "All the inconveniences, the anomalies, the errors, the disorders, found in the family, in the state, in social and religious relationships, etc., are provoked by the economic situation in which society finds itself. . . ."[1]

Civil Status. In the communistic villages of Russia it is advantageous for the father of a family to have many children, for the work in the common fields is then performed more easily. Hence the marriages of persons less than 20 years old are numerous. In the rest of Europe the situation is entirely different. By marrying, a man makes himself worse off, and at the birth of each child his cares increase. Hence marriages are put off (especially among professional men) when the man cannot provide for the needs of his family. For analogous reasons some deny their sexual desires and contract a marriage to better their position. In both cases economic conditions exercise an unfavorable influence. When his income is not sufficient to support himself and his family properly, the workman is obliged to labor longer than his strength permits; he and his family are not well enough fed, their dwelling is bad; consequently their physical condition deteriorates. The effects are not only diseases, like scrofula, pellagra, phthisis, anemia, etc., but also a great predisposition to contract them. Poverty undermines the organism and exhausts its strength.

[1] P. 404.

In consequence of present economic conditions it is possible to amass enormous wealth; but wants are still further increased relatively, which brings it about that frauds, embezzlements, etc., are often committed by persons of means, especially since the moral sentiments are lost when one thinks only of gaining money. But wealth is inconstant; he who has plenty today may be very poor tomorrow. This is what causes the disquiet and agitation that characterizes the bourgeoisie, and the neuroses that often follow. Finally the author dwells upon the work of women and children, so harmful to morality and to health.

Alcoholism. The inevitable consequence of poverty is the abuse of alcoholic drinks. One who works too much and eats too little, who is badly housed and ill-clad, and has no intellectual occupation, finds in alcohol a means of forgetting his poverty. The life led by a great part of the bourgeoisie leads also to alcoholism. The harmful consequences of alcoholism are numerous, especially as regards criminality, because, first, it leads directly to violent crimes, and, secondly, it indirectly favors degeneracy.

Fatherhood. It is only for economic reasons that legal marriage, its indissolubility, and all that belongs to it, are maintained. If each of the parents kept his or her economic independence, there would be no reason to take up the matter of legal regulation, and thus the question of whether the father of the child is or is not the legal husband of the mother would no longer concern the State.

Prostitution. Most prostitutes come from the lower strata of society. Like the criminals they present signs of degeneracy, and from the sole fact of degeneracy have taken on larger proportions in the proletariat than in the other classes, though the chance that these women will recruit themselves in this class is already greater. The other causes of prostitution are of an economic nature, such as exploitation by parents, bad housing, etc. In consequence of prostitution syphilis spreads and in its turn favors degeneracy. Further, from the weakening of their moral sentiments prostitutes are more easily led to commit crimes.

Ignorance. The cause of the great ignorance of the working-people — an important factor in criminality — is of an economic nature. The workers have to exhaust their strength, and have neither the leisure nor the means, for mental development.

Laxity of morals. In indigent families all the members sleep in one room, often even in one bed. Hence it comes that sexual morality is lacking. The parents, often absent on account of their work, leave their children to their fate.   These latter do not know how to look after themselves, and easily learn bad habits from other children. The education of the children of the bourgeoisie is no more favorable. Often they learn only that they must make money, or acquire a social position, or make a "good" marriage, a thing which leads them to all sorts of deceits and intrigues to arrive at their end.

Plutocracy.   The great armaments and wars of European powers are the consequence of the present system of competition, which obliges the constant search for new outlets for commerce.

Plutocracy of the Church.   It is only upon its economic resources that the great power of the Church rests.

Corollary.   Poverty alone causes many moral situations from which crime must logically result.   The majority of criminals are in fact recruited among the less privileged classes.

But the bourgeoisie is not happy simply because the proletariat is unhappy.   The cause of the unhappiness of both is in the present economic conditions, by which the great majority of the population vegetate in the blackest misery, while the others are immersed in idle luxury.   There is only one remedy for this injustice; it is to divide the total product of labor among the workers, and not among the capitalists.

III.

N. Colajanni.

The whole of the first volume and the first chapters of the second volume of "La sociologia criminale"[1] contain a criticism of the theses of the Italian school.   The author denies the correctness of these, since he believes that we must consider the anthropological and physical causes as having little or no importance.   This he demonstrates in detail.   In his last chapters Dr. Colajanni treats of social and economic factors.

While admitting that economic conditions are of the highest importance in the development of the whole social life, and consequently in the matter of criminality, the author does not agree with Marx and Loria, who consider every social occurrence, whether political, or religious, or æsthetic, or moral, as the unique and direct product of an economic phenomenon.[2]

---

[1] See also his, "La delinquenza della Sicilia e le sue cause", and "Socialismo e criminalità."

[2] Dr. Colajanni is in error here.   Marx never formulated so strange a theory.

According to the author, this assertion is carried too far, since the feelings and passions of superior people, who do not think of material profits, influence the masses at certain moments.

A great number of philosophers, moralists, poets, statisticians, and economists have seen in economic conditions the "causa causarum" of morality, and consequently also of crime.   Pietro Ellero, among others, says very decisively: "From private property are derived all crimes, or almost all.   Property engenders cupidity and haughtiness on the one side and depravity on the other, even when it does not produce the perfect tyranny of the one class and the degradation of the other.   It is the cause of most of the evil passions, faults, and crimes that are committed, of the troubles, anxieties, sadness, and rancor from which both rich and poor suffer alike. The immoral influence of property is continued afterwards, and that terribly, in the present organization of the family, constructed, as it is, almost always upon the basis of calculation!" [1]

It is incontestable that economic conditions have a direct influence upon the origin of crime.   The lack of the means of satisfying the numerous wants of a man is already a goad to incite him to procure these means in any way whatever, honest or dishonest.   And it is the dishonest way that one will choose by preference when society makes it difficult or impossible to act otherwise.   A London pickpocket gets $1500 a year on the average; on the other hand, the misery of those who wish to earn their living honestly is indescribable. Further, the honest man's chance of being killed or becoming incapable of working is greater than the thief's chance of being punished. Honest work results in fewer advantages and more dangers than dishonest work.

The *indirect* influence is not less important than the direct.   War, our present industry, the family, marriage, political institutions, revolutions, vagrancy, prostitution, education, etc. are important causes of crime, but they can all be reduced to economic causes. According to many persons education is the one means of preventing moral evils, but John Stuart Mill has already said: in our present society the poor have no education, and that of the rich is bad. There is no possibility of a good education if a certain material well-being is lacking.   Hence those who expect everything from education under the present conditions are wrong.

But where does well-being cease and poverty begin?   Both are only relative conceptions; consequently we cannot fix their limits.

[1] Pp. 456, 457.

In order to attain the minimum of criminality in any given society there must be the *certainty* of the means of subsistence, *stability* of economic conditions, and *equality* in the distribution of wealth.

Some authors deny that political revolutions have their causes in economic conditions. Lombroso and Laschi, for example, attempt to explain them chiefly by physical influences; which is the more astonishing, because in the general opinion it is from economic causes that they are derived. They adduce, among other things, to support their opinion, the fact that out of 147 revolts that took place in Europe between 1793 and 1880, only a third were attributable to economic conditions. It goes without saying that this does not at all prove the correctness of their thesis, since in all these cases the authors are speaking only of direct causes, while most military revolutions, revolts against the royal power, etc., spring from economic conditions, even if indirectly. It is true that in the 19th century the direct revolutionary influence of crises and famines has decreased, because of the measures taken by the governments. This does not however prevent there having been revolts occasioned by such conditions (Lyons in 1831, etc.). The frequent revolts in Belgium and France, rich countries, do not furnish any proof against the thesis of Dr. Colajanni; for notwithstanding the great wealth of these countries, nothing proves that it is equally divided. As soon as the poverty of a people has passed certain limits, we see in that country neither crimes, revolutions, nor suicides, since all energy is then extinct.

Another question is this: how far is there a correlation between *the progress made by socialism* and the increase of criminality.[1] Several authors, like Garofalo, are of the opinion that there is an intimate connection between the two. But they do not furnish any facts as proofs in support of their assertion, to which, on the contrary, the facts give the lie.

The countries where socialism is most widely spread do not show the greatest criminality; rather the contrary. The German and Italian districts where there are the most socialists are no longer the most criminal. How could it be otherwise? While socialism is the conscious and collective reaction against the existing order, crime is the unconscious and individual reaction against that order.

Next, Dr. Colajanni turns his attention to *idleness and vagrancy*, which are both causes of crime. Out of 32,943 thefts in Paris in 1882, 57 % were committed by vagrants.

---

[1] For further details see Dr. Colajanni's report to the Fifth Congress of Criminal Anthropology.

But are idleness and vagrancy considered in themselves also offenses? Any man is harmful to his species, says Féré, when he does not collaborate, either materially or intellectually, in production. According to Dr. Colajanni, idleness and vagrancy, viewed from such a high social point of view, are really offenses. But then the idle rich are also guilty of these offenses. Finally, what are the causes of these crimes? Spencer, Féré, and Sergi say : the vagrants are the weak, the degenerate, the parasites of society. The question is this, then : do these phenomena find their origin inside or outside of the human organism? Romagnosi says that vagrancy and idleness ought to be punished only when they are not excusable. To make them inexcusable it would be necessary to procure employment for every man who was willing to work. Spencer, Sergi, and Garofalo, on the contrary, are of the opinion that these crimes are almost always to be imputed to the same persons. However, Spencer should not have forgotten that in his own country, aside from industrial crises, numerous occurrences have forced a great number of persons to become idlers and vagrants through no fault of their own, as for example, the Irish and Scotch farmers driven from their lands by the landlords.

And Garofalo should have known that it is capitalism that has made the work of men superfluous by employing women and children, and that the cause does not rest with those who suffer from it ; on the contrary, the cause of economic crises is not in their victims, but in the system that is in force.

An examination of the causes of these two phenomena obliges us to distinguish between habitual and accidental, or forced, vagrancy. However — and this is too often forgotten — the latter transforms itself into the former, for the taste for work is, like morality, an acquired social product. This is why this quality is lost when one is long without work.

One of the most important causes of the possible transformation of a worker into a vagrant is a long illness. Having lost the habit of work, and being enfeebled, a man will find great difficulty in going to work again. If he does not succeed he descends step by step until he comes finally to mendicity. But it is chiefly the economic transformations, inventions, overproduction, that must be called the "causa causarum" of the phenomena cited above.[1]

Prostitution, which occupies so important a place in the etiology of

---

[1] See pp. 494–500, where the author proves this with the aid of numerous quotations.

crime, in almost every case finds its origin in poverty, in a bad education, in a corrupting environment, as is proved by the official investigations and the writings of specialists, like Parent-Duchatelet, Fiaux, Agagneur, and many others.[1]

The correlation that exists between crimes against property and economic conditions is very evident, and is direct. This causality appears also with regard to crimes against persons. Only it is then indirect. The influence of poverty upon criminality is especially great when it has been of long duration. Proudhon is quite right when he says: "Hunger that is every instant present, during the whole year, during the whole life, hunger which does not kill in a day, but is composed of all deprivations and all griefs, and unceasingly consumes the body, ruins the spirit, demoralizes the conscience, corrupts the race, generates all vices and diseases (drunkenness, among others), and an aversion towards work and thrift, baseness of spirit, callousness of conscience, laziness, and prostitution together with theft." [2]

The fact that the number of thefts of provisions is relatively small has little importance, since the thief always tries to steal some article of small bulk and great value. Also it must not be forgotten that little thefts of food often pass unnoticed, or without complaint being made, because the party injured does not consider the act a crime, since committed from necessity.

Another convincing proof of the influence of economic conditions is the incontestable fact that it continually happens that a person will declare himself guilty of a crime that has not been committed, with the sole purpose of obtaining a lodging in jail. The great percentage made up of crimes committed from cupidity, as well as the fact that the number of recidivists is greater for crimes against property than for others, shows the great influence of economic conditions.

The study of the *morality of primitive peoples* shows us that the crimes of abortion, for example, of infanticide, and homicide upon the aged, have their origin in economic conditions exclusively, the means of subsistence not being sufficient to support a large population. When these crimes occur among civilized peoples they have the same causes. For example, cases of infanticide are very common in Trevise, one of the poorest provinces in Italy. The lack of education or the influence of other factors opposed to education are the reason why the corrupting influence of which we have been speaking often rages in the lower classes with all its force.

To prove the assertion that economic conditions have little influ-

[1] See pp. 504–510.   [2] P. 513.

ence upon criminality, some authors cite the fact that England, with
its great wealth, shows a greater number of crimes against property
than Italy, which is much poorer. He who reasons in this way forgets that the absolute wealth of a country may be very great, but
the distribution of that wealth not proportional. England gives
us the proof of this; in no other country is the difference between
rich and poor more pronounced, and without the presence of other
important and opposing factors, the criminality would be much
greater than it is now.

One might also bring up the difference between the criminality of
Ireland, which is smaller despite the proverbial poverty there, and
the great criminality of Italy.   However, when we study conditions
in the two countries we find that those in Italy are still more undesirable than those in Ireland, which explains the greater criminality
against property in Italy.   The mysterious assassinations of large
landholders and their agents in Ireland have also their cause in the
bad distribution of the land.   In Belgium criminality is greatest
where well-being is least (in Flanders).   According to the researches
of Liszt and Starcke, the poorest districts of Germany are also those
that are most criminal, etc.

Upon the *economic condition of criminals* the author gives the following data: In 1870–71 there were among the prisoners at Neuf-
châtel 10 % who had some property, and 89 % who had only their
work for their support (in the non-criminal population the percentage
of these is much smaller).   According to the data of Stevens the
prisoners in Belgium were divided as follows: 1 % of well-to-do persons, 11 % of persons with some income, and 88 % of indigent persons.

The statistics of recidivists in Sweden from 1870 to 1872 give the
following information:

Well-to-do   0.64 %
With sufficient means of subsistence 10.08 ”
   ”   insufficient   ”   ”   ”   43.54 ”
   ”   miserable   ”   ”   ”   45.63 ”

Marro, in his "I caratteri dei delinquenti", gives us the following:

	CRIMINALS.	NON-CRIMINALS.
Without property	79.6 %	43.4 %
Minor children of well-to-do parents	4.1 ”	10.5 ”
With a little property.	6.7 ”	18.4 ”
With considerable property	9.4 ”	27.6 ”

At the time that they committed their crimes 43 % of these criminals in general, and more than 50 % of the criminals against property were without work.

All that has been given above has to do with *statics;* what follows has to do with dynamics. The rule universally observed is this: modifications in economic conditions are followed by modifications in criminality. When the former grow worse, the number of crimes (and especially of those against property) increases, and vice versa. It is especially the proletariat, who have no means of resisting the unfavorable influence of crises, a rise in the price of food, etc., who are hardest hit in these cases.

The author gives some data. In Italy in 1880 a great increase of crime coincided with a lack of work and with a rise in the price of provisions. The gradual diminution in criminality must be attributed to the good harvest and the large emigration. In Belgium the number of prisoners rose during the crisis of 1846 from 6750 to 9884. In Norway, in consequence of the depression of 1869, crimes against property reached the maximum. The number of prisoners in Sweden rose from 1835 to 1839, chiefly because of poverty, from 12,799 to 18,357. A great increase in crime took place in England in consequence of the crises of 1826, 1830, 1847, and others. In the United States there were in 1884 not less than 400,000 workingmen without work, which explains the following figures:

	1883	1884
Homicides	1,494	3,377
Cases of lynching	92	219
Suicides	910	1,897

In consequence of the economic crises of 1839, 1840, 1843, 1847, 1867, 1876, and 1881, the number of murders increased in France.[1]

The maximum stability and the minimum lack of proportion in the distribution of wealth is the best preservative against crime. The correctness of this rule is proved by the facts. The small number of crimes among the Irish is explained by their altruistic sentiments, which are the consequence of their social institutions from before the conquest of their country by the English. Among Mohamme-

[1] With regard to Starke, from whom Dr. Colajanni takes these figures, see Chap. II of this work.

dans crime is rare.   Also there may be remarked among them a true democracy, based upon equality and fraternity.   The Yorubas (in Eastern Africa) have a mild character, and they are benevolent and true to their word; with them the land is considered as common property, etc., etc.

"These are facts which speak clearly: the collectivism of the Javanese *dessa*, of the Berber *diema*, the Russian *mir*, the Slav *zadrouga*, and the village community of the early Aryans and North American Indians, produces everywhere, with all climates, among all races, identically the same results — morality and solidarity.

"It is to be noted also, that everywhere and at all times, whether in the temperate or the frigid zone, in the North, in the South, or at the equator, laws and institutions which aim to insure certainty of subsistence and to maintain a certain equality, go far to cut down crime; and they do it in such a way as to make those who live under them more moral than those who are subject to different institutions and laws.   We have clear examples of this among the Hebrews, Iroquois, Peruvians, Chinese, Berbers, etc., although they differ greatly as to the grade of civilization they have reached." [1]

IV.

A. BEBEL.

In "Die Frau und der Socialismus" the author gives the following pages to the relation between the present social organization and crime: "The increase of crime of every description is intimately connected with the social conditions of the community, little as the latter is inclined to believe it.   Society hides its head in the sand, like the ostrich, in order not to be forced to recognize a state of things that bears witness against it, and silences its own conscience and others' with the lying pretense that laziness and love of pleasure on the part of the workmen and their want of religion is accountable for everything.   This is hypocrisy of the most revolting kind.   The more unfavorable and depressed the condition of society, the more numerous and grave do crimes become.   The struggle for existence then assumes its most brutal and violent shape, it throws man back into his primæval state, in which each regarded the other as his deadly enemy.   The ties of solidarity, not too firm at the best of times, become daily looser.

[1] Pp. 562, 563.   See also Chap. XIII, in which Dr. Colajanni treats of the influence of militarism upon criminality.

"The ruling classes, who do not and will not recognize the causes of things, attempt to effect a change by employing force against the products of these conditions, and even men whom we should expect to be enlightened and free from prejudice, are ready to support the system. Professor Haeckel, for instance, regards the stringent application of capital punishment as desirable, and harmonizes in this point with the reactionaries of every shade, who on all other subjects are his bitterest enemies. According to his theory, hopeless criminals and ne'er-do-wells must be rooted out like weeds, which deprive the more valuable plants of light, air, and soil. If Professor Haeckel had occupied himself even to a slight degree with the study of social science, instead of limiting himself to natural science, he would have discovered that all these criminals could be transformed into useful, valuable members of society, if society offered them more favorable means of existence. He would have found that the annihilation of the criminal has just as little effect on crime, *i.e.* on the development of fresh crimes, as if on a number of farms the ground were superficially cleared of weeds while the roots and seeds remained undestroyed. Man will never be able absolutely to prevent the development of noxious organisms in nature, but it is unquestionably within his power so to improve the social organism created by himself, that it may afford equally favorable conditions of existence and an equal freedom of growth to all; that no one may be forced to gratify his hunger or his desire of possession or his ambition at the expense of someone else. People only need to investigate the causes of crime and to remove them, and they will abolish crime itself.

"Naturally those who seek to abolish crime by abolishing its causes cannot take kindly to measures of brutal suppression. They cannot prevent society from protecting itself against crime in its own way, but they demand all the more urgently the radical reformation of society, *i.e.* the removal of causes." [1]

"The relationship between social conditions and crime has often been pointed out by statisticians and sociologists. One of the offenses that comes closest to us — for our society, in spite of all the Christian teaching about charity, regards it as a crime — in times of business depression, is mendicity. We learn from the statistics of the kingdom of Saxony, that in measure as the last great commercial

[1] [To this point Dr. *H. B. Adams*, *Walther's* translation, "Woman in the Past, Present, and Future", (Lovell, 1886) has been followed. The remainder of the quotation is matter added by *Bebel* since the publication of the edition from which the above translation was made. — TRANSL.]

crisis grew worse, beginning in Germany in 1890 with the end not yet in sight, the number of persons sentenced for mendicity also increased. In 1889, in the Kingdom of Saxony 8566 persons were punished for this offense, 8815 in 1890, 10,075 in 1891, and in 1892 as many as 13,120, a very great increase. The impoverishment of the masses on the one hand, with increasing wealth on the other, is the chief mark of our period. In 1874 there was one poor man to 724 persons, while in 1882 the number had reached 1 to 622.[1] Crimes and misdemeanors show a similar tendency. In 1874, there were 308,605 persons sentenced in Austria-Hungary, and 600,000 in 1892. In the German Empire in 1882 there were 329,968 persons sentenced for crimes and misdemeanors against the laws, *i.e.* 103.2 persons to 10,000 of the population over 12 years old; in 1892 the number of those sentenced reached 422,327, or 143.3 to the 10,000, an increase of 39%. Those convicted of crimes and misdemeanors against property were:

1882   169,334 persons, or 53.0 to the 10,000 over 12
1891   196,437   ”   or 55.8 ”   ”   ”   ”   ”

" We think that these figures speak volumes, that they show how the deterioration of social conditions increases and multiplies poverty, need, misdemeanors and crimes." [2]

V.

P. LAFARGUE.

The first part of the study, "Die Kriminalität in Frankreich von 1840–1886", is taken up with an examination of the trend of criminality during these years. The author comes to the conclusion that during this period crime has increased, and that the line that shows this increase is made up of a succession of curves, alternately concave and convex.

In the second part, he treats of the causes of crime. He first points out that the belief that the proclamation of liberty, equality, and fraternity in the French Revolution would be speedily followed by a diminution in crime, was not borne out by the facts. Then he takes up the idea, so widespread in the first half of the 19th century, that one of the most important causes of criminality is the lack of education. This hypothesis has been generally recognized as false,

[1] [A decimal point is plainly lacking after the first figure in each of these two numbers. — TRANSL.]   [2] Pp. 295–297.

in consequence of an examination of the facts. According to Lafargue, who is entirely in agreement with Quetelet on this point, it
is necessary not only to examine the qualities of the individual, but
also especially to analyze society, and to try thus to discover the
sources of crime. Next the author shows the results of the researches
of Quetelet with regard to the influence of the season, age, and sex
upon criminality, and sets forth and criticises briefly the theories
of Lombroso and his partisans with regard to the criminal man. We
should run to too great length if we gave more fully his refutation
which is as brilliant as it is accurate.

Some statisticians connect the returns of the harvests and vintages
with criminality. An investigation upon this point as regards
France, gives the following results: the years 1847, 1854, 1868, and
1874, which are characterized by a great increase of crime, were
preceded by years of bad harvests.

The average of the crops of grain was:

> from 1840 to 1853 about 80 million hectolitres
> ”   1856 ” 1885   ”   100   ”   ”

the crop rose:

> in 1846 to 61 million hectolitres
> ” 1853 ” 63   ”   ”
> ” 1867 ” 83   ”   ”
> ” 1873 ” 84   ”   ”

However, the bad harvests of 1855, 1861, and 1879 did not have
these results, and with the good crops of 1847 to 1852 crime increased. Here there were, therefore, other factors. Consequently,
although the price of grain can partially explain the fluctuations of
criminality, it does not account for the general increase from 1840
to 1886.

The author combats further the opinion of Professor Lacassagne
that crimes against persons are especially under the influence of the
production and consumption of wine. If this were the case the wine-
growing departments ought to furnish the highest figure for crimes
against persons, which is not the case. On the contrary, Lafargue
is of the opinion that in this respect, the consumption of brandy is
of more importance. The continually increasing abuse of alcohol
(*i.e.* of spirituous drinks like brandy) which in its turn is due to the
miserable condition of the proletariat, is one of the causes of the increasing criminality.

Quantity of alcohol consumed:

YEAR.	TOTAL (HECTOLITRES).	PER CAPITA (LITRES).
1850	585,200	1.46
1855	714,813	2.00
1860	851,825	2.27
1865	873,007	2.34
1875	1,010,052	2.82
1880	1,313,849	3.64
1885	1,444,342	3.86

In the third part Lafargue makes special investigations with regard to the correlation between economic conditions and criminality. If the theory of Lombroso were correct, criminality ought to decrease; bad harvests no longer explain the increase, and the climate has not changed. However, the increase of criminality coincided with the enormous increase in the productive forces in France.

	1840	1860	1880	1884
Horse-power of steam engines used in manufacturing and agriculture	34,350	177,652	544,152	683,090
Consumption of coal (in tons) .	4,256,000	14,270,000	28,846,000	30,941,000
Production of iron (in tons) . .	· 585,000	1,430,000	2,790,000	2,747,000
Production of steel (in tons) . .	8,262	30,000	389,000	503,000
Exports and imports (in millions of francs)	1,442	4,174	8,501	7,575
Increase of inheritances (in millions of francs)	1,608	2,724	5,265	5,244
National wealth (in millions of francs)	64,320	108,960	210,600	209,760

There is a close correspondence, then, between the development of the economic forces and the increase of criminality. Must we regard this as simply chance, or is there causality between the two? Quetelet has already pointed out that the poorest districts, *i.e.* those in which the absolute wealth is not great, but where the contrasts are not very marked, furnish fewer criminals than the wealthier provinces. According to Lafargue this has become still more striking with the development of capitalism.

"The colossal development of the productive forces and the national wealth does not lead to the increase of the well-being of all the members of society, but to enormous fortunes on the one hand, and on the other to misery and need, for the great majority of the population." [1]   If the multiplying, grading, and perfecting of punishments have been incapable of checking the upward progress of crime, this proves that crimes and misdemeanors against the common law are the necessary products of conditions, and are closely bound up with the form and fashion of the creation of social wealth in capitalistic society.

"The development of the capitalistic mode of production is not uniform; at times it is over-rapid, and then slows up again and undergoes crises that destroy the living of thousands and millions of individuals. If it is correct that modern criminality is a necessary consequence of the method of the production of wealth in capitalistic society, then the fluctuations of crime must correspond with the variations in production. The number of offenses must increase in times of crisis, and decrease when economic conditions improve; in other words, criminality is determined by the flourishing or depression of the capitalistic mode of production." [2]

As a means of measuring comparative economic conditions, Lafargue has taken the annual number of failures. He has also traced a curve for the price of flour.[3]

Examining the first plate we see that lines I and II, although not entirely parallel with V, follow it in general. According to Lafargue there are three counter-determinants that caused the deviations: first, changes in the price of flour; second, political events; third, extraordinary industrial activity. Thus, for example, it was the political events of 1848–52 that prevented the decrease of crime during those years, though the failures and the price of flour went down; and at the close of 1854 a feverish economic development recommenced, which, with the fall of the price of flour in 1856–59, caused a decrease of criminality during those years. At the same time the failures rose a little; but the line would doubtless show a different course if it were drawn with reference to the ratio of failures to the total number of commercial and industrial enterprises in this period. The low price of flour in 1869 neutralized the increase of failures and even diminished the criminality. From 1874 to 1878 a new industrial revival kept crime stationary or reduced it. Since 1876 the failures have increased greatly and crime follows at a little interval; the falling price of grain (1881–1885) certainly exerted an influence.

[1] P. 107.   [2] Pp. 108, 109.
[3] In examining the statistical tables it must be remembered that they give no real picture of criminality during the years 1870–71, on account of the effect of the war.

PLATE I.

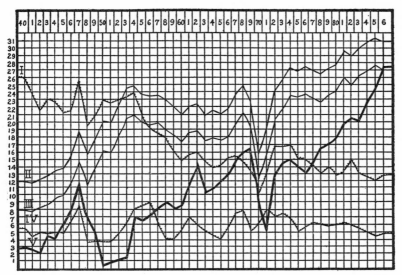

I. Crimes against Persons and Property, tried at the Assizes. II. General Criminality (Crimes and Misdemeanors). III. Offenses against the Common Law, tried by the Correctional Tribunals. IV. Price of a Sack of Flour in the Markets of Paris. V. Number of Failures.

PLATE II.

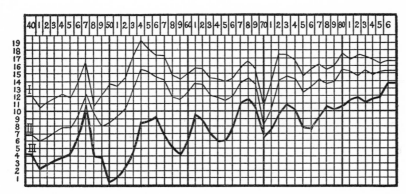

I. Thefts with Aggravating Circumstances, tried by the Assizes, and Simple Thefts, tried by the Correctional Tribunals. II. Theft, Fraud, Embezzlement, tried by the Correctional Tribunals. III. Number of Failures and the Price of Flour Combined.

The curves are almost constantly parallel; the deviations are caused by political events and by the industrial revival.[1]

Vagrancy and mendicity take the same course as failures; they increase, however, from 1848 to 1852 in consequence of the political troubles of those years. From 1878 on, failures, and vagrancy and

PLATE III.

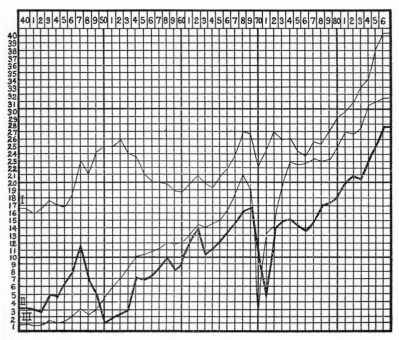

I. VAGRANCY AND MENDICITY. II. FAILURES. III. RECIDIVISTS SENTENCED
BY THE ASSIZES OR THE CORRECTIONAL TRIBUNALS.

mendicity increase and are parallel. In the periods of industrial revival (1854–59 and 1874–76) vagrancy and mendicity decline sharply. In examining the curve of recidivism it must be remembered that since 1884 many recidivists have been transported.

Here we see a result contrary to that on the preceding charts: If the failures increase the rapes generally decrease, and vice versa.

[1] Lafargue's idea of combining the curves of failure and of the price of flour is ingenious, but in my opinion does not give a correct notion of the truth, since it is upon the mistaken notion that the effect of these two factors is equal.

PLATE IV.

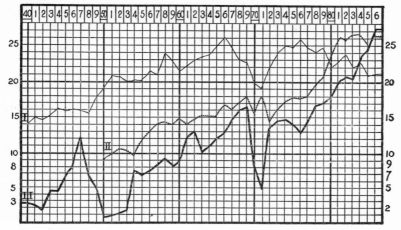

I. Rape.   II. Consumption of Alcohol.   III. Failures.

According to this plate the consumption of alcohol has no relation to crimes against morals.

At the end of his study the author comes to the following conclusion: "The effect of bankruptcy upon criminality and politics is undeniable; it furnishes one of the most striking proofs of the correctness of the historical theory of Karl Marx, that the phenomena of literature and art, of morality and religion, of philosophy and politics, in human society, lead back to the phenomena of economic development." [1]

VI.

H. Denis.

Professor Denis begins his report to the 3d Congress of Criminal Anthropology, entitled "La criminalité et la crise économique", by calling attention to the effect that the crisis of 1846–47 had upon criminality. The crops of wheat, rye, and especially potatoes had been bad, and the price of these articles of food had accordingly risen. The breaking up of household labor and the introduction of machines brought about a revolution in the linen industry at the same time. So the figures for crime indicate an enormous increase during these years, and at the close of the period a continuous decrease.

[1] P. 116.

Years.	Number of Delinquents to the 10,000 Inhabitants.	Years.	Number of Delinquents to the 10,000 Inhabitants.
1845	28.8	1850	19.8
1846	47.9	1851	19.8
1847	65.3	1852	19.2
1848	42.4	1853	19.7
1849	25.–		

Then the author treats of the effect produced upon criminality by the crises of 1874 and the years following. The price of grain no longer giving, in consequence of importation, an exact picture of the economic conditions, he adds to the chart which he uses, the "nombres indicateurs" (of 28 of the more important articles of commerce). The curve of these numbers shows a fluctuating rise during the period from 1850 to 1865, and a fluctuating decline during the period following the years 1874–75. During the first period, in which the economic conditions were favorable (the years 1870 to 1873 being characterized by an economic development that was even feverish), criminality remained fairly stationary. Only during the years 1856–57 and 1861–62 was there an increase, and this is probably to be ascribed to the high price of grain. The economic depression that commenced after 1874 was severely felt, and crime continually increased without the low price of grain being able to prevent it.

Professor Denis closes his report with the following words: "The solution of the problem of criminality must be in part sought in economic conditions; and the more regular and constant the social movement of wealth, the more we approach a normal equilibrium of collective functions, the more we instil justice into our economic institutions, the more shall we be able to gain the mastery over criminality.

"An Italian criminologist, Ferri, studying the evolution of criminality in France in relation to the income of the most numerous class, has shown that with a general rise in wages we see a decrease in certain kinds of crime. The general increase of prosperity is a sure pledge of a decrease in criminality. But there is another, and that is a decrease in those more or less marked oscillations, in the economic world, whose periodic return is certainly one of the gravest aspects of the modern state.

"In the second place, the economic causes that affect the tendency to crime reveal an immense solidarity, which continues to extend

itself into space, as heredity plunges its roots into time.   The great
fluctuations in prices are common to the whole world, and the individual whom these perturbations drive to crime by a series of shocks,
comes into conflict with a great number of other individuals, without
being conscious of this infinite solidarity.   But science must endeavor
to collect the evidence of it.   Finally these great economic influences
tend, on the one hand, to reduce the field of the individual responsibility, and on the other, to give a precise character to the responsibility of society in this connection.   It is responsible, in fact, within
the limits within which it might have restrained the economic fluctuations and corrected their effects, but has not done so.   Here the
terrible saying of Quetelet is still true : society herself has put the
weapon into the hand of the criminal." [1]

VII.

H. Lux.[2]

In the chapter, "Die degenerirenden Einwirkungen des Kapitalis-
mus", this author treats of the question of criminality and its relation with present economic conditions.

"The property-holders, those who enjoy the benefits of all the
political and social institutions, alone have the right to exist.   Those
without possessions do not have this right, despite the fiction of the
Prussian code with regard to the matter.   The simple instinct of
self-preservation causes them to engage in a continual attack upon a
legal system that protects only the stronger.   It is this attack which
those who are in possession of power, those who have drawn up the
laws for the purpose of protecting their power, characterize as a
breach of the law, as crime. . . .   This is the simplest relationship between the form of society and crime.   Naturally, complications
come in. . . .   The stronger those without property, the outlawed,
themselves become through some chance, the more do they modify
the law that was set up by those who were formerly stronger, the more
do complications arise in the primitively simple right of property, the
right to the protection of social institutions, and the law of marriage,
and the greater and more complicated becomes the circle of crimes." [3]

[1] Pp. 370, 371.   "Actes du troisième Congrès international d'anthropologie
criminelle."   See, by the same author, "L'influence de la crise économique
sur la criminalité et le penchant au crime de Quetelet", "Le socialisme et
les causes économiques et sociales du crime", and "Les index numbers
(nombres indices) des phénomènes moraux."
[2] "Sozial politisches Handbuch."   [3] Pp. 143, 144.

After having next spoken briefly of free will, and having shown that it is incorrect to connect criminality with a single social phenomenon alone, since the social mechanism is too complicated, the author begins to treat of the *crimes against property*.   In the first place he gives the following tables :

Germany.[1]

| YEARS. | PRICES. | | | | | To 10,000 INHABITANTS OVER 10 YEARS OLD. | |
| | In Marks per 1,000 Kilogr. | | | In Pf. per 1 Kilogr. | | | |
	Of Bread.	Of Peas.	Of Potatoes.	Of Beef.	Of Pork.	Crimes Against Property.	Theft.
1881	198	251	43.5	114	128	—	—
1882	171	236	56.5	116	128	52.9	32.6
1883	155	241	45.5	120	128	51.0	31.6
1884	145	229	47.0	120	120	50.7	30.1
1885	147	212	38.0	119	120	48.6	27.9
1886	130	209	39.5	117	119	48.1	27.2
1887	135	198	41.5	113	115	47.1	26.0
1888	144	219	59.0	112	114	45.9	25.4
1889	162	209	42.0	117	128	49.3	28.1

Hungary.

	1881	1882	1883	1884	1885	1886	1887	1888
Convicted of theft . . .	19.	26.7	25.7	23.4	32.2	22.0	21.7	22.3
Crop of maize per hectare .	16.1	20.0	16.8	17.2	20.5	15.5	14.2	18.0
" " potatoes per hectare	81.8	110.7	109.9	80.1	92.0	77.2	79.0	85.4

Finally, Dr. Lux cites some statistics from Kolb's "Handbuch ver vergleichenden Statistik", which show the close connection between crimes against property and economic conditions.

Political crimes.   "In the case of crimes against the State, public order, and religion, the dependence upon the form of society is immediately apparent.   The 'classes', *i.e.* the property-owners as a whole, see in the institutions that they have set up, the strongest support of the capitalistic system, which must be maintained at any cost.   The property-owners have the power to uphold their unique

---

[1] In the last two columns " crimes " was later corrected by the author himself to "criminals".   See "Neue Zeit", 1892–1893, II, p. 179, and 1893–1894, I, pp. 184 and 535.

position by laws directed against those who would break down that power. And if the laws are no longer sufficient, their place is taken by judicial interpretations in the interests of the classes. This is only the logical consequence of the whole spirit and aim of legislation. The greater become the rights founded upon property, the more do those without property feel themselves to be deprived of their rights, — in the fullest sense of the word — in jeopardy as to their existence, their full life; the more energetic is the reaction against the laws, which are felt as despotism; and the more serious is the attack upon those laws, — a characteristic phenomenon of all periods of transition as to the form of society." [1]

The question which presents itself now is this: how far are these factors connected with existing economic conditions? But before entering upon this the author calls attention to *the environment in which the children of the proletariat* live, and especially of the lower proletariat, an environment in which misery and vice contend for the preëminence. There it is nearly out of the question to learn ethical conceptions. Whence it comes also that in our days criminality among the young has greatly increased. However, alcoholism must also be named as one of the most important causes of psychical perturbations.

It is not only the non-possessers, but also the possessors who are driven to commit crimes as a consequence of existing economic conditions. "But not only for those without property, for the proletariat, does capitalism furnish the psychically prerequisite conditions for crime . . . but for the property-holders themselves. Entirely aside from business practices and tricks of the trade, which stand upon the hairline between right and wrong, apart from the frauds, forgeries, etc. that are evoked by too tempting opportunity, there are more general effects of the capitalistic system. The hurried chase for gain, the accelerating of commerce by railroad, steamship, telegraph, and telephone, the multiplication of commercial crises, which earlier came at intervals, but now are a permanent accompaniment of the social life, bring about a nervousness running through all circles of society, that is continually increasing, and is the forerunner of more serious psychoses. The terrible increase of cases of insanity (in Prussia, to the 10,000 of the population, in 1871, 5.94 cases; in 1875, 7.28; in 1880, 9.87), appears to be thus directly caused by capitalistic society." [2]

However, there act in man as counter-determinants, combating

[1] P. 150.   [2] Pp. 156, 157.

the factors called criminogenous, the *ethical factors* ("ethische Hem-
mungsvorstellungen"), which are determined by education, character, the fear of punishment, etc.   Those who do not wish to investigate the deepest causes of criminality, are of the opinion that the
best way to combat crime is by increasing the penalties.   The persons who speak thus forget that the so-called ethical factors have no
longer any effect when the conditions have reached a certain degree
of seriousness.

Crimes against persons.   It is the industrial workers who form the
greatest contingent of criminals against persons.   "The continually
changing conditions of earning a living, the desire for drink, the slight
influence of the family, the being crowded together with persons of
defective education and little training . . . these all necessarily
breed crimes of violence; entirely aside from the habitual rowdyism
of the bully ["Zuhälter",] which is to be regarded as the consequence of
prostitution.[1]

Besides the external conditions named above, *the person of the criminal* is also to be noticed.   We may consider it as proved that in some
cases of crime one of the causes is a mental perturbation (for example,
that caused by drunkenness).   These perturbations play a great part
in sexual crimes (perverted instincts).   What characterizes most of
these mental anomalies is that they blunt the social instincts.   But
there is another cause of psychic degeneracy.   "It is a universally
valid psycho-physical law that man, 'the more he depends upon an
agreeable stimulation for the satisfaction of his senses, demands ever
stronger stimuli, even to secure the same degree of pleasure.'   Pleasures, especially sensual pleasures, must always become more intense,
more titillating, in order to afford satisfaction, but the more their
intensity increases, the more do the nerves become irritated and exhausted, and the more quickly is the ground prepared for mental
diseases either in the individual himself or in his descendants. —
It must be emphasized, however, that such an increase in the stimulus is only possible to the rich, and accordingly it is with reference to
them chiefly that these sources of mental disturbances are to be
taken into consideration." [2]

After having called attention to the great amount of recidivism
among female delinquents, to the great increase of crime in our own
day, and to the great percentage of young people among the criminals,
the author closes with the following words: "Crime belongs in a
society founded upon capitalism just as necessarily as do prostitution,

---

[1] P. 152.   [2] P. 159.

the destruction of countless human lives through economic exploitation, etc."

VIII.

P. HIRSCH.

After having shown in the first chapter of his work, "Verbrechen und Prostitution",[1] the relation between criminality and prostitution, and the increase of the two at the same time, the author gives, in his second chapter, a short exposition of the doctrine of criminal anthropology, and in the third chapter he takes up the doctrine of the social environment.

Here he treats first of the *encouragement of prostitution and crime by the marriage restrictions*. Marriages increase or decrease as economic conditions grow better or worse. So, for example, in Prussia there were, from 1866 to 1870, 1605 marriages to 100,000 of the population; this number rose to 1896 in the period of prosperity between the years 1870 and 1875, only to fall, in 1888, to 1624. In bad times the number of illegitimate births makes a consequent increase. It is very comprehensible that natural children furnish a greater number of criminals than legitimate children, since they have more difficulty in enduring the combat of life than the others.

Then he sets forth as a cause of crime the *influence of domestic relations*. When the parents belong already to the class of criminals, it is almost inevitable that their children should fall into the hands of justice while still young. And the present system of production brings it about that the education of the children of the proletariat is almost nil, since it obliges the father, and very often the mother also, to work away from home during a great part of the day and often of the night. The situation is still more unfavorable for the children who have lost their parents when they were still quite young. Starke says that about 57 % of the legitimate children among the juvenile prisoners in Plötzensee were orphans or had been abandoned by their parents.

The third part has to do with *the housing conditions of the proletariat*. "A lodging fit for a human being is the first requirement for the bodily and mental welfare of the family; it is the prerequisite for a well-regulated family life, and for the rearing of the children to be moral men and women. The improprieties resulting from the exigencies of insufficient lodgings are innumerable, and this condition

[1] In 1907 a second edition appeared, revised and corrected.

is an inexhaustible source of crime, prostitution, and vice of every kind." All the data prove that the proletariat, who, of all classes, pay the highest rent, are the most miserably housed. In Berlin, for example, the poorest classes have been shown to spend on an average a quarter of their income for rent. In Hamburg the part of the income that had to go for rent among the class whose income was from 600 to 1200 marks, in 1868 was 18.77 %, in 1874 20.90 %, in 1882 23.51 %, and in 1892 24.71 %, while the percentage remained the same or decreased for all other classes. In order to make up the resulting deficit, resort is often had to night-lodgings. "The disadvantages of subletting are obvious. 'Children of both sexes have to sleep with their parents, and often with strangers, in the same room, often even in the same bed; the advantages of domesticity are lost; the tavern offers more pleasant entertainment than being crowded together with wife and children in one room that must be shared with strangers, and in which the opportunity for quarreling and fighting, in consequence of the narrow quarters, is constant. It is the bad housing conditions that are the cause of the increasing alcoholism, of the break-up of the family life, and of the lack of education for the youth.' (Braun)." [1]

The chapter that concerns us next treats of *the subsidiary businesses engaged in by school children.* It goes without saying that in the cases where the wages of the father of the family must be increased by the labor of the mother, the children also must be put to work at an age at which they ought to have their leisure time for play. For though child-labor in factories is a little limited by legislation, it is still commonly practiced in household industry. Further most of the children of the proletariat must, in their free hours, do all kinds of work harmful to their physique and their morals. "It is plain to be seen how greatly the school-children are injured by engaging in additional work. Entirely aside from the harm they suffer in the matter of health, and from the fact that the tired children cannot give sufficient attention to the words of the teacher and that for many of them their instruction is as good as lost, is the great fact that their morals are in the highest degree endangered. Under the pressure of necessity, these children learn to grasp every advantage, whether allowable or not, and — not through their own fault, but through that of society — are precociously familiar with vice." [2] "Any one who examines these conditions will not be surprised that according to the statement of Superintendent Schönberger, out of 100 juvenile prisoners in the Plötzensee prison near Berlin, 70 had been employed during school days as breakfast-carriers, newsboys, messengers, bowling-alley-boys, etc., early in the morning, from half past four on, and in some cases still earlier, until school time, and in the afternoon either the whole time, or from four till half past seven or half past eight at night." [1]

Next, Hirsch examines *the influence of economic crises.* He quotes, among other things, the following from the researches of J. S(chmidt). During the economic depression from 1875 to 1878 the number of punishments inflicted by the "Ordnungspolizei" in the country of Baden rose from 16,218 to 22,264, and that of the penalties inflicted by the "Sittenpolizei" (having surveillance of prostitution) from 1995 to 4485. There were increases, therefore, of 40 % and 125 %. In the period of prosperity from 1882 to 1885 these figures fell from 22,765 to 18,856 (16 %), and from 4106 to 4007 (3 %). During the critical years from 1889 to 1892 the number of recidivists convicted of theft rose 18 %, and the number of other thieves convicted 6 %. In the period from 1875 to 1878 (years of crisis) the number of offenses against property rose 17.4 %, and decreased 13 % in the years 1882 to 1885 (a period of prosperity).

In conclusion the author points out the fact that there are also criminals who are predisposed to crime by their physical constitution (mental disorders), and treats of "the repression of crime and prostitution." [2]

[1] P. 54.
[2] See also: *P. Kropotkine,* "Paroles d'un révolté", pp. 241 *ff.,* and "The Coming Anarchy", p. 161 ("Nineteenth Century", 1887); *J. Stern,* "Einflusz der sozialen Zustände auf alle Zweige des Kulturlebens", pp. 24 *ff.;* *E. Belfort Bax,* "Ethics of Socialism"; *T. W. Teifen,* "Das soziale Elend und die Besitzenden Klassen in Oesterreich", pp. 132–137, 170–171; *J. S(chmidt),* "Einflusz der Krisen und der Steigerung der Lebensmittelpreise auf das Gesellschaftsleben", pp. 16–19, 23; *H. Wetzker,* "Die Zunahme der Verbrechen" ("Sozialistische Monatshefte", 1902, II); *E. Reich,* "Kriminalität und Altruismus"; *E. Gystrow,* "Social-pathologische Probleme der Gegenwart" ("Soc. Monatshefte", V, 1901).
See also Chapter I, in which I have treated of several socialists, who had to be placed there because they wrote before the rise of modern criminology.
[NOTE TO THE AMERICAN EDITION: See also *E. Fischer,* "Laienbemerkun-. gen zur Reform des Strafrechts" ("Soc. Monatshefte", X,[1] (1906); Dr. *S. Etlinger,* "Das Verbrecherproblem in anthropologischer und sozialogischer Beleuchtung", which, resting upon the socialist theory, criticises especially the anthropological school; and *Robert Blatchford,* "Not Guilty", an original and popular exposition of the theory of the environment.]

CHAPTER VIII.

CONCLUSIONS.

HAVING come to the end of my exposition, I have still to sum up the different chapters. As we have seen, a very small proportion of the authors who have taken up the subject, deny the existence of the relation between criminality and economic conditions, and in my opinion they have not proved the correctness of their position.

The great majority of authors are of the opinion that economic conditions occupy a more or less important position, but that other factors besides these are also at work. I have tried to show that as far as these factors are of a cosmic or religious nature, this thesis cannot be correct; that as far as they are of an anthropological nature, they play a rôle only with regard to a part of criminality.

Finally, we have seen that a small number of authors are of the opinion that the influence of economic factors is sovereign. I have been able to find no inaccuracies in the foundations of their theses.

Nearly all the authors — later I shall speak of the exceptions — have this in common, that they give a very limited meaning to the words "economic factors", under which they include only poverty and wealth, and that they do not inquire whether these phenomena do not themselves need explanation, and whether economic conditions have not a great influence upon the whole social organization. They consider them as being phenomena of the same value as the other sides of the social life. In other words, most authors have omitted to explain the present mode of production and its consequences.

However, economic conditions, in my opinion, occupy an entirely different place; they are the foundation upon which the social structure rests. To make my thought clear I will once more call attention to the classic formula of this doctrine, originated by Marx and Engels, taken from the preface to the work, "Zur Kritik der politischen Oekonomie", which I have already quoted in treating of the theories of Professor Ferri.

"In the social production of their life men enter into fixed, necessary relationships in production, independent of their will, relationships which correspond to a definite stage in the development of their material powers of production. The sum total of these relationships forms the economic structure of society, the real basis upon which the juristic and political superstructure is erected, and to which definite forms of social consciousness correspond. The form of production of the material life conditions the social, political, and intellectual life-process in general. It is not the consciousness of mankind that determines their being, but their social being that determines their consciousness." [1]

In the second part of this work I will try to sketch a treatment of the question according to this theory. As regards economic conditions I shall limit myself, for different reasons, to the present system, *i.e.* modern capitalism.

These reasons are the following:

First. A really scientific examination of the causes of criminality is only possible since the existence of criminal statistics, *i.e.* since the beginning of the 19th century.[2]

Second. Criminality has increased greatly under capitalism, and is of the greatest importance to the whole social life.

Third. An examination of historic criminality is very interesting; that of our own day is still more so. However, social science is not simply a means of solving interesting problems, but also, and chiefly, a means of pointing out to society the way to protect itself from scourges like criminality, or if possible, to get rid of them entirely. Here the saying of Marx applies: "The philosophers have only interpreted the world differently; the important thing is to alter it."

Above I have already remarked that some authors have an opinion that differs from that of the majority, and are in agreement with the theory cited. Among these must be cited Engels, one of the two founders of this theory, and most of the authors of whom I spoke in the last chapter. However, Engels has only made, in passing, some observations upon the influence of capitalism on crime among the

---

[1] P. xi.
[2] I do not mean to deny the importance of historical researches into crime, such as the famous book of *Pike*, "History of Crime in England", or the "Documents de criminologie rétrospective" of *Corre* and *Aubry*. They can give us valuable information with regard to the etiology of crime, but in my opinion it is indubitable that the historic method never permits us to give the complete etiology of a social phenomenon, like criminality, for example.

workers in factories; Hirsch, in his interesting brochure, has pointed out only certain sides of the economic life; and although the studies concerning this question published by Lafargue and by Lux are more complete than those of the first two authors, there are nevertheless important points which these last have not examined, or to the bottom of which they have not gone, as it seems to me. And it is quite comprehensible that it should be so; for the work of Lafargue is only a magazine article, and that of Dr. Lux is one of the subdivisions of a social-political manual, in which he treats of crime among other social phenomena. The works of the other authors noticed in Chapter VII, do not make the study of the question in the manner noted, useless.

I am of the opinion, then, that while the works quoted have made considerable progress, there is still much to be done. It therefore appears to me that it will not be without profit to take up the subject.

The theory of Marx and Engels results in our having a method of investigation already marked out. While most authors who have published studies upon the question, have thought it unnecessary to give an exposition of the economic system in which we live, or perhaps have given a little attention to it along with other social conditions, I shall begin by setting forth the present economic system as that upon which the other parts of the social life rest. These I shall treat in their turn, in so far as they are connected with criminality. It is obvious that this will be only a sketch, for if one wished all the details, it would be enough to refer to the special literature upon the subject. Then I shall investigate the question of how far criminality, under its different forms, is the consequence of the conditions we have found.

[NOTE TO THE AMERICAN EDITION: According to some criticisms of my book it should have been my task not only to give a sketch of the economic theory of Marx, but also to prove it "in extenso" and to refute the criticisms of it, since it is not universally accepted.

It is true that this theory has not been generally accepted — a thing that would be impossible from the social consequences of such acceptance — but I claim that of all the economic theories, that of Marx is the only one that daily wins more adherents, and more and more interpenetrates all social science — even in the case of authors who are the bitterest opponents of this theory.

To require that a book like mine should once more set forth and defend the theory of Marx "in extenso", is as impossible as to require that a modern biologist, who proceeds upon the basis of the Darwinian theory, should prove over again that his basis is sound. That there may be more or less error in detail in the theory of Marx, as in that of Darwin, is possible, but in general they have resisted, like a wall of bronze, all attacks in the most pitiless of contests, that of opinions.

Let the adversaries of Marx's theory judge without prejudice whether that theory does not constitute a great step in advance in criminology!]

PART TWO.

BOOK I.

THE PRESENT ECONOMIC SYSTEM AND ITS CONSEQUENCES.

CHAPTER I.

THE PRESENT ECONOMIC SYSTEM.[1]

IN order to provide for his needs man has always been obliged to work, and this work has always depended upon the physical environment and especially upon the means of production. It is not our province to enquire how or why the means of production were developed. It is enough to show that because of their development the products which man had at his disposal were multiplied. Now when these products become too abundant for one group of producers, a surplus results, which may be exchanged for products of a different sort of which the first group of producers are deprived by reason of their circumstances. These products, which are not destined for personal use but for exchange are called commodities. Consequently it is its social qualities and not its natural qualities that make a commodity of any given product. That an exchange may be made, then, two conditions must be satisfied:

First, There must have been a division of labor; for there would be no point in the exchange of identical products. The objects to be exchanged are those which have no immediate usefulness for the person who possesses them, while they are useful to those who do not possess them.

Second, The persons who are exchanging must have full power to

[1] This sketch is based upon *Karl Marx's*, "Kapital" and *K. Kautsky's* works primarily, with some indebtedness to *Marx's* "Oekonomischen Lehren", and "Das Erfurter Programm."

dispose of their products — in other words, they must be the possessors of the product which they wish to exchange.

In the beginning the relative quantities of the products exchanged
for each other must have varied greatly. But in course of time the
exchange of commodities took place in a ratio fixed for any one place
and time; ten hatchets, for example, being equivalent to five bows, etc.
These commodities must have a common quality which makes a
comparison possible; and it is this common quality which we call
their value. The first problem to be solved, then, is this: "What
constitutes the value of commodities?"

To become a commodity anything must provide for some need
of man; it must have the value of usefulness. Without this value a
product can never be a commodity. However, it is impossible that
the quality which different commodities have in common, and on the
basis of which they are compared, should be their usefulness, that is
to say, their natural qualities. For it is just because of their difference in usefulness [to their possessors] that goods are exchanged.

"As regards their use-value goods are primarily of different quality;
as regards their exchange-value they can only be of different quantity,
without including a particle of use-value." [1]

Since usefulness does not count in exchange there is only one quality of the commodity that remains, that of being the product of labor.
And as we have withdrawn the consideration of usefulness in estimating exchange-value, we must do the same for different kinds of work,
so that the only quality which remains to a commodity is that of
being the product of the labor of man in general. Any commodity,
then, derives its value only from the circumstance that it represents
a certain amount of labor of man in general.

The value of a commodity is determined by the quantity of labor
it represents, measured by the time required. Naturally by "work"
is to be understood here not individual work, but social work; or as
Marx says: "It is . . . the quantity of work socially necessary, or
the time socially necessary for the production of a commodity, which
determines its value." [2]

In measure as the division of labor is developed, production for
personal use diminishes, and the production of commodities increases,
until it finally becomes the universal form of production, and one
commodity (money) is developed as a universal equivalent. As a

[1] *Marx*, "Kapital", I. p. 4.
[2] "Kapital", I, p. 6. It is plain that in this exposition it is needless to
add why this law is discarded under a developed system of capitalism.
The exception in no way diminishes the fundamental truth of the proposition.

consequence of the development of the production of merchandise, the purchase and sale of goods becomes a special profession. The merchant buys for a different reason from that which influences his customers. While the latter buy for consumption, the former buys to sell again and make a profit out of the transaction. The commodity which serves for this purpose is called capital.

Consequently capital comes into existence at the moment when the production of commodities has attained a certain degree of development. Private property, the basis of the production of commodities, begins from that point to show its capitalistic character, at first in an imperceptible manner, which nevertheless becomes more and more developed. The income of the artisan depends primarily upon his personal qualities; that of the capitalist — as such — depends in the first place upon the amount of his capital. The working power and capacity of an individual are limited, so that the quantity that he can produce is also limited; while money can be heaped up without limit. The larger the sum of money anyone uses as capital, the more the money can produce. But the reverse of the medal is not so pretty. Side by side with the possibility of accumulating a fortune there is that of becoming poor. This fact was not prominent at the entrance of capitalism into the field, when poverty was not yet a general phenomenon, but it increased more and more, so that at present we live in a society in which the greater part of the population is poor.

In the Middle Ages the trades were developed in Europe; the division of labor increased; tools were perfected; and commerce was developed, chiefly as a consequence of the improvement of the means of communication. The maritime route to India was discovered as well as the American continent. Enormous sums of money, acquired by means of commerce and pillage, flowed into Europe. With the discovery of these countries the outlets for trade correspondingly increased. The trades, however, not being in a position to furnish the great quantity of commodities required, the merchants determined themselves to undertake the wholesale production of articles intended exclusively for sale.

There was no lack of money to procure the raw materials and the tools, to establish workshops and to hire workmen. The only difficulty to be overcome was that of procuring these last. The workman who has in his own possession the means of production will not sell his labor. To attain their end the capitalists had to seek for persons who, having no means of production, were obliged to sell their productive energy or die of hunger.

For certain reasons it was possible for the needs of the capitalists to be satisfied. On account of the development of the market in the cities the demand for food, and for raw materials of every kind, such as wood, wool, etc., increased, and agricultural production for the purpose of sale increased, so that the peasants began to have money. This latter fact complicated the relation between them and the feudal lords. So long as the rent was paid in kind the lord demanded only as much as he could consume; but from the day that the rent began to be paid in money the landowner began to press the peasant more and more, since money can always be used, and no one ever has enough. From this fact arose so severe an exploitation that many peasants left the country to take refuge in the towns.

The second reason why a large number of workmen were obtainable was that the lords themselves began to produce commodities for city markets, especially wool and wood. This took fewer laborers than agriculture, but required more land, so that many peasants were driven from their farms and, like the others, went to swell the population of the cities.

Thus there was no further obstacle to wholesale production, and from then on raw materials were purchased, workshops established, and the labor of the proletariat procured. Human labor thus has become a commodity, corresponding exactly to definition: first, it has no use-value for the possessor if he has not the means of production, and, on the other hand, has such a value for the person possessing these means; second, the possessor of labor has the free disposition of it.

The contract is made; the proletariat on the one side furnishes the commodity — labor — and the capitalist on the other gives the equivalent of it. Now how much must be given for this commodity? In other words what is the value of the labor delivered? The value of a commodity is determined by the labor-time socially necessary for its production, in this case necessary for the proletarian and his family to live; for the workman being mortal, and capital having need of new forces, the wage must be sufficient to raise a new generation of workers. The standard of the workman's needs is subject to variation according to time and place (the causes of which variation we need not examine here), but it is fixed for a certain country, time, and category of workers.

Let us suppose now that the process of production has a normal course, that is to say, that it comes out as the capitalist wishes. He has begun with a sum, A, and ends by possessing $A + a$. We must now explain this surplus *a*, which, in the terminology of capitalistic production, is called *surplus-value*. The surplus obtained from the labor of slaves is easily explained. The owner leaves the slaves a part of the product of their own labor to live on. The rest is his. His surplus springs from the labor of others. The relation of the serf and his lord is, if possible, even clearer. The serf works part of the week for himself and on the remaining days for his master. The explanation of the surplus produced by capital employed at usury or in primitive commerce (the most ancient forms under which capital was employed) no longer offer any great difficulties. The usurer appropriated to himself the possessions of the borrower little by little and so ruined him completely. The primitive merchant made himself a surplus by selling dear something that he had bought at a trivial price, a transaction which involved no increase in value. Now it is just this increase in value that is to be explained upon the basis of the law that things of equal value are exchanged, and not, as in the cases cited above, upon the exceptions to the law.

If we represent the transaction of one who buys, not to make a profit, but to exchange something which has no use-value for him for something which has such a value (the simple circulation of commodities), by the formula $C - M - C$, in which C stands for commodities and M for money, we can represent the transaction of the capitalist by $M - C - (M + m)$. In this formula *m* stands for the surplus-value accruing to the capitalist at the end of a successful operation. The latter formula is composed of the factors $M - C$; the purchase of the commodity, and $C - (M + m)$, the sale. According to the law of the circulation of commodities the value of M ought to be equal to C, but C in turn must be equal to $M + m$, a thing which is possible only if C is a commodity which, while it is being consumed, produces a value greater than what it has. However, there is no value without labor; consequently the formula cited can harmonize with reality only if labor is itself a commodity. And, as we have seen above, it is such from the moment that the economic development has reached a certain point.

What is now the course of the production of the surplus-value? The capitalist has fitted up a factory, has procured tools and raw material, has hired labor, and the process of production commences. Suppose that the necessaries of life for the workman and his family may be produced by six hours of work socially necessary; by making him work, then, six hours the capitalist will have a product equal to that of the raw material used, increased by that which is given it by the tools and by the labor which the workman has put upon it. This value, however, has been entirely paid out by the capitalist; he has no surplus left; the transaction has failed. But ordinarily the process succeeds in procuring profits for the capitalist, since in the contract between him and the laborer it is not stipulated that the latter shall work only the number of hours necessary to produce enough for his own needs. On the contrary the workman is compelled to labor as long as his strength will permit. The value produced by the workman after the time necessary for the production of the equivalent of his needs falls to the capitalist, and this it is which constitutes the surplus-value, the value derived from work not paid for.

The aim of the capitalist is to procure for himself as large a surplus-value as possible. He can attain his end at once by forcing the laborer to work as long a time as it is possible for him to work. From this springs the irreconcilable conflict between the interests of the proletariat and those of capital, the combat over the length of the working-day. The day has its natural limits (it is necessary that certain hours be left to the workman for food and rest), its legal limits (decreed too late by the state, driven on one side by the workers themselves, and on the other by the plain certainty that without this protection the working class would become enfeebled), and finally its limits fixed by the pressure of the labor unions.

However, there is still one other way in which the surplus-value is increased, as I shall explain by what follows. Let us suppose the length of the working day to be twelve hours, and the time necessary for the production of the equivalent of the workman's needs to be six hours. We can then represent the day as follows:

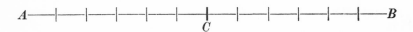

CB is consequently the time in which the surplus-value is produced. The aim of the capitalist, then, is to protract the period CB as much as possible, and this he can accomplish in two ways: first, that of which we have just spoken, the prolongation of AB; second, the shortening of AC in order that CB may be as long as possible, or in other words, the shortening of the time necessary for the production of the necessaries of life for the workman and his family. When the productivity of labor rises, the value of the commodities falls; and when the value of the commodities which the workman needs for his

support falls, the value of labor falls also. However, the increase of
the productivity of labor is only possible through the improvement of
the means of production and the methods of working, so that capitalism modifies its manner of production unceasingly. In general the
capitalist does not take account of the fact that the more cheaply
commodities are produced for sale, the more the value of labor falls,
and, other things being equal, the more the surplus-value increases.
The capitalist strives constantly to make improvements in his methods
of production in order to surpass his competitors. Supposing that,
by the employment of a new method of working, he succeeds in producing in half an hour an article up to that time generally made in an
hour, he will then obtain an extra profit as long as his competitors
do not employ this method. But as soon as the latter have improved
their production in the same way, the time socially necessary falls
from an hour to half an hour, and the extra profit of the man who
first introduced the method ceases. The result that remains is this:
the value of labor has decreased, and the relative surplus-value has
consequently increased, in so far as the commodities whose value has
declined are destined to provide for the needs of the workmen.

Before entering upon the consideration of some of the methods for
shortening the necessary hours of labor, attention must be fixed upon
the fact that, aside from this method, the capitalist tries above all
to lower the price of labor below its value, while the workers, for
their part, oppose this tendency and try to obtain the contrary;
whence there results a new cause for an inexorable struggle between
labor and capital, side by side with that over the length of the working-day.

Let us now examine the methods of abridging the labor-time necessary, beginning with coöperation. As we have seen above the capitalistic method of production begins when the capitalist has in his service
a sufficiently large number of workmen. In the days of the guilds
the master had also paid workers, but the surplus-value which he
procured from them was not great, since their number was small, a
fact which obliged him to work with them, since without this his
income would have been too small. The true capitalist is he who is
permitted by the amount of the surplus-value which he receives to live
according to his rank, without working with his laborers, reserving
to himself only the direction of affairs.

The difference, therefore, between capitalistic production and that
at the time of the guilds is in the first place only quantitative, but
there come in qualitative differences as well. In the first place the

differences in the individual capacities of the workmen disappear; the ability of one neutralizes the smaller ability of the other, so that the capitalist can count upon an average amount of labor. Next there is economy in the new arrangement; because a structure to hold twenty-five workmen working together costs less than twenty-five structures with one workman in each. Finally, and most important of all, by having a number of men working together, each doing his own share toward the common end, we bring about a systematic working together, that is to say, coöperation, which brings into being a new collective force greater than the sum of the individual forces. Not only does coöperation permit the accomplishment of work requiring a greater expenditure of energy, but it also raises the productivity of labor. The direction necessary for this joint labor falls to the capitalist as such. Submission of the workman to the capitalist is, then, an indispensable condition of the capitalistic method of production.

We come now to another method for increasing the relative amount of the surplus-value, the manufactory proper, a more developed form of coöperation, which became general between the middle of the sixteenth century and the end of the eighteenth. This comes from two causes. On the one side it is due to the combination of different trades, up to that point independent of each other. The manufacture of a carriage, for example, requires the work of a wheelwright, a harness-maker, a painter, etc., who all exercise their trades independently of each other. The capitalist unites them all in one trade, that of carriage-maker, in which the occupation of each becomes more limited, more specialized. The painter, for example, becomes especially a painter of carriages. On the other side the manufactory is due to the bringing together of workmen of the same trade into a single workshop, and to the division of labor made possible in this way. Thus, for instance, in the manufacture of pins, each pin is no longer made by a single workman but by several, each of whom does only a special part of the work.

It is clear that through the introduction of manufactory methods the productivity of labor has been enormously increased, so that the time necessary for the production of the necessaries of life for the workmen has become shorter, and the surplus-value correspondingly augmented. The part taken by the workman in the process of production is quite different from what it was in the time of the guilds. The different operations that he performed in making the complete product are now replaced by the monotonous and repeated production of a single one of the parts. From this point dates the division of workmen into skilled and unskilled laborers. The latter are those whose work is such as to require little or no apprenticeship, and they are the cause of a new lowering of the price of labor.

We have still to take up the question of the introduction of machinery and of manufacturing on a large scale. Although at the period of the early manufactories the workman was obliged to perform a monotonous task, which in so far may be called "mechanical", yet this task was performed, though with the aid of tools, by his own hands. But in the eighteenth century the machine was invented, that is to say, a mechanism which took the place both of the workman and of his tools. Machines were introduced because they saved hand-work, and consequently lowered the price of the product and relatively increased the surplus-value.

Each developed mechanism is composed of three parts : the motor, the transmission, and the operating part. It is to the development of this last that the economic revolution of the eighteenth century is due. However, there was needed a motive power greater and more regular than those then available. The steam-engine, invented by James Watt, provided for this need and, in its turn, led to new developments of operating machinery. The steam-engine was capable of running many operating machines at the same time, and thus the modern factory was established. In branches in which the product requires a series of different manipulations, a system of machines has been contrived of which one furnishes the material to the next without the intervention of hands, so that a system of automatic mechanism has been produced.

The revolution caused by the introduction of machines in one branch of industry necessitated its introduction into another, etc. The means of communication and of transportation were extended. The steamboat, the railroad, and the telegraph were invented. Because of important inventions in the manufacture of machines it finally became possible to produce the necessary quantity of machines of all kinds.

What are the most important consequences of the new system of production ? In the first place stands the introduction of the labor of women and children, since tending machines generally does not require great muscular strength. The advantages which accrue to the capitalist from the employment of women and children are obvious. Since the price of the workman's labor is determined by the time necessary for the production of the necessities of life not only for himself, but also for his family, as soon as the whole family are compelled to sell their labor, the price of that labor will simply equal that of the labor of the workman alone. Ordinarily the income of the family will rise a little under these circumstances, but, because of the absence of the wife from the household, expenses will increase also. The increase of the surplus-value, obtained by the labor of women and children, is therefore important. Besides, the women and children have less power to resist the capitalist than men have, while the men, in their turn, are weakened by the competition of women and children.

In the second place the introduction of machines produces in the mind of the capitalist a desire to prolong the working day as much as possible, for the following reasons among others. The greater the number of hours each day in which the machine is in operation, the more quickly it will return its cost through the product, and, other things being equal, the shorter will be the time required for the capitalist to gain the same amount of surplus-value. Suppose A works his machines for 8 hours a day, and B works as many machines for 16 hours; B's machines will return their cost through the product in half the time needed by A's. Consequently B will gain double the surplus-value in the same time, so that A also will be driven to work his machines for 16 hours. And since a machine deteriorates even when it is not in use, there is, when the machines are stopped, a loss of value which the capitalist cannot retrieve. Hence the tendency to prolong the working-day. In the third place every capitalist runs the danger of seeing his competitors introduce new machines which save still more work and so diminish the value of his own. The more quickly a machine returns its cost, the less the danger just mentioned becomes.

Finally, I have still to notice the following cause for the prolongation of the working-day. The object of the employment of machines is the increase of the surplus-value through their use. This increase, however, is possible only through the diminution in the number of workmen employed by the capitalist. But since the surplus-value is created only by the workmen, any diminution in their number is to the disadvantage of the capitalist. In order to overcome this he attempts to prolong the day.

The more machinery is developed, the more the attention which the workman must give to his work increases; in other words, the more intense the labor becomes. The tendency of the capitalist to increase the intensity of labor reaches its apogee as soon as the working time is limited, for different reasons. In order that the surplus-value may be equal to what it was formerly, the workman, for example, must produce as much in eleven hours as he formerly produced in thirteen hours. The means by which the intensity of labor is increased (not to enter into unnecessary details) are; first, the manner of fixing wages — piece-work, and second, the practice of making the workmen tend more machines than formerly, and of driving the machines faster, so as to force the workmen to a greater intensity of labor.

The contest between the large manufacturing establishments and the small factories and workshops has led gradually but infallibly to the destruction of the latter. They are forced to maintain the competitive struggle by incredibly long hours of labor, by an unlimited exploitation of the labor of women and children, etc. In this way it is often possible to resist competition for some time, but finally the large manufactory triumphs all along the line.

Agriculture also, though to a less degree than manufacturing, has been revolutionized by the introduction of machines. Rural workers who have become superfluous have betaken themselves to the cities, and there go to swell the population already enormously increased by industrialism.

The exposition which I have just given of the origin of the surplus-value is sufficient for this work. It is not necessary for our subject to stop to consider the fact that a part of the surplus-value is destined to become capital, while the other part is consumed by those who have appropriated the whole. As has been shown above, the employment of machines, etc., has increased in every branch of industry, and this has brought it about that the capital necessary to any manufacturing establishment increases continually under the pressure of competition. Hence it follows that capitalism itself forces the capitalist to invest as new capital part of the surplus-value acquired by him. But aside from this, it is capitalism also that produces the capitalist's penchant for always investing more capital, which, in its turn, produces a greater surplus-value than the original capital, etc. And since the accumulation of capital has no limits, the greediness of the capitalist has none, and he is driven to increase his capital incessantly, even when his income is so great that it permits him to satisfy every possible need.

However, the group of capitalists of which we have been speaking is not the only one that gains surplus-value. Industrial capital is obliged to share the total surplus-value with commercial capital, the capital consisting of money, and that consisting of real estate. In the first place, a part of the surplus-value is claimed by commercial capital. For the economic system in force would not be able to operate without commerce. The development of capitalism has led to an extensive division of labor in the class of capitalists (banks, insurance companies, etc.), and the capital invested in these enterprises must equally have its share of the total surplus-value. Capital in the form of money plays an increasingly important part in modern capitalism, and so must have its share of the surplus-value.

The owners of the soil also appropriate a considerable part. The land is the most indispensable means of production, and is incapable of being increased at will. As capitalism increases, the demand for territory becomes greater and greater. This causes the ground rents in general to rise, which means that the share of the total surplus-value which the land-owners appropriate becomes greater and greater. It is especially in the cities, which are highly developed under capitalism, and in which, consequently, the demand for land is great and the supply relatively small, that ground rents have risen to an unheard of degree, and this to the prejudice of the health and happiness of the less privileged classes.

Up to this point we have been necessarily supposing that the capitalist succeeds in making a profit. But, as we know, it often happens that he does not attain his end, that his capital produces no added value, that he even loses it entirely or in part. This case being important for the subject in hand we must stop to consider it for a moment. As has been shown above, the capitalist begins by purchasing labor and the means of production in order to set in motion the process of production. For him the difficulty then consists of selling the manufactured product at its value and of thus realizing the added value which is a part of this. At times, aided by circumstances, he succeeds in selling the product above its value, and so makes an extra profit. On the other hand, he runs the risk of having to sell the product below its value, or of not being able to sell it at all.

The causes of the poor success of the process are of different kinds. In the first place, the capitalist may not have the ability necessary for the direction of the process of production. For example, the product made under his management may be inferior to that of his competitor, though the cost of production is the same; the means of production may be purchased at too high a price; he may not have been in touch with the tastes of consumers, etc.; reasons all of which render his product unsalable, or salable at a loss.

In the second place, circumstances independent of his own act may present themselves which have the same result. Let us look at some of them. To begin with, the unforeseen cessation of payment on the part of one of his important debtors may oblige him to sell his goods at a sacrifice in order to satisfy his creditors. Again, he may lack the capital necessary to meet competition. For the amount of capital necessary in every branch of industry or commerce becomes greater and greater, and the man who cannot procure this capital is forced little by little to give ground to his competitors and finally to give up business altogether.

In the third place, it very often happens that, as a result of competition, there is an oversupply of commodities, which from this very fact are unsalable, or must be sold for less than their value. In the periods of prosperity this case is not general. But it is the rule in crises. Because of their great importance to the relation between criminality and economic conditions, it is necessary to pause here to examine the cause and origin of these crises.

Economic crises, that is to say periods in which the economic life is greatly disturbed, are due to various circumstances; for example, to a war which puts obstacles in the way of the regular continuance of international commerce. But aside from such causes there are others which are natural to the present economic system itself, and which bring on these crises periodically. It is these causes, which are the more important, of which it is necessary to treat here.

A crisis is the result of overproduction. This does not imply that in every case overproduction will bring about a crisis. If one who is producing for his own consumption happens to produce more than he can consume, the result will be that during a certain period he will proceed to produce less, and the equilibrium will be reëstablished. But when one manufactures not for himself but for the market the situation is entirely different. Each manufacturer of commodities produces separately, that is to say without any understanding with his fellow-manufacturers, articles of which he himself has no need, but which he attempts to exchange for money in order to obtain what he does need. If he does not succeed in selling his commodities he is left without money to buy the commodities that are necessary to him. Overproduction can thus have very harmful results for those who hold commodities.

Now how does it happen that the capitalistic mode of production causes periodically a production greater than the possible consumption? (It goes without saying that this phrase is not to be taken to mean that the consumers are physically incapable of using the product, but merely that there are not enough buyers.) As has been shown above, capitalistic production is carried on for the sake of the added value, that is to say, the value of the unpaid labor. In other words, the working class produces more than it consumes. In feudal society the surplus was entirely consumed by the class which appropriated it; at present, on the contrary, the owning class use part of the surplus to form new capital. For this comes a continually increasing accumulation of capital, and consequently a greater and greater quantity of products which in the end find no buyer. For the extension of production increases the number of workmen necessary, and consequently increases the demand also, but these workmen produce in their turn more than they consume. The overproduction is not, then, neutralized by a greater consumption. On the contrary it furnishes the material for an overproduction still greater. Hence capitalism causes crises periodically as the result of an overproduction caused by too small a consumption on the part of the working class.

Since the mass of capital increases without cessation it is indispensable to find new investments, and to broaden the market. From this it results, among other things, that the capitalist class is forced to take up the policy of political expansion and to conquer countries where capitalism has not yet become rooted. If it succeeds in finding a new outlet, then, production increases enormously, existing factories are enlarged, new ones are established, etc., and the new market is inundated with goods. But in the end this market ceases to be able to absorb the continually increasing mass of products, so much the more since the production of the country itself also increases as capitalism gains foothold there. The commodities remain, then, unsold, and a crisis is begun. Production must be stopped or decreased; the stock of commodities being thus made smaller the equilibrium begins little by little to reëstablish itself; after which the movement is repeated. But since the capitalistic method of production little by little spreads itself over the whole earth, it becomes increasingly difficult to find countries where capitalism has not been implanted. Hence overproduction tends to become chronic.

Besides the cause already set forth there is still another circumstance which can produce a crisis or aggravate one already existing; I refer to the lack of order in the present mode of production. Suppose that the demand for iron is great at any given moment. The production will then increase so quickly, and in such a degree (each manufacturer ignoring what his competitors are doing), that the supply will far exceed the demand. As a result manufacturing will be checked. As soon as overproduction occurs in as important a branch of industry as the manufacture of iron, there will follow also a stoppage of production in other branches, and a general crisis will ensue.

The consequences of a crisis for the capitalist class are well known. Many are forced to stop producing, are no longer able to pay their creditors, and draw many of their debtors in their train. Because of the complexity of the present system of production the consequences of a crisis are very far reaching. It is naturally the small capitalists who are stricken first, whence it follows that during crises there is a great concentration of capital.

Just as in the first part of this discussion I proceeded on the assumption that the capitalist always attains his end, *i.e.* gains the surplus-value, just so I have also been speaking as if the workman always sold his labor. Let us look now at the case of the man who does not succeed in selling it. In order that a contract be entered into between capitalist and workman it is necessary that labor be desired and offered. If the workman for his part cannot deliver the labor contracted for, or not enough of it, whether from sickness or from weakness, it is perhaps but a question of exchange, and the workman is abandoned to his fate. Capitalism rests upon this fact that there is a class of men, much more numerous than any other, who are deprived of everything and consequently are forced to sell their labor; otherwise no workman would care to close a contract.

Let us look at the other side of the question, when the supply of labor exceeds the demand. Those who do not succeed in selling their labor are then equally abandoned to their own resources. From what causes in the capitalistic method of production does it happen that the supply of labor is in excess of the demand? Are these causes to be found in too great an increase in the population, or in the method of production itself?

It has been shown above that the composition of capital changes incessantly. Machinery becomes more and more developed and a great part of capital is composed of machines. The introduction of machines has taken place because they economize labor. Thus a certain number of workmen find themselves without occupation. It is true that there is a mitigating circumstance, namely that there is an increased demand for labor in other branches (manufacture of machines), but this demand can never be as great as the amount of labor rendered superfluous by machinery, for otherwise machines would never have been introduced. However short the apprenticeship required by modern industry, it is nevertheless impossible for a

workman to change from one branch to another at short notice. Thus
the consequences for workmen thrown out of employment continue
to be serious notwithstanding the increased demand in another branch.
The only case in which the introduction of machines will occasion no
unemployment will be when the demand for commodities increases
extraordinarily, as, for example, when a new market is opened up.

However there are still other causes of forced unemployment.
Such are the introduction of the labor of women and children, the
migration of rural workers to the cities, immigration from backward
countries, and the supplanting of small businesses, by which members
of the lower middle class are forced down into the proletariat.

The causes of overpopulation are found, then, in the system of production itself, and not in a too great increase of the population; a
conclusion to be drawn also from the fact that as far as actual productivity of labor is concerned each produces more than enough for his
needs. There are, then, always a number of persons who desire to
work but cannot find employment. In periods of crisis the number of
these increases enormously. The so-called "reserve army of labor"
is a condition indispensable to capitalism. Without it sudden development in periods of prosperity would be impossible. Without it
also the power of organized labor would become so great that the
surplus-value would run serious danger. It is just because the supply
of labor exceeds the demand that the power of the capitalists over
the workmen is so great, and also that it happens so often that the
interests of the workmen are thwarted.

We come now to the end of my exposition. For our subject it is
unnecessary to continue it further. I should like, however, to draw
attention to two more points. The continually increasing concentration of capital has as a consequence that the conduct of the business
under the direction of the capitalist himself more and more gives
place to the stock company, which combines the capital of numerous
persons, and gives the direction to a salaried employe. Following
this, concentration drives the owners in one branch of industry to
combine for the purpose of eliminating competition, and thus of
increasing profits; in this way the "trusts" come into being. Competition, the fundamental principle of capitalism, is changed into its
opposite, monopoly.

CHAPTER II.

SOCIAL CONDITION OF THE DIFFERENT CLASSES.

LET us pass now to the social condition in which the different social classes live in consequence of the place they occupy in the economic system.

A. THE BOURGEOISIE.

After a long and difficult struggle against feudalism the bourgeoisie, the class possessing the means of production, came out victorious. It has grown and become more powerful, and in almost all the countries where capitalism exists it is still the directing class.

The bourgeoisie is divided into three groups. The first comprises the capitalists who direct their business themselves. As has been shown in the preceding pages the power of this group is based upon its monopolizing the surplus-value. The idea which predominates among the bourgeoisie in general, and particularly among the first group, is to gain money, always more money. This thirst for gold is not quenched when the man has arrived at a point where he can live a luxurious life and gratify all his caprices. Thanks to capitalism it is possible to amass wealth without limit, so that the capitalist is never satisfied, however enormous may be the sums which he has gained. The consequence is that in general he is little developed in other directions, uses all his time in attaining the end he wishes for, has a mind only superficially cultivated, and if he is interested in art he regards it simply as a pastime which he procures for money.

Next to this group comes that of the persons whose sole occupation consists in appropriating a part of the surplus-value to increase their capital and in spending the rest for a luxurious life. It is unnecessary to set forth here the regrettable consequences of idleness and too easy a life. Doubtless there are in this group some persons who work and do not squander their income. But the fact remains that the present economic system produces a class who are not forced to work and can dissipate what others produce. The luxury displayed by the bourgeoisie has injurious consequences for the whole population. Not only do many persons aid this class in spending a part of the surplus-value, but further, as a consequence of the uninterrupted increase of luxury among the bourgeoisie (the result of the continued increase in the surplus-value), desire becomes so much the greater among the other classes as they have the less possibility of satisfying it.

The development of capitalism (the growth of stock companies) is the reason why the above-mentioned group of capitalists increases in comparison with the first group. The control of affairs is more and more abandoned to salaried employes. With these we come to the third and last group; the so-called liberal professions, in which men provide for their needs by intellectual labor. They are not capitalists in the strict sense of the term, for they live by selling their labor; but as they are recruited principally from the bourgeoisie, and in general have nearly the same standard of living as the bourgeoisie, it will be best to treat them here. Under the capitalistic system those who cultivate science or the arts are obliged to sell their products. There was a time when their number being limited their products brought a high price. However the development of capitalism has been the cause of a continually increasing demand for these persons. The task of the state and municipality becoming constantly greater requires an increasing number of functionaries; the larger application of science to industry demands more engineers, chemists, etc.; the multiplication of stock companies puts the direction of affairs more and more into the hands of salaried employes; etc., etc.

The extension of university education produced a greater supply, and this occasioned a considerable fall in the price of the commodity. In the end the supply began to exceed the demand; in this territory also there is an overproduction. Thence it happens that the price of this commodity often falls below its value, and thus a sort of scientific proletariat is formed. Just as the merchant on account of overproduction in his branch can dispose of his goods only by taking advantage of every possible method, so men of the liberal professions must at times have recourse to similar means if they wish to attain a great success or even to support themselves.

Although I speak of these persons under the head of "bourgeoisie" this is not an exact classification. Not only does their material condition sometimes differ from that of the bourgeoisie, but in other regards they cannot be treated under the same head. Many of them are descendants of those who have practiced the same profession; others have come from among the bourgeoisie proper, and have chosen the profession in question from inclination and natural disposition. These circumstances as well as the influence of the profession itself bring it about that for the last group the gaining of money is not the principal end as with the first, but that other motives also impel them.

In the next place we must fix our attention upon a matter which concerns the entire body of the bourgeoisie : the uncertainty of the future, for no one, not even the richest, is sure of it. In the exposition of the economic system which we have been considering the principal causes of this state of things have been indicated; it is therefore useless to go over the details again. It is not only those who lack capital or the ability to direct an enterprise, whose position is uncertain. A manufacturer can be ruined by an invention which makes his product unsalable; an unforeseen fall in price may have the same effect upon a merchant; etc., etc. This uncertainty reaches its height during crises, and, as a consequence of the complexity of economic life at present, the fall of one has disastrous consequences for those who have relations with him. From this it happens that to the agitation and weakness which are the consequences of competition, is added the fear of losing one's position.

The cause of this fear is obvious. The capitalist who is ruined, and the stock-holder whose securities become valueless, see themselves thereby deprived of everything that makes life worth living, power, luxury, importance, etc., while the possibility of recovery without capital seems very small. This is especially true of the first two groups of the bourgeoisie. Nevertheless the position of the liberal professions is not very stable, though it is somewhat more so than that of the other groups.

Whence does the bourgeoisie recruit itself? In great part from the descendants of the bourgeoisie, in a less degree from the other classes. If a "petit-bourgeois" or a proletarian finds himself incorporated into the ranks of the bourgeoisie it is by virtue of extraordinary circumstances. They may reach this station because they have qualities which especially fit them to direct capitalistic enterprises; but in this case circumstances must arise to bring their capacity to light and give them a chance to develop it.

Although a relatively small number succeed in passing from another class to that of the bourgeoisie, this does not prevent nearly all from having an ardent desire to enrich themselves and from seizing every opportunity which may help them attain this end. (The only exception is found in those workers who understand that the historic task of the working class is to found a society where there shall be neither rich nor poor.) A man will often start a factory or a shop without having either capital or ability, in the hope of raising himself in the social scale; and unless the circumstances are extraordinarily favorable failure follows almost immediately. This applies also quite as strongly to the capitalists who for one reason or another have failed in business; they try to gain success in another branch at any cost, even if capital and ability are lacking. But such a course can only retard their fall, and they end infallibly by sinking permanently to the rank of the proletarian.

What I have just been saying brings out strongly the character of the present process of production. Production is not undertaken for the sake of consumption, but for profit, so that the man who believes that he has a good chance to improve his condition goes to work to produce, without asking himself whether there is need of his products, or whether he can meet the required conditions.

As to the relation of the bourgeoisie, as a class, to other classes, and especially to the proletariat, a few words will suffice after the exposition I have given of present economic conditions. "In every nation there are two nations." These words describe the relations in question. From their mode of life the bourgeoisie and the proletariat remain strangers to one another.[1] The bourgeoisie, having arrived at a wrong idea of the present system, do not consider the proletariat as the class which sustains society by its toil, but as a necessary evil. According to the bourgeois every strike is a diminution of his rights, an encroachment upon his property. In the political field the bourgeoisie, notwithstanding its intrinsic divisions, acts as a unit against the proletarians; a fact which does not prevent there being opposing interests within the class : in the first place the contest of the different groups of capitalists (manufacturers against agrarians, etc.) and then the opposing interests of the manufacturers within each group.

---

[1] In his work " The Condition of the Working-class in England ", *F. Engels*, after speaking of the condition of the English proletariat, says, " The working-class has gradually become a race wholly apart from the English bourgeoisie. The bourgeoisie has more in common with every other nation of the earth than with the workers in whose midst it lives. The workers speak other dialects, have other thoughts and ideals, other customs and moral principles, a different religion, and other politics than the bourgeoisie. They are two radically dissimilar nations." (P. 124. [In original, p. 127].)

B. The Petty Bourgeoisie.

In reality the line of demarcation between the bourgeoisie and the petty bourgeoisie is not drawn with the precision desirable for a theoretical exposition. Just as there are numerous gradations in the bourgeoisie, so are there in the petty bourgeoisie.

It is the petty bourgeoisie which has among its different classes the most ancient traditions. There was a time when it was strong and powerful. But the development of capitalism has changed all that. Industrialism has arisen and undermined the petty bourgeoisie. In the combat the small capitalist must eventually go down. He has not, like his adversaries, scientific forces at his disposal, has no great credit, cannot, in consequence of the insufficiency of his capital, make use of new inventions; in short, his arms are inferior to those of his antagonists. All this does not make him renounce the contest at once; on the contrary, it arouses him to bring all his forces into play. In consequence of his position in the economic life he has no breadth of view. He cannot comprehend that what earned bread for his ancestors during so many years will some day fail. This is the reason that, as soon as large capital enters into the competition, the small manufacturer overdrives himself, and not only himself but his workmen also, and further, attempts to lower wages, lengthen the working day, and introduce women and children to take the place of men. Competition forces the merchant to take advantage of his customers in all sorts of ways, a fact which gives commerce its character; for the art of commerce is to buy cheap and sell dear. Hence there is opposition between the merchant and the manufacturer on the one hand, and between merchant and customer on the other. This is why the merchant is led to depreciate the article he buys, and to praise that which he is selling. This tendency naturally becomes stronger as competition becomes fiercer. Advertising, a system of deceit, is invented to draw purchasers at any cost; and the point is even reached where men no longer give exact weight ("My competitors do not give it," says the merchant to himself), and sell goods of poorer quality than represented. This is why commerce has a moral code of its own.

However, notwithstanding their desperate resistance, the situation of the petty bourgeoisie becomes worse and worse, and this has important social consequences, for example, the increase of the labor of women outside of their own homes. Whole groups of the petty bourgeoisie are so fallen into decadence that the plane of their existence has become the same as that of the proletariat, or has even fallen below it. Finally the contest with the large capitalist means not simply degradation to the petty bourgeois, but absolute ruin. When a crisis comes the small capitalists are the first to feel the shock. Their ruin may come in various ways; their business may be annihilated altogether — in which case they are permanently reduced to the ranks of the proletariat — or it may become dependent upon great capital under the name of home industry, *i.e.* wage labor masked under the appearance of independence. Only those who have been able to save a part of their capital from the wreck can try fortune once more in another branch of industry where great capital has not yet begun to compete, but they are sure to be pursued and finally overtaken by their enemy.

As in the case of the bourgeoisie, the relations which the different members of the petty bourgeoisie have among themselves are determined by the economic system; fierce competition, life in a little circle where ideas cannot be broadened, all this breeds envy, hatred, and meanness.[1]

As to intellectual culture a great part of the petty bourgeoisie takes rank between the bourgeoisie and the proletariat. Generally the children of this class are better taught than those of the proletariat. But since the field of their ideas is very restricted and the struggle for existence requires all their time, their intellectual level remains in general much below the average level of the bourgeoisie. Others still who are of the lowest stratum of the petty bourgeoisie have the same development as the proletariat.

The petty bourgeoisie is recruited from the descendants of the same class, then from among the bourgeois who have failed in business, and finally from former proletarians. These last are those who cannot sell their labor for some reason, and try to gain a livelihood by making an insignificant capital of value in trading. Their plane of living does not differ from that of the proletariat unless by being lower.

As to the relation of the petty bourgeoisie to the other classes, it is naturally hostile to the bourgeoisie, since it is that class which has deprived it, or is still depriving it, of its influence. This hostility is, however, of a different kind from that which the working class feels toward the bourgeoisie. The petty bourgeoisie envies the bourgeoisie; it desires also to become rich, and thereby powerful.

---

[1] Upon the petty bourgeoisie see the excellent article of Dr. *N. Schönlank*, "Zur Psychologie des Kleinbürgerthums" ("Neue Zeit", 1890).

On the other hand it feels no community of interest with the working class, whose fixed determination to be free from the wage system it holds in abhorrence.   The political position of the petty bourgeoisie, placed as it is between the bourgeoisie and the proletariat, has necessarily become an equivocal one.

C. The Proletariat.

The proletariat, that class of persons who do not possess the means of production and who can exist only by the sale of their labor, dates from modern times.   Between the independent artisan and the modern proletarian comes the journeyman as a link in the chain.   The difference, however, between the journeyman and the proletarian is great.   The journeyman generally lodged with his master, worked with him, and was considered as a member of the family.   And since the means of production necessary were still quite limited, the journeyman by saving his wages had a chance some day to become master. With this hope he came to consider himself as having common interests with his employer.

The situation of the proletarian is entirely different.   His work is entirely separate from that of his employer; the lengthening of the working-day does not imply that the capitalist works longer also.   The workman lodges apart, and it makes little difference to the employer how his employes are housed and fed.   The means of production being very dear, and the knowledge necessary to direct any business being lacking, the proletarian can almost never become an employer.

As has been shown it is the ruined members of the petty bourgeoisie who have formed the first stock of the proletariat.   But although this class is still reinforced in the same way the greatest part of the proletariat is now composed of the descendants of proletarians.

We can easily comprehend the situation of the proletariat provided we do not lose sight of the basis of the present economic system, that is, the fact that the object of production is to gain for some the largest possible surplus-value at the expense of the rest of the population.   The child of the proletarian is set to work at an age when the child of the bourgeois parents is still leading a care-free life, with nothing to do but to develop his powers.   When taken to the factory the young proletarian finds himself in the midst of ignorant and coarse men caring nothing for him, and soon picks up their bad habits.   It is in this environment that the proletarian will pass the greatest part of his life without hope of ever raising himself above it.

The greater part of the trades practiced have an unfavorable effect, frequently even very harmful to the health of the workmen (on account of great heat, too much dust, injurious gases, etc.) These prejudicial influences might be checked or prevented, but it costs money to make a factory sanitary, with no immediate return, and hygienic suggestions are therefore generally not followed. A number of trades constantly threaten the workers with death or mutilation; but although safety devices can almost always remove the danger, for the reason above stated they are still many times left untried.

As regards the length of the working-day; moderate work is a pleasure, excessive work mere torment. Except in so far as the laws and the labor unions have intervened, the day has been prolonged until there is left only the time absolutely necessary for food and sleep. Many workmen are not even given the night for sleeping, for in many factories the night force succeeds that on duty in the daytime. We may read in the holy Scriptures that a day has been set aside for rest, but this does not prevent Sunday from being a day of work under the capitalistic system, even though we are supposed to be living in a Christian society.

In general the work in factories is very monotonous, and hence brutalizing; and further, fatiguing from its great intensity. Moreover a vexatious discipline is sometimes maintained. However harmful may be the results of factory labor upon the physical, intellectual, and moral condition of the worker, they are less so than the results of sweat-shop labor. For sweat-shop hours are still longer than those of the factory; and the work is done in a place which is both kitchen and bedroom, so that not only is the workman injured but his family as well.

Let us now take up the question of wages. It is necessary that the wage should be enough to procure what is strictly needful, and in fact wages generally do not rise above this standard. Further the workman buys at a high price goods of low quality, for he who cannot spend much is powerless in dealing with the producers. Since the workman does not draw his wages till he has done the work, he must get credit for the necessaries of life (often being obliged to add to his debts on account of sickness or unemployment). His wages prevent his paying his debts, and force him, therefore to continue to trade with his creditor, who cheats him at every turn. Again, in some branches of industry he is obliged to buy what he wants from the capitalist, or from the foreman (truck-system), or to live in a house which belongs to the capitalist (cottage system) — and then gets poorer quality at a higher price than elsewhere.

Let us take up next the dwellings of the proletariat.   Capitalism is the cause of a great congestion of persons in a limited area.   An enormous rise in the price of land in the cities and consequently a similar rise in rents have been the result.   No class spends a larger part of its income in rent than the laboring class.   The proletariat is not only lodged expensively but badly.   All those who pass through the laborers' districts know the monotonous rows of houses, ill-built, uniform and simple.   But the internal arrangement of these buildings is much more miserable ; the stairs and landings are narrow, the rooms small, badly lighted and ventilated, and often must serve for kitchen and bedroom combined.   But notwithstanding the limited space, the number of inmates often is further increased by taking lodgers, in an attempt to make both ends meet.   For all these reasons the house of the working-man is not a real home in which he can be at ease.

As if these consequences of capitalism were not serious enough, the labor of married women is added.   By this the life of the family, already damaged in so many ways, has been destroyed.   Furthermore the physical effect upon the woman, and even more upon the child with which she is pregnant, is most prejudicial, without reckoning that her moral condition suffers equally.

Up to this point I have been speaking of the proletarian on the supposition that he has been able to sell his labor-power.   But, as we have seen already, when this sale is not possible, he and his family are left to their fate.   This then is what freedom of labor means, a freedom that the slave never knows, freedom to die of hunger.   No one guarantees to the workman or his family the means of subsistence if, for any reason, he is not able to sell his labor.   The slave-owner had an interest in taking care of a sick slave, for the slave represented value which he did not care to see diminished.   But if a workman is sick he is discharged and replaced by another.   The sickness and death of the laborer do not harm the capitalist at all.

I have set forth above the numerous causes which prevent the workman from selling his labor.   Forced idleness has become chronic little by little, reaching its acute stage in times of crisis.   Then seasonal trades make the work of thousands dependent upon the weather. Aside from general causes, which affect whole groups, there are also individual causes.   A workman displeases his employer, it may be because he is one of the leaders of a union, or for some other reason ;

he is discharged, and runs, especially in times of economic depression, the risk of not being able to find employment elsewhere. If the worker falls ill or is injured (this often happens as a consequence of an unhealthful or dangerous trade), or when he reaches old age (and hard work ages men quickly), he is condemned. If the period of idleness lasts long the workman loses his ability and the habit of working (for working is above all a habit), and the time is not far distant when he will become altogether incapable of working.

The intellectual condition of the working class is easily understood. In his youth the child learns but little. The circle of his ideas remains restricted, since his parents have ordinarily neither the knowledge, the opportunity, nor the desire to supplement the little that is learnt at school. At the age when the child begins to think for himself, and his aptitudes begin to manifest themselves, he is put to work. The little that the proletarian has learned in his childhood is quickly forgotten under the pressure of the long, monotonous toil, which dulls his intelligence and makes him thus less sensitive to higher impressions. Even if this were not the case, the long duration of labor fatigues the workman too much, his domestic life does not permit him to develop himself, and further he has no money for intellectual pleasures. The pleasures of the workman belong to his kind of life. Consequently his amusements are rough and coarse. Alcohol and sexual intercourse are often the only pleasures he knows.[1]

The life of the working-man is less retired than that of the bourgeois. He sees continually the misery of his companions, which is also his own, he feels himself more at one with them, but the demand for labor always remaining below the supply, competition among the workers arouses antagonistic feeling among them. The possibility of some day becoming rich being almost entirely cut out, the working-man is less avaricious than the bourgeois, and less economical; he lives from day to day, and if he happens to get a little more than usual at any time he spends it at once.

The situation may be summed up as follows: under the capitalistic system the greater part of the population, the part upon whose labor the entire social fabric is based, lives under the most miserable conditions. The proletariat is badly clothed, badly fed, miserably housed, exhausted by excessive and often deleterious labor, uncertain as to income, and ignorant and coarse.[2]

---

[1] Alcoholism being of great importance for criminality I shall treat the etiology of this social phenomenon separately (see Chap. IV).

[2] It is plain that I cannot cite proofs in support of this exposition; I should go beyond the proper limits of this discussion of the present economic

However, the sketch given above shows only one side of the question. At length the workers have perceived that the interests of the employer are opposed to their own, that the cause of their poverty lies in his luxury. They have begun to set up opposition when they learn that by organizing themselves into labor unions they gain a power by which they can ameliorate their lot. The work no longer being done separately as in the time of the guilds, but together, there has been this consequence for the workmen, that being now in the same position with regard to the capitalist, and in the same social condition, they have gained in the feeling of solidarity and in disci-

system and its consequences. Furthermore it would be useless; for those of my readers who do not know from having seen it that the situation is as I have stated, can be convinced by reading the rich literature upon the subject. I will refer here only to the more noteworthy books; For England: *F. Engels*, "The Condition of the Working-Class in England" (1845); *K. Marx*, "Das Kapital" (1867); *M. Schippel*, "Das moderne Elend und die moderne Ueberbevölkerung" (1888); *Chas. Booth*, "Life and Labor of the People in London" (1892–1897); *R. Blatchford*, "Merrie England" (1894), and "Dismal England" (1901); *B. S. Rowntree*, "Poverty, A Study of Town Life" (1901). For Germany: Dr. *H. Lux*, "Sozial-politisches Handbuch" (1889); *P. Göhre*, "Drei Monate Fabriksarbeiter" (1891); Dr. *R. Hirschberg*, "Soziale Lage der arbeitenden Klasse in Berlin" (1897); *H. Herkner*, "Die Arbeitsfrage" (1894), treating also of Austria and Switzerland. For Austria: *T. W. Teifen*, "Das soziale Elend und die besitzenden Klassen" (1894). For Holland: "Rapport der Commissie belast met het onderzoek naar den toestand der kinderen in fabrieken arbeidende" (1872); "Enquête betreffende werking en uitbreiding der wet van 19 September 1874 en naar den toestand van fabrieken en werkplaatsen" (1887); "Enquête gehouden door de staatscommissie benoemd volgens de wet van 19 Jan. 1890" (1890–1894); "Een vergeten hoofdstuk" (1898); *H. Roland-Holst*, "Kapitaal en arbeid in Nederland" (1902).

Upon the conditions of women's work see: *L. Braun*, "Die Frauenfrage." Upon the housing of working-men in the great cities see: *A. Braun*, "Berliner Wohnungsverhältnisse"; *E. von Philippovich*, "Wiener Wohnungsverhältnisse" ("Archiv f. soz. Gesetzgeb." u. Stat. VII).

[NOTE TO THE AMERICAN EDITION: The literature upon the social condition of the proletariat has increased considerably in recent years. It would be impossible and also superfluous to cite the whole of this literature; I note only certain works that seem remarkable for one reason or another.

For England: *L. G. Chiozza-Money*, "Riches and Poverty" (1905). For Germany: *K. Fischer*, "Denkwürdigkeiten und Erinnerungen eines Arbeiters" (1903–04); *M. W. Th. Bromme*, "Lebensgeschichte eines modernen Fabrikarbeiters" (1905); and *Fr. Rehbein*, "Das Leben eines Landarbeiters." For the United States: *R. Hunter*, "Das Elend der neuen Welt" (1908). For Russia: *K. A. Pashitnow*, "Die Lage der arbeitenden Klasse in Russland" (1907). For the Netherlands: *J. J. Moquette*, "Onderzoekingen over Volksroeding in de gemeinte Utrecht", 1907; "Arbeidesleven in Nederland" (1908); "Onderzoekingen naar de toestanden in de Nederlandische heimindustrie", 1911–1912. Upon the condition of working-people in general see especially the very interesting and original work of *Niceforo*, "Anthropologie der nichtbesitzenden Klassen" (1910). Upon the condition of working-women, see "Die Jugendgeschichte einer Arbeiterin" (1909); *R. Kempf*, "Das Leben der jungen Fabrikmädchen in München" (1911); the official investigation into the work of married women in the factories in the Netherlands (1911). Upon child-labor: "Das proletarische Kind."]

pline, two conditions which are essential to victory in the struggle. Little by little the workers have learned that their enemy is not their own employer simply, but the whole capitalist class. The strife has become a strife of classes. And capitalism being international the conflict of the working class has become international also.

The means by which the working class attempt to better their position are of various kinds. First there are the unions, which undertake the contest for the shorter day and higher wages. Then there is coöperation; and finally, and above all, politics. The movement for unions, which could not exist without liberty of the press, of meeting, and of forming associations, forces the working-men to take part in politics.

At first, when they still had no clear idea of the position they occupied in society, the working-men permitted other political parties to make use of them. But coming to understand that the laborers form a class apart, whose interests are different from those of other classes, they have formed an independent working-man's party. Finally, the contest of the working class could not limit itself to improvements brought about within the frame-work of the existing economic system; if they wished to free themselves permanently they saw themselves obliged to combat capitalism itself. Thus modern socialism was born; on one side from an ardent desire of the working class to free itself from the poverty caused by capitalism; on the other side from the development in the manner of capitalistic production, in which small capital is always conquered by large capital. The conviction becomes more and more general that capitalism has fulfilled its historic task, the increase of the productive forces, and that the means of production must belong to all if we are effectively to deliver humanity from the material and intellectual miseries which result from capitalism. The labor movement blends itself with socialism, then, and thus social democracy becomes the political organization of the working class.

What have been the results of the opposition made by the working class to the misery imposed upon them by capitalism? When we compare the condition of the proletariat in the first half of the nineteenth century (see, for example F. Engels, *op. cit.*) with that of today, we cannot help recognizing that it has been improved. Forced (in order to avoid worse things) by the labor agitation and also by the ravages which capitalism had caused in the working class, incapacitating them for the work required of them, the bourgeoisie decided to put forth laws limiting the work of women and children, etc. The unions, consisting principally of skilled workers, have been and still are able to obtain increase of wages and a shortening of the working-day, by making use of the weapons at their disposal (strikes, etc.). Coöperation also has raised the standard of living somewhat for those who have taken part in it.

From the fact that the working class, in so far as it has been organized, has improved its condition, the conclusion has wrongly been drawn that the distance between the two parties, the possessors and the non-possessors, has been diminished. Those who draw this conclusion forget that during this period the totality of wealth has been enormously increased, and that the proletariat has obtained only a part, while the rest has fallen to the bourgeoisie. And so far as I know, no one has yet been able to prove that the part falling to the bourgeoisie must be smaller than that obtained by the proletarians.[1]

Besides the material consequences of the labor conflict, its spiritual consequences are also of very high importance. The contest has obliged the working-men to develop themselves, has taught them that they occupy an important place in society, and thus has increased their confidence in themselves. It is socialism especially which, by giving the hope of a better future to a whole class oppressed and poor, has had the effect of little by little elevating the proletariat intellectually and morally.

D. THE LOWER PROLETARIAT.[2]

I must speak now of the fourth and least numerous group of the population, that of the very poor. Not possessing the means of production, and not being able to sell their labor, these people occupy no position in the economic life properly speaking, and their material condition is therefore easy to understand. Everything that has been said upon this subject with reference to the proletariat applies here, but in a much larger degree. The manner in which these people are fed, clothed, and housed is almost indescribable. The middle class have no idea of such a life; they believe that the pictures of

---

[1] See the proof cited by *K. Kautsky* in his " Sozialreform und soziale Revolution " (pp. 22–25), in support of the assertion that the distance between the bourgeoisie and the proletariat has increased.

[2] What the Germans call "Lumpenproletariat." [The French is "le bas Proletariat." "Submerged class" is perhaps our most common English equivalent. — TRANSL.] With the lower proletariat we must include prostitutes and a part of the criminals. These two groups we shall naturally treat in detail later.

these conditions sometimes painted for them are exaggerated, and that charity is sufficient to prevent their passing certain limits. From these limits we understand that the bourgeoisie does not mean to be incommoded by the poor. If charity were to go farther it would require sums so great that the increase of capital and expenditures for luxury would be interfered with. That would be quite out of the question.

In order to depict these conditions I wish to give but one quotation, taken from an interesting article, "Englands industrielle Reserve-armée" in which account has been given of the researches of certain clergymen in the poorest quarters of London. And everything that is here said of London applies in general to other great cities. For capitalism produces the same effects everywhere.

"Think of the condition in which the poor live. We do not say the condition of their dwellings, for how can those holes be called dwellings, when in comparison with them the lair of a wild beast would be a comfortable and healthful place. Only a few who read these lines have any conception of what pestilential places these nests are, where tens of thousands of human beings are herded together among horrors that recall to us what we have heard of slave-ships between decks. To reach these abodes of misery we have to find our way through hardly passable courts, impregnated with poisonous and evil-smelling gases, which rise from the heaps of offal strewn around, and from the dirty water flowing underfoot — courts, into which the sun seldom or never penetrates, through which no breath of fresh air ever blows, and which seldom have the benefit of a cleaning. We have rotten stairs to climb, which threaten to give way at each step, and in some places have given way, leaving holes that endanger the lives and limbs of those who are not accustomed to them. We are obliged to feel our way along dark and dirty passages swarming with vermin; then, if we are not driven back by the intolerable stench, we may enter the holes in which thousands of beings, of the same race as ourselves, lodge together. Have you, dear reader, ever pitied those poor creatures whom you found sleeping in the open under railway arches, in wagons or hogsheads, or under anything that would afford them shelter? You will learn that these are to be envied in comparison with those who seek refuge here. Eight feet square is the average size of very many of these 'living-rooms.' Walls and ceiling are black with the accumulation of dirt which has become fastened there through the neglect of years. It falls down from the cracks in the ceiling, sticks out of the holes in the walls, in short, is everywhere.   What goes by the name of a window is half stuffed up with rags or nailed up with boards, in order to keep out the wind and rain, while the rest is so smeared and darkened that no light can get in, nor is it possible to see out.   If we climb up to an attic room, where at least we may expect a breath of fresh air through an open or broken window, and look down upon the roofs or cornices of the stories below, we shall discover that the already tainted air which might find its entrance into the window, has come thither over the decayed bodies of cats, birds, or still more nauseous things.   The buildings themselves are in such miserable condition that the thought naturally arises, 'Will they fall down upon the heads of the inmates?'   And furniture?   We shall perhaps discover a broken down chair, the rickety remains of an old bedstead, or the mere fragments of a table; more often, however, as a substitute for these we shall find only rough boards resting upon bricks, an old warped trunk, or a box; and more often still nothing but rags and rubbish.

"Every room in these rotten, damp, fetid houses is occupied by one, and often by two families.   A sanitary inspector reports that he found in a cellar a man, his wife, three children, and four hogs. In another room a missionary found a man sick with small-pox, his wife just recovering from child-birth, and the children half naked and covered with dirt.   Here seven persons live in a cellar-kitchen, and a dead child lies between the living.   In another room a poor widow was living with three children, and one child who had already been dead thirteen days.   Her husband, a cab-driver, had committed suicide a short time before. — Here lives a widow and her six children, including a daughter of 29, another of 21, and a son of 27.   Another room contains father, mother, and six children, of whom two are sick with scarlet fever.   In another live, eat, and sleep nine brothers and sisters from 29 years old down.   Here is a mother who sends her children out on the street from early evening till late after midnight, because she rents her room during this time for immoral purposes. Afterwards the poor worms may creep back to their dwelling if they have not found some scanty shelter elsewhere.   Where there is a bed it consists of nothing but a heap of dirty rags, refuse, or straw, but mostly there is not even this, and the miserable beings lie upon the dirty floor.   The renter of this room is a widow, who takes the only bed herself and sublets the floor to a married couple for two shillings sixpence a week." [1]

[1] Pp. 213–215. ("Neue Zeit", 1884).

"However miserable these rooms may be they are yet too dear for many, who wander about all day seeking to get a living as well as they can, and at night take shelter in one of the common lodging-houses, of which there are so many. The lodging-houses are often the meeting place of thieves and vagabonds of the lowest sort, and some are even kept by the receivers of stolen goods. In the kitchen men and women may be seen cooking their food, doing their washing, or lounging around smoking and gambling. In the sleeping room there is a long row of beds on each side, as many as sixty or eighty in a single room. In many lodging-houses the two sexes are permitted to lodge together without any regard for the commonest decency. Yet there is still a lower step. Hundreds cannot procure even the twopence necessary to secure the privilege of passing a night in the stuffy air of these dormitories; and so they lie down on the steps and in the passage ways, where it is nothing uncommon in the early morning to find six or eight human beings huddled together or stretched out." [1]

We may limit ourselves to this sketch of the habitation — all the other living conditions conform thereto. With so miserable a material life there can be no question of the intellectual life. Continual poverty and the permanent fear of dying of hunger destroy all that is noble in man and reduce him to the condition of a beast, without any aspiration for higher things; for those who have come to this state from the more favored classes become more and more degraded and have soon lost the little knowledge they acquired in earlier periods. Servility and lack of self-respect are necessary to the poor if they are to get the alms they need to keep them alive, since they occupy no place in the economic life. Between them and the workers there is an enormous difference; they have no feeling of solidarity in the social life.

What is the origin of the lower proletariat, from what classes is it recruited? If we are to believe many criminologists and sociologists the answer to this question ought to be that their poverty is not due to social conditions but exclusively to themselves; that they are inferior by nature. But to get a true answer we must put the question in this way: do the existing social classes form the groups into which men would be classified according to their qualities?

---

[1] *Op. cit.* p. 215. See also, as regards the condition of the lower proletariat in Germany, Dr. *H. Lux*, "Sozialpolitisches Handbuch", pp. 32 *ff.*; for Austria: *T. W. Teifen*, "Das soziale Elend, etc." IV, pp. 122 *ff.*; for Russia: *O. Zetkin*, "Die barfüszige Bande" ("Neue Zeit", 1885); for England: *Ch. Booth*, "Pauperism" and "Life and Labour of the People in London", VIII; for all Europe: *L. M. Moreau-Christophe*, "Du problème de la misère," III; for North America see *R. Hunter*, "Das Elend der Neuen Welt", pp. 51 *ff.*

Those who give an affirmative answer to this question reason as follows: men differ enormously among themselves in their innate capacities. The largest division of them is made up of people of moderate worth, a small number rise above this, and the rest are inferior. Circumstances have little influence upon the development of these capacities. If any man has great abilities circumstances cannot keep him from the place to which they entitle him. He who has little ability also arrives at the place which that fact makes his own. In other words (to confine myself to capitalism) the bourgeoisie, the ruling class, is composed of persons predestined to rule; next comes the petty bourgeoisie, followed by the proletariat, predestined to rough work; and finally lower proletariat, a class predestined to succumb in the struggle for existence, since incapable of meeting its requirements.[1]

An attentive examination of this theory, which is an application to society of the Darwinian theory of selection, shows at once — even supposing it to be correct — that there is an important difference between the struggle for existence in nature and that in society. In nature the conquered are either annihilated, or are prevented from reproducing themselves, while in society the lower classes multiply much faster than the higher. It is no longer a question of the survival of the most fit, and the annihilation of the rest, as in nature.

Who is it then who remains victor in the struggle for life in society? To answer this it is necessary first to answer another, Are the chances the same for all? If this is not the case then it cannot be a question of the triumph of the best.

There are few questions upon which opinions differ as much as upon this. Generally these opinions are only conjectures, for they are not based upon an examination of facts. For this reason I wish to set down here briefly the very important conclusions of Professor Odin in his "Genèse des grands hommes", a work noteworthy not simply from the wealth of documents of which the author made use, but also from his very scrupulous care in examining them. Professor Odin has made studies of the educational environment, the economic environment, the ethnological environment, etc., of all the men of letters born in France between 1300 and 1830, to the number of 6382.

---

[1] There may be found in Dr. *L. Woltmann's* "Die Darwinische Theorie und der Sozialismus" (pp. 81–135) a detailed résumé of the works of the authors who hold this opinion. *Cf.* also *Herkner*, "Die Arbeiterfrage", pp. 178 *ff.*, where also the literature upon this point is to be found.

As to educational environment, the author has been able to procure exact information with regard to 827 persons; a good education had been given to 811, or 98.1 % and 16, or 1.9 % had had a poor education. "All this forces us to admit that education plays a rôle not only important, but capital, decisive, in the development of the man of letters." [1]

The economic environment in which the men of letters had passed their youth could be discovered in the case of 619. Of these, 562, or 90.7 %, passed their youth sheltered from all material care, while 57, or 9.3 %, passed their youth in indigence or insecurity. In consequence the author makes the following observation: "As it appears, only the eleventh part of the literary men of talent have passed their youth in difficult economic conditions. This ratio, already very small in itself, appears much more striking when we strive to represent the numerical relation which ought to exist for the whole population between well-do-do families and those that are not. It is impossible to say, doubtless, what this relation has been on the average for the whole modern period. But it is clear that we shall be well below the truth if we admit that the families of the second category are three or four times as numerous as those of the first. That is to say, from the mere fact of the economic conditions in which they are born, the children of well-to-do families have at least forty or fifty times as much chance of making a name in letters as do those who belong to families that are poor, or are simply in a position of economic instability." [2]

Further, the author shows that the fifty-seven men of letters who passed their youth in an unfavorable economic environment were by chance put in a position to develop their capacities. (Only five of them received a poor education.)

Finally the social environment from which the literary men have sprung:

SOCIAL CLASSES.	NUMBER OF LITERARY MEN OF TALENT RELATIVELY TO THE TOTAL POPULATION OF EACH SOCIAL CLASS.
Nobility.	159
Magistracy.	62
Liberal professions.	24
Bourgeoisie.	7
Manual labor.	0.8

[1] P. 527, op. cit. I. [2] P. 529, op. cit. I.

Upon examining these figures we see that of two persons of the same innate qualities the one who has sprung from the nobility has about 200 times as much chance of becoming a person of importance as the one who comes from the laboring class.   The struggle of our day has been characterized as a race with a handicap, in which one runs on foot with a burden on his back, another rides a horse, while the third takes an express train.   The reality, however, is still stronger.

Doubtless we must not forget that the researches of Professor Odin include in part a period that differs in many respects from our own (hence the small contingent of the bourgeoisie), and that since this time education has become more solid and more general, a fact which increases the chances of success of a gifted man sprung from a poor environment.   In the second place it was literary men and not capitalists who were the subject of investigation, and since the former doubtless must have greater natural aptitudes than the latter, it may well be that it is easier for anyone without money to acquire capital, than would be suggested by the figures applying only to men of letters.   Nevertheless, all this does not overthrow the fact that the researches of Professor Odin have proved that the fact of being born in a class where youth is without care, and enjoys a good education, procures an enormous advantage in the struggle for existence.[1]

In order to prevent erroneous interpretations I will add Professor Odin's own conclusion, from which it is plain that he does not deny absolutely that men's innate capacities differ widely (which, indeed, is disputed by few, and may be considered settled).   "Heredity and environment," he says, concur with one another in the development of talent.   We may characterize as follows their respective spheres of action : where the hereditary qualities are identical — to suppose an impossible case — it is the environment which causes all the difference between individuals; where the environment is identical, it is heredity.

"Put in these terms the proposition is banal.   What is less so, since this has been established here with certainty for perhaps the

---

[1] As is well known, *Galton* is one of the authors who denies this thesis. One of the rare examples which he produces as proof is d'Alembert, who, notwithstanding an unfavorable educational environment, became a celebrity. (See "Hereditary Genius," pp. 34–39).   Unfortunately for Galton Professor *Odin* proves that d'Alembert received an excellent education and was brought up in relatively favorable economic conditions.   (See "Genèse des grand hommes," p. 538, I.)   See also Professor *Odin's* criticism of Galton (pp. 192 ff., *op. cit.*, I).

first time, is that heredity alone can do nothing.   However strong may be the natural disposition given by heredity, it can only develop itself in a favorable environment.   Thrown into an unfavorable environment it will become weakened in the degree in which the environment is contrary to it, and may even end by being atrophied to the point of being no longer perceptible.   The supposed omnipotence of heredity is only an illusion, resulting from an elementary confusion between heredity and simple parentage.

"This is not all.   We have been able to determine more nearly what is the indispensable environment for the development of literary talent.   It is a good education, made possible by certain circumstances which are advantageous socially and economically, in other words, a proper social environment." [1]

As a second form of the handicap we must speak of inheritance. It is impossible to estimate this advantage in figures, but it is incontestable that the man who has become rich in this way has no need of great knowledge or great intelligence in order to remain rich.   Provided he does not speculate or squander his money, he should be able to have the enjoyment of it all his life.   The struggle for existence is unknown to him; at the very start of the race his foot is nearly at the goal.

We see already that these two circumstances have as their result that the classes do not correspond exactly to the groups into which men are separated according to their capacities.   However we must now leave the cases in which one has a start of another, and give an answer to the question, "In what do the conquerors in the contest excel?"

In the first place, attention must be drawn to a group of capitalists who have acquired their wealth without having their abilities called into play, but who are entirely indebted to chance, i.e. the speculators, the winners of the great prizes in lotteries, the men who make rich marriages, etc.   Next we may mention the other capitalists, the great manufacturers and merchants.   Wherein are they distinguished?   First for energy and activity, next for a great talent for organization, especially as shown in the choice of their chief employes, and finally for a need of luxury, not too great, lest the building up of their capital be interfered with, nor too restrained, lest the suspicion be aroused that their fortune is in danger.   The first of these aptitudes must certainly be considered as the most favorable; the

[1] *Op. cit.*, I, p. 562.

talent for organization especially is of the highest importance, for it is without contradiction a factor in social progress. It is because of this talent and not for their fabulous wealth alone that the names of Pierpont Morgan, of Rockefeller, and of other directors of trusts will not be entirely forgotten after they are dead. But these are not the only capacities which these people must display. To direct a capitalistic enterprise it is necessary among other things to have a fair portion of insensibility as well toward workmen as toward customers; then it will not do to be too scrupulous about truth (in advertising, etc.), nor to show too much character (however impertinent his customers may be the capitalist takes it all through fear of seeing them go over to his competitors).

Nevertheless, he who displays all these qualities, still is not entirely sure of being able to improve his position, or even to maintain himself in it; crises, as has been shown, are inevitably bound up with capitalism itself, and strike at times the most substantial and energetic capitalists. By a new invention or a new manner of working the most active and intelligent manufacturer may see himself outstripped by a competitor. And aside from all fortuitous circumstances, in society as it exists today the struggle for existence is a struggle between those best armed, those who have the best machines, etc. But the manufacturer who can procure the best machines, who can bring his establishment up to the latest technical requirements, who can procure the services of the ablest technicians, etc., is the man who has most capital. The struggle is not a struggle of men but of capital.

In his work, "Die Darwinische Theorie und der Sozialismus" Dr. L. Woltmann has brought out clearly the difference between the combat in nature and that which takes place in society. He says: "The history of the civilization of the human race also proceeds upon the basis of the great biological principles of adaptation, transmission, and perfection in the struggle for existence. But between the application of these principles among the lower animals and in the world of man there are the following essential differences. In the first place in the animal world the struggle for existence takes place through the adaptation of organic means to organic ends, while with men technical tools and economical means of production enter in, things which are not within the power of separate individuals, but are made possible by association. In the second place hereditary transmission in the case of animals is organic, while in the case of human beings there is added an external and legally determined hereditary transmission of technical tools and of capital. In the animal kingdom, in the third place, the struggle for existence is a rivalry of organic production and reproduction, while among men, especially under the capitalistic order, there takes place a competition in commodities and places, a contest for profit, which has hardly anything in common with natural selection." [1]

Thus we see clearly who it is that can rise from the class of non-possessors to that of possessors: it is those to whom fortune is peculiarly favorable, or who, possessing the qualities necessary for the capitalist, meet with the opportunity of putting them in evidence. Those who are dropped from the capitalist class are those who have been unfortunate or who do not possess the qualities necessary for capitalists.

The answer to the question proposed, "Are the present classes also the groups where men can be ranked according to their qualities", must be decidedly negative. The bourgeoisie is not the ruling class because the most intelligent and energetic persons are found among its members. There are also included in this class persons without energy, stupid people, of minor importance in short, just as in the petty bourgeoisie and the proletariat very capable persons may be met with. The fact of being excluded from the class of possessors is not a proof of inferiority. If the superior persons were those who led society they would be the great thinkers, the savants, for it is they who have made society progress and who have desired its well-being. For even if capitalists, more than others, have aided progress, it is by chance, for they have always had in view only their own profit. [2]

I could easily cite a number of celebrated authors who are unanimously of the opinion that the conquerors in the present struggle are not such because they are naturally superior. [3] I will confine myself to recalling the opinion of one whose authority no one will contest, namely, Charles Darwin. Here is what Wallace says: "In one of my last conversations with Darwin he expressed himself as having very little hope of the future of humanity, and this upon the

---

[1] P. 80.

[2] *Cf.* especially the excellent refutation of the pseudo-Darwinian theory by Professor *Bücher* in the chapter "Arbeitsgliederung und Soziale Klassenbilderung" from his "Entstehen der Volkswirtschaft."

[3] See *Woltmann, op. cit.*, pp. 32–81 and pp. 334 *ff.*, where he cites a number of authors who are of this opinion. Upon the whole subject see Dr. *A. Ploetz*, "Die Tüchtigkeit unsrer Rasse und der Schutz der Schwachen", and Dr. *D. van Embden*, "Darwinisme en Demokratie."

basis of his observation that in our modern civilization natural selection does not occur, and the fittest does not survive. The victors in the struggle for gold are by no means the best or the most intelligent, and it is a well known fact that our population reproduces itself in each generation much more rapidly among the lower than among the middle and upper classes." [1]

An examination of the struggle for existence in the middle class shows that everything which happens in the bourgeoisie on a large scale is reproduced here on a small scale. He who has little capital is surpassed by a competitor who has more, even though the former may be entirely fitted for his business; crises have the same ruinous influence here, and strike skilful and unskilful alike. The difference, as far as the struggle for existence is concerned, between the class in question and the bourgeoisie, consists in this: the less energetic, the less intelligent of the middle class runs more danger of falling back out of the ranks than a member of the bourgeoisie who is his equal.

Finally, we come to the proletariat. Here also there is an elimination of individuals not because they are incapable, but because they are superfluous in the present mode of production, as well as of those whom sickness or old age render unfit for labor. Here we must take account of a factor which is of less importance in the other classes, bodily health and strength. While the proletarian has need neither of much knowledge or great intelligence to carry on his trade, he has a powerful weapon for the struggle in his muscular strength and health. Unfavorable conditions have a strong influence upon him, and the one who is weak and ailing must, other things being equal, yield in the present struggle for existence to a competitor who is stronger and in better health. And finally, in this contest also the less active, the less persevering among the workers will have the smaller chance of success, supposing conditions to be equal.

So we return to the point from which we set out, the lower proletariat. This class is not composed, then, as has sometimes been claimed, of beings inferior by nature, of persons who are fit for nothing. In the great majority of cases social conditions and not their lack of aptitude, are the exclusive and direct causes of their position. In support of this I will give some figures, which also show the relative importance of the causes compared among themselves.

[1] "Menschliche Auslese", p. 10 (Zukunft, 1894).

German Empire.

To the Hundred Poor Persons Assisted (Total of 1,592,386).

Injuries to the person assisted	By Accident.	1.04
" " " breadwinner of the family		0.09
Death of " " " " "		0.36
" " " " " " "	Not by Accident.	8.35
Sickness of the person assisted or of one of his family		15.24
Bodily or intellectual infirmities		8.97
Weakness of old age		12.32
Large number of children		1.34
Forced unemployment		2.23
Alcoholism		0.88
Laziness		0.71
Other causes designated		4.09
" " not designated		0.06
" Co-assisted " [1]		44.32
		100.00 [2]

This table shows that 44.32 % of the persons assisted were "co-assisted"; that 8.8 % have become indigent through the death or injury of the bread-winner of the family; that there are, therefore, 53.12 % of those assisted the cause of whose indigence is not to be found in the persons themselves, but in their social environment. (Generally such persons are spoken of as not being poor through their "own fault", a term so vague that it would be well to discontinue its use.) 1.34 % are persons with a large family, whose wages are too small to support so many; 2.23% are out of employment, *i.e.* they wish to work but can find nothing to do; 12.32 % are prevented from working by old age. Consequently we reach the figure of 69.01% for those who have become indigent through causes which do not depend upon themselves. Finally come 25.25% of those assisted who have been injured, or are sick, or have bodily or intellectual infirmities.

Further, there are social causes which play a great part in the etiology of the cases we have been discussing (bad housing conditions favoring tuberculosis, lack of protective devices for dangerous machines, causing injuries, etc.). Others of these persons are born weak

---

[1] Under this heading are included all the children below 14, and the women who live with the person assisted. It is enough to point out that the indigence of these co-assisted persons does not proceed from any cause in the persons themselves, but in their circumstances.

[2] "Statistisches Jahrbuch für das Deutsche Reich", X, 1889, pp. 206–208.

or sickly, in which case we may speak of individual causes of poverty, although social conditions have contributed in their turn by their influence on the parents to make the children wretched.

It is, however, a social phenomenon that the sick and weak of the proletariat are left to shift for themselves. They find themselves in that condition only because they do not possess the means of production, and are no longer in a condition to sell their labor. Many times we read in treatises upon morals how shameful it is that nomadic peoples abandon or kill their sick and aged, and how by these customs they give proof of their inferior morality. But those who speak in this way forget how, notwithstanding our present civilization, a great number of persons still pass their old age in the direst poverty; they forget also that the manner in which the nomadic peoples live forces them to rid themselves of their sick and aged, because it would be impossible to take them with them; they forget also that, on account of the limited power that nomads have over nature, they find themselves in exceedingly difficult material circumstances, so that their manner of acting is not judged immoral by any of their own families who suffer by it; [1] finally they forget that the productivity of labor is so enormous at present that all the sick and aged could be supported; a part of the money spent in superfluous luxuries would be ample for this purpose.

We have still to examine the last two headings, laziness and alcoholism. As the figures given above show, these form a very small part of the causes: together only 1.59%.[2] Among the causes which have brought these persons to the point where they are, there are social factors also. Later on I shall speak of the relation between the present economic system and alcoholism. But at this point we may say as regards the 0.71% of persons who do not wish to work

---

[1] Read the following taken from "Illustrations of the Manners, Customs, and Conditions of the North American Indians", by *G. Catlin*: "This cruel custom of exposing their aged people, belongs, I think, to all the tribes who roam about the prairies, making severe marches, when such decrepit persons are totally unable to go, unable to ride or to walk, — when they have no means of carrying them. It often becomes absolutely necessary in such cases that they should be left; and they uniformly insist upon it, saying as one old man did, that they are old and of no further use — that they left their fathers in the same manner — that they wish to die, and their children must not mourn for them." (I, p. 217.)

[2] The figures given by *J. S.* in "Aus den Ergebnissen der sächsischen Armenstatistik" ("Neue Zeit" 1894–95, II,) confirm those in the table I have given, if we do not lose sight of the fact that J. S. does not give the "co-assisted" persons separately. The figures of *Charles Booth* in his "Pauperism" show that alcoholism forms a more important factor in the two districts that he has studied (12.6% and 21.9%); for laziness the figures are

that a part of them — it is impossible to say just how many — have grown up in a bad environment, where they have never been given the habit of working regularly and diligently, so that they have become totally incapable of doing so.

There is still another social factor that may be named; the disagreeable character of many kinds of work, made worse by long hours and low wages. To adduce but one example: the miner is obliged to work in a vitiated atmosphere, often in a painful position, and constantly surrounded by dangers, and this for very low wages. If we stop to think of this we are more astonished at the millions of workers who pass their lives under similar conditions, than at the comparatively few who refuse to work.

However, taking all this into account, it is certain that there are among the proletariat persons who are predisposed to idleness by their congenital constitution. It is indubitable that these persons are invalids, who would be cared for in a well-organized society, but in ours are abandoned to their fate. Professor Benedikt says, in speaking of physical neurasthenia: "It represents not so much absolute weakness as speedy exhaustion coupled with a painful feeling of weakness. We make in our childhood more muscular movements than is necessary, and out of the pleasurable feeling which comes from these develop the first elements of pleasure in work. If, however, the child quickly becomes weary, and the muscular action soon begets a lively feeling of discomfort, there arises from this discomfort laziness or physical neurasthenia." [1]

1.9% and 10.6%. Statistics of the Netherlands confirm in general those of the German Empire:

ASSISTED TEMPORARILY.	1898	1899	ASSISTED CONTINUOUSLY.	1898	1899
Causes of Indigence.	%	%	Causes of Indigence.	%	%
Illness, etc.	42.3	45.1	Illness or bodily defects	18.6	18.9
Lack or shortage of work	30.7	28.9	Old age	45.4	47
Alcoholism	2.6	2.6	Death of breadwinner .	20.0	19.2
Other causes	24.4	23.4	Alcoholism	1.8	1.5
	100.0	100.0	Other causes	14.2	13.4
				100.0	100.0

(Verslagen over de verrichtingen aangaande het armbestuur over 1898 en 1899. Bijlage E. Handelingen 2e Kamer der Staten-Generaal 1899–1900, 1900–1901.)

[1] P. 490. "Biologie und Kriminalistik." ("Zeitschr. f. d. ges. Strafrechtswissenschaft", VII.)

The number of those the cause of whose poverty is to be found in themselves is not, then, very considerable. Nevertheless it is a little greater than the statistics given would lead one to suppose, for there are also certain of the bourgeoisie and petty bourgeoisie, ruined in consequence of the lack of the qualities required for success, who have gone down little by little and have finally become incorporated with the lower proletariat.

But is this class of poor persons absolutely fit for nothing? It seems to me that (leaving the sick out of consideration) the answer must be decidedly in the negative. It is true that a part of this group succumbs in the struggle because it is inferior. But it would be as absurd to say of the runner who comes in last in a race that he cannot run at all, as to say of the man who goes under in the struggle for existence that he is fit for nothing. Those who do not succeed in life are in great part those who through accident of birth have not obtained the place for which their talents fitted them. How many among the bourgeoisie are ruined from their incapacity for directing a business enterprise, while they would have become useful members of society if they had been able to follow their true vocation? And how many proletarians have fallen lower and lower through not being fitted for the trade to which their birth destined them, while their innate qualities predestined them to a different form of work? [1]

Side by side with these there are individuals who are really inferior, who have little energy, intelligence, etc. It would be absurd to claim that these persons are capable of doing great things, even in the most favorable circumstances. But there is a great difference between not being able to do great things, and being absolutely useless, as are the members of the lower proletariat under present conditions. These persons have need of being guided, cannot stand up without support, and in order not to perish need to find themselves in a favorable environment. If their neighbor comes to their assistance they can assuredly become sufficiently useful, and in any case need do no harm. Anyone who will look about him may be convinced of the truth of this; for many persons of just this sort, happening to belong to the bourgeoisie, have succeeded very well.

Ethnology points out also that classes have not their origin in the universal fact that men differ in their innate qualities. For if this were true classes would be as old as humanity itself. This, however, is not the case; it has been proved that in the evolution of society

[1] See *K. Kautsky's* "Das Erfurter Programm", p. 64.

there has been a stage (that it was a long time ago makes little difference) when riches and poverty were unknown, and classes did not
exist.[1] The assertion that the "war of all against all" is a natural
phenomenon, is absolutely false, and proves a very great lack of sociological knowledge. It is certain that classes have long existed, but
a society like that of our time, in which we can apply the adage of
Hobbes, that "man is a wolf to his fellowman", is of comparatively
recent date.

Our conclusion, then, is this: the groups into which the population
of capitalistic countries is divided do not originate in the circumstance
that men differ in their innate capacities, but in the system of production that is in force; it is chiefly chance that determines to which
class an individual belongs; there are inferior beings in each group,
but among the lower proletariat they are more numerous than elsewhere; but these inferior beings may still be useful enough on condition that they be placed in a favorable environment.

[1] Upon the period without class see, among others, *L. H. Morgan*, "Ancient
Society", and upon the origin of classes *H. Cunow*, "Arbeitstheilung und
Frauenrecht" ("Neue Zeit", 1900–01, I, p. 178 *ff.*).

CHAPTER III.

THE RELATION OF THE SEXES AND OF THE FAMILY.

A. MARRIAGE.

As between the two commonplaces, "There have always been poor people", and "The present institution of marriage springs from human nature itself and is as old as society", it is hard to say which is repeated oftenest, but it is quite certain that one is no more exact than the other. Sociology has proved that marriage, as it exists at present, is the result of a long process of evolution, and every serious observer must be convinced that its present form will be no more constant than those which preceded it, and that the ideas concerning it have undergone important modifications.

The question to solve is this: "How has monogamy taken its rise?" With the aid of sociology I shall endeavor to give the answer as summarily as possible.[1] It will, however, be necessary to recall the ancient forms of marriage, without which it would be impossible to grasp the origin and evolution of the present form. Most sociologists are of the opinion that primitive man lived in promiscuity, which, if true, must have been in the most remote period, when man was hardly distinguishable from the anthropoid apes. Other authors,

---

[1] It is well known that sociological studies upon the subject of marriage date from 1861, when *Bachofen's* "Das Mutterrecht" came out. Since then a very extensive literature on the subject has appeared, without by any means exhausting the subject. (See Dr. *Steinmetz*, "Die neueren Forschungen zur Geschichte der menschlichen Familie", "Zeitschr. für Sozialwissenschaft," 1899.)

[NOTE TO THE AMERICAN EDITION: The literature upon the origin and evolution of marriage and the family has recently been considerably increased. The following books seem to us to be the most important: *H. Schurtz*, "Altersklassen und Männerbünde"; *M. Weber*, "Ehefrau und Mutter in der Rechtsentwicklung"; *A. Vierkandt*, "Das Problem der Familien- und Stammesorganisation der Naturvölker"; *E. Westermarck*, "Ursprung und Entwicklung der Moralbegriffe", II; *F. Müller-Lyer*, "Formen der Ehe", "Die Familie", and "Phasen der Liebe"; *H. Cunow*, "Zur Urgeschichte der Ehe und Familie."]

on the contrary, have attempted to show that such a state of things has never existed.[1] However, the only thing proved is that no case of promiscuity has ever been established among peoples observed by serious ethnologists. But all these peoples, however far removed they may be from us, had already attained a certain degree of development, and were by no means in their primitive state. No amount of observation can prove whether or not primitive man really lived in a state of promiscuity, and we can only take refuge in hypotheses.

We shall be getting at the truth when we come to an agreement as to the meaning of the word "promiscuity." Do we mean by this a state like that in which dogs live, where after copulation the male and female do not remain together at all ? Then it is very likely that human beings have never lived in that state, inasmuch as such promiscuity exists rarely or not at all among the animals most approaching man.[2] If, on the contrary, we mean by promiscuity a state in which rules concerning the sexual life are lacking, but where life in common for a longer or shorter period is not excluded, then, since man is part of the animal kingdom, it is most probable that there has been a time when this state has existed, and that it is only little by little that objective rules have appeared.[3] Let us now leave the domain of hypothesis and examine the real facts.[4]

The most primitive of the peoples who have been observed in detail have been named "lower hunters"; they include the Australian aborigines, the Veddhas, the Botocudos, etc. Among these peoples the men hunt while the women gather fruit and roots. They are forced to wander in small groups in order to provide for their needs, as otherwise the game and fruit would soon fail. Their limited control over nature is a frequent cause of famine and distress generally, and thus prevents any considerable increase in the population.

As to their sexual relations, there could not be any question of

---

[1] *Westermarck* (in his "History of Human Marriage", pp. 51–133) has led the opposition to the promiscuity theory. It is also combated by *Starcke* in his "Die primitive Familie" and by *Grosse* in his "Die Formen der Familie und die Formen der Wirthschaft." (pp. 41–45). For a résumé of the arguments for and against see Dr. *C. J. Wynaendts Francken*, "De Evolutie van het huwelijk" (pp. 57–65).

[2] See *Ch. Letourneau*, "L'évolution du mariage" (pp. 46–48).

[3] See *Fr. Engels*, "Der Ursprung der Familie, des Privateigenthums, und des Staats" (pp. 17–18) [Translated as "The Origin of the family, etc." Page references are to the original.] ; and *C. de Kelles-Krauz*, "Formes primitives de la famille" (pp. 303–304 of the "Revue Internationale de Sociologie", VIII).

[4] The following discussion is based upon material drawn from *Grosse* (*op. cit.*), and from *H. Cunow* ("Die ökonomischen Grundlagen der Mutterherschaft" ("Neue Zeit", 1897–98).

promiscuity among these peoples.   Each horde is divided into three age-classes, and the union of a member of one of these classes with a member of another is forbidden.   The cause of this prohibition is not certain.   Grosse [1] (as well as other authors [2]) is of the opinion that it lies in the fact that these peoples discovered the unfavorable effects of consanguineous unions upon the children, and that this discovery led to the prohibition.[3]   Other authors believe that the hordes which practiced this exclusion, without suspecting its importance, ran less danger of extinction than those which did not practice it.[4]

The hordes being composed of but few persons, this exclusion would force the men more and more to seek wives from outside the horde, thus little by little becoming a group of consanguineous persons with whom union is forbidden.   If a man has procured a woman by capture he becomes her absolute owner, can maltreat her, abandon her, do what he likes in short.   The power of the man over his wife is less great if he has acquired her by purchase or exchange, since her family then exercises a certain control.

The relation of the sexes is sufficiently explained by the mode of production.   When these savages are on the march the woman carries the little that they possess, erects the tent, and searches for fruit; the man on the other hand by his natural qualities is fitted for hunting and for the defense of the hunting ground.   Hunting being the princi- pal resource, and in this period bodily strength being of the highest importance, it is natural that the man should rule.

The so-called "higher hunters", among whom we must reckon the North American Indians of the northwest coast and some peoples of northern Asia, have reached a higher stage of social evolution.   The difference between these and the preceding class is only quantitative, and results from the circumstance that they have been able to settle themselves in countries that are rich in game and fish.   This permits

---

[1] *Op. cit.*, pp. 60–61.

[2] *L. H. Morgan,* "Ancient-Society", p. 424;   *Fr. Engels, op. cit.,* p. 21; and others.

[3] Westermarck believes that there is an innate aversion to sexual rela- tionships between persons who have lived together from childhood; and that the sexual aversion that exists between near blood-relations is in consequence of the fact that these persons have always lived together.   This instinct would thus have been acquired by natural selection, since those who did not have it would run more danger than the others of disappearing in consequence of the injurious effects of such unions.   (*Op. cit.,* chaps. xiv and xv.)   Cunow on the other hand makes the point that there cannot be an innate aversion between persons who have been raised together, for marriages between such persons do take place, and are not thought at all immoral or contrary to nature. ("Die Verwandtschaftsorganisationen der Australneger," pp. 184 *ff.*)

[4] See *Steinmetz, op. cit.,* p. 817.

them to be more sedentary, to live in larger groups, and to attain a higher development.

As with the lower hunters there is among them a division of labor between men and women : The man hunts, fishes, and constructs the tools that he has need of; the woman gathers roots and herbs, prepares the food, and gives herself up to the duties of the household. Some of these peoples are capable of producing more than they need, a fact which occasions commerce of some importance, and produces at times a great inequality of fortune.

At this stage of development the woman is of great use, which brings it about that the father does not give his daughter but sells her. Since the man, then, has bought his wife she has become his property, and he can do with her as he wishes; her infidelity is punished with death. If the husband has received gifts of value from his father-in-law, he is a little limited in his power, since, if he wishes to repudiate his wife, he is obliged to return the gifts. However repudiation is rare, since the woman is very useful to the man and he has ordinarily paid very dear for her. This is also why polygyny, though permitted almost everywhere, is rare. Only the very rich can permit themselves the luxury of more than one wife.

The position of the wife is rather better when, instead of following her husband, he comes to live at her father's house. This happens sometimes when the man cannot pay the whole purchase price, sometimes when the father-in-law is much richer than he. In this latter case the son-in-law prefers to profit by the wealth and power of his wife's father, who, for his part, asks nothing better than to keep his daughter at home, since, in this manner, instead of losing a worker from the household he gains one by the coming of the husband.

We come now to the "pastoral peoples", living principally in Asia and Africa. Just as hunting is not the sole resource of the preceding groups, so the raising of cattle is not the exclusive occupation of this group, but simply the principal one; hence their name. The raising of cattle is naturally the work of the men, seeing that it proceeds genetically from hunting, while the women in this class, as in the preceding, gather fruits and herbs and attend to the work of the household. Although the land is held in common, there are great diversities of wealth, since cattle, the principal form of possession, are individual property, and since war and pillage are also frequent sources of wealth.

Polygyny is permitted, and nomads take as many wives as they can pay for and support. Only the rich, however, can afford to purchase more than one wife, for the fathers demand a good price.

Once purchased the woman becomes the absolute property of the man, who can exploit her in any manner, or abandon her, and when he comes to die can leave her to his heirs with the rest of his possessions. Adultery on the part of the woman is severely punished, while the man is free. Often under polygyny only one of the women is considered the legitimate wife and her children have the sole right to inherit, while the other women are considered only as concubines. The position of the legitimate wife towards her husband does not prevent her being as much of a slave as the other women. Nowhere else has the woman as humble a place as among these pastoral peoples, and nowhere else is the rôle of the man as important as here.

Let us next examine the "lower agriculturists" (among whom are to be found the greater number of the North American Indians, and a great number of the peoples of Africa and the East Indies). When hunting peoples, through chance circumstances (wealth of game for example), have ceased to wander continually, they may easily pass into agriculturists.[1] Agriculture in its turn brings it about that those who practice it become more and more sedentary.

The cultivation of the soil developed in connection with the gathering of fruit and roots, so that it originally formed part of woman's sphere of labor; hence the economic importance of women increased, and a father became less and less disposed to give his daughter in marriage for a small equivalent. The future husband is obliged to acquire his wife at a considerable price, perhaps may have to win her by serving his father-in-law temporarily. Thus, although polygyny is permitted it is only the rich and the chiefs who can procure more than one wife.

Since agriculture requires many hands, the parents try to keep their children with them as long as possible.[2] Thus the custom grows up of several families living in the same house, and the husband comes to live with his wife's family when he is unable to pay the purchase price. Even if this is not the case, a close relationship exists between the wife and her family, so that she returns to it with her children when her husband dies. The more important the position of the woman in the family becomes, the more it comes to pass that the married woman remains in her own family and the husband in his, and that the union consists only in more or less frequent visits paid by the man to his wife.

It is easy to see why the position of woman at this stage is in general

---

[1] Upon the origin of agriculture see *H. Cunow*, "Arbeitstheilung und Frauenrecht" ("Neue Zeit", 1900–1901; I, pp. 102 *ff.*).
[2] See *C. N. Starcke*, "Die primitive Familie", pp. 106–107.

better than at those which preceded.   Ordinarily it is the woman who tills the soil and cares for the household, while the man hunts and prepares the necessary tools; and since agriculture gives a more regular and surer production than hunting, it follows that the position of woman is improved.   The woman becomes less dependent upon the man, to such a point that, for example, she is able to break the marriage, a condition very different from those in which the wife was the property of her husband.   (The somewhat numerous exceptions are explained by the fact that in those cases the man takes part in the cultivation of the soil.)   This is especially the case when a domestic community is formed in which the women govern (matriarchate).[1] Thus a situation is developed at times in which the women have an important position even outside of the family (gynecocracy).

As the preceding considerations show it is not the family which, at this stage of development, takes the first place.   During the periods which I have examined before this the clan (in Latin "gens", in German "Sippe"), a group of persons descended from a common ancestor, is of importance only inasmuch as members of the clan are forbidden to marry among themselves.   Among the lower agriculturists, however, the clan is developed into a consanguineous group living in a community, and in most cases the clan is maternal — that is, descent and the right of succession are reckoned in the maternal line.

However as soon as agriculture increased greatly in importance, especially when the raising of cattle, commerce, and industry grew up beside it, the relation between the sexes became considerably modified. The man gave up hunting, always a less important resource at this stage, and applied himself more and more to agriculture and other branches, and the woman only seconded him in these occupations. In consequence of the continually increasing productivity of labor, the man could produce more than he needed for consumption.   The possession of slaves then became advantageous, slavery took on greater and greater proportions, and in this way the woman's part in the economic life became less important.   Thus the man becomes anew the principal factor and his authority resumes the force it had in the earlier periods.   It is no longer the man who lives with the woman and her family but she lives with him.   We have seen above

---

[1] The "metronymic" system by which the mother has the right to transmit her name to the child (Mutterrecht) is quite distinct from the matriarchate.   As to the origin of the matriarchate see *Dr. L. v. Dargun*, "Mutterrecht und Vaterrecht", pp. 67 *ff*.

that among the lower agriculturists it is the clan, and especially the maternal clan, that holds the first place. Through the economic development the maternal clan is made to give place to the paternal clan. In the clan there was equality, since the soil, the most important means of production, and the dwelling were possessed in common; but the disappearance of this equality followed the development of commerce and industry, for the products of these were, from the first, private property. This inequality was increased still more because private property in land began to grow up side by side with property in common. In the second place, the booty in war was not the same for all warriors, and furthermore war brought about the existence of a class of persons (slaves) whose interests were opposed to those of the conquerors. This development of private property leads necessarily to a gradual change from the maternal clan to the paternal. For in the first case a father had to leave his property to the members of his clan (we have seen that it was the man who became the possessor of private wealth); and since his children belonged always to another clan than his own, the clan of their mother, the children did not inherit from their father. Hence the change to the paternal clan.[1]

But this was not all. Through the great modifications in the mode of production of which I have already spoken, the importance of the clan diminished more and more, and at length disappeared entirely. As long as there was equality among the members of the clan, as long as the social relationships were little complicated, the clan and the organizations that sprang from it (mere combinations of clans) sufficed for the purposes of social organization. But such an organization, being purely democratic in its nature, was no longer adapted to a society in which there were rich and poor, freemen and slaves, in which, therefore, there was a large group of persons oppressed and a small group of oppressors.

The clan and the combinations of the different clans were replaced by the state. This was an organization which had for its principal end the maintenance of order as far as possible, in a society in which the interests of different groups, like those of individuals, were opposed to each other, and the regulation of this conflict of interests.[2] This organization is consequently entirely different from the clan, the object of which was to take the interests of the community to

[1] L. H. Morgan, "Ancient Society", p. 345; Dargun, op. cit., pp. 131, 132.
[2] See Morgan, op. cit., Pt. II, chap. X and XIII, and F. Engels, "Origin of the Family, etc.", chap. V, VI, VIII; Gumplowicz, "Grundriss der Soziologie," pp. 190 ff.; and F. Oppenheimer, "Der Staat."

heart. It is evident that in an organization like this it is the most important and influential class which comes first.

On the one hand, then, the clan loses itself in the state; on the other hand the family, which played but a secondary part while the clan system was at its height, became of greater importance. The clan is divided into "great families" ("Grossfamilien"), *i.e.* husband, wife, and their unmarried children as well as their male descendants, with their wives and children; and the father is the master of all these persons and all their property. However it is only little by little, and in proportion as we get away from the clan, that the authority of the father becomes unlimited. This form of the family has continued even down to our own day in China and Japan, and was general during the early days of ancient Rome.

In China the woman, whose work is entirely limited to household occupations, has a position which, according to all accounts, is only that of a subordinate. Her whole life is under the direction of her husband; she can never obtain a divorce, while her husband can dissolve the marriage without cause; if he takes her in the act of adultery he has the right to kill her, while he himself may keep concubines. In Japan the position of woman is much the same, and in ancient Rome also, though in the course of time the situation of the Roman woman was improved.

As the method of production became more elaborate and the social life was modified as a consequence, the "great family" disappeared, to be replaced by the modern family, consisting of the husband and wife with their unmarried children. Through the increasing extension of the division of labor the sons could more easily provide for their own needs and withdraw themselves in this way from the paternal authority, and the increasing power of the state favored this tendency by limiting the authority of the father.

The best sources for the study of the first phases of monogamous marriage are furnished by ancient Greece. There absolute submission of the woman to the man still prevailed. After the decease of the husband the woman was under the guardianship of his son. The man could repudiate his wife or give her to another. While he had full liberty to have intercourse with other women, the woman who committed adultery was severely punished. The occupations of the woman were confined to spinning, weaving, and housekeeping; her life was concentrated within the house, though even there her authority was very limited, while outside it had no force whatever.

In comparing the position of woman during the period in question with that in the earlier periods (excepting the lower agricultural period) we see that in general her condition is but little ameliorated. Monogamy existed in reality for one of the parties only, since the man was free to keep concubines, while he took every means in his power to prevent the infidelity of his wife, by isolating her from the outer world. Hence it is not true, as some would have us believe, that monogamy is the consequence of an instinct, nor that it is due to a higher degree of culture, made possible by the increased productivity of labor.[1] On the contrary, among the lower agriculturists, much less civilized than the ancient Greeks, the position of women was better than with the latter; being more free, the woman enjoyed in general a higher degree of consideration.

The origin of monogamy is explained only by the modifications that the mode of production has undergone. Through these the man has again taken the most important place in the economic life, it is he who governs and the woman has only to obey him. Thus it is that through the continual increase of private property monogamy sprung up, that is to say the union of a man and a woman with the object of producing legitimate children who might inherit the property of the father.[2]

Since that time monogamy has persisted to our own day. However important the modifications which the method of production has undergone since the rise of monogamy, the fact remains that a certain part of the work necessary to existence belongs still to the work of housekeeping, which, as at other times, is performed by the women. The more important labors, those which give the greater social power to him who executes them, fall upon the man, and from this fact his preponderance still persists.

Though the position of the married woman may be somewhat improved when compared with that at the beginning of civilization, nevertheless a study of existing civil codes (especially of the French civil code and of those for which it has served as a model) shows that the married woman is in general still in a state of great dependence. The woman must obey her husband and follow him wherever he wishes; except where otherwise stipulated in the marriage contract the husband has the management of his wife's fortune and the income from it belongs to him; it is the man who exercises parental authority; the woman cannot appear in a lawsuit without the assistance of her husband; etc.

[1] *Engels, op. cit.,* p. 51. [Paging of original.]
[2] See *Engels, op. cit.,* pp. 47 *ff.* [Paging of original.]

The difference between the position of the married woman of today and that of former times consists principally in that the consent of both parties is necessary to conclude the marriage, that the husband can no longer repudiate his wife, but can only dissolve the union for important reasons (adultery, cruelty, etc.), and that the woman also, for the same reasons, can obtain separation or divorce.

This raises the question as to why a marriage should not be dissolved as soon as for any reason the union becomes intolerable to either party. The answer must be as follows. From the dominant position of the man in the economic life it is clear that the woman would not be able to loose the bonds of marriage at her pleasure, except in the case provided by law, inasmuch as the man could not permit so grave an assault upon his authority. From this point of view monogamy and the ancient forms of marriage are alike, for the woman has never been able to secure a divorce at her own pleasure except among the lower agriculturists, where, on account of her importance in the economic life she enjoyed the same rights as the man. The present organization of society prevents the man, for his part, from getting a divorce except in certain cases provided by law, for if it were possible for the husband to break the marriage at will, society today would not have the necessary solidity and stability; marriage would be a very hazardous enterprise for the woman, since, from the nature of her occupation, she is generally not in a position to provide for her own needs by herself; and the support and education of the children by their parents would also be less assured. But even this is not all. As we have seen, monogamy was created as soon as private property became general. Reciprocally monogamy is one of the causes which support and increase the spirit of property in men. It is in the narrow circle of the family, away from the contact with society, that a keen desire to possess is developed among children.

The deepest roots of marriage as it exists today are found in our present state of society, based as it is on private property; and, in its turn, marriage is a support for that society. Here is also the reason for the disapprobation of free unions felt by the majority, even if the motives of these unions are the most noble. And this also is why the more conservative a man is as to the institution of private property, the more he holds to the existing form of marriage, a fact otherwise inexplicable.

An examination of the modifications made during the last century in the matrimonial law and in matters pertaining to it, shows that the position of the married woman has improved gradually. To cite only a few examples, the French civil code gave to the married woman the right of divorce in the case of adultery on the part of her husband only if he kept a concubine in the common dwelling (art. 230).   In 1884 this article was modified so that the woman now has the same right of divorce in case of adultery as the man.   (Article 337 of the penal code, however, punishes the adulterous wife by an imprisonment of from three months to two years, while article 339 punishes the adulterous husband only if he has been keeping a concubine in the common dwelling, and then only by a fine of from one hundred to two thousand francs.)   In England before 1870 the married woman was in a position of dependence.   The right of possession of personal property as well as the administration of real estate and the benefit of revenues from it devolved upon the husband.   Since 1870 and 1882 there has been a great change in the matrimonial law, to the great advantage of the woman who has become, among other things, the sole owner of her fortune, etc.[1]   In the countries where there have been no modifications in the last century, public opinion is such that we may be sure that the condition of women will be better in case of an eventual revision of the matrimonial law.

In searching for the causes of the changes of opinion upon this question we discover that here again they are due in the last analysis to the economic life.   This springs from the fact that the number of women who work independently, who gain their own bread, increases continually.   The causes which bring this about are of diverse kinds but can be reduced to the following.   In the first place, the number of marriages contracted is in general diminishing, and this decrease is due to the continually diminishing number of marriages among the moneyed classes, and to the fact that these marriages take place later in life than formerly.[2]   It is not difficult to see that a retrograde movement in the marriages of the bourgeoisie must tell.   Marriage brings an increase of expenses indeed, but among the proletariat it brings also an increase of revenue (the woman may earn something by working away from home, or save by doing the work of the house herself).   Among the bourgeoisie, on the other hand, it brings with it pecuniary disadvantages only, at least if we except those cases in which the wife is more or less rich.   The struggle for existence be-

---

[1] See *A. Bebel*, "Die Frau und der Sozialismus", pp. 265 *ff*.
[2] See "Neue Zeit", 188, p. 239; *G. v. Mayr*, "Statistik und Gesellschaftslehre", II, p. 384; *F. v. d. Goes*, "Socialisme en Feminisme" ("Tweemaandelijksch Tijdschrift", VI, 1900) pp. 430–445; *Braun*, "Die Frauenfrage", pp. 166 *ff*.; *C. Zetkin*, "Geistiges Proletariat, Frauenfrage und Sozialismus", pp. 4, 5.

comes more and more difficult, and especially among the members of the petty bourgeoisie and those who practice the liberal professions marriage does not take place until later in life, and in general the number of marriages diminishes.[1] To this it is still necessary to add the fact that in Europe and in some of the states of North America the number of women exceeds that of the men.[2]

The diminishing opportunity for women of the more or less well-to-do classes to marry forces them to earn their own living. The change that housekeeping has undergone and is still undergoing must also be taken into consideration. The importance of housekeeping continually decreases in consequence of the extension of manufacturing, which absorbs the special tasks of the household one after another. While formerly clothes were made at home, bread was baked there, etc., at present there remains for the work of the household only the care of the house and the preparation of the food. And even these occupations may soon be taken out of the house.[3] Unmarried women of the bourgeoisie used formerly often to be able to find a home with members of their family, since they were able to be of service. At present they are in general only superfluous persons in the household.

Even the married women of the bourgeoisie find themselves more and more forced to contribute to the revenues of the family by working for money,[4] and this for reasons already cited in speaking of unmarried women : the increasing difficulty of the struggle for existence, and the diminution of the importance of household occupations. Outside of those whose economic situation forces them to work for money, the number of women who seek to earn something is becoming greater and greater. With these it is not necessity that forces them, but the spirit of independence awakened in them by the example of the others. If, on the one hand, the supply of women's labor increases, on the other hand the demand is increasing also; for though it has been asserted that women are incapable of anything beyond housekeeping, they have proved their aptitude for many of the professions. And besides, the labor of women is much sought after, for not being yet organized like men, the wages they can obtain are not so large.

[1] See *Bebel, op. cit.,* chapter entitled "Ehehemmnisse und Ehehindernisse"; *v. d. Goes, op. cit.,* pp. 445–458; *Braun, op. cit.,* pp. 166–170; *Zetkin, op. cit.,* pp. 5–6.
[2] See *Bebel, op. cit.,* p. 159; *v. d. Goes, op. cit.,* pp. 458 *ff.*; and *Braun, op. cit.,* pp. 165, 166.
[3] See *Bebel, op cit.,* pp. 223 *ff.*; *v. d. Goes, op. cit.* (Année VII 1901), pp. 120 *ff.*; *Zetkin, op. cit.,* pp. 3, 4, and "Die Arbeiterinnen- und Frauenfrage der Gegenwart", pp. 3 *ff.*   [4] See *Braun, op. cit.,* p. 181.

And if the women of the bourgeoisie are engaging more and more in paid labor, the women of the proletariat were forced into it long ago. The labor of women became possible through the development of mechanical processes, as our exposition of the present economic system has shown. Since then this form of labor has assumed larger and larger proportions. The unmarried women of the proletariat are all obliged to provide for their needs, while the married women also often are, and the number of these is continually increasing.[1]

By what has gone before it has been indicated how important a change has taken place and is still taking place in the economic position of women. This change is in the last analysis the reason why women have revolted more and more against the inferior position in which the law places them, and why their opposition has already taken the form of deeds. This is the reason also why the legal position of woman is best in general in those countries where she has freed herself most by her independent work, as, for example, in the United States.

Up to this point we have examined only the legal side of the question. We must go on to add some observations concerning the material side. The civil codes rest, among other things, upon the fiction that all persons are equal. No mention is made of the division into distinct classes; and it is the same with marriage. Before the law all marriages are equal, while in reality they are not so. It is necessary, therefore to treat of the conjugal conditions of the different classes.[2]

In the first place take marriage *in the bourgeois class*. The conditions of life for the two sexes are different before marriage. Leaving out of account the fact that the number of women who provide for their own needs is increasing (they are still in the minority), it is incontestable that the aspirations of the women of the bourgeoisie tend toward marriage, the earliest and best marriage possible, in order that their future may be assured. And since the possibility of making a good marriage is becoming less, husband-hunting with all its unfortunate consequences becomes more and more eager. While the whole education of women looks only to marriage, that of the great majority of young men has as its object the attainment of

---

[1] See *Braun, op. cit.* Pt. II, chaps. IV and V.

[2] [NOTE TO THE AMERICAN EDITION: There has appeared, especially recently, an extensive literature criticising the conditions of modern marriage. *Cf.* among others: *Forel*, "Die Sexuelle Frage"; *M. Weber, op. cit.*, chap. vi; *T. Bloch*, "Das Sexualleben unserer Zeit", chap. x; *Havelock Ellis*, "Geschlecht und Gesellschaft", II, chap. x; *A. Moll*, "Handbuch der Sexualwissenschaften"; *F. Müller-Lyer*, "Die Familie" and "Phasen der Liebe."]

wealth or an important position as soon as possible. Even when the marriage is contracted in consequence of a reciprocal inclination, the differing conceptions of life held by the two parties contain the germs that may render it unhappy. In speaking of these very frequent cases Mme. Dr. Adams-Lehman very justly says: "Neither understands the other. Sundered in everything that belongs to life, from childhood up, nature succeeds in uniting them at one point for a short time only. From this point on their paths diverge. The husband complains often and bitterly that his wife does not understand him. What would he have, when she belongs to an entirely different civilization? She has her own virtues, her own failings and vices, but they are not those of her husband, and serve principally to set her at variance with him. And the same is true of the man, over whose lack of understanding his wife just as often and bitterly laments. Different systems of culture, different aims, different ideals, — in such an atmosphere how should harmony thrive?" [1]

But these causes are further strengthened when economic motives have influenced the marriage more or less. If the two parties have frankly made their union on this basis they will not be too exacting, and will know how to submit to the inevitable; but when, as is ordinarily the case, the marriage has been contracted under false pretenses, the situation is much worse.[2]

It is plain, then, from this how little the legal form shows the reality. In order that the marriage may be contracted, the consent of the two parties is necessary, no matter how that consent is obtained. It is very often the parents who have made the choice, being guided by calculation alone. Such is the reality, and the formal *free* consent is only the appearance.

Weighty causes, sprung from social conditions, then, often bring it about that the married life is one of hate and discord. Aside from the reasons cited there is yet another which does not proceed from social conditions. Even when the marriage has been brought about through mutual inclination, there is no guarantee that this inclination will last. Not only may the parties be deceived as to each other's character and temperament, but their feelings may change, and the marriage bond become insupportable.

---

[1] "Das Weib und der Stier." ("Neue Zeit", 1900–1901, II, p. 6–7.)
[2] Upon marriage in the bourgeoisie see *Fourier*, "Théorie des quatre mouvements" (Complete Works, I, pp. 162 *ff.*); *A. E. F. Schäffle*, "Bau und Leben", etc., III, pp. 36, 50; *Nordau*, "Die conventionnellen Lügen der Kulturmenschheit", pp. 263 *ff.*; *Bebel, op. cit.*, pp. 103 *ff.*; and *Dr. E. Gystrow*, "Liebe und Liebesleben im XIX Jahrhundert", pp. 26 *ff.*

The law permits divorce only in certain fixed cases; and since divorce brings with it serious economic disadvantages for the woman, and sometimes for the man as well, it is not often resorted to. The fear of losing the good opinion of one's friends may also prevent divorce. And this fear of blame where a divorce is desired proves once more how little real love has to do with the origin of monogamy.

If it is difficult, then, if not impossible, to break a marriage, the consequence is bound to be adultery, especially on the side of the man, since his manner of life gives him easy opportunity for it, and he does not fear the consequences as a woman does. The difference between monogamy and the more ancient forms of marriage is not great. Before the law monogamy alone is recognized and polygamy prohibited; but in reality polygamy always exists.

Let us go on now to marriage among *the proletarians*.[1] Here there can be no question of a different education for the boy and the girl; both are put to work while still children, and their relations are quite free. Among the working classes marriage usually takes place at an early age, because the workman early reaches the maximum of his earning capacity, and as a consequence it is useless for him to wait long before marrying; besides which he reaches maturity sooner than the bourgeois. Often marriage is contracted after it has been consummated and the sexual intercourse has had results. This is easy to understand when one observes the life of the proletariat, their housing conditions, their work in common, etc.

While it is not true that the marriages of the proletariat are always marriages of inclination, as has been asserted (for material interests play some part here also), yet they are oftenest of this kind. One of the causes, then, which often make marriages among the bourgeoisie unhappy does not exist here. On the other hand there are other causes which can bring about the same result. In the first place, this inclination is in many cases of a sexual nature only, without there being any sympathy of character. If this inclination dies out, therefore,— a thing which happens very often, since marriages in the proletariat are made at an early age, and the women soon grow old because of their hard life — there is no longer any basis for a happy marriage. There is a lack of that intellectual development which may render the difficulties of married life supportable. In consequence of this lack the slightest differences may result in great altercations,

[1] It is unnecessary to go into the question of marriage in the petty bourgeoisie, which does not differ fundamentally from that which we have been treating. See Dr. *B. Schoenlank*, "Zur Psychologie des Kleinbürgthums", pp. 123–124 ("Neue Zeit", 1890).

and the causes of unhappiness are sought in the person and not in the circumstances of which the person is but the victim. Then in the next place there are the heavy cares of the struggle for existence. If a laborer's family have already enough difficulty in making both ends meet, in the case of sickness or forced unemployment their misery is extreme, and it is often this misery which causes disputes and even blows. Further, the labor of women, the bad housing conditions, and alcoholism all tend to the same result. And because of hard work and many cares the wife of the workman soon grows old. In the proletarian class, therefore, marriages are threatened by many causes.

There is besides all this a very important difference between the marriages of the bourgeoisie and those of the proletariat as to their bases. The preponderating power of the man, which is strongly marked in bourgeois marriages, is less so in the proletarian, especially in those families where the woman provides for herself by paid labor. And private property, one of the "raisons d'être" of legal monogamy with the bourgeoisie, is lacking among the proletariat. This "raison d'être" is found with the latter in the necessity that the man should be charged with providing for the material needs of the children. Thus, in the proletariat the free union between a man and a woman generally meets with disapprobation only when there are offspring. The consequences are, first, that conjugal unions without legal sanction are not as much frowned upon by the proletarians as by the other classes; second, that the decision to dissolve the union, whether free or legal, is much more easily made among proletarians than among the bourgeoisie.[1]

With regard to marriage among the *lower proletariat* a word or two will suffice. Persons who have recently fallen to this class keep the ideas of the class from which they came. But when the persons have been born in the lower proletariat, or when their poverty has lasted for a long time, they become demoralized, and the relations between men and women show the effects of it.[2]

We come, then, to the end of our exposition. It seems to me that it has been shown that the different forms of marriage are in the last instance determined by the respective modes of production. Hence the origin of monogamy, the most recent form of marriage, is not to be found in the innate desire of the man and the woman to be united

[1] *Engels, op. cit.*, pp. 59, 60, and Dr. *A. Blaschko*, "Die Prostitution im XIX Jahrhundert", p. 12.
[2] See "Englands industrielle Reservearmee", pp. 215–216 ("Neue Zeit", 1884).

for the whole of their lives, a desire which the law is supposed to sanction. Quite on the contrary men are not all monogamous, and still less monogamous during the whole of their life; a circumstance because of which the present economic conditions have produced the legal marriage, obliging two persons to remain together; if it were otherwise the law would not concern itself with the relations between man and woman.

Some important modifications have taken and are taking place in this matter. The bases upon which the present marriage system rests are changing. This is due to different reasons. In the first place woman is coming little by little to occupy a higher and more independent social position. Next, the importance of housekeeping in the economic life is diminishing. The only moral basis for marriage is little by little coming to be mutual love and sympathy, for true love can only exist between persons free and equal.[1] There is a constantly increasing number of persons who, in place of stigmatizing as immoral a union that is non-legitimate, but contracted because of mutual love and sympathy, consider it, on the contrary, as superior to a legal marriage contracted for economic reasons.

Finally, it is to be noted that the present economic and social life has bound up the sexual life with the economic life, by making marriage possible only for those who have the necessary means at their disposal, and consequently has caused the compulsory celibacy of millions of men and women.

B. THE FAMILY.

In the preceding pages we have fixed the attention principally upon the relation between the man and the woman, and it now remains to treat of the position of the children born of their union.

It is a biological fact that the mother is designed by nature to have the care of the child during its first years, and consequently this care persists through all phases of the social development. It is, then, superfluous to speak of it in a sociological treatise.

The relations between parents and children have not always been the same in the different phases of social development, and it is therefore impossible to speak here of relations instituted by nature. A glance at the respective situations in the different periods shows that among the "lower hunters", where the woman is considered as the property of the man, the children born are also in the absolute power

[1] *Engels, op. cit.,* pp. 63–74 [paging of original].

of their father, who has the right of life and death over his children, and whose power over them ceases only when he has sold his daughters to their husbands, or when his sons, having become adults, are recognized as members of the tribe.[1]

Among the upper hunters and the pastoral peoples it is, as with the peoples named above, to the father, in general, that the children belong, or to whom they owe obedience. The mother, herself in subjection to the father, has little or no authority over the children.[2]

Among the lower agriculturists the conditions in question differ relatively very much. As has been shown in the considerations upon marriage among these peoples, the position of woman is often quite other than during the preceding periods. She is not at all in so subordinate a situation, her position is even not without importance, thanks to the place which she occupies in the economic life. And this importance shows itself also in her relations with her children. In general it is to the mother that the education of the children falls, while the influence of the father is little or nothing. In these last cases a greater or less power belongs to the mother's brother (under the matriarchate the grandfather and father of the children belong to another clan, and the maternal uncle and the children belong to the clan of the mother).[3]

As has already been said above conditions among the higher agriculturists were patriarchal. The father had unlimited power over his unmarried daughters, and over all his sons with their descendants.[4] It is from these so-called "great families", that the present form of the family springs (husband, wife, and their not yet emancipated children) as a consequence of the fact that the adult sons have been able to emancipate themselves on account of the modifications that the economic life has undergone. From this time especially the affection for children in general which is found among almost all people, takes on an exclusive character, and becomes limited to one's own children. For monogamy is before all a consequence of the desire of the man, which came in with private property, to leave his possessions to the children of his legal wife, whose father he knew himself to be.[5]

In its essence this form of the family has been maintained down to the present day. The modifications it has undergone may be reduced

---

[1] *E. Grosse*, "Die Formen der Familie und die Formen die Wirthschaft", pp. 49–53.
[2] See *Grosse, op. cit.*, pp. 78–82, 120–123.   [3] *Grosse, op. cit.*, pp. 183–186.
[4] See *Grosse, op. cit.*, pp. 220–223, 226–228, 230–234.
[5] See *v. Dargun, op. cit.*, p. 12.

to the two following.[1] In the first place, in consequence of her improved position as wife, the mother has obtained a greater influence over the education of her children, though her power is, under the law, still subordinated in every way to that of her husband. In the second place the state manifests a continually increasing tendency to exert an influence over the relations between parents and their children. To begin with, the state imposes upon married parents the task of supporting and bringing up their children, and prohibits by the penal law slaying or abandoning them. The origin of these requirements must be found in the fact that the state is interested in having the children cared for, in order that the population may be as numerous as possible. (The state being once formed, while the causes of infanticide among primitive peoples have almost disappeared, the law has no occasion to make any great change in the existing situation.) If the married parents were not forced by the state to support and bring up their children [2] it would be necessary to impose this task upon other institutions which do not exist in our present society. The state is not an institution for the public well-being; it is chiefly a means of maintaining the external order in the disorder which results from the complicated and muddled system of capitalistic production; it is before all a system of police. If it were otherwise, the state would consider it as one of its first duties to deprive parents of their rights over their children, if they did not perform their task, or did it badly, and would itself undertake the care and training of these children, as well of those whose parents were dead or otherwise absolutely unable to care for them. For society as a whole, as well as the children themselves, has a very great interest in this matter.

However, the state in general does not assume any duty towards abandoned or neglected children, and only in a hesitating way intervenes to punish or to take away the parental authority of those who have been guilty of such acts.[3] Little by little, as the ideas upon the duties of the state become modified however (principally under the influence of organized labor, which aims at transforming the state into an organized community), it interests itself more in the person of the child. As to the care of the child's *property* all the codes are already very much detailed !

[1] See *M. Kovalewsky*, "Tableau des origines et de l'évolution de la famille et de la propriété", pp. 150–161.
[2] The law does not produce much change in the situation which would exist without it, since most parents would perform this duty without being compelled.
[3] *L. Ferriani*, "Entartete Mütter", pp. 24–50.

There are two points with regard to which the state quite generally has an influence over the lot of the child. First, it prohibits or limits his paid labor; and second, it obliges parents to send their children to school.

We have already spoken of this prohibition, which is made necessary from the fact that the physical condition of the working classes is becoming worse, and because the labor movement exercises a pressure upon the state. Compulsory education has its origin, on one side, in the fact that, in some occupations, capitalism cannot make use of workmen who are altogether ignorant; on the other side, in the fact that without compulsory education the youth of the working class would be even more brutalized than at present. The opposition to compulsory education on the part of whatever is conservative is another clear indication of what an intimate connection there is between the individual family and the present economic system. The economic position of the man as breadwinner for his wife and children is the cause of his desire to be limited in his power as little as possible.

Up to this point we have been treating of conditions past and present only in so far as they are regulated by law (the formal side); we must now go on to treat conditions from the material side. Here we must consider three subjects: physical education, intellectual education, and moral education. In treating of criminality, however, we have, naturally little to do with the first two, while the third is of the highest importance for us.

As to physical education it is enough to say that it is the "conditio sine qua non" of the two others. The intellectual and moral qualities of a child that is badly cared for physically, can never be entirely developed. The parents (and the child himself) use up all their energy in providing for their bodily necessities, so that there is none left for the other needs. Dr. A. Baer says: "Children of this kind (*i.e.*, of the poor classes) already at an early age bear the cares and sorrows that life imposes upon them; they early become acquainted with the claims and demands of life, and not infrequently are very early influenced by living-conditions which will necessarily affect them long afterward." [1]

It is only among the bourgeoisie and the relatively well-to-do portion of the petty bourgeoisie that there can be any sufficient physical education for the children. Among the proletarians, and

---

[1] "Der Selbstmord im kindlichen Lebensalter", p. 48.

those of the petty bourgeoisie who are in a similar situation as regards material conditions, it is insufficient, and worse, if possible, among the lower proletariat. However, if there is a lack of it among these last, there is at times a superabundance among the bourgeoisie. There children are often brought up in such luxury that they are early made blasé and rendered unhappy for the future. Dr. Baer says upon this subject: [1] "It is through other circumstances and causes that the children of the rich and well-to-do classes are brought to a condition of precocity, accompanied by sickly irritability and arrogant self-conceit. Here are good-living, luxury, and the superabundance of bodily enjoyments, the early familiarity with the theater, balls, and outside social life in general, which make them incapable of the harmless pleasures of childhood. Improper education in the family is responsible for the fact that children in widely separated social classes are already at any early age left to themselves and fall into evil ways. 'One must have lived in a great city,' says von Krafft-Ebing, 'and have visited the hovels of the poor, and the palaces of the rich to know what mistakes in the bringing up of children are committed there, where the children of the poor, amidst dirt and drink, and those of the rich, amidst arrogance and rascality, are going to ruin physically and morally. . . . Every day may be seen children falling asleep at the theater or other places of amusement to which their parents' folly and desire for pleasure have dragged them. Other parents provide for their children the doubtful happiness of children's balls and soirées. Is it any wonder, then, if we now, especially in the great cities, very seldom meet with any real children?'"

In the countries where education is compulsory, it is guaranteed that all the children will acquire a certain amount of knowledge. It is unnecessary to say that in general this amount of knowledge is very small in the case of the children of the poor, and consists of the rudiments of reading, writing, and arithmetic, so that there is no real intellectual education. For the children of the bourgeoisie quite a different preparation is made; here there is rather an over- than an undersupply of the means of education. The great competition in present day society, the superabundance of intellectual forces, the ardent desire to see their children succeed in spite of everything, all this obliges parents to crowd their children's intellectual capacities, even to the detriment of their other qualities. "The thing which in our modern life conduces most to the giving of a one-sided, inharmonious development to the child, is the fact that too little weight

[1] *Op. cit.* This quotation follows directly upon the one given above.

is given to the development of the disposition, and too much to the development of the understanding. Because there is no influence exerted upon the spiritual and emotional life, the mind of the child is often from early youth turned toward the material and sensuous, the life of pleasure, and comes to bend its thought wholly to the practical and utilitarian." [1]

Thus we arrive at the very subject we have in view, moral education. As I have already remarked, one of the characteristic differences between education among the primitive peoples and that of our own day is this, that as a consequence of the great complexity of our present society, and the numberless conflicts between individual interests, the task imposed upon the educator is now much broader and more onerous. [2]

The first condition, without doubt, that might be demanded of one who is to make a child into a moral man, a man of character, is surely this, that he should be himself a man of character. It goes without saying that no person can give more than he has. Leaving aside for the moment the criminal class, of whom I shall treat later, it is clear that no one without character, or weak in character, can ever train children to have well developed moral sentiments. He may be able, it is true, to teach them to distinguish good from bad, but such lessons concern only the intellectual part of the nature and not the moral part, and they cannot transform children into persons who *feel* morally. It cannot be denied that the number of persons who do not feel morally is great, and that these have children. Without forgetting the fact that it is the father to whom the law gives especially the parental authority, we must recognize that it is the mother upon whom the task of education generally rests, because the father is almost always away from home. But the inferior position of woman, maintained now for centuries, has been extremely harmful to her character, and thus it often happens that this lack of character passes to the children as well. [3]

A second condition without which successful education is impossible is that educators shall have the innate qualities necessary for their task. We should doubt, and not without reason, the common sense of anyone who dared to assert that every person was capable of becoming a good sculptor or even carpenter. Just so no one could say

[1] *Dr. A. Baer, op. cit.*, p. 49. See also pp. 58, 59.
[2] [NOTE TO THE AMERICAN EDITION: *Cf. M. Kauffmann*, "Die Psychologie des Verbrechens", pp. 235 *ff.*]
[3] *C. Zetkin*, "Die Arbeiterinnen- und Frauenfrage der Gegenwart", pp. 23–39.

that everyone possesses the qualities necessary for an art as difficult as that of education.

To be a good educator it is necessary to be very fond of children, to have much patience and zeal, to know how to put one's self on a plane with the child, to have a clear and practical intellect, especially when the teacher has a great affection for the child, since without intelligence the excess of affection will only be harmful. There are parents who possess these qualities in a very high degree, and it is only to be regretted that they teach only their own children, and not those also of parents in whom the teaching faculty is entirely lacking. Next comes the group of those who have a modicum of the requisite qualities, and finally a smaller group who have little or no aptitude for the task. The least fit to give a good education, however, are psychopathic individuals, because of their changeable disposition, their quick fits of temper, etc.

Just as educators differ greatly in their innate fitness for teaching, so different children need to be guided in different ways. If there are children who require little care in order that they may presently be able to adapt themselves to the requirements of society, others, who form the great majority, require more; while there remains a second minority who, if they are to be made fairly useful men and women, must have constant and minute attention. Among these last are to be classed the victims of heredity. If they have parents without great teaching ability, as is often the case with these psychopathic individuals, the results are even worse.

Aside from innate fitness it is necessary that an educator should have received the necessary education. The teacher without notions of psychology, of pedagogy, etc., often deceives himself, even if he has all the necessary innate qualities, and consequently warps the character of his pupils.

The instructor must learn his trade, and if this is so, why should not the educator in charge of the moral education of the child need an apprenticeship, since moral education is a task no less difficult than intellectual education (which is about all that our present schools undertake)? However, it is incontestable that in all classes of society today moral education is practiced in dilettante fashion, as was formerly the case with intellectual education.[1]

Finally, there remains the condition that the teacher should have the time necessary to perform his task, for without this the most

[1] See *J. Stern*, "Thesen über den Sozialismus", p. 24; and *C. Zetkin, op. cit.*, pp. 30 *ff.*

capable cannot attain good results.   Having now laid down the general conditions, let us go on to examine in a few words education as it is actually practiced in the different classes.

Let us begin with the bourgeoisie.   As has already been remarked, the children in this class are often spoiled by the great luxury that surrounds them, and further by the fact that their intellect is developed at the expense of their moral qualities.   As my remarks concerning capacity, character, etc., apply to all classes, it is unnecessary here to speak of them more fully.   Only it must be observed that, as far as positive knowledge of pedagogy is concerned, the bourgeoisie is much superior to the proletariat, from which there follows among other things a corresponding superiority of the bourgeois education. The character of the bourgeois woman, who occupies, like all women, a lower rank in society, has generally suffered still more from her easy mode of life, and her weakness of character is transmitted to her children if she brings them up herself.   This condition must be added, for society life, or in other words, the habit of doing nothing at all, is often the cause of mothers' having their children brought up by some one who has neither natural aptitude nor acquired capacity for this task, but only takes charge of the children for the sake of a place.   There are even children who are not suckled by their mothers but by nurses, since the mothers are afraid of diminishing their own charms.   This proves once more the weakness of the allegation that the parents are the natural educators of the child; for we see in this case that the social environment can lead to the renunciation of duties that are really natural.[1]

The moral education of the children of the bourgeoisie is generally superficial, and has especially in view the task of teaching the children to conduct themselves according to the proprieties, much more than that of developing their real moral nature.[2]   In the second place this education develops among them a very strong feeling of class, so that they consider the members of the proletariat as inferior beings, born by nature to serve the bourgeoisie, in place of seeing in them only their own fellows, who have become different merely because of fortuitous circumstances.

In the third place, our present educational system makes children egoistic, those of the bourgeoisie more than those of the proletariat. This assertion contradicts, it is true, the numerous authors who are convinced that our present education in the family is a source of

[1] C. Zetkin, op. cit., p. 24.
[2] L. Ferriani, "Schlaue und glückliche Verbrecher", pp. 34, 35.

altruism.[1] They are right when they say that altruistic sentiments *between the members of the family themselves* have their rise *within* the circle of the family. For a long time the life within the family constituted a man's whole life (as it still does for a very great number of women), but in the society of today a great part of the time is passed outside of the family circle, and for this reason the opinion of these authors, though shared by many persons, is not correct. In the family circle the child, especially when he has neither brothers nor sisters,[2] soon discovers that his own interests come first, that the outside world is his enemy, and that when he grows up he must make himself as large a place there as possible. It matters little that the interests of others will then be injured. It must be added further, that if on the one side the family is an economic unity, and that the interests of the members of the family are so far parallel, on the other hand there exist opposing interests, such as inheritance, which may destroy the homogeneity of interest.

It may be objected here that in our present society, consisting as it does for the most part of adherents of Christianity, most children are taught to love their neighbor as themselves. This is true, but in a society such as ours, where the interests of all men are opposed, the effect of this commandment cannot be great, or will be practiced only in words and not in acts, and so end in hypocrisy. He who wants to follow this commandment to the letter sees himself at once defeated in the conflict of life, unless he changes his opinion.[3]

No one known to me has better characterized the existing educational system than Owen. "As society is now constituted," he says, "no children can by possibility be really well educated. The fundamental errors upon which it has been based, filling the early mind with error and hypocrisy and all manner of conflicting ideas, opposed to facts and to nature, render it impracticable for any child to be rationally trained or treated by society. And the more education of this kind is given to children, the more they are estranged from a knowledge of themselves, or of human nature generally, and the less competent will they be to understand what society has been made to be, and yet less what it ought to be, and how it may be made what it is desirable that it should be, for the happiness and well-being of all.

---

[1] To name one among many: *M. Kovalewsky.* See his "Tableau des origines et de l'évolution de la famille et de la propriété", pp. 160, 161.

[2] The number of births is constantly decreasing, and the consequent decrease in the size of families accentuates the tendency to develop egoism in the child.

[3] Compare, among others, *E. Key*, "Das Jahrhundert des Kindes", p. 316.

"Mothers and fathers thus taught, are incompetent to teach and educate their children in the spirit, manner, and conduct, which should, for the benefit of all, be given to all children. Their affections also, especially the strong natural animal affections of the mother, are, in almost all cases too strong for the very limited powers of judging accurately respecting their own children and those of other parents, which females now acquire from their present mal-education.

"The individual family arrangements confining the child to the limited number of ideas among them — to their early deep impressions in favor of family interests and supposed rights — to the narrow and partial experience of a family and its usual small connections, are equally destructive of a good sound practical education or well-training of children.

"The individual system of society which has so long prevailed in all nations, and amongst all peoples, is also a strong barrier to the proper education of beings intended to be made rational. The individual system of society is injurious to man now, under every point of view in which it can be considered; but especially in the education of children of all classes. It confines all their strongest feelings to self first, then to family, afterwards to kindred, and then to small neighborhoods and districts, regularly and systematically training each child to become at maturity a merely localized, ignorantly selfish animal, filled with family and geographical prejudices.

"As long as this individual system shall be continued, it will be vain to expect that any child can be well educated, or properly trained to become a rational being — a man with the full physical and mental powers of humanity, intelligent, moral, and virtuous. The isolated character formed by the individual system will, as long as children shall be educated under it, and in accordance with all its innumerable errors in practice and principle, render it impossible for any child to be so educated and placed in society as not to become, more or less, a cause of anxiety to its parents. Every child under this system comes into society, at its birth, opposed by the capital and experience of society; and as it advances in its progress, and has to take part in the jostle, bustle and business of life, it has to contend for itself, often, not only against these general powers of society, but on the death of parents, or sometimes even before, with brothers and sisters, for individual property or other advantages.

"Besides, children before they have any resisting powers of mind, being forced to receive the errors of their parents and other early instructors, respecting their supposed faculties of believing and disbelieving, loving and hating, are by this process, placed through life in direct opposition to nature; and, as vice has been made, by the gross errors of our ancestors, to consist in acting in accordance with nature, and virtue in acting in opposition to it, and as nature continually impels the individual to desire to act in accordance with its own laws, in defiance of man's unwise and unjust laws, the great probability is that children will be more liable to obey nature than man; and thus, where there are children, they must be a source of constant anxiety to parents; and that anxiety must be injurious to the best formation of the organization of the remainder of the infants that may be born to them." [1]

We have still to fix our attention upon the sexual education of the children of the bourgeoisie. In our society the Christian sexual ethics is dominant, often even among non-Christians, without their being conscious of it. According to this system the whole sexual life proceeds from the evil one, and man would be better without any sexual instincts.[2] This is why children are generally raised in an absolute ignorance upon this subject, or even have lies told to them about it. As nature cannot be suppressed it follows that the curiosity of the child only becomes the more inflamed, and that the conduct of men in this regard becomes hypocritical.[3]

Secondly, let us take up education in the petty bourgeoisie. Upon this point we can be very brief. A part of this class joins on to the proletariat from the conditions of its life, and another part to the bourgeoisie. It is unnecessary, therefore, to speak of it at length. It is only the core of the petty bourgeoisie who, having kept the traditions of their class, show any differences in this regard. Here there is no danger of the demoralizing influence of the luxurious surroundings of the rich, and the surveillance of the father is greater, and thus the education more severe; but the limited conception of life, and the continual efforts of the parents, eager to procure advantages for their families, develop egotism among their children in a high degree.

With regard to the proletariat it has already been shown that the material advantages necessary for a sufficient education are lacking in the case of this class. Housing conditions are here of the greatest importance. Generally there is not room enough for the children at home, so that they spend the greater part of the day in the street.

---

[1] "The Book of the New Moral World", Pt. III., pp. 9–11.
[2] *K. Kautsky*, "Die Entstehung des Christenthums" ("Neue Zeit", 1885).
[3] *L. Ferriani*, "Schlaue und glückliche Verbrecher", p. 48.

Then again the housing conditions are responsible for the fact that the children often are thrown with persons whose influence is harmful to them (prostitutes, etc.). And finally the small apartments bring it about that the children are too early instructed in sexual matters, and this in a bad way (through sleeping in the same small room with their parents, or in the same bed with children of the opposite sex, etc.).

Then children need to grow up in an environment not poisoned by cares, one in which poverty does not harden the heart, and extinguish all gayety, and where the knowledge necessary for education is not wanting. Further, in this class the father has generally no opportunity to busy himself with the education of his children in consequence of the long duration of his hours of labor outside of the home. A great many working men have to leave home in the morning to go to work long before their children are awake, to return only after the little ones have already been put to bed; and the situation is much the same where the laborer works at night, and consequently sleeps during the day.

The development of capitalism has led to the paid labor of married women, and consequently to one of the most important causes of the demoralization of the children of the working class. When there is no one to watch a child, when he is left to himself, he becomes demoralized. In his work, "The Condition of the Working-Class in England", F. Engels has put the situation briefly: "The employment of the wife [in the factory] dissolves the family utterly and of necessity, and this dissolution, in our present society, which is based upon the family, brings the most demoralizing consequences, both for parents and for the children. A mother who has no time to trouble herself about her child, to perform the most ordinary loving services for it during the first year, who scarcely indeed sees it, can be no real mother to the child, must inevitably grow indifferent to it, and treat it unlovingly, like a stranger. The children who grow up under such conditions are entirely ruined for later family life, can never feel at home in the family which they themselves found, because they have always been accustomed to isolation, and they contribute therefore to the already general undermining of the family in the working class." [1]

---

[1] P. 144 [In original, p. 147]. See also *L. Braun*, "Die Frauenfrage", pp. 318 *ff.*; *C. Zetkin, op. cit.*, p. 26; *Herkner, op. cit.*, pp. 36 *ff.*; and especially *Rühle*, "Das proletarische Kind" pp. 42 *ff.* Upon the education of children of the working class in general, see also: *G. Schönfeldt*, "Die heutige Arbeiterfamilie und die öffentliche Erziehung vorschulpflichtiger Kinder" ("Neue Zeit", I, 1898–1899).

Finally, when, through death or otherwise, the parents are no longer in a position to support and raise their children, they are left to their fate, unless there are charitable persons or benevolent institutions that wish to take charge of them.   For the state, for reasons shown above, does not lay upon itself the duty of caring for such children.

It remains now to speak of the lower proletariat, among whom prostitutes and criminals are included.   The education of these persons is not only much neglected, as is often the case with the children of the proletariat, of whom it may be said that they receive a negative education — but these receive in addition a positive education in evil.   It might be possible to dispute the advantages of a good education, but it is indisputable that children brought up by immoral people, or even incited to evil (prostitution or crime) run the greatest risk, unless exceptional circumstances present themselves, of becoming persons hurtful to society.

In this connection it is necessary to fix our attention, finally, upon the situation in which illegitimate children find themselves.   Since marriage, at once the consequence and support of existing social conditions, is the only form of sexual union legally recognized, illegitimate children are legally and socially treated as pariahs.[1]

It is difficult to form an idea of the great number of children who, in our present society, are neglected or abandoned.   The following passage may help form some conception of it: "If the reader will imagine a procession of 109,000 children marching past him, and notice attentively child after child as it goes by, he will get some idea of the extent of the suffering of children with which the 'National Society for the Prevention of Cruelty to Children in England' has actually had to do during the first ten years of its existence.

"The first 25,437 are sufferers from injuries inflicted upon them with boots, crockery, pans, shovels, straps, ropes, pokers, fire, boiling water, in short with every imaginable instrument that came to the hand of the brutal and vindictive parents — covered with wounds and bruises, burned, scalded, and covered with plasters and bandages.

"Then come 62,887 sufferers from neglect and starvation — covered with dirt, eruptions, and sores, trembling, in rags, half-naked, pale, weak, faint, feeble, pining, starving, dying — many of them borne in the arms of the nurses of the hospitals.

[1] [NOTE TO THE AMERICAN EDITION: Upon the situation of illegitimate children see *Rühle, op. cit.* pp. 63 *ff.*, and especially the interesting works of *Dr. Spann*, "Untersuchung über die uneheliche Befölkerung in Frankfurt a/M " and "Die unehelichen Mündel des Vormundschaftsgerichtes in Frankfurt a/M."]

"Then come 712 funeral processions, where the maltreatment ended fatally.

"Then come 12,663 little beings, their sufferings displayed to turn the lazy and cruel benevolence of the street to those who are answerable for their pallor, leanness, and coughs — most of these, too, are still in arms, but in the arms of vile drunkards and vagabonds.

"Then come 4460 pitiable girls, victims of the lust of human monsters.

"Then come 3205 little slaves of unsuitable and harmful occupations and dangerous performances, untimely births in traveling vans, acrobats at fairs, trapeze performers and tight-rope walkers in circuses, laboring under too heavy a load, and suffering the most diverse outrages. The procession is 60 miles long and takes 24 hours to pass by."[1]

The society spoken of above is a private institution. The extent of its labors is very limited, which is why it has not taken cognizance of a great number of the children who have been thus treated. At the time when the report containing the above figures had just appeared, it had only been in operation ten years — during the last five more effectively, as a part of the first five was taken up with the organization of its service. Finally the field of its labors includes only the United Kingdom, while capitalism reigns over a great part of the world and has everywhere the same consequences. In consideration of these facts we can form an idea of the great destitution in which a multitude of children are found, and what sort of persons children so treated are likely to grow up to be.

To sum up what has been said, we see that the system of education for the child has not always been what it is now, and that we cannot therefore speak in this connection of institutions created by nature, except as regards the relation between mother and child during the first years of the latter's life. It has been shown, I think, that the present system of education is closely bound up with the method of production of the day. No one can deny that in this regard also we are far from living in the "best of possible worlds." [2]

---

[1] *Dr. C. Hugo,* "Kind und Gesellschaft", p. 562 ("Neue Zeit", 1894–1895, I). See also *L. Ferriani,* "Entartete Mütter."

[NOTE TO THE AMERICAN EDITION : At this moment I have before me the "Annual Report, 1912–1913", where it is shown that the total number of children for whom the society in question has cared has increased to 2,101,130 in 29 years, an annual average, therefore, of about 75,000. For the year of the report the number was 159,000.

Cf. Rühle, op. cit., and especially the report upon Austria of *Dr. J. M. Baernreither,* "Die Ursachen, Erscheinungsformen und die Ausbreitung der Verwahrlosung von Kindern und Jugendlichen in Oesterreich."]

[2] For a criticism of the present educational system see *A. C. F. Schäffle,*

C. Prostitution.[1]

By prostitution must be understood the social fact that there are women who sell their bodies for the exercise of sexual acts, and make a profession of it. The putting of one's body at the disposal of another for the purpose of sexual intercourse constitutes then at times the sale of merchandise. To find the cause of prostitution in our present society it is necessary to begin by asking: "What are the causes for the demand for this merchandise?" These causes may be reduced to the following:

a. The difficulty or impossibility of marrying found by many men. We have already seen that in our present society there is a continually increasing number of the petty bourgeois and of those who practice the liberal professions who, in consequence of the insufficiency of their incomes, cannot marry, or only at a rather advanced age. As we have seen, also, this is not in general the case with the proletariat. They reach the maximum of their wages while still quite young, and are less exacting as regards their material needs. All this brings it about that they marry sooner and so have less recourse to prostitution. (Soldiers and seamen, who are often forced to remain unmarried, form an exception.)

b. Besides those of whom I have been speaking, those also must be mentioned who do not wish to attach themselves for life to a single woman. Further, separate education, inducing a different life for the two sexes, is often an obstacle to the easy meeting of two persons

"Bau und Leben des socialen Körpers", I, p. 262; *Ch. Letourneau*, "L'évolution du mariage et de la famille", p. 444; *E. Key*, "Das Jahrhundert des Kindes", pp. 109 *ff.*; *Th. Schlesinger Eckstein*, "Die Frau im XIX Jahrhundert", pp. 54–56.

[1] [NOTE TO THE AMERICAN EDITION: There has also appeared in recent times a considerable literature upon the etiology of prostitution. We note the following: *A. Forel*, "Die sexuelle Frage", chap. x; *P. Kampffmeyer*, "Die Prostitution als soziale Klassenerscheinung und ihre sozialpolitische Bekämpfung"; *T. Hermann*, "Die Prostitution und ihr Anhang"; *T. Bloch*, "Das Sexualleben unserer Zeit", chap. xiii, and "Die Prostitution", I (chiefly historical); *A. Pappritz*, "Die Welt von der man nicht spricht"; *H. Arendt*, "Menschen die den Pfad verloren"; *M. Minovici*, "Remarques sur la criminalité en Roumanie"; *C. K. Schneider*, "Die Prostituirte und die Gesellschaft"; *G. Schnapper-Arndt*, "Sozial-Statistik", chap. viii; *Quiros* and *Aguinaliedo*, "Verbrechertum und Prostitution in Madrid"; *R. Hessen*, "Die Prostitution in Deutschland"; *A Blaschko*, "Prostitution" ("Handwörterbuch der Staatswissenschaften", VI); *H. Ellis*, "Geschlect und Gesellschaft", II, chap. viii; "The Social Evil in Chicago" ("Report of the Vice Commission of Chicago"); *A. Moll*, "Handbuch der Sexual-Wissenschaften", chap. iv; *E. von Grabe*, "Prostitution, Kriminalität, und Psychopathie"; *A. Neher*, "Die geheime und öffentliche Prostitution in Stuttgart, Karlsruhe, und München."]

who might make a marriage of inclination. Many men renounce marriage because the intellectual plane of women is altogether different from theirs, as a consequence both of their education and of their manner of life, and also because with them the thought of improving their economic position by marriage predominates.[1]

The larger contingent of men who have recourse to prostitutes is made up of bachelors,[2] and the smaller of married men. Whence springs the following cause:

c. Often the marriage is not contracted from inclination, but for financial reasons, which brings it about that the men often indemnify themselves with prostitutes. But this is applicable also to those cases where the marriage has not been made for the reasons named, but in which, for any cause, an antipathy has sprung up between the couple, without the dissolution of the marriage, either because of the difficulty of securing a divorce, or from motives of expediency. Since monogamy does not proceed from an innate inclination, prostitution is a necessary correlative of marriage.

d. The keeping of extravagant mistresses is a pastime for those who have been demoralized by a life of luxury and ease, and at the same time is a means by which these people can get rid of their incomes.

e. Finally, prostitution is a means whereby rich perverts satisfy their inclinations.

Before leaving the causes of the demand for prostitutes there is one further matter to consider. Those who have recourse to prostitutes must necessarily have a low opinion of woman, whom they consider only as an object existing for pleasure, and thus bound to be ready, as soon as a man wishes, to furnish him what he desires, for money, and not because of affection. This vile fashion of regarding women has been universal for centuries, and is still pretty general. It is to be explained from the long-continued inferior social position of women. We have seen that this position has been improved little by little, and that the result of this improvement has been an increase in the

---

[1] C. Zetkin, "Geistiges Proletariat, Frauenfrage, und Sozialismus", pp. 5, 6; Dr. J. Jeannel, "De la prostitution dans les grandes villes au XIXe siècle", pp. 187, 188.

[2] Each consequence becomes in its turn a cause; as in this case, for, while prostitution is largely a consequence of the impossibility of marrying, prostitution in its turn becomes, through the demoralizing influence of the prostitutes, a reason why some men do not marry although their means would permit it.

number of men who have a higher opinion of woman, and who wish to have sexual relations with a woman only when there is a mutual affection between them.   These persons form even today only a small minority, however.

In the presence of a majority still thinking quite differently it is absurd to preach total sexual abstinence to all unmarried young men, as certain moralists do (Tolstoi, for example).   Though there are men who abstain without injury to their health, these moralists forget that the satisfaction of the sexual desires is one of the most important needs of the majority of men (the life of our day certainly increases these desires), and that present social conditions are the cause of men's considering woman their inferior.   Dr. Blaschko, in his work "Die Prostitution im XIX Jahrhundert", rightly says: "The sexual requirement in the case of mankind as of all other beings is an entirely natural one.   To be sure, it is not so strong and compelling as the necessity of food and drink; it can be suppressed in the case of anyone for a time, and with many permanently, without injury to the health.   But what is true of this or that person does not hold for the mass of mankind, for whom sexual intercourse is doubtless a necessity." [1]

It is now necessary to inquire why there is a sufficient supply to meet this demand.   Before beginning, however, one remark must be made.   The point of departure of the etiology of prostitution must be the incontestable fact that modesty is not an innate but an acquired quality.   The problem is chiefly, then, what are the causes why the feeling of modesty is not sufficiently developed among certain women.   The following are the principal causes:

a.   Immoral environment.   We shall examine this first in so far as it affects children.[2]   In running over the statistics which mention the age of prostitutes one is particularly struck by the fact that a great number of them are still very young.   To cite some examples: Dr. G. Richelot gives the following figures in his work "La Prostitution en Angleterre": [3]

---

[1] See also by the same author: "Die moderne Prostitution", pp. 14, 15 ("Neue Zeit", 1891–92, II), and "Hygiene der Prostitution und venerischen Krankheiten" p. 39; *Dr. V. Augagneur:* "La prostitution des filles mineures" ("Archives d'anthropologie criminelle", III, p. 224).

[2] [NOTE TO THE AMERICAN EDITION: Upon the demoralization of poor children see the works of *Baernreither* and *Rühle* already cited, and *H. Arendt,* "Kleineweisse Sklaven."]

[3] This study may be found in the second volume of *Parent-Duchatelet's* work: "De la Prostitution dans la ville de Paris."

London, 1836–1854.

Prostitutes Sentenced in Cases of Summary Jurisdiction.

AGE.	TO THE 10,000.
From 10 to 15 years	27
" 15 " 20 "	2,463
" 20 " 25 "	3,623
25 and over	3,887

Edinburgh, 1835–1842.

Prostitutes Admitted to " Lock Hospital."

AGE.	TO THE 1000.
Below 15	42
From 15 to 20	662
" 20 " 25	199
25 and over	97

In the "Reports from the Select Committee of the House of Lords on the Law Relating to the Protection of Young Girls"[1] the following figures may be found:

England, 1881–1882.

Received into an " Asylum for Girls and Women."

AGE.	NUMBER.	PERCENTAGE.
12 to 14	8	
14 " 16	6	
16 " 18	28	55
18 " 20	34	
20 " 23	9	
23 " 25	25	45
25 " 39	27	
	137	100

In his work "De la Prostitution dans la ville de Paris" Parent-Duchatelet gives the following figures:[2]

[1] P. 39 (Session 1882).   [2] Vol. I, pp. 91, 92.

Paris, 1831.

Registered Prostitutes.

AGE.	NUMBER.	PERCENTAGE.
12 years	1	
13 "	3	
14 "	8	
15 "	17	
16 "	44	23.6
17 "	55	
18 "	101	
19 "	115	
20 "	216	
21 "	204	
22 "	249	
23 "	240	
24 "	207	76.4
25 "	193	
26 and over	1,582	
	3,235	100.0

C. J. Lecour gives the following table : [1]

Paris, 1855–1869.

Registered Prostitutes.

AGE.	NUMBER.	PERCENTAGE.
Below 18 years	513	8
From 18 to 21	1,704	26.6
Over 21	4,190	65.4
	6,407	100.0

Dr. Augagneur gives the following ages for prostitutes admitted to the hospital : [2]

Lyons.

YEARS.	OLDER GIRLS.	YOUNGER GIRLS.	TOTAL.
1877	520 (65.5 %)	274 (34.0 %)	794
1887	144 (68.2 %)	67 (31.8 %)	211
	664 (66.07 %)	341 (33.73 %)	1,005

---

[1] "La Prostitution à Paris et à Londres", p. 125.   [2] *Op. cit.*, p. 211.

S. Sighele gives the following figures : [1]

Italy.

Registered Prostitutes.

YEAR.	AGE.	NUMBER.	PERCENTAGE.
1875	From 16 to 20	2,455	26.98
	" 21 " 30	4,766	52.50
	31 and over	1,867	20.52
		9,088	100.00
1881	From 17 to 20	2,953	31.90
	" 21 " 30	5,456	58.92
	31 and over	850	9.18
		9,259	100.00
1885	Under 20	3,228	27.76
	From 20 to 30	4,589	54.70
	31 and over	1,471	17.54
		8,388	100.00

Dr. L. Fiaux gives the result of an official enquiry, as follows : [2]

Russia, 1889.

Out of a Total of 17,603 Prostitutes.

AGE.	PERCENTAGE.	
15 and under	0.3	
From 15 to 16	1.3	
" 16 " 17	3.5	
" 17 " 18	6.9	69.9
" 18 " 19	8.8	
" 19 " 20	10.8	
" 20 " 25	38.3	
25 and over	30.1	30.1
	100.0	100.0

Dr. A. Baumgarten gives the following figures : [3]

[1] "Le Crime à Deux.", pp. 205, 206. For figures for Berlin see *Dr. B. Schoenlank*, "Zur Statistik der Prostitution in Berlin," pp. 335, 336 ("Archiv für soziale Gesetzgeb. u. Stat.", VII.).
[2] "La prostitution en Russie", p. 195 ("Progrès médical", 1893).
[3] "Die Beziehungen der Prostitution zum Verbrechen", p. 8 ("Archiv f. Kriminal Anthropologie u. Kriminalistik", XI.).

Vienna.
Prostitutes Not Registered.

AGE.	NUMBER TO THE 1,000.
13	4
14	19
16	94
17	97
18	111
19	119
20	83
	527

As these figures show, there is a considerable portion of the prostitutes who are minors, but they do not tell us of the number of adults who embraced the profession while they were yet under age. As to this point, Dr. Bonhoeffer gives the following, showing the age at which the prostitutes whom he examined began the practice of their profession : [1]

Breslau.

16 years old or under	30	
Between 17 and 18 years	44	54%
" 19 " 20 "	28	
" 21 " 50 "	88	46%
	190	100%

Parent-Duchatelet gives the following table : [2]

Paris.

AGE AT THE TIME OF REGISTRATION.	NUMBER.	PERCENTAGE.
10	2	
11	3	
12	3	
13	6	
14	20	
15	51	50.4
16	111	
17	149	
18	279	
19	322	
20	389	
21	303	
Over 21 years	1,610	49.6
	3,248	100.0

[1] "Zur Kenntnis des groszstädtischen Bettel- und Vagabundentums," p. 188 ("Zeitschr. f. d. ges. Strafrw.", XXXIII).   [2] *Op. cit.* I, pp. 92, 93.

Dr. Fiaux gives the following figures : [1]

Russia.

AGE AT THE TIME OF REGISTRATION.	PERCENTAGE.	
11 or younger	1.2	
13 to 15	9.0	
15 " 16	12.9	80.5
16 " 18	30.8	
18 " 21	26.6	
21 and over	19.5	19.5
	100.0	100.0

A large majority of prostitutes, then, have been placed upon the registers of the police while still under age. We may very well say, moreover, without fear of mistake, that a great part of those who are registered at a later period of life have already been among the clandestine prostitutes. Dr. Augagneur says : "How many of these women, devoted indefinitely to the life of a common prostitute, would not have fled all its horrors if a society, careless of the interests of its members, had furnished them with sufficient means of defense up to the age at which they all have succumbed, — under 21 years? *When a woman has not prostituted herself before 21, she will not prostitute herself later.* Look for exceptions to this rule and you will find that they are very few. The woman who is older and more experienced knows the consequences of her acts; less passionate, less weak, and less impressionable, she resists better a first temptation whose consequences she is fully aware of.[2]

However this may be, it is certain that a very great proportion of the prostitutes have taken up their profession, or have been seduced, while they were still very young. Upon this latter point the following figures enlighten us : [3]

[1] *Op. cit.*, p. 210.
[2] *Op. cit.*, pp. 215, 216.
[3] "Reports of the Select Committee", Appendix B, p. 52.

England.

Age at which Prostitutes Were Seduced.	Number.	
11	3	
12	5	
13	16	
14	79	
15	189	
16	184	58%
17	247	
18	221	
19	297	
20	280	
21	256	
22 and over	1,299	42%
	3,076	100%

In his work, "La prostitution clandestine", Dr. L. Martineau informs us that the age at which the prostitutes whom he observed were deflowered is distributed as follows : [1]

France.

Age	Number.	Age.	Number.
5	1	15	86
9	2	16	87
10	2	17	115
11	2	18	93
12	5	19	50
13	11	20	37
14	31	21	27
			549

90% of a total of 607.

The facts already brought out give rise to the presumption that the ranks of prostitutes are in a very large measure recruited from the less well-to-do classes, where the neglect of children has assumed enormous proportions, and not from the more favored classes where the children are carefully guarded and kept away from unfavorable influences. The correctness of this conclusion is shown by a further examination. According to figures given in the "Reports" quoted above, only 44 out of 3,076 prostitutes, or 1.4 %, came from the well-

[1] Pp. 42–44 and 46–66.

to-do classes.[1] In his "Sozialpolitisches Handbuch" Dr. Lux publishes the following table:[2]

Berlin, 1871–1878.

PROFESSION OF THE PARENTS OF PROSTITUTES.	NUMBERS.	PERCENTAGE.
Artisans	1,015	48
Factory hands	467	22
Lower officials	305	14
Commerce and transportation	222	11
Agriculture, etc.	87	4
Soldiers	26	1
	2,122	100

Dr. Bonhoeffer found that the fathers of the prostitutes whom he examined practiced the following professions:[3]

Breslau.

Manufacture and trades	72	42
Unskilled workmen	32	19
Lower officials	24	14
Commerce	13	8
Transportation	12	7
Lodginghouse-keepers	6	3.5
Agriculture	8	5
Traveling musicians	2	1
Higher officials	1	0.5
	170	100.0

Dr. Fiaux gives the following figures:[4]

Russia.

CLASSES FROM WHICH PROSTITUTES ARE RECRUITED.	PERCENTAGE.
Peasants	47.5
Bourgeois	36.3
Wives and daughters of soldiers	7.2
Other classes	4.7
Foreign subjects	1.5
Nobles and daughters of employes	1.8
Merchants and considerable citizens	.5
Daughters of members of the clergy	.5
	100.0

---

[1] Appendix B, p. 52.   [2] P. 133.   [3] *Op. cit.*, p. 108.   [4] *Op. cit.*, p. 196.

As the table given above shows, the Russian prostitutes are recruited in greater numbers from the bourgeoisie than in the other
countries of Europe.   The Russian bourgeoisie, however, cannot be
compared with that of other countries.   It is more like the petty
bourgeoisie, as the following quotation given by Dr. Fiaux proves:
"The committee considers that the great mass of the women registered belong to the lower classes."   The fact that, of 100 prostitutes,
83 come from poor families, 16 from well-to-do families, and one
from a rich family, proves the same thing.

After having given the professions of 3,332 fathers of prostitutes,[1]
Parent-Duchatelet arrives at the following conclusion: . . . "prostitutes born in Paris all proceed from the artisan class, and . . . it
is not true, as some persons have assured me, that there are to be
found among them a number belonging to very distinguished
families; . . ." [2]

In speaking of the prostitutes born outside of Paris he says:
". . . there is a mass of facts more than sufficient to prove to us that,
as far as the class of society from which prostitutes come is concerned,
the departments do not differ in any way from Paris; we see upon the
last table as upon the first, only working people and those little
favored by fortune, who consequently cannot take care of the education of their daughters, nor watch them, and still less provide for their
needs when they have reached a certain age, . . ." [3]

We must particularize these unfavorable environmental influences.
And the first fact that we meet is that a part of the young prostitutes
have been incited to the profession by their parents.   Parent-Duchatelet mentions 16 cases in which mother and daughter were both
registered prostitutes [4]; and von Oettingen quotes the following
from Dr. Tait: [5]

---

[1] *Op. cit.*, I, pp. 67–70.
[2] *Op. cit.*, I, p. 68.
[3] *Op. cit.*, I, p. 71.   The data of the same author show that out of 3,095
fathers of prostitutes, 1,078 (35%) could not sign their names.
[4] *Op. cit.*, I, p. 108.
[5] "Moralstatistik", p. 216.   Upon this cause of prostitution see also:
Dr. G. Richelot, *op. cit.*, pp. 582, 583; Dr. C. Röhrmann, "Der sittliche Zustand von Berlin", pp. 45, 46; "Die Prostitution in Berlin", pp. 86, 87;
L. Faucher, "Études sur Angleterre", I, p. 74; Lecour, *op. cit.*, pp. 202–204;
Carlier, *op. cit.*, pp. 35, 36; G. Tomel and H. Rollet, "Les enfants en prison",
pp. 156 ff.; L. Ferriani, "Entartete Mütter", p. 161; Dr. O. Commenge,
"La prostitution clandestine à Paris", pp. 33–35.

Edinburgh.

There were found among the prostitutes :

2 mothers with 4 daughters each, or	8 in all,
5 " " 3 " " " 15 " "	
10 " " 2 " " " 20 " "	
24 " " 1 daughter " " 24 " "	
41 mothers with	67 daughters in all

In the second place it is necessary to speak of the abandonment of the children of the poor classes.   No scientist of consequence admits that the moral ideas are innate, but simply that the new-born infant is more or less fitted to appropriate such ideas.   It follows that one cannot expect much from a child whose moral education has been neglected in youth, however great natural capacity he may have been endowed with.   From this it follows that where there is lack of education and care because of the death of the mother, or the alcohol-ism of the father, or because the father and mother are both at work away from home a great part of the day, or where the morality of the parents themselves is not great, the children run great risk of being lost.   The following figures support this assertion :

Von Oettingen shows that, according to Dr. Ryan, 12,000 to 14,000 prostitutes in London became such as a consequence of a neglected childhood.[1]   In the "Reports of the Select Committee," etc., the fol-lowing figures are found :[2] of 3,075 prostitutes 1,481 (48 %) were orphans, and 921 (29 %) were half-orphans.   In his "La prostitution clandestine à Paris", Dr. Commenge gives the following figures con-cerning the 2,368 prostitutes whom he observed during the years from 1878 to 1887 :[3]

> 692 (29 %) were orphans ;
> 456 (19 %) had lost their mother ;
> 811 (35 %) ”   ”   ”   father.

Out of a total of 190 cases Dr. Bonhoeffer shows 72 (38 %) in which the education had been positively bad (criminality or prostitution on the part of the parents, neglect, lack of surveillance, etc.) ; 106 cases (56 %) in which the education had been probably bad ; and only 12 cases (6 %) in which it was proved that the education had been good.[4]

For Russia Dr. Fiaux gives the following figures :[5] 3.6 % of the

[1] *Op. cit.*, p. 216.   [2] Appendix B, p. 52.
[3] P. 42.   [4] *Op. cit.*, p. 108.   [5] *Op. cit.*, p. 197.

prostitutes still had father and mother; 47.5 % had parents who were separated, and 18.5 % were without any family.

With regard to the cause given for prostitution Dr. Augagneur says as follows: "The majority of prostitutes are born to prostitution at the same time that they are to puberty. Their moral sense, if such may be called that which no one has ever tried to awaken, is not shocked by their situation; they have prostituted themselves without shame and without regret. They have left normal and respectable society without being really aware of its existence, without the desire of ever returning thither. They have lacked the things necessary to make them respectable women — instruction in virtue, the example of their relatives, the suspicious surveillance of their mothers, and material well-being. The daughters of the people are not, at the day of their birth, of a clay inferior to that of the daughters of the bourgeoisie or of the nobility; they are naturally no less intelligent, no more perverse. And yet if you examine the civil status of a hundred prostitutes, you will find that 95 at least have sprung from the lowest strata of society. The existing social inequality, that is to say, is alone responsible for this unequal distribution." [1]

Finally I will cite once more the opinion of Parent-Duchatelet, which is of great value, since this author is the most able sociologist who has treated of this subject. He says: "The misconduct of parents, and the bad examples of every kind which they give to their children, must be considered with regard to many girls, and especially those of Paris, as one of the causes determining their mode of life. The dossiers of each girl constantly make mention of disorder in the household, of fathers who are widowers living with concubines, of lovers of mothers widowed or married, of fathers and mothers separated, etc. What surveillance can such parents exercise over their children, and if they judge it proper to give a reprimand, or give good advice, what authority could such observations have in their mouths?

"Thus the depravity, the indifference, the necessitous position of many people of the last class provoke, or do not or cannot prevent, the corruption of the children; we may say in general with regard to a good number of prostitutes, what observation continually teaches us of criminals, that they have for the most part an ignoble origin." [2]

---

[1] *Op. cit.*, I, p. 102.
[2] *Op. cit.*, I, p. 102. Upon this cause of prostitution see further: Dr. *Richelot*, *op. cit.*, pp. 574, 575; Dr. *Fr. S. Hügel*, "Zur Geschichte, Statistik, und Regelung der Prostitution", pp. 206, 207; Dr. *Jeannel*, *op. cit.*, pp. 145, 146; A. C. *Fr. Schäffle*, "Bau und Leben des sozialen Körpers", I, p. 261;

In the third place, we must name as a cause of the demoralization in youth bad housing conditions. One of the most pronounced characteristics of the child is his propensity to imitate. Hence it follows that the fact that a whole family must live and sleep in one or two rooms has the most harmful consequences for the sexual morality of the children. Sexual life has no longer any secrets for the child of the poor classes at an age at which this life is still a thing unknown to the children of the well-to-do classes.

I will give here some figures to show how small the dwellings of this class are. According to an investigation made in Berlin in 1895 there were 4,718 dwellings without fireplaces, and occupied by 13,700 persons; more than 200,000 dwellings consisted of a single room with a fireplace, and 22,160 of these were occupied by more than 6 persons. There was the following percentage of "overcrowding" (in official statistics this means more than 6 persons in one room with fireplace, and more than 8 persons in two rooms with fireplace, or in one room with kitchen attached): in Königsberg 10.6; in Halle 10.3; in Breslau 9.9; in Lübeck 8.75; in Görlitz 6.91; in Leipzig 7.85; in Altona 7.62; in Munich, 4.41; in Kiel 4.46; in Mannheim 11.8. In 1890 there were living in overcrowded dwellings the following number of persons to the 1,000: in Berlin 784; in Munich 533; in Breslau 754.[1]

According to the investigation made in 1890 there were in Vienna 23,921 dwellings consisting of a single room, with 64,621 occupants, and 103,433 dwellings of two rooms, with 411,314 occupants. These two groups include 44 % of the dwellings and 35 % of the population. Professor von Philippovich, in the article from which these data have been taken, shows that in the districts inhabited by the Viennese workingmen, Ottakring, Meidling, and Favoriten, 29.3 %, 30.8 %, and 31.26 % respectively of the dwellings of one or two rooms were "overcrowded" (i.e. 3 to 5 persons in a room).[2]

The 1899 census of the Netherlands gave the following results: There were 307,937 dwellings consisting of one inhabited room each, and occupied by 1,172,014 persons (22.7 % of the population); and there were 334,355 dwellings consisting of two rooms each (including

H. Stursberg, "Die Prostitution in Deutschland und ihre Bekämpfung", pp. 44, 45; Dr. E. Laurent, "Les habitués des prisons de Paris", pp. 585–589 (description of types); G. Schönfeldt, "Beiträge zur Geschichte des Pauperismus und der Prostitution in Hamburg", p. 269.

[1] A. Pappritz, "Die wirthschaftlichen Ursachen der Prostitution", p. 14.

[2] "Wiener Wohnungsverhältnisse", pp. 221–223 ("Archiv f. soz. Gesetzg. u. Statist." VII).

kitchens, alcoves, and covered passages), occupied by 1,497,353 persons (29 % of the population).[1]

The detailed statement shows the situation still better.   There were 45,641 dwellings of only one room, with 4 persons in each; 62,548 dwellings of more than one room with 5 or 6 persons; 41,877 dwellings of only one room, occupied by 6 or more persons; 45,363 dwellings of 2 rooms which were occupied by 3 or 4 persons; 20,582 dwellings of two rooms with from 4 to 6; and 706 dwellings of two rooms with 6 occupants or more.[2]

What is often lacking besides is space to place a sufficient number of beds, or even the means of procuring them.   In a great number of cases children of different sexes must sleep together in one bed, or even with adults.   It also often happens that the inhabitants of these already insufficient dwellings are obliged to take night-lodgers.   There are the following percentages of dwellings with lodgers: in Leipzig, 17.5; in Breslau, 12.5; and in Berlin, 15.8.[3]   In Vienna 6.4 % of the population are night-lodgers, and in Berlin 6.1%[4].

It goes without saying that among these persons lodging together there are some who are demoralized and dangerous to children.   In his work, "Verbrechen und Prostitution", P. Hirsch depicts these dangers as follows: "Think in how narrow a space an entire family is penned up together, so that at times a separation of the sexes is scarcely possible, at a time when the sexual instinct of the growing children is already beginning to develop.   The children unhappily only too often are present at the most intimate occurrences and early lose all feeling of shame.   How can decency and good morals be learned by children whose parents are obliged to take prostitutes as lodgers?   Who shall protect these unfortunates from moral contamination?   Often a word will be spoken in their presence, or an occurrence take place, which they are not yet, perhaps, able to understand.   But the childish nature is receptive to such impressions, and what happens in their presence falls upon fruitful soil, and what has remained fixed in their memory from earliest youth, will, if later their sensuality is once aroused, bear terrible fruit.   We are astonished when we hear a twelve or thirteen year old girl use language which we are accustomed to hear only from prostitutes who have followed their trade for years; we are astonished at the sophistication of persons still quite young, and are inclined at once to pass an unfavorable judgment

---

[1] " Bijdragen tot de Statistiek van Nederland XXIV, Uitkomsten der woning-statistiek ", p. 52.   [2] *Op. cit.*, p. 98.
[3] *Pappritz, op. cit.*, p. 15.   [4] *v. Philippovich, op. cit.*, p. 222.

upon them. Truly our judgment would be quite different, we should have sympathy with them, and should be made to reflect, if we came to know the holes in which these poor creatures passed their childhood." [1]

As a cause of the demoralization of young girls we must note, finally, child labor. In the first place there are children who are sent to sell flowers, matches, etc., and this causes them to be neglected and to frequent bad company. With regard to this Hirsch says: "One has only to get into conversation with the children who sell flowers, matches, and the like on the streets of the great cities in the evening, or to overhear their talk, to be astonished at their sophistication. One would hardly believe with what shamelessness such boys speak of sexual matters with growing girls in the same situation, without blushing and quite as a matter of course, since they have been accustomed to it from earliest childhood. It is no wonder that from these circles a considerable contingent is furnished to the ranks of prostitution and crime. . . ." [2]

A second cause is work in factories, by which girls are brought into contact with adults who, from their often coarse manners and language, and their lack of moral sentiments, corrupt these children for their whole lives. After having spoken of the other dangers which threaten the morality of children, Lecour says: "If she has escaped these dangers the child, placed too young as an apprentice, will meet other perils. There will be the contact with girls who are older and already corrupted, and workmen who respect neither youth nor innocence, who boast of debauchery, propagate immorality, and dishonor the daughters of their comrades. There will be, perhaps, the impure domination of the proprietor or foreman." [3]

[1] P. 42. See also: *Richelot, op. cit.,* pp. 573, 574; *W. Acton,* "Prostitution Considered in its Moral, Social, and Sanitary Aspects", pp. 131 *ff.; Jeannel, op. cit.,* p. 143; *Lecour, op. cit.,* p. 246; "Reports of the Select Committee, etc.", p. 39 (Session of 1882); *Stursberg, op. cit.,* pp. 46, 47; *Commenge, op. cit.,* p. 32.
[NOTE TO THE AMERICAN EDITION: *Cf. Th. M. Raest van Limburg,* "In den strijd tegen de ontucht." *P. Kampfmeyer,* "Das Wohnungselend der Grossstädte und seine Beziehungen zur Verbreitung der Geschlechtskrankheiten und zur Prostitution", and "Die Wohnungsmissstände im Prostitutions- und im Schlaf-gängerwesen und ihre gesetzliche Reform"; *Pfeiffer,* "Das Wohnungselend der grossen Städte und seine Beziehungen zur Prostitution und den Geschlechtskrankheiten."]
[2] *Op. cit.,* p. 54.
[NOTE TO THE AMERICAN EDITION: *Cf.* especially the "Report of the Departmental Committee on the Employment of Children, Oct., 1903."]
[3] *Op. cit.,* p. 247. See also *Parent-Duchatelet, op. cit.,* I. p. 103; *Röhrmann, op. cit.,* p. 44; *Jeannel, op. cit.,* pp. 146–148; "Reports", etc. (Session of 1882), pp. 15–17; *K. Strunz,* "Die Erwerbmäszige Kinderarbeit und die Schule", pp. 183 *ff.* ("Neue Zeit", 1898–1899, I).

Let us now look at the influences which demoralize adult women. In the first place we must speak of the influence of profession. The following figures serve to show which are the professions from which prostitutes are recruited most : [1]

Berlin, 1855.

Factory-workers	73 ⎤	
Seamstresses, laundry-workers	16 ⎥	61 %
Day-laborers	23 ⎥	
Workers at home	32 ⎦	
Domestics	22	9 "
Without declared profession	70	30 "
	236	100 "

(Industrial workers)

1873.

Factory workers	355 ⎤	
Workers at home and saleswomen	936 ⎥	64.3 %
Caretakers of stores	139 ⎦	
Domestics	794	35.7 "
	2,224	100.0 "

(Industrial workers)

1898.

Workwomen, seamstresses, and saleswomen	66	43.4 %
Domestics	78	51.3 "
With their parents	7 ⎤	5.3 "
Nurses of children	1 ⎦	100.0 "

In the "Reports of the Select Committee, etc." we find the following : [2]

England.

Domestics	1,589	60.7 %
Seamstresses, dressmakers, and other industrial professions	967	36.9 "
Barmaids	64	2.4 "
	2,620	100.0 "

Breslau, 1901.[3]

Domestics	72	38 %
Factory workers	37	20 "
Seamstresses	28	15 "
Saleswomen	14	7 "
Dressmakers	8	4 "
Barmaids, flower-girls, hairdressers	13	7 "
Dancers	4	2 "
Without profession and living at home	14	7 "
	190	100 "

In Parent-Duchatelet's "La Prostitution à Paris" figures are found showing that domestic servants, in proportion to their number,

---

[1] *Dr. A. Blaschko*, "Die Prostitution im XIX Jahrhundert", p. 22; "Hygiene der Prostitution", pp. 40, 41.
[2] Appendix B, p. 52.   [3] *Dr. Bonhoeffer, op. cit.*, p. 109.

furnish the largest contingent of prostitutes, and that working-women who try to provide for their needs with the needle furnish also a very great proportion.[1]   Dr. Jeannel shows that in 1859, out of 298 prostitutes registered in Bordeaux, 40% had been domestics, and 37% workwomen who had tried to live by sewing.[2]   Out of a total of 6,842 clandestine prostitutes in Paris (from 1878 to 1887) Dr. Commenge found that 2,681 (39.18%) had been domestics, and 1,326 (19%) seamstresses.[3]

Dr. Baumgarten gives the following table of percentages for 1,721 prostitutes:

Vienna.

Servants	58.00
Working by the day	16.00
Cashiers	14.00
Factory workers	5.50
Office employees	0.38
Children's nurses	0.36
Singers	0.28
Hairdressers and models	5.48
	100.00

Dr. Fiaux gives the following figures:[4]

Russia.

Servants	45.0 %
Seamstresses	8.4 "
Factory workers	3.7 "
Laundresses	1.4 "
Governesses and nurses	1.3 "
Merchants, bakers, and others	1.3 "
Cigar-sellers	0.7 "
Singers, circus-performers, and other artists	0.3 "
Practicing different trades and professions	2.7 "
Kept mistresses	2.0 "
Without fixed profession	6.4 "
Living upon the labor of their husbands	1.7 "
Living in their family, or with their parents more or less remote.	22.3 "

These statistics show that a quite considerable number of the prostitutes have been workwomen in factories. (In Russia manufacturing is very little developed — hence the low figures there.) We may accept it as indisputable that this labor has in general very disadvantageous consequences for the morality of the workwomen.

In his work, "The Condition of the Working Class in England", Engels depicts these consequences in the following terms: "The collecting of persons of both sexes and all ages in a single workroom,

---

[1] See the detailed statistics, *op. cit.*, I, pp. 79–84.
[2] *Op. cit.*, p. 148.   [3] *Op. cit.*, p. 336.   [4] *Op. cit.*, p. 197.

the inevitable contact, the crowding into a small space of people to whom neither mental nor moral education has been given, is not calculated for the favorable development of the female character. The manufacturer, if he pays any attention to the matter at all, can interfere only when something scandalous actually occurs; the permanent, less conspicuous influence of persons of dissolute character, upon the more moral, and especially upon the younger ones, he cannot ascertain and consequently cannot prevent. The language used in the workshops was characterized by many witnesses in the report of 1833 as 'indecent', 'bad', 'filthy', etc. (Cowell, evid., pp. 35, 37, and in many other places). It is the same process upon a small scale which we have already witnessed upon a great one in the great cities. The centralization of population has the same influence upon the same persons, whether it affects them in a great city or in a small factory. The smaller the mill, the closer the packing, and the more unavoidable the contact; and the consequences are not wanting. A witness in Leicester says that he would rather let his daughter beg than have her go into a factory; that they are perfect gates of hell; that most of the prostitutes of the town had the mills to thank for their present condition (Power, evid., p. 8). Another in Manchester 'did not hesitate to assert that three-fourths of the young factory employees of from 14 to 20 years of age were unchaste' (Cowell, evid. p. 57). Commissioner Cowell expresses it as his opinion, that the morality of the factory operatives is somewhat below the average of the working class in general (p. 82). And Dr. Hawkins says (Rept. p. 4), 'An estimate of sexual morality cannot readily be reduced to figures, but if I may trust my own observations and the general opinion of those with whom I have spoken, as well as the whole tenor of the testimony furnished me, the aspect of the influence of factory life upon the morality of the youthful female population is most depressing.' " [1]

And then it happens at times that the proprietors or their foremen by abusing their power force the working-girls who please them to yield to their desires. Engels says of this: "It is a matter of course that factory-servitude, like any other, and to an even greater degree, confers the 'jus primæ noctis' upon the master. In this respect also the employer is sovereign over the persons and charms of his employees. The threat of dismissal suffices to overcome all resist-

[1] Pp. 148, 149 [in original, pp. 151, 152]. See also: *L. Faucher*, "Études sur l'Angleterre", I, pp. 276, 277; *M. de Baets*, "Les influences de la misère sur la criminalité" pp. 35, 36; *Stursberg, op. cit.*, pp. 49, 50; *Commenge, op. cit.*, pp. 13–15; *L. Ferriani*, "Schlaue und glückliche Verbrecher", p. 467.

ance in nine cases out of ten, if not in ninety-nine cases out of a hundred, in girls who, in any case have no strong inducements to chastity. If the master is mean enough, and the official report mentions several such cases, his mill is also his harem; and the fact that not all manufacturers use their power, does not in the least change the position of the girls. In the beginning of the manufacturing industry, when most of the employers were upstarts without education or consideration for the social hypocrisy, they let nothing interfere with the exercise of their vested rights." [1]

Besides factory workers domestics form a very considerable percentage of the prostitutes. As the Berlin statistics cited above show the percentage of workers has diminished and that of domestics has increased. According to Dr. Blaschko the cause of the diminution of the percentage of factory workers is to be found not only in the fact that, the year 1898 being very prosperous, poverty did not come in as an important factor in the same measure as formerly, but also in the raising of the intellectual and moral plane of the Berlin working-women. It is impossible to speak of a similar raising of the plane of the domestics. The nature of their occupations prevents their forming associations; they are therefore deprived of the moral effect of the trades union.[2] The causes of the importance of the contingent furnished to prostitution by the domestics are of different kinds. Besides the reason I have just mentioned, the fact is to be noted that it is not from among the most intelligent and best of the working classes that domestic servants are ordinarily drawn. For these prefer the less dependent position of working-woman to that of domestic. In the second place there is the influence of the occupation itself. (There are still others, of which I shall speak later.)

It is easy to understand how the occupation of domestic has a demoralizing influence. Not only do young girls, often ignorant and without education, come to live in surroundings of a sort to pervert them, but there is also their dependence upon people who only demand that their work shall be well done, the lack of civilizing influ-

---

[1] *Op. cit.*, p. 149 [in original, p. 152]. For analogous cases see *A. Bebel*, "Die Frau und der Sozialismus", pp. 195–197; "Les Scandales de Londres", pp. 235–238; "Enquête betreffende werking en uitbreiding der wet van 19 September 1874 en naar den toestand van fabrieken en werkplaatsen" 1887, deel V, p. 77; *Dr. H. Lux*, "Sozialpolitisches Handbuch", pp. 135, 136; *Hirsch, op. cit.*, pp. 46–48; *Commenge, op. cit.*, pp. 15–17; *G. S.*, "Die weibliche Lohnarbeit und ihr Einflusz auf die Sittlichkeit und Kriminalität", p. 748 ("Neue Zeit", 1899–1900, II); *L. Braun*, "Die Frauenfrage", p. 308.
[2] See "Die Prostitution im XIX Jahrhundert", pp. 23, 24.

ences, and the isolation that deprives them of contact with their fellows, all of which lowers their moral plane.[1]

Aside from the two groups cited there are still other occupations which may exercise a demoralizing influence, such as that of barmaid, etc.[2]

Before closing our observations upon demoralizing environment as a cause of prostitution, we must fix our attention upon the evil influences to which many women are exposed, those, that is, who must provide for their own needs and do not live at home. The smallness of their wages does not permit them to rent a room by themselves but they are obliged to content themselves with a bed simply. This brings at once great moral disadvantages. But further, this arrangement drives the persons in question into the street when not at work, since often the landlords do not allow them in the house except during the night. The harmful consequences of this are sufficiently obvious.[3]

b. The maternity of girls and concubinage are among the causes of prostitution. Parent-Duchatelet gives the following figures:[4]

Paris.

Having come from the provinces to conceal themselves in Paris and to find resources there	280
Brought to Paris and abandoned by soldiers, traveling salesmen, students, and other persons	404
Domestics seduced by their masters and dismissed by them	289
Simple concubines during a longer or shorter period who have lost their lovers, and do not know what else to do	1,425
Total	2,398

46 % of a total of 5,183.

In the "Reports of the Select Committee", etc. we find given as cause of prostitution:[5]

---

[1] *L. Braun*, "Die Frauenfrage", pp. 409–411; *G. S.*, *op. cit.*, pp. 754–756.
[NOTE TO THE AMERICAN EDITION: Upon servants *cf.* further: *O. Spann*, "Die geschlechtlich-sittlichen Verhältnisse im Dienstboten und Arbeiterinnenstande"; and *R. de Ryckère*, "La servante criminelle", ch. IX.]
[2] *Hirsch, op. cit.*, pp. 48–50.
[NOTE TO THE AMERICAN EDITION: *Cf.* further: *C. Jellinek*, "Kellerinnenelend" and *Dr. H. Peters*, "Zur Lage der Kellerinnen im Grossherzogtum Baden." Upon prostitution in the theater see *V. v. Lepel*, "Prostitution beim Theater."]
[3] *Stursberg, op. cit.*, pp. 55, 57; *Hirsch, op. cit.*, pp. 42, 43; *Pappritz, op. cit.*, pp. 13, 14.
[4] *Op. cit.*, I, p. 107.
[5] Appendix B, p. 52.

England.

Concubines abandoned by their lovers	360
Girls seduced under promise of marriage	806
	1,166

37.9 % of a total of 3,076.

In his "Minderjährige Verbrecher" L. Ferriani gives the following :[1]

Italy.

Seduction by a lover	1,653
" " employer	927
	2,580

24.7 % of a total of 10,422.

The statistics cited show, then, that the cause named occupies a quite considerable place in the etiology of prostitution. This cause is entirely a consequence of the existing social conditions, which maintain the dependent position of woman, and of marriage, which brings it about that every woman living with a man as with a husband is despised, even when the union is due to inclination, and that life is made very hard for her, especially if a child is born of the union. However, it must be added, that this applies especially to the women of the middle classes, and that "free love" and the child that is the fruit of it, are not at all so despised among the proletariat, for, as we have seen above, the bases of the present legal monogamy have not so great an importance there.[2]

However this cause of prostitution only makes itself felt when the woman to whom it applies is also deprived of all pecuniary means. And so we come to the third category in the etiology of prostitution.

c. Poverty. As the statistics already cited have shown, almost all prostitutes spring from the classes without fortune, and the great majority of them have been at first working-women or domestics, and consequently have belonged to families without fortune. If such women, for any reason whatever, cannot find work, they are thrown into poverty. As this happens constantly in society, poor women find themselves forced into prostitution. The facts are there to prove it. In treating of the etiology of prostitution Parent-Duchatelet gives the following figures :[3]

---

[1] P. 169.

[2] H. *Frégier*, "Les classes dangereuses de la population dans les grandes villes", I, p. 97; *Lecour, op. cit.*, p. 244; L. *Taxil*, "La corruption fin-de-siècle", p. 42; *Commenge, op. cit.*, pp. 17–20; A. *Aletrino*, "Over eenige oorzaken der prostitutie", pp. 21, 22; E. *Gystrow*, "Liebe und Liebesleben im XIX Jahrhundert", p. 22.   [3] *Op. cit.*, I, p. 107.

Paris.

Excess of poverty, absolute destitution	1,441
Loss of father and mother; expulsion from home; complete desertion	1,255
To support aged and infirm parents	37
Eldest of the family having neither father nor mother, to support brothers and sisters, and sometimes nieces and nephews	29
Widows and deserted wives, to raise a large family	23
	2,785

53 % of a total of 5,183.

The author says among other things: "Poverty, often pushed to the most frightful extreme, is still one of the most active causes of prostitution. How many girls abandoned by their families, without parents, without friends, unable to find refuge anywhere, are obliged to have recourse to prostitution in order not to die of hunger! One of these unfortunates, still susceptible to feelings of honor, strove to the last extremity before taking up a part which she regarded as extreme, and when she came to register herself it was shown that she had not eaten anything for three days." [1]

"One would hardly believe that the career of prostitution has been embraced by certain women as a means of fulfilling their duty as daughter or mother; yet nothing is more true. It is not unusual to see married women who have lost their husbands or been deserted by them, become prostitutes with the sole purpose of not leaving a numerous family to die of hunger. It is still more common to find young girls who, not earning by their labor enough to provide for the wants of their aged and infirm parents, ply the trade of prostitute in the evening to make up what is lacking. I have found the marks peculiar to these two classes of prostitutes too often not to be convinced that they are more numerous in Paris than one would believe." [2]

In the "Reports of the Select Committee, etc.", which I have already quoted several times, are found the following figures: [3]

England.

To provide for the needs of her mother	11
" " " " " " idle husbands	35
As a consequence of poverty or lack of work	164
	210

6.8 % of a total of 3,076.

---

[1] Op. cit., I, p. 99. [2] Op. cit., I, pp. 104, 105.
[3] Session 1882, Appendix B, p. 52.

(We must take into consideration the fact that in the case of many of the 37.9% who are put down in this same set of tables as seduced, poverty was a contributory cause.)

Ferriani gives the following table:[1]

Italy.

Deserted by husband, parents, or other members of the family	794
Death of husband, parents, or other persons contributing to their support, or other cause of poverty	2,139
To provide for the wants of children, parents, or other sick or needy members of the family	393
	3,326

31.9 % of a total of 10,422.

Dr. Blaschko shows that the forced idleness among garment makers during some months of each year causes an increase of prostitution.[2]

As we have seen in the first part of this work, it has been proved at various times that crime against property increases or diminishes according as the economic situation is favorable or unfavorable. If poverty is one of the causes of prostitution it must follow that the number of prostitutes will vary at the same times as the general condition. Statistics prove that this is what does actually happen. However, we need only take into consideration the figures for registered prostitutes; if we had at our disposal the figures for clandestine prostitution they would naturally show still greater modifications.

Berlin.[3]

Year.	Number of Prostitutes Registered.	To 100,000 of the Population.	Year.	Number of Prostitutes Registered.	To 100,000 of the Population.
1869	1709	223	1882	3900	326
1870	1606	203	1883	3769	306
1871	1625	197	1884	3724	293
1872	1701	198	1885	3598	273
1873	1742	195	1886	3000	230
1874	1956	210	1887	3063	216
1875	2241	232	1888	3392	231
1876	2386	242	1889	3703	244
1877	2547	248	1890	4039	255
1878	2767	262	1891	4364	273
1879	3033	277	1892	4663	288
1880	3186	284	1893	4794	292
1881	3465	298			

[1] *Op. cit.*, p. 169.
[2] "Die Prostitution im XIX Jahrhundert", pp. 17, 18. See also *B. Schönlank*, "Zur Lage der in der Wäschefabrikation und Konfectionsbranche Deutschlands beschäftigen Arbeiterinnen", pp. 126, 127 ("Neue Zeit", 1888); *Hirsch, op. cit.*, p. 46; *Pappritz, op. cit.*, p. 10.   [3] *Hirsch, op. cit.*, p. 57.

Leaving aside the abnormal years, 1870 and 1871, we perceive that the prosperous years 1872 and 1873 give very low figures. After this period times become worse and worse, while the number of prostitutes sustains a considerable increase. From the year 1882 economic conditions began to improve, and the figures for prostitution correspondingly fell, to rise again very noticeably during the unfavorable years 1889 to 1892.

In his work "Statistik der gerichtlichen Polizei im Königreiche Bayern und in einigen anderen Ländern", Dr. Mayr also gives convincing proofs of the parallelism between the changes in the economic situation and prostitution.[1]

However it is not only forced unemployment leading to great poverty that is one of the causes of prostitution; we must also consider as such the fact that the wages paid to women are often so small that it is imposible for them to pay even their necessary expenses, and are thus obliged to find some supplementary source of income.

In his work already quoted, "Die wirthschaftlichen Ursachen der Prostitution", Pappritz fixes the minimum that a working woman in Berlin must have for her strictly necessary expenses at 600 marks a year. Most of the women working in factories generally earn but 500 marks. The average earnings in 1897 were 457 for dressmakers, and 354 for those who made the button-holes (hand labor). And yet the wages paid in Berlin were not the lowest — the average for all Germany was 322 marks.[2]

It will not be very difficult to quote several authors who, in treating of this subject as regards Germany, have expressed themselves in the same way. But I must be brief, and hence shall content myself with citing a passage from Dr. Frankenstein's "Die Lage der Arbeiterinnen in den deutschen Groszstädten", in which he sums up the result of his studies upon this subject; "A very great proportion of the working-women of our great cities receive wages that are not sufficient to provide the most indispensable necessities of life, and find themselves for this cause in the dilemma either of seeking a supplementary trade in prostitution, or of falling into the unavoidable consequences of bodily and spiritual destruction." [3]

It is evident that the same thing is true of all the countries where capitalism reigns. Here is what Faucher, for example, says in his

[1] P. 161. See also *Faucher, op. cit.*, I, p. 277; *Bebel, op. cit.*, p. 194; and *Schäffle, op. cit.*, I, p. 261. *Cf. Neher, op. cit.*, pp. 13 *ff.*
[2] Pp. 8, 9.
[3] P. 188 ("Jahrbuch für Gesetzgebung, Verwaltung, und Volkswirthschaft", XII, 2). See also *L. Braun*, "Die Frauenfrage", pp. 227 *ff.*, and 287 *ff.*

"Études sur l'angleterre" : "Work with the needle is so poorly paid in London that the young persons who give themselves up to it earn only three or four shillings a week, working sixteen or eighteen hours a day. The wages of a fancy needle worker, for a hard day, are from 50 to 60 centimes, while linen workers generally get 30 centimes for stitching a shirt. Nothing more frightful could be imagined than the existence of these poor girls. They must get up at four or five o'clock in the morning, at all seasons of the year, to go to work, or to receive the orders of the merchants. They work without relaxation until midnight in small rooms, where they are crowded together by fives and sixes for economy in the use of fuel and light. If they are admitted to a dressmaker's or linen draper's establishment, they are ill-fed, and under pretext of pressure of business are kept at their task day and night, with only four or five hours of sleep, which are further regularly limited on Saturday. This sedentary life and constant confinement ages them before their time, when phthisis spares them. Is it to be wondered at if some, frightened and disheartened at finding the way of virtue so hard, hold out their arms to prostitution?" [1]

Against these long, hard days and small wages are to be set the easy life and often quite considerable returns — at least in the beginning of their career —which prostitutes enjoy. Moreau-Christophe in his "Du Problème de la Misère" says that in London there are prostitutes who earn $100 to $150 a week, and that the average earnings are $10 a week.[2]

To conclude I wish to call attention to the opinion of Parent-Duchatelet concerning this state of things in Paris. He says: "Of all the causes of prostitution, particularly in Paris, and probably in the other large cities, there is none more active than the lack of work, and the poverty inevitably consequent upon insufficient wages. What do our dressmakers, seamstresses, menders, and in general all those who work with the needle, earn? If we compare the wages of the most capable of them with what those of only moderate abilities can make, we shall see that it is not possible for these last to procure the mere necessaries of life. And if we then compare the price of their labor with that of their dishonor we shall not be surprised that so great a number fall into a life of shame made all but inevitable." [3]

---

[1] I, p. 65.
[2] III, p. 168. See also "Reports of the Select Committee," etc. (Session 1882), pp. 15, 16.
[3] *Op. cit.*, I, pp. 103–104. See also; *Richelot, op. cit.* pp. 577–579; *Frégier,*

Not only does poverty, taken in the sense of the lack of the actual necessaries of life, act as a cause of prostitution, but also that relative poverty which prevents women from enjoying luxuries which seem necessities, like jewelry and fine clothes. With these same women laziness also plays a part.

Now the general opinion with regard to these factors is that they belong exclusively to the individual nature, that they are innate to some women, and that they consequently have nothing to do with the social environment. In my opinion this is entirely erroneous. Mankind are born with certain needs. The non-satisfaction of these needs causes death or the wasting away of the organism. These needs are what we call the strict necessities. All the other wants are awakened by the environment : that is to say, each possesses them in germ, but they are latent as long as the surroundings do not develop them. For example, no one would suffer from abstaining from tobacco if he did not.see someone smoking; no woman would want expensive clothes if others did not wear them ; etc. The desire to dress expensively, to wear jewelry, etc., is not at all, then, an individual quality of certain working-women; the germ of this want is innate in each individual, without any exception though in different degrees. The present order of society, by permitting certain women to spend immense sums for senseless luxury, awakens in others the desire to imitate them as far as possible. Since these last have not the means necessary to shine, they seek them where they may find them, and as there is only the way of prostitution, many follow it. We may add to this that a great number of men use their money and their distinguished manners to decide those who hesitate. This is, therefore, also one of the reasons why the ranks of prostitution are so often recruited from among dressmakers and domestics, *i.e.* from among those who come into direct contact with the luxury of

---

op. cit., I, pp. 97, 98; *Ducpetiaux,* "De la condition physique et morale des jeunes ouvriers", I, p. 315; "Die Prostitution in Berlin" (Anon.), pp. 84, 85; *Loewe,* "Die Prostitution", pp. 135, 136; *Röhrmann, op. cit.,* pp. 24, 25; *Moreau-Christophe, op. cit.,* III, pp. 167, 168; *Acton, op. cit.,* pp. 180 *ff.*; *Hügel, op. cit.,* p. 208; *Jeannel, op. cit.,* pp. 140–142; *Lecour, op. cit.,* p. 248; *Müller,* "Die Prostitutie", pp. 10–11; *du Camp,* "Prostitution à Paris", pp. 257, 258 ("Journal des économistes", 1872); *Kühn,* "Die Prostitution im XIX Jahrhundert", pp. 37, 38; *Schäffle, op. cit.,* p. 261; *von Oettingen, op. cit.,* pp. 212, 213; *Domela Nieuwenhuis,* "Zur Frage der Prostitution", pp. 254 *ff.* ("Neue Zeit", 1884); *Stursberg, op. cit.,* pp. 51–53; *Lux,* "Die Prostitution", pp. 10–12; *Schönfeld, op. cit.,* pp. 269 *ff.*; *Teifen,* "Das Soziale Elende und die besitzenden Klassen in Oesterreich", pp. 150 *ff.*; *Taxil, op. cit.,* pp. 33–38; *De Baets, op. cit.,* pp. 36, 37; *Commenge, op. cit.,* pp. 28, 29, 36, 37; *Blaschko,* "Die Prostitution im XIX Jahrhundert", pp. 16–21.

others.[1] Another cause which makes women desire expensive and
useless things is their low degree of culture, which shows them nothing more preferable than the possession of luxury. And where women
who have all the leisure and the means necessary to busy themselves
with more serious matters set the example of frivolity, we ought
not to be surprised that those without the same advantages try to
follow their example.

The same is true of idleness. If each person who is capable of
it would do a certain amount of work, any normal individual would
be ashamed to pass the day doing nothing. But the fact that
there are women who are esteemed though they remain idle,
awakens in other women, who are obliged to work long and hard,
the desire to do nothing also. As prostitution opens to them the
means of remaining unoccupied, they have recourse to it to satisfy
their desire.

The irony which comes out so often in the social life shows itself
here; the rich women who despise prostitutes never suspect that
they themselves are in part the cause of the fall of the others, and
that placed in the same poor surroundings they themselves would
not act differently.[2]

All those who rank the causes last cited among individual factors
base their opinion upon the thesis, equally strange and false, that
there are two kinds of persons: those who by birth are destined to
command and to enjoy, and those who are destined only to obey,
to work, and not to enjoy at all. Looked at from this point of view
the person who rejects these conditions constitutes an individual
anomaly.

Perhaps it will be objected that without admitting the existence
of individual causes it will be impossible to explain why, though a
great number of women live under the conditions named, only a
small fraction prostitute themselves. Those who reason in this way
commit the error already spoken of, of thinking circumstances the
same when they really differ. There are no two persons who live
under *exactly* the same conditions, how much less thousands. To
give one example only: all the women who earn only the strict necessities of life have not been raised in the same environment. Those
who have grown up in favorable surroundings have perhaps so great
an aversion to prostitution that they prefer a life of poverty to one of
abundance procured by prostitution. It is possible that these women

---

[1] *L. Braun, op. cit.,* p. 555; *Röhrmann, op. cit.,* pp. 46, 47; *Pappritz,
op. cit.,* p. 12. [2] *Kühn, op. cit.,* p. 38.

would prefer suicide to selling themselves, if they came to a state of complete destitution. Secondly it is necessary that a woman should not be too ugly, or the possibility of her earning her living by prostitution is excluded. No one would claim, however, that feminine beauty is one of the causes of prostitution; placed in another environment a woman would not prostitute herself simply because of her beauty.

Although the reasons already given refute in great measure the supposed objection, it must be confessed that the question is not thus entirely answered. Just as all the beings of a certain species differ among themselves, so these women differ naturally as to their innate qualities. The one will have more decided and more numerous wants than the other, she will be less laborious, more frivolous, etc. (qualities which in themselves have nothing to do with prostitution), and, other things being equal, she will be more exposed to the temptation to become a prostitute. All this is perfectly true, but it has nothing to do with the etiology of a social phenomenon like prostitution. For we are here in the presence of two distinct problems; why, of two persons placed in the same situation (supposing that to be possible), the one is more in danger of becoming a prostitute than the other; and, second, what are the causes of the social phenomenon which is called prostitution? The answer to the first question must be that in part at least it is because people differ as to the intensity of their characteristics and of their appetites. The answer to the second is the social conditions.

When two persons of different height are fording a river, and the shorter steps into a hole and is drowned, should we have the right to say that the difference between the height of persons is one of the reasons why people are drowned? I think not. The only reason why there are people who are drowned is that a man cannot live in water — which in no way excludes the fact that a short person runs more danger of drowning than a tall one.

Now as to prostitution — the atmosphere in which certain women live is the cause of their fall, which does not prevent its being true that some of them run more risk than others. The truth of this assertion may be proved by an observation of the facts. Among women who are not prostitutes also there are more who are lazy, frivolous, etc. than those who are not. And though the former have not prostituted themselves, if they had lived in bad surroundings and in poverty they would have run more risk than the latter. If all women were exactly equal prostitution would be as general as it is now; only in this case it would be in every case the environment which would decide what woman became a prostitute, whereas in reality there are, alongside of the environment, individual differences which determine which ones run more risk than the others.

Those who believe that there are here individual causes at work always take the point of view that society is not an organism but a collection of individuals, and that consequently an examination of the individual will suffice to explain social phenomena. It is by the study of prostitution, for example, as a social phenomenon that we bring out the fact that individual differences do not play any part in the etiology of prostitution.

d. Among the causes of prostitution must not be forgotten the fact that many persons have pecuniary interests in it. Without this many women would never have become prostitutes or would not have remained such, and the opportunity for a man to procure the services of a prostitute would not be so good. Capital has settled down on this as upon every place from which profits are to be drawn. The profession of the keeper of a house of ill-fame being extremely lucrative, great sums have been invested in it. In order to furnish the necessary material for these capitalists an international commerce has been created, whose ramifications extend over almost the whole world, and in which large sums are employed, the "white-slave trade." [1] Often before their entrance into these houses the prostitutes have already plied their trade, but many innocent girls become the dupes of the false promises of these traffickers and are given over to the keepers of houses of prostitution. In his "Der Mädchenhandel" Dr. Hatzig says: "The girls, in so far as they do not give themselves up voluntarily as objects of traffic, are generally enticed with illusory promises of a glittering future. . . . Advantageous positions in foreign countries are as a rule offered to them, while nothing is said of the unchaste object of the business. To this especially is to be ascribed the enormous exportation of Hungarian girls into Russia, to whom engagements as dancers in St. Petersburg are promised. When the unhappy victims have once arrived at their destination they would hardly venture to escape from the hands of the slave-trader. In helpless case, deprived of the pro-

[1] *Hatzig,* "Der Mädchenhandel", p. 514 ("Zeitschr. f. d. ges. Strafw." XX); *Bebel, op. cit.,* pp. 190–192; "Reports of the Select Committee", etc. (Session 1881); "Les scandales de Londres" *passim; Collard,* "De Handel in blanke slavinnen", pp. 4–56.

[NOTE TO THE AMERICAN EDITION: *Cf.* further: *A. Mackirdy* and *W. N. Willis,* "The White Slave Market"; *Willis,* "The White Slaves of London"; and *H. Wagener,* "Der Mädchenhandel."]

tection of friends and country, they submit to their fate and are sold to houses of prostitution." [1]

Once fallen into the hands of the keeper of such an establishment it is almost impossible for these women to free themselves. He holds them in all sorts of ways. For example, he will exchange their clothes for others not proper to wear in the street, and will charge them so high a price that they are in his debt; often they do not understand the language of the country; etc. Legally slavery is abolished, but in reality it always exists for these women.[2]

e. The ignorance of a part of the women, a consequence of the environment in which they were brought up, is also one of the causes of prostitution, and no inconsiderable one. Dr. Richelot gives the following figures: [3]

London (1837–1854).

Prostitutes Arrested.	
Not able to read or write	34.98 %
Able to read only or to read and write imperfectly .	61.29 %
Able to read and write well	3.51 %
Having a higher education	.22 %
	100.00 %

Manchester (1840–1855).

Unable to read or write	51.61 %
Able to read only, or to read and write imperfectly .	47.60 %
Able to read and write well	.78 %
Having a higher education	.01 % (?)
	100.00 %

In the "Reports of the Select Committee, etc." the following table is given: [4]

England.

Unable to read and write.	1,213	40 %
Able to read only	464	15 %
Able to read and write imperfectly . .	1,016	33 %
Able to read and write well	371	12 %
	3,064	100 %

---

[1] Pp. 514, 515.

[2] *Collard, op. cit.*, pp. 13–15. Upon the procurer's trade in general see: *Parent-Duchatelet, op. cit.*, I, pp. 430–436; *Richelot, op. cit.*, pp. 583–588; *Acton, op. cit.*, p. 165; *Lecour, op. cit.*, pp. 195–202; *Carlier, op. cit.*, chap. II; *Stursberg, op. cit.*, p. 53; *Commenge, op. cit.*, pp. 60–90; *Blaschko*, "Hygiene der Prostitution und venerischen Krankheiten", pp. 37, 38.

[3] *Op. cit.*, pp. 600 and 637.   [4] P. 52 (Session 1882), Appendix B.

Parent-Duchatelet gives the following figures: [1]

Paris.

Unable to sign their name	2,503	56%
Able to sign, but badly	1,868	42%
Able to sign well	110	2%
	4,481	100%

Dr. Commenge gives the following: [2]

Paris (1878–1887).

UNREGISTERED PROSTITUTES.		
Able to read and write	4,297	68.12%
Able to read and sign their name . . .	988	15.66%
Able to read but not to write or sign . .	11	0.18%
Unable to read or write	1,012	16.04%
	6,308	100.00%

From an examination of the statistics given it is evident that the number of illiterates is very large, however they may be decreasing in number now that primary education for the children of the poorer classes is becoming more and more general. Knowing how to read and write, however, proves very little as to the culture of the individual. The statistics only show the number of prostitutes who are totally illiterate, and we must certainly count many of the others as well among the ignorant.

It is clear that ignorance alone does not lead to prostitution. But it is clear that many prostitutes would not have become such, or would not have lent an ear to the flattering offers of good positions, etc., if they had known what an abominable life awaited them.

Among the secondary causes of prostitution must certainly also be classed:

f. Alcoholism. Not only have many women been seduced when they had drunk too much, and so have become prostitutes, but the demoralization which is the result of the constant abuse of alcohol may have the same effect.[3]

g. Degeneracy. According to some physicians (among whom

---

[1] *Op. cit.*, I, p. 86. 　　　　　　　　[2] *Op. cit.*, p. 334.
[3] *Richelot, op. cit.*, pp. 664, 665; *Acton, op. cit.*, p. 165; *Pappritz, op. cit.*, pp. 17, 18.

are Professors Lombroso and Tarnowsky, to cite only the most famous) the cause of prostitution is not to be found first in the environment, but in a pathological (or atavistic) condition. These authors
have examined a certain number of prostitutes, and have drawn
from this examination the conclusion that the stigmata of degeneracy often found in them indicate a state which is the cause of their
misconduct; prostitution is in large part kept up by born prostitutes.[1]

There is one objection to be made to such a manner of proceeding,
namely that we must in the very beginning give a precise definition
of the social phenomenon which is called prostitution. This definition, which can perhaps be given only by the sociologist and not by
the biologist, will show us at the outset that it is very difficult to represent anyone as born with a tendency to commit sexual acts *for economic reasons*. So Professor Lombroso understands a totally different
thing by prostitution from what it really is. He says: "Sometimes
in the beginning marriage does not even exist and prostitution is
the general rule"[2] and as an example he cites that the Naïrs live
in complete promiscuity. According to Professor Lombroso, then,
everywhere that there is no marriage there is prostitution. In other
words, according to him all nature is one grand brothel, in which,
aside from the married women, all the females would be prostitutes!
Truly Professor Lombroso has some sociological views all his own.

These authors claim, then, that prostitutes often present stigmata of degeneracy. An examination of the figures shows, however,
that 63 % of all the prostitutes examined show almost no such stigmata.[3]

For 63 % of them then degeneracy cannot be the cause, nor does
it follow that it is the cause in the remaining 37 % of cases. For
many women with these stigmata are not found at all among the
ranks of prostitution. To bring out the real import of the researches
in question we must put beside them the results of an examination
of non-prostitutes. It is for this reason that I wish to call attention
to the work of Dr. P. Näcke, "Verbrechen und Wahnsinn beim
Weibe", in which the author arrives at the result that only 3 % of
the normal women examined by him failed to show signs of degeneracy.[4] It seems to me, then, that when we find figures so low among
normal women the thesis of Professor Lombroso is not proved.

[1] *Tarnowsky*, "Prostitution und Abolitionismus", pp. 108 *ff*.
[2] *Lombroso* and *Ferrero*, "La femme criminelle et la prostituée", p. 212.
[3] *Op. cit.*, p. 581.   [4] P. 132.

If his conclusion were true, prostitutes would be drawn from all classes of society, for degeneracy is present in all classes. But, as we have seen above, they are drawn almost exclusively from the poorer classes. Professor Lombroso thinks he has refuted this argument (which is enough to overthrow his whole theory) by saying: "The woman who, coming from the lower classes, ends by becoming the inmate of a brothel, in the upper classes becomes an incorrigible adultress. . . ." [1] Consequently according to Lombroso there is no difference between a prostitute and an adultress. It is not necessary to combat such singular ideas: they refute themselves.

Nevertheless the theory named is not without importance for the problem of prostitution. The following quotation, taken from a recent study of Dr. Bonhoeffer shows what its importance is: "We have no more right to speak of prostitution as inborn than we should have to speak of a born drinker. The disposition brought about through the defective psychical condition is inborn. But whether a psychically defective female individual will become a prostitute is in a certain sense dependent upon chance and external conditions." [2]

There are persons who are born with psychic defects. These persons adapt themselves to their environment only with difficulty, and have a smaller chance than others to succeed in our present society, where the fundamental principle is the warfare of all against all. Hence they are more likely to seek for means that others do not employ (prostitution, for example). If the defect of a woman has relation especially to the sexual sphere, so that she feels, for example, extraordinary sexual desires, the danger of her becoming a prostitute is very great. [3] Even when the environment in which such persons live is very favorable, it is nevertheless certain that their actions will be different from those of others, though it does not at all follow that they will infallibly become prostitutes. It is certain that these morbid cases are rare in general, and very rare among prostitutes. [4] Parent-Duchatelet says: "Finally there are girls who give themselves up to prostitution in consequence of a licentiousness which one can explain only by the action of a mental disease . . .; but in general these Messalinas are rare; I have only found one opinion upon

---

[1] *Op. cit.* p. 574.

[2] *Op. cit.*, pp. 118, 119.

[3] See some typical examples cited by *Dr. Magnan* in his report to the second Congress of Criminal Anthropology: "De l'enfance des criminels dans les rapports avec la prédisposition naturelle au crime." ("Actes," pp. 60–63.)
    [NOTE TO THE AMERICAN EDITION: *Cf. H. F. Stelzner* "Die psychopathischen Konstitutionen und ihre sociologische Bedeutung."]

[4] *Commenge, op. cit.*, p. 107.

this fact, and it has been abundantly confirmed by my own researches." [1]

This theory, that the principal cause of prostitution is to be found in innate psychic defectiveness, contains, as Dr. Blaschko says (in his "Die Prostitution im XIX Jahrhundert"), "a small grain of truth in a mass of exaggerations." It is only a very small proportion of prostitutes who have gone into the profession for this reason, and it is certain that they would not have done so if circumstances had not contributed to bring it about.[2]

We have now arrived at the end of our observations upon prostitution. In our opinion it has been shown that it is partly the inevitable complement of the existing legal monogamy, and partly the result of the bad conditions under which many young girls grow up, the consequence of the physical and mental misery in which the women of the proletariat live, and the consequence also of the inferior position of woman in our present society. When we make exception of a few cases where a certain degeneracy enters in beside the effect of the unfavorable environment, the prostitution of today is, then, the consequence of existing social conditions, which, in their turn, spring from the economic system of our time.

It may be objected that prostitution has presented itself under other economic systems. I am not ignorant of this, but I know also that $3 \times 4 = 12$, and $2 \times 6 = 12$ also; that is to say that two different causes may produce the same result. The prostitution of our day may be the consequence of capitalism while that of earlier periods may have been the consequence of the mode of production of those times. Further, an examination of the epochs in which prostitution was a general phenomenon (it never reached proportions as great as under capitalism) [3] shows us that they did not differ much from our own in those matters which concern the question in hand, namely, the inferior position of woman, and the strong contrasts in fortunes.

Many authors who have taken up the question of prostitution declare that it is as old as humanity itself. If we understand by prostitution what it really is, and not what imagination makes it out to be, this assertion is absolutely false. Prostitution is of very ancient

---

[1] *Op. cit.*, I, p. 106.

[2] See further against Lombroso's theory: *R. Calwer*, "Die erbliche Belastung der Prostituirten" ("Neue Zeit", XII, 2); *Hirsch, op. cit.*, pp. 15 *ff.*; *Pappritz, op. cit.*, pp. 3–6.

[NOTE TO THE AMERICAN EDITION: *Cf. Näcke*, "Die Ueberbleibsel der Lombrosischen kriminalanthropologischen Theorien."]

[3] See for example *Blaschko*, "Die Prostitution im XIX Jahrhundert", p. 9.

date, but it has not always existed.   Westermarck, one of the authors best qualified to pronounce an opinion upon this matter, says : "Prostitution is rare among peoples living in a state of nature and unaffected by foreign influence.   It is contrary to a woman's natural feelings as involving a suppression of individual inclinations." [1] I advise those who, in spite of everything, wish still to maintain that prostitution belongs to all time and all places, to investigate the peoples among whom the matriarchate exists. If they are so unfamiliar with sociology, let them look for prostitution in the country.   They will find none; prostitution exists only in the cities.

[1] "The History of Human Marriage", pp. 70, 71.

CHAPTER IV.

ALCOHOLISM.[1]

WE understand by alcoholism the social phenomenon which consists of the chronic abuse of alcoholic beverages.[2] Before touching upon the etiology of this phenomenon we must decide the biological question, why does a man consume alcohol? Always and everywhere it has been established that the liking for narcotics is natural to man. Those who believe that human nature is inclined to evil, and that the tendency to excess is innate, find the solution of the problem very simple. They reason as follows: "by alcohol this innate desire is satisfied; man is inclined to excess, — ergo . . . alcoholism." Those who deny the evil nature of man find here on the contrary the crux of the problem. For, say they, the facts are there to prove that man has not always and everywhere been intemperate; there must then be other causes than this so-called sinful instinct.

Alcoholic beverages are consumed first, because they are agreeable to the taste (at least some of them); second, and especially, because aside from the taste they have the power of awaking agreeable sensations. In his work "Der Alkoholismus" Dr. A. Grotjahn expresses himself thus upon this point: "Narcotics act . . . not primarily through their agreeable taste, but influence directly the cerebral cortex and awaken pleasurable sensations which are completely independent of the activity of the senses or of pleasure-producing perceptions of the outer world. There is no other means of producing pleasurable sensations independent of the perceptions

---

[1] [NOTE TO THE AMERICAN EDITION: Notable recent works are: *E. Vandervelde*, "Le socialism et l'alcool" ("Essais socialistes"); *E. Wurm*, "Die Alkoholfrage"; *A. Pistolese*, "Alcoolismo e delinquenza"; and *A. Diz*, "Alkoholismus und Arbeiterschaft."]

[2] The *abuse* of alcohol is much more extensive than is generally believed. Dr. Grotjahn gives as the amount that a normal man can take without being injured by it, 30–45 grams of absolute alcohol, the amount contained in a liter of beer, or a half-liter of light wine. ("Der Alkoholismus", p. 143.)

arising from the outer world, and independent of the functions of the senses. Only in this way is it to be explained that the need for the use of narcotics has attained so wide a dissemination, and struck such deep roots when once mankind had learned their use." [1]

If alcohol is used regularly, then, to drive away disagreeable sensations, the consumption must necessarily increase if the individual wishes to attain the same psychical condition, for use continually weakens the effect.

Here, as in the case of the etiology of other social phenomena, we must treat the different causes of alcoholism separately, although it often happens that a number combine to make a man alcoholic. We shall begin with the causes which lead to alcoholism among the proletariat, for it is in this class that the abuse of alcohol is most widespread and produces the greatest ravages, first because the quality of the drinks consumed is very bad, and secondly, because alcohol has more harmful effects upon a badly nourished system.

a. There are occupations which, by their nature, lead the workmen who follow them almost inevitably to the abuse of alcohol. Dr. Grotjahn says: "The mental condition suffers when the temperature is too high or too low, more than the capacity for work. The great discomfort while at work may be removed by regulating the things which influence the temperature (clothing, housing, heating, ventilation) or the uncomfortable feelings may be blunted through copious draughts of spirituous beverages. Hence the peculiar custom of taking alcohol against great heat and great cold both, a thing which would be absurd if alcohol worked specifically against the one extreme of temperature or the other, and did not simply moderate the unpleasant sensations produced by abnormal temperatures. " [2]

In the second place come the industries in which much powder or gas are produced. To quote Dr. Grotjahn again: "The dust, which those working in the open air have at times to endure, but which those who work in closed rooms must almost always put up with, brings about, through directly irritating the mucous membrane of the mouth, a highly annoying thirst, which greatly induces the drinking of beer and brandy. We hear it on all sides from workmen who outside of working hours are entirely moderate or even abstemious, that the thirst which is excited by dust is not nearly so well quenched by water or any 'soft drink' as by the use of alcoholic beverages. Experience shows that in the callings which are dust-producing there is a marked tendency to beer- and brandy-drinking, and to a quick passage from

[1] Pp. 126, 127.   [2] Op. cit., pp. 287, 288.

moderate to immoderate use of alcohol. This is the case with masons, carpenters, cabinet-makers, but especially with grinders and quarry-men. The production of irritating vapors in chemical works has a similar effect, but more intense than that of ordinary dust." [1]

In the third place there are the industries in which the workmen are brought into direct contact with alcohol. Thus there are, for example, the workmen in distilleries,[2] breweries, alcohol-warehouses, etc.; then wine tasters, those who have to use alcohol in their business, and finally those whose business takes them into establishments where alcoholic drinks are sold, such as commercial travelers, and the tenants of the establishments themselves.[3]

b. The too great length of the working-day. Workers who are forced to work much longer than the human organism can stand are inclined to the abuse of alcohol for two reasons. In the first place they find in it the means of repairing temporarily the diminution of force caused by great fatigue. Since alcohol gives only a temporary increase of capacity, its continued use, and consequently its abuse, is therefore almost inevitable.[4] This is the cause of the great development of alcoholism among longshoremen, who often work for twenty-four hours or even longer at a stretch.

In the second place immoderately prolonged labor produces a veritable torture, which can be assuaged by large quantities of alcohol. Those who have an interest in having the workman toil as long as possible have always tried to prevent the shortening of the working-day by claiming that it would increase the abuse of alcohol. The facts have shown, however, that just the contrary is true. It has been proved that it is not the shortening of the working-day, but its too great extension that is one of the important causes of the abuse of alcohol. So it is not by chance that the retailers of alcoholic beverages are among the most zealous opponents of the shortening of the day.[5]

---

[1] *Op. cit.*, p. 288.

[2] *Holst,* "Arbeiders en Alkohol" ("Nieuwe Tijd", VII), p. 527, and *Grot-jahn, op. cit.*, p. 225.

[3] *Verhaeghe,* "De l'alcoolisation", pp. 215, 216.

[4] *Grotjahn, op. cit.*, pp. 35–41.

[5] See *J. Rae,* "Der Achtstunden-Arbeitstag", pp. 249, 250, where mention is made of the opposition of public-house keepers in Australia to the movement for an eight-hour day. Upon the shortening of the day and the decrease in the use of alcohol, see pp. 96, 107, 108 in the same work; *Lux,* "Socialpoli-tisches Handbuch", pp. 328–329; *Dr. G. M. den Tex,* "Verkorting van den arbeidsdag", pp. 28, 29, 34, 80, 117–120, 140; "Onmatig lange arbeidstijd en misbruik van sterke drank" (Anon.), pp. 17–20; *Grotjahn, op. cit.*, pp. 288–289; *Roland Holst, op. cit.*, pp. 530–532; *Augagneur,* "Les vraies causes et les vrais remèdes de l'alcoolisme", pp. 76–77 ("Mouvement Socialiste", 1900); *Verhaeghe,* "Le parti socialiste et la lutte contre l'alcool", pp. 25–26 ("Mouvement Socialiste", 1900).

c. **Bad** and insufficient nourishment. There are many workers not sufficiently nourished for the support of the body. For the purpose of removing the feeling of discomfort arising from this they make great use of alcoholic drinks. In these cases the nourishment is insufficient both objectively (considered from a physiological point of view) and subjectively (it does not satisfy the individual). Besides these there are those who are able to procure a sufficient quality of food but lack the means to vary the dishes and to replace foods that are bulky and difficult to digest (potatoes, bread, cereals, etc.) by others less bulky but more nutritious (especially meat). The persons who rely upon persuasion in combating alcoholism, fix the attention upon the enormous sums expended for spirituous drinks, and then figure how much bread, how many beds, and other useful things could have been bought with this money. All this is well and good, only in reasoning in this way they make the capital error of representing a workman as a sort of machine who says to himself: "I do not earn enough for the support of my family — let us not buy alcohol, then, for it is harmful but rather eat more potatoes. It is true that the discomfort will persist, but . . . I shall at least be nourished as well as *possible*." However, since the working-man is, no more than other men, a being who is content to reason, but who feels, the calculations of these Utopists fall to the ground.

Aside from the bad quality and insufficient quantity of the food, very often the working family do not know how to give an agreeable taste to the dishes they eat; and in families where the married woman herself is employed away from home they often have to content themselves with cold viands. In these cases spirituous drinks serve to counteract the discomfort of the monotony and bulkiness of the food. Among a number of proofs which may be brought in support of what has been said above, we may cite the researches made by a Swiss inspector of factories, M. Schuler, upon the relation between alcoholism and the food of the working-classes.[1] In this investigation the following facts appear.

In the cantons of Geneva, Vaud, and Neufchatel the condition of the people with regard to food is the best; a small consumption of potatoes and a large consumption of meat. Little brandy is drunk there, the use of alcohol being mainly limited to a large consumption of wine. The workmen in the canton of Neufchatel, except those employed in watch-making, live in poor circumstances, eat many potatoes and also drink much brandy.

[1] Given in detail in *Grotjahn, op. cit.*, pp. 277–283.

In the cantons of Berne and Lucerne the living conditions of the working class, and especially their food, are very bad; they consume much grain and little meat, and in these districts they drink an extraordinary quantity of brandy. In Aargau there is a great difference between the condition of the industrial proletariat and that of the proletariat engaged in agriculture. The food of the former is insufficient, potatoes forming the main resource; furthermore the working day is very long, and the consumption of brandy is correspondingly great. The food of the agricultural laborers, on the other hand, is much better (a greater consumption of meat and of milk) and the consumption of brandy is much less than among the factory hands. In the canton of Zurich the conditions are much the same as those in Aargau.

All this shows clearly that it is the bad material condition of the proletariat which causes alcoholism, for everywhere that the condition of the industrial worker is raised above that of the agricultural population (as, for example, among the skilled workmen at Winterthur), the consumption of brandy is less among the factory people. Just so the material condition of the small rural proprietors in the canton of Zug is worse than that of the factory hands, and the consumption of brandy there is considerable.[1]

d. Bad housing conditions. These conditions often bring it about that the workman, returning from his work, goes to the dram-shop instead of to his home. The dwelling is ordinarily small, too small for a large family, without comfort or attractiveness, gloomy, and often cold in winter, whereas in the dramshop there is light, warmth, and gaiety; comrades are there, and other topics of conversation than the perpetual cares of life; and, above all, for a little money there may be procured the means of forgetting for the moment the miseries of life.[2]

e. The uncertainty of existence and forced unemployment. The continual difficulties, the anguish of not knowing what the future

---

[1] See also *Colajanni*, "L'alcoolismo", pp. 153 *ff.*; *Zerboglio*, "L'alcoolisme: causes et remèdes", pp. 123, 124 ("Devenir Social", 1895); *Vandervelde*, *op. cit.*, p. 260, and "Die ökonomischen Faktoren des Alkoholismus", pp. 747, 748 ("Neue Zeit", 1901–1902, I); *Verhaeghe*, *op. cit.*, pp. 203–205.

Upon the fact that the abuse of alcohol has consequences much more injurious for the badly nourished man than for others, see: *A Baer*, "Der Alkoholismus", p. 286; *Colajanni*, *op. cit.*, p. 183; *Grotjahn*, *op. cit.*, p. 273; *Verhaeghe*, "De l'alcoolisation", p. 203.

[2] *Colajanni*, *op. cit.*, pp. 177, 178; *Braun*, "Berliner Wohnungsverhältnisse", p. 22; *Grotjahn*, *op. cit.*, pp. 290–292; *Verhaeghe*, "De l'alcoolisation", pp. 205–208 and 217; *Vandervelde*, "Die ökonomischen Faktoren des Alkoholismus", p. 747.

has in store, produce a depression which may be driven away for the moment by the consumption of alcohol. In the article by Richard Holst already cited, is found the following answer given by a workman to the question: What are the principal causes of alcoholism? "One of the principal factors is the difficulty of earning a living for one's family, and also — *and especially* — care, the eternal care for the morrow, which fastens upon the life of the working-man like a bur, and which, as work becomes more rare, drives him to desperation. This is the principal cause of alcoholism. Remove this care and men will drink much less alcohol, for then the heart can open itself to joy instead of deadening itself, as is at present almost a necessity. For many persons this deadening is the only, although the fatal, means of ridding one's self for a moment of the terrible thought, 'What will happen if I have the misfortune to be thrown out of work, or fall sick?'" [1]

Unemployment leads often to alcoholism. "Idleness is the mother of all the vices", says an old adage; but among all the vices, that which arises most directly from idleness is without doubt drunkenness. What can a man do in the long hours when he has no work? The rich man, educated, well brought up, finds the means of passing his time agreeably; but the poor man has only the dram-shop, and is drawn thither irresistibly. The first time he goes for a change from boredom; then from habit, and finally from a necessity now become instinctive to his organism, which at a given moment feels the need of something to stimulate the nerves. It is in alcoholic drinks that he finds what he lacks.[2]

f. Ignorance. The lack of other means of enjoyment. One of the lesser causes of alcoholism, but important enough to be named, is ignorance. There are a great many persons who think that the regular consumption of great quantities of alcohol is not harmful, who even believe that alcohol has nutritive value, and that consequently the consumption of it is even useful.[3]

From another point of view, however, ignorance, the lack of culture, emptiness of life, are very important causes if not the most important causes of alcoholism. The desire for pleasure is innate in every man, including the working-man, whose life is a hard one in every way. But for him there are almost insurmountable difficul-

---

[1] P. 533.
[2] *Zerboglio, op. cit.*, p. 125. See also *Verhaeghe*, "De l'alcoolisation", p. 212; *Colajanni, op. cit.*, pp. 181, 182.
[3] See upon this subject *Colajanni, op. cit.*, pp. 168, 169; *Verhaeghe, op. cit.*, pp. 222, 223; *Holst, op. cit.*, p. 528.

ties in enjoying all that is truly beautiful, all that nature, art, and science can offer to man. This is due first, and principally, to material difficulties. In our present society one can enjoy these things only with plenty of money. The wages of the working-man are not enough for this. Often he is too tired when the day is over to take up anything which requires effort, and his abode is too small and too badly arranged for reading or any other form of distraction. However, the principal reason why the proletarian enjoys the products of civilization but little is that his intelligence is not prepared for it. His capacities have not been cultivated in this direction, for capitalism has developed in a great number of people only the capacity for manual work to the detriment of everything else. Dr. Augagneur, in his article already cited, has expressed it as follows: "The true cause of alcoholism is entirely of the intellectual and moral order; it is the insufficiency of cerebral activity, the intellectual indigence and distress, the mental unemployment.

"Every individual who, after the business of his calling is completed, is incapable of busying himself with something else, is a fruitful soil for alcoholism. How many, aside from their technical efficiency, are unfitted to think, to comprehend, to explain anything whatever. When the workman, after ten or twelve hours of mechanical work, leaves the factory, he is confused, does not know how to kill the time that must elapse before he goes to bed; he drinks. . . .

"Sundays and holidays ordinary labor is suppressed, the laborer wanders about the streets, objectless, adrift, embarrassed by his liberty, and runs fatally aground upon the dram-shop. The days of rest are days of drunkenness.

"Our society suffers from this intellectual inaction, which is the true cause of alcoholism. Most men, as soon as their trade no longer makes them work their arms and in some cases their brains, know not which way to turn. Alcohol is their refuge, because it procures for the nervous system sensations which take the place of the absent ideas." [1]

It is for this reason that the abuse of alcohol is greatest among unskilled laborers [2] and that it decreases everywhere that the workmen begin to organize in unions and political parties, since these lead to the amelioration of conditions, material, intellectual, and moral. In other words, drinking diminishes wherever the prole-

---

[1] Pp. 75, 76. See also *Colajanni, op. cit.*, pp. 169–173; *Grotjahn, op. cit.*, pp. 289–298; *Verhaeghe*, "De l'alcoolisation", pp. 225–227.
[2] *Holst, op. cit.*, pp. 534, 535.

tariat is animated by an ideal. And it is also among those workmen who foresee the future of their class and know what there is to do, that the ranks of total abstainers are mainly recruited.[1]

There are persons who maintain the thesis that poverty is not the principal cause of alcoholism among the working classes. As a proof they say that the laborers who earn the least (farm hands among others) are not those who drink the most, and that an increase in wages often brings about a higher consumption of alcohol. They are deceived, however. They lose sight of the fact that most agricultural laborers earn so little that they cannot consume alcohol regularly, that beside the material poverty there is an intellectual poverty, and that a slight amelioration of the one does not produce simultaneously a diminution of the other. The abuse of alcohol has, on the contrary, decreased regularly everywhere that the labor movement has brought about a continuous amelioration of material and intellectual conditions.[2]

To close these remarks upon alcoholism among the workers I will quote the following from Engels in which the causes are concisely set forth : "All possible temptations, all allurements combine to bring the workers to drunkenness. Liquor is almost their only source of pleasure, and all things conspire to make it accessible to them. The working-man comes from his work tired, exhausted, finds his home comfortless, damp, dirty, repulsive; he has urgent need of recreation, he *must* have something to make work worth his trouble, to make the prospect of the next day endurable. His unnerved, uncomfortable, hypochondriac state of mind and body arising from his unhealthy condition, and especially from indigestion, is aggravated beyond endurance by the general conditions of his life, the uncertainty of his existence, his dependence upon possible accidents and chances, and his inability to do anything towards gaining an assured position. His enfeebled frame, weakened by bad air and bad food, violently demands some external stimulus; his social need can be gratified only in the public-house, he has absolutely no other place where he can meet his friends. How can he be expected to resist temptation? It is morally and physically inevitable that, under such circumstances, a very large number of working-men should fall into intemperance. And apart from the chiefly physical influences which drive the working-man into drunkenness, there is the

---

[1] *Kautsky*, "Der Alkoholismus und seine Bekämpfung" ("Neue Zeit", 1890–91, II); *Vandervelde*, "Het alkoholisme en de arbeidsvoorwaarden in België," pp. 268, 271, 272; *Holst, op. cit.*, pp. 528–536.
[2] See, among others, *Grotjahn, op. cit.*, pp. 296–298.

example of the great mass, the neglected education, the impossibility of protecting the young from temptation, in many cases the direct influence of intemperate parents, who give their own children liquor, the certainty of forgetting for an hour or two the wretchedness and burden of life, and a hundred other circumstances so mighty that the workers can, in truth, hardly be blamed for yielding to such overwhelming pressure. Drunkenness has here ceased to be a vice for which the vicious can be held responsible; it becomes a phenomenon, the necessary, inevitable effect of certain conditions upon an object possessed of no volition in relation to those conditions. They who have degraded the working-man to a mere object have the responsibility to bear." [1]

As for the causes of alcoholism in the lower proletariat they are the same as for the proletariat (if we except the two first named), only they are much more intense. A very insufficient diet, frightful housing conditions, the demoralization consequent upon inaction, ignorance, and the absolute lack of any intellectual life have made of the man a brute who can forget his misery only by drinking.

The same is true of prostitutes, among whom the abuse of alcohol is very wide spread. Parent-Duchatelet says: "The taste of these women (prostitutes) for strong drink may be considered to be general, although in different degrees; they contract it early, and this taste ends by plunging some into the last state of brutishness. All the information that I have gathered proves that they began drinking only to blunt their sensibilities; gradually they become accustomed to it, and in a little while the habit becomes so strong that it resists any return to virtue; . . ." [2]

Dr. Bonhoeffer says: "In many cases alcoholism is the result of the manner of life of prostitutes." [3]

The etiology of the abuse of alcohol in the well-to-do class is principally as follows:

a. A part of the well-to-do class, those who live exclusively upon the income from their invested capital, consider one of their occupa-

---

[1] "Condition of the Working Class", pp. 102, 103 [in original pp. 105, 106]. See also: *Ducpetiaux,* "De la condition physique et morale des jeunes ouvriers", I, pp. 352 *ff.*; *Battaglia,* "La dinamica del delitto", pp. 415–417.

[2] "De la prostitution dans la ville de Paris", I, p. 139.

[3] "Zur Kenntnis des groszstädtischen Bettel- und Vagabondenthums. Zweiter Beitrag; Prostituirte", p. 119 ("Zeitsch. f. d. ges. Strw.", XXIII). See also: *Logan,* "The Great Social Evil", pp. 55–56, 59; *Ladame,* "De la prostitution dans ses rapports avec l'alcoolisme, le crime et la folie", pp. 7–14; *Colajanni, op. cit.,* p. 179; *Lombroso* and *Ferrero,* "La femme criminelle et la prostituée", p. 538.

tions to be the spending of a part of the surplus-value that they receive. Among the means they make use of for this end is alcohol, which has also the faculty of dissipating the ennui resulting from the emptiness of their existence.

"Many persons, belonging for the most part to the well-to-do classes, have no fixed occupation and feel the need of none. These persons do not know what it is to love work for work's sake. Having all that they need to live upon they imagine that work exists only for those who have to earn their bread, and they themselves are created for 'dolce far niente.' Unfortunately the 'far niente' is not always sweet! Having nothing to do, these individuals do not know how to use their time; they are bored, they seek distractions and pleasures. Alcohol presents itself to them as procuring the pleasure sought for, but as this enjoyment is only momentary, they are forced to renew it and to prolong it . . ." [1]

b. Another part of the bourgeoisie is composed of those who pass their lives in the fierce combat of competition, who are bent under the burden of material cares, and whose mind is occupied with a single idea, that of getting money. This is why in these surroundings also they frequently have recourse to alcohol to dissipate their vexations, especially when things go badly.

Having treated of alcoholism among the idle portion of the bourgeoisie, Kautsky says in the study quoted above: "Not all, of course, and perhaps not even the majority, of the moneyed class are idlers. Many work as long and hard as any working-man, even if the work they do is often superfluous. But it is always one-sided nervous work. Muscular exercise among the property-holding class has been constantly pushed ever further into the background since the sixteenth century, and the demands upon the nervous system have correspondingly increased. Besides the continual struggle with the working-class, from whom the surplus-value is taken, there is going on an equally uninterrupted battle of the spoilers among themselves for a share of this surplus-value. All these battles are carried on today by nervous, not muscular, energy, and the contests become constantly more bitter, the crises more tremendous, the battlefields more colossal, the forces involved more incalculable.

"Thus the nerves of the bourgeoisie become wrecked through their activity as well as through their idleness. . . . If part of the bourgeoisie befuddle themselves out of wantonness, another part grasp

[1] *Verhaeghe*, "De l'alcoolisation", p. 211; see also *Colajanni, op. cit.,* p. 183; and *Kautsky, op. cit.,* p. 50.

for stimulants or for means of benumbing themselves, alcohol, morphine, cocaine, any thing to take away their feeling of sickness, to conquer their pains, to make them forget their cares; and as it is with the proletariat, so is it with the moneyed class, the power of resistance to these agents declines." [1]

Finally, we must notice some causes of alcoholism which influence the whole population.

a. Imitation. This is reckoned among the important causes. In the first place there are many children (for whom alcohol even in small quantities is extremely harmful) who are accustomed to the use of alcohol as a consequence of the example set by their families. Dr. R. Frölich mentioned the following facts at the 8th International Congress against Alcohol at Vienna: [2]

Out of 81,187 children from 6 to 14 years of age going to school in Vienna, there were:

49.5 % who already drank beer and	32.1 % who drank beer regularly	
82.1 % " " " wine	11.2 % " " wine "	
94.2 % " " " brandy	4.1 % " " brandy "	

But imitation is also important among those who have attained their full development. In the course of time certain circles have taken up the habit of drinking, and any one who frequents these circles must do the same under penalty of being looked down upon. However, I think that the importance that abstainers give to imitation is exaggerated. The number of those who are guilty of the *abuse* of alcohol from force of example and *nothing else* is certainly not very great. The other factors which have been at work at the same time to bring about this result are not so obvious. Finally we must not forget that imitation is not an independent factor; what does not exist cannot be imitated, and consequently there must be other causes primarily responsible.

b. The climate. Although so much importance is not attached to climate as formerly, it is nevertheless certain that a cold climate, especially if damp, favors the consumption of alcohol, since this dissipates temporarily the discomfort resulting from cold and humidity. It is for this reason that the inhabitants of the northern countries (for example, England, Denmark, and Holland) consume on

[1] Pp. 50, 51. See also *Battaglia, op. cit.*, pp. 418–420, and *Zerboglio, op. cit.*, p. 125.
[2] " Ergebnisse einer Umfrage über den Alkoholgenuss der Schulkinder in Nieder-Oesterreich ", p. 82. See also *Ducpetiaux, op. cit.*, pp. 367–370.

the average greater quantities of alcohol than southern countries (like Spain and Italy). However the facts show that the social environment is a much more important factor, and is apt to modify or overcome entirely the influence of climate. In Sweden and Norway, for example, the consumption per capita is smaller than in countries farther south, like Denmark and Holland. The great changes which occur at different times in the same country, where the climate remains a constant factor, are a further proof of the truth of this. And notwithstanding the climate the abuse of alcohol increases greatly in the southern countries in which industrialism becomes more and more prevalent (like northern Italy).[1]

   c. Race.   There are many persons who attribute much importance in the etiology of alcoholism, as in other social phenomena, to the influence of race. Where two nations differing racially have not the same consumption of alcohol, they think they can explain the difference by race. But in reasoning thus they forget that two nations may present great differences in their manner of life, and that the greater or less consumption of alcohol may be explained better by these than by race (without counting that racial difference in the tendency to alcoholism is still to be accounted for somehow). To cite an example; the peoples of the Germanic race are more intemperate, than the peoples of the Latin race (a fact already explained by the climate, and further accounted for by the cheapness of wine); this difference it is said is to be explained in part by race. And yet the use of brandy in northern Italy increases with increasing industrialism, northern industrial France gives a very high figure for brandy-consumption, and the Belgians of the Latin race do not yield to their Germanic compatriots in the use of alcohol.[2] The proverbial temperance of the Jews is often attributed to their race, while we should ask whether this temperance is not rather to be attributed to their manner of life, which differs from that of other peoples. It is probable that the Jewish industrial workers, for example, who have broken with the habits of their coreligionists, have also become consumers of spirituous beverages. As far as the diamond-cutters of Amsterdam are concerned this fact is at least averred.[3] The tend-

---

[1] See *Baer, op. cit.*, pp. 144, 145; *Colajanni, op. cit.*, pp. 139–142; *Grotjahn, op. cit.*, pp. 178, 179; *Verhaeghe,* "De l'alcoolisation", pp. 209–211; *Vandervelde,* "Die ökonomischen Faktoren des Alkoholismus", pp. 741, 742.

[2] *Grotjahn, op. cit.*, pp. 300, 301.

[3] *Holst, op. cit.*, p. 530.

[NOTE TO THE AMERICAN EDITION: *Cf.* further upon alcoholism among the Jews, *Dr. L. Cheinisse,* "Die Rassenpathologie und der Alkoholismus bei den Juden."]

ency which is observed among the Slavic peoples of becoming intoxicated periodically in an extraordinary fashion, is attributed to race, but the same thing is observed in other countries where wages are very low, thus preventing regular drinking, and limiting the consumption of alcohol to paydays.[1]

I believe that the influence of race upon alcoholism is enormously exaggerated, which does not, however, imply that I deny its influence. The slight expansion of the use of alcohol among the Mongolians (among whom, it is to be added, this is replaced by other narcotics, principally by opium) is to be explained in part perhaps, by race.

d. The psycho- and neuro-pathic condition of some persons enters into the etiology of alcoholism in three ways. In the first place, the regular use of small quantities of alcohol may, with the said persons, result in alcoholism. Secondly, quantities of alcohol which have results imperceptible in the normal man, may cause drunkenness in a very neuropathic person. Thirdly, alcoholism is present as the principal symptom with dipsomaniacs, and as a secondary symptom in the case of persons suffering from mania, melancholia, or paralytic dementia.[2]

After what we have said concerning the causes of the *consumption* of alcohol, we must add something about the production of it. As is the case with most articles, the production of alcohol is capitalistic, that is to say, for the sake of profit. Consumption is only a condition for attaining this end. If the profits could be greater without production it would cease.[3] Aside from the producers, the state also has a great interest in the consumption of alcohol, since it derives considerable revenue from it.

The consequences of the fact that the production of alcohol is capitalistic have a great social importance. To instance only some of these :

First. The number of places where liquor may be drunk is very great. The more there is consumed, the more profit there is for the producers and for the retailers. As a consequence there is much advertising, and many dram-shops, in which the wages are often

---

[1] *Vandervelde*, "Die ökonomischen Faktoren des Alkoholismus", pp. 742, 743.

[2] See *Zerboglio, op. cit.*, pp. 125–127; *Grotjahn, op. cit.*, pp. 149–155; *Verhaeghe, op. cit.*, pp. 187–189.

[3] This has actually happened, certain distilleries in the whisky trust being closed to increase the profits.

paid and workmen hired. These two things increase the profits of the dealer, but exercise an indirect pressure upon the working-man to make him drink.[1]

Second. The constantly decreasing price of alcohol. As we have seen above there is a tendency in the present economic system to lower the price of commodities, since each producer tries to increase his profits, if only temporarily, by seeking to improve the processes of production. This is applicable to alcohol also.

Third. The adulteration of alcoholic drinks. Under the capitalistic system the object of production is not to furnish as perfect a product as possible, but to make as great profits as possible. Hence comes the tendency among producers to adulterate their wares, to deliver goods of poorer quality than they are supposed to be, for the purpose of gaining greater profits. The adulteration so frequent with alcoholic beverages has physical and psychical consequences most harmful to the consumers.[2]

The exposition which I have just given of the etiology of alcoholism points out the principal causes of it, and proves that they are to be found in the last instance almost wholly in the present constitution of society. It is possible that some one will interpose the objection that this cannot be the case, that there must be, besides pathological causes, individual causes, since it happens that among persons living in the same environment some become alcoholics and others do not.

This last fact is incontestable, but it is partly to be explained by the fact that, while there are persons who live in environments that are very similar, there are no two individuals whose surroundings are exactly the same. Take, for example, two workmen. The one may have passed his youth in circles where they drink little or no alcohol, and where it is pointed out to him that abstinence is very salutary, while the other sees only examples of intemperance. It may be that here is the explanation of the fact that the first has remained temperate, while the second has not, although the two live in surroundings almost alike.

But suppose that the environment is and has always been exactly the same for a group of persons, we shall see then that the tendency toward alcoholism is not the same for each individual. No one will be able to dispute the fact, however, that it is the environment

[1] See *Vandervelde*, "Het alcoholisme en de arbeidsvoorwaarden in Belgie", p. 268.   [2] See *Grotjahn, op. cit.*, pp. 219–221.

that is the cause of the abuse of alcohol. Individual differences bring
it about that one man is more drawn to the use of alcohol than
another, but circumstances explain why the first has *become* alcoholic.
These differences can never explain why, at a certain period, the
abuse of alcohol has, or has not, become an almost universal phenomenon.

The proofs are plain. In examining, for example, a period like
that in which capitalism took its rise in England, as it is described
by Engels in his "Condition of the Working Class", a period, that is
to say, in which the working class found itself in very disadvantageous material and moral conditions, we see that the workers, with
rare exceptions, were consumers of alcohol, and largely abused it.
Since that time conditions have improved. The moral and material
plane having been raised, those whose tendency toward alcohol was
less strong and who had more marked innate moral qualities, ceased
misusing alcohol. As conditions improve still further those who are
weaker follow little by little the same road to temperance. This
process may be observed going on among unorganized workmen,
with whom the tendency to drink is generally great. As soon as
they begin to organize, and in measure as their organization is developed, we see that first the most intelligent, etc., among them become temperate, and that little by little these are followed by the
others.

It is a biological fact that men always and everywhere present
qualitative differences. But this constant factor does not give an
explanation of the changes which society undergoes, and is not, therefore, of great importance to sociology, which, while taking it into
account, has for its task the explanation of the changes in question.
And it is just those changes in the use of alcoholic beverages which
have taken place during the course of the centuries, which show that
the social environment is the principal cause of alcoholism.

In ancient times alcoholism was unknown. It is true that among
the Israelites, for example, the abuse of alcohol at times occurred,
but the fact that no importance was attached to it proves that alcoholism properly speaking did not exist.[1] Nor was it to be met with
among the ancient Greeks. At every meal, and at their reunions
they drank wine diluted; it is unnecessary to say that these "sym-
posia" were not looked down upon by the Greeks, but on the contrary
were highly regarded. "Greek opinion found nothing improper in
intoxication, only a certain self-control in drunkenness was held to

[1] See *Grotjahn, op. cit.*, pp. 5–12.

be indispensable. Gross and violent conduct was, like the drinking of unmixed wine, a custom of the barbarians, and unworthy of a Greek." [1] Nor was ancient Rome any more acquainted with alcoholism, though among the Romans, coarse in comparison with the Greeks and demoralized by their immense wealth, the abuse of alcohol was often met with. But it was only the very small group of the rich who were addicted to it. When the barbarians annihilated the ancient world they were not capable of assimilating the civilization of the peoples whom they had just subjugated, while they adopted their pleasures, a thing which did not require so high a state of development. This is the cause of the great abuse of alcohol among the Germans.[2] The uncertainty of existence, and the miserable conditions during the migrations of these peoples were favorable to this abuse.

In the fifteenth and sixteenth centuries the abuse of alcohol had reached a high degree of development among the rich. The cause of this was the birth of capitalism, by which great wealth was accumulated in the hands of a few without their having occasion to place a great part of it as new capital. To this fact was joined a low degree of culture, and it thus came about that the wealthy of the period spent enormous sums for eating and drinking.[3]

The discovery in the middle of the sixteenth century of the distillation of spirits from grain brought about a considerable cheapening in the price of strong drink, which thus came within the reach of the poor. (Arab physicians had long before discovered how to extract brandy from wine, but this in the beginning was only used medicinally.) The great poverty occasioned by the Thirty Years' War increased the use of liquor enormously, and the birth of the industrial proletariat contributed equally to the same result. Mention is made for the first time of the regular use of liquor *to increase the amount of work done*, in 1550 among the Hungarian miners, the first category of workmen who lived under conditions almost identical with those of the modern industrial proletariat. With the continually increasing development of capitalism King Alcohol began his triumphal march, which has continued without any great obstacle to the present day. Alcoholism has its deeper causes in the material

---

[1] *Grotjahn, op. cit.*, p. 9. See also: *Hirschfeld*, "Die historische Entwicklung des Alkoholmisbrauchs" (VIII Intern. Cong. gegen den Alkoholismus).

[2] The assertion that the Germans were addicted to alcohol before the invasion is erroneous. Agriculture was not sufficiently developed among these peoples for a regular consumption of alcohol. See *Kautsky, op. cit.*, pp. 46, 47, and *Grotjahn, op. cit.*, pp. 13–15.

[3] See *Kautsky, op. cit.*, p. 47, and *Grotjahn, op. cit.*, pp. 20 *ff.*

intellectual and moral poverty created by the economic system now in force. It is with reason that Professor Gruber has said: "We cannot shut our eyes to the truth that alcohol is not without basis in our present order of society. Without it life would long ago have become unendurable for the suffering part of the population."

CHAPTER V.

MILITARISM.

WE may be very brief upon the correlation of militarism and the present economic system. This correlation is so clear that there are few persons who deny it. The motives which, under all earlier modes of production, have engendered wars are principally of an economic nature. But besides these there have been at times others; but we have not to enquire here what was in the last analysis their correlation with the mode of production of that day. The relation between capitalism and war is always so close that we can find in the economic life the direct causes of the wars waged under the empire of capitalism.

As we have seen above in our exposition of the present economic system, a part of the surplus-value that comes to the moneyed class is invested as new capital. The continually increasing amount of capital does not readily find investment in full in a country where capitalism is already in force. This is why the moneyed class desires to invest a part of the surplus-value in countries whither capitalism has not yet penetrated. If the inhabitants of the country chosen as field of operation are opposed to this, or if the same country is coveted by other capitalistic powers, the resulting antagonism generally leads to war.

In the second place, the producers can sell in their own country only a part of the increasing quantity of their products; whence come their efforts to find an outlet into other countries. But as capitalism expands with increasing rapidity over the whole world, the difficulty of finding a country in a position to buy, or to which capitalism has not yet penetrated, becomes greater and greater. Encounters with other capitalistic powers pursuing the same end are the inevitable consequence.

It is upon the State that the task is imposed of finding new territories where capital may be invested, or new outlets for goods which do not find purchasers in the country where they are produced. Beside the duty of the State to maintain a certain order in a society confused and complicated through the nature of our economic life (civil and criminal jurisprudence), there is its more important duty of warding off other groups of competitors, or even at need attacking them by force of arms.

But the army serves not only to act against the foreigner, it has equally a domestic duty to fulfil. In the cases where the police cannot maintain order the army reinforces them. The army must especially then be active at the time of great strikes, when so-called free labor is to be protected, that is when employers are trying to replace the striking workmen with others who, in consequence of their poverty, or their lack of organization, put their personal interests above those of their comrades. Also it has its part to play in connection with great political movements, like that to obtain universal suffrage, for example.

Our present militarism is, therefore, a consequence of capitalism. The double duty of the army proves it; for its function is to furnish the bourgeoisie with the means of restraining the proletariat at home, and of repulsing or attacking the forces of foreign countries.

BOOK II.

CRIMINALITY.

CHAPTER I.

GENERAL CONSIDERATIONS.[1]

A. DEFINITION OF CRIME.[2]

CRIME belongs to the category of punishable acts. However, as the term is applicable to only a part of such acts, it is necessary to be more exact. The best way to do this, in my opinion, is to exclude successively all the groups of acts which are punishable without being crimes.

The first exclusion is in connection with the question, "Who is it that punishes?" You cannot call that a crime against which one or several individuals take action of their own motion, and where the social group to which they belong does not move as such. In this case the word "punish" is an improper term, for the act in question is one of personal vengeance. Nor can you apply the name of crime to the act of a group of persons forming a social entity, against an analogous group. The reaction of the second group called forth by such act is not properly punishment, but "blood-" or "group-vengeance", and is in reality nothing but a kind of war.[3]

The second exclusion concerns the nature of the punishment. Acts

---

[1] [NOTE TO THE AMERICAN EDITION: *Cf.* upon the whole subject of this chapter: *J. Makarewicz*, "Einführung in die Philosophie des Strafrechts."]

[2] [The author disregards the legal distinction between the words *crime* and *delit* as being "without interest in a sociological work." The latter word will appear in this translation as "misdemeanor" or "offense" according to the context. — TRANSL.]

[3] See upon this subject: *Post*, "Die Geschlechtsgenossenschaft der Urzeit und die Entstehen der Ehe", p. 156; *Steinmetz*, "Ethnologische Studien zur ersten Entwicklung der Strafe", I, pp. 365 *ff.*; *Makarewitz*, "Evolution de la peine", p. 137 ("Archives d'Anthropologie Criminelle", XIII). Upon the vengeance of blood see especially *Kohler*, "Shakespeare vor dem Forum der Jurisprudenz."

[NOTE TO THE AMERICAN EDITION: *Cf.* also *H. Berkusky*, "Die Blutrache" ("Zeitschr. f. Socialwissenschaft", XII).]

which bring no other punishment than moral disapprobation are not reckoned as crimes. They are not so called unless they are threatened with something more severe than this.

The provisional result is, then, as follows: A crime is an act committed within a group of persons that form a social unit, and whose author is punished by the group (or a part of it) as such, or by organs designated for this purpose, and this by a penalty whose nature is considered to be more severe than that of moral disapprobation. This definition, however, considers only the formal side of the conception of crime; it says nothing as to its essence. It is proper, then, to consider next the material side.

Crime is an act.[1] The question which presents itself first of all is this: Is crime considered from a biological point of view an abnormal act? The answer to this, which is of the highest importance for the etiology of crime, must be negative. From a biological point of view almost all crimes must be ranked as normal acts. The process which takes place in the brain of the gendarme when he kills a poacher who resists arrest is identical with that which takes place in the brain of the poacher killing the gendarme who pursues him. It is only the social environment which classes the second act rather than the first as a crime. From the biological point of view homicide is not an abnormal act. Sociology and history prove that men have always killed when they thought it necessary. No one would maintain, for example, that those who take part in a war are biologically abnormal.

The same observation may be applied to assaults. No anthropologist would maintain that a policeman clubbing a mob of strikers was performing a biologically abnormal act, or that the strikers were abnormal because they did not choose to let themselves be maltreated without defending themselves. It is only the social circumstances which class this defense as a crime, and cause the action of the policeman to be considered otherwise.

The same thing is true with regard to theft. For centuries it was considered the right of the soldiers to pillage the country of the conquered (and in colonial wars it is still done at times). Soldiers are not, however, from this fact considered to be biologically abnormal individuals. And yet there is no biological difference between these acts and those of the ordinary thief; for anthropology does not ask whether one steals on a large scale or on a small.[2]

---

[1] The so-called offenses of omission are so few and unimportant that they may be left out of account.

[2] *Albrecht*, "Actes du I congrès d'anthr. crim.", pp. 110 *ff.*; *Battaglia*,

Continuing our researches into the essence of crime, it is obvious that it is an immoral act, and one of a serious character. Why do we find any act immoral? This question cannot be answered by asking of each individual separately, Why do you think such and such an act immoral? Moral disapprobation is primarily a question of feeling; ordinarily we take no account of why any given act is approved or disapproved by us. Sociology alone can solve the problem by taking the acts considered as immoral in relation with the social organization in which they take place. And in treating the matter thus we observe that the acts called immoral are those which are harmful to the interests of a group of persons united by the same interests. Since the social structure is changing continually, the ideas of what is immoral (and consequently of what is or is not criminal) change with these modifications.[1]

Considered in this way from the material side, a crime is an antisocial act, an act which is harmful in a considerable degree to the interests of a certain group of persons. This definition is not yet complete, however, for many acts of this nature are not crimes.

The best thing to do in order to find what is lacking in this definition is to examine a concrete case. A short time ago there was added to the Dutch penal code a new article threatening with a penal term of some years the railroad employe who went out on a strike. The proposal of this law, presented after a partial strike of the railroad employes, aroused great indignation on the part of organized labor, while the bourgeoisie in general regarded a strike as an immoral act which would henceforth be followed by a severe penalty. Notwithstanding the violent opposition on the part of the deputies of the labor party the plan was accepted.

It is clear that what must be added to our definition (already contained implicitly in the formal definition) is that the act must be prejudicial to the interests of those who have the power at their command. If, in the case cited above, the deputies of the proletariat had had the majority the Dutch penal code would contain no penalties against railroad employes on a strike. Power then is the necessary condition for those who wish to class a certain act as a crime.

It follows that in every society which is divided into a ruling class and a class ruled penal law has been principally constituted according

"La dinamica del delitto", pp. 201, 202; "Genesi e funzioni delle legge penali", pp. 211, 212; *Manouvrier*, "Genèse normale du crime", pp. 451, 452 (see also Part One of the present work, on Manouvrier); *Näcke*, "Verbrechen und Wahnsinn bein Weibe", p. 96.

[1] *A. H. Post*, "Bausteine für eine allgemeine Rechtswissenschaft", I, p. 224.

to the will of the former.   We must at once add that the present legal
prescriptions are not always directed against the class of those ruled,
but that most of them are directed against acts that are prejudicial
to the interests of both classes equally (for example, homicide, rape,
etc.).   These acts would without doubt continue to be considered
criminal if the power were to pass into the hands of those who are at
present the governed.   However, in every existing penal code hardly
any act is punished if it does not injure the interests of the dominant
class as well as the other, and the law touching it protects only
the interests of the class dominated.   The rare exceptions are
explained by the fact that the lower classes are not wholly without
power.

Before closing our observations we must put the question, What is
the object of punishment?   It seems to me that there are elements of
different nature in punishment as prescribed in our present penal
codes.   To begin with the object of punishment is to be found in the
feelings of vengeance excited by the crime, for which satisfaction is
desired.   But after this punishment has three things in view:

First, To put the criminal where he can do no further harm, either
permanently or for a certain period.

Second, To inspire the criminal, and other persons as well, with a
fear of committing crime.

Third, To reform the criminal as far as possible.

Most criminologists do not admit that punishment is still in great
part a manifestation of the desire for vengeance (although regulated).
Nevertheless it is indubitable that he who desires that some one shall
be punished solely because he has committed a misdeed, and without
his punishment's being of any use to the criminal or to others, wishes
simply to satisfy his feelings of revenge.   The most subtle theories
cannot refute this fact.   Those who from the height of their knowledge
disdain the primitive peoples who practice the rule of "eye for eye,
tooth for tooth", are nevertheless on the same plane in this matter,
as those they scorn.[1]

It is unnecessary to say that the minority that wishes to exclude all
idea of vengeance from the penal code, and sees in it only a means of
securing the safety of society, and, if possible, of reforming the
criminal, is at present still very small, so that the ideas of this group
are almost never realized in our present penalties.[2]

---

[1] *Steinmetz*, "L'ethnologie et l'anthropologie criminelle" ("Compte rendu
du Ve Cong. d'anthr. crim.", p. 105).

[2] It is unnecessary to treat of the origin of punishment.   For this subject

This is our conclusion, then, that a crime is an act committed within a group of persons forming a social unit; that it prejudices the interests of all, or of those of the group who are powerful; that, for this reason, the author of the crime is punished by the group (or a part of the group) as such or by specially ordained instruments, and this by a penalty more severe than moral disapprobation.

To find the causes of crime we must, then, first solve the question: "Why does an individual do acts injurious to the interests of those with whom he forms a social unit?", or in other words; "Why does a man act egoistically?"

B. The Origin of Egoistic Acts in General.[1]

What are the causes of egoistic acts? How does it happen that one man does harm to another? The answers that have been given to this primeval question may be divided into two groups. The first group attributes the cause to the man himself, the second to his environment.

The great majority of persons who treat of this question settle it in favor of innate egoism. They are of the opinion that man is egoistic by nature and that environment can produce no change in this (this is implied in the Christian doctrine of original sin). This opinion, in order to be accepted as true, needs facts to prove that egoism has always and everywhere been the same among men.

Others, among whom are most of the well-known sociologists, also consider egoism as a fundamental trait of man, but are at the same time of the opinion that little by little egoism has decreased, that altruism has developed, and that this process continues.[2] For this hypothesis to be correct it must be shown by the facts:

First. That the peoples of a much lower degree of social evolution than ours show much more egoistic traits of character.[3]

Second. That the animals from whom man has descended are inveterate egoists.

This theory is naturally of the highest importance for criminal

the works of Steinmetz and Makarewitz already cited may be consulted, together with *Westermarck's* "Der Ursprung der Strafe" ("Zeitschrift für Socialwissenschaft", 1900).

[1] [Note to American Edition: Recent works of importance are: *P. Kropotkin*, "Mutual Aid"; *L. T. Hobhouse*, "Morals in Evolution"; *K. Kautsky*, "Ethik und Materialistische Geschichtsauffassung"; *E. Westermarck*, "Ursprung und Entwicklung der Moralbegriffe."]

[2] [Note to the American Edition: *Cf. Ch. Vallon* and *G. Genil-Perrin*, "Crime et altruisme" ("Archives d'anthr. crim." XXVIII).]

[3] See, among others, *Spencer*, "Principles of Sociology", I, p. 79, where he says "Sociality, strong in the civilized man, is less strong in the savage man."

science, and it becomes still more so from the fact that, according to Professor Lombroso, crime is a manifestation of atavism, that is, that some individuals present anew traits of character belonging to their very remote ancestors. The criminal would thus be a savage in our present society. We must therefore examine to see whether the said theory is correct.

We have only to consult one of the standard works on zoölogy to perceive that there is no basis in this science to uphold the theory. There are some animals that are complete egoists. Two harpies (South American birds of prey) for example, upon meeting will attack each other at once and will fight till one is conquered. Other animals, on the contrary, show very altruistic traits of character. The following extract from Darwin's "Descent of Man", is one of many proofs which might be adduced: "Animals of many kinds are social; . . . We will confine our attention to the higher social animals; and pass over insects, although some of these are social, and aid one another in many important ways. The most common mutual service in the higher animals is to warn one another of danger by means of the united senses of all. Every sportsman knows, as Dr. Jaeger remarks, how difficult it is to approach animals in a herd or troop. Wild horses and cattle do not, I believe, make any danger-signal; but the attitude of any one of them who first discovers an enemy, warns the others. Rabbits stamp loudly on the ground with their hind-feet as a signal; sheep and chamois do the same with their fore-feet, uttering likewise a whistle. Many birds, and some mammals, post sentinels, which in the case of seals are said generally to be the females. The leader of a troop of monkeys acts as the sentinel, and utters cries expressive both of danger and of safety. Social animals perform many little services for each other: horses nibble, and cows lick each other, on any spot which itches: monkeys search each other for external parasites; and Brehm states that after a troop of the Cercopithecus griseo-viridis has rushed through a thorny brake, each monkey stretches itself on a branch, and another monkey sitting by, 'conscientiously' examines its fur, and extracts every thorn or burr.

"Animals also render more important services to one another: thus wolves and some other beasts of prey hunt in packs, and aid one another in attacking their victims. Pelicans fish in concert. The Hamádryas baboons turn over stones to find insects, etc.; and when they come to a large one, as many as can stand round, turn it over together and share the booty. Social animals mutually defend each other. Bull bisons in North America, when there is danger, drive the cows and calves to the middle of the herd, whilst they defend the outside. . . . In Abyssinia, Brehm encountered a great troop of baboons, who were crossing a valley: some had already ascended the opposite mountain, and some were still in the valley: the latter were attacked by the dogs, but the old males immediately hurried down from the rocks, and with mouths widely opened roared so fearfully, that the dogs quickly drew back. They were again encouraged to the attack; but by this time all the baboons had reascended the heights, excepted a young one, about six months old, who, loudly calling for aid, climbed on a block of rock, and was surrounded. Now one of the largest males, a true hero, came down again from the mountain, slowly went to the young one, coaxed him, and triumphantly led him away — the dogs being too much astonished to make an attack. I cannot resist giving another scene which was witnessed by this same naturalist; an eagle seized a young Cercopithecus, which, by clinging to a branch, was not at once carried off; it cried loudly for assistance, upon which the other members of the troop, with much uproar, rushed to the rescue, surrounded the eagle, and pulled out so many feathers, that he no longer thought of his prey, but only how to escape. . . .

"It is certain that associated animals have a feeling of love for each other, which is not felt by non-social adult animals." [1]

Later I shall treat of the question why some species of animals show altruistic proclivities while others do not. At present I wish to inquire whether peoples showing a much lower degree of civilization than our own are much more egoistic.

Nansen, the celebrated explorer, in speaking of the Eskimos, among whom he sojourned for some time, says: "The Greenlander is of all God's creatures gifted with the best disposition. Good-humor, peaceableness, and evenness of temper are the most prominent features in his character. He is eager to live on as good a footing as possible with his fellow-men and therefore refrains from offending them and much more from using coarse terms of abuse. He is very loth to contradict another even should he be saying what he knows to be false. If he does so, he takes care to word his remonstrance in the mildest possible form, and it would be very hard indeed for him to say right out that the other was lying. He is chary of

[1] Chap. iv, pp. 97–99. See also *Kautsky*, "Die sozialen Triebe in der Tierwelt" ("Neue Zeit", 1883); *Letourneau*, "L'évolution de la morale", pp. 59–64; and *Kropotkin*, "Mutual Aid among Animals" ("Nineteenth Century", 1890).

telling other people truths that he thinks will be unpleasant to them; in such cases he chooses the vaguest expressions, even with reference to such indifferent things as wind and weather. His peaceableness even goes so far that when anything is stolen from him, which seldom happens, he does not as a rule reclaim it even if he knows who has taken it. The result is that there is seldom or never any quarreling among them.[1]

"The only thing that makes him [the Eskimo] really unhappy is to see others in want, and therefore he shares with them whenever he has anything to share."

"The Greenlander is, on the whole, like a sympathetic child with respect to the needs of others; *his first social law is to help his neighbor*." [2]

"One of the most prominent and attractive traits in the Eskimo's moral character is certainly his integrity. . . . It is of special importance for the Eskimo that he should be able to rely with confidence upon his neighbors and his fellow-men; and it is the first condition of this mutual confidence, on which depends all united action in the battle for life, that every man should be upright in his dealings with his neighbors. The Eskimo therefore regards it as in the highest degree dishonorable to steal from his house-mates or from his fellow-villagers, and it is very seldom that anything of the sort occurs." [3]

"The worst thing that can happen to a Greenlander is to be made ridiculous in the eyes of his fellows, and to be scoffed at by them." [4]

With regard to the American Indians living in the region of the Columbia river, Dr. Waitz makes the following statement: "The qualities regarded as virtues by these peoples are honesty and love of truth, courage, obedience to parents and chiefs, and love of wife and child; and the Salish, whose moral ideals are here especially indicated, in general come up to these requirements very well. With them and with their cousins, the 'Pends-d'Oreilles' and Spokane, crimes are very rare, and a mere rebuke, administered by the chief, is of great effectiveness. Old age, too, finds among the Salish benevolent support and care, though children who have the misfortune to lose their fathers have often a sad lot, their property being frequently taken from them. Most of these peoples are upright and honest, live together in the most peaceable fashion, and have friendly intercourse with the whites." [5]

[1] "Eskimo Life", p. 101.
[2] *Op. cit.*, p. 106.
[3] *Op. cit.*, p. 158.
[4] *Op. cit.*, p. 187.
[5] *Op. cit.*, II, pp. 342, 343.

G. Catlin, one of the authors who are best informed upon everything concerning the North American Indians, says of their character:

"I have roamed about from time to time during seven or eight years, visiting and associating with, some three or four hundred thousand of these people, under an almost infinite variety of circumstances; and from the very many and decided voluntary acts of their hospitality and kindness I feel bound to pronounce them, by nature, a kind and hospitable people. I have been welcomed generally in their country, and treated to the best that they could give me, without any charges made for my board; they have often escorted me through their enemies' country at some hazard to their own lives, and aided me in passing mountains and rivers with my awkward baggage; and under all of these circumstances of exposure, no Indian ever betrayed me, struck me a blow, or stole from me a shilling's worth of my property that I am aware of.

"This is saying a great deal, (and proving it too, if the reader believe me) in favour of the virtues of these people; when it is borne in mind, as it should be, that there is no law in their land to punish a man for theft — that locks and keys are not known in their country — that the commandments have never been divulged amongst them; nor can any human retribution fall upon the head of thief, save the disgrace which attaches as a stigma to his character, in the eyes of his people about him.

"And thus in these little communities, strange as it may seem, in the absence of all systems of jurisprudence, I have often beheld peace and happiness, and quiet, reigning supreme, for which even kings and emperors might envy them. I have seen rights and virtue protected, and wrongs redressed; and I have seen conjugal, filial and paternal affection in the simplicity and contentedness of nature. I have unavoidably, formed warm and enduring attachments to some of these men which I do not wish to forget — who have brought me near to their hearts, and in our final separation have embraced me in their arms, commended me and my affairs to the keeping of the great Spirit." [1]

In treating of the question of which of the two are the happier, the civilized nations or the peoples he visited, the same author says:

"I have long looked with the eye of a critic, into the jovial faces of these sons of the forest, unfurrowed with cares — where the agonizing feeling of poverty had never stamped distress upon the brow. I have

[1] " Illustrations of the Manners, Customs, and Conditions of the North American Indians", pp. 9, 10.

watched the bold, intrepid step — the proud, yet dignified deport-ment of Nature's man, in fearless freedom, with a soul unalloyed by mercenary lusts, too great to yield to laws or power except from God. As these independent fellows are all joint-tenants of the soil, they are all rich, and none of the steepings of comparative poverty can strangle their just claims to renown. Who (I could ask) can look without admiring, into a society where peace and harmony prevail — where virtue is cherished — where rights are protected and wrongs are redressed — with no laws, but the laws of honour, which are the supreme laws of their land. Trust the boasted virtues of civilized society for awhile, with all its intellectual refinements, to such a tri-bunal, and then write down the degradation of the 'lawless savage' and our transcendent virtues."

Lewis H. Morgan, after passing a great part of his life among the Iroquois, says with regard to them : "All the members of an Iroquois gens were personally free, and they were bound to defend each other's freedom; they were equal in privileges and in personal rights, the sachem and chiefs claiming no superiority; and they were a brother-hood bound together by the ties of kin. Liberty, equality, and fraternity, though never formulated, were cardinal principles of the gens. These facts are material, because the gens was the unit of a social and governmental system, the foundation upon which Indian society was organized. A structure composed of such units would of necessity bear the impress of their character, for as the unit so the compound. It serves to explain that sense of independence and per-sonal dignity universally an attribute of Indian character."[1]

He describes the hospitality of the peoples mentioned as follows : "Among the Iroquois hospitality was an established usage. If a man entered an Indian house in any of their villages, whether a villager, or a stranger, it was the duty of the women therein to set food before him. An omission to do this would have been a discourtesy amount-ing to an affront. If hungry, he ate; if not hungry, courtesy required that he should taste the food and thank the giver. This would be repeated at every house he entered, and at whatever hour in the day. As a custom it was upheld by a rigorous public sentiment. The same hospitality was extended to strangers from their own and from other tribes. Upon the advent of the European race among them it was also extended to them. This characteristic of barbarous society, wherein food was the principal concern of life, is a remarkable fact. The law of hospitality, as administered by the American aborigines,

[1] "Ancient Society", pp. 85, 86.

tended to the final equalization of subsistence. Hunger and destitution could not exist at one end of an Indian village or in one section of an encampment while plenty prevailed elsewhere in the same village or encampment.[1]

A. R. Wallace speaks as follows of the primitive population of South America and the Indian Archipelago: "I have lived with communities of savages in South America and in the East, who have no laws or law courts but the public opinion of the village freely expressed. Each man scrupulously respects the rights of his fellow, and any infraction of these rights rarely or never takes place. In such a community, all are nearly equal. There are none of those wide distinctions, of education and ignorance, wealth and poverty, master and servant, which are the product of our civilization; there is none of the wide-spreading division of labor, which, while it increases wealth, produces, also conflicting interests; there is not that severe competition and struggle for existence, or for wealth, which the dense population of civilized countries inevitably creates. All incitements to great crimes are thus wanting, and petty ones are repressed, partly by the influence of public opinion, but chiefly by that natural sense of justice and of his neighbor's right, which seems to be, in some degree, inherent in every race of man." [2]

In his work, "Village Communities in the East and West", H. S. Maine says:

"Whenever a corner is lifted up of the veil which hides from us the primitive condition of mankind, even of such parts of it as we know to have been destined to civilisation, there are two positions, now very familiar to us, which seems to be signally falsified by all we are permitted to see — All men are brothers, and all men are equal. The scene before us is rather that which the animal world presents to the mental eye of those who have the courage to bring home to themselves the facts answering to the memorable theory of Natural Selection. Each fierce little community is perpetually at war with its neighbour, tribe with tribe, village with village. The never-ceasing attacks of the strong on the weak end in the manner expressed by the monotonous formula which so often recurs in the pages of Thucydides, ' they put the men to the sword, the women and children they sold into slavery.' Yet, even amid all this cruelty and carnage, we find the

---

[1] "Houses and House-life of the American Aborigines." For the facts with regard to the North American Indians east of the Rocky Mountains, see *Waitz, op. cit.*, III, pp. 160 *ff.*

[2] "The Malay Archipelago", II, p. 283; see also *Waitz, op. cit.*, III; *Spencer*, "Descriptive Sociology", No. 6 ("American Races"), pp. 31, 32.

germs of ideas, which have spread over the world. There is still a place and a sense in which men are brothers and equals. The universal belligerency is the belligerency of one total group, tribe, or village, with another; but in the interior of the groups the regimen is one not of conflict and confusion but rather of ultra-legality. The men who composed the primitive communities believed themselves to be kinsmen in the most literal sense of the word; and surprising as it may seem, there are a multitude of indications that in one stage of thought they must have regarded themselves as equals." [1]

Scores of pages might be filled with facts proving that the primitive peoples of all races and in all parts of the world were not only not egoistic in their relations with the people they lived among, but rather the contrary. In conclusion I wish to note the opinions of two distinguished sociologists, Steinmetz and Kovalewsky, opinions which derive significance from the great ethnological knowledge of these authors.

At the Fifth Congress of Criminal Anthropology Dr. Steinmetz, in speaking upon the explanation of crime by the hypothesis of atavism, says: "It is not at all probable that our true born-criminal resembles the normal savage. The former is characterized by his ferocious egoism, while the latter is nothing if not a devoted member of the group whose customs he respects and whose interests he defends; the savage is very tender toward the children whom the criminal abandons; the savage is only cruel toward the enemy, the criminal toward all the world." [2]

After having cited different altruistic traits of primitive peoples Kovalewsky says: "The enumeration would wear out your patience if one were to cite all the proofs that travelers give of the care that savages and barbarians have for their mutual welfare, and the fulness of their charity. To these facts, which indicate the prolonged existence of a sort of communism, others correspond. . . ." [3]

I am of the opinion that no one, taking the above facts into consideration, will maintain that man has always and everywhere shown the same egoistic traits, or that there has been a gradual evolution from egoism towards altruism.

It would be a mistake, however, to suppose that primitive peoples

---

[1] Pp. 225, 226.
[2] "L'ethnologie et l'anthropologie criminelle", pp. 100, 101.
[3] "Tableau des origines et de l'évolution de la famille et de la propriété", p. 58. See also *Kautsky*, "Die sozialen Triebe in der Menschenwelt" ("Neue Zeit", 1884); and *Kropotkin*, "Mutual Aid among Savages" ("Nineteenth Century", 1891), and "Mutual Aid among the Barbarians" (*ibid.*, 1892).

present under all circumstances the altruistic characteristics that I have mentioned. I have already remarked that the position of woman is in general very dependent. In general the primitive peoples are very fond of their children and give them very tender care. Nevertheless infanticide is not uncommon among those who are at a low stage of civilization. And I have already remarked that among nomadic peoples the sick and aged were often abandoned. Here are then contradictions which it is necessary to explain.

Apparently — but only apparently — an evolution from egoism towards altruism has really taken place and has not yet ceased. This appearance is the effect of the alteration in the character of the egoism under the present economic system; it has become less *violent* than at earlier periods. The fight is no longer carried on with fire-arms or cold steel, but with other weapons no less dangerous, and this is what is generally lost sight of. We note that in ancient times the prisoners were killed; that later they were sold into slavery; that slavery was superseded by serfdom, which in its turn gave place to free labor.

But it is not always a growing altruistic sentiment that has been the motive in these changes. The life of prisoners of war has not been spared from reasons of humanity, but because the extension of the productivity of labor made it more profitable to make a prisoner work than to kill him. And slavery was not abolished because slave-owners had become less egoistic, but because it was more profitable to make free laborers work than to make slaves do so.[1] We cannot speak of the diminution of egoism, but of the moderating of violence in the course of time. It cannot be maintained that a capitalist who tries by a lock-out to force his workmen to break with their union, in order that he may escape the danger of a decrease in his profits through a strike, and who in this way condemns them and their families to hunger, is less egoistic than the slave-owner driving his slaves to harder labor. The former does not use force — it is useless — he has a surer weapon at his command, the suffering with which he can strike his workmen; he *seems* less egoistic, but in reality is as egoistic as the latter. The great speculator who, by manipulating the market, forces thousands of persons to pay more for the necessaries of life, and to become his tributaries as it were, is not less egoistic than the robber-baron of the middle ages who, arms in hand, forced the travel-

---

[1] See *Morgan*, "Ancient Society", p. 505.
[NOTE TO THE AMERICAN EDITION: Upon the origin of slavery *cf. H. J. Nieboer*: "Slavery as an Industrial System."]

ing merchants to pay him tribute. The difference is merely that the former attains his end without using violence like the latter. Capitalism is a system of exploitation in which, in place of the exploited person's being robbed he is compelled by poverty to use all his powers for the benefit of the exploiter.[1]

The same thing is true of colonial history. At first the aborigines of the countries explored by the Europeans were often pillaged and massacred. This system has long been abandoned, not from altruism however, but because it is more profitable to make a conquered people work than to pillage and exterminate them. When they do not submit voluntarily, force is used as heretofore.

The apparent improvement has yet another cause. Christianity preaches "Thou shalt love thy neighbor as thy self." And since this maxim has been often preached and many Christians have it always in their mouths, men come to believe that it is really put into practice. The contrary is true. The fact that the duty of altruism is so much insisted upon is the *most convincing proof that it is not generally practiced* or it would not be so much spoken and preached about. There are many persons in our days who ask nothing better than to see men act altruistically, but they preach in the wilderness; their wish has not come true. Present society is moulded by egoism. The egoism is less violent, however, and more disguised.

Before speaking of the real causes of egoism and altruism it may be well to attempt to answer the question, Whence come these inexact ideas? It is not difficult, in my opinion, to explain how it comes about that many men believe that the "homo homini lupus" of Hobbes has been true always and everywhere. The adherents of this opinion have studied principally men who live under capitalism, or under civilization; their correct conclusion has been that egoism is the predominant characteristic of these men, and they have adopted the simplest explanation of the phenomenon and say that this trait is inborn.

If they had known the periods anterior to civilization, they would have noted that the "homo homini lupus" is an historical phenomenon applicable during a relatively short period,[2] and that consequently it is impossible that egoism should be innate in man. However great have been the social modifications during the period of civilization, the principal aim of men has always been, and still is, to acquire

[1] [NOTE TO THE AMERICAN EDITION: *Cf. Kautsky, op. cit.*, pp. 99, 100.]
[2] See *Maine, op. cit.*, pp. 227, 228.

personal wealth, and men still remain divided into classes, that is into groups whose economic interests are contrary. This is why an examination of the earlier periods is of such high importance for sociology.

An erroneous interpretation of the Darwinian theory has also contributed to bring about the strange notion of the eternal character of the struggle of all against all. Darwin himself maintains nothing of the sort. In his "Origin of Species" he says in the clearest terms that the struggle between the individuals of the same species does not at all happen in every species: "There must in every case be a struggle for existence, either one individual with another of the same species, or with the individuals of distinct species, or with the physical conditions of life." [1]

The explanation of the second hypothesis, that of the evolution from egoism towards altruism, is more complicated. In the first place the facts adduced in support of it are not numerous, and they serve rather to illustrate a theory than to furnish the materials by which it may be justified. In the second place a part of the ethnological materials in relation to the question it has been impossible to utilize. They have been collected partly by persons convinced beforehand of the superiority of Christian morality to every other system, and who consequently disapprove of everything opposed to it, and partly by persons whose own conduct has caused the enmity manifested by the peoples with whom they have come into contact. No part of the history of civilization offers a more hideous spectacle than that of colonization. [2] In the third place it is necessary to exclude peoples that have had much contact with Europeans or other civilized peoples. In the fourth place we often lose sight of the fact that primitive peoples show great differences of development, and consequently cannot be placed in the same rank. [3] For example, if peoples despotically governed show strong egoistic tendencies, we have no right to declare that all primitive peoples are egoistic.

Finally it is of the highest importance in studying primitive peoples to make the distinction between the acts which have to do with persons of the same social group, and those which have to do with strangers. One of the principal causes of the charge of egoism made against primitive peoples is to be found in the fact that this dualism of ethics

---

[1] P. 50.

[2] See *Kautsky*, "Die sozialen Trieben in der Menschenwelt", and also "Die Indianerfrage" ("Neue Zeit", 1885) by the same author.

[3] See *Steinmetz*, "Classification des types sociaux et catalogue des peuples" ("Année sociologique", III).

is forgotten. In the passages I have cited (those from Maine and Steinmetz, for instance) the great difference between acts committed within and without the group is brought out. We have seen that the Indians of North America, although very altruistic toward those who form the same group with them, as also toward their guests, are the most pitiless enemies of those who attack their independence or their hunting ground. Now it has been by these last acts that these peoples have been generally judged, a wholly wrong method, since the "dualism of ethics" has always existed. Great would be the astonishment if any one were to maintain that the South African war proved that the English were a nation of murderers and incendiaries. Yet this is just the sort of reasoning that is applied to primitive peoples.[1]

How does it happen that some animal species are social while others are not? It is impossible to maintain with some authors that sociability increases according to the degree of development attained by the animal.[2] Certain insects, for example, are endowed with pronounced social feelings, while the cat tribe and some kinds of birds are on the contrary unsocial. Nevertheless the latter occupy a higher place in the scale than the former. The explanation, then, must be sought elsewhere.[3]

There are divers reasons that draw a more or less considerable number of animals to one place — the fact of being born in the same locality, for example. Most animals are social when they are young, even those which are no longer so when full-grown, like the arachnids. Another cause that brings animals together is emigration towards a country because of great changes of temperature. A third cause, probably the most important, that unites animals of the same species is the abundance of the food-supply of certain countries.

However, the occasional assembling of animals does not explain why certain animals are social while others are not. Lions, for example often meet in places where they come to drink, and yet do not become social. It is not probable that there are animals who have *remained* together because they have comprehended the advantages

---

[1] Upon the dualism of ethics see: *Kulischer*, "Der Dualismus der Ethik bei den primitiven Völkern" ("Zeitschr. f. Ethnologie", 1885); *Kropotkin*, "Mutual Aid among Savages", pp. 558, 559; *Kovalewsky*, "Les origines du devoir", pp. 85 *ff*. ("Revue internationale de sociologie", II).

[2] See *Sutherland, op. cit.*, I, x, for example, and compare *Letourneau*, "L'évolution de la morale", p. 55.

[3] In the discussion which follows I have made large use of *Kautsky's* "Die sozialen Triebe in der Tierwelt."

of a life in common, for this would suppose an intelligence on their part which it is difficult to attribute to them. In order that these animals should remain together they must find it agreeable, and disagreeable to be isolated.

When we study the social species of animals we notice that the life in common is in general *one of their most powerful weapons in the struggle for existence*, a weapon without which it would be nearly or quite impossible for them to maintain the fight. Consequently the animals for which the life in common is advantageous and which possess social instincts stronger than others, have, when brought together by any cause whatever, a greater chance to survive.[1] Per contra the animals who have to stalk their prey have more chance of surviving when life in common is disagreeable to them. It is therefore by survival that social feelings are developed in some species of animals and not in others.[2] Habit, and the tendency to imitate increase these feelings considerably.

The advantages to certain species of animals resulting from life in common are of two kinds; in the first place a better defense against their enemies, and in the second place greater ease in procuring subsistence. Wild cattle give us an example of the first case; while the wolves who in winter gather into packs for purposes of the chase, because food has become scarce, furnish us an example of the second. For other animals (like the simians) social sentiments are helpful in both ways.

It is unnecessary to amplify further upon the two ways in which life in groups is of advantage to certain species of animals. We have yet to turn our attention to the qualities developed by the group struggle for existence.

One of the principal characteristics of social animals is the pleasure they experience in living in common, so that a social animal is unhappy if he is separate from those of the group in which he lives. Further it is necessary that the animal that cannot live alone, and is happy with his group, should also feel a sympathy with that group. Pleasure or its opposite felt by any individual reacts upon the whole group. A social being will try then to favor the interests of his fellows as far as he can, and in so far as he comprehends these interests. This sympathy will not extend to the whole species but only to the group.

[1] See *Galton*, "Inquiries into Human Faculty and its Development", pp. 68–82.

[2] See *Darwin*, "Descent of Man", p. 102; *Sutherland, op. cit.*, I, x; *Ammon*, "Der Ursprung der sozialen Triebe" ("Zeitschr. f. Socialwissenschaft" IV); *H. Schultz*, "Altersklassen und Männerbünde", I, 2.

The general interest of the group does not permit the sympathy to embrace the whole species, but on the contrary requires one group to fight the other if, for example, the latter interferes with its food-supply. And even within the limits of the group the general interest may demand that a sick or wounded individual be abandoned, when by its presence it would for example, attract beasts of prey, and thus put the existence of all in danger.

Highly developed sympathy produces the spirit of sacrifice, which impels the individual to assist his companions sometimes even at the risk of his life.[1] This quality is reinforced by the desire of gaining the praise and avoiding the blame of companions, which desire in its turn is brought about only by the life in common. For the one that lives in conjunction with others, and takes pleasure in doing so, whose interests are those of the members of the group, must be sensible of the approval or disapproval of his acts felt by others, since their feelings of pleasure or displeasure react upon himself. The lack of the power of speech among animals, however, limits the force of praise or blame among them.

We come now to the question: what are the causes of altruism among men?[2] It must be considered as certain that man has always lived in groups more or less large, and it is even very probable that he is descended from animals equally social.[3] A study of the means man has of sustaining the struggle for existence proves that they are of such a nature that he would have succumbed if he had lived in isolation. Kautsky puts it thus: ". . . man . . . whose mightiest and most effective, almost whose only weapon, indeed, in the struggle for existence, is association. He is, to be sure, distinguished above other animals by his intelligence, but this too is to the fruit of society, for in isolation he becomes dull and stupid. All man's other weapons in the struggle for existence are less efficient than those of the beasts. He has no weapons of attack like the beasts of prey, nor is he pro-tected by his size like the elephant, hippopotamus and rhinoceros. He lacks the quickness of the squirrel and deer, and cannot repair his losses through superabundant fertility."[4]

It is therefore on account of his constitution and of the struggle

---

[1] See the quotation from Darwin earlier in this section, in which he speaks of cases of self-sacrifice among animals.

[2] I make great use here of *Kautsky's* "Die sozialen Triebe in der Men-schenwelt."

[3] See *Darwin*, "Descent of Man", p. 105.

[NOTE TO THE AMERICAN EDITION: Upon the social origin of man see *Müller-Lyer*, "Die Familie", pp. 12 *ff.*]

[4] "Die sozialen Triebe in der Tierwelt", p. 27.

that he has had to sustain for his existence that man is a social being; in other words, those who showed social instincts stronger than the others ran less danger of succumbing in the contest for life, and had more chance of transmitting their leanings to their posterity. As man has greater intellectual capacities than the animals he is more capable of understanding the joys and sorrows of his fellows, and so is better able to assist the one and avoid the other. In the second place he has a developed language at his command, through which a great influence can be exercised upon conduct by blame and praise.[1]

The fact that man is born with social instincts does not, however, explain altruism sufficiently, for among animal species there is not one whose individuals have done so much harm to one another as men, who, though they are social beings, are capable of committing the most egoistic acts. How shall we explain these contradictions?

We have seen above that primitive peoples, to whom we have referred showed very altruistic traits of character. The members of a group extend mutual aid, and, in their relations with one another, are benevolent, honest, truthful, and very susceptible to the opinions of others,[2] etc.

It is impossible to explain this either by the race to which these peoples belong or by the climate in which they live, for they are of different races (for example North American Indians and the Hindoos of the delta of the Ganges) and live under different climates (as the Eskimos and the South American Indians). Besides this some of these peoples show towards strangers, qualities directly contrary to those they display toward members of their own group. Thus, as we have already remarked, the North American Indians are most cruel enemies, most pitiless toward those who are not of their group, while they are quite the reverse toward their own fellow-tribesmen. It is plain, then, that their altruistic sentiments have nothing to do with race or climate.

Consequently the cause can only be found in the social environment, which is determined in its turn by the mode of production. What follows will show that in the last instance it is the mode of production that is able to develop the social predisposition innate in man (not in the same measure for each individual, which is a question that I shall return to) or prevent this disposition from being developed, or may even destroy it entirely. Upon examining the modes of production in force among the peoples cited we see that they are characterized

[1] See *Darwin*, "Descent of Man", pp. 95, 96, 106.
[2] See *Maine*, "Village Communities", p. 68.

by the following traits, very different from those of the present system.

The first of these characteristic traits is this: *production takes place among these peoples for personal consumption and not for exchange as with us.* It has often been claimed that the primitive peoples lived in a state of communism. Taken in the sense of a communism in production this assertion is true only in part; except for hunts undertaken in common, production was not carried on in common but was individual. The weapons and utensils of the hunt were private property, while the hunting-ground was held in common. Just so as soon as architectural technique made some progress the houses often became common property. At its inception agriculture was not practiced in common. It was only when it had attained a certain development that this was sometimes the case.[1] But if we take communism in the sense of consumption in common, then the assertion becomes much more exact. I do not mean to say that consumption always took place in common, (though several primitive peoples took their food in common), but when from whatever cause some members of the group had failed to produce, the other members who had been more fortunate provided for them. The productivity of labor was still small; there was not generally any surplus of labor. Even if there had been there could not have been any possibility of exchange, since the division of labor was very slight, and consequently each one was capable of making for himself what others would have been able to offer in exchange.

The second characteristic of the modes of production of the peoples in question is bound up with the first, namely that *there was neither wealth nor poverty.* If there was privation (through scarcity of game, for example), all suffered; if there was abundance, all profited by it.[2]

The third fact to be noted is that *the subordination of man to nature was very great,* so great that we, who have so largely subjugated the forces of nature, can have no idea of it. If primitive men were very weak in their contest with nature even when joined together in a single group, individually they were absolutely unable to maintain the struggle, and were thus forced to unite.

If we consider the characteristics of the primitive modes of production it becomes clear, it seems to me, why the primitive peoples were not more egoistic. They had neither rich nor poor; their economic

---

[1] *Dargun,* "Egoismus und Altruismus in der Nationalökonomie", pp. 100, 101.   [2] See *Dargun, op. cit.,* p. 34.

interests were either parallel or equal (the latter in the case of production in common); the economic life, therefore, did not arouse egoistic ideas — they were not led into temptation. Where the economic system does not produce egoistic ideas it accustoms men to being unegoistic, and if their interests do happen occasionally to conflict, the matter is looked at altruistically and not egoistically. And since the economic life is the "conditio sine qua non" of life in general, and thus occupies the important place in human existence, it stamps the whole life with its non-egoistic character. Since the struggle for existence must be sustained in common against nature, if it is to be efficacious it binds human interests so closely together that they are inseparable; the interest of one is the same as that of his comrade.

We shall now understand why primitive men feel themselves to be first of all the members of a unit; why they not only abstain from acts harmful to their companions, but come to their aid whenever they can; why they are honest, benevolent, and truthful towards the members of their group, and why public opinion has so great an influence among them — characteristics which the quotations that I have already made have established. The cause of these facts is to be found in *the mode of production, which brought about a uniformity of interest in the persons united in a single group, obliged them to aid one another in the difficult and uninterrupted struggle for existence, and made men free and equal, since there was neither poverty nor riches, and consequently no possibility of oppression.*

It is only in such an environment that the social instincts innate in man can be developed, and the more the mode of production binds men's interests together the greater will this development be. It is a truth as old as the world that one respects the interests of others and does not deceive them, only when these others do not make life more difficult, but aid in supporting it. If not, social instincts will be suppressed and the contrary instincts formed. The development of the social feelings is based upon reciprocity. When this is lacking these feelings lie dormant, but when reciprocity exists they grow stronger by constantly reacting from one to the other.[1]

There is still another reason which helped strengthen the solidarity among the members of the same group. The primitive peoples, who practiced agriculture little or not at all, needed an immense territory to provide for their needs. Lands whose population would seem small to the Europeans of our day, had in reality as dense a population as the mode of production would permit. From this there sprang

[1] See *Letourneau*, "L'évolution de la propriété", pp. 72–75.

continual wars between groups disputing the possession of a certain territory. The necessity of defending as a body the territory acquired, or of conquering it anew, resulted in drawing always tighter the bonds uniting the members of the same group.

The same mode of production which drew the members of a group into an altruistic solidarity, forced these same persons into a position of excessive egoism toward those who did not belong to their group and opposed them in obtaining what they needed. The same act, killing an enemy for example, is the most egoistic act possible from the point of view of the enemy but a very altruistic act from the point of view of the slayer, since he has increased the security of his group. The development of the social feelings is, then, only determined by the form of the struggle for existence.

How then shall we explain certain egoistic acts directed against members of the same group? How, for example, can the infanticide so common among primitive peoples be explained? In seeking for a solution we shall see that this egoistic act does not result from innate insensibility toward children (the contrary is true, as we have seen above), but from the fact that the limited control over nature makes a great increase in the population impossible. The children were killed immediately after birth; no one dreamed of ridding himself of a child of greater age. Further, the nomadic life prevented the carrying along of a great number of children.[1]

It is for the same reason that the sick and the aged were sometimes abandoned by the primitive peoples. They were driven to this because these feeble persons were unable to make long journeys, and because their economic means did not allow them to support those who could no longer work. Here again there could be no question of innate insensibility.[2] In these cases then, there was an opposition of interests; the act that was egoistic toward the individual was altruistic toward the group. If different action had been taken in such cases all would have succumbed. Thus these acts have fallen into desuetude as the productivity of labor has developed.

The continual development of the productivity of labor has modified the structure of society greatly. As soon as productivity has increased to such an extent that the producer can regularly produce more than he needs, and the division of labor puts him in a position to exchange the surplus for things that he could not produce himself, at this moment there arises in man the notion of no longer giving to

[1] See *Kropotkin*, "Mutual Aid among Savages", pp. 552, 553; and *Sutherland, op. cit.*, I, vi. [2] See *Kropotkin, op. cit.*, pp. 553, 554.

his comrades what they need, but of keeping for himself the surplus of what his labor produces, and exchanging it. Then it is that the mode of production begins to run counter to the social instincts of man instead of favoring it as heretofore.

In his work already quoted Nansen has described the influence exercised by exchange upon the character of the Eskimos studied by him. (The fact that this commerce has been developed by the coming of the Europeans makes no difference. Among primitive peoples exchange must have developed in the same way, only more slowly.) He says: "How baneful to them has been the introduction of money! Formerly they had no means of saving up work or accumulating riches; for the products of their labor did not last indefinitely, and therefore they gave away their superfluity. But then they learned the use of money; so that now, when they have more than they need for the moment, the temptation to sell the overplus to Europeans, instead of giving it to their needy neighbors, is often too great for them; for with the money they thus acquire they can supply themselves with the much coveted European commodities. Thus we Christians help more and more to destroy instead of to develop their old self-sacrificing love of their neighbors. And money does still more to undermine the Greenland community. Their ideas of inheritance were formerly very vague, for, as before mentioned, the clothes and weapons of a dead man were consigned with him to the grave. Now, on the other hand, the introduction of money has enabled the survivors to sell the effects of the deceased, and they are no longer ashamed to accept as an inheritance what they can obtain in this way. This may seem an advantage; but, here, too, their old habit of mind is upset. Greed and covetousness — vices which they formerly abhorred above everything — have taken possession of them. Their minds are warped and enthralled by money." [1] Thus are born avarice and rapacity, which, opposed in the beginning by altruistic sentiments developed earlier, become stronger from one generation to another.[2]

However, this is only one side of the question. Through the development of exchange not only does man become egoistic towards those who for any reason are unable to provide for their needs, but exchange itself is an entirely egoistic act for the two parties who enter into it. Each tries to get as much profit for himself as possible, and consequently to make the other lose. The existence of economic laws which in many, and even in most cases prevent the two parties from injuring each other, does not change the fact at all. Commerce

[1] Pp. 335, 336.   [2] Compare *Morgan*, "Ancient Society", p. 527.

weakens the social instincts of man ; the loss of one becomes the gain of another. When two persons are trading there springs up a tendency on the part of each to overvalue his own property and to disparage that of the other ; commerce is one of the important causes of lying. In addition to this tendency another arises, that of giving goods of quality inferior to that agreed upon ; the constant attention to one's own interests produces and develops fraud.

The more production for one's own use decreases, and the greater becomes the production for exchange, the more do habit and tradition produce in men the characteristics mentioned. As soon as exchange has developed to a certain point commerce begins to be a special trade. The merchant is much more exposed to the conditions named than those who trade only occasionally. Not only does he pass a great part of his life in exchanging but he is by profession egoistic in two directions ; toward the producer from whom he buys, and toward the consumer to whom he sells.[1]

When it reaches a certain height the continually increasing productivity of labor brings a further important modification in the social structure, namely slavery. For this springs up when production is so advanced that man can regularly produce more than he actually needs for himself, and when it is possible for him to exchange the overplus for things which he can use but cannot make. Prisoners of war are no longer killed as formerly, but are obliged to work for the profit of the conquerors. In this way is formed a considerable opposition of interest between two classes of individuals who together form a social unit : on the one hand those who, deprived of one of the most important factors of human happiness, liberty, are obliged to exhaust themselves for the benefit of others, and have only the strict necessaries of life ; and on the other hand those who profit by the enslavement and excessive labor of the first.

Slavery (with the other forms of forced service, serfdom and wagelabor) is one of the most important factors that undermine the social instincts in man. Slavery, runs the saying, demoralizes the master as well as the slave. It arouses in the master the notion that the slave is not a thinking and feeling man like himself, but an instrument destined exclusively to be useful to him. In the slave himself it kills the feeling of independence ; lacking the arms which the free man has at his disposal, the slave has recourse to dissimulation to defend himself against his master.

[1] See *Dargun*, "Egoismus und Altruismus in der Nationalökonomie", pp. 36, 37 ; *Jhering*, "Der Zweck im Recht", I., p. 117.

The overplus which one person can obtain by his own labor must always remain limited. Without the rise of slavery the great wealth of a single individual would not have been possible. To the difference between master and slave is now added that between rich and poor, and the envy and hatred of the poor for the rich, and the pride of the rich and their desire to dominate over the poor. Since the division of society into rich and poor the aristocracy has been formed, which does not owe its origin to the excellence of its members, as one might imagine from this inaccurate name, but to their wealth.

The period of civilization during which the social modification mentioned above has taken place is generally lauded to the skies, as compared with preceding epochs. In certain relations this is justifiable. Technique has made immense progress and especially during the last phase of civilization, capitalism; the power of man over nature has advanced greatly; the productivity of labor has been so increased that one class of men, exempted by this from permanent care for their daily bread, are able to devote themselves to the arts and sciences. All this is indisputable. But the development of the arts and sciences and of technique has only an indirect importance for the etiology of crime. The question first of all to be asked is this: What influence has this modification in the economic and social structure had upon the character of man? And the answer to this question can only be the following: this modification has engendered cupidity and ambition, has made man less sensitive to the happiness and misery of his fellows, and has decreased the influence exercised upon men's acts by the opinions of others. In short, it has developed egoism at the expense of altruism.

C. Egoistic Tendencies Resulting from the Present Economic System and from its Consequences.

The etiology of crime includes the three following problems;
First. Whence does the criminal thought in man arise?
Second. What forces are there in man which can prevent the execution of this criminal thought, and what is their origin?
Third. What is the occasion for the commission of criminal acts. (As the occasion may be one of the causes of the criminal thought, problems one and three at times form but one.)
For the moment we are still occupied with general considerations with regard to crime; it is clear then that the first and third questions

will be examined only when we are treating of crimes according to the groups into which they must be divided because of the great differences which their nature presents.

It is otherwise with the second question. As we have seen in the preceding pages, it is certain that man is born with social instincts, which, when influenced by a favorable environment can exert a force great enough to prevent egoistic thoughts from leading to egoistic acts. And since crime constitutes a part of the egoistic acts, it is of importance, for the etiology of *crime in general*, to inquire whether the present method of production and its social consequences are an obstacle to the development of the social instincts, and in what measure. We shall try in the following pages to show the influence of the economic system and of these consequences upon the social instincts of man.

After what we have just said it is almost superfluous to remark that the egotisic tendency does not *by itself* make a man criminal. For this something else is necessary. It is possible for the environment to create a great egoist, but this does not imply that the egoist will necessarily become criminal. For example, a man who is enriched by the exploitation of children may nevertheless remain all his life an honest man from the legal point of view. He does not think of stealing, because he has a surer and more lucrative means of getting wealth, although he lacks the moral sense which would prevent him from committing a crime if the thought of it occurred to him. We shall show that, as a consequence of the present environment, man has become very egoistic and hence more *capable of crime*, than if the environment had developed the germs of altruism.

a. *The present economic system* is based upon exchange. As we saw at the end of the preceding section such a mode of production cannot fail to have an egoistic character. A society based upon exchange isolates the individuals by weakening the bond that unites them. When it is a question of exchange the two parties interested think only of their own advantage even to the detriment of the other party. In the second place the possibility of exchange arouses in a man the thought of the possibility of converting the surplus of his labor into things which increase his well-being in place of giving the benefit of it to those who are deprived of the necessaries of life. Hence the possibility of exchange gives birth to cupidity.

The exchange called simple circulation of commodities is practiced by all men as consumers, and by the workers besides as vendors of their labor power. However, the influence of this simple circulation of commodities is weak compared with that exercised by capitalistic exchange. It is only the exchange of the surplus of labor, by the producer, for other commodities, and hence is for him a secondary matter. As a result he does not exchange with a view to profit, (though he tries to make as advantageous a trade as possible) but to get things which he cannot produce himself.

Capitalistic exchange, on the other hand, has another aim — that of making a profit. A merchant, for example, does not buy goods for his own use, but to sell them to advantage. He will, then, always try, on the one hand, to buy the best commodities as cheaply as possible, by depreciating them as much as he can; on the other hand, to make the purchaser pay as high a price as possible, by exaggerating the value of his wares. *By the nature of the mode of production itself* the merchant is therefore forced to make war upon two sides, must maintain his own interests against the interests of those with whom he does business. If he does not injure too greatly the interests of those from whom he buys, and those to whom he sells, it is for the simple reason that these would otherwise do business with those of his competitors who do not find their interest in fleecing their customers. Wherever competition is eliminated for whatever cause the tactics of the merchant are shown in their true light; he thinks only of his own advantage even to the detriment of those with whom he does business. "No commerce without trickery" is a proverbial expression (among consumers), and with the ancients Mercury, the god of commerce, was also the god of thieves. This is true, that the merchant and the thief are alike in taking account *exclusively* of their own interest to the detriment of those with whom they have to do.

The fact that in our present society production does not take place generally to provide for the needs of men, but for many other reasons, has important effects upon the character of those who possess the means of production. Production is carried on for profit exclusively; if greater profits can be made by stopping production it will be stopped — this is the point of view of the capitalists. The consumers, on the other hand, see in production the means of creating what man has need of. The world likes to be deceived, and does not care to recognize the fact that the producer has only his own profit in view. The latter encourages this notion and poses as a disinterested person. If he reduces the price of his wares, he claims to do it in the interest of the public, and takes care not to admit that it is for the purpose of increasing his own profits. This is the falsity that belongs inevitably to capitalism.

In general this characteristic of capitalism has no importance for

the morality of the consumer, who is merely duped, but it is far
otherwise with the press, which is almost entirely in the power of the
capitalists. The press, which ought to be a guide for the masses, and
is so in some few cases, in the main is in the hands of capitalists who
use it only as a means of making money. In place of being edited by
men who, by their ability and firmness, are capable of enlightening
the public, newspapers are carried on by persons who see in their
calling only a livelihood, and consider only the proprietor of the sheet.
In great part the press is the opposite of what it ought to be; it
represents the interests of those who pay for advertisements or for
articles; it increases the ignorance and the prejudices of the crowd;
in a word, it poisons public opinion.[1]

Besides this general influence upon the public the press has further
a special place in the etiology of crime, from the fact that most newspapers, in order to satisfy the morbid curiosity of the public, relate all
great crimes in extenso, give portraits of the victims, etc., and are
often one of the causes of new crimes, by arousing the imitative
instinct to be found in man.[2]

As we have seen above the merchant capitalist makes war in two
directions; his interests are against those of the man who sells to him,
and of the man who buys from him. This is also true of the industrial
capitalist. He buys raw materials and sells what he produces. But
to arrive at his product he must buy labor, and this purchase is "sui
generis."

Deprived as he is of the means of production the working-man sells

[1] *Lassalle*, "Die Feste, die Presse und der Frankfurter Abgeordnetentag"
II, p. 646; *Schäffle*, "Bau und Leben des sozialen Körpers", I, pp. 461–466,
and IV, pp. 68–70; *Mandl*, "Die Wiener Preszkorruption" ("Neue Zeit",
1884); *Stern*, "Einflusz der sozialen Zustände auf alle Zweige des Kulturlebens", pp. 33–37.

[2] *P. Moreau* (of Tours), "L'homicide commis par les enfants", p. 80; *Cué-
noud*, "La criminalité à Genève au XIXe siècle", pp. 93–96; *Aubry*, "La
contagion du meurtre", pp. 84–106; "De l'influence contagieuse de la publicité des faits criminels" ("Archives d'anthropologie criminelle", VIII);
Ferriani, "Minderjährige Verbrecher", pp. 106, 107 and 282, 283; *Lombroso*, "Crime, its Causes and Remedies", pp. 54, 55.

[NOTE TO THE AMERICAN EDITION: Besides the influence of the sensational
press, and harmful literature, we must now mention the cinematograph.

From the literature upon the whole subject we select the following: *S.
Türkel*, "Einfluss der Lektüre auf die Delikte phantastischer jugendlicher
Psychopathen" ("Archiv f. Krim. anthr. u. Krim." XLII); *S. Sighele*,
"Littérature et criminalité", chap. v; *M. Homburger*, "Der Einfluss der
Schundlitteratur auf jugendliche Verbrecher und Selbstmörder" ("Monat-
schr. f. Krim. psych. und Straf.", VI); *F. Fenton*, "The Influence of News-
paper Presentations upon the Growth of Crime and Other Anti-social
Activity"; *A. Hellwig*, "Die Beziehungen zwischen Schundlitteratur, Schund-
films, und Verbrechen" ("Archiv f. Krim. anthr. u. Krim.", LI); *Meyer*,
"Schundlitteratur und Schundfilm" ("Arch. f. Krim. anthr. u. Krim.", LIII).]

his labor only in order not to die of hunger. The capitalist takes advantage of this necessitous condition of the worker and exploits him. We have already indicated that capitalism has this trait in common with the earlier methods of production. Little by little one class of men has become accustomed to think that the others are destined to amass wealth for them and to be subservient to them in every way. Slavery, like the wage system, demoralizes the servant as well as the master. With the master it develops cupidity and the imperious character which sees in a fellow man only a being fit to satisfy his desires. It is true that the capitalist has not the power over the proletarian that the master has over his slave; he has neither the right of service nor the power of life and death, yet it is none the less true that he has another weapon against the proletarian, a weapon whose effect is no less terrible, namely enforced idleness. The fact that the supply of manual labor always greatly exceeds the demand puts this weapon into the hands of every capitalist. It is not only the capitalists who carry on any business that are subjected to this influence, but also all who are salaried in their service.

Capitalism exercises in still a third manner an egoistic influence upon the capitalistic "entrepreneur." Each branch has more producers than are necessary. The interests of the capitalists are, then, opposed not only to those of the men from whom they buy or to whom they sell, but also to those of their fellow producers. It is indeed claimed that competition has the effect simply of making the product better and cheaper, but this is looking at the question from only one point of view. The fact which alone affects criminality is that competition forces the participants, under penalty of succumbing, to be as egoistic as possible. Even the producers who have the means of applying all the technical improvements to perfect their product and make it cheaper, are obliged to have recourse to gross deceits in advertising, etc., in order to injure their competitors. Rejoicing at the evil which befalls another, envy at his good fortune, these forms of egoism are the inevitable consequence of competition.

Following the same classification that we employed in the preceding chapter we come now to that part of the bourgeoisie which, without having any occupation, consumes what has been made by others. Not to feel obliged to contribute to the material well-being of humanity in proportion to one's ability must necessarily have a demoralizing influence. A parasite, one who lives without working, does not feel bound by any moral tie to his fellows, but regards them simply as things, instruments meant to serve and amuse him. Their example is a source of demoralization for those about them, and excites the envy of those who see this easy life without the power of enjoying it themselves, and awakes in them the desire to exchange their painful existence for this "dolce far niente."

The egoistic tendencies work less strongly in the third group of the bourgeoisie, those who practice the liberal professions. However, the products of the arts and sciences having become commodities, the egoistic influence of exchange here too is not to be neglected. Then competition arising from overproduction is a great cause of demoralization, for where there is competition men become egoistic. So in the domain of the liberal professions competition often forces those who do not find a field of activity in accordance with their ideas, to work that is contrary to those ideas. Thus it is quite right to speak of a prostitution of the intellect.

Before concluding these observations upon the bourgeoisie there is still something to be said about politics. As we have seen above the state owes its origin to the formation of opposition of interests in society; the first task of the state being, therefore, the maintenance of a certain amount of order. This requires above all the holding of the great mass in subjection. As long as this mass is weak the dominant class has no need to resort to trickery; but as soon as the oppressed class can oppose the domination of the others, as soon as brutal power no longer gives the desired result, the dominant class changes its tactics. It attempts to create the impression that the concessions it has been forced to make are acts of charity; and presuming upon the ignorance of the oppressed, it pretends that their condition is not so bad, etc. Many of those engaged in politics play this part without being conscious of their duplicity. However, the contest between the classes exercises its baleful influence upon them also, for they involuntarily distort the facts, whereas the evolution of society has reached such a point that a new social order is necessary.

The power in the State sometimes passes from one party of the ruling class to another. All profit by the temporary opportunity not only for the realization of their political program, but also to procure advantages for their partisans. This struggle for power is carried on partly by means prejudicial to the character of those interested, while the end aimed at by some parties can be frankly avowed. It is for the same reason that international politics is such a source of lying and hypocrisy, the states not being able to avow their real intention — the weakening of their neighbors.

The proletariat. To be thorough we begin by making mention of one of the consequences of the economic position of the proletariat, of which we have already treated briefly, namely the dependence in which persons of this class find themselves in consequence of their lacking the means of production, a state which has a prejudicial influence upon character. The oppressed resort to means which they would otherwise scorn. As we have seen above, the basis of the social feelings is reciprocity. As soon as this is trodden under foot by the ruling class the social sentiments of the oppressed become weak towards them.

We come now (following the order adopted in the first chapter of Part II) first to the consequences of the labor of the young. The paid labor of the young has a bad influence in several ways. First, it forces them, while they are still very young, to think only of their own interests; then, brought into contact with persons who are rough and indifferent to their well-being, they follow these only too quickly, because of their imitative tendencies, in their bad habits, grossness of speech, etc. Finally, the paid labor of the young makes them more or less independent at an age where they have the greatest need of guidance. Even if the statistical proof of the influence of the labor of children and young people upon criminality were totally wanting, no one could deny that influence. Child labor is entirely a capitalistic phenomenon, being found especially in the great manufacturing countries like England and Germany. And then one of the most salient facts of criminality is the amount of juvenile crime, which is so enormous that England, followed by other countries, has established a special system to combat this form of criminality. Certainly this increase of juvenile crime is chiefly due to the influence of bad domestic conditions (wage-labor of married women, etc.), but the labor of the young people themselves also plays its part.

Although figures upon the relation in question are not totally lacking, they are, as far as I know, quite rare. In the first part of this work I have given the figures furnished by P. Hirsch, to which I refer the reader.[1] The director of the "Erziehungsheim am Urban" at Zehlendorf near Berlin, mentions that 80 % of his pupils had formerly practiced a trade.[2]

The following figures are given for the Netherlands:[3]

---

[1] P. 242.

[2] "Fürsorgeerziehung" (Woche V, No. 51).

[3] From " Crimineele Statistiek" for the years given, and "Uitkomsten der achste tienjaarlijksche volkstelling" and "Uitkomsten der beroepstelling van 1899."

Years.	Total Sentenced 10 to 16 Years Old.	Practicing a Trade.[1]	Percentage Sentenced who Practiced a Trade.	Percentage of Children in General 10 to 16 who Practiced a Trade.
1899	791	363	45.8	18.5
1900	671	347	51.7	—
1901	674	344	51.0	—
1902	712	331	46.4	—
1903	671	344	51.2	—
1904	702	347	49.4	—

These figures are very significant. Among the young delinquents there are two or three times as many persons following a trade as among non-delinquents.

I do not know of any other statistics giving information upon this point directly.[2]

As to statics (the geography of crime) we encounter great difficulties of a technical nature. The statistics in which we can compare juvenile delinquency with the local extent of child labor are rare, often taking no account of the figures for the non-criminal population.[3] On this point the statistics of Germany, Italy, and Austria are the best.[4]

Since the work of young people has increased enormously, and in general is still increasing, we may expect an increase in juvenile crime also, unless there are other determining factors, such as special laws, which work in the opposite direction.

In order to give an example of the extent of child labor we take from one of the best sets of statistics of occupations the following figures.

In the census of occupations in the German Empire in 1895 it was shown that whereas in 1882 16.46 % of the population under 20 had some occupation (other than that of domestic servant), in 1895 there were 17.97 % so employed, an increase of 9.1 %.[5] The absolute figures are the following. In 1882 the number of persons below the

[1] This number is below the reality; they have classed among persons without trade those whose trade was unknown.

[2] [NOTE TO THE AMERICAN EDITION: For North America cf. *Fehlinzer*, "Erwebsarbeit und Kriminalität von Kindern u. Frauen in den Vereinigten Staaten."]

[3] See "Kriminalstatistik für das Jahr 1898", I, pp. 52 ff., and "Notizie complementari alle statistiche giudiziare penali degli anni 1890–1895", pp. xlix, l.

[4] [NOTE TO THE AMERICAN EDITION: For Germany the "Kriminalstatistik" of 1891, 1901, and 1902 contain data upon this point; see II, p. 32. For Austria, cf. *Herz*, "Verbrechen und Verbrechertum in Oesterreich", pp. 121 ff.]

[5] "Die berufliche und soziale Gliederung des Deutschen Volkes nach der Berufszählung vom 14 Juni, 1895" ("Stat. des Deutschen Reichs. Neue Folge", Band 111).

age of 20 at work was 3,333,791; in 1895 it was 4,161,600, an increase of 827,809.

In 1895 the number of persons at work below the age of 20 was divided among the different ages as follows: [1]

Below 12   having paid occupation   32,687
From 12 to 14   "   "   "   148,766
"   14 " 16   "   "   "   1,131,723
"   16 " 18   "   "   "   1,397,161
"   18 " 20   "   "   "   1,451,263

If the paid labor of young people has really an influence, then, upon juvenile criminality, statistics must necessarily show an increase in this criminality, unless other factors exercise an influence in the other direction.

The following figures have a bearing on this subject: [2]

Germany, 1882–1896.

OFFENSES.	NUMBER CONVICTED AT 12 TO 18 YEARS OF AGE TO 100,000 OF THE POPULATION OF THE SAME AGE, IN THE YEARS:														
	1882.	1883.	1884.	1885.	1886.	1887.	1888.	1889.	1890.	1891.	1892.	1893.	1894.	1895.	1896.
Crimes in general	568	549	578	560	565	576	563	614	663	672	729	686	716	702	702
Theft and embezzlement	370	353	358	335	337	337	334	369	391	392	430	376	393	380	373
Assaults . . .	63	65	78	81	84	86	82	88	99	101	108	118	121	126	130
Malicious mischief . . .	31	27	31	33	30	34	32	34	40	38	40	41	45	41	46
Fraud . . .	20	20	21	20	21	22	22	26	27	28	31	26	28	28	26
Insults . . .	10	10	12	13	13	13	13	13	16	15	17	19	20	19	19
Rape, etc. . .	12	10	11	11	11	12	11	12	12	13	14	14	16	15	15
Domiciliary trespass . .	7	6	9	7	9	8	8	8	11	11	12	12	14	14	14
Forgery . . .	5	6	6	6	6	6	7	7	8	9	10	9	9	9	10
Rebellion . .	4	5	5	5	4	6	4	5	5	5	5	6	7	7	8
Arson . . .	3	3	3	3	3	3	2	2	2	3	3	3	2	2	3
Crimes against life	1	1	1	1	1	1	1	1	1	1	1	1	1	1	1
Counterfeiting .	0.3	0.3	0.4	0.3	0.3	0.3	0.4	0.2	0.3	0.5	0.4	0.2	0.5	0.5	0.3

Consequently, in Germany there is a great and constant increase in juvenile criminality, both as to crime in general and also in each crime separately.[3]

[1] *Op. cit.*, pp. 143 and 144.
[2] " Kriminalstatistik für das Jahr 1896.   Erläuterungen ", I, pp. 22, 23.
[3] [NOTE TO THE AMERICAN EDITION: Juvenile criminality in Germany in-

The following table gives a comparison between the criminality of the young and that of adults.[1]

Germany, 1882–1896.

OFFENSES.	NUMBER OF PERSONS FROM 12 TO 18 YEARS OF AGE TO THE HUNDRED, CONVICTED IN THE YEARS:															
	1882.	1883.	1884.	1885.	1886.	1887.	1888.	1889.	1890.	1891.	1892.	1893.	1894.	1895.	1896.	1882 to 1896.
Arson	24	21	22	26	26	27	29	32	30	37	31	37	29	28	35	28
Offenses against morals	23	19	22	20	18	21	21	22	23	24	25	24	24	22	21	21
Theft and embezzlement	17	16	17	17	18	19	19	20	22	21	21	21	21	21	21	19
Malicious mischief	14	13	13	13	12	14	15	15	17	17	17	16	17	15	16	15
Forgery	8	10	10	10	11	10	12	12	13	14	13	13	12	11	12	11
Fraud	9	9	9	9	9	9	9	10	10	10	10	8	6	9	8	9
Counterfeiting	6	6	8	8	7	9	12	6	10	14	10	6	15	10	8	9
Crimes in general	9	9	9	8	8	9	9	9	10	11	11	10	10	9	9	9
Assaults	5	5	6	6	6	6	6	6	7	7	7	7	7	7	7	6
Crimes against life	5	4	5	5	4	5	4	6	6	6	6	6	5	5	6	5
Domiciliary trespass	2	2	3	2	3	2	3	3	3	4	4	4	4	4	4	3
Rebellion	1	1	1	2	1	2	1	2	2	2	2	2	2	2	2	1.6
Insults	1	1	1	1	1	1	1	1	2	2	2	2	2	2	2	1.4

If we remember that in 1890 persons from 12 to 18 years of age formed 12.75 % of the population,[2] the study of this table will show how large a part the young play in certain crimes, and in crime in general. Still it must not be forgotten that criminal statistics include only a part of the crimes really committed, and that this affects particularly the figures for juvenile crime, since the persons injured make complaint against the young less readily, on account of pity.[3]

According to the figures given below (which, it is true, only cover a short period) juvenile delinquency in England has remained almost stationary.[4] Here we must remember: first, the great number of acquittals; second, that the criminality of the young is nowhere

creased up to 1906, when a fairly regular decrease began. The law upon the "Fürsorgeerziehung" dates from the beginning of the century.]

[1] Calculated from the work cited, I, pp. 18–21.
[2] "Statistisches Jahrbuch für das Deutsche Reich", 1896, p. 5.
[3] *Morrison*, "Juvenile Offenders", p. 5.
[4] [NOTE TO THE AMERICAN EDITION: According to recent statistics juvenile delinquency in England has decreased rather than increased.]

better combated than in England with its system of Industrial and Reformatory Schools; third, that industrialism has been prevalent in England longer than elsewhere, and that the increase of criminality during the period designated cannot be as great as in other less industrial countries.

England, 1893–1899.[1]

CONVICTED UNDER 21 YEARS OF AGE.	1893.	1894.	1895.	1896.	1897.	1898.	1899.
Convicted	42,926	43,950	38,994	38,637	39,821	43,538	39,111
Sent to the Industrial schools	3,180	3,703	3,311	4,658	4,289	4,635	4,981
Correction made for those discharged under the S. J. A.[2]	4,255	4,543	5,125	5,955	6,640	7,114	7,547
Total	50,361	52,196	47,430	49,260	50,750	55,287	51,639
To the 100,000	169.39	173.63	156.05	160.26	163.33	175.98	162.57

Finally, the following table shows of what crimes the young are guilty in England: [3]

England, 1893–1899.

	NUMBER OF PERSONS UNDER 21 TO THE 100 CONVICTIONS.							
YEARS	1893.	1894.	1895.	1896.	1897.	1898.	1899.	1893 to 1899.
Simple theft	45.51	47.31	44.73	44.54	44.14	45.27	43.19	44.95
Theft by domestics . . .	41.07	43.17	40.26	43.12	42.60	42.71	40.70	41.80
House-breaking	41.27	40.65	36.83	36.67	38.83	38.30	39.86	38.91
Theft upon the person . .	32.93	29.73	27.53	28.77	28.95	26.85	27.68	28.93
Malicious mischief . . .	21.51	25.95	22.89	19.98	27.22	29.29	26.82	24.80
Extortion	26.61	28.99	25.35	27.22	16.42	23.26	21.60	23.92
Crimes against morals . .	25.44	23.73	23.57	23.07	23.22	22.23	21.96	23.32
Crimes committed with violence	20.48	22.33	22.76	25.82	24.69	23.82	22.77	23.23
Forgery	14.01	15.56	18.62	14.34	10.63	16.74	14.64	14.93
Obtaining money by false pretenses	14.12	13.98	14.75	13.80	14.04	11.56	12.02	13.46
Counterfeiting	24.39	10.10	11.53	11.76	9.19	20.17	7.61	13.53
Assaults	14.74	14.20	13.22	12.93	12.39	13.44	11.57	13.21

[1] "Judicial Statistics, England and Wales, Part I, Criminal Statistics, 1899", p. 64.
[2] The "Summary Jurisdiction Act" gives the English judges the right not to convict, even though the proof may be sufficient, when they deem the offense not grave enough. 20 % of those so discharged are added to the figures to allow for this.
[3] *Op. cit.*, p. 65.

If we take into consideration the fact that generally about 23 % of the population are between the ages of 10 and 21, this table shows that persons at this age have a large part in certain of the crimes.

Austria, 1881–1899 (Crimes).[1]

YEARS.	NUMBER OF YOUNG PERSONS CONVICTED.			
	11 to 14 Years.	14 to 20.	Total.	To the 1000 Convicted.
1881	460	5405	5865	17.5
1882	525	5258	5783	18.0
1883	525	5256	5781	19.0
1884	579	5538	6117	19.9
1885	566	5249	5815	18.8
1886	546	5287	5833	19.6
1887	625	5358	5983	20.8
1888	593	5241	5834	20.8
1889	614	5617	6231	21.8
1890	578	6001	6579	22.6
1891	650	5779	6429	22.2
1892	803	6238	7041	22.8
1893	842	5959	6801	23.2
1894	826	6378	7204	23.9
1895	766	5976	6742	23.5
1896	818	5945	6763	23.5
1897	812	6473	7285	24.5
1898	1026	7569	8595	24.9
1899	1015	6665	7680	22.8

Consequently there is here, too, both in absolute numbers and in proportion to adult crime, an increase in juvenile criminality (about 23 % in 18 years). Estimates of the number of non-criminal minors are wanting to give us a complete picture. It must not be forgotten that Austrian law ranks simple theft, fraud, assault, and the like as "contraventions", and that these do not figure in these statistics. The total figures for young criminals are consequently much higher.[2]

The following table shows of what crimes the young are guilty :

[1] *P. L.* "Die Ergebnisse der Strafrechtspflege in den im Reichsrathe vertretenen Königreichen und Ländern im Jahre 1899."

[2] [NOTE TO THE AMERICAN EDITION : After the period cited juvenile crime in Austria has increased further. *Cf. Herz, op. cit.*, pp. 107 *ff.* See also *Hoegel*, "Die Grenzen der Kriminalstatistik", pp. 414 *ff.*]

Austria, 1882–1889.[1]

| CRIMES. | CONVICTED FROM 1882 TO 1899. | | |
| | Total. | Persons from 14 to 20 Years of Age. | |
		Absolute Numbers.	To the 100 Convicted.
Rape etc.	17,187	5,534	32.2
Aggravated theft	268,686	67,106	25.0
Extortion	2,257	547	24.2
Counterfeiting	642	113	17.6
Infanticide	1,734	302	17.4
Assassination	4,209	611	14.5
Serious assaults	85,055	12,202	14.3
Defamation	3,139	410	13.0
Homicide	2,478	312	12.6
Fraud	51,487	5,651	10.9
Leze-majesty	5,369	380	7.0

Belgium, 1861-1885.[2]

YEARS.	PERSONS ACCUSED.	UNDER 16.	16 TO 21.	UNDER 21.	PERCENTAGE OF ACCUSED PERSONS UNDER 21.
1861	24,673	1,043	2,429	3,472	14.1
1862	25,357	1,224	2,355	2,579	14.1
1863	24,133	1,206	2,456	3,662	15.1
1864	24,185	1,245	2,307	3,552	14.6
1865	24,236	1,115	2,483	3,598	14.8
1866	24,608	1,141	2,396	3,537	14.3
1867	25,041	1,220	2,750	3,970	15.8
1868	27,469	1,500	3,064	4,565	16.6
1869	27,883	1,107	2,923	4,030	14.9
1870	26,507	1,298	3,075	4,373	16.4
1871	28,819	1,550	3,344	4,894	16.9
1872	28,047	1,336	3,255	4,597	16.3
1873	29,569	1,448	3,451	4,899	16.5
1874	31,653	1,261	3,408	4,669	14.7
1875	30,867	1,371	3,767	5,138	16.6
1876	33,366	1,445	4,363	5,808	17.4
1877	37,964	2,183	5,096	7,279	19.1
1878	37,348	1,994	5,245	7,239	19.3
1879	36,614	1,873	5,074	6,947	18.9
1880	41,653	2,546	5,680	8,226	19.7
1881	44,361	2,634	6,271	8,905	20.0
1882	45,895	2,695	6,487	9,182	20.0
1883	45,325	2,681	6,942	9,623	21.2
1884	45,665	3,325	7,063	9,388	20.5
1885	46,479	2,398	7,279	9,677	20.8

[1] Op. cit., pp. l–li.
[2] Calculated from "Administration de la Justice criminelle et civile de la Belgique, période de 1881–1885. Résumé statistique", p. 81.
[NOTE TO THE AMERICAN EDITION: In Belgium no criminal statistics ap-

In Belgium, therefore, a great increase in the criminality of the young has taken place.

For France we take the following figures showing the trend of criminality from 1881 to 1900 : [1]

France, 1881–1900.

Court of Assizes.   Accused.

Age.	1881–1885.		1886–1890.		1891–1895.		1896–1900.	
	Absolute Number.	%	Absolute Number.	%	Absolute Number.	%	Absolute Number.	%
Under 16 . .	32	0.7	31	0.7	31	0.7	26	0.7
16 to 21 . .	750	17.1	618	14.5	631	15.6	574	16.8
Under 21 . .	782	17.8	649	15.2	663	16.3	600	17.5

When we take into consideration the fact that the population of France has increased a little during the period in question, this table shows a slight diminution in juvenile criminality. Nevertheless, this diminution is smaller than that of criminality in general.

France, 1881–1900.[2]

Correctional Tribunals.   Accused of Misdemeanors.

Age.	1881–1885.		1886–1890.		1891–1895.		1896–1900.	
	Absolute Number.	%	Absolute Number.	%	Absolute Number.	%	Absolute Number.	%
Under 16 . .	5,846	3.0	6,980	3.4	6,903	3.2	5,776	2.9
16 to 21 . .	28,688	15.1	27,309	13.6	31,119	14.8	80,415	15.7
Under 21 . .	34,534	18.1	34,289	17.0	38,022	18.0	36,261	18.6

Here, then, we have once more a slight diminution in juvenile criminality, but less great than that of criminality in general.

We should deceive ourselves if we saw in these figures the conclu-

peared from 1886 to 1897. For the period after 1898 see *Jacquart,* "La criminalité belge." Here there appears rather a decrease than an increase of juvenile delinquency for this period.]

[1] Figured from p. cix, Table No. 3 of the "Rapport sur l'administration de la justice criminelle de 1881 a 1900." (Compte general de l'administration de la justice criminelle pendant l'année 1900.)

[2] Figured from *op. cit.,* p. cxvi, Table No. 8.

sive proof that criminality on the part of the young was decreasing. We must not overlook the fact that these figures do not include those delinquents whose prosecution was not pushed, whether because they were thought not to have understood the nature of their acts, or because the offense was considered as too light. It is well known that judges incline more and more to the opinion that it is better not to convict youthful delinquents, but to send them to a house of correction, or to place them under the care of a guardian.[1] What the figures given above show is that the increase of juvenile criminality has not been as great in France as it has been in Germany. (I have not the figures for child labor in France, but probably the increase is not as great as it has been in Germany, which is more of an industrial country. The difference, then, in the juvenile crime of the two countries would be explained, at least in part.)[2]

Finally, the following figures will show of what crimes and misdemeanors the young delinquents are guilty:

France, 1900.[3]

CRIMES.	TOTAL ACCUSED.	NUMBER UNDER 21.	PERCENTAGE UNDER 21.
Aggravated theft	1300	367	28.2
Rape and indecent assault upon adults	65	18	27.6
Counterfeiting	120	27	22.5
Infanticide	95	21	22.1
Assaults	203	33	16.2
Homicide	620	100	16.1
Arson	157	19	12.1
Rape etc., upon children	383	42	10.9

[1] See *Grosmolard*, "Criminalité juvénile" ("Archives d'athr. crim.", XVIII), and *Albanel*, "Le crime dans la famille", p. 194.

[2] [NOTE TO THE AMERICAN EDITION: Upon France cf. especially *Dr. G. Jacquelty*, "Étude statistique de la criminalité juvénile en France." According to this study the crimes of minors under 16 years of age have remained stationary as regards crimes against persons, and have decreased as regards crimes against property; misdemeanors, however, have increased. The crimes committed by minors between 16 and 20 have remained the same in comparison with the criminality of adults; on the other hand there has been a constant increase of misdemeanors. The increase of crimes and misdemeanors of violence committed at this age has been considerable. See also: *G. L. Duprat*, "La criminalité dans l'adolescence."]

[3] According to the "Compte Général de l'administration de la justice criminelle pendant l'année 1900", p. 32, Table XVI.

France, 1900.[1]

Correctional Tribunals. Persons Arraigned.

MISDEMEANORS.	Total Arraigned.	Number under 21.	Percentage under 21.
Thefts	42,127	12,483	29.6
Sexual offenses	2,939	643	21.8
Rebellion	3,315	676	20.3
Assaults	36,592	6,600	18.0
Vagrancy	11,804	1,914	16.2
Obtaining money under false pretenses	3,179	376	11.8
Mendicity	9,057	778	8.5

As in most countries it is theft, violence, and sexual offenses of which the young delinquents are most often guilty in France.

Italy, 1887–1889.[2]

	PERSONS CONVICTED UNDER THE AGE OF 21.												
	Up to the Age of 14.			From 14 to 18.			From 18 to 21.			Total.		
YEARS.	Absolute Number.	To the 100 Persons Convicted.	To the 1000 of the Population from 9 to 14.	Absolute Number.	To the 100 Convicted.	To the 1000 of the Population of this Age.	Absolute Number.	To the 100 Convicted.	To the 1000 of the Population of this Age.	Absolute Number.	To the 100 Convicted.	To the 1000 of the Population under 21.
1887	4,566	1.48	1.60	22,361	7.24	10.55	36,871	11.93	24.52	63,798	20.65	9.85
1888	5,743	1.72	2.01	22,991	6.90	10.84	42,436	12.73	28.23	71,171	21.35	10.99
1889	6,426	1.88	2.25	24,229	7.08	11.43	38,697	11.30	25.24	69,352	20.26	10.71

This table shows that the increase of delinquents under 18 is quite large, and that there is an increase followed by a decrease of criminality among those between the ages of 18 and 21. However, the period is too short for conclusions of much significance.

[1] According to *op. cit.*, p. 54, Table XXIX.
[2] " Statistica giudiziaria penale per l' anno 1899 ", p. cxvii.

Italy, 1890–1895.[1]

YEARS.	PERSONS CONVICTED.							
	From 9 to 14.		14 to 18.		18 to 21.		9 to 21.	
	Number.	%	Number.	%	Number.	%	Number.	%
1890	2,920	2.23	12,208	9.31	14,980	11.42	30,108	22.96
1891	3,605	2.50	14,287	9.95	16,166	11.25	34,058	23.70
1892	3,354	2.25	13,952	9.36	16,896	11.34	34,202	22.95
1893	3,008	2.12	12,998	9.18	15,800	11.16	31,806	22.46
1894	3,838	2.54	13,948	9.21	17,826	11.77	35,612	23.52
1895	4,026	2.40	15,468	9.21	19,615	11.67	39,109	23.28

This table shows (except for 1893) an increase in the number of young delinquents (about 30 % in 6 years), a phenomenon by no means accounted for by the increase in the population.

The following figures show the crimes of which the young delinquents are especially guilty.

Italy, 1891–1895.[2]

CRIMES.	To 100,000 OF EACH AGE GROUP.		
	9 to 14.	14 to 18.	18 to 21.
Simple theft	59.50	278.89	302.86
Minor assaults	14.64	83.40	215.04
Aggravated theft	30.95	128.96	157.28
Rebellion	1.25	24.94	83.58
Serious assaults	5.22	28.56	82.07
Threats	1.11	15.10	47.71
Obtaining money under false pretenses etc.	1.54	13.96	30.00
Homicide	0.49	3.97	15.78
Rape	1.02	6.36	9.62
Extortion, blackmail	0.41	3.55	9.07
Offenses against chastity of minors and against public decency	0.38	2.93	5.70
Offenses against public order	1.01	2.14	4.95
Assassination	0.07	0.75	3.55
Infanticide	0.01	0.02	0.36

[1] "Notizie complementari alle statistiche giudiziarie penali degli anni 1890–1895", p. xli. In the period from 1896–1900 juvenile criminality increased further in a striking manner.

[2] *Op. cit.*, p. xlvii.

We will close the series of statistics concerning juvenile criminality with some figures from the Netherlands.[1]

Netherlands, 1896–1900.[2]

YEARS.	CONVICTED.				
	Total.	Under 16.	16 to 21.	Under 21.	% under 21.
1896	15,567	683	2,941	3,624	23.2
1897	16,086	666	3,024	3,690	22.9
1898	15,662	712	2,967	3,679	23.4
1899	15,390	619	2,895	3,514	22.4
1900	14,488	537	2,670	3,207	22.8

Netherlands, 1901–1910.[3]

YEARS.	CONVICTED.		
	Total.	Under 16 Years of Age.	Percentage Under 16.
1901	13,917	651	4.7
1902	14,205	683	4.8
1903	13,673	645	4.7
1904	14,056	667	4.7
1905	13,310	592	4.4
1906	12,311	589	4.7
1907	12,182	588	4.8
1908	13,563	544	4.1
1909	13,361	649	4.8
1910	13,790	800	5.8

Juvenile criminality has not changed much, then, as compared with the criminality of adults. As I have already observed above, there is reason to suppose that the real facts are different, especially after

[1] I have not been able to get data for the United States. The American criminologist, A. Drähms, says that the criminality of the young is increasing in the United States ("The Criminal", p. 279), and W. D. Morrison makes a similar statement ("Juvenile Offenders", p. 17).

[2] From "De Gerechtelijke Statistiek van het Koninkrijk der Nederlanden" for the years 1896 to 1899, and from "Bijdragen tot de Statistiek van Nederland, Nieuwe volgreeks XVII, XXVII. Crimineele statistiek over de jaren 1900 en 1901."

[3] Taken from "Crimineele Statistiek over het jaar 1901." In the criminal statistics of the Netherlands the system was changed in 1901. Before this year convictions were counted, and from that year on, individuals convicted.

1905, when the new law with regard to juvenile crime was put into effect.

The following figures show what crimes are most often committed by the young delinquents.

Netherlands, 1896-1901.

| CRIMES. | AVERAGE FOR THE PERIOD 1896-1901. | | |
| | Number Convicted. | | Percentage under 21. |
	Total.	Under 21.	
Aggravated theft	894	416	46.4
Sexual offenses	202	63	31.1
Theft	1,713	526	30.7
Malicious mischief	756	226	29.9
Assault	3,927	1,030	26.2
Domiciliary trespass	318	72	22.6
Rebellion	1,056	216	20.4

Keeping constantly in mind that in our days juvenile criminals are less often sentenced than formerly, we shall find that the foregoing statistics show:

First. That juvenile crime is increasing.

Second. That this increase is considerable in the countries like Germany, Austria, and Belgium, where there is a continuous industrial development; while in countries less developed industrially the increase is less.

Third. That England, where the capitalism is very intense, shows a great amount of juvenile crime.

The figures we have given have in general, in my opinion, gone to support the incontestable truth, that there is a relation between child labor and juvenile criminality. Although it is of smaller importance than the lack of care of the children among the proletariat, it is still one of the factors in the etiology of crime.[1]

[1] See also *Ducpetiaux*, "De la condition physique et morale des jeunes ouvriers", Bk. I, ch. 2; *Starke*, "Verbrechen und Verbrechen in Preuszen", pp. 210, 211; *Ferriani*, "Minderjährige Verbrecher", pp. 144 *ff.*, 177–185; "Entartete Mütter" and "Schlaue und glückliche Verbrecher", pp. 443, 444, 458–475; *Agahd*, "Die Erwerbsthätigkeit schulpflichtiger Kinder im Deutschen Reiche" ("Archiv für soziale Gesetzgebung und Statistik", XII); *Strunz*, "Die erwerbmässige Kinderarbeit und die Schule" ("Neue Zeit", 1898–1899, I); *Dix*, "Die Jugendlichen in der Sozial- und Kriminalpolitik"; *Albanel*, "Le crime dans la famille", pp. 41–43; *Aschaffenburg*, "Das Verbrechen und seine Bekämpfung", pp. 119–123; *Joly*, "L'enfance coupable", pp. 24, 25, 126.

[NOTE TO THE AMERICAN EDITION: *Cf.* the following recent works: *Baern-*

Following the order adopted in Part II, chapter I, we come now to the influence of long hours of labor. It has rightly been said that work has a strong moral influence. But it is also true that immoderate labor has the contrary effect. It brutalizes a man, makes him incapable of elevated sentiments, kills as Key says (in "das Jahrhundert des Kindes"), the man in the beast, while moderate labor ennobles the beast in the man.[1]

The housing conditions of the proletariat have also a significance as regards criminality, and for the special group of sexual offenses their importance is very great. We shall speak of this more fully when we treat especially of these offenses, and will, for the moment, note simply their general consequences.

The disorder and squalor of the home communicate themselves to the inmates; the lack of room obliges the children to live, during a great part of the day, on the streets, with the result that they are brought into contact with all sorts of demoralizing companions. Finally, the living together of a great number of uneducated persons in one small dwelling is the cause of constant quarrels and fights. The situation of those who are merely night-lodgers is especially unfortunate, as we have already seen.

In Part I we have quoted from authors who have laid stress upon the importance of the question of housing conditions in the study of criminality (Hirsch, for example), and we have indicated the gravity of this cause in speaking of prostitution and alcoholism.

It would be possible to quote a number of authors who have taken up the effect of housing conditions upon morals.[2] However, it is naturally very difficult to express this influence in figures. As far

---

reither, op. cit., passim; P. Pollotz, "Die Psychologie des Verbrechers", pp. 112 ff.; Duprat, op. cit., pp. 125 ff.; M. Homburger, "Ueber den Zusammenhang zwischen den Zahlen der in den Fabriken beschäftigten Personen unter 18 Jahren und der Zahl der Verbrechen solcher Personen"; H. W. Gruhle, "Die Ursachen der jugendlichen Verwahrlosung und Kriminalität", pp. 104 ff.]

[1] See also Engels, "The Condition of the Working Class in England," pp. 118, 119.

[2] See: Brace, "The Dangerous Classes of New York", pp. 51 ff.; O. S., "Die Verbrecherwelt von Berlin", pp. 120 ff. ("Zeitschr. f. d. gesammte Strafrechtswissenschaft", V); Földes, "Einige Ergebnisse der neueren Kriminalstatistik", p. 548 (ibid., XI); Lux, "Sozialpolitisches Handbuch", pp. 58 ff.; Philippovich, "Wiener Wohnungsverhältnisse", p. 264 ("Archiv für soziale Gesetzgebung und Statistik", VI); Dix, "Sozial-Moral", pp. 15–18; Ferriani, "Schlaue und glückliche Verbrecher", pp. 444 ff.; Liszt, "Das Verbrechen als sozial-pathologische Erscheinung", p. 22; Th. Holmes, "Pictures and Problems from London Police Courts", pp. 70 ff.; Albanel, op. cit., pp. 11 ff.; Aschaffenburg, op. cit., p. 115.

[NOTE TO THE AMERICAN EDITION: Cf. Baernreither, op. cit., passim.]

as I know it is Dr. E. Laspeyres who (in "Der Einflusz der Wohnung auf die Sittlichkeit") gives the most significant data upon this subject. I borrow from him the following figures: summarizing part of the results of a study of "Furnished Rooms" in 2,360 dwellings: [1]

Paris, 1849.

TABLE I.

ARRONDISSEMENTS.	GOOD DWELLINGS. %	CONDUCT OF THE INMATES.			
		Men.		Women.	
		Good. %	Very Bad. %	Good. %	Very Bad. %
The 6 arrondissements with the smallest number of good dwellings	35	46	10	20.4	19
The 6 arrondissements with the largest number of good dwellings	44.5	50	2.5	21.7	14
The 12 arrondissements together	39	48	6.4	21.0	16.6
The figures cited above in proportion to all Paris = 100	89 114	96 104	156 39	97 103	114 86
	100	100	100	100	100

TABLE II.[2]

ARRONDISSEMENTS.	VERY BAD DWELLINGS. %	CONDUCT OF INMATES.			
		Men.		Women.	
		Very Bad. %	Good. %	Very Bad. %	Good. %
The 6 arrondissements with the greatest number of very bad dwellings	13.6	9	45	20.2	21.3
The 6 arrondissements with the smallest number of very bad dwellings	6.0	2.2	52	11.7	21.0
The 12 arrondissements together	11	6.4	48	16.6	21.0
The figures cited above in proportion to all Paris = 100	124 55	141 34	94 108	122 70	101 100
	100	100	100	100	100

[1] P. 10.   [2] P. 12.

TABLE III.[1]

ARRONDISSEMENTS.	GOOD AND RATHER GOOD DWELLINGS. %	CONDUCT OF INMATES.			
		Men.		Women.	
		Good and Rather Good. %	Bad and Very Bad. %	Good and Rather Good. %	Bad and Very Bad. %
The 6 arrondissements with the smallest number of good and rather good dwellings . . .	75	70	30	50	50
The 6 arrondissements with the greatest number of good and rather good dwellings . . .	86	81	19	58	42
The 12 arrondissements together	80	74.5	25.5	53	47
The figures cited above in proportion to all Paris = 100 .	{ 94 / 107	94 / 109	118 / 71	96 / 109	106 / 91
	100	100	100	100	100

Although the division according to good and bad conduct is somewhat arbitrary, and although it is impossible to separate the effect of bad housing from other influences operative at the same time, yet these figures say plainly : there is a relationship between housing and conduct. It is evident that there is a reciprocal effect between the condition of the dwelling and the conduct of the inmates, but this fact does not diminish the influence of the dwelling.[2]

Finally, we add some figures upon the influence of furnished rooms as residence, summarizing the results of an inquiry into industries in Paris, made in 1860 and including 400,000 persons : [3]

Paris, 1860.

I. MEN.

OCCUPATIONS.	IN FURNISHED ROOMS.	CONDUCT DOUBTFUL OR BAD.
	%	%
90 occupations	5	3
90 "	14	9
90 "	28	12
270 occupations	20	9

[1] P. 12.   [2] See *Laspeyres*, pp. 86–91.
[3] *Laspeyres, op. cit.*, pp. 19 and 21.

Proportion to all the occupations = 100.

90 occupations	25	13
90 "	70	100
90 "	140	133
270 occupations	100	100

II. WOMEN.

OCCUPATIONS.	IN FURNISHED ROOMS.	CONDUCT DOUBTFUL OR BAD.
	%	%
110 occupations	—	3
60 "	4	6
60 "	14	15
230 occupations	7	9

Proportion to the Average of the 230 occupations = 100.

110 occupations	0	33
60 "	59	68
60 "	206	169
230 occupations	100	100

The evil influence of living in furnished rooms comes out plainly in these figures.

As has already been said at the beginning of these observations as to the influence of the economic life upon the development of social feelings on the part of the proletariat, the egoistic side of the human character is developed by the fact that the individual is dependent, that he lives in a subordinate position, and that he feels himself poor and deprived of everything. However, in so far as the proletarian sells his labor he is guaranteed against famine, however miserable his condition, and conscious of the utility of his rôle in society, he feels himself, notwithstanding his poverty, a man who, except for his employer, is independent of all men. But if work is not to be found, or if the proletarian, sick and infirm, is not able to work, it goes without saying that the resulting unemployment is very demoralizing. The lack of steady work, the horrors of the penury into which he and his fall, and the long train of evils which result from both, kill the social feelings in a man, for, as we have seen above, these feelings depend upon reciprocity. Let one familiarize himself with the thought of the condition of the man who lives in the greatest poverty, *i.e.* the man who is abandoned by all, and he will understand how egoistic must be the feelings of such.

From the position in which the proletarians find themselves it follows that, towards each other, it is rather the altruistic than the egoistic feelings that develop; living less isolated than the bourgeois, they see the misfortune that strikes their neighbor, and have felt the same themselves, and above all, their economic interests are not opposed. Forced idleness — at present chronic, and acute in times of panic — modifies these conditions at times; it makes competitors of the workers, who take the bread out of each other's mouths.[1]

The proletarian is never sure of his existence: like the sword of Damocles unemployment is constantly hanging over his head. Upon this subject Engels says:

"But far more demoralizing than his poverty in its influence upon the English working man is the insecurity of his position, the necessity of living upon wages from hand to mouth, that in short which makes a proletarian of him. The smaller peasants in Germany are usually poor, and often suffer want, but they are less at the mercy of accident, they have at least something secure. The proletarian, who has nothing but his two hands, who consumes today what he earned yesterday, who is subject to every chance, and has not the slightest guarantee for being able to earn the barest necessities of life, whom every crisis, every whim of his employer may deprive of bread, this proletarian is placed in the most revolting, inhuman position conceivable for a human being." [2]

This uncertainty of existence is one of the reasons which explain why, in relatively prosperous times the workingman often spends his wages as soon as he receives them, for he knows that the economies possible to him are so small that he could never be saved from misery in case of unemployment.

Finally we must speak of ignorance and lack of training on the part of the proletariat, as a factor of criminality. As we know, this question of education is one of those which are most debated in criminal sociology. Certain authors have prophesied that each new school would make a prison superfluous, while on the other hand it has been claimed that ignorance and the lack of civilization have nothing to do with the etiology of crime, but that on the contrary knowledge and civilization are even factors of crime. Although these extreme

[1] See *Engels*, "Condition of the Working Class in England", pp. **76** *ff*.
[2] "Condition of the Working Class in England", p. 116.

opinions are hardly ever expressed nowadays, the ideas upon the point in question still differ widely.[1]

In my opinion, no really decisive arguments have ever been adduced for the opinion that the intellectual condition of men has no influence upon criminality. In general the reasoning is as follows: ignorance is decreasing; crime on the contrary increases; ignorance cannot therefore be a factor. Such a line of argument is very superficial, for ignorance is surely not the only cause of crime. Its influence may therefore be neutralized by other factors. And further, from the point of view of statistics it is not permissible to use the indirect method when the direct method is practicable. In most criminal and prison statistics the percentage of the illiterate among the criminals is given, and we have only to put beside these figures those for the illiterate among the non-criminal population to be convinced of the existence or absence of the connection in dispute.

We shall begin, then, by giving the figures that we know.

United States, 1890.[2]

	To 82,329 Prisoners there were		To 100 of the Population over Age of 10 Years.
	Absolute Number.	%	
Illiterate	19,631	23.83	13.3

Austria, 1881–1899.[3]

Years.	To 100 Persons Convicted of Crimes.		
	Unable to Read or Write.	Able to Read and Write	Having a Higher Education.
1881–1885	46.2	53.5	0.2
1886–1890	41.0	58.7	0.3
1891–1895	37.5	62.2	0.2
1896	33.0	60.3	0.7
1897	34.9	64.4	0.7
1898	33.2	66.1	0.7
1899	33.0	66.2	0.8

[1] For the different opinions see *Dr. L. DelBaere,* "De invloed van opvoeding en onderwijs op de criminaliteit", pp. 23 *ff.,* and *Földes,* "Einige Ergebnisse der neueren Kriminalstatistik", pp. 552–559 ("Zeitschr. f. d. ges. Strw." XI).

[2] The figures for prisoners are from *Drähms,* "The Criminal", p. 74; those in the last column from "The Statesman's Year-Book", 1902, p. 1203.

[3] From "Die Ergebnisse der Strafrechtspflege in den im Reichsrate vertretenen Königreichen und Ländern im Jahre 1899", p. xlviii.

England and Wales, 1894–1900.[1]

YEARS	PRISONERS FOUND GUILTY.																PERCENTAGE OF PERSONS WISHING TO MARRY WHO WERE UNABLE TO SIGN THEIR NAMES.	
	Unable to Read or Write.				Able to Read, or to Read Poorly and Write.				Able to Read and Write Well.				Having a Higher Education.					
	Men.		Women.		Men.		Women.		Men.		Women.		Men.		Women.		Men.	Women.
	Absolute Number.	%	Absolute Number.	%	Absolute Number.	%	Absolute Number.	%	Absolute Number.	%	Absolute Number.	%	Absolute Number.	%	Absolute Number.	%		
1893	—	—	—	—	—	—	—	—	—	—	—	—	—	—	—	—	5.0	5.7
1894	20,760	18.4	11,457	27.4	86,639	76.6	29,620	70.7	5,554	4.9	797	1.9	102	0.1	3	0.0	0.0	—
1895	18,840	18.2	11,143	27.8	80,409	77.9	28,511	71.2	3,879	3.8	386	1.0	89	0.1	2	0.0	0.0	—
1896	19,377	18.1	11,844	28.5	85,199	79.2	29,261	70.6	2,806	2.6	307	0.7	52	0.1	2	0.0	0.0	—
1897	18,588	17.4	11,783	27.8	84,777	79.7	30,290	71.4	2,980	2.8	344	0.8	68	0.1	4	0.0	0.0	—
1898	18,591	16.6	12,092	26.8	86,675	77.3	32,350	71.6	6,680	6.0	726	1.6	158	0.1	7	0.0	0.0	—
1899	17,703	16.3	11,483	25.3	84,854	78.4	35,114	73.0	5,658	5.2	740	1.6	84	0.1	6	0.0	0.0	—
1900	16,583	16.6	11,519	25.3	77,967	77.8	33,169	73.5	5,460	5.5	420	0.9	81	0.1	5	0.6	2.9	3.4

[1] Taken from the "Judicial Statistics of England and Wales", Part I, Criminal Statistics, 1894–1900. The last two columns are taken from "The Statesman's Year-Book", 1892, p. 39.

The following table gives the figures for the different crimes:

Austria, 1899.[1]

CRIMES.	To 100 Persons Convicted.			
	Illiterate.	Able to Read.	Able to Read and Write.	Higher Education.
Arson	44.2	2.6	53.2	0.0
Libel	41.7	0.8	57.1	0.4
Assault	40.5	1.4	58.0	0.1
Infanticide	39.5	2.6	57.9	0.0
Homicide	39.3	3.1	57.4	0.2
Robbery	35.0	1.6	63.4	0.0
Theft	32.6	1.2	65.7	0.5
All crimes	31.7	1.3	66.2	0.8
Fraud	30.8	1.3	66.2	2.7
Extortion	27.3	1.5	70.4	0.8
Malicious mischief . . .	21.6	1.1	77.3	0.0
Threats	21.0	1.7	76.9	0.4
Leze majesty	19.7	1.6	76.2	2.5
Rape, etc.	17.2	1.7	79.3	1.8
Criminal breach of trust .	6.0	0.2	86.4	7.4

Belgium, 1899–1901.

YEARS.	Persons Convicted.				
	Illiterate.	Able to Read or Write Imperfectly.	Able to Read and Write.	Having a Higher Education.	Total.
1899	588	1389	424	144	2545
1900	626	1444	521	176	2767
1901	619	1581	604	218	3022
1899–1901	1833	4414	1549	538	8334
%	22.—	53.—	18.6	6.4	100.0

According to the census of 1900, 18% of the total male population over 15 years old were completely illiterate.[2]

In 1907 1.32% of the men and 1.75% of the women out of the total population could not sign their names.[3]

[1] Figured from the table F. A II of the "Ergebnisse der Strafrechtspflege in den im Reichsrate vertretenen Königreichen und Ländern", 1899. The number of illiterates in the total population 16 and over, was about 24%.
[2] Taken from Jacquart, op. cit., p. 104.
[3] "Statesman's Year Book", 1910, p. 31.

France, 1882–1898.[1]

Years	Illiterate.		Able to Read.		Able to Read and Write.		Able to Read, Write and Cipher.		Having a Complete Primary Education.		Having an Education Higher than Primary.		Number of Persons to the 100, who could not sign their Names when they Married.	
	Men.	Women.	Men.	Women.	Men.	Women.	Men.	Women.	Men.	Women.	Men.	Women.	Men.	Women.
1882	27.60	38.04	12.62	15.41	30.56	32.36	21.17	18.01	6.24	0.87	1.81	0.31	14.4	22.6
1883	30.08	36.11	11.91	16.78	30.48	30.60	19.00	15.28	6.60	0.87	1.93	0.36	14.2	22.4
1884	27.54	42.61	10.14	15.02	31.71	30.57	21.67	9.93	5.72	1.39	2.18	0.46	13.6	22.2
1885	28.44	40.25	10.19	16.15	30.02	33.53	23.55	9.17	5.33	0.69	2.47	0.21	12.7	20.2
1886	26.63	39.93	11.20	14.52	31.19	36.64	22.81	8.06	5.63	0.85	2.54	—[2]	11.6	18.7
1887	26.51	37.49	12.49	14.31	33.89	38.90	21.04	8.88	4.05	0.92	2.02	—	10.7	17.0
1888	24.90	32.29	14.05	12.92	32.50	42.43	22.50	10.77	4.18	1.59	2.17	—	10.6	16.2
1889	22.50	35.13	14.18	27.22	30.06	27.78	24.99	7.70	5.80	2.17	2.47	—	9.8	15.2
1890	20.12	34.94	14.19	26.34	30.76	29.71	25.97	6.47	6.34	2.54	2.52	—	8.8	13.6
1891	20.05	33.32	12.79	22.44	31.14	33.39	26.52	8.37	6.57	2.06	2.93	0.42	8.4	12.6
1892	20.38	33.80	13.24	24.89	28.29	30.60	28.30	7.34	6.33	2.64	3.46	0.73	8.1	12.1
1893	22.08	29.78	11.19	24.75	28.03	32.75	27.33	9.22	7.51	2.82	3.86	0.68	—	—
1894	20.89	31.14	13.15	22.57	27.64	35.86	27.84	7.42	6.70	2.47	3.78	0.54	6.8	10.4
1895	20.50	30.43	13.80	18.82	26.66	38.39	30.15	9.80	6.41	2.32	2.48	0.24	—	—
1896	20.91	28.58	11.97	17.09	31.00	38.70	23.78	12.04	10.40	3.22	1.94	0.37	—	—
1897	21.09	28.57	10.59	15.67	27.77	40.48	30.40	12.10	8.15	2.48	2.00	0.69	—	—
1898	23.70	31.65	9.11	8.70	31.05	46.67	27.77	8.69	6.81	3.65	1.56	0.69	4.5	7.2

[1] The last two columns are taken from "l'Annuaire Statistique de la France" xvi ff.; the others from the "Statistique Pénitentiaire," 1882–1898.

[2] From 1886 to 1891 women and men are reported together under this heading.

Scotland.[1]

| | PRISONERS. | | | |
| | Men. | | Women. | |
	Absolute Numbers.	%	Absolute Numbers.	%
Illiterate	3,807	12.0	2,635	20.5
Able to read and write .	27,849	87.9	10,245	79.5
With a higher education	46	0.1	1	0.0
Total	31,702	100.0	12,881	100.0

France, 1896–1900.[2]

CRIMES.	PERCENTAGE OF ACCUSED PERSONS COMPLETELY ILLITERATE.	CRIMES.	PERCENTAGE OF ACCUSED PERSONS COMPLETELY ILLITERATE.
Arson	26	All crimes	14
Infanticide	21	Aggravated theft . . .	12
Poisoning	20	Parricide	10
Rape and indecent assault upon children	20	Assaults upon parents, etc.	10
		Fraudulent bankruptcy .	10
Serious assaults . . .	16	Highway robbery . . .	8
Murder	16	Counterfeiting	7
Homicide	15	Forgery, etc.	2
Rape, etc. upon adults . .	14	Breach of trust	2

Ireland, 1905.

| | PRISONERS. | | | | | |
| | Men. | | Women. | | Total. | |
	Absolute Numbers.	%	Absolute Numbers.	%	Absolute Numbers.	%
Illiterate	4,321	22.5	3,264	32.5	7,585	25.9
Able to read, or read and write imperfectly . . .	3,804	19.8	1,983	19.8	5,787	19.8
Able to read and write well	11,003	57.2	4,757	47.4	15,760	53.9
With a higher education .	93	0.5	32	0.3	125	0.4
Unknown	2	0.0	—	—	2	0.0
Total	19,223	100.0	10,036	100.0	29,259	100.0

[1] After Table XXIV of the "Report of the Judicial Statistics of Scotland for the Year 1910."

[2] "Rapport sur l'administration de la justice criminelle de 1881 à 1900."

According to the census of 1901 the percentage of illiterates was 12.2 for the men, 13.1 for the women, and 12.7 for the total population 12 years old and over.[1]

Italy, 1881–1889.[2]

YEARS.	CORRECTIONAL TRIBUNALS.				ASSIZES.			To 100 MARRIED THERE WERE THE FOLLOWING WHO WERE ILLITERATE.	
	To 100 Arraigned there were				To 100 Convicted there were				
	Illiterate.	Able to Read.	Able to Read and Write.	Having a Higher Education.	Illiterate.	Able to Read and Write.	Having a Higher Education.	Men and Women.	Men.[3]
1881	68.38	1.74	27.38	2.50	63.40	34.87	1.73	59.07	48.24
1882	67.93	1.61	27.59	2.87	59.05	38.11	2.84	57.43	46.68
1883	66.45	1.82	28.74	2.99	57.64	40.00	2.36	56.67	45.79
1884	64.61	1.71	30.10	3.58	58.99	38.76	2.25	55.81	44.97
1885	60.93	1.80	32.90	4.37	61.24	36.75	2.01	54.92	44.28
1886	61.34	2.20	33.15	3.31	59.66	38.25	2.09	53.31	43.19
1887	59.25	—	37.07	3.68	59.34	37.04	3.62	52.83	42.83
1888	61.48	—	34.51	4.01	69.14	31.99	3.87	52.08	42.27
1889	60.98	—	35.31	3.71	63.75	33.14	3.11	50.83	41.21

The following figures shed light upon the intellectual condition of those accused of certain important classes of crime:

Italy, 1889 (Assizes).[4]

CRIMES.	To the 100 Accused of Each Crime there were		
	Illiterate or Nearly So.	Able to Read and Write.	Having a Higher Education.
Infanticide	92.9	7.1	0.0
Perjury	86.8	11.3	1.9
Highway robbery	75.5	24.2	0.3
Homicide	72.5	26.5	1.0
Serious assaults	68.8	30.6	0.6
Rebellion, etc.	65.9	34.1	0.0
All crimes	63.8	33.1	3.1
Rape	63.6	32.7	3.7
Aggravated theft	59.7	38.4	1.9
Counterfeiting etc.	50.9	46.9	2.2
Offenses against public decency etc.	47.6	38.1	14.3
Sexual crimes against nature	43.8	45.8	10.4
Forgery	10.4	36.2	26.4

[1] "Judicial Statistics, Ireland," 1905, I, "Criminal Statistics," p. 24.
[2] The last two columns are taken from the "Annuario Statistico Italiano", 1900, p. 214; the others from the "Statistica giudiziaria penale", 1881 to 1889.
[3] Men playing a larger part in crime than women, I have thought it well to give the figures for illiterate men also.
[4] Figured from Table XXVIII of the "Statistica giudiziaria penale" 1889.

New York State, 1881–1897.[1]

| YEARS. | To 100 PERSONS ENTERING ELMIRA REFORMATORY. | | | |
	Illiterate.	Able only to Read and Write.	Primary Education.	Higher Education.
1881	19.0	59.3	16.5	5.2
1882	18.5	58.7	18.0	4.8
1883	19.3	57.5	18.6	4.6
1884	19.3	56.1	20.2	4.4
1885	18.3	55.7	21.9	4.1
1886	19.9	53.2	23.0	3.9
1888	19.8	50.1	26.2	3.9
1889	19.5	49.9	26.9	3.7
1890	19.1	50.8	26.9	3.2
1891	18.7	48.6	29.4	3.3
1892	19.3	48.8	28.6	3.3
1893	19.0	45.6	31.8	3.6
1894	18.8	43.8	33.8	3.6
1896	18.3	41.3	37.0	3.4
1897	18.3	43.3	35.2	3.2

Netherlands, 1865–1900.[2]

| YEARS. | UNABLE TO READ OR WRITE. | | YEARS. | UNABLE TO READ OR WRITE. | |
	Convicts at Time of Incarceration. %	Militia-men. %		Convicts at Time of Incarceration. %	Militia-men. %
1865	38	18.2	1894	20	5.0
1870	30	16.3	1895	20	5.4
1875	25	12.3	1896	20	4.7
1880	25	11.5	1897	19	4.0
1885	22	10.5	1898	19	3.6
1890	24	7.2	1899	18	2.8
1892	25	5.4	1900	16	2.3
1893	22	5.4			

[1] From the "Year-Book of the New York State Reformatory", for the years in question. In "The Dangerous Classes of New York" (p. 32), *Brace* mentions that in 1870 about 31% of the adult criminals in the State of New York were illiterate, while of the adult non-criminals of the population only 6.08% were illiterate.

[2] Taken from the "Jaarcijfers voor het Koninkrijk der Nederlanden. Rijk in Europa", 1901, p. 47.

Netherlands, 1903–1905.[1]

	OUT OF 100 CONVICTED THERE WERE					
	1903.		1904.		1905.	
	Men.	Women.	Men.	Women.	Men.	Women.
Without elementary instruction .	7.57	24.70	6.61	18.26	6.36	13.33
With elementary instruction . .	91.43	74.71	92.20	80.62	92.50	85.34
" secondary education . . .	0.74	0.33	0.84	0.22	0.80	0.47
" higher education	0.07	0.00	0.12	0.00	0.11	0.00
Unknown	0.15	0.26	0.23	0.90	0.23	0.86
Total	100.00	100.00	100.00	100.00	100.00	100.00

The following figures give an estimate with regard to some specified crimes : [2]

Netherlands, 1901.

CRIMES.	To 100 CONVICTS UNABLE TO READ OR WRITE.	CRIMES.	To 100 CONVICTS UNABLE TO READ OR WRITE.
Marauding	16.6	Defamation and kindred offenses	6.9
Vagrancy	10.0		
Simple theft	9.9	Offenses against public decency	6.5
Malicious mischief, etc.	9.4		
Aggravated theft . .	9.1	Embezzlement	5.8
All crimes	8.6	Rebellion	5.7
Assaults	7.9	Rape and other sexual crimes	4.3
Domiciliary trespass .	7.5	Obtaining money under false pretenses	1.7
Receiving stolen goods	7.4		

Prussia, 1894–1897.[3]

	OUT OF 18,049 RECIDIVISTS IN PRUSSIAN PRISONS.				TO THE 100 RECRUITS.
	Without Education.	Very Little Education.	Primary Education.	Higher Education.	Without Primary Education.
Number	1,491	8,589	7,782	187	—
Percentage . . .	8.3	47.6	43.1	1.0	0.23

[1] de Roos, op. cit., p. 108.
[2] Figured from Table II of the "Crimineele Statistiek", 1900.
[3] Evert, "Zur Statistik rückfälliger Verbrecher in Preussen" ("Zeitschr. des Kön. Preuss. Stat. Bureaus", XXXIX), p. 197; the last figure from "Stat. Jahrb. f. d. Deutsche Reich", 1896, 1897, and 1898.

Switzerland, 1892–1896.[1]

EDUCATION	MEN.		WOMEN.	
	Number.	%	Number.	%
Illiterate	352	3	82	5
Primary education	8,665	87	1,580	92
Secondary and higher education . .	856	9	45	2
Unknown	109	1	15	1
Total	9,982	100	1,722	100

The figures for those who have had a primary education are divided up as follows : [2]

STATE OF EDUCATION	MEN.		WOMEN.	
	Number.	%	Number.	%
Good	4,394	51	764	48
Mediocre	4,125	47	750	48
Reading only	146	2	66	4
Total	8,665	100	1,580	100

The redactor of the official statistics of Switzerland observes that there are no figures to determine the number of illiterates among the non-criminal population, but the statistics of recruits for the years 1891 to 1895 show that about 19% of the recruits had a higher education.

I am of the opinion that the statistics which I have quoted,[3] including, as they do, millions of criminals, are very significant : the illiterates supply, in general, a great proportion of the criminals, a proportion much greater than that of the illiterates in the general population. (In countries with a relatively small number of illiterates, like England, the Netherlands, and Prussia, for example, the difference is naturally much greater than in a country like Italy where the percentage of illiteracy is great. In Prussia for instance, there are

[1] "Die Ergebnisse der Schweizerischen Kriminalstatistik während der Jahre 1892–1896", p. 38 ("Schweizerische Statistik", Pt. 125).
[2] Ibid.
[3] [NOTE TO THE AMERICAN EDITION: Upon the Balkan states see Wadler, op. cit., pp. 176 ff.]

thirty-six times as many illiterates among the recidivists as among the recruits.)

However, most of the statistics, aside from the figures for illiteracy, give others which show how many persons really educated are to be found among the criminals. And then we note that a very great majority of criminals are ignorant and untrained. In England, for example, there is among male criminals only 1 to 1,000 who knows more than how to read and write well, and among the women not even 1 to 1,000; in Austria there are a little more than 4 to 1,000; and in France a little more than 20 to 1,000 among the men, and between 4 and 5 among the women. The relation between ignorance and criminality cannot, then, be contradicted. But it is impossible to fix exactly the extent of the influence of the one upon the other, or it is difficult to separate ignorance from other factors with which it is ordinarily found, as poverty, for instance.

The ancient idea that crime is only a consequence of ignorance need not be treated of, for morality and intellect are two distinct parts of the psychic life, even though there exists a certain relation between them.

The first reason why ignorance and the lack of general culture must be ranked among the general factors of crime is this: the person who, in our present society, where the great majority of parents care very little for the education of their children, does not go to school, is deprived of the moral ideas (honesty, etc.) which are taught there, and ordinarily passes his time in idleness and vagabondage.

The second reason which makes ignorance a factor of crime, is that generally an ignorant man is, more than others, a man moved by the impulse of the moment, who allows himself to be governed by his passions, and is induced to commit acts which he would not have committed if his intellectual equipment had been different.

In the third place, it is for the following reasons that ignorance and the lack of training fall within the etiology of crime. The mind of the man whose psychic qualities, whether in the domain of the arts, or of the sciences, have been developed, has become less susceptible to evil ideas. His intellectual condition constitutes thus a bridle which can restrain evil thoughts from realizing themselves; for real art and true science strengthen the social instincts. The figures cited above furnish only a slight contribution to this question. There is no doubt that if we had figures showing how many criminals there are any part of whose life is taken up by art or science, we should find the number very small. It could not be objected that the cause of this is in the innate qualities of the criminals; certainly one man is born with greater capacity than another, but everyone is born with some capacities which, if developed, may become a source of happiness; and a happy man, says the proverb, is not wicked.

Finally ignorance is in still another way a factor in crime. Very often the author of a crime conceives and executes it in so clumsy a fashion and with so little chance of success, that we may be certain that he would not have committed it if he had not been an ignorant person, without knowledge of the forces with which he had to do.

When the Italian school is reproached with making their researches upon prisoners only, and not upon criminals and their free equals, the implication is that it is only the stupid and ignorant criminals that are in prison, while the others, the shrewd and tricky, remain at liberty. There is assuredly much truth in this assertion.

The lower proletariat. In the preceding pages I have already spoken of the influence exercised by bad material surroundings upon a man's character; I have pointed out the moral consequences of bad housing conditions, and also that he becomes embittered and malicious through lack of the necessaries of life. All this applies to the proletariat in general, but much more strongly still to those who do not succeed, for any reason, in selling their labor, that is the lower proletariat.

If the dwellings of the working-class are bad, those of the lower proletariat are more pitiable still. There are, through sickness or lack of work, periods of dire poverty in the life of almost every worker — for the lower proletariat these periods are without intermission. Its poverty is chronic. And when the poverty makes itself felt for a long time together, the intellectual faculties become blunted to such a point that there remains of the man only the brute, struggling for existence.

Although the material and intellectual poverty of the lower proletariat is much greater than that of the proletariat, the difference between them is only quantitative. In one connection, however, there is also a qualitative difference, and a very important one, namely that the working-man is a useful being without whom society could not exist. However oppressed he may be, he is a man who has a feeling of self-respect. It is different with the member of the lower proletariat. He is not useful, but a detriment. He produces nothing, and tries to live upon what others make; he is merely tolerated. He who has lived long in poverty loses all feeling of self-respect, and lends himself to anything whatever that will suffice to prolong his existence.

In short, poverty (taken in the sense of absolute want), kills the social sentiments in man, destroys in fact all relations between men. He who is abandoned by all can no longer have any feeling for those who have left him to his fate.

b. *The proportion in which the different classes are guilty of crime.* After having treated of the direct consequences of the present economic system upon the different classes, I shall take up this question, which is an important one for the problem of criminality, before touching upon the indirect consequences.

As I have already observed in Part I, the opinions with regard to this proportion are very divergent. There are authors (Garofalo, for instance) who are of the opinion that the bourgeoisie commits as many crimes, in proportion to its numbers, as the proletariat. On the other hand there are those who maintain that the prisons hold only the poor. That Garofalo's conclusion does not hold good for Italy has been proved by the statistics of Fornasari di Verce and those of Dr. Marro, quoted in Part I of this book. The figures given by Fornasari di Verce have to do with the persons sentenced by the assizes, the correctional tribunals, and the justices of the peace. They show that 56 % of the convicts were indigent, that 31 % had only the strict necessities of life, 10 % were moderately well off, while 2 % were well-to-do or rich; while among the non-criminal population about 40 % were rich or more or less well-to-do, and the other 60 % indigent or having only the necessaries of life. But the figures for non-possessors become much greater if we take only the number of those sentenced by the court of assizes, — the real criminals.

Italy, 1887–1889 (Assizes).[1]

CONDITION.	1887.	1888.	1889.
	%	%	%
Indigent	79.57	79.62	77.58
Having the necessaries	9.39	10.21	13.31
Passably well off	7.35	6.62	6.12
Well-to-do and rich	3.69	3.55	2.98
	100.00	100.00	100.00

The following figures give the economic condition of persons convicted for different crimes:

[1] Taken from "Statistica giudiziaria penale", 1887, 1888, 1889.

Italy, 1889 (Assizes).[1]

CRIMES.	To the 100 Convicted of the Crimes Given there were:			
	Indigent.	Having the necessaries.	Passably well off.	Well-to-do or rich
Infanticide	88.1	7.1	4.8	0.0
Theft of every kind . . .	81.5	13.4	3.3	1.7
Counterfeiting, etc. . . .	80.3	10.4	7.7	1.6
Rebellion, cruelty, etc. . .	79.5	11.4	0.0	9.1
Homicide of every degree .	79.0	10.8	6.8	3.4
Serious assaults	78.7	12.4	7.4	1.5
Highway robbery	77.8	17.5	4.0	0.7
Rape and other sexual offenses	77.3	14.8	5.6	2.3
Extortion	74.7	13.1	7.8	4.4
Forgery	47.5	24.7	11.1	16.7

Italy not being a rich country, it is evident that the headings "passably well-off" and "well-to-do or rich" have been given a liberal interpretation, otherwise they would never include almost 40 % of the population. But even taking account of this fact, these figures show that the indigent, that is, the lower proletariat, and the proletariat without work, form a much higher proportion of the criminal class than of the population as a whole.

Other figures confirming these conclusions for Italy have been produced by Dr. Colajanni (see Part I of this work). Further than these, statistics concerning the financial condition of convicts are not numerous so far as I know. Here are those that are known to me:

[1] Figured from Table XXVIII of the "Statistica giudiziaria penale", 1889.

Austria, 1881–1899.[1]

YEARS.	CONDITION (%).		
	Without Money.	With a Little Money.	Well-to-do.
1881–1885	89.1	10.4	0.3
1886–1890	90.0	9.4	0.4
1891–1895	89.6	9.9	0.4
1896	86.7	13.0	0.3
1897	86.0	13.5	0.5
1898	85.9	13.7	0.4
1899	86.7	13.0	0.3

The following figures give us the proportions of the different crimes :

Austria, 1899.[2]

CRIMES.	THERE WERE TO THE 100 CONVICTS GUILTY OF THE CRIMES MENTIONED:					
	Without Fortune.[3]		Little Fortune.		Well-to-do.	
	Men.	Women.	Men.	Women.	Men.	Women.
Robbery	96.6	100.00	3.4	0.0	0.0	0.0
Theft	92.0	94.7	7.8	5.3	0.2	0.0
Rape, etc. . . .	91.2	100.0	8.6	0.0	0.2	0.0
Leze majesty, etc. .	90.1	93.1	9.6	6.9	0.3	0.0
Threats	90.0	81.5	9.9	18.5	0.1	0.0
Rebellion, etc. . .	87.3	74.9	12.4	24.8	0.3	0.3
Crimes in general .	86.4	88.4	13.2	11.4	0.4	0.2
Extortion . . .	86.2	80.0	13.5	20.0	0.3	0.0
Serious assaults . .	79.0	70.2	30.6	29.8	0.4	0.0
Fraud	74.8	75.1	23.6	24.3	1.6	0.6
Murder, homicide .	73.0	87.2	26.7	12.8	0.3	0.0
Infanticide, abortion	0.0	90.8	0.0	9.2	0.0	0.0

I have not been able to procure the figures showing the financial condition of the Austrian population. But it may be considered as certain that there are more well-to-do persons in Austria than about 3 % of the population, and also that there are more persons with a little money than the percentage of criminals shown under that

[1] From "Die Ergebnisse der Strafrechtspflege in den im Reichsrate vertretenen Königreichen und Ländern im Jahre 1899", p. xlviii.

[2] [Figured from Table F. a. II in "Die Ergebnisse der Strafrechtspflege in den im Reichsrate vertretenen Königreichen und Ländern im Jahre 1899."

[3] ["Fortune" here has not exactly the connotation of our English word, but as "money" and "property" would be equally inexact it seems better to keep the author's term. TRANSL.]

heading. Therefore, as in Italy, the poor there are more guilty of crime than the well-to-do (and much more so of certain crimes). It is interesting to note that well-to-do women are not guilty at all of most crimes.[1]

Prussia, 1894–1897.[2]

AMONG RECIDIVISTS WERE FOUND															
With incomes of												Indigent.			
Less than 900 marks.				900 to 2,000 marks.				2,000 to 5,000 marks.							
Men.		Women.		Men.		Women.		Men.		Women.		Men.		Women.	
Number.	%	Number.	%	Number.	%	Number.	%	Number.	%	Number.	%	Number.	%	Number.	%
13,931	90	2,424	96.5	1,424	9.2	66	2.6	46	0.3	2	0.1	74	0.5	18	0.8

There were no rich persons then among the recidivists; no one with an income of more than 5,000 marks. On the other hand, those of very limited income are exceedingly numerous, especially among the women. It is a pity that the first group was not further subdivided, for "less than 900 marks" leaves the group still very large.

The following figures give a picture of the financial situation of the Swiss criminals.

Switzerland, 1892–1896.[3]

THERE WERE PRISONERS:	Number.	%
With fortune	589	5.0
With expectations	1,140	9.7
With neither	9,569	81.8
Condition unknown	406	3.5
	11,704	100
Having a savings-bank book	202	1.7
Without " " "	9,608	82.1
Unknown	1,894	16.1
	11,704	100

[1] [NOTE TO THE AMERICAN EDITION : Upon Austria *cf. Herz, op. cit.* pp. 8 *ff.*]
[2] Figured from the table on p. 199 of Evert's "Zur Statistik rückfälliger Verbrecher in Preussen."
[3] From "Die Ergebnisse der Schweizerischen Krimmalstatistik während der Jahre 1892–1896", p. 37.

All the statistics cited [1] show then that the poor supply a very great proportion of the convicts, in every case a greater proportion than they bear to the population in general, and the well-to-do form only a small part.

There are still other ways of inquiring what part the different classes take in criminality. One consists in an examination of the statistics of the intellectual development of the convicts, for the illiterate and those who have received only a primary education belong, almost without exception, to the classes without fortune. These statistics have already been given, and they confirm entirely the conclusions to be drawn from the figures for the financial condition of the convicts.

The third way of solving the problem is by a study of the statistics of the occupations of those convicted. Here, however, great difficulties present themselves. In the first place not all the criminal statistics make the distinction between the employer and the workman in such and such an occupation. And it is just this information that we need. In the second place we need beside statistics for the occupation of the criminals, others showing the occupations of the population in general, and the two classified in the same way. Even in this case the picture given by these statistics will not be exact, for there are among the employers many persons who are not really independent (workers at home, etc.), or persons who, while being employers, are, as far as their plane of living is concerned, only the equal of the proletarian, and not of the bourgeois.

Upon this question we have the following figures:

[1] Concerning Hungary *Prof. Földes* says (without giving the year) that 92 % of the crimes are committed by persons without fortune, while these represent only 85% of the population in general ("Einige Ergebnisse der neueren Kriminalstatistik", Zeitschr. f. d. ges. Strw., XI, p. 545).
[NOTE TO THE AMERICAN EDITION: Upon the Balkan States *cf. Wadler*, *op. cit.*, pp. 164 *ff.*]

Germany, 1894-1896.[1]

Groups of Occupations.	To 10,000 Persons Over 12 Years of Age in Each Group of Occupations there were:															
	Crimes in General.	Theft.	Aggravated Theft.	Embezzlement.	Fraud.	Rape, etc.	Incest.	Insult.	Violence and Threats against Public Functionaries.	Domiciliary Trespass.	Perjury.	Serious Assaults.	Homicides.	Malicious Mischief.	Arson.	Infanticide.
I. Agriculture:																
a. Independent	75.1	7.1	0.2	1.5	1.7	0.21	0.10	19.1	1.5	2.9	0.22	14.1	0.02	2.3	0.08	0.03
b. Workers	142.1	28.9	3.1	4.8	6.0	1.67	0.18	9.8	3.1	6.8	0.31	36.4	0.05	6.5	0.36	0.37
II. Manufacturing:																
a. Independent	129.9	7.1	0.5	5.1	5.4	1.20	0.17	27.8	3.3	5.3	0.32	17.5	0.02	3.2	0.09	0.05
b. Workers	234.5	32.7	5.8	10.2	10.2	2.98	0.20	19.4	13.1	13.3	0.32	57.5	0.06	12.0	0.19	0.14
III. Commerce and transportation:																
a. Independent	275.5	10.4	0.7	8.8	16.4	1.35	0.11	49.4	5.9	7.4	0.59	21.8	0.04	3.4	0.10	0.01
b. Workers	222.6	35.2	6.7	22.0	18.3	2.22	0.09	20.8	10.3	8.8	0.32	26.3	0.05	6.1	0.06	0.05
IV. Domestics	52.8	27.1[2]	2.0[2]	3.1[2]	4.0[2]	0.06	0.15	2.4	0.4	0.8	0.20	1.4	0.01	0.6	0.12	0.31
V. Public service and lib. profess.	79.3	5.9	1.2	4.8	5.6	1.69	0.06	20.0	2.0	2.2	0.14	6.6	0.01	1.6	0.02	0.00
VI. Population over 12	120.1	19.2	2.5	5.2	5.4	1.17	0.13	14.7	4.5	5.5	0.22	22.3	0.03	4.6	0.13	0.09

[1] Taken from Prinzing, "Soziale Faktoren Kriminalität" (Zeitschr. f.d. ger. Strafsw. XXII). The figures for criminality are the average figures for the years 1894-1896. The figures for the occupations are those of the census of occupations of June 14, 1895. [2] Servants only.

Germany, 1896.[1]

Groups of Occupations.	To 100,000 Persons Over 12 Years of Age and having Occupation there were to Each Group:															
	Crimes in General.	Theft.	Aggravated Theft.	Embezzlement.	Robbery.	Extortion.	Fraud.	Forgery.	Rape upon Children, etc.	Insult.	Assaults.	Serious Assaults.	Violence and Threats against Public Functionaries.	Domiciliary Trespass.	Perjury.	Homicide.
Agriculture	1,208.7	238.1	26.2	35.8	1.2	1.1	54.1	9.0	12.1	127.2	84.1	299.8	24.6	55.0	2.8	0.42
Manufacturing	2,144.3	304.3	58.4	86.6	2.3	2.6	97.9	19.0	26.3	225.3	141.8	496.1	105.3	120.0	3.2	0.51
Commerce and transportation .	2,566.2	276.9	40.1	159.3	1.2	6.3	154.5	50.5	19.5	353.4	126.3	256.8	84.8	80.1	4.0	0.64
Workman and day-laborers[2]	10,402.6	2,622.7	439.3	514.7	20.8	15.3	459.7	88.8	107.8	829.8	669.5	1,679.5	664.2	439.5	9.7	1.60
Domestics	530.3	305.7	25.3	29.4	0.23	0.45	46.8	9.2	0.83	24.8	7.4	13.4	4.3	10.0	2.2	0.08
Public service and liberal professions .	798.6	70.7	13.1	48.9	0.63	1.6	65.3	18.7	17.1	193.0	33.2	70.8	19.7	21.4	2.1	0.13
Professors, physicians, employees .	418.6	19.2	1.7	9.9	0.00	0.71	19.8	6.8	12.4	120.0	14.3	25.8	8.6	7.8	0.99	0.14
Persons of income, students, persons supported .	224.5	17.3	0.71	4.3	0.00	0.65	9.2	1.8	4.6	65.7	14.8	30.6	8.3	12.7	0.59	0.06

[1] Taken from "Kriminalstatistik für das Jahr 1896" (Erläuterungen) II, pp. 38, 39.

[2] This category includes the unskilled workmen, as the author of this table says himself, this heading is not very exact, since it includes those who without following a fixed occupation call themselves working-men.

[NOTE TO THE AMERICAN EDITION: The "Kriminalstatistik 1908" gives the statistics of the criminality of the different occupations, figured from the census of occupations of 1907.]

These statistics, probably the best upon the subject, tell the whole story to those who know how to read the figures.   They constitute a proof of the enormous influence of the social factors in the etiology of crime.   It is impossible to maintain that the influence works the other way, that the moral disposition influences the choice of a profession.   Dr. Prinzing rightly says in the article cited : "It is quite impossible that those engaged in the three great groups of occupations, agriculture, manufacturing, and commerce, are persons of different kinds of moral traits.   On the contrary, the supposition that the moral endowment of each group is nearly the same is completely justified by the movements that are continually going on under our own eyes, through which the countryman becomes a city-dweller, and the man who has grown up in the practice of agriculture, a workman or assistant in manufacturing and commerce." [1]

According to the first table the workmen are implicated, in a much greater degree than the independents, in all the crimes except that of

England and Wales, 1894–1900.[2]

OCCUPATIONS.		AMONG THE PRISONERS CONVICTED THERE WERE:							AVERAGE.	
		1894.	1895.	1896.	1897.	1898.	1899.	1900.	Number.	%
Domestics	M.	948	729	832	651	662	667	604	729	0.7
	W.	1,876	1,530	1,417	1,369	1,424	1,986	2,042	1,663	3.9
Workmen, housekeepers, seamstresses	M.	75,539	69,944	72,725	73,264	77,321	75,220	69,168	73,311	68.0
	W.	11,083	10,596	10,574	12,394	14,376	14,960	14,179	12,594	29.2
Factory workers . . .	M.	3,763	2,420	3,212	2,855	3,019	2,590	2,331	2,941	2.7
	W.	3,755	3,127	2,926	2,762	3,086	3,367	3,498	3,217	7.5
Mechanicians and skilled workman	M.	20,702	18,747	19,216	19,179	20,914	20,351	19,726	19,870	18.4
	W.	677	646	1,220	1,342	1,527	1,348	1,480	1,177	2.7
Foremen, inspectors . .	M.	80	75	65	64	60	75	61	68	0.1
	W.	2	3	4	5	2	1	2	2	0.0
Store and office clerks . .	M.	2,869	2,652	2,805	2,506	2,877	2,677	2,550	2,705	2.5
	W.	125	83	77	84	102	161	237	124	0.3
Merchants	M.	4,054	4,045	4,410	3,984	4,352	4,052	3,461	4,056	3.7
	W.	4,127	4,004	4,249	4,087	4,820	4,513	4,179	4,282	9.9
Liberal professions . .	M.	239	231	208	223	194	209	204	215	0.2
	W.	24	23	34	23	33	24	28	27	0.1
Soldiers, sailors and marines		3,620	3,338	3,433	3,227	3,202	3,082	3,327	3,318	3.1
Prostitutes		5,132	5,105	7,411	6,746	6,413	6,092	6,715	6,230	14.5
Without occupation . .	M.	1,369	746	644	550	518	391	320	648	0.6
	W.	15,067	14,910	13,494	13,606	13,361	12,888	12,745	13,725	31.9
	Total { Men								107,861	100.00
	{ Women								43,041	100.00

[1] Pp. 585, 586.

[2] Figured from the "Judicial Statistics, England and Wales, Pt. I Criminal Statistics", 1894–1900.

[NOTE TO THE AMERICAN EDITION : The English Criminal Statistics for 1905 contain a table upon the occupations of prisoners convicted during the years 1896–1905.]

insult (which is explained by the fact that this crime is one of those which are prosecuted only after complaint laid, and that working-men decide to lay complaint much less quickly than the bourgeois). Certain crimes, indeed, are more often committed by the independent merchants than by the workingmen of the same class, but here it is necessary to remember that many of the small merchants are on the same plane of living as the working-men. The liberal professions, on the contrary, show very low figures, a fact which is to be plainly noticed in the second table, where the attention is caught by the very low figures of the group of students and person with incomes. The participation in all crimes by unskilled workmen is very great, even if we allow for the figures' being exaggerated.

I have not been able to procure statistics concerning the occupations of the whole population of England. Nevertheless, it seems to me to be worth while to mention the figures concerning the occupations of the criminals, for, considered by themselves, they show clearly that the classes without means play a very large part in crime. At least 95 % of the men are in this condition, as well as at least 5 % of the women (a part of the merchants must be added in both cases) while of the 31.9 % without occupation it is certain that a large number are also poor.

France, 1898–1900.[1]

GROUPS OF OCCUPATIONS.	NUMBER OF PERSONS ACCUSED TO 100,000 OF EACH GROUP.		
	1898.	1899.	1900.
Agriculture	8	9	8
Manufacturing	20	22	24
Commerce	29	33	27
Domestic service	16	16	13
Liberal professions and public service	15	15	15

Since this table makes no distinction between independents and dependents, it does not advance the matter much, and the only important observation that can be drawn from it is that agriculture and the liberal professions give the lowest figures. A clearer idea is given by the following table :

[1] From the "Rapport au Président de la république française sur l'administration de la justice criminelle de 1881 à 1900", p. xxvi.

France, 1890–1895.[1]

TO THE 100 PRISONERS IN PENITENTIARIES AND HOUSES OF CORRECTION.

OCCUPATIONS.	1890.		1891.		1892.		1893.		1894.		1895.	
	Men.	Women.	Men.	Women.	Men.	Women.	Men.	Women.	Men.	Women.	Men.	Women.
Property owners, persons of income	0.58	1.10	0.62	2.21	0.62	0.99	0.66	1.45	0.66	1.78	0.65	2.07
Liberal professions	2.36	1.03	2.92	1.66	2.64	1.42	2.41	1.90	2.64	1.62	2.50	1.33
Employes	5.00	0.55	5.40	0.34	5.07	0.36	4.81	0.30	5.26	0.62	5.49	1.33
Merchants, manufacturers	3.77	4.47	3.25	4.80	3.49	4.35	3.39	3.81	3.64	4.71	3.19	5.72
Alimentary professions	3.12	1.24	3.41	0.92	3.53	0.85	3.60	1.52	4.31	1.78	4.27	1.82
Workmen in shops and factories	8.39	13.14	8.93	12.03	8.73	12.17	7.86	15.16	9.46	16.08	9.39	15.34
Building and furnishing trades	16.76	0.21[2]	16.09	0.28[2]	17.11	0.49	17.68	0.23	17.51	1.23	17.92	0.66
Agricultural and day laborers	48.31	62.45	48.85	61.02	47.94	63.17	49.52	56.44	45.71	56.03	44.93	54.15
Nomadic occupations	3.99	4.68	3.89	4.63	4.19	4.77	3.79	4.72	3.77	4.79	3.82	4.48
Soldiers and sailors	2.41	—	2.23	—	2.29	—	1.94	—	1.75	—	1.60	—
Vagabonds and mendicants	1.48	4.74[3]	0.82	4.65[3]	0.94	4.77	1.03	5.71	1.27	4.95	1.52	5.14
Individuals in the care of their families	3.83	6.39	—	7.46	3.45	5.66	3.31	8.76	4.02	6.41	4.72	7.96
	100.00	100.00	100.00	100.00	100.00	100.00	100.00	100.00	100.00	100.00	100.00	100.00

[1] From the "Statistique pénitentiaire", 1890–1895.
[2] Furnishing trade only.
[3] Vagrants and prostitutes.

Although there are no statistics of the occupations of the corresponding non-criminal population, the figures are well worth noting. We discover that the unskilled laborers form a large proportion of the prisoners, in every case a larger proportion than they bear to the population in general; and that the merchants and manufacturers form a much smaller part of the prisoners than they do of the population as a whole, for they certainly constitute more than 5.45 %, especially in France, a country where small industries still flourish.

Italy, 1891–1895.[1]

GROUPS OF OCCUPATIONS.	CONVICTS. Annual Average to 100,000 of Each Group of Occupations.
Agriculture	1,009.03
Manufacturing, arts and trades	855.78
Commerce, transport, navigation and fishing	1,677.46
Domestic service	410.96
Employees, liberal professions, capitalists, pensioners .	288.58

These figures show that in Italy also the capitalists and liberal professions furnish a figure for criminality below that of the other groups. The same is true of the following table:

Italy, 1891–1895.[2]

GROUPS OF PROFESSIONS.	CONVICTS. Annual Average to the 100,000 of the Population.	
	Proprietors or Managers.	Dependents.
Agriculture	307.43	1,368.99
Manufacturing, arts and trades	678.56	861.57
Commerce	1,278.11	1,585.03

[1] "Notizie complementari alle statistiche giudiziarie penali degli anni 1890–1895", p. lxi. As the calculations are based upon the census of 1881 the accuracy of the table is not absolute.
[2] *Op. cit.*, p. lxxxii.

The following table is more detailed for certain occupations:

Italy, 1891–1895.[1]

OCCUPATIONS.	CONVICTS.	
	Annual Average to 100,000 of Population.	
	Proprietors or Managers.	Dependents.
	Men.	
Building trade	1,654.52	1,895.18
Manufacturing { textile, mechanical, chemical, alimentary, arts and trades } . . .	837.80	1,443.22
Shoemaking	1,080.95	2.254.63
Meat business	3,925.95	3,900.61
Cafés, etc.	1,542.12	914.68
Sale of food and fuel	1,035.58	2,411.66
Other kinds of commerce	1,649.80	1,383.12
Navigation, fishing	259.11	1,769.94
	Women.	
Manufacturing { mines, building, tobacco, textile, alimentary, arts and trades }	133.70	193.38
Seamstresses, dressmakers, milliners	285.00	138.15
Sale of food and fuel	460.46	511.49
Other kinds of commerce	2,403.88	3,113.34

We have now arrived at the end of our observations upon occupations among criminals. Other statistics are available, but either it is impossible to compare them with statistics of the non-criminal population, or they are without significance for some other reason. At any rate it seems to me that those I have given are enough to show that proportionately the non-possessors are more guilty of crime than the possessors.[2]

The thesis set forth above is confirmed, then, in three different ways.

[1] *Op. cit.*, pp. lxxxiii–lxxxiv.

[2] [NOTE TO THE AMERICAN EDITION: *Cf.* the recent works upon the relation between occupation and criminality: for Germany: *Aschaffenburg, op. cit.* pp. 56 *ff*; *H. Lindenau,* "Beruf und Verbrechen"; *Peterselie, op. cit.,* pp. 106 *ff.*; *Wassermann,* "Beruf, Konfession, und Verbrechen"; *Galle, op. cit.,* pp. 93 *ff.*; *Stöwesand, op. cit.,* pp. 99 *ff.*; for Austria: *Hoegel, op. cit.,* pp. 449 *ff.*; and pp. 134 *ff.*; for the Balkan States; *Wadler, op. cit.,* pp. 137 *ff.*; for the Netherlands: *de Roos, op. cit.,* pp. 132 *ff.*; *Verrijn Stuart, op. cit.* II, pp. 244 *ff.*; for France: *G. Bertrin,* "De la criminalité en France dans les congrégations, le clergé et les principales professions."]

The question still remains to be answered, to what must we attribute the greater criminality among the non-possessors?

As was remarked at the beginning of this section (on the egoistic tendency of the present economic system, and its consequences), there are three questions which present themselves in connection with the etiology of crime; first, what is the origin of the criminal idea? Second, what are the forces in man which prevent this idea from coming to realization? Third, the occasion for committing the crime. For the moment we shall concern ourselves with the second question only; and we shall ask ourselves the question, is the explanation that these forces are weaker with non-possessors than with others? It is very difficult, if not impossible, to give an answer to this question, for it is very complicated. In the first place it is necessary to prove that the environment of the non-possessors arouses thoughts for which that of the possessors offers no place. The circumstances in which the well-to-do live are in general of such a nature that the moral force has no need of offering combat, since the criminal thought does not exist. For example, in economic offenses one of the principal provocatives of criminal ideas is poverty, which is unknown to the bourgeoisie. It follows that nothing definite can be said about the relative force of the moral sentiments in these two groups of the population in counteracting criminal ideas. Other examples could be added, and I am of the opinion that this influence of the environment will be by itself sufficient to explain the difference in the criminality of the two groups.

It is impossible to decide with certainty whether, aside from the above-mentioned influence of the environment, the present economic system and its consequences have a harmful influence upon the social sentiments that is stronger in the case of non-possessors than it is in the case of possessors. It must be considered as certain (and the figures which I shall give farther along also show it) that the circumstances in which children and young people live among the proletariat is a cause of their being much more demoralized than the children of the bourgeoisie. The influences acting upon the adults of the two classes differ so much in nature and intensity that it is impossible to contrast their effects.

It is unnecessary to say that in what has preceded the possessing class has been contrasted with the proletariat alone, and not with the lower proletariat. It goes without saying that the environment in which the latter live makes them the class most destitute of the moral sense in the whole population.

c. Marriage. To form an idea as to whether there is a relation between crime and marriage, and in this case, as to what its nature is, we must have recourse to statistics. Almost all the criminal statistics give information upon the civil status of criminals (England is the sole exception, I believe).

We shall commence with :

Austria, 1881–1899.[1]

STATUS.	YEARS.						
	1881–1885.	1886–1890.	1891–1895.	1896.	1897.	1898.	1899.
Unmarried	56.8	59.9	60.7	62.2	62.9	61.7	61.3
Married	39.9	36.9	36.2	34.7	34.1	35.3	35.3
Widowers and widows . . .	3.2	3.1	3.0	3.1	3.0	3.0	3.3

Here the unmarried are more numerous than the married. It is different, however, in a neighboring country :

Hungary, 1888.[2]

STATUS.	To 100 CONVICTS.			
	Men.		Women.	
	Assizes.	Corr. Tribun.	Assizes.	Corr. Tribun.
Unmarried	42.89	32.99	33.51	18.03
Married	54.66	62.31	53.08	69.29
Widowers and widows	2.36	4.06	13.08	11.46
Divorced	0.09	0.64	0.33	1.22

Here, then, the married persons far outnumber the unmarried. However, neither of these tables has much value, for first, nothing shows that from the total number of the unmarried those who have not yet reached marriageable age has been subtracted, and second, the corresponding figures for the non-criminal population are lacking, so that a comparison of the two is impossible.

[1] "Die Ergebnisse der Strafrechtspflege in den im Reichsrate vertretenen Königreichen und Ländern im Jahre 1899 ", p. lxviii.
[2] *Prinzing*, " Der Einflusz der Ehe auf die Kriminalität des Mannes ", p. 41 ; and " Die Erhöhung der Kriminalität des Weibes durch die Ehe " (" Zeitschrift f. Sozialwissenschaft ", II), p. 437.

In these respects the following figures are better :

Italy, 1891–1895.[1]

STATUS.	ANNUAL AVERAGE NUMBER (OF CRIMINALS) TO 100,000 OF THE POPULATION IN EACH GROUP OVER 14.
Unmarried	978.47
Married	622.27
Widowers and widows	291.84

But as the Hungarian figures have already shown it is necessary to make a division for sexes, for first, women have a much lower figure for criminality than men, and second, the whole population is not equally divided between men and women.

The defects so far noted have been avoided in the following tables :

France, 1881–1900.[2]

STATUS.	To 100,000 OF THE SAME STATE OF LIFE THERE WERE ACCUSED AT THE ASSIZES :			
	Men.		Women.	
	1881–1885.	1896–1900.	1881–1885.	1896–1900.
Unmarried	62	41	8	5
Married	18	12	3	2
Widowers and widows . . .	24	14	5	3

Netherlands, 1899.[3]

STATUS.	MEN.		WOMEN.	
	To 100 Men of Marriageable Age there were :	To 100 Male Convicts of Marriageable Age there were :	To 100 Women of Marriageable Age there were :	To 100 Female Convicts of Marriageable Age there were :
Unmarried	34.8	59.1	36.2	36.7
Married	58.8	36.7	52.4	52.6
Widowers, widows, divorced	6.4	4.2	11.4	10.7

[1] "Notizie complementari alle statistiche giudiziarie penali degli anni 1890–1895", p. lii.

[2] "Rapport au Président de la République française sur l'administration de la justice criminelle de 1881–1900", p. xxiii.

[3] Figured from "Uitkomsten der achste tienjaarlijksche volkstelling", and the "Gerechtelijke Statistiek over 1899."

Switzerland, 1892–1896.[1]

STATUS.	MEN.		WOMEN.	
	To 100 of Population Over 12 Yrs. Old there were:	To 100 Prisoners there were:	To 100 of Population Over 12 Yrs. Old there were:	To 100 Prisoners there were:
Unmarried	49.3	64.0	45.7	48.5
Married.	44.8	26.6	41.9	33.0
Widowers and widows .	5.5	5.7	11.7	11.6
Divorced	0.4	3.7	0.7	6.9

These tables show that the unmarried men (but not the women) are in general more criminal than the married. However it is necessary to be careful as to this point. All these tables fail to connect civil status with age, a fact which reduces their importance almost to nothing, first because the tendency to crime differs much with age; and secondly, because the percentage of married persons is not the same for different ages. It is, therefore, necessary to compare the married and the unmarried at the same age. The German statistics are the only ones which furnish the necessary materials, and the conclusions to be drawn from these are the only ones which give us certain information as to the relation between crime and marriage. These statistics have served as the basis for the two studies of Dr. Prinzing's already quoted from which we take the following tables.

First the relation between marriage and crime among men. But it must first be remarked that married men are acquitted oftener than bachelors, as a consequence of which the unmarried men are made, in the tables, to seem more criminal than they are — as the following table shows:

[1] "Die Ergebnisse der Schweizerischen Kriminalstatistik während der Jahre 1892–1896", p. 21.

Germany, 1886–1890.[1]

Age.	Number Acquitted out of 100 Accused of Each Category of Age and Civil Status.		
	Unmarried.	Married.	Widowers and Divorced.
18–21	15.0	20.7	—
21–25	15.8	18.4	—
25–30	15.9	20.1	16.1
30–40	15.1	22.3	16.0
40–50	13.4	23.7	15.2
50–60	13.4	24.9	18.0
Over 60	14.2	28.1	22.3

Germany, 1888.[2]

Crimes in General.

Age.	Number of Convicts to 100,000 Persons of Each Category.			
	Unmarried.	Married.	Wid. and Div.	Total.
18–21	2,994.5	5,413.0	—	3,009.2
21–25	3,107.0	3,566.3	—	3,163.8
25–30	2,950.9	2,504.7	4,273.7	2,746.7
30–40	2,880.9	1,961.2	3,797.2	2,171.5
40–50	2,205.7	1,487.8	2,626.3	1,599.8
50–60	1,241.9	1,009.8	1,267.8	1,052.5
Over 60	494.6	490.1	342.7	450.5

It appears, then from this table, first, that in general the bachelors commit more crimes than the married men; second, that the contrary is true of the period between 18 and 25; third, that the criminality of married men is very great.

The following figures have to do with some important economic crimes.[3]

[1] *Prinzing,* "Soziale Faktoren, der Kriminalität", pp. 556–557.
[2] "Der Einflusz der Ehe auf die Kriminalität des Mannes", p. 42.
[3] *Op. cit.* p. 117. The figures for criminality are the average figures for the years 1882–1893. They all give the number to 100,000 persons of each category.

Simple Theft.

Age.	Unmarried.	Married.	Widowers, Widows and Divorced.	Total.
18–21	551.7	1,418.3	—	555.3
21–25	427.7	685.9	627.2	457.7
25–30	382.6	412.6	572.1	398.5
30–40	411.9	296.9	550.0	323.0
40–50	365.0	216.2	420.0	237.4
50–60	233.1	151.6	231.1	164.6
Over 60	109.2	84.0	67.2	81.2

It is, then, in the period between 18 and 30 that married persons are more often guilty of theft than the unmarried; after 30 the parts are changed, except that under the last two age-classes the widows, widowers, and divorced persons show high figures.

Embezzlements.[1]

Age.	Unmarried.	Married.	Widows, Widowers and Divorced.	Total.
18–21	123.2	338.7	—	124.4
21–25	131.6	163.6	295.6	135.5
25–30	139.7	109.8	291.6	126.1
30–40	161.8	86.1	279.6	103.4
40–50	128.0	61.1	168.8	71.3
50–60	66.2	37.7	71.3	42.7
Over 60	28.3	16.6	13.9	16.7

In this crime also there is a greater criminality among married persons between 18 and 25 than among the unmarried, and the opposite for the later periods. The situation is entirely different in the case of the crime which follows : [2]

Fraudulent Bankruptcy.

Age.	Unmarried.	Married.	Widows, Widowers and Divorced.	Total.
18–21	0.3	33.9	—	0.3
21–25	3.3	21.3	—	4.5
25–30	3.9	14.8	—	9.8
30–40	4.3	9.9	15.9	9.0
40–50	2.2	6.6	7.2	6.2
50–60	1.1	4.0	4.1	3.7
Over 60	0.4	1.7	1.4	1.5

[1] *Op. cit.*, p. 117.   [2] *Op. cit.*, p. 119.

Here we have a higher degree of criminality among the married persons of all ages.

It is unnecessary to give the figures for all the economic crimes and it will be enough simply to give the general results for the rest. Unmarried persons are guilty of the following crimes more often than married persons: aggravated theft (at all ages); robbery and extortion (except between the ages of 21 and 25); fraud and criminal breach of trust (except between the ages of 21 and 25) forgery (except between 21 and 25, and over 60); and counterfeiting. The following offenses are more often committed by married persons than by unmarried: being accessory to theft, and receiving stolen goods (except between 30 and 40); violation of secrets; usury; and procuration. It must be added that widows, widowers and divorced persons show very high figures for economic offenses.

As to sexual crimes we have the following figures: [1]

| | INCEST. | | | | DEBAUCHING THROUGH ABUSE OF CONFIDENCE. | | | |
AGE.	Unmarried.	Married.	Widows and Divorced.	Total.	Unmarried.	Married.	Widows and Divorced.	Total.
18–21	0.7	—	—	0.7	0.03	—	—	0.03
21–25	0.8	1.4	—	0.9	0.20	0.4	—	0.20
25–30	1.0	0.9	—	1.0	0.30	0.3	—	0.30
30–40	1.0	1.4	22.7	1.7	0.20	1.5	2.3	0.40
40–50	0.9	1.7	26.3	2.5	0.40	0.4	1.2	0.50
50–60	0.8	1.2	12.4	2.1	0.20	0.3	0.7	0.30
Over 60	0.2	0.4	1.9	0.8	—	0.1	0.1	0.10

Consequently, as regards these crimes, the married persons are more often guilty than the unmarried, but the widowers, widows and divorced persons occupy the first rank.

| | RAPE, ETC.[2] | | | |
AGE.	Unmarried.	Married.	Widowers and Divorced.	Total.
21–25	26.3	24.1	—	26.1
25–30	26.2	15.7	—	21.2
30–40	39.7	12.8	61.4	18.6
40–50	44.5	9.9	56.2	14.8
50–60	36.8	8.4	28.3	12.3
60–70	28.3	6.8	18.7	11.1
Over 70	18.7	5.6	10.3	8.6

[1] *Op. cit.*, p. 111. [2] *Op. cit.*, p. 112.

Here the unmarried persons are guilty oftener than those married, and widowers and divorced persons oftenest of all. As for debauch contrary to nature it is the unmarried persons who are the most often guilty.

Here, finally, are figures for the more important remaining crimes:

Age.	Rebellion.[1]			
	Unmarried.	Married.	Widowers, Widows and Divorced.	Total.
18–21	130.5	211.7	—	130.8
21–25	199.0	143.6	—	192.0
25–30	228.2	113.8	258.0	174.2
30–40	262.6	83.1	236.2	119.4
40–50	206.6	55.6	160.4	73.6
50–60	92.0	34.2	59.6	40.8
Over 60	25.2	14.5	11.2	14.3

Age.	Insults.[2]			
	Unmarried.	Married.	Widowers and Divorced.	Total.
18–21	111.1	444.5	—	112.5
21–25	173.3	279.0	448.0	186.7
25–30	222.9	270.6	381.4	249.3
30–40	277.4	316.2	377.3	312.8
40–50	240.7	311.3	317.3	307.3
50–60	158.1	237.7	187.5	229.4
Over 60	66.4	122.9	66.6	103.7

Here the married persons have the highest figures at all ages.

Age.	Assaults.[3]			
	Unmarried.	Married.	Widowers and Divorced.	Total.
18–21	1,084.2	1,778.2	—	1,087.3
21–25	1,132.5	1,051.5	1,344.0	1,124.1
25–30	904.6	692.9	964.7	803.3
30–40	552.6	434.1	602.3	459.7
40–50	262.9	268.1	316.1	269.6
50–60	117.7	161.9	144.6	157.2
Over 60	43.5	68.6	40.9	59.0

[1] *Op. cit.*, p. 109. [2] *Op. cit.*, p. 113. [3] *Op. cit.*, p. 114.

The unmarried show in general higher figures than the married persons (except for the period between 18 and 21).

Age.	Murder and Homicide.[1]			
	Unmarried.	Married.	Widowers and Divorced.	Total.
18–21	2.2	—	—	2.2
21–25	3.1	2.1	—	3.0
25–30	3.1	2.0	—	2.6
30–40	3.3	1.4	13.6	1.9
40–50	1.8	0.9	6.0	1.9
50–60	0.8	0.5	2.1	0.7
Over 60	0.2	0.3	0.2	0.3

Here it is the widowers, widows and divorced persons who are most involved, and then the unmarried.

For some other crimes we shall give only the results. Married persons are more often guilty of the following crimes than the unmarried; domiciliary trespass (except between 25 and 50); perjury (except between 21 and 25, and between 30 and 40) and other offenses against the obligation of taking oath; false accusation; unintentional homicide (except between 25 and 30); offenses against personal liberty (except between 30 and 50); and crimes and misdemeanors committed by public officials.

For the following crimes, on the other hand, the unmarried hold the first rank: offenses against public worship (except between 21 and 25); malicious mischief (except between 18 and 21); and arson. It is to be noted that for nearly all the above the widowers, widows and divorced persons show very high figures.

After an examination of the results found it is impossible to say that the married persons show absolutely a criminality less in degree than that of the unmarried; there is a variation for offenses as well as for ages. Only considered in general, the tendency to crime is less in the case of the married than of the unmarried.

As the following figures prove the connection between crime and marriage is quite different in the case of women. It is necessary, however, to show the following table before giving figures in support of this assertion.

[1] *Op. cit.*, p, 114.

Germany, 1886–1890.[1]

Age.	Number of Acquittals to 100 Accused Persons of Each Age Group.		
	Unmarried.	Married.	Widowed and Divorced.
18–21	15.1	25.6	—
21–25	16.8	24.5	24.1
25–30	16.7	24.2	19.7
30–40	17.3	23.4	19.6
40–50	18.2	24.2	21.7
50–60	18.2	25.8	24.4
Over 60	19.8	27.0	27.7

As in the case of men there are, then, a greater percentage of acquittals among the married than among the unmarried.

Germany, 1882–1893.[2]

Crimes in General.

Age.	To 100,000 Persons of Each Age Group there were Sentenced:		
	Unmarried.	Married.	Widowed and Divorced.
18–21	415.2	602.5	—
21–25	417.5	469.9	1339.3
25–30	440.7	454.5	1149.2
30–40	446.2	500.0	1029.9
40–50	334.7	468.2	709.9
50–60	221.5	299.5	369.2
Over 60	102.2	133.4	111.2

While married women of all ages lead the unmarried in general criminality, the highest figures are shown by the widows and divorcées.

The following tables have to do with the more important crimes, beginning with those affecting property : [3]

[1] *Prinzing*, "Soziale Faktoren der Kriminalität", p. 559.
[2] "Die Erhöhung der Kriminalität des Weibes durch die Ehe", p. 437.
[3] This table and those which follow all belong to the period from 1882 to 1893, and are figured for 100,000 of each category. They are taken from the work cited, pp. 438–444.

Simple Theft.

Age.	Unmarried.	Married.	Widows and Divorcées.	Total.
18–21	210.6	209.3	—	210.6
21–25	177.1	147.8	385.7	169.3
25–30	158.5	132.0	318.5	144.0
30–40	136.6	127.1	265.9	135.1
40–50	92.2	104.0	175.9	111.6
50–60	61.2	64.4	88.6	70.3
Over 60	32.0	31.1	28.0	29.5

The married women show, then, figures a little lower than those of the unmarried women, except between 40 and 60, and the widows and divorcées give the highest figures.

Age.	Embezzlement.				Receiving Stolen Goods.			
	Unmar.	Mar.	Wid. and Div.	Total.	Unmar.	Mar.	Wid. and Div.	Total.
18–21	25.3	35.2	—	25.8	9.2	33.7	—	10.7
21–25	25.9	23.4	92.8	25.4	10.6	26.3	48.2	15.3
25–30	26.0	20.3	80.7	23.2	12.6	23.9	52.4	20.2
30–40	25.3	21.6	63.4	24.2	17.2	32.6	61.3	31.4
40–50	18.6	18.3	40.3	21.1	16.1	36.4	56.4	36.6
50–60	11.0	10.3	17.2	12.2	11.4	22.6	29.6	23.3
Over 60	4.4	4.3	4.6	4.4	4.5	8.8	7.4	7.6

Under the head of "embezzlement" the unmarried women show figures a little higher than those of the married women (except between 18 and 21); in the crime of receiving stolen goods the married women are more guilty than the unmarried; while in both offenses it is the widows and divorcées who lead.

Procuration.

Age.	Unmarried.	Married.	Wid. and Div.	Total.
18–21	0.6	5.2	—	0.9
21–25	2.1	8.2	33.8	3.9
25–30	6.4	10.1	47.5	9.2
30–40	10.9	11.7	47.3	13.2
40–50	7.6	9.7	28.4	11.7
50–60	3.5	4.5	10.4	5.9
Over 60	1.1	1.8	2.5	2.2

Here also the highest figures are found with the widows and divorcées and the lowest with the unmarried women.   In the following economic offenses it is the married women who are oftenest guilty : aggravated theft (except between 18 and 21 and after 60) ; fraudulent bankruptcy ; forgery (except between 25 and 50) ; and violation of secrets.   We must once more note that the widows and divorcées show very high figures.

As to sexual crime we have the following :

Age.	INCEST.			
	Unmarried.	Married.	Widows and Divorcées.	Total.
18–21	2.7	1.4	—	2.6
21–25	2.1	0.6	—	1.7
25–30	2.3	0.2	8.0	1.1
30–40	2.5	0.2	6.2	0.8
40–50	0.6	0.1	1.2	0.3
50–60	0.1	0.1	0.6	0.2
Over 60	0.1	0.02	0.1	0.07

Here the widows and divorcées are at the head and the married women last.   The other sexual crimes give figures for women too small to be of any value for our purpose.

Certain of the crimes which remain show the following figures :

Age.	INSULTS.			
	Unmarried.	Married.	Widows and Divorcées.	Total.
18–21	24.3	88.5	—	27.9
21–25	34.9	85.7	157.1	50.0
25–30	44.2	99.8	137.1	76.7
30–40	57.3	116.8	138.4	108.1
40–50	58.4	121.4	121.7	114.5
50–60	43.6	84.8	77.1	78.5
Over 60	22.4	38.3	26.7	30.2

The highest figures are those for widows and divorcées (except over 50), and the lowest for the unmarried.

Age.	Domiciliary Trespass.			
	Unmarried.	Married.	Widows and Divorcées.	Total.
18–21	5.4	16.9	—	6.0
21–25	6.9	13.3	28.6	8.9
25–30	8.6	15.2	28.2	13.0
30–40	11.1	21.2	32.7	20.1
40–50	10.6	23.9	27.2	22.8
50–60	6.2	15.3	15.9	14.4
Over 60	3.0	6.0	4.2	4.7

The highest figures are for the widows and divorcées, the lowest for the unmarried.

Age.	Assaults.			
	Unmarried.	Married.	Widows and Divorcées.	Total.
18–21	20.4	67.5	—	23.0
21–25	24.9	61.1	96.4	35.7
25–30	29.8	58.7	88.9	48.3
30–40	29.9	61.0	70.2	56.4
40–50	21.3	55.3	46.8	50.4
50–60	13.9	33.9	25.7	29.5
Over 60	7.0	14.2	8.6	10.4

Here the highest figures are those for the married women except between the ages of 21 and 40 when they fall to the widows and divorcées.

Age.	Crimes against the Life of a Child.			
	Unmarried.	Married.	Widows and Divorcées.	Total.
18–21	5.6	4.3	—	5.5
21–25	9.8	1.7	7.1	7.4
25–30	9.3	1.4	16.1	4.5
30–40	5.4	1.1	12.5	2.4
40–50	1.3	0.8	3.4	1.2
50–60	0.5	0.5	0.7	0.6
Over 60	0.1	0.3	0.2	0.2

In this regard the widows and divorcées show the greatest criminality, the married women the lowest.

Finally, we may add the results for some other crimes. The married women are more guilty than the unmarried in the following : rebellion [1] (except between 21 and 40) ; violation of factory laws ; crimes against individual liberty ; and malicious mischief (except between 25 and 40). In the following the unmarried women lead the married : perjury, false accusation, homicide and murder (except for the ages over 50), unintentional homicide (except after 50), and arson. It is to be noted that the widows and divorcées are at the head.

The conclusion to be drawn is that the married woman commits more crimes than the unmarried, but that this does not apply to all crimes nor to all ages.

So much for the figures themselves ; now for their explanation.

It is very difficult, in examining the influence of marriage upon criminality, to separate the moral consequences from other factors. We are mistaken, for example, if we attribute to the moral influence of marriage the fact that married persons are less often guilty of the great majority of economic crimes than the unmarried. The fact that anyone marries is ordinarily an indication that he is in a material situation more or less good. The danger that he will commit an economic offense becomes, then, much less great than when he is in a less comfortable condition. The correctness of this position is clearly shown by the statistics given, according to which married men still young give a higher figure than that furnished by the bachelors. The reason is that proletarians marry while still young. The material cares of these husbands are then much greater than later on when their children have already left home, or are at least earning their own living.[2] If we examine the figures for insults we shall see that married men and women both are more guilty than the unmarried. It would be very erroneous to conclude that marriage increases the tendency to this offense. The explanation is to be found in the fact that when a single dwelling (or barrack rather) is the common habitation of several workmen's families, living conditions easily become a permanent source of disputes. In this case it is not marriage but bad housing conditions which appear as a factor in the etiology of crime. If it were possible to separate these conditions

[1] ["Rebellion" has a wider significance in French than in English, any violence to public officials being so designated. The word is retained, however, for brevity. — Transl.]

[2] *Cf.* F. *Prinzing,* "Ueber frühzeitige Heiraten, deren Vorzüge und Nachteile." See also *Dürkheim,* "Le suicide", pp. 186 *ff.*

or these material consequences of marriage from its moral consequences, the difference between the criminality of the married and the unmarried would not appear very great. Especially is this true if we keep sight of the fact that the bourgeoisie generally marry at a more advanced age than the proletariat. This brings it about that there are more of the bourgeois among the older married people than among the younger; and since, from other causes, the bourgeoisie commit fewer crimes than the proletariat, the influence of marriage seems greater here than it really is.

As for the criminality of women it must be noted that the unmarried women of the bourgeoisie represent a greater proportion of the whole number of unmarried women than the women of this class do of women in general. And since from other causes the criminality of the women of this last class is very small, marriage seems to have a less favorable effect than it really has.

As for the consequences of marriage upon morality, I believe they are the following. In the first place marriage has a tendency to increase the feeling of responsibility, especially if there are children. Then when man and wife understand one another, when they are happy in their union, no one will deny that marriage has a strong moral influence, for, according to the proverb, happy people are not wicked. The proof of this is that married men participate less than bachelors in the crimes of rebellion, assault, homicide, murder, etc., while widowers are more often guilty of them, becoming addicted to alcohol after the death of their wives, or becoming demoralized in other ways. However, it would be more accurate to speak of the moral influence of love than of marriage in the sense of legal monogamy. Happy married couples do not owe their happiness to the legal sanction. Without it their happiness would be as great. On the other hand if the couple is ill-assorted for one reason or another, then marriage has a very demoralizing influence. Legal monogamy comes into play in such cases by rendering difficult the separation of persons who do not understand each other, or of whom one or the other conducts himself badly.

The great power of a man over his wife, as a consequence of his economic preponderance, may equally be a demoralizing cause. It is certain that there will always be abuse of power on the part of a number of those whom social circumstances have clothed with a certain authority. How many women there are who now have to endure the coarseness and bad treatment of their husbands, but would not hesitate to leave them if their economic dependence and the law did not prevent. Holmes, the author of "Pictures and Problems from London Police Courts", who for years saw all the unfortunates who came before these tribunals, says in this connection: "A good number of Englishmen seem to think they have as perfect a right to thrash or kick their wives as the American had to 'lick his nigger.' Yes, and some of these fellows are completely astonished when a magistrate ventures to hold a different opinion. I well remember a great hulking fellow, with a leg-of-mutton fist, being charged with assaulting a policeman. After all the evidence had been given, the magistrate inquired whether the prisoner had been previously charged. 'Yes, your worship, he was here two months ago, charged with assaulting a female.' As the prisoner declared this was false, and indignantly denied that he had ever assaulted a female, the gaoler brought in his book and proved the conviction. The prisoner then looked up in astonishment, and said: 'Oh, why, it was only my own wife!' Only their own wives; but how those wives suffer! Is there any misery equal to theirs, any slavery to compare with theirs? If so, I never heard of it. I have seen thousands of them, and their existence is our shame and degradation." [1]

Further it goes without saying that a marriage entered into for reasons of self-interest is demoralizing.

Although the above consequences of marriage must be mentioned, that our discussion may be as complete as possible, and although they may have a certain importance for the etiology of crime, yet their influence is not very great. There are causes of criminality much more important, which may put those that have been named entirely in the shade.[2]

Before taking up the criminal consequences of the family, I am of the opinion that this is the best place to fix our attention for a moment upon the criminality of women. In treating above of the origin of marriage as it exists today, we have at the same time spoken of the social position of woman.

d. The criminality of women. In order to give an idea of its extent and nature we must begin with some statistics.

[1] P. 40.
[2] NOTE TO THE AMERICAN EDITION: *Cf.* the following recent works upon the relation between marriage and criminality: for Germany: *Aschaffenburg, op. cit.,* pp. 139 *ff.* ; *Pollitz, op. cit.,* pp. 34 *ff.*; for Austria: *Hoegel, op. cit.,* pp. 16 *ff.* ; *Herz, op. cit.,* pp. 127 *ff.*; for the Balkan States: *Wadler, op. cit.,* pp. 128 *ff.*; for Belgium: *Jacquart, op. cit.,* pp. 80 *ff.*; for the Netherlands: *de Roos, op. cit.,* pp. 122 *ff.* See further *N. Muller,* "Biografisch-aetiologisch onderzoek over occidivie, etc."

Germany, 1886–1895.[1]

CRIMES.	To 100,000 Persons Over 12 of the Same Sex, There was an Average Number of Persons Sentenced of:	
	Men.	Women.
Simple theft	352.49	132.25
Aggravated theft	57.95	7.19
Embezzlement	80.97	18.25
Robbery and extortion	2.44	0.10
Receiving stolen goods	28.21	16.33
Fraud	88.06	19.50
Forgery	18.78	3.75
Perjury	6.83	2.31
Threats	46.36	2.65
Procuration	5.21	7.23
Rape, etc.	20.63	0.15
Insults	204.32	69.52
Domiciliary trespass	90.38	12.25
Malicious mischief	80.37	4.85
Arson	2.43	0.54
Violence and threats against officials . . .	77.45	5.90
Minor assaults	118.30	12.71
Serious assaults	256.86	25.99
Murder	0.56	0.13
Homicide	0.75	0.15
Crimes in general	1847.03	380.42

This table shows that women have a general criminality from 4 to 5 times less than that of men. The figure for women exceeds that for men in the case of one crime only, procuration; for the others it is smaller, and for some very small (*e.g.* assaults, assassination, etc). The following table gives an idea still clearer and more detailed.

Germany, 1896.[1]

CRIMES.	Number of Persons Convicted to 100,000 of Same Sex.		Number of Women Convicted to Each 100 Men Convicted.
	Men.	Women.	
Abandonment of children	0.02	0.1	800.0
Abortion	0.4	1.7	437.3
Procuration	6.0	9.2	167.7
Receiving stolen goods (repeated recidivism) .	0.07	0.1	158.3
" " " (simple)	26.5	13.1	53.9

[1] "Kriminalstatistik f. d. Jahr 1896", Erläuterungen, II, p. 33.
[Note to the American Edition: The "Kriminalstatistik für das Jahr

CRIMES.	NUMBER OF PERSONS CONVICTED TO 100,000 OF SAME SEX.		NUMBER OF WOMEN CONVICTED TO EACH 100 MEN CONVICTED.
	Men.	Women.	
Simple theft	274.6	100.8	40.1
Perjury	3.1	1.2	38.7
Insults	223.7	76.5	34.2
Simple theft (repeated recidivism)	51.7	14.4	30.5
Homicide	0.5	0.1	22.0
Arson	2.2	0.5	21.8
Embezzlement	85.6	17.6	20.6
Fraud	101.7	20.4	20.1
Crimes in general	2177.07	388.9	17.9
Extortion	3.0	0.4	14.3
Aggravated theft	45.0	5.6	13.5
Domiciliary trespass	103.8	12.3	11.8
Minor assaults	138.3	15.4	11.1
Aggravated theft (repeated recidivism) . .	14.4	1.2	9.1
Serious assaults	448.4	32.8	7.3
Violence, etc. against officials	88.3	5.6	6.3
Violence and threats	60.7	3.6	5.9
Malicious mischief	93.6	5.4	5.8
Robbery	2.4	0.07	2.9
Crimes against morals upon children . . .	25.3	0.2	0.7

The country upon which we are about to fix our attention is :

England and Wales, 1893–1900.[1]

YEARS.	NUMBER OF WOMEN TO THE 100 PERSONS SENTENCED FOR:	
	Offenses tried on Indictment.	Offenses tried Summarily.
1893	13.07	23.39
1894	12.95	23.50
1895	13.26	23.94
1896	11.75	23.58
1897	12.00	23.99
1898	11.82	23.66
1899	11.70	23.89
1900	11.51	24.67

1903" contains very important data bearing upon the period 1882–1902, with regard to feminine criminality in Germany.]

[1] "Judicial Statistics, England and Wales, Pt. I, Criminal Statistics, 1899", p. 55, with separate calculations made for 1900.

When we examine this table, as well as the one that follows, it must be noted that the women constitute more than half of the population (51.5 % according to the census of 1901).[1]

The following table shows the relative proportion for the more important groups of offenses:

England and Wales, 1893–1894.[2]

CRIMES.	NUMBER OF WOMEN TO 100 PERSONS SENTENCED.	
	1893.	1894.
Abortion and failure to report birth . . .	91	86
Kidnapping and cruelty to children . . .	70	57
Counterfeiting, etc.	18	21
Malicious mischief	15	20
Crimes against property without violence .	19	19
Other crimes	16	16
Crimes of violence against persons . . .	11	13
Robbery and extortion	10	11
Forgery	9	8
Domiciliary trespass, etc.	3	4
Sexual crimes	4	3

These statistics show, then, that in England also the criminality of women is not as great as that of men. However there is great divergence in the crimes taken separately.

[1] "The Statesman's Yearbook, 1902", p. 14.
[2] "Judicial Statistics, England and Wales, Criminal Statistics, 1894," p. 19.

Austria, 1899.[1]

CRIMES.	OF 100 CONVICTED OF EACH CRIME THERE WERE:	
	Men.	Women.
Abandonment of children	7.1	92.8
Abortion	10.7	89.2
Murder	69.6	30.3
Fraud	79.1	20.8
Theft	80.4	19.5
Defamation	80.9	19.0
Arson	85.2	14.7
Crimes in general	86.1	13.9
Rebellion	89.5	10.4
Leze-majesty	91.6	8.3
Criminal breach of trust	93.4	6.5
Crime against religion	94.8	5.1
Robbery	95.1	4.8
Serious assaults	95.8	4.1
Sexual crime	96.7	3.2
Malicious mischief	96.8	3.1
Homicide	97.3	2.6
Blackmail	97.4	2.5

In connection with this table we must note that, according to the census of 1890, 51.6 % of the population over 14 are women.

France, 1881–1900 (Persons accused).[2]

	1881–1885.		1886–1890.		1891–1895.		1896–1900.	
	Average Annual Number.	%	Average Annual Number.	%	Average Annual Number.	%	Average Annual Number.	%
Before the Assizes								
Men	3,767	86	3,589	85	3,389	84	2,900	85
Women	615	14	646	15	631	16	500	15
Before the Correctional Tribunals:								
Men	162,573	86	172,162	86	179,194	86	165,586	86
Women	26,330	14	27,719	14	29,992	14	28,049	14

[1] "Die Ergebnisse der Strafrechtspflege in den im Reichsrate vertretenen Königreichen und Ländern im Jahre 1899", p. xlix.

[2] "Rapport au président de la république française sur l'administration de la justice criminelle de 1881–1900", pp. xix, cxvi.

As the two following tables show, the part which women take in different crimes varies greatly, as in the countries cited above.

France, 1900 (Assizes).[1]

CRIMES.	To 100 ACCUSED THERE WERE:	
	Men.	Women.
Infanticide	5	95
Abortion	12	88
Domestic theft	82	18
Murder	84	16
Fraudulent bankruptcy	84	16
Arson	84	16
Counterfeiting	85	15
Serious assault	86	14
Crimes in general	86	14
Homicide	90	10
Other aggravated thefts	91	9
Parricide	92	8
Forgery	92	8
Concealment or false attribution of parentage	93	7
Rape and indecent assault upon children . .	98	2
Breach of trust	98	2
Theft with violence	98	2

For the correctional tribunals the figures are as follows:

France, 1900 (Correctional Tribunals).[2]

OFFENSES.	To 100 PERSONS ARRAIGNED THERE WERE:	
	Men.	Women.
Concealment of parentage	5	95
Offenses against chastity	29	71
Adultery	50	50
Defamation and insult	75	25
Theft	80	20
Fraud	83	17
Offenses against public decency	85	15
All offenses	87	13
Criminal breach of trust	88	12
Assaults	89	11
Mendicity	89	11
Domiciliary trespass	91	9
Rebellion	92	8
Vagrancy	95	5

[1] Figured from "Compte général de l'administration de la justice criminelle pendant l'année 1900", pp. 30–31.
[2] *Op. cit.*, pp. 54–62, Tab. XXIX.

It is only in some few crimes that women play a larger part than men (infanticide, abortion, concealment of parentage, offenses against chastity — including procuration); in all others they play a smaller part, and in some cases much smaller, than the men.

We turn now to Italy:

Italy, 1894–1895.[1]

YEARS.	NUMBER OF WOMEN CONVICTED.							
	Justices of the Peace.		Correctional Tribunals.		Assizes.		Total.	
	Number.	%	Number.	%	Number.	%	Number.	%
1884	46,683	18.31	—	—	304	6.00	—	—
1885	48,063	17.58	—	—	304	5.91	—	—
1886	51,199	18.23	—	—	297	6.38	—	—
1887	45,598	17.58	4,690	9.30	265	5.11	50,553	16.05
1888	49,125	17.38	4,482	8.56	290	5.81	53,897	15.86
1889	53,690	18.38	4,910	9.08	272	5.68	58,872 [2]	16,78
1890	—	—	—	—	—	—	23,984	18.29
1891							26,182	18.23
1892							25,638	17.21
1893							22,959	16.21
1894							26,274	17.34
1895							28,502	16.96

The following table shows us to what extent the women are guilty of the different crimes:

Italy, 1891–1895.[3]

OFFENSES.	To 100 SENTENCED FOR EACH OFFENSE THERE WERE:	
	Men.	Women.
Infanticide	7.70	92.30
Procuration	19.11	80.89
Abortion	21.65	78.35
Defamation	53.70	46.30
Insults	54.78	45.22
Offenses against morals and order of the family	58.27	41.73
Abandonment of children, abuse of means of correction	62.85	37.15

[1] For the years 1884–1889 taken from the "Statistica giudiziaria penale per l'anno 1889", and for the years following from the "Notizie complementari alle statistiche giudiziarie penali degli anni 1890–95."

[2] The fact that a new penal code went into effect in 1890 makes a noticeable change in the total figures.   [3] *Op. cit.*, p. xxxvii.

Italy — *Continued*.

OFFENSES.	To 100 SENTENCED FOR EACH OFFENSE THERE WERE:	
	Men.	Women.
Simple theft	75.63	24.37
Fraud in commerce and industry	79.46	20.54
Offenses in general	82.81	17.19
Minor assaults	83.32	16.68
Corruption of minors and offenses against decency	84.80	15.20
Fraud, etc.	85.74	14.26
Aggravated theft	88.77	11.23
Threats	90.68	9.32
Rebellion and insults to public officials	90.95	9.05
Forgery	92.49	7.51
Serious assaults	93.61	6.39
Murder	93.91	6.09
Counterfeit money	95.02	4.98
Homicide	96.74	3.26
Offenses against public order	97.70	2.30
Robbery, etc.	97.77	2.23
Rape, etc.	99.04	0.96

According to the census of 1901 the population over 9 years old consisted of 49.4 % men and 50.6 % women.[1]

Finally some figures for the Netherlands:

Netherlands, 1896–1900.[2]

YEARS.	NUMBER SENTENCED.			
	Men.		Women.	
	Number.	%	Number.	%
1896	13,964	89.6	1,625	10.4
1897	14,483	90.0	1,613	10.0
1898	14,018	89.5	1,646	10.5
1899	13,928	90.5	1,463	9.5
1900	13,234	91.3	1,254	8.7

[1] "Statesman's Year Book", 1910, p. 948.
[2] Taken from "de Gerechtelijke Statistiek van het Koningrijk der Nederlanden", 1896–1899, and "de Crimineele Statistiek", 1900. For more detailed information upon the Netherlands see *Loosjes*, "Bijdrage tot de studie van de criminaliteit der vrouw", pp. 8–30.

Women participate in the different crimes in the following proportions:

Netherlands, 1901.[1]

CRIMES.	To 100 SENTENCED THERE WERE:	
	Men.	Women.
Debauch of a minor (as principal or accessory)	6.2	93.8
Simple insults	64.9	35.1
Simple theft	79.0	21.0
Fraud	80.0	20.0
Offenses against public decency	81.8	18.2
Homicide	89.5	10.5
Aggravated theft	90.5	9.5
Embezzlement	91.1	8.9
Receiving stolen goods	91.8	8.2
Forgery	92.1	7.9
Assault	93.5	6.5
Serious assault	94.7	5.3
Malicious mischief	95.5	4.5
Mendicity and vagrancy	96.5	3.5
Assaults upon officials	97.3	2.7
Domiciliary trespass	98.1	1.9
Rebellion	98.7	1.3

The whole population being divided in 1901 into 50.5 % women and 49.5 % men, the figures given above make the criminality of woman appear a little greater than it really is.

Here, then, are the facts, which may be reduced to this, that in all the countries named the criminality of women is much less than that of men. However, it is greater than we should suppose from the figures, since almost all the figures (except those for France) have to do with persons convicted, and acquittal is much more common in the case of women than in that of men. We have already given the figures for Germany in regard to this matter. In England the percentage of convictions is 82 % for men and 79 % for women.[2]

[1] Figured from "Krimineele statistiek over het jaar 1901."
[2] "Criminal Statistics, 1899", p. 27. See in the same place the reason for thinking that the figures quoted for the number of women acquitted are too small. *Morrison* says that in England one woman in four is acquitted, and one man in six. ("Juvenile Offenders", p. 46.)

In France the differences are still greater :

France, 1881–1890 (Assizes).[1]

SEX.	PERCENTAGE OF ACQUITTALS.			
	1881–1885.	1886–1890..	1891–1895.	1896–1900.
Men	25	25	26	28
Women	45	47	50	52

1896–1900 (Correctional Tribunals).[2]

SEX.	PERCENTAGE OF ACQUITTALS TO EACH AGE-CATEGORY.		
	Under 16.	16 to 21.	Over 21.
Men	57	6	5
Women	58	9	7

These figures lead to the presumption that in other countries also women are more apt to be acquitted than men.

Other reasons why the criminality of women seems smaller than it really is are the following: As is shown by the statistics cited, the offenses of which women are most often guilty, are also those which it is most difficult to discover, namely those committed without violence. Then, those who have been injured are less likely to bring a complaint against a woman than against a man.[3] But even when we take account of all these things, the criminality of women remains much smaller than that of men. This may be explained as follows :

First. An examination of the tables shows that women participate less in the crimes which require strength or courage. The first cause is to be found in the fact, then, that the average woman of our time has less strength and courage than the average man, and consequently commits on the average fewer crimes than he.

Second. It is clear that women take small part in sexual crimes (for procuration is not a sexual crime but an economic one), which is to be explained by the fact that most sexual crimes cannot, from their

[1] "Rapport", etc., p. xxxiv.
[2] *Op. cit.*, p. lvi.
[3] See *Colajanni*, "Sociologia criminale", II, p. 83 ; *Földes, op. cit.* pp. 630, 631 ; and *Morrison, op. cit.*, p. 46.

nature, be committed by women. Another reason is that the rôle of women in the sexual life (and thus in the criminal sexual life) is rather passive than active.

Third. The small part played by women in economic crimes committed because of poverty or even of greed, is explained by prostitution, which generally yields greater and more certain returns than crime, and avoids the risk of prison.

Fourth. A comparison of the criminal statistics of different countries has not much value for the different reasons already given (Pt. I, Ch. II, sec. XIX). Only when the figures are very different may one draw a conclusion from them. A comparison of the tables brings out the fact that the criminality of women does not differ much in the countries named. However, when we fix our attention upon the crimes and misdemeanors more or less grave in the Italian statistics (assizes and correctional tribunals) we discover that there is a considerable difference between England, for example, on the one side, and Italy on the other. While the former country shows about 12 % (offenses tried on indictment) and 23 % (offenses tried summarily) of women among those convicted, the figures are 5 to 6 % (assizes) and about 9 % (corr. trib.) in the latter country. This difference shows that the direction in which the principal reason for woman's small part in crime must be sought, is in her social position. This differs less from that of the man in England than in Italy. However, there are figures much more significant than those I have just cited. Between 1893 and 1899 the percentage of convicts in prison in Scotland was between 36 and 37.[1] In Denmark from 1876 to 1885 about 26 % of the convicts were women.[2] It is an incontestable fact that Denmark and Scotland are countries where the social position of women approaches most closely that of men. Let us set in opposition to this now a country like Algeria where the life of woman is entirely different. It appears that there between 1881 and 1900 3 % of those arraigned before the assizes were women, and 4 % of those arraigned before the correctional tribunals.[3]

An examination of the criminality of women in the different parts

[1] "Criminal Statistics of England and Wales, 1899", p. 54.
[2] *Loosjes, op. cit.,* p. 50.
[3] Figured from Tables 23 and 24 of the "Rapport au président de la république française", etc.
[NOTE TO THE AMERICAN EDITION: Wadler tells us that in Servia the percentage of feminine criminality is between 3.71 (1893) and 6.25 (1903); in Greece, about 2 (1899–1902); in Bulgaria, about 3.2 (1899–1906); in Bosnia and Herzegovina, between 5.07 (1899) and 6.69 (1902) (*op. cit.,* pp. 94, 102–104). In Rumania, Minovici tells us, the percentage is 2.42 (1874–1890).]

of the same country, Germany for example, shows that the highest figures for female criminality are furnished by the great cities and the countries most developed economically.

Germany, 1897–1898.[1]

CITIES OR COUNTRIES.	PERCENTAGE OF WOMEN AMONG THE CONVICTS.	
	1897.	1898.
Berlin	27.8	27.6
Hamburg	24.7	25.3
Saxony	22.0	21.7
Prussia	21.8	21.5
Germany as a whole	20.6	20.3
Bavaria	18.6	18.6
Alsace-Lorraine	17.3	18.1
Wurtemberg	16.7	15.8
Hesse	15.2	14.4
Baden	13.8	12.1

As regards England, Morrison says that of misdemeanors 25 % are committed by women in London (Metropolitan Police District), and 33 % in Manchester; while women commit only 10 % of the misdemeanors in Surrey, and about 14 % in Lancashire.[2] The high percentages come then in the places where the social position of woman is most nearly equal to that of man.

Dr. H. Hoegel gives the following table for Austria. As the author says it proves that the country where the woman takes the greatest part in the economic life gives the highest figures for female criminality.

As to the movement of the criminality of women the data that I have given, and others that I have at my disposal, are not significant enough to lead to a definite conclusion. In England it has been made out that there is a small diminution of serious crimes and a slight increase of minor offenses, though the period of observation is very short. Between 1881 and 1900 the relative criminality of men and women remained constant. In Italy there was between 1890 and 1895 a slight increase in the absolute number, and a slight, but fluctuating, diminution in the relative number. In the Netherlands the proportions remained pretty constant from 1896 to 1901.

[1] "Kriminalstatistik für das Jahr 1898", II, p. 73.
[2] "Juvenile Offenders", p. 47.

Austria, 1889–1893.[1]

COUNTRY.	NUMBER OF WOMEN TO		NUMBER OF CONVICTIONS FOR CRIME TO 10,000 OF POPULATION.
	100 of Population.	100 Convicts.	
Moravia	52.5	18.0	15.9
Silesia	52.5	17.8	17.8
Salzburg	50.9	17.6	17.6
Bohemia	52.0	17.2	8.9
Lower Austria	51.4	16.7	14.1
Upper Austria	50.9	16.1	13.9
Austria	51.4	14.9	12.6
Carinthia	51.6	14.7	18.5
Galicia	51.0	13.7	13.7–10.4 [2]
Tyrol and Vorarlberg .	51.4	13.5	10.5–12.0 [3]
Styria	50.7	12.9	17.3
Bukowina	50.0	11.8	13.3
Littoral of Trieste . .	50.2	8.8	14.2
Carniola	52.5	7.5	19.5
Dalmatia	50.0	6.8	13.9

The following are the figures for Germany and Austria:

Germany, 1888–1900.[4]

YEARS.	NUMBER CONVICTED.		NUMBER OF WOMEN CONVICTED TO EACH 100 MEN CONVICTED.
	To the 100,000 Men over 12.	To the 100,000 Women over 12.	
1888	1,821.7	358.0	19.7
1894	2,164.3	374.9	18.7
1896	2,177.7	388.9	17.9
1898	—	—	19.5
1900	—	—	19.3

There was, then, an increase in the criminality of women, but a smaller increase than that of men (except in 1898).

[1] "Die Straffälligkeit des Weibes", p. 253 (Archiv f. Krim. Anthr. u. Kriminalstatistik, V).
[2] Galicia, Western and Eastern separately.
[3] Tyrol and Vorarlberg separately.
[4] From "Kriminalstatistik", 1888, 1894, 1896, 1898, and 1900.

Austria, 1881–1899.[1]

Percentage of Persons Convicted who were Women.

1881–1885.	1886–1890.	1891–1895.	1896.	1897.	1898.	1899.
14.8	14.6	14.7	14.1	14.4	13.5	13.9

Here, then, there was a slight but fluctuating diminution in the criminality of women in proportion to that of men.

It must be conceded that the figures given do not contribute much to the support of the thesis that it is especially the social position of women which is the cause of their being less criminal. This position has been modified during the years to which the figures given refer. Women participate much more than formerly in the whole economic and social life. One would accordingly naturally look for a great increase in the criminality of women. Nevertheless these figures cannot, it seems to me, be used to refute the thesis in question, for the following reasons :

In the first place the figures given cover a short period only. They do not show very much, therefore ; for, notwithstanding the continual increase of the importance of the rôle of woman in the economic life, the modification of her position in the whole social life is not made so quickly that one can expect much of an increase in female criminality in the criminal statistics of the last few years.[2]

In the second place, most of the figures give the ratio of the crimes of women to those of men ; they do not then show whether the decrease in the percentage is due to a decrease in the criminality of women, or rather to an increase in that of men. This latter is the case, for example, in Germany.[3]

In the third place the statistics at my disposal are not sufficiently detailed with regard to the movement of the criminality of women, so that it is impossible to tell whether there are changes in the qualitative character of the crimes even though its quantitative character remains about the same.[4]

[1] " Die Ergebnisse etc.", p. xlviii.

[2] [NOTE TO THE AMERICAN EDITION : Wadler points out that in the Balkan States the percentage of feminine criminality is rapidly increasing.]

[3] See *Loosjes, op. cit.*, pp. 11, 12.

[4] See *Loosjes, op. cit.*, p. 12, where he demonstrates that the decrease in the percentage of female criminality is in great measure due to the diminution of mendicity.

[NOTE TO THE AMERICAN EDITION : French and German statistics bearing

A very conclusive proof of the thesis that the social position of woman is what explains her lower criminality, is as follows. The difference in the manner of life of the two sexes decreases as we descend the social scale. If the social position of woman is then an important determinant of her lower criminality, the figures ought to show that the criminality of men differs more from that of women in the well-to-do classes than in classes less privileged. Now the figures already given (pp. 482 *ff.*) upon the intellectual development of criminals confirm our hypothesis completely. Just so the tables upon the financial situation of criminals (see pp. 493, 494); in Austria, for example, 0.2 % of the women convicted in 1899 came from the well-to-do classes, and 0.4 % of the men. There were no well-to-do women at all among those convicted of the graver crimes. Just so again, in the table of Prussian recidivists the women form 4 % of the well-to-do convicts and 14 % of the poor convicts.

Finally the figures for the influence of marriage upon criminality show (see p. 513 *ff.*) that the criminality of widows is very great. This proves that the smaller criminality of woman is not to be sought in innate qualities, but rather in the social environment. For widows are generally forced to come into contact with the economic and social life of the world more than other women.

We have still to explain how social position is a cause of a lower degree of criminality. As to economic offenses, it must be remarked that the small part that woman plays in the economic life has the result that the desire to be enriched at some one else's expense is less aroused in her than it is in man, and that the opportunity to accomplish the desire is presented to her less often than to him. As to crimes committed for vengeance etc., since women live more retired lives they enter less quickly into conflict with others, and hence are less in danger of committing such crimes. Then the fact that women are less addicted to alcohol must be taken into account. The almost wholly negligible participation of women in political life explains why they are almost never guilty of political crimes, a kind of crime rare enough in any case.

After the long detour that we have made (in order to comprehend what follows), we come now at last to the subject which especially

upon a long period show that the economic criminality of woman tends to decrease, and that against persons to increase. The last fact corresponds, therefore, with the thesis that the social situation of woman explains her criminality. The first fact is explained perhaps by the decrease of poverty resulting from the greater participation of woman in the economic life.]

concerns us in this section, the influence of the economic and social life upon the social sentiments of women.

It results from this examination that, on the one hand, women feel generally less than men the direct harmful influences of the present economic system, and those of alcoholism; that the influence, very significant for criminality, of the environment in which she passes her youth, acts as strongly upon her as upon a man; and that militarism has no influence upon her, nor has prostitution itself upon the majority of the sex.

Then woman has lived for ages in a state of oppression injurious to the development of the social instincts, which forces her to have recourse to lying and hypocrisy, those two defensive weapons of the oppressed. Just so also her retired life has been an obstacle to the development of her feeling of solidarity with reference to persons outside of the family.

In looking the whole field over I see nothing to justify the opinion that the less criminal character of women indicates a higher morality, whether innate or acquired. The consequences of her manner of life, in so far as they are harmful to the formation of character, are probably counterbalanced by those which are favorable. Her smaller criminality is like the health of a hothouse plant; it is due not to innate qualities, but to the hothouse which protects it from harmful influences. If the life of women were like that of men their criminality would hardly differ at all as to quantity, though perhaps somewhat as to quality.[1]

e. The family. Here we have to take up the question of how far the family in which the criminal has been raised has contributed to make him such. It will be well to begin with some theoretical observations upon the question, what is the effect of moral education upon

[1] For opinions of other authors see *Loosjes, op. cit.,* pp. 75–108.

[NOTE TO THE AMERICAN EDITION: Upon feminine criminality in general see further the following recent works: for Germany: *Aschaffenburg, op. cit.,* pp. 135 *ff.*; *Wulffen, op. cit.,* I. pp. 402 *ff.,* and II, pp. 258 *ff.*; O. *Mönkemüller,* "Korrectionsanstalt und Handarmenhaus"; *Galle, op. cit.,* pp. 68 *ff.*; *Stöwesand, op. cit.,* pp. 23 *ff.*; *Sauer, op. cit.,* pp. 57 *ff.* For Austria: *Herr,* "Die Kriminalität des Weibes nach den Ergebnissen der neueren österreichischen Statistik" ("Archiv f. Krim. anthr. u. Krim.", XVIII), and *op. cit.,* pp. 78 *ff.*; *Hoegel, op. cit.,* pp. 410 *ff.* For the Balkan States: *Wadler, op. cit.,* pp. 93 *ff.* For Belgium: *Jacquart, op. cit.,* pp. 67 *ff.* For France: *C. Granier,* "La femme criminelle"; *de Lanessan, op. cit.,* pp. 145 *ff.*; *H. Lacaze,* "De la criminalité féminine en France"; *H. Leale,* "De la criminalité des sexes" ("Archives d'anthr. crim.", XXV). For the Netherlands: *de Roos, op. cit.,* pp. 76 *ff.*; *Verrijn Stuart, op. cit.,* pp. 190 *ff.* For Rumania: *Minovici, op. cit.* Upon female criminality in relation to special occupations, see: *R. de Rijcken,* "La servante criminelle."]

a child (in the larger sense of moral surroundings), and how far does this education in the end affect the adult?

It is unnecessary for us to tarry long upon this. The facts which we shall cite below are more convincing than all the theoretical observations, and they show clearly how great this influence is. Nevertheless some brief observations are necessary. It is not far from the truth, it seems to me, to say that the power of moral education upon the character, and that of intellectual education upon the intelligence, are equal. The thesis has been maintained that the intellectual capacities of all men are equal, and that education is the sole cause of the great differences which exist. No reasonable person would maintain this theory; men differ enormously in their innate intellectual capacities; some have great intellectual power, others have very little, while between the two extremes is found the general average. What now is the rôle that education has to play?

Those who have small intellectual capacity naturally never become superior men, even if their education is the best possible; though by virtue of proper education they might become fairly useful. Those who have great intellectual capacity also need education (though less so than the run of mankind), for otherwise their faculties will remain dormant. Darwin would never have made his great discovery if he had been born and reared in the slums of a great city and had learned nothing (even supposing that, with his poor health, he had not succumbed to such an environment). His acquaintances would have doubtless thought him intelligent, but the scientific world would never have heard of him.

It must be much the same with the moral faculty. We are not born with moral precepts in our heads, but only with a greater or less predisposition to become moral. If this predisposition, even though it be very strong, is not cultivated, there is no question of morality.

The child, even more than the man, is an imitator, and responds to suggestion in everything, but especially in morals. If we put the question: how does it happen that there are honest persons? the answer must be: largely because in their youth they have become accustomed to be honest.[1] In his "Descent of Man", Darwin says: . . . "Habit in the individual would . . . play a very important part in guiding the conduct of each member; for the social instinct, together with sympathy, is like any other instinct, greatly strengthened by

[1] *Liszt,* "Die gesellschaftlichen Ursachen des Verbrechens." (See discussion of this work in Pt. I of the present work.)

habit, and so consequently would be obedience to the wishes and judgment of the community." [1]

A great proportion of the whole number of criminals have become such through the evil example of those about them, or have even been deliberately trained to crime. Even those who are endowed with great innate moral capacities cannot withdraw themselves from these influences. One of the men most competent to speak on this subject, M. Raux, director of one of the penitentiary districts in France, and author of one of the best books upon juvenile criminality says, after speaking of the miserable environment in which young criminals are brought up: "Let no one attempt to tell us after these revelations that the child, born in surroundings which asphyxiate him morally, can escape from vice. No nature would resist such demoralizing agencies. In order to convince ourselves of the truth of this it would only be necessary to try an experiment, which, it if were possible, would not fail to be conclusive.

"The method would be to transport some children of the middle or wealthy class, neither of which furnish any inmates to our reformatories, into families considered as types of those from which our young delinquents come, and to substitute for them in their former homes the children of poor families. This double substitution would have immediate effects. Little time would be needed, very little, we are convinced, for the former group of children to lose all trace of their early education and to become thoroughly bad characters. As to the other group, a moral movement in the other direction would be produced in them, but much more slowly. Vices are like diseases, they take hold quickly, and let go with difficulty. There would long remain to the second group a taste for vagabondage and gross pleasures. But when even these habits and impressions of childhood are painfully eradicated, well-being, advice, and care would always keep the child away from the possibility of theft, and after a certain time of probation passed in the bosom of well-to-do and respectable families the public would certainly regard our subjects, grown to be men, as upright and worthy of all confidence. Thus we should have transformed children of good character into malefactors, and of the malefactor we should have made an honest man.

"This experiment, which no good family would consent to try for fear of the result, would prove on the one hand, that any child placed in the living conditions of most of our young delinquents would inevitably become vicious and criminal, and on the other that if

[1] P. 96, chap. IV.

circumstances easily make a malefactor of a child well brought-up, it is much more difficult to transform a bad character into an honest man." [1]

In consequence of what we have just said we may put two questions; first, do all those who are brought up in such an environment inevitably become criminals; second, is there, then, no difference as to morality between two persons of whom one is born with a strong and the other with a weak moral disposition (supposing that both live in the same unfavorable moral environment)?

The answer to the first question must be that there may be sometimes those who succeed notwithstanding the very bad surroundings of their youth. (As we have seen, an expert like Raux denies this possibility.) But such cases are very rare and prove nothing against the theory of environment, for it may readily happen that such persons fall in with a better environment (at school, for example) which puts them on the right track, if they have a strong moral disposition by nature.

To the second question the answer must be made that one endowed with a strong moral disposition, but raised in unfavorable surroundings, will perhaps become criminal, and yet need not be as bad as another with a weak moral disposition, raised in a like environment.

There are criminals and criminals. Anyone who has given himself the trouble of reading the biographies of great criminals knows that all have not been entirely corrupted. It is with morals as with intelligence; in unfavorable circumstances Darwin would not have become a genius, but even in such environment he would nevertheless have been recognized as intelligent; so a child with great moral capacity would not become an honest man when brought up in the company of thieves and assassins, but in his own circle would have been considered as a good boy.

Beside very bad environments there are the great mass of those that are neither the one thing nor the other, in which the children neither have bad examples, nor are, properly speaking, deserted, but in which, nevertheless, they do not receive an education positively good. What is the influence of such environments? They are absolutely insufficient for children with little moral disposition. These have need of a strong and well-taught guide, without which they run much danger of leaving, sooner or later, the straight path. It is evident that an education such as that in question, is insufficient for the great middle class. The future lot of these young people will depend

[1] "Nos jeunes détenus", pp. 24, 25.

especially upon the circumstances in which chance shall place them.
The surroundings spoken of will be enough for those who have great
moral capacities, in the sense not that a better environment would
not have had a better effect upon them but in the sense that they
are more susceptible to the good than to the evil influences and —
except in rare circumstances — they will cause less trouble to their
fellows.

Finally, how far does the effect of a good education extend? What
can a good education do for a person born with weak social instincts?
This is the well-known controversy. For no one denies that those
who are endowed with strong social instincts, as well as those who
have them only in moderation, and who constitute the great majority,
do not become bad when they are brought up in a good environment.

It will perhaps be impossible to give a decisive answer to this
question. For, since we cannot make experiments with living persons, we cannot get sure results. And then an education really
good is so great a rarity that the number of cases where children with
little moral disposition are excellently brought up is certainly very
small.[1]

We may consider it as certain that children not well endowed will
never become very altruistic even if brought up under the best conditions imaginable. But on the other hand no one would doubt that
a favorable environment would develop, however little, their weak
social instincts (for no one is wholly without such instincts). For the
moment we cannot decide how far this influence may extend.

After this introduction we come to the organization of education in
present-day society. Before stating the facts we must sum up what
has been said above (see Ch. I., Sec. III, B, of this part). The organization of our present social system charges the legitimate parents of
the child with his support and education. Most authors who treat
of the family wax so enthusiastic that they lose all critical sense.
They note that there are parents who love their children, perform all
their duties towards them, etc., and they wish to make themselves
believe that this is the general rule. But the subject must be considered in cold blood. Certainly it would be ridiculous to deny the
social importance of the family; we may even say without hesitation
that without the family our present society could not exist. But
all this would not be a reason for not seeing its defects.

Are there not many who are bad, even aside from criminals? Is
not the majority of mankind made up of those weak in character?

[1] See what is said in criticism of Professor Ferri in Pt. I of this work.

Are there not many alcoholics? Are there not persons who do not love their children at all? Are not the persons numerous who have little patience and tact to guide children, or who are lacking in other pedagogic qualities? Is it not true that nearly everyone is ignorant of psychological and pedagogical principles? And have not most men their whole time taken up with the struggle for existence, so that they are not able to concern themselves with the education of their children?

These are the questions that we must ask ourselves; and the answer to all of them is categorically; yes. And have not all these persons offspring? Most certainly. Then the results may be imagined. It will be of the highest importance to know how many children receive an education that is really good. I do not know of any statistics covering any very great number of children. But it will not be far from the truth to infer that the following figures are applicable, not simply to a limited number, but in general to all children. These figures are given by Ferriani: [1]

To each 100 children between 8 and 12 years of age:

Good education	5
Education fair	10
" superficial	20
" partially neglected	17
" entirely "	42
" bad	6
	100

One of the characteristics of our present education is that it makes children egoistic. It is to be expected. The organization of society obliges men to be egoistic, and "like father, like son." An apparent morality is the consequence. Children are taught that they ought to do or leave undone this or that, not because it is needful to help their fellows or not to injure them, but because it will be advantageous to them to act morally, or because otherwise they will be punished. It is unnecessary to say that brought up in such a manner, the individual will not recoil from crime because of any moral restraint, when the opportunity presents itself of making a profit, or when the risk of being punished is not great.

As to education among *the well-to-do classes*, there it is especially egoistic. The children — speaking of course in a general way — are

[1] "Schlaue und glückliche Verbrecher", p. 34. See the whole section "L'hypocrisie dans l'education" (pp. 29–49), where the author criticises contemporary education severely.

brought up with the idea that they must succeed, no matter how; the aim of life is presented to them as getting money and shining in the world. Such principles are incompatible with a really moral education, and the education of this class aims only at an apparent morality instead of a real one.[1]

Whatever may be the defects of this education, it is at least an education; the children are watched, prevented from getting into bad society, etc. The consequence is that the children of the well-to-do almost never get into the courts. This sad monopoly is reserved for the children of the poor.[2] This is not to say that the defects of education among the well-to-do classes are not among the causes of the criminality to be met with in the adults of these classes. When a poor devil appears in court it will often happen that his counsel in defending him will draw attention to the fact that the environment in which his client has grown up is one of the causes of his fall; but it does not often happen that the advocate makes a similar appeal when his client is from the well-to-do. It is generally believed that nothing is wanting in the moral education of one who has not known poverty, and has not been neglected; but this is a mistake. There can be no doubt that one of the factors of criminality among the bourgeoisie is bad education.

The figures of the following tables show that it is almost exclusively the children of the poor who are guilty of crime.

England and Scotland.

According to the English law the parents of children placed in a "Reformatory" or an "Industrial School" must, if they are able, contribute toward their children's expenses. The following table shows the assessments due in 1882 (in shillings per week).[3]

---

[1] See *Corre*, "Crime et Suicide", pp. 327, 328, and *Ferriani*, "Minderjährige Verbrecher", pp. 284–295, 372, 373.

[2] There are other reasons for this, of course, besides better education: the absence of poverty, pleasures within easy reach, etc.

[3] Taken from *Morrison*, "Juvenile Offenders", p. 160.

	Total.	Exempt.	Less than 1 Shilling.	1 Shill. and More.	2 Shill. and More.	3 Shill. and More.	4 Shill. and More.	5 Shillings.
Reformatories								
Absolute numbers	6,601	3,858	257	1,818	573	66	15	14
Percentage . . .	100.0	58.5	3.9	27.5	8.7	1.0	0.2	0.2
Industrial Schools								
Absolute numbers	17,641	10,406	600	3,904	2,316	301	67	20
Percentage . . .	100.0	59.1	3.4	22.2	13.1	1.7	0.4	0.1

A little less than 60 % of the parents, then, were unable to make any contribution, 25 to 30 % of them were able to pay less than two shillings, while the remaining 10 or 15% were working people not at all well-to-do.[1]

France.[1]

The French "statistique pénitentiaire" gives information with regard to the financial condition of the parents of the children received into the "Etablissements d'éducation correctionelle." The following figures covering the years 1878 to 1882 [2] will give a sufficiently accurate notion, as figures for a longer period would lead to the same results.

Children Belonging to Parents	1878.		1879.		1880.		1881.		1882.		1878–1882 Average Percentage.	
	Boys.	Girls.	B.	G.	B.	G.	B.	G.	B.	G.	B.	G.
Well-to-do	81	32	75	60	61	3	50	4	43	5	0.9	1.2
Living by their own labor	5,874	1,254	5,799	1,177	5,800	1,224	5,455	1,154	5,300	1,090	79.3	68.7
Mendicants, vagabonds, prostitutes	923	421	956	433	809	429	726	395	697	349	11.5	23.6
Unknown, disappeared, deceased	707	133	684	138	545	102	546	84	486	101	8.3	6.5
Total	7,585	1,840	7,514	1,808	7,215	1,758	6,777	1,637	6,527	1,545	100.0	100.0

After 1882 the penitentiary statistics no longer mention the financial condition of the parents, but their occupation. The results confirm those that we have just cited.

[1] Morrison, op. cit., p. 159.
[2] Figured from "L'annuaire statistique de la France", V–IX.

France, 1890–1895.[1]

CHILDREN BELONGING TO PARENT	1890.		1891.		1892.		1893.		1894.		1895.		1890–1895 AVERAGE PERCENTAGE.	
	Boys.	Girls.	B.	G.	B.	G.	B.	G.	B.	G.	B.	G.	B.	G.
Property owners or possessing incomes	29	2	36	1	36	1	36	2	34	2	29	0	0.6	0.1
Practicing liberal professions . . .	31	2	28	0	31	0	30	0	42	17	46	0	0.8	0.0
Agricultural .	1,000	125	1,192	105	1,199	101	1,252	138	893	102	929	115	20.8	10.0
Industrial . .	1,252	193	1,186	179	1,059	163	1,237	240	1,304	300	1,317	304	23.7	20.1
Miscellaneous .	2,084	572	1,937	493	2,130	413	1,866	373	2,199	311	2,120	327	39.8	36.4
Mendicants, vagabonds, prostitutes .	391	201	434	224	423	287	440	294	403	286	333	300	7.8	23.3
Unknown or disappeared	364	91	342	133	347	136	374	129	325	95	263	106	6.5	10.1
Total	5,151	1,186	5,155	1,135	5,225	1,101	5,235	1,176	5,200	1,131	5,037	1,152	100.0	100.0

These figures show clearly that it is only an insignificant number of young criminals who come from the well-to-do classes.[2]

I have been able to procure only a few data from other countries; their results, however, are identical with those for England and France.

Italy.

Of the 2,000 young criminals examined by Ferriani, there were 1,758, or 87.9 %, coming from families where a profound poverty reigned, and only 148 (7.4 %) from families that had never known poverty.[3]

Prussia.

77.8 % of the children received in the correctional educational institutions during the year 1901–02 came from very poor families.[4]

[1] Figured from the " Statistique pénitentiaire," 1890–1895.
[2] *Raux* (" Nos jeunes détenus") and *Grosmolard* ("Criminalité juvénile", p. 199) come to the same conclusion.
[3] "Minderjährige Verbrecher", pp. 76 and 440.
[4] *Plasz*, "Fürsorgeerziehung" (Woche V, No. 51). According to the statistics upon the "Fürsorgeerziehung" there were between 1901 and 1906 among the parents of the children on an average: 7.1% without income, 71.5% with an income under 900 marks, 14.1% with an income between 900 and 3000 marks, 0.1% between 3000 and 6000 marks, and 7.2% with income unknown. See *F. Frank*, "Das Fürsorgeerziehungsgesetz in Preussen", ("Neue Zeit", XXVII, p. 460).

It is then the poorest classes that furnish the greatest number of juvenile criminals.

We come now to education among the *proletariat*. Here we meet first, insufficiency of the pecuniary means which education requires; second, bad housing conditions, which oblige the children to pass a great part of the day in the street; third, the total absence of pedagogical ideas; fourth, the absence during the greater part of the day of the father of the family, and in many cases even of the mother. The number of married women who work away from home is continually increasing. In 1882 there were in Germany, for example, 507,784 married working-women, and by 1895 this figure had risen to 807,172 — an increase of 299,388 (59%) in 13 years. In 1882 17.3% of the working-women were married; in 1895 21.5%.[1] There are no official figures but Braun[2] calculates that in Germany there are 500,000 children under 14 years of age, whose mothers are working-women. In Austria 44.6% of the working-women are married, and in France 20.6%.[3] We have seen above (pp. 409 *ff.*) that juvenile criminality is increasing. This is explained in part by the increase in the labor of married women, from which it results that an increasing number of children are brought up without the proper care.

Among the working classes there is no question of education properly speaking. We can consider the children as fortunate if their parents do not set them a bad example, are not continually engaging in disputes, and are not given to alcohol. It is plain that all this does not make up a proper education; and yet how many children there are who do not have even so much of an education as this![4]

In the *lower proletariat* the situation is naturally worse. Not only is there a total lack of care and surveillance, but children are even brought up to crime.

Up to this point we have supposed the parents to be living. From the present organization of society it follows that the condition of the children of the poor becomes very bad as soon as the parents or even

---

[1] *L. Braun,* "Die Frauenfrage", pp. 279–280.

[2] *Op. cit.,* p. 320.

[NOTE TO THE AMERICAN EDITION : *Cf. W. Feld,* "Die Kinder der in Fabriken arbeiten den Frauen und ihre Verpflegung."]

[3] *Braun, op. cit.,* p. 278.

[4] See *Ducpetiaux,* "De la condition physique et morale des jeunes ouvriers", pp. 199 *ff.,* and *Corre,* "Crime et Suicide", pp. 330–332.

one of them dies. Often private or public charity intervenes, but generally the community does nothing for the orphan.

As a last consequence of the present system it must be noted that children born of illegitimate unions are in a still more precarious situation, since it is only the mother who has to protect them.

The community (in this case the state) concerns itself little with the education of children; it makes education compulsory (at least in some countries) and deprives parents of the charge of their children when they neglect them too much (this again in some countries only).

Now we come to the facts. They prove that the surroundings in which many children live are an important factor in the etiology of crime. The figures at my disposal are not as numerous as I could wish, but official statistics are not yet as full as is desirable for sociological purposes.

In reading the statistics which follow we must not lose sight of the fact that when it is stated that a certain percentage of children were brought up in a bad environment, it does not follow that all the others had a good education. The figures record only the very grave cases, as, for example, where the parents have been convicted, or the children entirely abandoned, etc. It is easier to prove, in making an investigation into the condition of a family, that the children do not receive a good education than it is to prove the contrary. Raux says that 36% of the parents of the juvenile criminals whom he had examined had a good reputation. The author adds, however, that this figure is too high for the following reason: "For certain officials charged with furnishing information on this point, every man who, without being absolutely irreproachable, has not been complained against, is a person of good character. So we have been made to add to the list of those of good reputation certain families where the father, drunken, idle, and unchaste, sets a very bad example to his son." [1]

Some readers will see in what follows only a tiresome mass of figures — quite wrongly, for those who know how to read the figures find in them a language much more convincing and more shocking than that which can be expressed in words.

Before beginning, the following remark must be made. We shall give, as far as possible, the percentages of criminals born of illegitimate unions together with the percentages of illegitimate births in general. We shall see that with some exceptions, even so, the percentage for criminals is much greater than that for the population in

[1] *Op. cit.*, p. 9.

general. However, to make the comparisons exact it is necessary to know the percentage of illegitimate persons among the population of an age to commit crime, and not among the newly born. This percentage is very much less, because, first, the mortality among illegitimate children is especially great, second, because a considerable number are legitimated. In general the percentage of illegitimate persons among the adult population is unknown. From researches by *Neumann* ("Die jugendlichen Berliner unehelicher Herkunft") and *Spann* ("Untersuchungen über die uneheliche Bevölkerung in Frankfurt a/M."), it appears that 3.6 times fewer illegitimate children in proportion, than legitimate, reach the age of 20 years! [1]

Austria, 1883-1889. [2]

The following figures have to do with illegitimacy among the criminals imprisoned in the years 1883 and 1884.

	1883.			1884.		
		Illegitimate.			Illegitimate.	
Sex.	Total Number of Criminals Imprisoned.	Absolute Number.	To 100 Prisoners.	Total Number of Criminals Imprisoned.	Absolute Number.	To 100 Prisoners.
Men . .	4,988	595	11.9	4,512	626	13.8
Women . .	781	149	19.0	751	156	20.7
Total .	5,769	746	12.9	5,263	782	14.8
			Recidivists.			
Men . .	2,719	392	14.4	2,353	366	15.5
Women . .	425	93	21.8	365	97	26.5
Total .	3,144	485	15.4	2,718	463	17.0

[1] In the following list I do not give the statistics for Germany as a whole, as I have been able to procure them for certain states, only. For Germany see: *Näcke*, "Verbrechen und Wahnsinn beim Weibe", pp. 161, 162; *von Liszt*, "Das Verbrechen als sozial-pathologische Erscheinung", pp. 22, 23; *W. Rein*, "Jugendliches Verbrecherthum" ("Zeitschr. f. Socialwissenschaft", III); *H. Wetzker*, "Die Zunahme der Verbrechen"; *Aschaffenburg, op. cit.*, pp. 107-116; see also the section on Hirsch in Pt. I of this work.

[NOTE TO THE AMERICAN EDITION: Besides the works of Neumann, Spann, Pöllitz, and Rühle, already cited, the following recent publications must be named: *Mönkemöller*, "Zur Kriminalität des Kindesalters" ("Archiv f. Krim. Anthrop. u. Kriminalstatistik", XL); *H. W. Gruhle*, "Die Ursachen der jugendlichen Verwahrlösung und Kriminalität"; *A. Hamburger*, "Lebensschicksale geisteskranker Strafgefangener".]

[2] "Statistisches Uebersicht der Verhältnisse der Oesterreichischen strafanstalten und der Gerichtsgefängnisse", 1883 and 1884, Table IV and IVa.

For the years 1896 and 1899 I have the following data, bearing upon the persons convicted of crime during those years.[1]

Sex.	1896.			1897.		
	Total Convicted.	Illegitimate.		Total Convicted.	Illegitimate.	
		Absolute Number.	To 100 Convicted.		Absolute Number.	To 100 Convicted.
Men . . .	24,833	2,095	8.4	28,984	2,838	9.7
Women . .	4,065	621	15.2	4,679	642	13.7
Total .	28,898	2,716	9.3	33,663	3,480	10.3

In order to be able to make a comparison we must have the figures for illegitimate births in the population in general. For Austria they are very high : in the period 1876–1880 13.84 % of the children born living were illegitimate, and in the period 1887–1891 14.67 %.[2] During the period between 1883 and 1892 the general mortality of children under a year old was 24.9% as against 30.3% for illegitimate children.[3]

Baden, 1887-1891.[4]

In 1887 correctional education (Zwangserziehung) was introduced into the Grand Duchy of Baden. The family conditions of the children received between 1887 and 1891 were as follows :

Years.	To Each 100 Children there were:			
	Illegitimate.	Full Orphans.	Motherless.	Fatherless.
1887	18.5	3.3	21.8	24.3
1888	17.0	4.7	16.2	30.2
1889	15.9	5.0	16.5	30.6
1890	15.0	4.8	16.6	32.8
1891	15.6	4.1	17.7	32.6

England and Scotland, 1887-1899.

With regard to the children received into the "Industrial Schools" during the years 1887 to 1891 there are the following data : 5 % were

[1] "Die Ergebnisse der Strafrechtspflege in den im Reichsrate vertretenen Königreichen und Ländern", 1896 and 1899.
[2] *Mayr*, "Statistik und Gesellschaftslehre", II, p. 197.
[3] *Mayr, op. cit.*, p. 282. [NOTE TO THE AMERICAN EDITION : Upon Austria, cf. *Baernreither, op. cit.*]
[4] *J. S.*, "Zur Verwahrlosung der Kinder in der kapitalistischen Gesellschaft" ("Neue Zeit", 1893–94, II).

illegitimate, while for the same period 4.52 % of all children born living were illegitimate.[1] Here we must take into consideration the greater mortality among illegitimate children. There are no recent data, but in England in 1875 this mortality was twice as great as that of legitimate children, and in some countries it is four times as great.

4 % were full orphans; 34 % half orphans, 20 % being fatherless and 14 % motherless; 6 % had been abandoned by their parents; and 2 % were the children of habitual criminals. 51 %, therefore, were living under unfavorable conditions. For the pupils of the "Reformatories" in the same period this percentage was 53.[2]

The following figures indicate also the relative numbers for the two sexes:

Industrial Schools, 1891.[3]

	Boys.		Girls.	
	Number.	%	Number.	%
Illegitimate	233	6.8	108	11.6
Full orphans	115	3.4	65	6.7
Fatherless only	532	15.6	181	18.6
Motherless only	535	15.7	171	17.6
Abandoned by parents	193	5.7	76	7.8
One or both parents perverted or criminal	118	3.5	53	5.5
Parents living and able to care for children	1,681	49.3	317	32.7
Total	3,407	100.0	971	100.0

It is interesting to note that with girls the influence of bad family surroundings is worse than it is with boys, more than two thirds living under abnormal circumstances.

However, confining ourselves to figures for the period 1887–1891, 49 % and 47 % of the children in the two classes of institutions respectively came from normal families. In what follows we see what their education was; different competent witnesses before the "Royal Commission on Reformatory and Industrial Schools" affirmed that the environment from which these children came was very unfavorable. The most important testimony was that of Mr. Macdonald, one of the officers who receive the contributions of the parents to the support of their children in the "Industrial Schools." Accord-

---

[1] *Mayr*, "Statistik und Gesellschaftslehre", II, p. 197.
[2] *Morrison*, "Juvenile Offenders", pp. 122–147.
[3] *Tönnies*, "Jugendliche Kriminalität und Verwahrlosung in Gross-Britannien", p. 904 ("Zeitschr. f. d. ges. Strw.", XIII).

ing to him only 6 % of the children came from homes favorable to their moral education.   In Manchester 68 % of the parents of children in the industrial schools had a bad reputation; 14.7 % were of doubtful character; and only 17 % conducted themselves well.[1]

Of 1,209 juvenile delinquents in the English prisons (1898–99) 90 (7.4 %) had had no education; 512 (42.3 %) had had very little; 496 (41 %) a fair education; and of 111 (9.1 %) only could it be said that their education was good.   211 (17.4 %) were without father or mother; 183 (15.1 %) had bad homes; 198 (16.3 %) had none at all; and 30 (2.4 %) slept in night-lodgings.[2]

If the environment in which the young criminals have lived is the cause of their fall, a considerable portion of them ought to return to the right way as a result of the education given in the schools in question.   If this is not the case with all, this proves nothing against the influence of environment, for the impressions received by the child in the surroundings in which he has lived before his conviction are too strong to be effaced by a comparatively brief stay in an educational institution (even if these reform-schools were perfect).   Finally, after they are set at liberty environment may once more contribute to recidivism.   The following figures show the facts in the case:[3]

| YEARS. | To Each 100 Released there were: | | | | | | | |
| | Boys. | | | | Girls. | | | |
	Good Conduct.	Doubtful Conduct.	Recidivists.	Conduct Unknown.	Good Conduct.	Doubtful Conduct.	Recidivists.	Conduct Unknown.
				a. Reformatory Schools.				
1882	76	3	14	7	72	7	6	15
1883	76	3	14	7	69	9	8	14
1884	78	2	14	6	70	9	6	15
1885	79	2	14	5	72	9	6	13
1886	77	3	14	6	73	11	5	11
1887	78	2	14	6	75	10	5	10
1888	76	1	17	6	75	9	6	10
1889	74	2	18	6	76	9	6	9
1890	78	2	14	6	73	10	7	10
1891	78	2	14	6	76	8	5	11

[1] *Morrison, op. cit.*, pp. 148–151.
[2] *W. H. Douglas*, "The Criminal; Some Social and Economic Aspects", p. 106 ("Proceedings of the Royal Philosophical Society of Glasgow", vol. XXXIII, 1901–1902).
[3] *Lenz*, "Die Zwangserziehung in England", p. 38.

| YEARS. | To Each 100 Released there were: | | | | | | | |
| | Boys. | | | | Girls. | | | |
	Good Conduct.	Doubtful Conduct.	Recidivists.	Conduct Unknown.	Good Conduct.	Doubtful Conduct.	Recidivists.	Conduct Unknown.
			b. Industrial Schools.					
1882	81	4	5	10	79	7	1	13
1883	80	4	5	11	79	7	2	12
1884	81	4	5	10	80	7	2	11
1885	81	3	5	11	81	7	2	10
1886	82.5	3	4.5	10	83	8	1	8
1887	83.3	3	5	9	84	7	1	8
1888	83	3	5	9	81	8	1	10
1889	83	3	5	9	82	8	1	9
1890	84	2	5	9	83	7	1	8
1891	85.5	2	4.5	8	84	7	1	8

The percentage of those who conduct themselves well is considerable, therefore, and indicates how great the influence of an unfavorable environment upon these children has been.[1]

France, 1890–1895.[2]

The following important data concern the children in the "établissements d'éducation correctionelle":

| CONDITION AS TO FAMILY. | 1890. | | 1891. | | 1892. | | 1893. | | 1894. | | 1895. | | 1890-1895 Average Percentage. | |
	B.	G.	B.	G.	B.	G.	B.	G.	B.	G.	B.	G.	B.	G.
Illegitimate . .	693	236	669	238	654	277	635	295	589	289	535	395	12.1	25.1
Half orphans . .	1,676	432	1,641	419	1,753	418	1,634	410	1,690	428	1,492	452	31.7	37.1
Full orphans . .	384	152	310	172	323	203	333	212	324	236	271	225	6.2	17.4
Parents: Convicted one or more times .	977	412	875	443	864	570	922	566	853	481	801	488	17.0	43.0
Mendicants, vagabonds, or prostitutes . . .	391	201	434	224	423	287	444	294	403	286	333	300	7.8	43.0
Unknown or disappeared . .	364	91	342	135	347	136	374	129	325	95	263	106	6.5	10.0
Total of juvenile delinquents .	5,151	1,186	5,155	1,135	5,225	1,101	5,235	1,176	5,200	1,131	5,037	1,152		

[1] With regard to England see also: *L. Gordon Rylands*, "Crime, its Causes and Remedy", pp. 18–19, 37–42.

[2] Figured from the "Statistique pénitentiaire", 1890–1895.

Out of 100 children born living 8.41 were illegitimate (1887–1891),[1] while the mortality in the first year of life rose to 28.8 % of the illegitimate children, and only to 16.7 % of the legitimate.[2]

The figures given above constitute a crushing accusation against present conditions. If we suppose that the number of persons born of illegitimate unions who have attained the age at which it is physically possible to commit a crime are 6 % of the whole population (a figure which is certainly rather too low than too high), it follows that a natural son runs twice as much danger of becoming a criminal as he would if legitimate, and that this danger is even four times as great in the case of a natural daughter. The other data are striking, especially those which deal with girls. There were 54 % who were orphans or half-orphans; 43 % had criminal parents; 33 % had parents who were vagabonds or prostitutes, or who had deserted their children ![3]

As the official statistics furnish no other data, we will pass on to some of those given by private individuals. In the work already more than once quoted, Raux gives the following table, based upon careful researches and dealing with 385 juvenile prisoners received in the "Quartier correctionel" at Lyons, to which the juvenile delinquents guilty of grave crimes are sent:[4]

JUVENILE PRISONERS.

Under normal surveillance	51	51	13 %
" weak "	90		
" impotent "	44	158	41 "
" brutal "	24		
Morally abandoned	98		
Completely "	47	145	38 "
Excited to crime by the example of parents	15		
Having committed crime under the instigation and with the complicity of parents	16	31	8 "
Total	385	385	100 %

Only 13 % among them enjoyed a normal education (and who could say how far it was really good?), while 87 % had an education

[1] *Mayr, op. cit.*, p. 197.
[2] *Mayr, op. cit.*, p. 282.
[3] *A. von Oettingen* says that in 1864 there were in France, out of 8,006 young prisoners, 60% who were illegitimate children or orphans, and 38.5% who were descended from criminals, vagrants, and prostitutes ("Moralstatistik", p. 335). [4] P. 17.

insufficient or bad. The author arrives at the following conclusion: ". . . the population of the 'quartier correctionel' of Lyons, more unfortunate than guilty, has been recruited for more than 16 years from families the majority of which bore within themselves, by reason of the vices of their constitution, the principle of disintegration; whose morality was detestable or very doubtful, and whose means of subsistence were insufficient or totally lacking.

"It is to these different causes that the young delinquents owe first their deplorable antecedents, then their recklessness at the moment of the crime, their perversity, their corruption, and finally, their arrest." [1]

The opinion of M. Grosmolard, of great value because of the competence of the author, who has been attached to the penal institutions of Lyons, is entirely in accord with what has just been quoted. After having spoken of the strong influence of poverty upon juvenile criminality, Grosmolard continues thus: "Besides material poverty, and as an auxiliary to this factor, we find the moral poverty of the home, manifested by the disorganization of the family. Whether it is due to the misconduct of the father or of the mother, or of both, the disruption, whether private through separation of the couple, or officialized by divorce, has no less deplorable consequences for the children. There is always the depressing spectacle of domestic disputes, the abandonment of the home, the weakening of parental discipline." [2]

Concerning 400 children in a parental school in Paris we have the following figures: [3]

There were:

Natural children	11.25 %
Half orphans	35.00 "
Full orphans	10.00 "
Children whose parents had disappeared or been convicted	13.25 "
Whose parents had separated or been divorced	16.25 "
Coming from a normal family	14.25 "
	100.00 %

These results agree, therefore, with those of the official statistics and of Raux. The normal families were those which did not present any of the *external* marks of demoralization, and it is more than probable that their "morality", in many cases was only apparent.

[1] *Op. cit.*, p. 48.   [2] *Op. cit.*, p. 201.
[3] *Joly*, "L'enfance coupable", p. 37. See the whole of chap. III.

Out of 600 families from which juvenile criminals had issued, studied by Dr. L. Albanel, 303 (50.5 %) had been disorganized by death, divorce, desertion, etc. In 268 (44.6 %) families the fathers and mothers worked away from home and the children were entirely neglected; 291 children (48.5 %) were confided to persons outside of the family; and 41 (6.8 %) were brought up by their grandparents, etc.[1]

Finally, there is the following fact about the children undergoing correction in Paris during the period 1874–1878: nearly 68 % of them received visits from no one at all, not even from their parents. What complete misery! Out of 100 children 68 in whom no one was interested, not even when they were in prison.[2]

The results obtained by correctional education (probably no more perfect in France than elsewhere) prove the correctness of what has been advanced. If the thesis that the environment is the cause of the criminality of minors is true, the conduct of most of those set free ought to be good. Here are the results obtained in the "Quartier correctionel" of Lyons:[3]

101 discharged prisoners led a good life, *i.e.*	60 %
20 conducted themselves passably, *i.e.*	12 %
24 were put down as bad, *i.e.*	14 %
24 disappeared (died, etc.), *i.e.*	14 %
169 discharged prisoners	100 %

As I have already remarked, the fact that all do not lead good lives proves nothing against the theory of environment, for it is quite possible that earlier evil influences have not been eliminated in a comparatively short detention. To prove how strong an influence the environment exercises anew upon discharged prisoners, let us look at the following figures, which also have to do with the pupils of the Lyons "Quartier correctionel":[4]

---

[1] "Le crime dans la famille", pp. 27, 38.
[2] *Motet*, "De l'éducation correctionelle", p. 186 ("Actes de IIe Congrès d'anthropologie criminelle").
[3] *Raux, op. cit.*, p. 181.
[4] *Raux, op. cit.*, p. 211. See also the following authors with regard to France: *Joly*, "La France criminelle", Ch. VI; *Corre*, "Crime et Suicide", pp. 485–490; *Tomel* and *Rollet*, "Les enfants en prison"; and *Aubry*, "La Contagion du meurtre", pp. 17–51.
[NOTE TO THE AMERICAN EDITION: *Cf.* further: *Duprat* and *de Lanessan, op. cit.; E. Laurent*, "La criminalité infantile"; *L. Manouvrier*, "Quelques cas de criminalité juvenile et commençante" ("Archives d'anthr. crim." XXVII); *E. Martin*, "Études sur l'enfance coupable" ("Archives d'anthr. crim." XXVIII).]

Discharged Inmates whose Parents:	Reformed.	Recidivists.
Had a good reputation	83 %	5 %
" " doubtful "	52 "	16 "
" " bad "	37 "	16 "
" been convicted	50 "	29 "

Ireland, 1891.

Among the children subjected to correctional education in 1891 there were: 1.2 % of illegitimate birth; 8.1 % who had lost their parents; 16.2 % without father; 19.3 % without mother; and 0.6 % who had been abandoned or whose parents were unknown.[1] 43.6 %, then, were entirely or partially orphaned. These figures have no great value since they relate to so small a number (160).

Italy, 1885–1889.

With regard to illegitimacy among criminals I have data for the years 1885, 1886, and 1889. In these years there were among those convicted at the assizes 2.35 %, 2.25 %, and 2.21 % respectively, of illegitimate birth.[2] The number of natural children in general in the years 1872–1889 was about 7 %;[3] the mortality among children in general in the first year was 19 %, and that among the illegitimate children 26 % (these percentages are the averages for the years 1884–1893).[4] Italy is an exception, therefore to the rule, good everywhere else, that a larger proportion of criminals than of the general population are illegitimate.

In his "Entartete Mütter", Ferriani says that more than 25 % of the 806 juvenile criminals examined by him had become such because of the depravity of their families.[5] In his "Minderjährige Verbrecher" he gives the following results from an examination of 2,000 juvenile criminals: 207 (10.3 %) came from families of which one or more members had been convicted; 53 (2.6 %) from families entirely demoralized; 701 (35.0 %) from families of bad reputation; and 169 (8.4 %) from families with a doubtful reputation — all together 56.3 %; while 896 (44.8 %) had been corrupted by bad examples.[6]

[1] *Lenz, op. cit.*, p. 70.
[2] From *Colajanni*, "Sociologia criminale", II, p. 107, and the "Statistica giudiziaria penale per l'anno 1889", p. CXV.
[3] "Annuario statistico italiano 1900", p. 95.
[4] *Mayr, op. cit.*, p. 282.   [5] P. 164.   [6] P. 76.

Dr. A. Marro gives the following figures : [1] of 507 criminals examined by him there were :

  19 (3.6 %) whose father or mother was a criminal
  98 (13.4 %) who had a criminal brother or sister
115 (22.6 %) whose father was immoral or violent
  56 (11.0 %)   "   mother "   "   "   "
209 (41.0 %)   "   father was alcoholic
  26 (5.1 %)   "   mother "   "
120 (24.1 %) had lost their father before the age of 16
  90 (18.1 %) "   "   "   mother   "   " " " "
and 36 (7.0) % were orphans before the age of 16.

Netherlands, 1896–1901.

The data concerning the Netherlands are limited to the following : [2]

Percentage of Persons of Illegitimate Birth.

YEARS.	CONVICTS.			RECIDIVISTS.		
	Men.	Women.	Total.	Men.	Women.	Total.
1896	1.5	3.4	1.7	2.2	6.8	2.4
1897	1.3	2.3	1.6	1.9	3.5	2.0
1898	1.3	1.9	1.3	1.6	1.6	1.6
1899	1.5	2.2	1.6	2.0	2.2	2.2
1900	1.8	2.0	2.0	1.9	1.4	1.9
1901	1.3	1.9	1.9	1.5	2.8	1.6

In the period 1887–1891 the number of illegitimate children to 100 born living was 3.2 [3]; the mortality among illegitimate children during their first year rose to 26.6 % as against 17.5 % among children in general (1885–1893).[4] It is not possible to calculate for

[1] "I caratteri dei delinquenti", pp. 237 and 250. For Italy see also : *Carrara*, "Les petits criminels de Cagliari" ("Compte rendu du Ve Congrès d'anthropologie criminelle").
[2] Figured from "Gerechtelijke Statistiek van het Koningrijk der Nederlanden", 1896, 1897, 1898, and 1899, and "Crimineele Statistiek", 1900 and 1901.
[NOTE TO THE AMERICAN EDITION: *Cf.* further the work of *de Roos* already cited, pp. 117 *ff.* *Dr. J. P. F. A. Noorduijn*, "De Observatie, na de invoering der Kinderwetten, etc." ("Tijdschrift v. Strafrecht", XXIII), and *J. Feith*, "Misdadige Kinderen."]
[3] *Mayr, op. cit.*, p. 197.   [4] *Mayr, op. cit.*, p. 282.

the population in general the number of individuals born of illegitimate unions and arrived at the age at which they are capable of committing crime, but it is certain that the mortality is greater among illegitimate children at each age than among legitimate children, and that the number of children legitimated is very considerable. The percentage of illegitimates to the whole population, then, is much smaller than 3.2. It is consequently probable that in Holland also illegitimate children are more likely to become criminals than legitimate children.

As to juvenile criminals there are the following figures to be gathered from the criminal statistics for the years from 1899 to 1901:

| YEARS. | To 100 of Each Category. | | | | | |
| | Boys. | | | Girls. | | |
	Illeg.	Orph.	Half-Orph.	Illeg.	Orph.	Half-Orph.
1899	0.5	0.8	18.8	4.3	2.2	27.2
1900	3.5	0.1	18.3	3.0	1.5	29.6
1901	2.5	0.8	15.0	1.5	1.5	19.6

New York (State), 1875-1897.

Dugdale gives the following figures in "The Jukes." They deal with 233 criminals imprisoned in New York in 1875. 40.77 % were orphans; 46.78 % had been neglected in their youth; 17.16 % were descended from criminal families, and 42.49 % from intemperate families.[1]

The following very interesting figures are taken from the annual reports of the Elmira Reformatory.

[1] P. 85.

YEAR.	To Each 100 Prisoners.							
	Parents Alcoholic.		Character of Home Environment.			Length of Stay at Home.		
							Left Home.	
	Plainly.	Probably.	Positively Bad.	Fair.	Good.	Before 10.	Between 10 and 14.	Soon after the Age of 14.
1881	33.8	18.0	47.7	44.0	8.3	5.4	7.6	22.5
1882	35.1	16.0	48.1	41.1	10.8	5.0	7.3	22.7
1883	35.6	14.1	49.3	39.1	11.6	5.2	7.0	23.6
1884	35.9	13.3	50.0	39.2	10.8	4.4	6.8	25.0
1885	36.4	12.8	50.6	38.9	10.5	4.9	6.8	25.5
1886	37.5	12.0	52.4	37.4	10.2	4.6	6.4	25.5
1888	38.4	10.9	52.1	38.9	9.0	5.2	6.3	29.5
1889	38.7	11.1	51.8	39.9	8.3	5.2	6.2	30.8
1890	38.4	11.4	52.0	40.4	7.6	4.7	5.8	29.5
1891	38.4	13.0	52.6	39.8	7.6	4.5	5.9	30.7
1892	38.3	13.1	54.1	38.3	7.6	4.1	5.8	32.0
1893	37.8	12.7	50.3	40.0	9.7	3.8	6.1	32.6
1894	37.5	12.1	49.0	40.6	10.4	3.8	6.1	31.8
1896	37.5	11.3	47.0	41.3	11.7	3.6	6.7	33.0
1897	37.6	51.7?	46.7	41.1	12.2	3.7	6.3	34.2

In round numbers then : 50 % of the criminals come from a corrupt environment, and only 10 % from a good environment; 40 % had left home before the age of 15 ; and further, 40 to 45 % had alcoholic parents.[1]

Norway, 1897–1900.[2]

The following figures deal with illegitimacy of birth among the prisoners in Norway.

| YEARS. | Persons of Illegitimate Birth to 100 Prisoners of Each Category. | | |
	Men.	Women.	Total.
1897–1898	12.7	14.7	13.0
1898–1899	11.8	17.2	12.6
1899–1900	—	—	12.0

[1] See *Drähms*, "The Criminal", Ch. XI.
[2] " Beretning om Rigets Strafarbeidsanstalter for 1897–1898, 1898–1899 ", and for 1899–1900 from *Weinberg*, "Der werdende Verbrecher", p. 16. ("Neue Zeit", 1902–1903, II).

During the years 1887–1891, out of 100 living births 7.33 were illegitimate,[1] while the mortality of natural children in the first year was 15.3 % and that of children in general 9.5 %.[2] Persons of illegitimate birth formed a much greater proportion of the prisoners than of the population in general.

Prussia, 1891–1900.[3]

To 100 Prisoners Born of Illegitimate Unions there were:					
In Houses of Detention. (1891–1900).		In Correctional Prisons. (1896–1900).		In Institutions for Correctional Education. (1895–1900).	
Men.	Women.	Men.	Women.	Men.	Women.
8.5	10.2	8.3	12.5	11.6	15.1

In the years 1887–1891 there were 7.81 illegitimate children out of each 100 living births; 35.7 % of the illegitimate children died in the first year as against 20.8 % of children in general (1884–1893).[4] In Prussia also, then, the influence of illegitimacy upon criminality is very marked.

The following table gives the figures for 18,049 recidivists in Prussian houses of detention in the years 1894–1897.[5]

	Absolute Numbers.	%	
Of illegitimate birth	2,218	11.2	
Had lost father before age of 14	3,230	17.8	
" " mother " " " "	2,116	11.7	35.1
" " both " " " "	1,027	5.6	
" " father after " " " but before 18 .	1,183	6.5	
" " mother after the age of 14 but before 18	880	4.8	12.2
" " both after the age of 14 but before 18	167	0.9	
" committed their first crime before the age of 14	1,150	6.3	
" committed their first crime between the ages of 14 and 18	4,936	27.3	33.6

[1] *Mayr, op. cit.*, p. 197.   [2] *Mayr, op. cit.*, p. 282.
[3] *Aschaffenburg, op. cit.*, p. 105.   [4] *Mayr, op. cit.*, pp. 197 and 282.
[5] Based on *Evert*, "Zur Statistik zurückfälliger Verbrecher in Preussen."

Consequently 47.3% had lost one or both parents before reaching the age of 18; 11.2% were of illegitimate birth — a total, therefore, of 58.5% brought up under abnormal home surroundings. And what was the environment under which the other 41.5% had lived? The table gives no answer to this question, but we may imagine it on the basis of the figures given above.

Switzerland, 1892–1896.

Among the 14,612 persons confined in the Swiss prisons during the years 1892–1896 there were 1,359 of illegitimate birth — 1,044 men (8.5%) and 315 women (13.9%).[1] In the period 1871–1890 there were only 5 illegitimate births to the 100, while the mortality during the first year was 24.0 to the 100 natural children as against 16.4 to the 100 children in general.[2] The influence of illegitimate birth upon criminality, therefore, is very great in Switzerland; an illegitimate child is at least three times as likely to become a criminal as a legitimate child.

As regards the education of criminals, 22% of the women and 17% of the men had been brought up by persons outside of the family. The following table bears upon the others, *i.e.* those who were brought up at home:[3]

	NUMBER OF PRISONERS.				
EDUCATION.	Men.		Women.		Illegitimate.
	Total.	%	Total.	%	%
Good . . .	4,696	57	586	44	37.6
Defective .	3,096	37	619	46	47.6
Bad . . .	481	6	141	10	14.8
Total	8,273	100	1,346	100	100.0

These figures show that the education of a very great number of criminals was very insufficient, and especially so in the case of illegitimate children.

The following table, dealing with the canton of Berne, gives still further details.[4]

[1] "Die Ergebnisse der Schweizerischen Kriminalstatistik während der Jahre 1892–1896", p. 34.
[2] *Mayr, op. cit.*, p. 282.
[3] "Die Ergebnisse etc.", pp. 35, 37, 38.
[4] *Weinberg, op. cit.*, p. 19.

CATEGORIES OF CONVICTS.	To 100 Convicts of Each Category the Education had been:			
	Good.	Defective.	Bad.	Not known.
Legitimate	33.0	54.0	11.0	2.0
Illegitimate	8.4	63.4	25.3	2.8
Brought up at home . .	38.0	11.0	49.0	2.0
" " in another family	9.0	17.0	73.0	1.0
" " " an institution	16.0	19.0	53.0	13.0

The figures concerning the bad education of illegitimate persons are very striking, as well as those brought up in families other than their own; of the latter only 9% had received a good education even as that term is used in the table.

Wurtemberg, 1877–1888.

The following figures have to do with 3,181 criminals in prison in Wurtemberg during the years mentioned:

Out of 100 in each group there were the following number of illegitimate births:

All prisoners	27.0
Habitual criminals	30.6
Occasional criminals	17.4
Thieves	32.4
Swindlers	23.1
Sexual criminals	21.0
Perjurers	13.0
Incendiaries	12.9

Between 1876 and 1885 there were 8.76% of illegitimate births in the general population; and while the general mortality of children in their first year was 26.1% (1884–1893) that of illegitimate children was 32%.[1] The influence of illegitimacy is very strong here, therefore.

To 100 persons of each category the following were brought up outside of their own family:

[1] *Mayr, op. cit.,* p. 283. The other data are taken from *Sichart,* " Ueber individuelle Faktoren des Verbrechens.'' ("Zeitschr. f. d. ges. Strafrw." X.)

Prisoners in general	.	.	.	.	.	.	.	16.0
Habitual criminals	.	.	.	.	.	.	.	19.3
Occasional criminals	.	.	.	.	.	.	.	7.6
Thieves	.	.	.	.	.	.	.	20.9
Incendiaries	.	.	.	.	.	.	.	11.0
Swindlers	.	.	.	.	.	.	.	10.8
Sexual criminals	.	.	.	.	.	.	.	9.4
Perjurers	.	.	.	.	.	.	.	6.0

To 100 persons of each category there were the following one or both of whose parents had led an immoral or criminal life:

Prisoners in general	.	.	.	.	.	.	43.7
Sexual criminals	.	.	.	.	.	.	51.7
Thieves	.	.	.	.	.	.	47.3
Swindlers	.	.	.	.	.	.	34.8
Incendiaries	.	.	.	.	.	.	31.0
Perjurers	.	.	.	.	.	.	23.0

Finally it must be mentioned that 16.2% of 1,714 in the detention prison had alcoholic parents.

We are now at the end of our statistical data and also of our observations upon the environment in which criminals are brought up; for it seems to me superfluous to make further comments: the great influence of environment is indubitable.

Tomel and Rollet close their work "Enfants en prison" with these words, which I make my own, and which are as applicable to adult as to juvenile criminals: "Has society done everything that it ought to spare children the prison? We believe that with ourselves [the reader] will answer, 'No!' Each child to whom we refuse protection will become a delinquent. It is a wolf that we are preparing for the sheep-fold. If tomorrow he makes his fellows pay his own arrears of injustice, if he steals, if he kills, he will not say, 'I commit a crime'; he will say, 'I make reprisals.'" [1]

f. Prostitution. Prostitution has a special importance for the etiology of sexual offenses and of procuration. However, it is not with this that we are concerned at present, but with the correlation between prostitution and criminality in general, in the sense, that is, that prostitution has a demoralizing effect upon the women who practice it and upon the men who have intercourse with them.

[1] P. 298.

Let us begin with the effect upon the prostitutes themselves.   And as with all observations upon the relation between certain social phenomena and criminality, these must be preceded by statistical data.

How large a quota do prostitutes contribute to crime?   This is a hard question to answer, because, first, most criminal statistics make no mention of the occupation of prostitute; second, when the statistics do mention prostitution they do not give the real truth, since the facts will often be concealed by the woman interested; third, the extent of prostitution is almost unknown, so that it is impossible to make the necessary calculations.

The following figures give us some information on the subject.

Austria, 1896–1898.

It is to the study of Dr. A. Baumgarten "Die Beziehungen der Prostitution zum Verbrechen", that I owe the following figures (which, I believe, bear wholly upon Vienna).   In the years 1896–98 there were 34 annually convicted out of a total of 2,400 prostitutes, or 1.4 %, not counting those who were punished for infraction of the regulations covering prostitution.[1]   The author thinks this degree of criminality very small.   I venture to be of a different opinion.   If we note that criminal statistics, those of Germany, for example, show that there are annually only 0.3 women over 12 years of age convicted to the 100, we shall see that the part that prostitutes take in crime must be called more than a small one.

England, 1836–1900.

The English penitentiary statistics show whether the female prisoners are prostitutes or not.   As we have seen above (p. 499) the percentage of prostitutes rose in the period between 1894–1900 to 15% of the total.   The figures bearing upon earlier years, however, show a much higher percentage; in the years 1836–1854 25.2 % of the women convicted (in London) were prostitutes [2]; in the years 1858–1862 prostitutes made up 24.7 % of the women arrested.[3]

However, when we examine these exceptionally high figures, we must not forget that, according to the "Vagrant Act", the fact of being a prostitute itself is a misdemeanor; a part of these women,

[1] P. 10.
[2] *Richelot*, "La Prostitution en Angleterre", p. 571.
[3] *Mayr*, "Statistik der gerichtlichen Polizei im Königreiche Bayern und in einigen andern Ländern", Table CXVIII.

therefore, were convicted for this and not for having committed some
other offense.   The following figure however, where this circumstance
is excluded, also shows a great criminality upon the part of prostitutes,
and gains added weight from the fact that many persons would not
care to make complaint for fear of scandal : to each 100 persons of
both sexes convicted in London between 1843 and 1854 of "theft
from the person", there were 36.0 prostitutes.[1]

France, 1890–1895.

In citing the figures upon the occupations of the prisoners (1890–
1895) we showed (p. 501) that about 5 % were prostitutes.   Compared with that given in the corresponding statistics for England
this percentage is small.   It must, however, be taken into consideration that a great number of occasional prostitutes figure in the penitentiary statistics under the head of another occupation.

Germany, 1885.

For this country I have been able to find only the following.
Among the 2,900 women imprisoned in the 16 great German prisons
there were found in 1885 500 (17.2 %) who had already been punished for professional prostitution.[2]   Although there are no positive
data upon the extent of prostitution, it is nevertheless certain that
much less than 17.2 % of women in general are prostitutes.   The
figure cited shows that prostitutes take a relatively large part in
crime.

Italy, 1891–1895.

1,949 (1.5 %) out of 126,717 women convicted in the years 1891–
1895 were prostitutes.[3]   Here also it must be taken into account
that this number is made up only of prostitutes by occupation, and
that those who follow it as an auxiliary calling are grouped under
other occupations.   Also, L. Ferriani, in his "Minderjährige Verbrecher", concludes that of the 460 young female criminals studied
by him, 243 (52.8 %) were prostitutes.[4]

What data I have been able to secure do not prove — but render

---

[1] *Parent-Duchatelet*, "De la prostitution dans la ville de Paris", II, p. 612.
[NOTE TO THE AMERICAN EDITION: The "Criminal Statistics, Ireland"
(1905) even gives a percentage as high as 38.5, of prostitutes among female
prisoners (p. 25).

[2] *G. S.*, "Die weibliche Lohnarbeit und ihr Einflusz auf die Sittlichkeit
und Kriminalität", p. 751 ("Neue Zeit", 1899–1900, II).

[3] After "Notizie complementari alle statistiche giudiziarie penali degli
anni 1890–95."   [4] P. 173.

exceedingly probable — the assertion that prostitutes show a high degree of criminality. In my opinion this phenomenon is to be explained as follows.

First. From its nature the profession opens a vast field for committing economic offenses.

Second. Prostitution has a very demoralizing effect upon those that practice it. Those who have not sufficiently taken account of the real causes of prostitution consider this a confusing of cause and effect, and believe that it is the demoralization which causes prostitution. In reasoning thus they forget that part of the prostitutes are forced by poverty to take up this profession, and that in such cases there is no need of supposing demoralization. Whatever may be the case with regard to the rest, the profession would increase the demoralization already existing.

All the authors who have taken up the question are agreed that this is really the case. It is impossible to imagine a more degrading situation than that of a prostitute. A woman who is continually forced to act in opposition to her feelings, who is obliged to enter into intimate relations with the first comer however abject he may be, who has become unaccustomed to all work, and who is despised, inevitably loses all respect for herself and falls lower and lower.[1]

A second bond of connection between criminality and prostitution is that it makes possible a category of persons who constitute a permanent danger to society, namely the "protectors." The unregistered prostitutes need a man who will look after them, and to whom they may attach themselves in their forlorn condition. In exchange for this protection the prostitute gives up a large part of her earnings. In examining the biographies of great criminals we see that a large number of them have belonged to this category. It is evident that only demoralized persons can lead such a life, but that this life in its turn increases their demoralization.[2]

---

[1] See further: *Parent-Duchatelet, op. cit.* pp. 139–142; *Faucher*, "Études sur l'Angleterre", I, pp. 77, 78; *C. L. Brace*, "The Dangerous Classes in New York", pp. 116, 117; "Einiges über die Prostitution in Gegenwart und Zukunft", p. 519 ("Neue Zeit", 1891–92, I); *Commenge*, "La prostitution clandestine à Paris", pp. 29–131; *Blaschko*, "Die Prostitution im XIX Jahrhundert", pp. 27, 28.

[2] Upon "souteneurs" and the part they play in crime see: *Parent-Duchatelet, op. cit.*, I, Chap. II, § 12; *Frégier*, "Les classes dangereuses", I, pp. 168–170; *Ladame*, "De la prostitution dans ses rapports avec l'alcoolisme, le crime, et la folie", p. 16; *Sichart*, "Ueber individuelle Faktoren des Verbrechens", p. 44; *Baumgarten, op. cit.*, pp. 17–19; *Stursberg*, "Die Prostitution in Deutschland und ihre Bekämpfung", pp. 76–82.

[NOTE TO THE AMERICAN EDITION: See further *Hermann, op. cit.* pp. 68 *ff.*; *Brusse, op. cit.*; and *H. Ostwald*, "Das Zuhältertum in Berlin."]

In the third place, prostitution has a demoralizing effect upon the men who come into contact with the prostitutes. We cannot lay it to chance that it is shown in many criminal procedures that guilty persons have had relations with the world of prostitution. This world includes only a relatively small number of persons; but the men who frequent it are numerous, and the demoralization which ensues is prejudicial to society. This demoralization is easily explained, as Dr. Lux shows in his "Sozialpolitisches Handbuch", in these words: "The venality of the delights of love debases the pleasure; the man learns to see in woman only a means of satisfying his lust; all higher regard for woman is lost to him, his thoughts become frivolous and cynical, his character continually more vulgar. Whoever has an opportunity to come to know the young men of the large cities, must, unless he is already tainted with their opinions himself, be shocked at the brutality and coarseness of their thought and speech. The whole conversational material of our gilded youth consists of filth and obscenities; they boast of things that a decent man would blush to be charged with. The young man is demoralized and depraved by association with prostitutes, of whose standard of morality he must beware lest he stifle in it every nobler feeling." [1]

g. Alcoholism. Here we have to take up but a single one of the ways in which alcoholism is connected with criminality. For while acute alcohol-poisoning enters into the etiology of sexual offenses and those committed in revenge, etc., it has almost no relation to the largest of the classes, namely economic crimes. Acute alcoholism, therefore, has no place among our general observations. With chronic alcoholism it is otherwise; for the man who is subject to this undergoes a general demoralization by which he is predisposed to crime even when he is not drunk. The manner in which this demoralization takes place is not a question within the province of

[1] P. 138. See also: *Engels,* "Der Ursprung der Familie, des Privateigenthums und des Staats", p. 63; *Stursberg, op. cit.,* pp. 28, 29; *Faure,* "Souvenirs de la Roquette", p. 360; *Baumgarten, op. cit.,* p. 20; *Blaschko, op. cit.,* pp. 28, 29.

Upon the relation between prostitution and criminality in general see: *Moreau-Christophe,* "Du problème de la misère", III, pp. 167–170; *Richelot, op. cit.,* pp. 610–615; *Avé-Lallemant,* "Das Deutsche Gaunerthum", II, pp. 28, 29, and 336, III, pp. 157 and 165; *Oettingen,* "Moralstatistik", pp. 224–232; *Ladame, op. cit.,* pp. 15 ff.; *Lombroso* and *Ferrero,* "La femme criminelle et la prostituée", pp. 535–538.

[NOTE TO THE AMERICAN EDITION: *Cf.* further the recent studies: *A. H. Hübner,* "Ueber Prostituiste und ihre strafrechtliche Behändlung" ("Monatschr. f. krim. Psych. und Strafrechtsreform", III); *O. Mönkmöller,* "Die Kriminalität der Korrigendin" ("Monatschr." etc. V) and "Korrectionsanstalt und Landarmenhaus", ch. III.]

sociology; it is sufficient for us that this consequence of chronic alcoholism is universally recognized.[1]

To show the influence of chronic alcoholism upon criminality we can use only the direct statistical method; that is to say, we must find the number of chronic alcoholics among criminals, and then place beside this the number among the non-criminal population, in order that we may compare them. If the latter figures are lacking, a comparison is impossible. However, as we shall see, the percentage of chronic alcoholics is so great among the criminals, that we can affirm that among the non-criminals the percentage is very small. Consequently the influence of chronic alcoholism, whether greater or less, is indubitably proved. Here are the statistics which we have at our disposal.

Belgium, 1874–1900.

M. Masoin tells us that out of 2,588 convicts (sentenced for 5 years at least) who entered the central institution at Louvain between 1874 and 1895, there were 1,157 (44.7 %) addicted to drunkenness. Out of 216 sentenced to hard labor for life there were 118 (54.6 %), and out of 202 sentenced to death 121 (60 %).[2]

In the prison of Mons Dr. Morel shows that out of 325 recidivists 181 (53.9 %) were given to alcoholic excesses.[3]

It appears from the "Statistique Judiciaire de la Belgique" of 1900, that in 1898, out of 19,169 recidivists (men) there were 5,976 (31.2 %) who had already been convicted of breaking the law against drunkenness, and out of 22,904 non-recidivists (men) 1,984 (8.7 %). Among the women the figures were 8 % (recidivists) and 1.1 % (non-recidivists).[4]

Denmark, 1871–1897.

Out of 2,982 prisoners received between 1871 and 1880 in the prison at Vridslöselille, 797 (27 %) were drunkards. The penitentiary statistics show us that during the years 1891–1897, among the non-recidivists 16.3 % of the men were drunkards, and 4.6 % of the women.[5]

---

[1] See among others: *Krauss*, "Die Psychologie des Verbrechens", pp. 68, 69; *Grotjahn*, "Der Alkoholismus", p. 87.

[2] "L'alcoolisme dans ses rapports avec la criminalité", pp. 411, 413, 415 ("Bulletin de l'académie royale de médecine de Belgique", 1896).

[3] "La prophylaxie et le traitement du criminel récidiviste", p. 64 ("Compte rendu Ve congrès d'anthropologie criminelle").

[4] *Löffler*, "Alkohol und Verbrechen", p. 511 ("Zeitschr. f. d. ges. Strafw." XXIII).

[5] *Dalhoff*, "Rapport sur l'influence de l'alcoolisme sur la criminalité", pp. 40, 41. ("Actes du Congrès pénitentiare internat. de Bruxelles", IV.)

England and Wales, 1858–1897.

The following figures are taken from the police statistics [1] :

Years.	Number of Persons Prosecuted.	Of whom there were Habitual Drinkers: [2]					
		Men.		Women.		Total.	
		Absolute Number.	%	Absolute Number.	%	Absolute Number.	%
1858	434,492	13,553	3.7	4,130	4.5	17,683	4.1
1859	419,929	18,440	5.6	5,303	5.9	23,743	5.7
1860	409,780	19,471	6.0	5,210	6.0	24,681	6.0
1861	421,891	19,475	5.8	4,960	5.7	24,425	5.8
1862	438,228	20,830	6.0	5,209	5.8	26,039	5.9
1894	689,761	19,224	3.3	6,557	5.3	25,781	3.6
1895	687,075	16,268	2.8	5,695	4.7	21,963	3.1
1896	728,374	17,308	2.8	6.015	4.7	23,323	3.2
1897	757,485	17,012	2.7	6,084	4.6	23,096	3.0

These figures have no great value; they represent the number of habitual drinkers to be less than it really is. The statistics cited divide all persons prosecuted into eight groups (habitual criminals, prostitutes, vagrants, etc.) and under the heading of habitual drinkers only those alcoholics figure who are not included under other headings. If a vagrant, for example, is also a habitual drinker, he will be counted among the vagrants and not among the habitual drinkers; hence this latter group is much larger than the figures would indicate. [3]

France.

At the penitentiary Congress in Brussels (1900), M. V. Marambat, well known for his studies on the relation between criminality and alcoholism, gave the following figures: [4]

[1] For the years 1858–1862 taken from *Mayr*, "Statistik der gerichtlichen Polizei im Königreiche Bayern und in einigen anderen Ländern", Tab. CXVIII; and for the other years from "Criminal Statistics", 1894–1897.

[2] In these tables the term "drinker" is used for one who drinks to excess.

[3] Upon England see further: *L. Gordon Rylands*, "Crime, its Causes and Remedy", pp. 17, 20–22; *J. Baker*, "Rapport sur l'influence de l'alcoolisme sur la criminalité", and *W. C. Sullivan, id.* ("Actes de Cong. pen. internat. de Brux." 1900, IV).

[Note to the American Edition: The "Report on the Judicial Statistics of Scotland for the year 1908" contains data upon criminality and alcoholism.]   [4] "Actes,". p. 112.

CRIMES AND MISDEMEANORS.	NUMBER OF CONVICTS.	NUMBER OF DRUNKARDS.	%
Murder, assault, and other crimes of violence	787	649	82.4
Malicious mischief, etc.	433	344	79.4
Theft and other economic offenses . .	3,359	2,156	64.2
Arson	42	26	61.9
Rape and other sexual offenses . . .	683	352	51.5
Other offenses	18	9	50.0
Total	5,322	3,536	66.4

At the same congress Dr. Malgat reported the following results of an investigation made by him in the prison at Nice: [1]

OFFENSES.	ENTERED.	DRINKERS.	%
Insults and violence to public officers .	138	91	65.9
Theft	579	357	61.6
Obtaining money under false pretenses	56	34	60.7
Assaults	275	160	58.1
Vagrancy	346	196	56.6
Indecent assault	52	29	55.7
Homicide	33	18	54.5
Expelled offenders	175	95	54.2
Breach of trust	63	33	52.3
Other offenses	133	80	60.1
Total	1,850	1,093	56.3

Germany.

An inquiry made by Dr. A. Baer with regard to the inmates of the German prisons, in the period after 1870, gives the following results: [2]

	NUMBER OF PRISONERS.	NUMBER OF DRINKERS.					
		In General.		Occasional.		Habitual.	
		Absolute.	%	Absolute.	%	Absolute.	%
Men . . .	30,041	13,199	43.9	7,071	23.5	6,128	20.4
Women . .	2,796	507	18.1	198	7.1	309	11'0
Total . . .	32,837	13,706	41.7	7,269	22.1	6,437	19.6

[1] "Actes", p. 106. See also upon France: *Laurent*, "Les habitués des prisons de Paris", pp. 297 *ff*.; *Corre*, "Crime et suicide", pp. 182 *ff*., and *Verhaeghe*, "De l'alcoolisation", p. 144.
[NOTE TO THE AMERICAN EDITION: See also the "Compte général de l'administration de la justice criminelle pendant l'année 1907", pp. xx *ff*.]
[2] "Der Alcoholismus", p. 348.

For the different crimes and misdemeanors the figures are as follows: [1]

Crimes and Misdemeanors.	Number of Prisoners (Men).	Drinkers.		Among the Drinkers there were:			
				Occasional.		Habitual.	
		Absolute Number.	%	Absolute Number.	%	Absolute Number.	%
A. Houses of Correction.							
Assaults .	773	575	74.5	418	72.7	157	27.3
Robbery, etc.	898	618	68.8	353	57.1	265	42.9
Homicide .	348	220	63.2	129	58.6	91	41.4
Rape, etc. .	954	575	60.2	352	61.2	223	38.8
Theft . .	10,033	5,212	51.9	2,513	48.2	2,699	51.8
Attempted homicide .	252	128	50.8	78	60.9	50	39.1
Arson . .	804	383	47.6	184	48.0	199	52.0
Murder . .	514	237	46.1	139	58.6	98	41.4
Various crimes	1,689	712	42.2	358	50.2	354	49.8
Perjury . .	590	157	26.6	82	52.2	75	47.8
B. Houses of Detention.							
Offenses against morals	200	154	77.0	113	73.3	41	26.7
Rebellion .	652	489	76.5	445	89.0	54	11.0
Assaults . .	1,130	716	63.4	581	81.1	135	18.9
Robbery . .	48	28	58.3	16	57.0	12	43.0
Domiciliary trespass .	411	223	54.2	210	94.2	13	5.8
Disturbance of public peace	34	18	52.9	12	66.6	6	33.3
Various misdemeanors	826	433	52.4	306	70.7	127	29.3
Arson . .	23	11	48.0	5	45.4	6	54.6
Theft . .	3,282	1,048	32.0	666	63.5	382	36.5
Obtaining money under false pretenses, forgery, embez.	786	194	24.7	111	57.2	83	42.8

Out of a total of 359 vagabonds and mendicants Dr. Bonhoeffer found 281 (78.2 %) alcoholics.[2]

[1] *Op. cit.*, p. 351.
[2] "Ein Beitrag zur Kenntnis des groszstädtischen Bettel- und Vagabondentums" ("Zeitschr. f. d. ges. Strw." XXI).

Italy.

Out of a total of 507 criminals examined by him Dr. Marro found 379 (74.7 %) addicted to excess in alcohol, and only eight (1.5 %) abstainers or "unknown." [1]

Netherlands, 1900–1901.

It was only in 1900 that the criminal statistics mentioned for the first time the number of habitual drunkards among the convicts. Here are the results:

CRIMES AND MISDEMEANORS.	PERCENTAGE OF HABITUAL DRUNKARDS IN EACH CATEGORY.
Obtaining money under false pretenses	16
Crimes against the public authority	13
Mendicity and vagabondage	10
Crimes of violence	10
Crimes against morals	10
All crimes	8.31
Assault	7
Theft	7
Receiving stolen goods	.5
Poaching	3

Among the recidivists the drunkards formed 11.6 %.

The data for 1901 are more detailed and also more worthy of confidence.

CRIMES AND MISDEMEANORS.	PERCENTAGE OF HABITUAL DRUNKARDS IN EACH CATEGORY.
Mendicity and vagabondage	26.51
Rebellion	21.16
Embezzlement	19.20
Obtaining money under false pretenses	18.26
Serious assaults	16.94
Malicious mischief	16.59
Insult to public official	16.10
Disturbing the public peace	14.33
Simple theft	11.61
Sexual offenses	10.84
Assaults	10.87
Insults	9.96
Aggravated theft	8.84
Poaching	1.46
All crimes	13.00

[1] "I caratteri dei delinquenti", p. 296.

Of the recidivists 21.96 % were habitual drunkards.[1]

New York (State), 1869–1870.

In his "Dangerous Classes of New York", C. L. Brace states that in 1870, out of 49,423 criminals in the prisons of New York City there were 30,507 (61.6 %) habitual drunkards, and 893 (81.6 %) of the 1,093 prisoners in the Albany penitentiary in the years 1869–70 likewise were drunkards.[2]

R. L. Dugdale gives the following figures for the 233 criminals examined by him : [3]

CRIMES.	PERCENTAGE OF HABITUAL DRUNKARDS.
Theft from the person	55.00
Robbery	47.36
Crimes against persons	40.47
Theft	39.28
All crimes	39.05
Crimes against property	38.74
Burglary	33.33

Prussia, 1894–1897.

Out of 18,049 recidivists in the houses of correction in the years 1849–1897, there were 4,930 (27.3 %) habitual drunkards, of whom 4,473 (28.7 %) were men, and 457 (18.2 %) were women.[4]

Sweden, 1887–1897.

Out of 27,452 inmates in the prisons during the years 1887–1897 there were 3,273 (11.9 %) addicted to drink, of whom 3,101 (12.7 %) were men and 99 (3.2 %) women.[5] These figures, however, are below the reality, since only those are counted as alcoholics who were drunk at the time they committed the crime. When we take into consider-

---

[1] [NOTE TO THE AMERICAN EDITION : "The criminal statistics of the Netherlands for 1904" contain data upon the subject in question. *Cf.* further *de Roos, op. cit.,* pp. 175 *ff.,* and "Parallelismen tusschen alcoholisme en criminaliteit" ("Tijdschrift v. Strafrecht", XXIII); *Verrijn Stuart, op. cit.,* pp. 204 *ff.* ; *A. Ariens,* "Criminaliteit en drankmisbruik."]

[2] P. 66.

[3] "The Jukes", p. 85.

[4] Evert, "Zur Statistik rückfälliger Verbrecher in Preussen", p. 198.

[5] *Wieselgren,* "L'influence of alcoolisme sur la criminalité", p. 164 ("Actes du Congr. pénit. de Bruxelles"), *cf. Kinberg,* "Alcool et criminalité" ("Arch. d'anthr. crim." XXVIII).

ation that the number of criminals who were in a state of intoxication when they committed their crimes was 52.6 %, we may be certain that a considerable number of them were habitual drunkards.

Switzerland, 1892-1896.

On the 1st of January, 1892, there were 2,201 persons in the 35 penitentiaries; 1,816 men and 385 women. Among these there were 880 drunkards (39.9 %); 762 (42 %) men, and 118 (31 %) women.[1]

In the years 1892-1896, the Swiss criminal statistics give alcoholism as the cause of crime in 23.1 % of the cases.[2] This figure, however, has no great value; not only are the statistics concerning alcoholism as a cause little worthy of confidence, as the author of them confesses (indeed, it is impossible to speak of "the cause" of a criminal act, since there are always several); but further there is no distinction made between acute and chronic alcoholism.

Wurtemberg, 1887-1888.

Among the 3,181 prisoners examined by Sichart in the years 1887-1888, there were 939 (29.5 %) habitual drunkards. The figures for some of the more important crimes are as follows:[3]

CRIMES.	PERCENTAGE OF DRUNKARDS IN EACH CATEGORY.
Crimes against morals	36.3
Arson	34.2
Theft	28.0
Obtaining money under false pretenses	25.7
Perjury	24.0

The data given above show sufficiently, it seems to me, what the relation is between chronic alcoholism and criminality. Notwithstanding their divergences the percentages in the different countries are generally very high, and in every case much higher than among the non-criminal population. The danger that these statistics are

[1] *Schaffroth*, "L'influence de l'alcoolisme sur la criminalité", p. 128 ("Actes du Cong. pén. intern. de Bruxelles").
[2] "Die Ergebnisse der Schweizerischen Kriminalstatistik während der Jahre 1892-1896", p. 36.
[3] "Ueber individuelle Faktoren des Verbrechens", p. 42.

based upon inaccurate data is not great, since the culprit has every reason to pretend that his act has been committed in a state of intoxication, in order that he may be less severely punished, and not that he is a chronic alcoholic.

There still remains the question as to what is the degree of influence which chronic alcoholism has upon crime. We should be exaggerating if we were to declare (as is sometimes done by total abstainers) that whenever a criminal is an habitual alcoholic, alcoholism is one of the principal causes of his crime. It is evident that in many cases it is only an accidental phenomenon. Nevertheless, the figures given above agree with the thesis that chronic alcoholism is a demoralizing agent and as such belongs to the etiology of crime. Its influence naturally cannot be exactly expressed in figures.[1]

h. Militarism. Although the influence of militarism upon criminality may not be an important factor in comparison with some others, it is still necessary to speak of it here briefly, and under two heads: its influence in time of peace, and its influence in time of war.

First, the influence of militarism in time of peace. The army is recruited in great part among those who do not volunteer, in other words among persons who have not the least taste for the military life and only serve for fear of incurring severe penalties. Then a great number of the volunteers have become soldiers only from necessity, because they could not find a place for themselves anywhere else. Finally one class of volunteers have enlisted very young, for a long term of service, perhaps at the instance of their parents, or drawn by the brilliant uniform, or other means of advertising peculiar to the army. It is unnecessary to add that for the last two classes the military service is often a deception, which makes them regret having engaged in it.

The first source of demoralization in an army is to be found in its composition. When you bring together a number of men, uneducated for the most part, with nothing to unite them but constraint, and when there are already certain bad elements among them, the

---

[1] [NOTE TO THE AMERICAN EDITION: *Cf.* besides the works of de Roos, Verrijn Stuart, Ariëns, and Kinberg, already cited, the following of recent date: *H. Hoppe,* "Alkohol und Kriminalität"; *A. Pistolese,* "Alcoolismo et delinquenza"; *Hoegel, op. cit.,* pp. 397 *ff.*; *K. W. F. Boas,* "Alkohol und Verbrechen nach neueren Statistiken; *Aull,* "Alkohol und Verbrechen"; *A. Ley* et *R. Charpentier,* "Alcoolisme et criminalité," *G. B. Gruber,* "Der Alkoholismus." All these authors recognize, though not all in the same degree, that the influence of alcoholism upon crime is great; Pistolese alone denies it almost wholly.]

demoralizing influence makes itself felt at once. No moral bond unites these men, but on the contrary a vague irritation begins to spread. And this demoralization is not counteracted by that great moral force, work; a great part of the time among the soldiers is passed in forced idleness, and the rest in learning things in which they have little interest, if indeed they do not feel an aversion to them.

It is naturally only by a discipline of iron that order can be maintained and the recruits taught their trade. As soon as a man is debased by excessive discipline to the rôle of a machine, his moral qualities deteriorate; the state of things thus created brings it about that the great power given to superiors often degenerates into a thirst for domination, and renders the subordinates servile, and yet of the opinion that anything is right for them so long as they are not found out.[1]

Since most soldiers are only under arms for a short time, the consequences named are not of great importance for them, but those consequences nevertheless exist for the professional soldier. The best known set of statistics upon the criminality among soldiers is that of Hausner,[2] who shows that it is 25 times as great as the criminality of civilians. These figures, however, have little value, because among the civilians are counted not simply the men of military age, but the whole population. Further, a statistical comparison of military and civil criminality will always meet with great difficulties, for, first, there are offenses of which only soldiers can be guilty; second, the number of the soldiers is not constant even in any one year. Although we cannot, therefore, express in figures the harmful influences of militarism, it exists, nevertheless. But even if we had the figures and they were to show — supposing a most improbable case — that criminality was no greater among soldiers than in civil life, even this would not contradict the evil influence of military life, since repression and the fear of punishment are greater among soldiers than among civilians, and abject poverty, one of the powerful factors in economic criminality, is totally lacking in the army.[3]

---

[1] The question must be looked at from the other side also, and it must be admitted that military service *can* have a favorable effect upon totally lawless individuals, who thus learn order and discipline; this, however, does not prevent the disadvantages from remaining.

[2] Quoted by *Oettingen* in his "Moralstatistik", p. 481.

[NOTE TO THE AMERICAN EDITION: *Cf.* further: upon Germany: *H. Dietz*, "Die Militärstrafrechtspflege in Lichte der Kriminalstatistik"; for France: *A. Corre*, "Aperçu général de la criminalité militaire en France"; for Italy: *L. Ferrero di Cavallerleone* and *C. Placido*, "Essais de criminologie militaire."]

[3] See also *Oettingen*, *op. cit.*, p. 687; *Colajanni*, "Sociologia criminale",

The question may be raised as to whether the disadvantages spoken of above are inseparable from every form of organization of the army. The answer must be that this is the case in part only. The harmful consequences will partially disappear when the army is adapted to the democratic spirit, and the service remains limited to the time strictly necessary to make a good soldier; but the fact that the great mass of which the army is composed has no sympathy with its aim and end but remains in service only by constraint, will continue to exist. This latter circumstance will disappear only in the country where the army is exclusively for the purposes of defense, to repulse an enemy that wishes to destroy democratic institutions.

We come now to the influence of war itself. That which, at ordinary times, is one of the gravest crimes, homicide, is commanded in war; ravages and burnings are the order of the day. It is inevitable that those who are driven to commit such acts, lose little by little their respect for the lives and property of their fellows. War arouses a spirit of violence, not only in those who take part in it, but in the whole population.

Happily wars are neither so numerous nor so long continued as formerly, so that the consequences have no longer so wide a scope.

Statistical research into the influence of war upon criminality is very difficult, for criminality diminishes in time of war in an abnormal fashion, first, because a great part of the male population of the age most disposed to crime is under arms; second, the repression of crime being less vigorous makes the degree of criminality appear smaller than it really is, which explains why the figures for the criminality of women and juveniles are less.

We often hear that war has also a good moral influence, since the whole nation is then animated with a single ideal. This is true only in the very rare cases where a war is really popular, in place of being the means of procuring material profits for a small minority, while the great majority remain indifferent. It goes without saying that even in these exceptional cases, the harmful consequences to the participants still remain.[1]

II, pp. 572–589; *Corre*, "Crime et suicide", p. 337; *Lux*, "Sozialpolitisches Handbuch", p. 250; *Wagner*, "Die Sittlichkeit auf dem Lande", pp. 77–81; *Lombroso*, "Crime, its Causes and Remedies", pp. 201–203; *Steinmetz*, "Der Krieg als sociologisches Problem", p. 37; *Bleibtreu*, *op. cit.*, p. 16; *Hamon*, "Psychologie du Militaire professionel", Chs. V–VIII.

[1] See also: *Corre*, "Essai sur la criminalité", p. 78 ("Journal des Economistes", 1868); *Colajanni*, *op. cit.* II, pp. 572–589; *Aubry*, "La contagion

We have examined the tendencies of the present economic system and of its consequences. Before concluding we must treat of the effect of

i. The penalty. The present codes give prominence to three kinds of penalties: fines, different kinds of imprisonment, and capital punishment. We naturally do not have to say anything of the first of these, since there can be no question raised as to its effect upon the person upon whom the fine is laid. All that we can say is that this penalty fails of its object since no account is taken of the financial condition of the person sentenced to it, and it follows that while the punishment involved is only trifling for the rich, it constitutes a heavy burden for the poor. Often a fine for a poor man who cannot pay is simply a sentence to a short imprisonment.

The death penalty also naturally is outside of our present discussion. I would simply observe that among the numerous arguments against this penalty it must be noted that it has no intimidating effect upon those who are present, as one would suppose, but on the contrary a demoralizing influence; besides which the attention of the ignorant class is drawn to the crime and the perpetrator of it. Those who are condemned to death have almost all been present at executions. Out of a total of 511 of whom we have information, there were only 15 (about 3 %) who had never witnessed an execution.[1]

In investigating the influence of punishment upon morality it is imprisonment alone, therefore, which must be taken into consideration, so much the more since even in the case of minor crimes it is almost always inflicted, while capital punishment is either altogether abolished, as in some countries, or else rarely pronounced and still more rarely executed.

The following table shows how many times imprisonment is inflicted in comparison with other forms of punishment.

du meurtre", pp. 247–249; *Prof. Fr. v. Liszt*, "Das Verbrechen als sozial-pathologische Erscheinung", p. 17.
[NOTE TO THE AMERICAN EDITION: See further upon the demoralizing consequences of war: *Steinmetz*, "Die Philosophie des Krieges", ch. III, 5, and my criticism of this book under the title "An apology for war" (" Nieuwe Tijd", XIII, pp. 488 *ff*.). Think of the horrible cruelties committed in the recent wars in the Balkans (see the report of the Commission of the Carnegie Foundation); no one can any longer deny the demoralizing consequences of war!] [It may be of interest to the reader to know that the author wrote the foregoing in the spring of 1914. — TRANSL.]
[1] *Aubry*, "La contagion du meurtre", p. 70; see also Ch. III, and *Aschaffenburg, op. cit.*, p. 229.

Germany, 1882–1895.[1]

YEARS.	PENALTIES TO EACH 1,000 PERSONS SENTENCED.			
	Death.	Imprisonment (All kinds.)	Fines.	Public Admonition.
1882	0.3	736.3	253	10
1883–87 } annual	0.2	697.4	291	11
1888–92 } average	0.1	660.2	323	17
1893	0.1	619.2	363	18
1894	0.1	607.2	375	18
1895	0.1	595.2	386	19

60% to 70% of the sentences, then, were deprivation of liberty. What is the effect of this? The answer to this question must be found in the statistics of recidivism. Here are the results for certain countries of Europe, which probably are not much different from those of other countries.

Germany, 1882–1900.[2]

YEARS.	NUMBER OF RECIDIVISTS TO 100 CONVICTS.	TO 100,000 OF THE POPULATION OVER 12 THERE WERE RECIDIVISTS WHO WERE CONVICTED			
		Once.	Twice.	3 to 5 Times.	6 Times and Over.
1882	24.9	115	56	64	23
1883	25.8	119	59	69	20
1884	26.3	127	63	72	22
1885	27.4	127	63	75	26
1886	28.0	129	65	79	30
1887	28.8	131	66	81	34
1888	29.3	127	65	80	35
1889	31.2	142	71	87	40
1890	32.7	150	76	93	43
1891	34.0	158	79	99	47
1892	34.7	169	87	107	54
1893	35.2	171	88	111	57
1894	36.9	181	93	120	65
1895	37.9	184	96	124	69
1896	38.8	183	96	129	75
1897	39.6	186	99	129	78
1898	40.1	189	100	133	83
1899	40.8	187	100	133	85
1900	41.2	180	96	131	86

[1] "Kriminalstatistik für das Jahr 1895", I, p. 31.
[2] "Kriminalstat. f. d. Jahr 1900", I, pp. 18–19.

Recidivism has regularly increased, then: a little more than 65% in 18 years.

It is present in different crimes in very various degrees. For the following crimes it is very great.

Germany, 1882–1895.[1]

CRIMES.	NUMBER OF RECIDIVISTS HAVING UNDERGONE IMPRISONMENT TO EACH 100 CONVICTS IN THE YEARS			
	1882.	1886.	1890.	1895.
Leze-majesty	40.7	41.3	43.2	52.8
Rebellion	31.8	41.3	46.8	52.7
Robbery and blackmail	44.4	45.6	51.5	50.9
False accusation	34.8	37.1	42.1	48.3
Crimes of fraud	32.9	38.9	42.9	45.4
Crimes against personal liberty . . .	26.6	32.3	37.8	42.8
Theft and embezzlement	32.1	35.2	37.2	40.4
Crimes against morals	24.1	31.3	35.9	38.3
Counterfeiting	28.5	31.1	35.1	38.2

The following figures give a picture of recidivism in

England and Wales, 1871–1900.[2]

YEARS.	PERCENTAGE OF RECIDIVISTS AMONG CONVICTS.	PERCENTAGE AMONG CONVICTS OF RECIDIVISTS WHO HAVE BEEN CONVICTED				
		Once.	2 to 5 Times.	6 to 10 Times.	11 to 20 Times.	Over 20 Times.
1871–77	40	—	—	—	—	—
1880–92	48	—	—	—	—	—
1894	54.5	15.2	18.3	7.7	6.2	6.9
1895	55.5	15.7	18.0	8.9	6.9	5.9
1896	57.3	14.8	19.1	9.0	7.7	6.6
1897	57.6	18.9	19.0	8.8	7.6	7.1
1898	59.9	16.2	20.0	8.9	7.5	7.1
1899	60.2	16.4	19.9	9.2	7.6	7.0
1900	59.3	15.8	19.2	9.2	7.7	7.4

Here also, then, as in Germany there is a great increase in recidivism; 72% in 29 years.

[1] "Kriminalstat. f. d. Jahr, 1895", I, p. 25.
[2] *Drähms*, "The Criminal", p. 228, and "Criminal Statistics", 1894–1900, Table XXXV.

For some offenses recidivism is more common than for others, as the following figures show.

England and Wales, 1899–1900.[1]

(Assizes and Quarter Sessions.)

YEARS.	NUMBER OF RECIDIVISTS TO 100 PERSONS CONVICTED OF THE FOLLOWING CRIMES.					
	Crimes against Persons.	Crimes against Property with Violence.	Crimes against Property without Violence.	Malicious Mischief.	Forgery and Counterfeiting.	Other Crimes.
1894	32.1	67.3	64.1	42.5	41.1	27.9
1895	35.2	67.3	66.1	51.8	38.5	24.4
1896	36.1	67.2	66.3	44.3	37.4	25.0
1897	38.0	68.7	66.4	51.1	40.0	28.1
1898	39.3	68.1	68.3	56.0	43.2	32.4
1899	37.7	69.9	67.4	58.3	40.0	35.2
1900	39.7	71.0	68.9	59.4	40.9	29.8

The following table has to do with

Austria, 1866–1899.[2]

YEARS.	PERCENTAGE OF CONVICTS WHO				
	Had been convicted of Crime Once Before.	Had been convicted of Crime Several Times.	Total.	Had been already convicted of a Misdemeanor or Contravention.	Were Recidivists.
1866–1870	11.9	15.5	27.4	17.5	44.9
1871–1875	11.6	14.2	25.8	17.9	43.7
1876–1880	10.9	14.6	25.5	22.2	47.7
1881–1885	10.6	14.2	24.8	25.2	50.0
1886–1890	10.9	12.9	23.8	27.9	51.7
1891–1895	11.1	12.5	23.6	28.9	52.5
1896	12.5	10.7	23.2	31.5	54.7
1897	12.7	10.6	23.3	30.4	53.8
1898	12.5	9.9	22.4	29.1	51.5
1899	12.4	10.1	22.5	29.8	52.4

[1] After "Criminal Statistics", 1894–1900, Table, IX.
[2] "Ergebnisse der Strafrechtspflege in den im Reichsrate vertretenen Königreichen und Ländern im Jahre 1899", p. li.

This table has only a little value for the problem of recidivism; it bears only upon those convicted of crime and leaves out of account those convicted of misdemeanors; and in the last two columns are included persons convicted of contraventions, who ought not to figure in statistics of recidivism.

The following figures have much greater value.

France, 1850–1900.[1]

YEARS.	PERCENTAGE OF RECIDIVISTS IN EACH GROUP OF CONVICTS.		
	Assizes.	Correctional Tribunals.	Total.
1850–1855	33	—	—
1856–1860	36	—	31
1861–1865	38	—	34
1866–1870	41	—	38
1871–1875	47	—	42
1876–1880	48	—	44
1881–1885	52	44	44
1886–1890	56	47	47
1891–1895	57	46	46
1896–1900	57	46	46

Here, then, is a steady increase, checked only in the last 15 years by the law of May 27th, 1885, upon recidivism.

The following table shows recidivism for certain offenses.[2]

CRIMES AND MISDEMEANORS.	PERCENTAGE OF RECIDIVISTS AMONG CONVICTS.			
	1881–85.	1886–90.	1891–95.	1896–1900
Drunkenness	81	79	79	86
Vagabondage	73	78	79	82
Mendicity	72	77	75	80
Assaults upon parents, etc.	69	63	55	80
Aggravated theft	73	77	79	79
Counterfeiting	50	54	57	55
Insults and violence to public officials	48	50	51	51
Obtaining money under false pretenses . . .	51	50	51	50

[1] The figures for 1850–1880 are taken from *Bournet*, "De la criminalité en France et en Italie", p. 31, for the Assizes, and from *Joly*, "La France criminelle", p. 166, for the others; the figures for 1881–1900 are from the "Rapport sur l'administration de la justice criminelle de 1881 à 1900", p. lxii.

[2] "Rapport etc.", pp. lxiv and lxv.

CRIMES AND MISDEMEANORS.	PERCENTAGE OF RECIDIVISTS AMONG CONVICTS.			
	1881–85.	1886–90.	1891–95.	1896–1900.
Homicide	42	50	52	50
Murder	46	44	44	48
Arson	53	50	52	46
Theft	47	51	47	46
Serious assaults	40	35	42	46
Domestic theft	47	45	42	44
Forgery	37	43	46	44
Fraudulent bankruptcy	33	26	31	44
Misdemeanor connected with fishing	35	39	39	41
Breach of trust	41	43	41	39
Offenses connected with hunting	26	32	34	38
Minor assaults	32	36	35	35
Offenses against morals	31	30	32	31
Maltreatment of children	32	25	21	25
Infanticide	7	6	8	7

Here are the figures for

Italy, 1876–1889.[1]

YEARS.	PERCENTAGE OF RECIDIVISTS AMONG THOSE ARRAIGNED BEFORE.		YEARS.	PERCENTAGE OF RECIDIVISTS AMONG THOSE ARRAIGNED BEFORE.	
	Assizes.	Correctional tribunals.		Assizes.	Correctional tribunals.
1876	10.4	—	1883	29.4	22.6
1877	11.2	—	1884	32.8	23.6
1878	13.2	—	1885	34.7	27.6
1879	20.7	—	1886	34.0	27.8
1880	21.5	—	1887	36.0	32.2
1881	26.5	20.2	1888	32.2	30.6
1882	28.8	21.1	1889	36.3	32.3

In Italy also, then, there is a constant increase of recidivism (except in 1888).

[1] After *Bournet* "De la criminalité en France et en Italie", p. 32, and "Statistica giudiziaria penale", 1881–1889. The criminal statistics for 1890–95 contain all those convicted including those brought before the justices of the peace, which makes them not comparable with those given above. The average figure for 1891–95 was 25.27%, and for 1896–1900, 30.19% ("Notizie complementari etc.", 1896–1900).

In conclusion, here are the figures for the

Netherlands, 1896–1901.[1]

YEARS.	CONVICTS.	RECIDIVISTS.	PERCENTAGE OF RECIDIVISTS.	PERCENTAGE OF CONVICTS WHO HAD BEEN CONVICTED.		
				Once.	2 to 5 times.	6 times or more.
1896	17,205	5,097	29.6	17.1	10.3	2.2
1897	16,832	5,566	33.0	19.6	11.6	1.8
1898	16,368	5,997	36.6	21.2	13.2	2.2
1899	15,631	6,092	38.9	20.7	15.4	2.8
1900	15,169	6,048	39.8	20.3	16.2	3.3

The imperfection of the present mode of combating crime is shown even by the evidence of the statistics we have given. It would be hard to imagine a more complete fiasco; in place of a decrease there has been an increase of recidivism; in place of making men better, the prison makes them worse.

Here is in brief the explanation of the fact. As we have already observed above in treating of the definition of crime, one of the important elements in the present system of punishment consists, for many people, in the desire to satisfy their revengeful feelings excited by the crime. Those who realize that the punishment must be especially aimed at the improvement of the criminal form only a small minority. The present forms of punishment and the manner in which they are inflicted are little if at all in accord with this latter point of view. At present the penalty is not much more than an evil inflicted upon the criminal to satisfy the vengeance of a great part of mankind, and at the same time to make it impossible for the criminal to do harm, either for a time or else forever, and finally to terrify him and other men into not committing crimes. *So long as punishment has this characteristic, so long as it does not aim at the improvement of the criminal, so long will it fail to effect a decrease in crime, but will rather bring an increase, as the facts prove.* No one, not even the most dangerous criminal is morally improved in the slightest degree by vengeance wreaked upon him. Vengeance engenders only vengeance and no other feeling. We can expect to see good re-

---

[1] After the "Jaarcijfers voor het Koninkrijk der Nederlanden", 1901, p. 121.

[NOTE TO THE AMERICAN EDITION: The general percentage of recidivism in the Netherlands had risen to 44.5% in 1908.]

sults from punishment only if the criminal, from the manner in which he is treated, perceives that those who have him in charge wish him well, are trying to improve him, and that his act was wicked and intolerable.

There are two types of imprisonment; imprisonment in common, and in separate cells. It is very easy to understand that a term of imprisonment served in common has disastrous consequences for the prisoner. It is because of this system that the prison has had the name of a school of crime, which would be a good joke if the facts were less serious. All kinds of criminals, young and old, those sentenced for minor offenses,[1] and those guilty of grave crimes, criminals against property and criminals against persons, all find themselves massed together, so that instead of leaving prison bettered, almost every one leaves it worse than he went in. No work is done, or at least only stupefying labors; a real trade is neither practiced nor learned.[2]

The disadvantages of this system have led to the cellular plan by which the contagious influences of the prison are gotten rid of. Much was hoped for from the change, but the statistics of recidivism show the hope to have been ill-founded; separate confinement improves the prisoner no more than the older type. This fact is not difficult to explain. Starting from the false theory that man has a free will, the non-determinists have believed, and unhappily still believe, that the criminal left to himself and to his own reflections will repent. As Sacker in "Der Rückfall" judiciously remarks, the criminal must not be left to his thoughts — if he has any — but must be given new ideas. It is unnecessary to remark that it is not life in a cell that will give them to him.

Man is a social being; without life among his fellows he is like an animal out of its element. How can he become better if he lives alone. The cell stupefies him, isolation and monotony make him a machine, which later will not be fit for a free life. I do not know a better description of the consequences of separate confinement than that given by the competent author of "Pictures and Problems from

[1] On short imprisonments for minor offenses see *von Liszt*, "Kriminalpolitische Aufgaben", V, "Die kurzeitige Freiheitsstrafe" ("Zeitschr. f. d. ges. Strw." IX).

[2] See *Gautier*, "Le monde des prisons" ("Archives d'anthropologie criminelle", III) p. 563; *Colajanni*, "Sociologia criminale", II, pp. 671–679; *Laurent*, "Les habitués des prisons de Paris", pp. 592–596; *Havelock Ellis*, "Verbrecher und Verbrechen", pp. 266–276; *Moreau*, "Le monde des prisons", pp. 280–282; *Aubry*, "La contagion du meurtre", Ch. II; *Lombroso*, "Les palimpsestes des prisons", pp. 379–381.

London Police Courts", Th. Holmes. He says: "How is it that a man's facial expression changes during a long detention? How is it that his voice becomes hard and unnatural? How is it that his eyes become shifty, cunning, and wild? It is no fault of the prison officials; they cannot help these things; from the governor downward they are not to blame. It is not because of hard work. From conversation with, and knowledge of, such men, I gather that some of them at any rate would be thankful for more work. It is the system that does it, the long-continued, soul-and-mind-destroying monotony, the long, silent nights in which for hours men lie awake thinking, thinking, thinking, driven in upon themselves and to be their own selves' only companion. No interchange of ideas is possible, no sound of human voices comes to call forth their own, and their own vocal organs rust. Nor does returning day bring change, nothing but the same duties, performed in the same way, at the same hour, and the same food, in the same quantities, served in the same demoralizing way. They become strangers to the usages of civilized society, and devour their food even as the beasts, but not with the wild beast's relish. To the use of knife and fork they become strangers; to a knowledge of their own lineaments they become strangers; to high thoughts, amiable words, courtesy, love of truth, and all that makes a man they become strangers, for these virtues cannot dwell with senseless monotony. But if these things die of atrophy, other but less desirable qualities are developed. A low cunning takes their place; the wits are sharpened to deceive or to gain small ends; hypocrisy is developed, and men come out of prison hating it, loathing it, but less fitted to perform the duties of life than when they entered it." [1]

Read further the opinion of Dostoievsky: "I am firmly convinced that the boasted cellular system pursues but a false, if specious, aim. It sucks the vital power out of a man, enervates his mind, weakens and cows him, and finally presents the desiccated mummy of a man made half mad, as a picture of reformation and repentance." [2]

It would be possible to fill these pages with the well-supported opinions of those who regard the cellular system as "an aberration of the 19th century" (Ferri).[3]

[1] Pp. 142, 143.   [2] *Op. cit.*, p. 22.
[3] I will mention the following: *Prins*, "Criminalité et répression", Ch. V.; *Ferri*, "La sociologie criminelle", pp. 546–554, and "Eine Verirrung des neunzehnten Jahrhunderts" ("Neue Zeit", 1898–1899, II); *Sacker, op. cit.*, pp. 70–74; *Roos*, "De strafmiddelen in de nieuwere strafrechtswetenschap", Ch. VIII; *Leuss, op. cit.*, pp. 176–193.
[NOTE TO THE AMERICAN EDITION: *Cf.* further: *G. Gradnauer*, "Das

To sum up then, we come to the conclusion that the system of imprisonment is not in a condition to arrest the tide of criminality, but further that it is even one of the causes of the increase of crime, since it makes the prisoners still worse. It may be that in consequence of what I have just said the reader will remark that there is no other expedient possible than imprisonment, whether in common or cellular. Although the question of the treatment of the criminal as it ought to be is not one of those with which we are at present occupied, I shall nevertheless say a few words on the subject.

It is possible to practice a third system, which takes its origin from the idea that the crime does not proceed from the free will, but from causes which it will be necessary to try to remove, in place of inflicting a useless punishment. It is to the credit of the State of New York that it should be the first to put in practice this sort of a system of combating crime (in the Elmira Reformatory). An effort is made to make a man of the criminal, to turn him into a strong and sound individual; he is taught a trade, his mind is elevated, his feeling of honor revived, in short, everything is done that is necessary to stimulate the development of what is human in the man. And the results prove that those who are following this method are surely on the right road.[1]

There is only one objection to this system; that many persons who have not committed crime lead a life which in various ways is worse than that of the criminals so treated. However, this very sound objection does not condemn the system, but rather the present organization of society, which obliges a great number of persons to drag out a miserable existence. The question of crime and the social question are inseparable; he who examines the first without the second will not do much toward solving it.

j. Imitation. Before concluding we must give our attention to one more factor: imitation. We have already pointed this out in speaking of the moral education of the young, but it is also of importance with adults (*e.g.* the influence of the press, etc.; see above, C., *a.*, in this chapter), though not to so great an extent. When society shows very egoistic tendencies imitation strengthens these considerably; when we see persons with whom we have to do, always acting in an egoistic manner, our anti-egoistic forces weaken little by little

Elend des Strafvollzugs ", and *A. Aletrino,* "Is celstraf nog langer geoorloofd en gewenscht?"]

[1] See the Reports already cited, and *Winter,* "The New York State Reformatory in Elmira."

and we end by doing as the others do.[1]   In the crime of mobs imitation plays an important part.

The proofs to support the power of imitation in the etiology of crime are to be found in the biographies of most great criminals; bad example plays generally a preponderant rôle in the drama of life.   I know only a single set of statistics giving exact information of the atmosphere in which criminals have lived, and so furnishing an idea of the influence of imitation.   It is that furnished by the "Elmira Reformatory."   According to the "Twenty-second Yearbook" (1897) the character of the people with whom the inmates had associated was as follows:[2]

CHARACTER OF ASSOCIATES.	PRISONERS.	
	Absolute Number.	%
Positively bad	4,511	54.2
Less bad	3,614	43.4
Doubtful	81	1.4
Good	113	1.0
Total	8,319	100.0

A second proof of the influence of the contagion of crime is found in the fact that the criminality in the cities, where people come more into contact with each other, is in general greater than that in the country.   Although it is evident that we cannot impute this exclusively to imitation (it is due, among other things, in part to the great differences of fortune found in the cities), it still plays an important part.[3]   The following figures give a picture of the criminality in the large cities and in the country.[4]

[1] As was pointed out in Part I, Tarde is the author who has drawn attention to the rôle of imitation in the etiology of crime; but see also: *Sighele*, "Le crime à deux", "La foule criminelle", and "La psychologie des sectes"; *Aubry*, "La contagion du meurtre"; *Ferriani*, "Minderjährige Verbrecher", pp. 203–211.
[2] P. 37.
[3] See Engels, "The Condition of the Working Class in England", pp. 120 *ff.*
[4] "Criminal statistics", 1894 and 1898, pp. 24 and 31.
[NOTE TO THE AMERICAN EDITION: In the "Crim. Stat. England and Wales, 1905" there is a special study of crime in some of the great cities (pp. 62 *ff.*).]

England and Wales, 1894–1898.

DISTRICTS.	CRIMES KNOWN TO THE POLICE, TO THE 100,000 OF THE POPULATION.							
	All Indictable Offenses.		Crimes Against Property.		Crimes Against Persons.			
					Crimes of Violence.		Sexual Crimes.	
	1894.	1898.	1894.	1898.	1894.	1898.	1894.	1894.
London	416.77	391.56	386.24	358.90	11.95	10.63	5.93	5.72
Mining districts . .	234.33	230.84	214.32	211.07	8.39	7.19	8.11	7.89
Manufacturing cities .	351.84	325.93	332.48	306.21	6.66	6.74	*4.43	4.00
Sea-ports	643.60	611.10	597.91	575.60	22.54	16.72	8.44	5.95
Watering places, etc. .	265.70	302.25	250.37	283.34	4.38	5.93	4.14	6.16
Agricultural districts divided into:								
1st. Eastern . .	128.20	120.23	119.06	107.84	3.76	3.22	3.63	5.45
2nd. South-eastern .	182.97	195.86	163.52	176.55	5.29	6.22	8.10	8.70
3rd. Around London	202.13	198.07	185.97	181.41	4.29	4.94	6.53	6.32
England and Wales .	296.70	284.20	275.93	262.83	7.28	7.39	6.09	5.94

The following table [1] relates to

Bavaria, 1883–1897.

CRIMES.	NUMBER OF CONVICTS TO 10,000 OF THE POPULATION OVER 12 YEARS OF AGE.					
	1883–1887.		1888–1892.		1893–1897.	
	City.	Country.	City.	Country.	City.	Country.
Assault	19.9	27.7	19.9	31.2	22.4	32.8
Theft	37.4	26.6	39.7	26.1	37.3	25.9
Fraud	10.2	5.0	12.1	6.9	12.5	6.9
Violence and threats against public officials	4.7	2.7	4.5	2.4	4.9	2.6
All crimes	137.1	114.0	133.7	119.6	139.4	123.1

As in England the criminality in the cities is in general greater than in the country.

We find the same picture in the figures for

[1] *Prinsing*, "Soziale Faktoren der Kriminalität", pp. 565, 566.

France, 1881–1900.[1]

RESIDENCE.	NUMBER OF PERSONS ARRAIGNED TO 100,000 OF THE POPULATION.	
	1881–1885.	1896–1900.
Urban	15.4	11.1
Rural	7.8	5.4

The following table gives figures for certain important crimes.[2]

CRIMES.	PERCENTAGE OF PERSONS ARRAIGNED.			
	Living in Rural Communes.		Living in Urban Communes.	
	1881.	1900.	1881.	1900.
Murder	64	50	36	50
Homicide	58	54	42	46
Assaults	50	56	50	44
Indecent assaults	55	53	45	47
Forgery	37	37	63	63
Breach of trust	35	14	65	86
Arson	77	74	23	26
Theft	33	21	67	79

In studying the preceding table it must be noted that in the two periods 34 % and 39 % of the population respectively were urban.

Netherlands, 1901.[3]

PLACES WHERE THE OFFENSE WAS COMMITTED.	PERCENTAGE OF CONVICTS WHO HAD COMMITTED THEIR CRIMES IN THE GROUPS OF COMMUNES DESIGNATED.					PERCENTAGE OF WHOLE POPULATION LIVING IN THE GROUPS DESIGNATED.
	Total.	Rebellion.	Simple Assaults.	Simple Theft.	Aggravated Thief.	
Communes of more than 20,000 inhabitants . .	38.3	45.3	21.2	41.7	50.4	36.8
Communes of less than 20,000 inhabitants . .	61.7	54.7	78.8	58.3	49.6	63.2

[1] "Rapport sur l'administration de la justice criminelle de 1881 à 1900", p. xxix.

[2] "Rapport etc.", p. xxx.

[3] "Crimineele statistiek over het jaar 1901", pp. xvii and xviii.

An examination of the statistics given shows that except for a few offenses the cities are more criminal than the country.[1] However, it must not be forgotten that the cities have proportionately a greater number of inhabitants at the age at which there is the greatest tendency to crime, and that the figures therefore give the criminality of the cities as a little greater than it is. On the other hand there is a greater proportion of crimes that are not prosecuted, or whose authors remain undiscovered. The English statistics, which do not speak of the persons arraigned or convicted, but of the crimes known to the police, are better in this regard.

It is unnecessary to treat more fully of the rôle of imitation in the etiology of crime; no one will deny it. As I have already noted, in Part I, in my criticism of the theory of Tarde, imitation is not an independent factor, but dependent upon others. In our present society, with its pronounced egoistic tendencies, imitation strengthens these, as it would strengthen the altruistic tendencies produced by another form of society. Man does not imitate that which is egoistic simply, but also that which is altruistic. It is only as a consequence of the predominance of egoism in our present society that the error is made of supposing the effect of imitation to be necessarily evil.

k. Conclusions. In recapitulating now the egoistic tendencies of the present economic system and of its consequences, we see clearly that they are very strong. Because of these tendencies the social instinct of man is not greatly developed; they have weakened the moral force in man which combats the inclination towards egoistic acts, and hence towards the crimes which are one form of these acts. To mention only the most important things, in a society in which, as in ours, the economic interests of all are in eternal conflict among themselves, compassion for the misfortunes of others inevitably becomes blunted, and a great part of morality consequently disappears. The slight value that is attached to the opinion of others is also a consequence of the strife of economic interests, for we can be responsive to that opinion only when we do not see adversaries in our fellows.

The fluctuations of the mind of the person in whom the criminal

[1] See also *A. Mayer*, "Die Verbrechen in ihrem Zusammenhang mit den wirthschaftlichen und sozialen Verhältnissen im Kanton Zürich."
[NOTE TO THE AMERICAN EDITION: *Cf.* further: for Germany: *J. Galle*, "Die Kriminalität in Stadt und Land in ihrer Beziehung zur Berufsverteilung"; for the Balkan States: *Wadler, op. cit.,* pp. 155 *ff.*; for Belgium: *Jacquart, op. cit.,* pp. 86 *ff.*; for the Netherlands: *de Roos, op. cit.,* pp. 222 *ff.,* and *Verrijn Stuart, op. cit.,* p. 239.]

idea is born may be compared with the oscillations of a balance; and it is upon sociology that must devolve the task of examining the forces which throw a weight on one side or the other. When the organization of society influences men in an altruistic way there is then a considerable force which can prevent the balance from inclining towards the egoistic side. In our present society, the organization of which does not exert an altruistic influence, this force is very weak, or does not exist at all. Since, however, in every society, man must abstain from a number of egoistic acts, substitutes have been devised to take the place of the weak or wanting social sentiments. The hope of reward (whether terrestrial or celestial) and the fear of being punished (whether by man or God) are charged with the duty of keeping men in order. As believers themselves know very well, most men are not very responsive to divine rewards and punishments — heaven and hell are too far off. Is it not believers who are the strongest partisans of rewards and punishments here below for human acts? However, this expedient is only a very insufficient one. We know too well that the rewards are very often lacking, and the punishments as well. This is why many persons take the risk of committing the crime they have planned.

The present environment exercises an egoistic influence upon all men. We all participate, for example, in exchange, which, as we have seen, is a great egoistic factor; and other similar factors could be named that act upon all. On the other hand there are other egoistic factors which exercise their influence only upon some of us.

Let us compare two totally different environments in which an individual grows up. Let us place him first in the slums of a great city; his father is alcoholic, his mother a prostitute; he has never attended school, passing his time in vagabondage up to the day when, still young, he has been committed to prison, where his education in crime is completed. Now let us suppose this same individual to have grown up in a healthy environment, where neither poverty nor extreme riches exercised their pernicious influence. He has been brought up by rational and loving parents, his mind has been developed, he has found later a good career, in which the greed of gold has not been aroused in him. We shall then have before us two extremes, between which a great many degrees are to be found. The environment is a very important cause of the great diversity among men. However, it is not the only one; we still must give our attention for a moment to:

D. Individual Differences.

Men differ in height, in strength, in weight, in intellectual capacity, in everything, in short. Apparently no regularity is to be seen in their diversity. If, for example, we look at a crowd with reference to the heights of the individuals composing it, there seems to be no regularity about them. However, this is only in appearance. By placing all the persons in a line according to their height, and drawing a line at the top of their heads we shall always get a curve differing little from the one below (the greater the number of persons, the lower the point

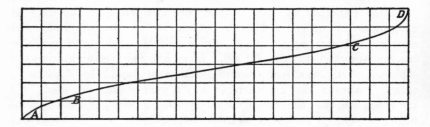

A, the higher the point *D*, and the more nearly horizontal the line *BC*).

The irregularity is, then, only apparent; there is regularity in this sense, that the persons of average height predominate very greatly in number, and that the very short and very tall persons form minorities. This regularity in the individual differences, discovered by Quetelet, has been recognized as a universal law, applicable to everything living. The scientist named has demonstrated this not only for the height of the human body, but also for its weight, strength, quickness, etc.

Galton has proved the existence of this law for the intellectual capacity of man, and a number of other scientists have done the same for the animal and vegetable kingdoms.[1] Hence, "uniformity in variability" for all living nature must be considered as a universal law.

The same thing must be true for men's moral qualities. In ranking any number of persons according to the intensity of their innate social sentiments (supposing it were possible to apply a measure to these), we should find that here also the law in question held good; with the great majority the social sentiments would have only a

[1] See, among others, *de Vries*, "Eenheid in Veranderlijkheid", pp. 3–6.

moderate intensity, while there would be one small minority in which they would be weak, and another in which they would be very strong. We have no need to revert to the influence of the environment, for we have seen that it gives to all an egoistic or altruistic impulse, differing naturally according to the individual.[1] Supposing that the environment were the same for all, there would still be great differences between men as to the intensity of their social sentiments.

What is now the importance of this fact for the etiology of crime? In my opinion, the answer to this question will not be different from those which have been given to analogous questions when we were treating of the etiology of prostitution and alcoholism (pp. 407, 408 and 428), namely, that in every society, everywhere and always, an individual, according as his social sentiments are weaker or stronger than another's, runs more or less risk than he of becoming a criminal, supposing the environment of the two to be the same in effect. The man who, according to the intensity of his social sentiments, would be placed in the line between A and B, would run more danger of becoming a criminal than the man who belonged between C and D. This point is of great importance for anyone who is investigating why the first falls into crime and not the latter. But it has little weight for criminal sociology, which concerns itself, not with definite persons, but only with general social facts.

The evidence that individuals differ quantitatively always and everywhere does not give the explanation of the problems whose solution sociology seeks, although they must be taken into account. *The task that is incumbent upon it is to explain why individuals who, as a consequence of their innate qualities, run more danger than others of becoming criminals, actually become so.* He who is born with weak social instincts runs more *danger* of becoming a criminal. But the *certainty* that he will become such does not exist — that depends upon the environment.

To sum up; I am of the opinion that individual differences are of great importance for one who is studying an individual by himself, but that they do not belong to the domain of the etiology of criminality.

[1] [NOTE TO THE AMERICAN EDITION: In present day sociology it is almost universally accepted that there is only a quantitative difference between criminals and other men, and that the "homo criminalis" does not exist. An interesting contribution to this question is given by Dr. *Finkelnburg* in his "Die Bestraften in Deutschland." His statistical calculations bring him to the conclusion that in Germany there *is one person out of every 12* (over 20 years of age) *convicted!*]

E. The Classification of Crime.

Before proceeding to the treatment of crimes separately, it is necessary to divide them into some main groups. It is a grave error (committed, however, by many criminologists) not to take account of the very different nature of crimes, if one is concerned with their etiology. It is, to be sure, permissible to treat conjointly moral forces which may prevent the execution of criminal ideas and which apply to all crimes. I have done so in the preceding pages. But we cannot treat the origin of the criminal idea itself in this same way. There are criminals and criminals. There are enormous differences between a professional thief, and a man who has been guilty of assault and battery in a state of intoxication, just as there are between a ravisher and a political criminal. And anyone who does not take account of these differences must necessarily limit himself to certain generalities.

I propose to treat of crimes divided into four categories in accordance with the motives which led their authors to commit them. Three of these categories form quite definite units, while the fourth is more heterogeneous.

The first is composed of crimes that have an economic aim (economic crimes). The greater part of the so-called crimes against property, such as theft, embezzlement, etc., belong to this category, but not all, for malicious mischief, for example, is generally dictated by a desire for vengeance. On the other hand some crimes against the person, like procuration, the object of which is economic and not sexual, belong here. As for crimes against the state, we must add counterfeiting to this category. Then there are other crimes that may be committed either for economic or non-economic reasons; for example, murder (for the purpose of robbery or for revenge), perjury (for the profit of winning a civil suit, or to prevent the conviction of a friend), arson (to get the insurance money, or for revenge), etc.

It may be urged here that, notwithstanding the similarity of their motives the crimes of any class still present many differences. This is true in part, and I have accordingly subdivided them. But on the other hand these differences are not very great *from the standpoint of criminal sociology*. For the jurist the difference between counterfeiting bank-notes, burning a house to get the insurance, and procuration is very important; but for sociology it is much less so. A man who knows how to make counterfeit bank-notes, will commit this crime, whenever he wishes for any reason to enrich himself in a dis-

honest fashion, but he will become neither an incendiary nor a procurer.   A former prostitute, on the contrary, will not think of making
banknotes, but will become a procuress.   The kind of economic crime
committed by the person who has a mind to commit such a crime,
depends principally upon chance (occupation etc.).

The second category includes sexual crimes, and the fourth political crimes — two categories quite distinct therefore.

The other misdemeanors and crimes form the third category, and
are more or less heterogeneous.   The principal motive of these
crimes is vengeance.   Among them are insults, malicious mischief,
assaults, homicide, etc.   Other motives are: the fear of shame
(infanticide, which, however, may also be committed for economic
reasons) ; then fear of falling into the hands of justice (perjury, rebellion) ; and some others beside.[1]

Finally, to give a picture of the quantitative proportions of the
principal crimes, I add here some figures upon criminality in some of
the countries of Europe.   These figures may at the same time serve
to show to those who are not acquainted with criminal statistics,
how regular a course crime has from one year to another.

It is crimes of vengeance, therefore, which form the largest group,
then come economic crimes, and then sexual and political crimes,
both with low figures.   If we do not count the very minor offense
of insult in the third group, the first and third groups will be
nearly of the same size.   There are, then, almost no political crimes
in England.   As in Germany, sexual crimes are very rare, and it is
the economic crimes and those committed out of revenge, etc., that
are the most important.   The latter preponderate even more in
England than in Germany.

---

[1] I speak neither of all the crimes nor of all the motives of those of which
I do treat.   For a complete enumeration of the motives of crimes, see *Starke*,
"Des éléments essentials qui doivent figurer dans la statistique criminelle
et des moyens de les rendre comparables", pp. 77, 78 ("Bulletin de l'institut
international de statistique", 1889), and *von Liszt*, "Die psychologischen
Grundlagen der Kriminalpolitik", pp. 490–494 ("Zeitschr. f. d. ges. Strw."
XVI).

Germany, 1896–1900.[1]

CRIMES.	NUMBER OF PERSONS CONVICTED OF THE FOLLOWING CRIMES IN					1896–1900 Average.	
	1896.	1897.	1898.	1899.	1900.	Absolute Number.	%
Theft and embezzlement . .	109,545	112,591	116,977	113,159	114,831	113,420	29.96
Receiving stolen goods and being accessory after the fact in general	8,164	7,922	8,490	8,124	8,068	8,153	2.15
Procuration, etc.	2,816	2,671	2,765	2,622	2,648	2,711	0.72
Counterfeiting	234	166	203	212	186	200	0.05
Perjury	1,523	1,450	1,478	1,316	1,198	1,393	0.37
Criminal breach of trust and obtaining money under false pretenses	28,649	25,169	26,546	26,580	26,079	25,604	6.76
Forgery	4,761	5,068	5,185	5,479	5,231	5,144	1.36
Robbery and extortion . .	1,048	995	1,114	1,114	1,009	1,056	0.28
Fraudulent bankruptcy . .	931	924	871	952	905	916	0.24
Total of economic crimes . .	—	—	—	—	—	—	41.89
Bigamy	76	72	64	70	64	69	0.02
Incest	462	381	397	411	448	419	0.11
Rape, etc.	4,483	4,182	4,507	4,597	4,762	4,506	1.19
Total of sexual crimes . . .	—	—	—	—	—	—	1.32
Insults	53,968	54,143	55,988	55,514	52,883	54,499	14.39
Malicious mischief	17,485	17,486	18,213	18,858	18,261	18,060	4.77
Arson	479	468	501	519	472	487	0.13
Assaults	116,613	117,864	122,561	126,490	124,646	121,632	32.12
Rebellion	18,377	18,484	17,968	19,817	17,951	18,393	4.86
Homicide	1,511	1,562	1,468	1,542	1,580	1,532	0.40
Total of crimes of vengeance, etc.	—	—	—	—	—	—	56.67
Political crimes	561	428	466	416	305	435	0.12
General total	—	—	—	—	—	378,629	100.00

[1] After the "Kriminalstatistik für das Jahr 1900", II, pp. 7–13.

England, 1881–1900.[1]

CRIMES.	NUMBER ARRAIGNED FOR EACH OF THE CRIMES GIVEN:					
	Annual Averages.				1881–1900 Average.	
	1881–85.	1886–90.	1891–95.	1896–1900.	Absolute Number.	%
Theft (of every kind) . . .	57,373	52,573	50,432	45,960	51,584	32.92
Embezzlement	1,475	1,345	1,335	1,387	1,385	0.88
Receiving stolen goods . . .	1,302	1,239	1,348	1,241	1,282	0.82
Burglary	1,464	1,530	1,665	1,630	1,572	1.00
Robbery and extortion . . .	320	322	310	278	307	0.20
Fraud	1,054	965	997	870	971	0.62
Counterfeiting, etc.	534	410	365	309	402	0.26
Perjury	100	85	78	77	85	0.05
Fraudulent bankruptcy . .	49	41	43	35	42	0.03
Total of economic crimes . .	—	—	—	—	—	36.78
Bigamy	116	99	104	103	105	0.07
Indecent assault upon girls under 16	—	305	258	236	249	0.16
Rape, etc. upon adults . . .	647	639	636	595	629	0.40
Total of sexual crimes . . .	—	—	—	—	—	0.63
Malicious mischief	21,779	19,646	18,484	17,470	19,594	12.51
Arson	155	133	117	104	127	0.08
Assaults	72,707	66,020	63,601	59,611	65,484	41.80
Assaults upon officers . . .	322	285	291	278	294	0.19
Homicide (including attempted homicide) . . .	13,223	11,850	12,626	12,524	12,555	8.01
Total of crimes of vengeance .	—	—	—	—	—	62.59
Political crimes	4	0	0	0	1	0.00
General total	—	—	—	—	156,668	100.00

France, 1881–1900.[1]

CRIMES.	NUMBER ARRAIGNED FOR EACH CRIME.					
	Annual Averages.				1881–1900 Averages.	
	1881–1885.	1886–1890.	1891–1895.	1896–1900.	Average Number.	%
Vagrancy . . .	15,629	19,050	18,449	14,148	16,819	11.17
Mendicity . . .	9,421	14,625	14,707	11,274	12,506	8.30
Aggravated theft .	1,668	1,715	1,517	1,308	1,552	1.03
Simple theft . .	44,596	47,941	49,145	43,750	46,358	30.78
Counterfeiting . .	98	141	134	111	121	0.08
Procuration . . .	341	361	406	304	353	0.23
Forgery	355	304	237	224	280	0.19
Obtaining money under false pretenses	41,210	4,422	3,898	3,496	4,006	2.66
Breach of trust .	4,106	4,495	4,488	4,834	4,480	2.98
Commercial frauds	3,221	3,015	2,607	2,931	2,941	1.95
Fraudulent bankruptcy	86	63	63	44	64	0.04
Simple bankruptcy	934	967	802	860	890	0.59
Perjury	126	126	151	136	134	0.09
Total of economic crimes	—	—	—	—	—	60.09
Bigamy	6	6	8	8	7	0.00
Adultery	1,038	1,758	1,838	2,212	1,711	1.14
Rape and indecent assault upon adults	103	76	95	70	86	0.06
Rape and indecent assault upon children . . .	717	592	584	452	586	0.39
Total of sexual crimes	—	—	—	—	—	1.59
Defamation and insults	3,513	2,918	2,940	2,877	3,062	2.03
Insults to officials .	13,492	13,728	15,258	13,450	13,982	9.28
Malicious mischief	3,291	4,876	4,530	4,382	4,269	2.84
Arson	207	245	263	213	252	0.17
Serious assaults .	187	155	178	183	175	0.12
Intentional assaults	27,768	28,971	33,443	36,158	31,585	20.97
Violence to officials	3,721	3,746	3,926	3,502	3,723	2.47
Homicide . . .	518	506	515	461	500	0.33
Infanticide . . .	191	191	157	118	164	0.11
Total of crimes of vengeance, etc. .	—	—	—	—	—	38.32
Political crimes . .	4	1	2	0	1	0.00
General total .	—	—	—	—	150,607	100.00

[1] After the "Rapport sur l'administration etc.", Tables 1, 2, and 7.

Here, also, the political crimes and the sexual offenses show the smallest figures. The economic crimes exceed considerably those committed out of revenge, etc., a fact to be accounted for in great part by the inclusion of vagrancy and mendicity among the economic crimes. These tables hardly lend themselves to international comparison, since certain acts are regarded as misdemeanors in one country, and as contraventions in another.

Italy, 1891–1895.[1]

CRIMES.	NUMBER CONVICTED OF EACH CRIME.						
						Average 1891–1895	
	1891.	1892.	1893.	1894.	1895.	Absolute Numbers.	%
Simple theft	44,380	38,750	35,343	37,022	41,875	39,474	29.07
Aggravated theft	14,512	15,103	15,230	15,238	17,132	15,441	11.37
Fraud (of every kind)	6,288	6,202	6,446	6,861	7,917	6,742	4.97
Counterfeiting, etc.	85	59	59	68	90	72	0.05
Forgery	788	626	683	726	839	732	0.54
Procuration	182	188	185	162	267	196	0.15
Robbery, extortion, etc.	683	719	824	879	966	814	0.60
Total of economic crimes	—	—	—	—	—	—	46.75
Rape, etc.	724	797	879	902	1,066	873	0.64
Corruption of minors and other offenses against morals and the order of the family	1,036	1,246	1,269	1,373	1,411	1,267	0.93
Total of sexual crimes	—	—	—	—	—	—	1.57
Defamation and insults	9,030	9,957	9,005	11,247	12,196	10,287	7.58
Malicious mischief	5,396	4,938	4,493	5,069	5,617	5,102	3.76
Arson	213	156	197	210	197	194	0.14
Minor assaults	24,275	27,617	23,740	27,479	28,924	26,407	19.45
Serious assaults	6,491	8,440	9,124	8,211	9,199	8,293	6.11
Threats	4,788	5,997	5,875	6,702	8,053	6,283	4.63
Violence, insults, etc., to officials	10,293	11,829	11,999	11,835	11,800	11,551	8.51
Homicide	1,686	1,946	2,145	2,035	2,049	1,972	1.45
Infanticide and abortion	60	59	54	64	81	63	0.05
Total of crimes of vengeance, etc.	—	—	—	—	—	—	51.68
Crimes against the safety of the state.	11	9	10	10	12	10	0.00
General total	—	—	—	—	—	135,773	100.00

[1] After "Notizie complementari alle statistiche penali degli anni 1890–1895", pp. x and xi.

The results of the Italian statistics agree in general with those that have gone before.

Netherlands, 1897–1901.[1]

CRIMES.	NUMBER OF CONVICTS FOR EACH CRIME.						
						Average 1897–1901.	
	1897.	1898.	1899.	1900.	1901.	Absolute Numbers.	%
Vagrancy and mendicity .	2,139	2,173	2,209	1,873	1,857	2,050	16.42
Simple theft	1,685	1,830	1,740	1,544	1,758	1,711	13.71
Aggravated theft	936	919	761	837	1,029	896	17.18
Receiving stolen goods . .	95	69	88	82	98	86	0.69
Embezzlement	320	262	295	309	269	291	2.33
Causing or being accessory to the debauch of a minor	14	6	10	14	16	12	0.10
Obtaining money under false pretenses	102	115	97	112	115	108	0.87
Extortion and blackmail .	8	12	6	9	5	8	0.07
Forgery	75	72	49	64	42	60	0.48
Perjury	29	18	15	22	18	20	0.16
Fraudulent bankruptcy . .	14	14	12	20	12	14	0.11
Total of economic crimes .	—	—	—	—	—	—	42.12
Rape and indecent assault upon adults	88	81	94	110	97	94	0.75
Rape and indecent assault upon children	13	5	13	6	18	11	0.09
Total of sexual crimes . .	—	—	—	—	—	—	0.84
Simple insults	356	319	330	288	291	316	2.53
Insults to officials . . .	549	508	431	421	440	469	3.76
Malicious mischief . . .	916	900	861	857	874	881	7.06
Arson	10	12	22	25	15	17	0.14
Rebellion, etc.	1,188	1,091	1,069	1,166	1,112	1,125	9.01
Assaults	4,241	4,020	4,101	3,814	3,715	3,978	31.87
Assaults upon officials . .	340	286	331	330	296	316	2.53
Homicide	16	16	12	14	19	15	0.12
Infanticide and abortion .	4	3	4	4	0	3	0.02
Total of crimes of vengeance, etc.	—	—	—	—	—	—	57.04
Political crimes	3	1	1	0	0	1	0.00
General total	—	—	—	—	—	12,482	100.00

[1] After the "Gerechtelijke Statistiek", 1897–1899, and the "Crimineele Statistiek", 1900–1901.

These figures thus confirm in general the results of the preceding tables. The most frequent crimes are those committed out of revenge etc. and the economic crimes. The sexual crimes only reach low figures, and the political crimes are negligible.

We have placed certain crimes, like homicide and arson, in all the tables, among the crimes of vengeance, etc., although they may also be committed from an economic motive. The French and Italian criminal statistics give information upon the frequency of the motives which lead to these crimes.

France, 1881–1900.[1]

PRESUMABLE MOTIVE OF THE CRIMES.	PERCENTAGE OF THE CRIMES OF HOMICIDE AND ARSON DUE TO EACH CAUSE.			
	1881–1885.	1886–1890.	1891–1895.	1896–1900.
Cupidity	26	28	31	26
Love, jealousy	2	2	6	3
Adultery	3	3	2	2
Concubinage, debauch	6	6	5	8
Hate, revenge	24	27	28	28
Domestic disputes	15	13	9	12
Drink-shop quarrels	2	1	1	1
Various motives	22	20	18	20

About 28 % of the crimes, then, had an economic motive, about 12 % had a sexual motive, and 40 % were committed out of revenge.

Italy, 1880–1881.[2]

PRESUMABLE MOTIVES OF THE CRIMES.	PERCENTAGE OF CRIMES OF BLOOD DUE TO EACH CAUSE.	
	1880.	1881.
Cupidity	9.2	9.98
Question of interests	4.2	8.76
Love, lawful or unlawful	7.5	8.76
Family relations and questions of honor . . .	2.6	3.11
Defense of life	4.9	3.04
" " property	1.7	1.89
Domestic disputes	3.0	4.43
Anger	30.3	23.67
Hate and revenge	26.5	28.46
Cruelty	4.1	2.72
Drunkenness	3.2	4.25
Politics	0.1	0.14
Various and unknown motives	2.6	0.79

[1] " Rapport sur l'administration etc." p. xxxvii.
[2] *Ferri*, "Atlante antropologico-statistico dell' omicidio", p. 328, for 1880,

Finally, it must not be forgotten that certain crimes of a different kind (leze-majesty and malicious mischief, for example) are sometimes committed simply that the author of them may get himself imprisoned, and hence should be classed as economic crimes.

We have now reached the question: how close a connection have the different crimes with economic conditions? We shall give only a detailed sketch of the subject; to treat it more fully would require extensive monographs. We shall limit ourselves to indicating the general lines.

and for 1881, from "Statistica giudiziaria penale perl' anno 1881", pp. xc and xɐi.

CHAPTER II.

ECONOMIC CRIMES.

It is necessary to divide these crimes into separate groups. Notwithstanding their partial similarity they differ too much among themselves to be treated together. I propose to speak of them under the four following heads: A. Vagrancy and mendicity; B. Theft, and analogous crimes; C. Robbery, homicide for economic reasons, etc., (that is to say, economic crimes committed with violence or directed against life); D. Fraudulent bankruptcy, adulteration of food, etc., (that is to say, economic crimes committed almost exclusively by the bourgeoisie, while those of the first three categories are committed almost exclusively by the poor). Some crimes, like that of embezzlement, belong to the second class as well as to the fourth (for example, a workman's making off with a bicycle loaned to him, and the embezzlement of deposits by a bank director).

It seems to me unnecessary to explain this division. It creates four fairly distinct groups, which contain all the economic crimes. However, I must point out why I treat vagrancy and mendicity in this way, while both are generally regarded not as misdemeanors but as contraventions.[1] Properly speaking they ought not, therefore, to appear in a work on criminality, but the following are the reasons why they nevertheless find a place here; first, they are the most important and the most common contraventions; second, there is a very close relation between vagrancy on the one hand, and criminality properly speaking on the other. This relation has been shown by many authors. As Professor Prins says in his "Criminalité et répression", vagrancy and mendicity are the novitiate of crime. I will only recall here the opinions of two writers, Josiah Flynt and E. Sichart. The former, the author of "Tramping with Tramps", has given up a part of his life to tramping for some years in America,

[1] [There seems no better way to designate a classification that does not exist in English than by taking over this French term. — Transl.]

Germany, and in other countries, in order to familiarize himself with the vagrant and the criminal; his conclusions accordingly have great value. He is of the opinion that the vagrants endowed with great energy become professional criminals, to fall again into vagrancy as soon as their physical and mental forces decline so as no longer to permit them to carry on their criminal trade with success.[1]

Sichart, the prison director, having examined 3,181 convicts, found that 28 % of them had been convicted before for vagrancy, and 27 % for mendicity — 55 % in all.[2] These figures differed according to the kind of criminal. There were to

each 100 thieves	44.2 vagrants,	35.0 mendicants
" 100 swindlers	11.1 "	20.2 "
" 100 sexual offenders	14.0 "	17.3 "
" 100 incendiaries	15.1 "	15.5 "
" 100 perjurers	4.2 "	4.7 "

For these reasons, then, it is necessary to treat of vagrancy and mendicity.

A. VAGRANCY AND MENDICITY.

In examining the etiology of these contraventions, we perceive that different causes lead to them. We shall treat them successively and endeavor to find their relation to the economic life.

First. As a first cause of vagrancy and mendicity is the fact that under capitalism there are always workmen who cannot sell their labor. The number of these persons increases greatly at the time of a crisis. When the men out of work have no resource in their family and no longer receive aid from their union, they are obliged to go from place to place looking for employment, and if they do not succeed in finding it must have recourse to begging in order not to die of hunger. Statistics furnish the proof that the army of vagrants and mendicants

[1] Pp. 6, 14–18.

[2] "Ueber individuelle Faktoren des Verbrechens", pp. 40, 41. On the relation between vagrancy and mendicity, and criminality see also: *Colajanni*, "Sociologia criminale", I, pp. 478, 479 (quoted in Part I of this work); *Kurella*, "Naturgeschichte des Verbrechers", pp. 206, 207; *Sacker*, "Der Rückfall", pp. 56, 57; *Fornasari de Verce*, "La criminalità e le vicende economiche d'Italia", p. 19; *A. Meyer*, "Die Verbrechen in ihrem Zusammenhang mit den wirthschaftlichen und sozialen Verhältnissen im Kanton Zürich", p. 59; *Ferriani*, "Minderjährige Verbrecher", pp. 144 *ff.*; *Bérard*, "Le vagabondage en France", pp. 609, 610 ("Arch. d'anthr. crim." XIII); *Florian* and *Cavaglieri*, "I Vagabondi", II, pp. 181–197; *Loewenstimm*, "Das Bettelgewerbe", pp. 124–128 ("Kriminalistische Studien"); *Rivière*, "Mendiants et vagabonds", pp. 227, 228.

is in fact made up in part of the unemployed who, though they wish to, cannot find work.

In the first place, vagrancy and mendicity increase in winter (as in general all economic criminality does), when forced unemployment is at its height, and needs are most pressing, while they diminish in summer. The following figures with reference to some of the German states show these facts.

Grand-Duchy of Baden, 1884–1891.[1]

Months.	Number Convicted of Vagrancy and Mendicity.	Number Convicted per Diem, the Minimum = 100.
January	7,232	364
February	6,315	336
March	4,816	235
April	2,945	148
May	2,743	133
June	2,475	124
July	2,540	124
August	2,410	118
September	1,989	100
October	2,672	130
November	3,857	195
December	5,310	259

Hesse, 1899–1900.[2]

Months	Number Convicted of Vagrancy and Mendicity.	
	Absolute Number.	Daily Average.
December–February	479	5.32
March–May	334	3.63
June–August	259	2.82
September–November	531	3.64

[1] "Neue Zeit", 1893–1894, II, p. 443.
[2] *Ostwald*, "Das Leben der Wanderarmen", p. 313 ("Archiv f. Kriminalanthr. u. Kriminalstat." XIII).

The following figures confirm those that have preceded.

Saxony, 1882–1887.[1]

YEARS.	NUMBER CONVICTED OF VAGRANCY AND MENDICITY.							
	First Quarter.		Second Quarter.		Third Quarter.		Fourth Quarter.	
	Absolute Numbers.	Percent-age of Annual Total.	Absolute Numbers.	Percent-age of Annual Total.	Absolute Numbers.	Percent-age of Annual Total.	Absolute Numbers.	Percent-age of Annual Total.
1882	6,752	36.1	4,220	22.6	3,181	17.0	4,546	24.3
1883	6,619	36.6	3,934	21.7	2,957	16.5	4,567	25.2
1884	6,641	37.6	3,855	21.8	2,721	15.5	4,462	25.2
1885	6,555	35.9	3,424	18.7	2,872	15.7	5,440	29.7
1886	7,139	41.5	3,507	20.4	2,654	15.4	3,900	22.7
1887	5,787	39.1	3,344	22.6	2,251	15.2	3,411	23.1

These statistics justify the conclusion drawn by Ostwald, from whom I have taken the figures for Hesse. This author is a competent witness, as he tramped as a vagrant for some time himself. He says: "These figures directly contradict the statement that antipathy to regular work forms the principal source of vagrancy and mendicity; especially as there is no inclination to frequent the highways in winter. It is the need that comes of unemployment that drives out these poorest of the poor; and whoever wishes to do away with vagrancy must make the economic existence of the working people secure, instead of visiting the victims of poverty with Draconian punishments." [2]

Another proof in support of the assertion that unemployment is a cause of mendicity and vagrancy, is to be found in the fact that the figures for vagrancy and mendicity rise considerably at the time of economic crises. The same phenomenon occurs more or less when the price of grain or bread goes up. Then those whose labor is only poorly paid must find some means of increasing their resources; and further when bread is dear less of other things can be bought, which brings about a decrease in production and consequently an increase in forced idleness.

In the first part of this work I have mentioned authors who have shown for different countries that the curve of vagrancy rises or falls as economic conditions become worse or better. I add here the data that I have been able to find elsewhere.

[1] "Neue Zeit", 1893–1894, II, p. 58.   [2] Ostwald, op. cit., p. 313.

England, 1856–1896.[1]

YEARS.	VAGRANTS CONVICTED.		YEARS.	VAGRANTS CONVICTED.	
	Absolute Numbers.	To 100,000 of the Population.		Absolute Numbers.	To 100,000 of the Population.
1856–57	19,270	99.7	1876–77	22,475	90.9
1857–58	21,473	109.9	1877–78	23,662	94.5
1858–59	16,401	83.0	1878–79	25,790	101.6
1859–60	16,374	82.2	1879–80	30,323	117.5
1860–61	17,496	86.9	1880–81	28,088	107.8
1861–62	20,636	101.4	1881–82	28,729	109.0
1862–63	21,758	105.8	1882–83	28,825	108.2
1863–64	20,414	97.7	1883–84	28,370	105.3
1864–65	20,307	96.7	1884–85	27,467	100.9
1865–66	19,607	91.8	1885–86	26,546	96.4
1866–67	21,071	97.5	1886–87	28,690	103.0
1867–68	24,125	110.2	1887–88	31,380	111.5
1868–69	29,890	134.8	1888–89	28,032	98.5
1869–70	28,367	126.3	1889–90	25,001	86.5
1870–71	24,902	109.4	1890–91	22,577	77.6
1871–72	21,325	92.4	1891–92	23,623	80.3
1872–73	19,433	83.2	1893	24,830	83.3
1873–74	19,582	82.8	1894	25,676	85.4
1874–75	17,692	73.5	1895	23,524	77.4
1875–76	19,841	81.4	1896	25,188	81.9

When we compare these figures with the course of economic events, we find the following: 1856 was a bad year economically, and 1857 and 1858 were still worse; in 1859 the situation improved, to become worse again in 1860, 1861, and 1862. The improvement was restored in 1863, while 1864 and 1865 were fair; in 1866, 1867, and 1868 conditions became worse again, but improved from 1869 to 1874. With 1875 things took a turn for the worse, and this condition lasted till 1879, when there was a slight improvement; 1880, 1881, and 1882 were fair, while 1883 was a passably good year. In 1884 a period of depression began, which lasted till 1888, following which there was an improvement until 1891, with the succeeding years up to 1894 not so good. In 1895 things once more took a turn for the better.[2]

[1] *Florian* and *Cavaglieri*, op. cit., II, pp. xl. and xli.
[2] See the works of *Fornasari di Verce*, *Tugan-Baranowsky*, and *G. Mayr*, cited in Part I.
[NOTE TO THE AMERICAN EDITION: In his "Statistik und Gesellschaftslehre", III, p. 653, G. V. Mayr gives statistics of vagrancy and mendicity for Germany (1877–1888), in which there appears a formidable increase during the years 1877–1880 (the end of the economic crisis), and a decrease after 1880. For Austria cf. Herz, op. cit., pp. 49 ff.]

With some exceptions the curve of vagrancy rises and falls, then, pretty much as the economic situation grows worse or improves.

Bavaria, 1835–1861.

Dr. G. Mayr has proved that during the period named there was a close connection between the movement of the price of grain and the figures for vagrancy. (See p. 42 of this work.) [1]

Flanders, 1839–1848.

Ducpetiaux had given proofs of the same correlation. (See pp. 33–37.)

France, 1840–1886.

Lafargue has proved that vagrancy and mendicity follow in general the curve for bankruptcies. (See p. 235.) [2]

Hesse, 1895–1900.[3]

YEARS.	NUMBER OF THOSE CONVICTED OF VAGRANCY AND MENDICITY.	
	Absolute Figures.	To 100,000 of the Population.
1895	2,583	21.96
1896	2,244	21.49
1897	1,968	18.49
1898	1,658	15.60
1899	1,267	11.82
1900	1,442	12.95

In this period the economic depression in Germany, dating from about 1890, began to decrease.

Netherlands, 1860–1891.

Since there are no statistical investigations of the course of vagrancy and mendicity I have composed the following chart from the official data.

[1] [NOTE TO THE AMERICAN EDITION: Upon Bavaria, cf. F. Knoblauch, "Bettel und Landstreicherei im Königreiche Bayern", 1893–99.]

[2] For France see also Bérard, op. cit., pp. 607, 608.

[3] Ostwald, op. cit., p. 313. Cf. upon the periods 1866–1870 and 1877–1884, H. Bennecke, "Bemerkungen zur Kriminalstatistik des Grossherzogtums Hessen", pp. 369 ff.

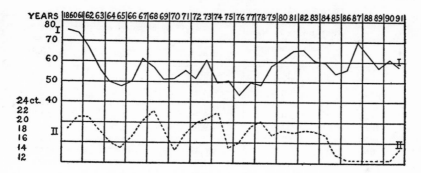

I. Number Convicted of Vagrancy and Mendicity to 100,000 of the Population. II. Price of Bread (in Centimes per Kilogram).

A comparison of the two curves shows that there is a parallelism, tolerably constant up to 1869. After this it ceases with some exceptions. The great fall in the price of bread, beginning with 1878 (as a consequence of the agrarian crisis), even coincides with a considerable increase in vagrancy and mendicity. To explain this we must consult the statistics of failures. These show that the great increase of vagrancy and mendicity coincide with an equally great increase in the number of bankruptcies, beginning in 1875 and lasting to 1882. For the following years there is no relation between the two phenomena apparent.

Prussia, 1854–1870.

I have composed the following table by means of the data given by Starke in his "Verbrechen und Verbrecher in Preuszen" (pp. 55 and 115).

Years.	Number of New Cases of Vagrancy and Mendicity.	Price of 50 Kilograms in Marks.		
		Wheat.	Rye.	Potatoes.
1854	14,619	12.90	10.40	3.17
1855	16,665	14.21	11.45	3.37
1856	20,414	13.51	10.64	3.13
1857	15,801	10.18	6.87	2.18
1858	15,318	9.08	6.38	1.91
1859	16,978	8.93	6.79	1.98
1860	16,320	10.48	7.65	2.41
1861	14,239	11.04	7.71	2.79
1862	12,846	10.68	7.97	2.47
1863	11,840	9.18	6.78	2.04
1864	12,026	7.95	5.69	2.10
1865	11,640	8.13	6.24	2.03
1866	13,664	9.80	7.30	2.05
1867	15,339	12.89	9.87	2.95
1868	14,801	12.48	9.84	2.62
1869	15,091	9.70	8.08	2.16
1870	13,320	11.04	7.78	2.58

Although the curves of the price of foodstuffs and of vagrancy do not exactly conform, the influence of the price is none the less evident. The three periods of high prices (1854–56, 1860–62, and 1867–68) coincide with high figures for vagrancy and mendicity. (It is to be noted that the effect of an economic depression does not always make itself felt the following year.)

Kingdom of Saxony, 1889–1892.

Bebel showed that mendicity increased greatly in the above period (a crisis of great intensity). (See pp. 228–229 of this work.)[1]

I am of the opinion that these data show sufficiently that the increase or diminution of vagrancy and mendicity are regulated by the economic situation; in other words, that a great many persons become guilty of these contraventions not because they are not *willing* to work, but *entirely* as a consequence of an unfavorable economic environment. There are some exceptions to this rule. Above (pp. 89–90) I have shown that these exceptions do not weaken the general conclusion; the unfavorable influence of the economic depression may be neutralized by counter-determinants. It must

[1] *Cf. K. Boehmert,* "Die Sächsische Kriminalstatistik mit besondere Rücksicht auf die Jahre 1882–1887."

further be remarked especially with regard to vagrancy and mendicity, that the application of the laws relative to these offenses is quite arbitrary, and it happens at the time of a crisis that the courts do not punish those who are guilty of them, whence it follows that the statistics do not give an accurate picture of the reality.[1]

It is impossible to fix exactly how far the influence of economic depressions extends; in other words, we cannot determine the number of vagrants and mendicants who become such *directly* through forced idleness. When it is necessary to record a certain number of convictions for vagrancy and mendicity, although the economic conditions are most favorable, we shall not even then be able to say that this proves that the convictions fell only upon persons who could have found work, but did not wish it.

Under the present economic system unemployment is chronic, that is to say, it is present even in times of economic prosperity. Consequently it has not been proved that those who are convicted during these periods are necessarily lazy and do not want to work. The only figure that I have been able to find with regard to the importance of this cause of vagrancy and mendicity is this: that in Germany, out of a total of 200,000 mendicants, there are 80,000 (40 %) who are really in search of work.[2] This figure being only approximate, its significance is not great.

Before leaving the subject of this cause, we must say something with regard to the objection that the workers who, on account of a long period of unemployment, fall finally into vagrancy, are inferior to the average, generally do not know a trade, and are often addicted to alcohol; and that consequently in this case an individual factor plays a rôle beside the economic factor.

It is true that most of the vagrants and mendicants do not know a trade, nor are worth much as workmen. In his study Dr. Bonhoeffer says that 55.4 % of the vagrants and mendicants examined by him had not learned a trade, or had learned it insufficiently.[3] This author also shows (we shall return to this later) that a great proportion of these people are also physically inferior to the average. This inferiority is in part not the cause but the effect of the conditions under which they have been living (insufficient food, etc.),[4] and in part congenital weakness.

However, supposing that each of these individuals knew a trade,

---

[1] See *Bérard, op. cit.*, pp. 605, 606.   [2] *Flynt, op. cit.*, p. 170.
[3] "Ein Beitrag zur Kenntnis des groszstädtischen Bettel- und Vagabondtums" ("Zeitschr. f. d. ges. Strafrw." XXI).
[4] See *Ostwald, op. cit.*, pp. 306, 307.

supposing also that they were all robust and healthy and in a condition to work regularly, would there then be fewer persons without work than there are now? *The answer to this question must be negative.* Even if every workman knew a trade, this fact would not increase the demand for skilled workmen. At any given time the labor market demands only a certain number of skilled workmen, and a certain other number of unskilled laborers; the number of unskilled laborers available has no influence. The same thing is true as to fitness for work; if all the workmen had the same energy, the same zeal, etc., this would not increase the demand for workmen; this demand is regulated by other factors.

In my opinion it cannot be a question of individual causes; individual differences explain partially who remain without work, and so become vagrants; but it is the economic system which causes the existence of persons without work. *Vagrancy and mendicity would be no less extensive even if all the workers knew a trade and were equal in zeal and energy.*

In the second place the world of vagrants and mendicants is composed of people too old to work, or more or less incapable of working, from physical or psychical causes, so that they are no longer employed. So far as I know the data concerning the age of vagrants and mendicants are not numerous; I can cite those that follow.

England, 1894–1900.[1]

		Of Whom there were of the Age of			
Years.	Number of Mendicants Convicted.	50 to 60 years.		Over 60.	
		Absolute Numbers.	%	Absolute Numbers.	%
1894	13,021	1,638	12	1,916	14
1895	10,497	1,387	13	1,490	14
1896	11,839	1,512	12	1,801	15
1897	10,735	1,338	12	1,701	15
1898	11,047	1,540	13	1,838	16
1899	9,308	1,374	14	1,667	17
1900	8,402	1,253	14	1,690	20

[1] After "Criminal Statistics", 1894–1900, Table XIII. In studying these figures it must not be lost sight of that in general a workman is soon worn out and after that is no longer hired.

Netherlands, 1896–1901.[1]

YEARS.	NUMBER OF PERSONS CONVICTED OF VAGRANCY AND MENDICITY.	OF WHOM THERE WERE OF THE AGE OF			
		50 to 60 years.		Over 60.	
		Absolute Numbers.	%	Absolute Numbers.	%
1896	2,181	541	24	273	12
1897	2,139	529	25	278	13
1898	2,173	534	24	291	13
1899	2,215	564	25	285	12
1901	1,857	491	26	257	13

Russia, 1897.

In the work of Loewenstimm already cited we find mentioned the fact that out of a total of 7,916 mendicants arrested in St. Petersburg, 1,185 (14.9 %) were between 50 and 60 years of age, and 982 (12.4 %) over 60.[2]

As has been said, a certain number of vagrants are weak or sickly, and consequently are nearly or quite unable to work. In "Les habitués des prisons de Paris", Dr. Laurent gives the following description of some vagrants observed by him, true types of this kind of individual. "I have known at the Santé in recent years an individual who has passed almost the whole of his life in prison, who was born and lived in misery. A natural child, his mother received him as a mistake and a burden and tried to destroy herself and him. Later, convulsions twisted him upon a hospital bed, and he has remained half-paralyzed. So far from knowing how to read or write he can hardly see clearly, for an opaque film covers his left eye. He has undergone more than twenty sentences for mendicity and vagrancy, and he is still only 37 years old. He leaves prison only to enter it again. So he complains bitterly and blames the judicial authorities, who, instead of placing him in an asylum, where he belongs, cast him into prison, because, says he, the food does not cost so much.

"An individual 29 years old, the son of a drunkard and a consumptive, has already been seven times sentenced for mendicity. He has been half-paralyzed since he was 13 months old and can walk only with crutches. Epileptic in addition, he drifts from prison to prison.

"These facts are very common, and it is impossible to estimate how

[1] After "de Gerechtelijke Statistiek", 1896–1899 and "de Crimineele Statistiek", 1901. [2] After pp. 30, 31.

many of these poor devils live in the prisons, which are a kind of refuge for them. Lately I saw a blind man who had been arrested for mendicity and sentenced to a fortnight in prison." [1]

The following figures, taken from the work just quoted, inform us as to the number of such individuals.

Breslau.

PHYSICAL AND MENTAL CONDITION.	ABSOLUTE NUMBERS.	%
Physical condition weak	337	91
Incapable of military service from physical weakness	236	64
Mental anomalies	322	87
Epilepsy	43	11
Imbecility	86	23
Total number examined	369	100

Here it must be noted that in the years 1896–97 there were on the average only 9 % of the conscripts of Silesia who were incapable of military service.

The other figures that are known agree with the ones I have just cited. Dr. Kurella found 20 % to 30 % of imbeciles or epileptics among the vagrants.[2] Dr. Mendel also found a great number of psychic abnormalities among the vagrants.[3]

All that I have just said demonstrates sufficiently, I believe, that the cause named above plays a considerable rôle in the etiology of mendicity and vagrancy. It is still necessary to give an answer to the question : do all the individuals who fall under the unfavorable conditions named under one and two, become vagrants or mendicants? It is evident that the answer must be negative. Three expedients offer themselves to one who has fallen into the blackest poverty ; mendicity, theft, and suicide. It is partly chance (opportunity etc.), and partly the individual predisposition which fixes what anyone under the conditions named will become, whether a mendicant or a thief. Generally those who have still some intelligence

---

[1] Pp. 40, 41.

[2] "Naturgeschichte des Verbrechers", p. 208.

[3] *Florian* and *Cavaglieri, op. cit.*, II, p. 22. See also the whole of Sec. 5, IV, Chap. 2, of the same authors.

[NOTE TO THE AMERICAN EDITION : Upon this subject *cf. K. Wilmanns,* "Zur Psychopathologie des Landstreichers", and *Stelzner, op. cit.*, pp. 92 *ff.*]

and energy become thieves, the rest vagrants.[1] The third expedient, suicide, also is frequently met with among the lower proletariat.[2] Those who have recourse to it are either those who have known better conditions and find that the miserable existence that mendicity procures is not worth the trouble of living, or those who have lost all energy. Sometimes persons commit suicide to escape the shame of begging or stealing. These have been called "the heroes of virtue"; but, considered from another point of view, they may also be called the "victims of vice", the vice of others, of course. These have been born with a very strong moral disposition and have lived in an environment where this disposition has been developed. These cases prove the degree of intensity that the social sentiments can attain; they are stronger than the fundamental desire to live, although those whom these "heroes" are unwilling to injure, reject these sentiments, by abandoning their fellows who find themselves in want.

Third. A third category of mendicants and vagrants is made up of children and young people. Let us see what relation there is between this fact and the economic and social environment. All those who have taken up this subject are agreed that a great proportion of the children are systematically taught to beg by their parents. Whatever may be the cause for which the parents act thus, these children are entirely the victims of the detestable atmosphere in which they are forced to live. Brought up in a wholesome environment they would become neither mendicants nor vagrants.[3]

Another part of the vagrant body is made up of children who are either illegitimate or orphans, or deserted by their parents, or forced by bad treatment to run away from home. Tomel and Rollet mention the following typical case. A girl of 16 was charged with vagrancy, and made this heart-rending statement of her case before the tribunal: "I went on Friday to find the police commissioner of the ward; I told him that I had been without a lodging place for 15 days, and that I had not eaten for 48 hours. I was employed at the house of a wine merchant, who, when my mother died three years ago, took me as a servant (at 13 years of age) at two sous a day as wages. But my employer failed, his shop was closed, and I had to go out and wander in search of work without finding anything. My father, sen-

---

[1] See *Dugdale*, "The Jukes", pp. 47 and 49; and *Flynt, op. cit.* p. 6.
[2] See *Florian* and *Cavaglieri, op. cit.*, II, pp. 34, 35, 177, 178.
[3] See *Tomel* and *Rollet*, "Les enfants en prison", pp. 55–76; *Puibaraud*, "Les malfaiteurs de profession", pp. 217–230; *Albanel*, "Le crime dans la famille", p. 88; *Loewenstimm, op. cit.*, pp. 89–99; *Joly*, "L'enfance coupable", pp. 60 *ff*.

tenced to hard labor for life, died in New Caledonia. I have no longer any mother, and since I did not wish to imitate my grown-up sister, who leads a bad life, I preferred to get myself arrested." [1]

It is difficult to tell how many of these children there are. The only figures that I know of are the following.

Italy, 1885–1889.[2]

Among the minors sent to a house of correction for vagrancy there were

DIVISIONS.	ABSOLUTE NUMBERS.	%
Illegitimate children	91	8.0
Orphans	498	43.8
Children whose parents were in prison	25	2.2
Other children	524	46.0
Total	1,138	100.0

We must now speak of another kind of vagrant and mendicant, those whom some criminologists have called born-vagabonds; children who run away from home to meet with adventures and to see something more than the neighborhood where they live. It makes little difference to us here whence comes this desire; everyone, especially every child, has it more or less (who is there who does not love to travel?) and there are those in whom it is very strong. "Who among us," say Tomel and Rollet, "at certain moments of existence, does not feel the desire to break with social conventions, or more simply, to break through the circle of his horizon, in order to depart in search of the unknown? Put money in the pocket of the tramp and you make a tourist. The sportsman and the delinquent are separated only by the thickness of some hundred-sou pieces." [3]

These authors have hit the truth of the matter. Such children are called born-vagabonds, but then we meet thousands of born-vaga- bonds who have never become vagabonds in reality. The children who have a great love of adventure are found in all classes of society, but only those who come from among the poor become vagrants. It is in

[1] Op. cit., pp. 31, 32.

[2] Florian and Cavaglieri, op. cit., II, p. 52. See also : Frégier, "Les classes dangereuses de la population dans les grandes villes", I, pp. 199, 200; Tomel and Rollet, op. cit., pp. 28–45; and Albanel, op. cit., p. 78.

[3] Op. cit., p. 2.

poverty then that we find the "casua efficiens"; the same inclination that brings poor children to prison, would perhaps lead them to a post of honor if they had lived in better surroundings. There are people of all kinds among criminals, and it cannot be denied that the majority of them are inferior in every way. But this does not apply to this class of little vagrants. Those who, as a consequence of years of experience, have a right to speak, are agreed that such children can be made useful members of society, if they are rationally guided.[1] They are bold and energetic lads. Could it be believed that all the boys who, in 1889, came on foot to Paris from all parts of France to see the Eiffel tower (there were some of them under seven years of age) were not brave and energetic? Brought up in another environment they would have become sailors or explorers, or would have undertaken long journeys as tourists — while now they get into prison, to descend later lower and lower.[2]

Fourth. Finally, the fourth category of vagrants and mendicants. This consists of those not included in the other three classes of people who are physically in a condition to work and who have opportunity to do so, but are not willing to work. It is hard to determine with certainty how large a part of the army of vagrants and mendicants they make up. But it seems to me certain that the facts given above prove that they are not as numerous as some authors and many other people believe. Besides, how is it that the philanthropic institutions where everyone admitted has to work, are always full, if it is true that most vagrants are persons who are not willing to work?

The vagrants of this class are then lazy persons, unwilling to work, but living at the expense of others, and consequently parasites. It is with reason that many authors have blamed such persons (though, as Dr. Colajanni says, justice would require that we should include all do-nothings, and not the poor only). But this does not advance the cause of sociology; her task is to find the causes of the phenomenon.

It is incontestable that the zeal and energy, evidenced by modern peoples in their work, are not innate but acquired. All sound individ-

---

[1] *Flynt, op. cit.*, p. 49; *Th. Holmes*, "Pictures and Problems of London Police Courts", p. 64; and others.

[2] Upon vagrancy and mendicity of children see further: *J. Délie*, "Le vagabondage des mineurs"; *Ferriani*, "Minderjährige Verbrecher", pp. 144–155; and Flynt, *op. cit.*, pp. 28–60.

[NOTE TO THE AMERICAN EDITION: Upon pathological children see *P. Schroeder*, "Das Fortlaufen der Kinder" ("Monatsschr. f. Krim. psychologie in Strafr. reform", VIII); and *E. Stier*, "Wandertrieb und pathologisches Fortlaufen bei Kindern."]

uals have, not in the same measure, it is true, an innate tendency to
exercise their muscles and their intellectual faculties, but without
external causes this inclination does not go very far. The primitive
peoples work no more than is necessary to provide for their very moderate needs. They find people laughable who work more than is
strictly necessary.[1] The enormous change which took place in the
method of production little by little induced men to produce a greater
and greater amount of work; on the one hand were the slaves, forced
to labor hard, and on the other hand the property owners driven to
work by the desire of profit. In our present society the case is almost
the same; the great mass are forced to work by fear of poverty, the
smaller number by the desire for gain. And then the great majority
of men have been accustomed to work from infancy; much work is
done from necessity, but much from habit, which causes a feeling of
uneasiness when one cannot work.

The first reason why there are people who do not want to work, is
that they have not been accustomed to it from childhood. In general
children, like primitive people, who are analogous to them in many
ways, show little zeal for work. It is necessary to train them for a
fairly long time before they set themselves to work assiduously.
What will all those children whose parents have neglected them, or
who have even taught them to beg, turn into when they are grown
up, if not into vagrants and mendicants? They have never learned
any trade, have never become accustomed to work, have never found
any pleasure in it, so that later in life they will never have any desire
to do anything.[2]

Part of those who have not been able to work for a long time go the
same road, they lose the habit of working, become lazy, and in the
end are not willing to do anything any more.[3] These, to be sure, are
the least diligent by nature, but that would not alone send them into
vagrancy if they had always been able to find work.

However, there is still one more thing to be said about the circumstances which give rise to this class of individuals. In the first place,
the long duration, the monotony, and the disagreeable features of the
work of the proletariat, which, as a consequence is rather hated than
loved.[4] In the second place: the small wages of a large part of the
workers, and the comparatively large amounts that clever beggars

[1] See *Florian* and *Cavaglieri, op. cit.*, II, pp. 11–14.
[2] See, for example, *Loewenstimm, op. cit.*, pp. 17 and 92.
[3] See *Bérard, op. cit.*, p. 605.
[4] See *Ferriani*, "Minderjährige Verbrecher", pp. 177 *ff.*, and "Schlaue
und glückliche Verbrecher", pp. 460 *ff.*

are able to secure. Flynt gives the following data as to the "earnings" of tramps; in New York, $1 a day; in the Eastern States generally, from 50 cents to $1 or $2, without counting food; in New Orleans a skilful beggar can "earn" $1 a day. He estimates that in Germany the daily receipts of a beggar are from a mark and a half to four marks, and food; in England most beggars get from 18 pence to two shillings, though some very clever ones even get as much as 10 shillings.[1] Loewenstimm tells that in Petrograd a skilful beggar has a daily income of three rubles.[2] Florian and Cavaglieri say that in Paris a beggar gets four francs, and if he is very clever, even as much as twenty-five francs, a day.[3]

In some cases, then, it is more profitable, and in all cases more easy, not to work. In consequence of these facts we read very often that the public ought not to give to these idlers. But the public cannot distinguish this class of mendicants from the others. It is certainly true that professional mendicity would diminish if nothing were given to mendicants; but on the other hand the great misery among the other poor would be aggravated still more. And I venture to doubt whether the advantage thus gained on one side would counterbalance the disadvantage created on the other.

And these laments upon the subject of the stupidity of the public are generally accompanied by anathemas upon those who prefer the life of the parasite to work. No one would naturally be inclined to excuse these individuals. But it is necessary to look at the question from both sides. If these people are blamed, blame must be attached also to a state of society *in which honest labor is so poorly paid that begging is often more lucrative.* These individuals are cunning egoists and as long as society is organized as it is, they are right from their point of view. To be sure, they have no feeling of honor, they attach no value to the opinion of others, but the feeling of honor is not innate but acquired. As the facts show, vagrants generally come from an environment where there can be no question of a development of moral qualities. Dr. Bonhoeffer shows, for example, that about 45% of the vagrants examined by him had been brought up in bad home surroundings (alcoholism of the parents, etc.). Then, as we have seen above, the social feelings can be developed only where there is reciprocity. I should like to know whether society really concerns itself with the fate of these unfortunates to such an extent that they in their turn care greatly for the opinion of this same society.

[1] *Op. cit.*, pp. 97, 103, 110, 182, and 244. [2] *Op. cit.*, p. 38.
[3] *Op. cit.*, I, pp. 111, 112.

Certainly not. They are pariahs, and since they are such the contempt of a hostile world is a matter of indifference.

As we come to the conclusion of our observations upon the etiology of vagrancy and mendicity, we have still but one category to consider, that of those who are indolent by nature. There are individuals in whom assiduous labor of any kind awakens a strong feeling of discomfort.[1] As we have already stated above, in speaking of poverty in general (see p. 288), the cause of this phenomenon is a species of neurasthenia, more especially physical. It is necessary to recognize that, while these individuals are out of harmony with society, they are sick and must be cared for if society is to avoid trouble. Besides, Professor Benedict, who was the first to point out physical neurasthenia, himself recognizes[2] that such sick persons need not become vagrants, if they are brought up in a favorable environment, and that later the struggle for existence will not be painful to them.

To sum up, it is evident that the principal causes of vagrancy and mendicity are lack of work, the want of care for the old, the sick, and the weak, the abandonment of poor children, the low wages and long hours of the workers. The persons who run most danger of being incorporated in the army of vagrants are the weak, whether mentally or physically, but this need not necessarily happen; the "causa causarum" is the environment.[3]

History proves this also. If vagrancy and mendicity sprang from the innate qualities of man, there would always have been vagrants and mendicants, which is not the case. The appearance of these is due to the economic structure of society. It is not possible to discuss this at length and the reader is referred to the work of Florian and Cavaglieri, "I vagabondi" (I, Part One). These authors show that the first type of vagrant was the runaway slave, and then the serf

---

[1] *Ferriani*, "Minderjährige Verbrecher", pp. 151–154. *Tomel* and *Rollet*, *op. cit.*, pp. 24–27.
[NOTE TO THE AMERICAN EDITION: *Cf. Haury*, "Laparesse pathologique" ("Archives d'anthrop. crim." XXVIII).]

[2] "Die Vagabondage und ihre Behändlung", p. 715 ("Zeitschr. f. d. ges. Strafrw." XI).

[3] [NOTE TO THE AMERICAN EDITION: Of the recent literature upon vagrancy and mendicity we would call attention to the following: *K. Wilmanns*, "Das Landstreichertum, seine Bekämpfung und Abhilfe"; *A. Aletrino*, "Handleiding bij de studie der crimineele anthropologie", II, ch. VI; *Rotering*, "Das Landstreichertum der Gegenwart"; *Riebeth*, "Ueber den geistigen und körperlichen Zustand der Korrigenden"; *de Roos, op. cit.*, pp. 151 *ff.*; *A. Marie* and *R. Meunier*, "Les vagabonds"; *Pollitz, op. cit.*, pp. 95 *ff.*; *A. Pagnier*, "Le vagabond": *Kauffmann, op. cit.*, pp. 97 *ff.*; *H. T. de Graaf*, "Karakter en behandeling van veroordeelden wegens landlooperij en bedelarij."]

who had fled from his lord's domain. In. the following periods the penalties with which vagrants were threatened (and they were very severe) were especially designed to force the proletariat to serve the purposes of the possessors of the means of production.[1] In measure as the number of available workers increases and the proletariat submits to the will of the capitalists, this cause becomes less important, and disappears almost completely in our own time. It is rather the contrary that takes place, since the army of vagrants and mendicants is now mainly composed of those who have not been able to find work. Vagabondage and mendicity are at present punishable because of the importunity of the mendicants, the losses experienced by persons living in the country especially, and also because of the danger to society from the fact that the dangerous criminals are partly recruited from this class.

B. Theft and Analogous Crimes.

Before examining the motives inducing the commission of theft (the most important crime of this group, the others being mostly modifications of it) we must first stop a moment to ask the question, "Is honesty an innate characteristic or is it acquired?"

In my opinion it is indisputable that honesty is as little innate as any other moral conception.[2] No child can distinguish between mine and thine, it is only little by little that he gains this concept. On the contrary he has the tendency to monopolize everything that he desires (the prehensory instinct, Lafargue names it).[3] It is just this instinct that must be combated to make a child honest. It would, therefore, be more correct to say that dishonesty is innate. Unless one takes account of this fact it is impossible to give the etiology of theft and crimes of the same nature.

The motives for these crimes with which we are now occupied we shall speak of under three heads. The first group includes the crimes committed from *poverty*, the second those that result from cupidity, and in the third group we shall treat of the criminals by profession.

---

[1] *Marx*, "Kapital", I, ch. xxlv, pp. 699 *ff*.

[2] Upon the impossibility of innate moral concepts see *Näcke*, "Die neuern Erscheinung auf kriminal-anthropologischen Gebiete und ihre Bedeutung", p. 342 ("Zeitschr. f. d. ges. Strafrw." XIV).

[3] "Der Ursprung der Idee des Gerechten und Ungerechten", pp. 470, 471. ("Neue Zeit", 1898–1899, II.)

a. THEFTS COMMITTED FROM POVERTY.

There are some needs which a man must satisfy, without which his existence is impossible. These are fundamental needs, independent of environment. If a man has not sufficient food, if he has not (at least in non-tropical countries) clothing to protect him against cold, if opportunity for rest is lacking, etc., his life is in danger. In our present society there are always a number of persons who are in want of the strict necessaries of life, and who are therefore obliged to steal if they do not wish to succumb to poverty. It is evident that the word "poverty" is not to be taken in the most limited sense, so that one who can still buy a morsel of bread, and yet steals, may still be considered as a thief from poverty.

We must make here one more observation before we enter upon the proofs of this thesis. We have defined crime as an egoistic act. However, the same act may be at once egoistic and altruistic, and this is the case with some crimes committed from poverty, when an individual steals in order not to have those in his charge die of hunger. What conflicts of duty our present society creates!

The proofs that absolute poverty provokes a number of thefts are of three kinds. The first two are based upon the dynamics of criminality.

First. In winter, when poverty is most pressing, the number of thefts etc. is much greater than in summer. This is a fact so well known that it is unnecessary to give detailed proofs of it, and I think it will be sufficient to give the following statistics dealing with two important countries for a great number of years.

Germany, 1883–1892.[1]

CRIMES.[2]		January.	February.	March.	April.	May.	June.	July.	August.	September.	October.	November.	December.
Simple theft	a	7,991	7,342	6,909	5,777	6,097	6,003	6,230	6,481	6,249	7,436	7,966	8,523
	b	113	115	98	85	87	88	88	92	92	106	117	121
Aggravated	a	913	877	830	777	840	856	879	866	818	956	971	996
theft	b	102	107	92	89	94	98	98	96	94	106	112	111
Embezzle-	a	1,539	1,358	1,454	1,397	1,505	1,485	1,583	1,551	1,459	1,604	1,573	1,659
ment	b	100	97	94	94	98	100	103	101	98	104	105	108
Receiving stolen goods	a	682	615	571	442	458	447	444	451	451	556	643	789
	b	123	122	103	82	82	83	80	81	81	100	120	142
Professional and habitual receiving of stolen goods	a	3	5	4	8	4	3	3	3	6	3	3	5
	b	71	130	94	195	94	73	71	71	146	71	73	118
Fraud	a	2,174	2,050	1,909	1,744	1,823	1,869	1,932	1,845	1,758	2,065	2,279	2,432
	b	107	111	94	89	90	95	95	91	90	102	116	120

There is, then, a pretty considerable increase as winter approaches, and a decrease with the summer months. I would call the attention of the reader especially to the fact that it is the crimes of simple theft and the receiving of stolen goods which show this change in the most marked way, while aggravated theft, embezzlement and the professional and habitual receiving of stolen goods show it in less degree. It is the two former crimes which have poverty as their cause, while the three latter are more apt to be committed from cupidity and by professional criminals.

[1] "Kriminalstatistik für das Jahr 1894", II, p. 53.
[2] The figures in the line a are the absolute figures (annual averages), those in the line b the relative numbers, i.e. what the daily average for that month would be if the daily average for the year were 100.

The following figures, taken from the criminal calendar composed by Professor Lacassagne, have to do with

France, 1827–1870.[1]

Number of Crimes Against Property for Each Month, Reduced to an Equal Duration of 31 Days.

JANUARY.	FEBRUARY.	MARCH.	APRIL.	MAY.	JUNE.	JULY.	AUGUST.	SEPTEMBER.	OCTOBER.	NOVEMBER.	DECEMBER.
16,350	15,400	14,250	13,450	13,625	13,450	13,225	13,425	13,875	14,400	16,100	16,825

We have here, then, as always, a great increase in fall and winter, and a corresponding decrease in spring and summer.

Second. A second proof of the importance of absolute poverty as a cause of crime etc. is furnished by the fact that there is a considerable increase of the crimes in question in times of economic depression (high price of bread, lack of work, etc.). In Part One I have cited many works in which this phenomenon is proved for a number of countries. I refer the reader, therefore, to the more important of these, and add other data here.

[1] "Marche de la criminalité en France, 1825–1880" ("Revue scientifique", 1881), to be found also in *Levasseur's* "La population française", II, p. 458.

Germany, 1882–1911.[1]

YEARS.	PRICE OF RYE IN MARKS PER 1000 KILOGR. (BERLIN.)	IMPORTS AND EXPORTS IN BILLIONS OF MARKS.	NUMBER OF PERSONS CONVICTED OF CRIMES GIVEN BELOW, TO 100,000 OF POPULATION OVER 12 YEARS OF AGE.				
			Simple Theft.	Aggravated Theft.	Receiving Stolen Goods.	Fraud.	Embezzlement.
1882	152.3	6.3	250	28	26	37	46
1883	144.7	6.5	241	25	24	38	46
1884	143.3	6.4	231	25	23	39	46
1885	140.6	5.8	214	22	22	38	45
1886	130.6	5.9	210	20	21	41	45
1887	120.9	6.2	198	21	20	43	44
1888	134.5	6.7	194	21	20	44	44
1889	155.5	7.2	211	23	21	49	47
1890	170.0	7.6	206	24	21	50	47
1891	211.2	7.7	216	25	22	54	50
1892	176.3	7.3	236	31	25	59	52
1893	133.7	7.3	202	26	22	58	51
1894	117.8	7.2	198	27	22	60	52
1895	119.8	7.6	192	24	22	61	53
1896	118.8	8.2	184	24	19	58	50
1897	130.1	8.5	188	23	18	61	51
1898	146.3	9.4	191	25	19	63	52
1899	146.3	10.0	179	24	19	63	53
1900	142.6	10.7	181	23	18	60	51
1901	140.7	10.2	190	26	19	64	52
1902	144.2	10.6	191	28	20	66	55
1903	132.3	11.4	182	26	19	64	54
1904	135.1	12.1	176	24	17	62	54
1905	151.9	13.2	175	25	17	61	56
1906	160.6	14.8 [3]	179	28	18	62	58
1907	193.2 [2]	15.5	178	28	18	61	60
1908	186.5	14.0	189	32	20	61	63
1909	176.5	15.1	182	33	20	62	65
1910	152.3	16.4	176	32	19	63	65
1911	168.3	17.8	169	30	19	63	65

If, in examining the preceding table, we do not lose sight of the fact that the rise or fall of the price of grain does not make itself felt immediately, and that in the criminal statistics of a certain year there appear also persons who have committed their crime in a preceding year, it is clear how enormous is the influence of the economic

[1] Taken from the "Kriminalstatistik", 1895, 1907, 1908 and 1911, and from the "Statistisches Jahrbuch für das deutsche Reich."
[2] The figures from 1907 on are not comparable with those preceding.
[3] The figures from 1906 on are comparable with those preceding, only with reserve.

movement upon economic crimes.   The price of grain had formerly
a decisive influence upon the trend of economic crimes; now, in industrial countries like Germany, it is rather the industrial situation,
without, however, the price of cereals losing all influence.[1]

England, 1823–1896.

Dr. Tugan Baranowsky proved for the periods 1823–1850 and 1871–
1896 the correlation between good and bad times and the decrease
and increase of criminality.

For the period 1858–1864 the same proof is given by Mayr (see
Part I); and for the years 1840–1890 by Fornasari di Verce (see
Part I).   The figures of the former have reference only to crime in
general, and do not, therefore, show sufficiently the effect upon crimes
that are merely economic.[2]

Grand-Duchy of Baden, 1875–1892.[1]

J. S(chmidt), the statistician, shows the parallelism of the two
curves for the period mentioned (p. 243).

Bavaria, 1835–1861.

Dr. G. Mayr was one of the first statisticians to show the influence
of the price of grain upon crimes against property (pp. 39–42).

Belgium, 1839–1890.

Dr. Weisz has proved the influence of the price of grain during the
period from 1841 to 1860 (p. 61) and Professor Denis that of the economic happenings for the period from 1840 to 1890 (pp. 235–237),
while Ducpetiaux draws attention especially to the enormous increase
of criminality in Flanders during the years of crisis, 1846–1847 (pp.
32–37).[3]

France, 1825–1886.

The influence of the price of grain upon crimes against property has
been shown for the periods 1845–1864, 1850–1864, and 1855–1864
respectively, by Drs. Weisz (pp. 60–61), Corne (pp. 48–49), and
Mayr (pp. 46–47).   Lacassagne and Lafargue have shown the correlation between the fluctuations of the economic life and those of eco-

---

[1] For details see my study already cited, "Verbrechen und Sozialismus."
[2] [NOTE TO THE AMERICAN EDITION: The English criminal statistics
for 1905 show an interesting diagram upon the connection between the trend
of economic crime and that of business from 1885 to 1905 (Int. p. 24).]
[3] [NOTE TO THE AMERICAN EDITION: Cf. Jacquart, op. cit. pp. 109 ff.]

nomic crime for the years 1825–80 and 1840–86 respectively (pp. 149 and 231 *ff.*).

Italy, 1873–1890.

For this period Fornasari di Verce has shown the parallelism between the curves of economic occurrences and of economic crime (pp. 138–143).

New South Wales, 1882–1891.

The same author has shown here also the same correlation (p. 144).

Netherlands, 1860–1891.

Since researches for this country upon our subject are lacking, I have composed the following diagram from the official data.

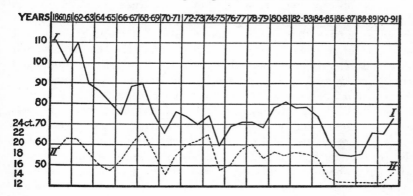

I. Number of those Convicted for Theft to 100,000 of the Population.
II. Price of Bread per Kilogram in Centimes.

The parallelism of the two curves is striking, there being simply a slight exception in the years 1871–1873. The increase of theft in the years 1879–1881 coincides with a very great increase in the number of bankruptcies, which continued until 1882.[1]

The same parallelism has also been shown for Prussia, Russia, Wurtemberg, and Zurich by Starke and Müller, Tarnowsky, Rettich, and Meyer, as quoted in Part I of this work.[2]

[1] [Note to the American Edition: For the period 1896–1908 I have shown in my study "Crime et Socialisme" the striking parallel between economic crime and the business situation.]

[2] There are still to be mentioned as authors who have treated the dynamics of criminality: *J. Sacker,* "Der Rückfall" (pp. 39, 40); *Aschaffenburg,* "Das Verbrechen und seine Bekämpfung" (pp. 89 *ff.*); and *H. Leuss,* "Aus dem Zuchthause" (pp. 228 *ff.*).

[Note to the American Edition: See further: for Austria: *Hoegel, op. cit.,* pp. 369 *ff., Herz, op. cit.* pp. 40 *ff.*; for Saxony: *Böhmert, op. cit.,*

Few sociological theses, it seems to me, have been proved as con-
clusively as the one of which we have just been speaking. The important influence of the trend of economic events upon that of economic criminality has been shown for thirteen different countries for
different periods of the nineteenth century. Some authors are of the
opinion that poverty cannot be the cause of crimes that are committed when economic conditions are most favorable, and when
economic crimes have consequently reached their minimum. This
assertion still needs fuller proof, as I have already pointed out, since
there are still many persons who are in want of the necessaries of life
even in times of prosperity.

I must say here a few words in answer to a final objection to the
preceding observation; namely, that the increase of theft etc., in
times of economic depression, is, in great part, a consequence, not of
absolute poverty, but of the impossibility of satisfying needs that
have sprung up in more favorable times; and that the increase will
be, therefore, in large measure due to an increase of crimes committed
from cupidity, and not from poverty. This may be true in some cases,
but not, in my opinion in the great majority of cases, for the following
reasons. When the economic situation is favorable, when earnings
are more than usual, and when, consequently, wants increase and
become more intense, can everyone satisfy the desires awakened in
him by the spirit of imitation? Surely not; even at such times of
prosperity there are still many individuals with whom desire is
awakened but who are not able to satisfy it in a lawful manner.
On the other hand, wants in general diminish in times of crisis;
cupidity is therefore less excited, and with a limited income men are
quite satisfied with having the means of subsistence, when there are
so many who lack the very necessaries of life. In my opinion, crimes
from cupidity increase rather than diminish in times of prosperity,
while in times of depression the opposite takes place. This cannot be
proved for each economic crime separately, since criminal statistics
do not show whether a crime is committed from poverty or cupidity.
However, embezzlement, fraud, and aggravated theft are committed
in a greater degree from cupidity than is simple theft, (and by professional criminals). Now statistics show that it is chiefly simple
theft that follows the course of economic events, the other crimes
named doing so much less; the same is true of the changes during the

and *Wulffen, op. cit.*, I pp. 390 *ff.*; for Servia: *Wadler, op. cit.*, p. 73 *ff. Cf.*
also in general: *V. Mancini*, "Le varie specie di furto nella storia e nella
sociologia", III 3, Ch. IV.]

different seasons. Finally, while absolute poverty in countries like Germany has decreased and simple theft also, luxury and cupidity have increased, together with the other crimes named.[1]

The third proof that poverty is a great factor in the etiology of theft is the enormous number of widows and divorced women who participate in these crimes (see pp. 452, 453). There is no reason to believe that these women are more covetous than married women or spinsters; but it is certain that their economic situation is often very burdensome.[2]

We shall not employ any further methods to establish our thesis; since for the reasons already stated they would lead to results of no great significance, and it seems that the accuracy of the thesis has been sufficiently shown by the proofs cited.

We have now come to the end of our consideration of the subject of thefts committed from poverty. There are two ways in which it is the cause of theft. On the one hand it incites directly the appropriation of the property of others, and on the other hand it exercises a demoralizing influence.

b. THEFT COMMITTED FROM CUPIDITY.

We have now to deal with crimes of persons who steal neither from absolute poverty, nor by profession. Those who are guilty of these crimes earn enough to satisfy their more pressing needs, and they steal only when the occasion presents itself (whence their name of occasional criminals) [3] in order to satisfy their desire for luxury.

The first question, then, which must be answered here is this; how do these needs arise? The answer can be brief; they are aroused by the environment. In a society where some are rich, who have more income than is needed to supply the fundamental necessities, and who create other needs for themselves, in such a society the cupidity of those who have not similar incomes at their disposal will be

---

[1] *Cf.* further: *Aschaffenburg, op. cit.*, pp. 98 *ff.*; *Eggert*, "Not und Verbrechen"; *Wulffen, op. cit.*, I, pp. 395 *ff.*; *v. Rohden* in "Zeitschr. f. Sozialwissenschaft", VII, pp. 522 *ff.*, and IX, pp. 229 *ff.*

[2] *Cf.* the recent study of *Prinzing*, "Die sozial Lage der Witwe in Deutschland" ("Zeitschr. f. Sozialwissenschaft", III).

[3] In general, criminals are distinguished as occasional, habitual, and professional. Habitual criminals, however, are also occasional criminals, for they do not seek the occasion for their crimes like criminals by profession, but profit by it whenever it presents itself. They are the bond of union between the first and third kind of criminals, and in my opinion, it is unnecessary to treat of them separately.

awakened.   The desires which the criminals of whom we are speaking
wish to satisfy by their misdeeds are not different from those of the
well-to-do.   It goes without saying that no one has ever desired any
luxury that he has not seen someone else enjoying.   It would be a
waste of time to discuss this.   Every need that is not strictly necessary, is not innate but acquired.   If one has much, the other, an
imitator, wants the same.   There is but one piece of advice to give
to those who are not convinced of this simple truth; that they read
some ethnological works treating of peoples among whom there are
neither rich nor poor.   They will then see that cupidity, with us a
universal quality, is there unknown.[1]

The division between rich and poor is many centuries old and does
not belong to capitalism alone, although under capitalism the distance
between the two has greatly increased and is still increasing.   The
greater this distance is, the more, other things being equal, cupidity
increases.[2]

The cupidity of those who can satisfy only the desire for the bare
necessities is not awakened in the same measure in each of them.
As has already been remarked by Guerry and Quetelet (see Part I),
economic crimes are most numerous in the countries where manufacturing and commerce are most developed, and where the contrasts of
fortune are consequently the greatest.   It is for this reason that the
cities, where the contrasts between poverty and wealth are greatest,
give also very high figures for crimes against property (see pp. 530–
531).

Those who live in the same country or the same city are not, in
spite of that, in the same environment.   Every great city has thousands of workers who, because of the character of their labor, have no
contact with luxury; others, on the contrary, have the desire for
luxury awakened in them by the fact that their work brings them in
touch with wealth.   Hence it is, for example, that so large a number
of economic crimes are committed by workers occupied in commerce
(see p. 446), and by servants.[3]   There are workmen who have never
been accustomed to more than they are able to earn at the time, but
there are also those who have known better days and to whom the
impossibility of satisfying needs previously acquired is a constant
source of suffering.

---

[1] See the passage from Mably, Pt. I, p. 14; also *Lassalle*, "Offenes Antwort-
Schreiben" ("Reden und Schriften", II, pp. 426–427).
[2] *Cf. Földes*, "Einige Ergebnisse der neueren Kriminalstatistik ", p. 548.
[3] *Cf. Ryckère*, "La servante criminelle", ch. III.

However, the contrast between rich and poor is not the only cause of the origin of cupidity. We must also sketch in addition to the above, especially the manner in which commercial capital tries to draw buyers. The times are long gone by when the producer worked principally to order. Modern industry manufactures enormous quantities of goods without the outlet for them being known. The desire to buy must, then, be excited in the public. Beautiful displays, dazzling illuminations, and many other means are used to attain the desired end. The perfection of this system is reached in the great modern retail store, where persons may enter freely, and see and handle everything, where, in short, the public is drawn as a moth to a flame. The result of these tactics is that the cupidity of the crowd is highly excited.[1]

After what has been said it is unnecessary to dwell longer upon the different ways in which cupidity is awakened in our present society. However we must note the following. Almost all the thefts of the class of which we are speaking (those committed by so-called occasional criminals) are thefts of articles of very small value (see the figures on p. 201); the exceptions are the thefts of large sums of money. The authors of these last are in general the employes of banks, etc., persons who, from the nature of their work, have the opportunity to appropriate other people's money. When we investigate the reasons for their committing their misdeeds, we shall see that nine times out of ten (I cannot prove it by figures, but no one will contradict me) the criminal is a speculator who has lost, or perhaps an individual who visits prostitutes, and hence has great need of money.

Cupidity is thus excited by the environment, but not in the same degree in every case, the environment not being the same for all. However, even supposing that the environment were exactly identical for a number of persons, cupidity would not be excited in the same measure in some as in others, since they are not alike, one being born with more intense desires than others (admitting that it is the environment that calls forth the desires). The more intense a man's desires, the more risk he runs, other things being equal, of falling foul of the law. As I have already remarked above, this is important for the person who is seeking the reason why A and not B has stolen, though both live in the same environment; for sociology this fact is only of

---

[1] As to the literature upon theft in stores, etc., see especially *Lacassagne*, "Les vols à l'étalage et dans les grands magasins" ("Compte rendu du IV Congrès d'anthr. crim.") and *Dubuisson*, "Les voleuses de grand magasins" ("Arch. d'anthr. crim.", XVI.); also *Lombroso* and *Ferrero*, "La femme criminelle et la prostituée", pp. 481, 482; *Albanel, op. cit.*, pp. 91–95.

secondary importance, for it does not ask "*Who* becomes criminal?" but rather "*How* does it happen that there are crimes?"

We have now examined one of the sides of the question; the principal cause of these crimes is the cupidity awakened by the environment. If the environment were different, cupidity would not be aroused and the crimes would not be committed. In my opinion most criminologists do not sufficiently appreciate the importance of this fact. It is very difficult for anyone who lives at ease to form an idea of what is passing in the mind of one who has only the bare necessaries of life and is deprived of every comfort and amusement, while he sees others who have too much, and yet often work less than he does.

Let us now examine the other side of the question. For this purpose let us make use once more of the figure of balances in describing the process that goes on in the brain of the man who hesitates. Upon one of the pans cupidity exercises its force, in different measure according to the person. What are the weights upon the other pan balancing the first? It is the moral forces which must be considered first. I have fully explained above how the economic environment has prevented the social instincts from being developed in man, and how this is especially true for certain classes of persons. It is unnecessary to repeat this here. It will be sufficient to note certain points which have a special importance for the kind of crimes with which we are occupied at the moment.

He who steals, prejudices the interests of another, does him harm, and at the same time injures society, the existence of which would become impossible were theft permitted. In my opinion, the present organization of society, of which the struggle of all against all is the fundamental principle, has reduced this moral factor to very small dimensions. In the economic domain each must be egoistic, for without egoism he would lose in the struggle for existence. In the case of theft and similar crimes, those injured are almost exclusively well-to-do persons, to whom the damage is disagreeable, but who, in general do not suffer much. The thieves, on the other hand, are almost exclusively persons who have to live on very little. How can we expect a poor man to take care not to do a small injury to the rich for fear of causing them a little discomfort, when most rich people are insensible to the suffering which without intermission, overwhelms the poor. The present organization of society is responsible for the fact that a slight sensibility to the misfortune of others offers only a trifling counterpoise to the tendency to realize one's desires in a dishonest manner.[1] The idea that society in itself is injured by theft cannot constitute any considerable counterpoise, since he who violates the eighth commandment cannot feel himself at one with a society which never has helped him when he was in difficulties.

After this general observation let us pass on to particular remarks that apply to certain classes of persons only. How does it happen that a great proportion of mankind are honest? To this question the answer must be, "because they have been accustomed to it from infancy." The opposite also is true; a great number of thieves are such because any moral education was out of the question in the environment in which they were brought up. They satisfy their "prehensory instinct" without being conscious of any ill-doing. With these the balance inclines to the side of dishonesty, unless a counterpoise of some magnitude is found. Above (pp. 489 *ff.*) we have seen that most criminals, especially thieves, come from a totally corrupt environment.[2]

This does not apply to another category of thieves; those who do not proceed from an absolutely corrupt environment — yet whose surroundings are not good and wholesome. Ferriani[3] and Aschaffen-burg[4] go so far as to say that almost every child has once stolen something. This may be a little exaggerated but it certainly has truth at the bottom of it. If the child has no one to take the trouble to teach him that he ought not to steal, it is more than likely that he will have to answer for theft later (occasional theft is committed by children and minors especially). It is true that all the children whose

---

[1] An interesting proof of the truth of this assertion may be found in an article by *Dr. P. v. Gizycki*, entitled "Wie urteilen Schulkinder über Fund-diebstahl?" ("Zeitschrift für Kinderforschung", VIII). One day this author gave young girls (between 11 and 15 years of age) in a school of the poor in Berlin, the following composition: "You are going to the Christmas fair without money, for your parents are poor. Your father is out of work. You find a pocket book containing a five-mark piece. What do you do with it?" The children had not been prepared for the subject and had received no indication of how they ought to treat it. Only five per cent. of the girls said that they would return the money, because they would pity the person who lost it, and *who might also be poor*. All the others among those who also wished to return the money (53%) had other motives. Those who, on the contrary, wished to retain the money, wanted, *without exception*, to use it to give their parents things they needed. Who will still dare to say that the children who wanted to keep the money (most of them believing in good faith that they had a right to it) in order to give it to others, had feelings less social than most of the rich who, without blushing, see the misery of the poor?

[2] Upon the bad surroundings of the childhood of thieves see further: *Raux*, "Nos jeunes détenus", p. 42, and *Ferriani*, "Minderjährige Ver-brecher", pp. 264 *ff*.

[3] *Op. cit.*, p. 28.

[4] "Das Verbrechen, etc.", p. 123.

education has been defective do not become thieves, nor even the majority of them; there are those for whom a single prohibition will be enough to make them respect the property of others for the rest of their lives. There are others of them, weak characters who, notwithstanding such prohibition, cannot resist when the temptation is strong. If their education had been good, the environment in which they were brought up more favorable, they would not have had to be turned over to justice. Hear the opinion of one of those most competent to judge of the matter, Raux, who, having put to himself the question whether the young people detained in the "Quartier correctionel" of Lyons have a real tendency to steal, answers as follows. "Evidently not. Without entering into the analysis of the circumstances which provoke crime, we shall give, in support of our assertion, an observation as simple as conclusive. Young prisoners condemned for theft have shown us upon different occasions a probity, a most praiseworthy disinterestedness, in the presence of things that they might have appropriated without exposing themselves to any reproof."[1]

We might close our observations upon theft from cupidity at this point if there were not fear of an objection drawn from what has just been said, namely the following. If the occasional thief has become such, on the one side because of the cupidity awakened in him, and on the other side in consequence of his lack of a good education, and if he differs, not qualitatively, but only quantitatively from the honest man, possessing less strength of character than the average — if all this is true, then the figures for theft should be higher than the statistics show. All of which would go to prove that it is wrong to deny that criminals constitute a biological anomaly.

Here is my reply. First. Moral forces do not constitute the only counterpoise to the tendency toward theft. Since the moral check often lacks efficacy, another has been created which acts in the same way to turn the egoist away from crime, namely the fear inspired by the possibility of punishment. Any one would be credulous indeed to fancy that those who have an opportunity to steal and do not profit by it are deterred by moral forces. Without punishment criminality would be much more extensive than it now is. Where the danger of being found out is not great, the number of transgressions is enormous (think, for example, of the cases of smuggling).[2]

Second. Many persons remain honest, not for moral reasons, but

---

[1] *Op. cit.*, p. 42.

[2] *Cf. Ferriani*, "Schlaue und glückliche Verbrecher", p. 39, and *Sighele*, "Psychologie des sectes", pp. 141, 142.

because they lack the courage, cleverness, or other qualities necessary for being otherwise, qualities which in themselves have nothing to do with crime.

Third. Still others remain honest for reasons based upon mature reflection. They find that it is too dangerous to commit an offense, but do not hesitate in the presence of acts *essentially* criminal, although they do not fall under the ban of the law.[1] No one is ignorant of this, and only certain anthropologists who examine no one but prisoners, have lost sight of it.

Those who compose the criminal world are by nature very diverse. Some are the most dangerous individuals that it is possible to imagine, others are rather weak than wicked. Among these last are ranged the occasional criminals, who, taken together, form a danger to society, but taken singly are not dangerous men in the strict sense. Leuss, who learned to know prisoners, not as judge, or as medical expert, but as a prisoner himself, says : "The great mass of prisoners are more good natured than the average man ; the good-nature of thieves corresponds with their weakness of will, that invincible obstacle to their maintaining themselves in the world of industry. Stress must constantly be laid upon the fact that these weak-willed, good-natured persons are the ones who swell the number of crimes." [2]

When we place beside the occasional thieves, those who never steal but commit all sorts of reprehensible (though not illegal) acts, the comparison is not to the advantage of the latter. Their trickery, their pitiless egoism, often make them more dangerous to society than the others ; which should be a reason for criminal anthropology not to build a system based solely upon investigations of prisoners.

Fourth. Finally many more crimes are committed than are mentioned by criminal statistics. Although I have already spoken of this (p. 84), I must return to it. In the first place, most criminal statistics give the figures only for those convicted. Those acquitted have no place, although, with few exceptions, a crime has nevertheless been committed. We know that the number of acquittals is very considerable. In Germany, there were 15 to 20 acquittals to 100 cases tried (1882–1896) ; [3] in Italy the number of acquittals ran as high as 51.37% (1890–1895).[4]

---

[1] *Ferriani, op. cit.* See also *Zerboglio*, "Les inconvénients de l'honnêté" ("Era nouvelle", 1894).

[2] "Aus dem Zuchthause", p. 122.

[3] "Kriminalstatistik f. d. Jahr 1896", I, p. 14.

[4] "Notizie complementari alle statistiche giudiziarie penali degli anni 1890–1895", p. viii.

In the second place, in many cases the prosecution is postponed for different reasons, with the result that there is neither an acquittal nor a condemnation. Then a great many cases never come to trial because justice cannot discover the authors of the crimes. In Germany, for example, of all the cases on the dockets in the criminal courts between 1881 and 1891, only 43 to 45% actually came before the judges.[1] During the period between 1886 and 1890, the examining judges dismissed on an average 8900 cases, either because the author of the crime was unknown, or because the proof was insufficient. During the same period and for the same reasons, 98,741 cases on the average were not prosecuted by the authorities.[2] The authors of about 25% of the crimes committed in Italy remained unknown (1887–1894).[3]

These two reasons by themselves show that the number of crimes is much greater than the statistics would generally lead one to suppose, even if one takes account of the fact that some of the complaints made to the prosecutors are false.

In the third place, we have been speaking so far of the cases that come to the notice of the officers, while in a great number of cases no complaint is made, especially in the matter of petty theft, either because the person injured wishes to avoid the annoyance of having to appear in the police court as witness, or because he wishes to spare the delinquent.

In the fourth place, a great many small thefts remain unknown even to the person injured, since he does not notice the loss that he has suffered.

All this goes to show that crime, taken in the strict sense, and especially theft, is much more extensive than one would expect at first, and the objection that might have been made to my thesis is hence without weight. It is evident that the number of criminals unpunished cannot be fixed with certainty. Dr. Puibaraud places it at 50%;[4] while Tarde believes that it is greater;[5] Yvernès, the well-known French statistician, says that 90% of the professional thieves remain unknown, and Dr. Thomsen, from whom I take this

---

[1] *Tönnies*, "Das Verbrechen als soziale Erscheinung", p. 334 ("Arch. f. Soz. Gesetzgeb. u. Stat.", VIII).

[2] *Tarde*, "Les délits impoursuivis", p. 207 ("Essais et mélanges sociologiques").

[3] "Statistica giudiziaria penale per l'anno 1894", p. lxxxii. See also the detailed statistics cited by *Ferriani, op. cit.*, pp. 112–118.

[4] "Les malfaiteurs de profession", 5. 139.

[5] "Les transformations de l'impunité", p. 167 (published by *Professor Lacassagne* in "Vacher l'éventreur et les crimes sadiques").

last fact, says that this applies to other cateogries of criminals also.[1] However this may be the number in any case is very considerable.

To sum up. I believe I have shown that the fundamental causes of theft and similar crimes committed from cupidity are, on the one hand, the cupidity aroused by the environment and, on the other, neglected childhood among the poor. It is especially those weak in character who run the greatest risk of becoming guilty of these crimes.

c. CRIMES COMMITTED BY PROFESSIONAL CRIMINALS.

In considering all the kinds of theft and analogous crimes, we note that the thefts committed by professional criminals represent only a minority. But as soon as we limit our consideration to the more serious forms of theft, such as burglary and similar crimes, we shall discover that they are committed almost exclusively by individuals whose principal or subsidiary occupation is theft, and who, in general, do not consider it shameful, and do not feel the slightest repentance.

The question arises, how it is possible for anyone to embrace so abject a profession, and thus become so harmful a parasite.[2] There are authors who would have us believe that there are persons who have chosen crime from pleasure in it. As Leuss observes in his work, "Aus dem Zuchthause", this opinion is so absurd that it would be a waste of time to consider it. No one of sound mind could possibly prefer so abominable a profession, and one so full of risks from the point of view of simple calculation. There must be other reasons for the existence of such persons.[3] If we wish to examine these causes we must divide professional criminals into separate groups.

[1] "Betrachtungen über ein Sammeln der verbrecherischen Motiven", p. 278 ("Zeitschr. f. d. ges. Strafw.", XVII). See also *Földes, op. cit.*, pp. 516–519.

[2] In a work upon the etiology of crime it is unnecessary to set forth in detail the numerous ruses that professional criminals make use of to dupe the public and the police. We merely note here a few important works dealing with this subject: *Frégier*, "Les classes dangereuses de la population dans les grandes villes", I, Part II, Chap. VII; *Avé-Lallemant*, "Das deutsche Gaunerthum", III, pp. 118–340; *O. S.*, "Die Verbrecherwelt von Berlin", III ("Zeitschr. f. d. ges. Strafw.", V); *Puibaraud*, "Les malfaiteurs de profession."

[NOTE TO THE AMERICAN EDITION: *Cf. Herz, op. cit.*, Ch. IV[a], and *E. Wulffen*, "Gauner, und Verbrecher typen."]

[3] *Cf.* the following passage from "Tramping with Tramps", by *Josiah Flynt*: "One more regret which nearly all criminals of the class I am considering have experienced at one time or another in their lives, is that circumstances have led them into a criminal career. Their remorse may be only for a moment, and an exaggerated indifference often follows it; but while it lasts it is genuine and sincere. I have never known a criminal well who has not confessed to me something of this sort; and he has often capped

The first category is composed of children. Sad as this is it is none the less true. It is plain that not a single child follows the profession of thief from pleasure, for a child prefers not to work at all. These children, then, are taught to steal by their parents. If they are not very numerous, in the great cities there are always some cases of this kind. Dr. Puibaraud, former police official in Paris, describes one of these as follows. "We recall that one day, on visiting the Petite-Roquette, we found in a cell a child scarcely eight years old, with a wide-awake face, a quick eye, but whose physiognomy was already very peculiar. It was a young pickpocket who had been found drunk upon the street, and who, being arrested by an agent and taken to the station, had confessed that the gold he had in his possession was the proceeds of a theft committed by him without the knowledge of his 'papa.' This capture ended by the whole family's being arested at their lodgings, near the Place Maubert.

"This gamin was very intelligent and gave the following account of himself, which was corroborated by what was brought out in the examination. 'My father showed me how to pick pockets, but so far I have only "done" ladies because that is easier. With gentlemen you may touch their leg when you stick your hand in their pocket and they turn round, and that's no joke! With ladies you do not get so close and they do not feel your hand. It isn't hard at all. Papa taught me well. We went every day together to the Palais Royal and Place de la Bastille omnibus stations. The Palais Royal is no good. The best is the Madeleine, but Mother G. works that and she quarrels with papa. We don't go there any more. Last week papa told me to wait for him at the Palais Royal omnibus stand. He didn't come, and, "ma foi!" I went to work by myself. I got a purse from an old lady. There were sixty francs in it. I drank a bit and then I was arrested.'" [1]

As we see this child found theft the most natural thing in the world (and any other child in the same environment would think the same); he "worked" with his father. If exceptionally favorable circumstances do not happen to present themselves to such children they will belong to the army of professional criminals all their lives.

Now, as for the others, those who have not been brought up for a life of crime, yet practice it as their profession — how can we explain

it with a further confidence — his sorrow that it was now too late to try anything else" (pp. 25–26).

[1] *Op. cit.*, pp. 131, 132. As regards the education of children in thieving, see also: *Faucher*, "Études sur l'Angleterre", I, pp. 89 *ff.*; *Tomel* and *Rollet*, "Les enfants en prison", pp. 195–197.

their manner of life? The answer to this question can be found only in the works of those who have familiarized themselves with the life of criminals, and who have lived in their midst in order to know them (like Flynt, for example), or who are in a position, because of their profession, to study them in detail, and become their confidants (like the well-known almoners of the Grande-Roquette: Crozes, Moreau, and Faure).[1]

Except for a few subsidiary circumstances the life of the professional criminal may be summed up as follows. With very rare exceptions he springs from a corrupt environment, perhaps having lost his parents while still very young, or having even been abandoned by them. Being misled by bad company, he commits an "occasional" theft while still a child, for which he must pay the penalty of an imprisonment; he may, at times owe his entrance into prison to a non-economic misdeed. This, however, is a very rare exception.[2] As we have remarked above, prison never improves him, and generally makes him worse. If he is in contact with the other prisoners, among whom there are naturally a number of out and out criminals, he hears the recital of their adventurous life, learns their tricks and all that he still needs to know to be thoroughly informed as to "the profession." Nor will the separate cell be any more profitable to him, brutalized as he already is by his earlier environment. Then after a certain time he is set at liberty and returned to society. The partisans of free will say that he has expiated his fault and can now commence a new life.

That is easy to say, and certainly justice will not concern itself with him any further until he commits a new offense. But this is not the same as saying that society pardons him and aids him, in order that he may remain in the right path. On the contrary, forgetting that we must forgive those who have trespassed against us, society makes life hard for him. It is almost impossible for him to find work; the fact that he has been in prison is enough to insure his being refused everywhere. Why should anyone hire an old prisoner when there are so many others who have never got into the courts? And then

---

[1] Although there are some works upon this subject, criminal sociology would derive great profit from the publication of a great number of biographies of criminals, and especially of great criminals.
[NOTE TO THE AMERICAN EDITION: Dr. N. Muller in his work already referred to, "Biografisch-aetiologisch onderzoek etc.", has made a noteworthy beginning in this field, by giving biographies of 24 great criminals. The "Verbrechertypen", edited by *Gruhle* and *Wetzel*, promises much.]
[2] See, among others, *G. Moreau*, "Souvenirs de la petite et de la grande Roquette", I. p. 27, and "Le monde des prisons", pp. 11, 16; *L. Gordon Rylands*, "Crime, its Causes and Remedy", pp. 18 *ff*.

most prisoners have never learned a trade, and this is one reason more why they cannot easily find employment. The liberated convict becomes a nomad, begins by losing all contact with the normal world (supposing he ever had any) and feels himself a social pariah. On the other hand he has relations more and more frequent with the "under world", with those who recognize no duty toward a society which is not interested in their fate. His moral sense comes to be more and more blunted until he becomes a criminal by profession, having a feeling neither of shame nor of repentance.

The ignorant public, who know nothing about the professional criminal except when he appears before the tribunal, is astonished to find that there are persons so abject. This astonishment is like that of some one who has never seen a house built, and cannot imagine how such a colossus can be put up. But he who has seen how the house has been erected by adding one small brick to another no longer feels any astonishment. It is the same with the professional criminal; he who has followed the story of the criminal's life recognizes with Dr. Havelock Ellis, that his crime is but the last link of a solidly forged chain.

Generally the professional criminal does not give the least sign of repentance. He does as much injury to society as he can, without having any shame about it. Yet he is not entirely deprived of moral sense, only it extends merely to those who are really his fellows. All the tales of the world of professional criminals which depict them as void of all sense of duty toward their fellows, proceed rather from the imagination of the authors than from facts really observed. The only competent authors are those who have been able to study the criminal *in his own environment*, and not in prison, where his true character makes itself known as little as that of an animal in a cage. Hear the opinion of Flynt, for example. "It is often said that his (the professional criminal's) lack of remorse for his crimes proves him to be morally incompetent; but this opinion is formed on insufficient knowledge of his life. He has two systems of morality : one for his business and the other for the hang-out." [1] There follows the description of the relations existing between him and society of which we have already spoken, after which the author continues as follows.

"In the bosom of his hang-out, however — and this is where we ought to study his ethics, — he is a very different man. His code of morals there will compare favorably with that of any class of society ; and there is no class in which fair dealing is more seriously preached,

[1] *Op. cit.*, pp. 21, 22.

and unfair dealing more severely condemned. The average criminal will stand by a fellow-craftsman through thick and thin; and the only human being he will not tolerate is the one who turns traitor. The remorse of this traitor when brought to bay by his former brethren I have never seen exceeded anywhere." [1]

After expatiating upon this subject, Flynt continues: "It is thought by criminologists that the good fellowship of the criminal is due to self-preservation and the fear that each man will hang separately if all do not hang together. They maintain that his good feeling is not genuine and spontaneous emotion, and that it is immaterial what happens to a 'pal' so long as he himself succeeds. This is not my experience in his company. He has never had the slightest intimation that I would return favors that he did me; and in the majority of instances he has had every reason to know that it was not in my power to show him the friendliness he wanted. Yet he has treated me with an altruism that even a Tolstoi might admire. At the hang-out I have been hospitably entertained on all occasions; and I have never met a criminal there who would not have given me money or seen me through a squabble, had I needed his assistance and he was able to give it. This same comradeship is noticeable in all his relations with men who are in the least connected with his life and business; and it is notorious fact that he will 'divvy' his last meal with a pal. To have to refuse the request of one of his fellows, or to do him an unkindness, is as much regretted by the criminal as by anyone else; and I have never known him to tell me a lie or to cheat me or to make fun of me behind my back." [2]

This is altogether different from what is generally said and written by those who allow themselves to be led away by their imagination. It is plain that the manner in which criminals act toward a society that is hostile to them will not fail to influence the relations they have with their fellows, just as war for those who take part in it cannot leave their moral sense as regards their compatriots unharmed. However, nothing permits us to put the actions of these persons among themselves in the same rank as those towards society. In my opinion this fact has great significance for the moralist and the criminologist; it is one of the forms of the dualism of ethics. It is of very high importance for the criminologist, for its shows that we are upon the wrong track, since it is precisely the more serious forms of crime that the present methods of repression favor.

[1] *Op. cit.*, p. 22.
[2] *Op. cit.*, pp. 23, 24. To the same effect see *O. S.*, *op. cit.*, pp. 136, 137.

In imprisoning young people who have committed merely misdemeanors of minor importance, and who have not yet lost all touch with normal society, and putting them in contact with inveterate criminals, or perhaps putting them into a cage like beasts, without striving to enlighten their darkened minds or teach them morality, and without making them capable of sustaining the struggle for existence by teaching them a trade, we are bringing up professional criminals. Punishment, as a means of intimidation, misses its aim in great part, for the professional criminals are recruited among individuals who are not easily intimidated.

We have now come to the question why a certain number only of those whose childhood has been neglected and who have committed a light offense, become professional criminals. In the first place there are those whom chance favors, since they are assisted, it may be by their families, it may be by some philanthropist, and so return to the right path. There are those also who have the advantage of being able to find work, since no one knows that they have been in prison.

Others have less chance; no one aids them, there is no work for them; all, however, do not become professional thieves. Those who become such are the more intelligent, energetic, ambitious, and courageous of these outcasts; the others become vagrants and mendicants. Here is the opinion of Flynt upon the criminal by profession, an opinion which agrees with that of other competent authors. "I must say . . . that those criminals who are known to me are not, as is also popularly supposed, the scum of their environment. On the contrary, they are above their environment, and are often gifted with talents which would enable them to do well in any class, could they only be brought to realize its responsibilities and to take advantage of its opportunities. The notion that the criminal is the lowest type of his class arises from a false conception of that class and of the people who compose it. . . .

"In this same class, however, there are some who are born with ambitions, and who have energy enough to try to fulfil them. These break away from class conditions; but unfortunately, the ladder of respectable business has no foothold in their environment. . . .

"Not all of these ambitious ones are endowed with an equal amount of energy. Some are capable only of tramp life, which, despite its many trials and vicissitudes, is more attractive than the life they seek to escape. Those with greater energy go into crime proper; and they may be called, mentally as well as physically, the aristocracy of their class. This is my analysis of the majority of the criminal men and women I have encountered in the open, and I believe it will hold good throughout their entire class." [1]

There are readers, perhaps, who will find that these qualities of the professional criminal give the lie to the environment hypothesis, since individual factors are recognized in a certain way. For myself I do not find it so. The qualities mentioned have nothing to do with crime as such; they can be utilized to the profit as well as to the detriment of society; it will depend upon the environment in which the individual endowed with them has been raised what direction he will take. It would not be difficult to name a number of historic celebrities (Napoleon, for example) who, if they had been born in the lower stratum of a great city, in place of in a favorable environment, would have had only the sad celebrity of criminals exceptionally endowed.

The psychology of this kind of criminals is not yet complete however. Besides intelligence, energy, and courage we find cupidity as their great characteristic. [2] They see others who can enjoy themselves without working hard, and it is their ambition to do the same, cost what it may. Since fate has made it impossible for them to attain it honestly they risk another method. This type of criminal is well delineated in the remark made by the notorious Lemaire, when he said to the president of the court: "If I were a property owner, I should not be here." [3]

To have invested funds, to spend plenty of money, not to have to work much, this is their ideal; to share the lot of the working-man, who, notwithstanding his long and hard labor, never succeeds in procuring for himself the pleasures of the rich, makes life insipid in their eyes. M. Gisquet, former prefect of police, gives in his memoirs the following declaration made by Leblanc, the notorious professional criminal. "If I were not a thief by vocation I should become one by calculation; it is the best profession. I have computed the good and bad chances of all the others, and I am convinced by the comparisons that there is none more favorable or more independent than that of thief, nor one that does not offer at least an equal amount of danger.

"What should I have become in the society of honest men?

---

[1] *Op. cit.*, pp. 5, 6; see also pp. 11–12. To the same effect: *Starke*, "Verbrechen und Verbrecher in Preussen", p. 221; *Havelock Ellis*, "Verbrecher und Verbrechen", pp. 24, 25; and *Leuss*, "Aus dem Zuchthause", p. 125.
[2] [NOTE TO THE AMERICAN EDITION: Muller mentions further as a result of his researches that criminals by profession show in general an adventurous and unstable character. *Cf. Kauffmann, op. cit.*, pp. 160 *ff.*]
[3] "Actes du II Congres d'Anthr. Crim.", p. 163.

A natural child, with no one to protect me or to recommend me, I could only choose a disagreeable trade, become a delivery-boy in a store, or at most reach the miserable place of shipping clerk in a warehouse; and there, a supernumerary for many years, I should have died of hunger before I reached a salary of six hundred francs. As a workman in any class whatever you exhaust yourself quickly through the fatigues of your labor, to earn a miserable wage, and to live from day to day; then when accident, sickness, or old age come you must go beg or die in the poorhouse. . . .

"In our condition we depend only on ourselves; and if we acquire skill and experience at least they profit ourselves alone. I know very well that we have risks to run, that the police and the courts are at hand, that the prison is not very far distant; but out of eight thousand thieves in Paris, you never have more than seven or eight hundred in jail; that is not a tenth of the whole. We enjoy, then, on the average, nine years of liberty to one in prison. Well, where is the worker who has not a dead season? Besides, what does he do when he is without work? He carries his possessions to the Mont-de-Piété; while we others, if we are free, lack for nothing; our existence is a continual round of feasting and pleasure." [1]

This is the type of the perfect egoist. In ranking men according to their social sentiments, such an individual would be put at the very lowest point in the scale. And then he has grown up under unfavorable circumstances (illegitimate birth, etc.). The innate egoism of this individual may perhaps be modified by the individual factor. But this in no way diminishes the truth of the environment hypothesis, for we are treating for the moment the question why this *particular individual* has become a criminal, and not that of the cause of the existence of professional criminals. And these two questions are far from being identical. The existence of individual differences is the reason why one *runs more danger* of becoming a professional criminal than another; but it is the environment which brings it about that the predisposed individual *actually* becomes such. The falsity of the environment hypothesis would be demonstrated if such individuals could be proved to become criminals *under all circumstances*. This is of course not the case. When individuals like these are not brought up in an atmosphere of poverty, they no longer see on the one side persons who enjoy everything while doing nothing, and on the other side those who, while toiling hard, live in poverty, — they will not

[1] IV., pp. 386–388. See also *Zerboglio*, "Les inconvénients de l'honnêteté", pp. 385 *ff.*

become examples of altruism indeed, but they will not become guilty of crime. They may even become very useful members of society, since they are generally more largely endowed with intelligence, energy, and courage than the average man. Rightly exercised, these qualities are very useful; but badly directed they are very harmful to society.[1]

So far we have been treating of the etiology of theft and analogous crimes; we shall conclude this section with some observations upon the causes that have led to the designating of these acts as crime.

Theft is a crime only because it is very harmful to society.[2] If in the majority of cases the individual does not take account of this, the assertion is nevertheless true. Everything that is harmful to society the individual considers as immoral. (*Why* this is so is a psychological question, with which we are not concerned here.) If we picture to ourselves present-day society, based as it is upon exchange, without the strict prohibition of theft, we shall see that it could not possibly exist. Life would be especially impossible in a society where the division of labor has attained a high degree of development, if it were permissible to take anything without giving an equivalent.

Since the human race has existed there has been private property, however trifling and unimportant it may have been. It is therefore very unlikely that theft has ever been permitted [3] (it is impossible to produce proofs in support of this), since it is difficult to imagine that anyone would consent to see himself stripped of things destined for his own use, to which, further he was more or less attached.[4] But there is a great difference between a prohibited act and a crime. It is proved that among primitive peoples theft is not reckoned among the crimes. Hear the opinion of one of the greatest specialists in this field, Dr. Post. "We find here and there a phenomenon very surprising from our modern point of view, namely that theft is not universally regarded as a misdemeanor, but the thief rather respected

---

[1] [NOTE TO THE AMERICAN EDITION: *Cf.* further (besides the works of *Muller* and *Kauffmann*): *Wulffen*, II, pp. 284 *ff.*; *Pollitz, op. cit.*, pp. 124 *ff.*; also *Brusse's* brochure, already cited, "Het rosse", etc.]

[2] *Cf. A. H. Post*, "Bausteine für eine allgemeine Rechtswissenschaft", I, p. 293, and "Grundriss der ethnologischen Jurisprudenz", II, pp. 421 *ff.*

[3] In his "Grundriss, etc.", II, p. 213, *Dr. Post* names different peoples who do not consider theft as blamable but as praiseworthy. It is very probable that this relates to theft committed to the detriment of another group, and not to the prejudice of the members of the thief's own group. It is plain that it is only the latter kind of theft that we treat of in a work upon crime. *Cf. Kovalewsky*, "Les origines du devoir", pp. 88, 89 ("Revue internationale de sociologie", II).

[4] To the same effect see *Kovalewsky, op. cit.*, pp. 88, 89, *note*.

for his cleverness. The maximum obligation that a theft lays upon the thief is simple restitution of the stolen property. The consequence of theft is thus simply the duty of restitution under the civil law. . . . Theft lies entirely outside of the province of criminal law." [1]

It is not difficult to explain the cause of this. Let the reader picture to himself the primitive forms of society, so different from those we have at present; contrasts of possessions were unknown, and the needs of men consequently less numerous; men produced only for their own consumption and not for exchange. If by chance more was produced than was needed, the surplus was given to others, for it was impossible to exchange it, or to preserve it for any great length of time, the necessary technique for this not having yet been acquired. "The law of hospitality" was universal and enjoined men to provide those in need with whatever they lacked.[2] It is quite comprehensible that at such a stage of development theft should not be in evidence, for the motives which drive men to it would be lacking. On the one hand cupidity was not awakened, and theft did not result from absolute poverty, since if there was poverty the whole group suffered together.[3] On the other hand the social instincts, being highly developed by the environment, constituted a restraint that would prevent the execution of a theft if the thought of it should occur. But even supposing that in such a society a theft, for no matter what cause, should nevertheless be committed, it would be little thought of, and certainly the thief would not be severely punished, for his act would not be very harmful to society.

As the social structure changed the ideas about theft changed equally; with the origin of the system of exchange and of the contrasts of property, came powerful motives for theft, and at the same time the social instincts grew weaker. Thus theft came to be considered a more serious matter than before, and the graded system of punishments for it, beginning with a fine, ended in capital punishment.[4] It is not our task to investigate the reason why the punishment for theft has not always been the same during the whole civilized period;

[1] "Bausteine etc.", I, pp. 286, 287. See by the same author, "Grundriss etc.", II, p. 429, and "Der Ursprung des Rechts", pp. 114, 115. *Cf.* *Steinmetz*, "Ethnologischen Studien zur ersten Entwicklung der Strafe", II, p. 252.
[2] *Cf.* the quotation from Morgan on p. 386 of this work.
[3] See *Dargun*, "Ursprung un Entwicklungsgeschichte des Eigenthums", pp. 81–83.
[4] *Cf. Post*, "Bausteine etc.", I, p. 288 *ff.*
[NOTE TO THE AMERICAN EDITION: *Cf.* further: *Westermarck*, "Ursprung und Entwicklung der Moralbegriffe", II ch. 24.]

it is enough for us to establish the fact that the act has always been considered as a grave offense, the perpetrator of which incurred severe penalties.

C. ROBBERY AND ANALOGOUS CRIMES.

As the figures reproduced above (pp. 535–542) have shown, the crimes with which we have now to concern ourselves are relatively rare. It is unnecessary to say that this has not always been so, but that there have been great changes in this regard. At one time robbery and similar acts of violence were the ordinary forms of professional crime. Happily for peaceable folk this is no longer the case; these crimes have been in large measure replaced by others less serious, like theft and fraud.[1] All modern states have not reached the same stage of development, nor all parts of the same state. There are those of them that, more than others, recall the past to us. So is it in regard to their criminality. While robbery may be said to have disappeared from the states of northern Europe, it is still very common in a country like Italy, and is met much less frequently in the modernized provinces of northern Italy than in the backward southern provinces, as the following figures show.[2]

Italy, 1887–1889.

PROVINCES.	AVERAGE TO 100,000 INHABITANTS.	
	Robbery, etc., with Homicide.	Robbery, etc., without Homicide.
Apulia	5.01	0.27
Basilicata	2.42	4.18
Sardinia	2.06	12.11
Sicily	1.22	14.56
Liguria	1.07	8.65
Calabria	0.97	6.36
Latium	0.89	17.15
Campania and Molise	0.71	8.08
Piedmont	0.63	4.67
Romagna	0.63	6.47
Abruzzo	0.58	2.07
Marches and Ombria	0.55	2.46
Venetia	0.33	2.58
Emilia	0.28	5.80
Lombardy	0.21	3.14
Tuscany	—	5.68

[1] *Cf. v. Liszt*, "Das gewerbmässige Verbrechen", pp. 126, 127 ("Zeitschr. f. d. ges. Strw." XXI).

[2] "Statistica giudiziaria penale per l'anno 1889", pp. cliv–clv.

[NOTE TO THE AMERICAN EDITION: *Cf.* further upon Austria: *Herz, op. cit.*, pp. 39 *ff.*; upon the Balkan states: *Wadler, op. cit.*, pp. 46 and 54.]

According to the figures given by Dr. Bosco, in the United States, also, the most backward states give the highest figures for homicide.[1]

The poorer classes have more resemblance to the people of a bygone day than have the well-to-do; it appears from the statistics (see pp. 438 *ff*.) that economic criminality takes a more violent form among the former than among the latter.[2]

An investigation into the causes of this change in the form of economic criminality will indicate also the principal causes of the persistent existence of this kind of crime, however it may have decreased in modern times. In my opinion these causes are as follows:

First. The opportunity for committing them presented itself more often formerly, since the means of communication were very primitive, travelers had to traverse uninhabited countries, etc., and in addition the states were not so well organized as at present, and had not the means of suppressing bands of brigands vigorously.

Second. While the opportunity to commit violent economic crimes successfully was diminishing, there was a constantly increasing opportunity to commit other economic crimes, such as theft, embezzlement, and fraud. The accumulation of great wealth in the cities, the development of credit, in short, the enormous extension of capitalism, has multiplied the opportunity for economic crimes without violence.

Third. One of the consequences of the development of society has been the gradual diminution of the importance of the rôle played by violence, and, since criminality presents itself always and everywhere under the same forms as the normal life, violent economic criminality has also commenced to form a smaller and smaller part in the totality of economic crimes. The assertion that violence has lost the importance of its rôle upon the human stage might surprise one, and appear ironical in times like ours when war is the chronic condition, when the military preparations of all the states have reached a degree hitherto unknown. Violence, however, has decreased in so far as it is exercised by the individual as such. The greater becomes the centralization of the state, the more it claims for itself the exclusive right to use violence in the cases where it judges it necessary, and the more it prohibits individual acts of violence.

It is not the development of the state that is alone to be considered in this regard; the economic system enters in also. Under capitalism

---

[1] "Della statistica dell'omicidio negli stati Uniti d'America" ("Bulletin de l'Institut intern. de statistique", X), pp. 40 *ff*.

[2] *Cf. Niceforo*, "Les transformations du crime et la civilisation moderne", pp. 642 *ff*. ("Scuola Positiva", XI).

violence is of no use; he who is master of the means of production attains his end, *i.e.* makes a profit, without the use of violence. Where it is necessary, however, modern man does not recoil from it, as the wars of expansion prove.

Fourth. Civilization (in the proper sense of the word) has become more general. Formerly the privilege of a few only, it now extends to a greater number. The great mass are still deprived of it, but primary instruction contributes to its development.

When we consider the gradual diminution in the number of economic crimes committed with violence, it clearly appears how false is the notion that anyone committing such a crime is for that reason a *biologically* abnormal being. Will anyone claim that the number of biologically abnormal persons has constantly diminished? The contrary is much more likely.

We need not concern ourselves with the details of this question, since it has already been thoroughly treated by Professor Manouvrier (see Pt. I of this work, pp. 168–171). He who uses violence to attain an economic end may perhaps, physiologically considered, be a perfectly normal man. How many children are there who do not use force to take a toy from a weaker child? Must we class them as abnormal on that account? And are those who voluntarily take part in a war abnormal? Certainly there is a great difference between those who take part in a war, and those who, for economic reasons, commit a crime, but this difference is of a *social* nature. Our ideas of war and homicide are not the same, but the act of killing one's neighbor remains identical. If homicide were the evident proof of biological abnormality the soldier also would be abnormal.

Scientific questions can be solved by reason alone, and not by sentiment. We who experience a profound repulsion at the thought of a murderer, hold him for a being apart, since we feel ourselves so remote from him. Scientific research tells us that this feeling is not innate but acquired, for we detest such acts because the environment in which we live has accustomed us to hate them. If our environment were different, our feelings would likewise be different. Besides, war proves that these feelings are not innate, by hardening the mildest persons in a very brief time.

With time the number of persons who have a horror of violence has increased. Does this prove that men have become better, or simply that they feel a repugnance to the act only and not to its effect? J. J. Rousseau once said: "If, in order to fall heir to the property of a rich mandarin living at the farthest confines of China, whom one had never seen or heard spoken of, it were enough to push a button to make him die, which of us would not push that button?"

It is certain that beside a great number of persons who would not wish to charge their consciences with such a crime, there would also be plenty who would commit it, and their number would be great enough to make the order of mandarins pass into legendary history. There is no reason to suppose that there are fewer persons in our day who would commit such acts, than formerly; if men are no longer as violent as they once were, they do not recoil any more than formerly when it is a question of suppressing, through the agency of a third party, those who oppose them; as witness the wars of expansion.

As the motives of these crimes are the same as those of economic crimes without violence, we shall treat first those that are caused by poverty; secondly, those that are committed from cupidity; and thirdly, those that are the work of professional criminals.

Statistics show that a part of the economic crimes of violence are committed from poverty, for their movement is influenced by the fluctuations of economic conditions. We take from the German criminal statistics the following table of the course of these crimes in the different months of the year.

Germany, 1888–1892.[1]

Number of Crimes a Day in the Different Months, on the Basis of an Average of 100 Crimes a Day throughout the Year.

CRIMES.	JANUARY.	FEBRUARY.	MARCH.	APRIL.	MAY.	JUNE.	JULY.	AUGUST.	SEPTEMBER.	OCTOBER.	NOVEMBER.	DECEMBER.
Robbery, etc.	100	87	78	84	94	98	99	106	84	120	132	116

The highest figures are shown in the winter months when poverty is at its height. (The slight increase from April to August, which appears also in the case of a number of other economic crimes, I am unable to explain.)

As we have seen in the statistics in Part One, the economic situation also exercises its influence upon the movement of these crimes during a period of years. We refer to them here while adding some others.

[1] "Kriminalstatistik für das Jahr 1894", II, p. 53.

Germany, 1882–1898.[1]

YEARS.	PRICE OF WHEAT AND RYE PER 100 KILOGR. IN MARKS.	To 100,000 INHABITANTS OVER 12 THERE WERE CONVICTED FOR	
		Robbery.	Extortion.
1882	185.19	1.3	1.7
1883	165.37	1.3	1.5
1884	159.73	1.4	1.5
1885	154.01	1.1	1.4
1886	147.26	1.3	1.3
1887	145.99	1.2	1.4
1888	155.43	1.2	1.3
1889	169.64	1.2	1.4
1890	181.32	1.3	1.4
1891	216.31	1.3	1.4
1892	184.00	1.4	1.8
1893	146.94	1.1	1.6
1894	127.10	1.3	1.7
1895	132.17	1.1	1.9
1896	139.29	1.2	1.7
1897	152.08	1.0	1.7
1898	170.55	1.3	1.6

Although there are exceptions, the influence of the price of grain makes itself felt. It should be remarked that the years 1889–1892 were years of crisis.

France, 1825–1882.

In his study "De la criminalité en France et en Italie" Dr. Bournet shows that in the period mentioned the maxima of assassinations coincide with the years of economic crises, namely : 1839, 1840, 1843, 1844, 1847, 1867, 1876, and 1881.[2] It should be remarked that assassinations are committed not simply from economic motives, but for other reasons, whence it follows that the parallelism cannot be as great as in the case of economic crimes that are not committed from other motives.

Italy, 1873–1890.

Dr. Fornasari proves that economic events have a great influence upon these crimes (see Part One, p. 143).

[1] *H. Berg*, "Getreide preise und Kriminalität in Deutschland seit 1882", pp. 10, 18.

[NOTE TO THE AMERICAN EDITION: After 1898, also, the influence of the economic situation made itself felt in these crimes.]

[2] P. 47. See plate, pp. 40, 41.

Prussia, 1854–1896.

Dr. Starke (see Part One, p. 64) and Dr Müller (see pp. 76–78) have proved that the changes of economic conditions are here also cause of an increase or diminution of these crimes.

Although these data are less numerous than we might desire, they show sufficiently that, in part, violent economic crimes are committed because of poverty.[1]

Above I have shown how it happens that only some of those who live in absolute poverty commit crime. We have only, then, to ask ourselves why one commits a crime with violence and the other without violence. The causes are of different kinds. Oftenest it is chance, *i.e.* opportunity, that is the cause. No one uses violence if it is not necessary, and since the opportunity of committing a successful theft is much greater than that of committing an economic crime with violence, it is the first that is most often practiced. Those who, when driven by abject poverty, commit an economic crime with violence, when the opportunity presents itself, are persons who lack neither the force nor the courage necessary, and in whom the environment in which they live has not inspired a great aversion to violence. Further, absolute poverty is so powerful a factor that it often neutralizes the important influences of education and environment.

From cupidity. The class of criminals who use violence or commit a homicide from cupidity is very small. They furnish only a minor part of violent economic crimes, the total number of which is not itself very great. To show how far the influence of economic environment goes I will cite some striking cases taken at random.

First. In 1892 a certain Scheffer was convicted at Linz (Austria) of attempted murder. His crime was the following. He and his wife could earn their living only by working hard. Chance brought a change. One of their relatives, a young girl who had lost her father and mother a short time before, came to live with them. The girl being very rich, the condition of the Scheffers was entirely changed; from then on they could live in abundance. Once habituated to this wealth they were filled with the fear that their relative would marry and the money pass to someone else. Little by little the idea came to them of persuading the girl to make a will in their favor, and then killing her, an idea which they rejected at first, but which nevertheless

---

[1] [NOTE TO THE AMERICAN EDITION: *Wadler* has shown the connection of these two phenomena for Servia (*op. cit.*, p. 83).]

became stronger and stronger. From unforeseen circumstances the crime was never consummated, but stopped in the attempt.[1]

Second. In a little village upon the frontier of Austria and Bavaria there was committed in 1893 a murder under the following circumstances. One evening, while returning by himself along a lonely road, a rich peasant who was in the habit of carrying a considerable sum of money with him, was killed and robbed. It was proved that his servant was the author of the crime. This man was a natural child, very poor, and had had to work very hard all his life. Seeing his strength going he was in great fear of being no longer able to earn a living. His sole enjoyment in his monotonous and toilsome life was getting drunk on Sundays. Like most of the inhabitants of his commune he was an ardent poacher.[2]

Third. In 1892 the wife of an employe of the post office was assassinated in her dwelling in Berlin, and all her money stolen. The criminals were two young workmen of 17 and 18 years of age, one of whom knew by chance that the woman had savings.[3]

These three cases, types of hundreds of others, have in common the opportunity which had excited, in an unusual degree, the cupidity of the criminals, and the fact that these were very poor. Whatever other causes may have entered in, it is certain that without the great difference of fortune between the authors of the crimes and their victims, the crimes would never have been committed.

Finally, we come to the influence of the environment upon the authors of the crimes. As we have seen, the conditions under which criminals are brought up are in general very unfavorable, and this is especially the case with dangerous criminals. Consider, for example, the second case (we know nothing of the environment of the criminals in the first). What a life this murderer had behind him. The influences which give most men their aversion to violence were entirely lacking. On the contrary his environment had brutalized him. A natural child, he had been brought up in very poor circumstances, and was stupefied by long and toilsome work, with a weekly intoxication as his sole relaxation. No one would assert that this same individual would have become an assassin if he had lived under totally different conditions.

Or look at the third case. One of the guilty parties had been

---

[1] Taken from *Sighele*, " Le crime à deux ", pp. 122–125.
[2] Taken from " Archiv für Kriminal-Anthropologie und Kriminalstatistik ", XI, pp. 307 *ff.*
[3] *Baer*, "Ueber jugendliche Mörder und Todtschläger" ("Archiv f. Krim.-Anthr. und Krim.", XI).

brought up under unfavorable conditions (of the education of the other we know nothing), both were forced, quite young, to earn their living and had been thrown with bad companions, and one of them had already been sentenced to imprisonment.

It is a mistake to believe that such a case is the exception instead of being the general rule. He who takes the trouble to read the biographies of these criminals knows that they have always been brought up in an unfavorable environment, that they have suffered imprisonment at an early age, and have fallen lower and lower. As far as I know there are no statistics upon this subject except those of Dr. Baer in his study already referred to. Out of 22 young assassins examined by him 9 (40%) had had a bad education, 11 (50%) a defective education, and only 2 (10%) a better education; 8 (36%) were orphans; 11 (50%) had been brought up in very poor circumstances and were obliged while quite young to contribute to the support of the family; 10 (45%) had grown up in the streets of a great city and had thus been exposed to demoralizing influences; and 13 (60%) had received an insufficient primary education.[1]

The researches of Dr. Baer have to do with Germany, but they hold good for other countries also. Take, for example, the opinion of Tomel and Rollet, who are authors of great experience. In speaking of the "criminal type" they say : "Well, no, this type does not exist, since we always find the same conditions in the genesis of the criminal temperament, and if these educational and environmental conditions had been absent, the destiny of the little assassin might have been quite different." [2]

We have still to fix our attention upon one side of the environment in which the authors of the crimes with which we are concerned at the moment, have lived. They come generally from an environment where,

First, education often consists simply in the administration of a sound beating to the child, a fact which habituates him to the idea that violence is an ordinary act, especially as he sees the members of the family often strike one another;

Second, the men ordinarily carry a knife, and do not hesitate to threaten with it, or even to use it in case of a dispute. It is evident that the influence of this upon character is great at the impressionable age of childhood. The tendency toward violence, combated among children of the well-to-do classes, is, on the contrary, often strengthened among the children of the poor. If later chance places

---

[1] *Op. cit.*, pp. 166, 167. [2] "Les enfants en prison ", p. 215.

in their way an opportunity to profit by violence they recoil from it less than others.[1]

The authors of violent economic crimes spring nearly always from the lower classes of the population; the exceptions are few in number. We will take up one of these exceptions which has attained considerable notoriety, an evident proof of the rarity of these cases.

In 1878 an old woman was murdered in Paris and all her papers of value were stolen. It was proved that Barré, a business agent, and Lebiez, a medical student, both of whom had passed their youth in a favorable environment, were the guilty persons. This is one of those very rare cases where objection can be made to the environment hypothesis with a semblance of truth, but a closer examination shows that environment nevertheless played its part in this frightful tragedy. The two criminals, sprung from fairly well-to-do provincial families, having gone to Paris, had been living in straitened circumstances. At the time of their deciding to commit the crime their pecuniary condition was very bad. In the second place, both had constant recourse to prostitutes; and in the third place both were ardent speculators. Because of his business Barré was in contact with those who gambled at the bourse, and seeing men enrich themselves without work he entered feverishly into speculation. He lost, drew his father into a new deal, and was still unfortunate. In order to go on and retrieve his losses he used money entrusted to him (his first crime), but still lost. Going from one malversation to another he finally, in order to extricate himself, had recourse to the crime narrated above. His accomplice was found in nearly the same situation.[2]

The effect of environment is to be discerned, then, as easily in this case as in those that have been referred to before. Limiting ourselves to the principal influence alone, we see that if these individuals had not been in contact with the world of speculation, their cupidity would not have been excited to such a point that they were induced to commit crime. Here the rôle played by chance in such cases clearly appears; if they had been fortunate in their speculations they would never have become criminals.

As with all crimes, the question presents itself as to how far individual factors were active, in other words, do the individuals who are guilty of such crimes differ from other men? Certainly, and that to a considerable extent. But in granting this we do not, however, recog-

[1] Cf. Ferriani, "Minderjährige Verbrecher", pp. 279 ff.
[2] Taken from Moreau, "Souvenirs de la petite et de la grande Roquette", II. ch. VIII. See also Joly, "Le crime", pp. 97 ff.

nize a *qualitative* difference between them and other men such as would make them *biologically abnormal*. The motives which have induced these persons to commit crime, are present, though only in small measure, in everyone. Those who commit these crimes have by nature very intense material needs; in the curve A D (see p. 534) they occupy the places near D. As regards their social sentiments they are ranged near the other end of the curve, and their repugnance to violence is very small. Further, they have the necessary courage and strength.[1] If we consider how little chance there is of finding all this united in one individual, it will become clear that few individuals are predisposed to these crimes, and when they are committed the criminal is found in a special environment. In my opinion there can be no question of individual factors, then; it is the environment that decides here. There will be persons always and everywhere who run more danger than others of committing such a crime; but it is the environment which will decide whether they will commit it or not.

Professional criminals. The great majority of violent economic crimes are committed by professional criminals. When an individual has fallen, from whatever reason, into the world of professional crime, sooner or later comes the time when he must use violence if he wishes to attain his end. Joly has very well said in his social study, "Le crime": "The man who has formed the habit of breaking into houses and bursting open safes, is forcibly drawn sooner or later to rid himself of witnesses who surprise him at this work, or of a victim who might perhaps recognize him." [2] It cannot be asserted of these individuals any more than of others, that they are born with a special tendency toward assassination, a tendency to be explained by atavism, or something approaching it. They have been living in an environment in which such acts are considered as a necessary evil inherent in their trade. Driven by the tendency to imitate, they do as others do. Certainly there are those of them who do not commit these crimes, but that proves nothing, for it may be that chance has favored them and they have never been under the necessity of using violence, or they have less courage and force than the average man, or, it may be, have an exceptional innate aversion to violence.

As Professor Manouvrier remarks, the case would be entirely different if such criminals killed without plausible motives, if they committed murder without anything but the act in view. The facts

---

[1] *Cf. Manouvrier*, "Les crânes des suppliciés" ("Arch. d'anthr. crim.", I), where he shows that the conformation of the skulls of assassins is simply of a coarser type than others.　　　　　　　　　　　　　[2] Pp. 47–48.

show that this is not so. Note the opinion of Flynt. "The taking of life is . . . [a] deed that he [the professional criminal] regrets more than he has been given credit for. One thinks of the criminal as the man who has no respect for life, as one who takes it without any twitchings of conscience; but this is not the general rule. The business criminal never takes a life, if he can help it." [1]

We need not treat here of the causes which have led to the designating of these acts as crimes; they are the same as those given above in connection with economic crimes without violence. The harm done by these crimes is naturally greater than in the case of crimes without violence, since they put life as well as property in danger. It is interesting to note here, once more, the dualism of ethics; many primitive peoples consider these acts as crimes when they are committed within the same group, but very honorable when once the act passes beyond the limits of the group. [2] Further, with modern peoples this difference still persists; colonial wars often resemble a colossal robbery.

D. Fraudulent Bankruptcy, Adulteration of Food, and Analogous Crimes.

We reach now the last group of economic crimes, those which are committed wholly, or in great part, by the bourgeoisie. The motives of these crimes are not all the same; here too it is necessary to make distinctions. The categories into which we must distribute the motives leading to these crimes are analogous to those which lead to theft etc., poverty and cupidity. And as in the case of theft it is necessary to add a third category, that of the great criminals, who can be compared with criminals by profession.

The first category may be compared with that of theft committed from poverty; those who fall into this class are persons who, for one reason or another, have seen their business decline, and not knowing any other way to escape from their difficulties, hope to retrieve their losses and save themselves by committing a misdeed. I take from Moreau's "Le Monde des Prisons" a typical case. After having described how a certain R. had succeeded in setting himself up in business and had been successful, the author speaks as follows.

[1] "Tramping with Tramps", p. 24. *Cf. Moreau*, "Le monde des prisons", p. 621, and *Kauffmann, op. cit.*, pp. 163, 164 and 203–206.
[2] *Cf. Post*, "Der Ursprung des Rechts", p. 116, "Bausteine etc.", I, pp. 300–302, and "Grundriss der ethnologischen Jurisprudenz", II, p. 444.

"Unhappily the panic caught him among the first. His business became worse and worse. In a few months he lost several thousand francs. Two of his traveling salesmen ran off with their goods. Orders ceased coming in. It was failure, dishonor. He fought, but was wrecked. . . ." [1] Finally, in order to escape ruin he committed a breach of trust; he was discovered and convicted.

We cannot say that it is absolute poverty that drives these persons to commit a crime, for generally they have enough left to keep them from dying of hunger. And if not, they are generally members of families who are in a position to keep them from the worst poverty. Further they can try to provide for their wants by paid labor. Nevertheless these cases are somewhat analogous to those of absolute poverty. Picture to yourself the state of mind of one who has led a more or less comfortable life, who has been independent, and enjoyed the esteem granted to a man who is well-to-do, and who sees that the time is approaching when all this will come to an end, and that there remains nothing for him to do but accept some minor poorly paid employment, and lead henceforth an existence that cannot satisfy him in any way. Imagine also that chance throws in his way an opportunity to commit a crime with good hope of success. It must be granted that we find here very powerful determinants to crime.

This cause of crimes of this class is of an entirely social nature. Under another mode of production, for example, under that of village communities, the idea of committing such crimes could not arise. For this reason we cannot say that social causes have often nothing to do with the matter, but that it is the man's own fault if his business goes to pieces. This is certainly true at times; but it is the present organization of society which makes it possible for a man to be in charge of an enterprise which he is not fitted to conduct, while another who is fitted for it cannot find employment for his talents. It is only in a society where complete anarchy reigns in the economic life, that it is possible for a man to think he is capable of directing a business merely because he happens to have capital.

Let us now examine the other side of the question. What are the forces capable of preventing these projects from being realized? First let us ask, what is the environment in which many of these individuals who are guilty of such crimes are brought up? Certainly they have learned that one must be honest, that it is wrong to pick pockets, etc., and they will not fail in this regard. But they have learned also that the principal end in life is to grow rich, to succeed.

[1] P. 318.

Too often this is contrary to the principle of probity. "Be honest, be honest, if possible, but . . . make money!" This is the principal rule imprinted upon the minds of the children in certain bourgeois environments. It is an honesty of a special kind that is inculcated, not a moral honesty, but an honesty for the sake of one's own interests. "Honesty is the best policy" says the quasi-moral precept. Those whose probity has this for a basis have only a weak check to prevent them from becoming criminal, when the thought of the wrong act arises within them. They remain honest so long as it is to their advantage, but woe to society when this is no longer the case.

But further, the environment in which these persons have lived after their youth has not contributed to reinforce the social sentiments, and consequently those that are working in an anti-criminal direction. "Every man for himself" is the principle of success in such an environment. It is evident that the social sentiments must be strongly opposed in their development if the maxim just given is that which dominates. To act morally implies sacrificing one's own advantage for the sake of the general good. He who is compelled always to have his own interests at heart can give very little thought to the interests of others.

As in the case of all crimes, it is necessary with regard to these also to put the question, are the individuals who are guilty of them, as regards their innate qualities, like those who have lived and still live under the same conditions? And as is the case with all crimes, the answer here must be in the negative. Those who are guilty of these crimes are, in general, those who are below the average in the strength of their moral qualities. They are rather weak than bad; they are conscious of the harm that they do to others and are ashamed of it, but they are too weak to resist the pressure of circumstances. As always it is the environment that is the cause of the crimes' taking place; it is the individual differences which explain in part *who* is the one to commit them. Adapting the well-known sentence of Quetelet we may say, "it is society that prepares the crimes, it is the men of inferior moral caliber who execute them." If the environment were entirely different the men of inferior moral caliber would not be guilty of crime.

It may be observed, perhaps, that if it is true that a special predisposition on the part of the individual is unnecessary for the explanation of these crimes, they ought to be more numerous than they are. This is true enough, but it does not refute the opinion which has been expressed. For, first, as is the case with all the others, these crimes are more numerous than the criminal statistics show; second, there are reasons why some men do not commit crime, although all circumstances lead to it, and their moral condition does not prevent. For example, there are those who, as a consequence of the struggle for existence, have lost all energy and all courage, and give up the fight, even the fight with dishonest weapons; others, prudent by nature, take into consideration the fact that, bad as their situation may be, it would be worse if the crime were discovered, etc.

Statistics prove that it is really the decline of business that is the cause of a great number of bourgeois crimes. In the first part of this work I have given some which show this correlation, namely:

Italy, 1873–1890.

For this country the statistics on this question (see p. 144) have been compiled by Dr. Fornasari di Verce. This author has shown that with the exception of fraudulent bankruptcy (an astonishing and inexplicable fact), commercial crimes are strongly influenced by economic happenings.

Prussia, 1854–1878.

Dr. Starke has proved that the curve of these crimes is parallel with that of economic events, (p. 65).

These statistics, to be sure, are not numerous, since the number of crimes committed by the bourgeoisie is small, and the other economic crimes, like theft, for example, are much more important, and hence draw the attention of statisticians more.[1]

We come now to the second category; bourgeois economic crimes from cupidity (as is always the case, the line of demarcation between this group and the preceding one is not distinctly traced, there being many gradations between the two). They are committed, not, as in the first category, by those whose business is declining, but by those whose affairs are more or less flourishing. The only motive, then, is cupidity; what they get by honest business is not enough for them, they wish to become richer. After what has been already said about cupidity it is unnecessary to go into detail here. It has been shown that it is only under certain special circumstances that this desire for wealth arises, and that it is unknown under others. It will be necessary only to point out the fact that although cupidity is a strong motive with all classes of our present society, it is especially so among the bourgeoisie, as a consequence of their position in the economic

---

[1] For Germany see also H. Berg, "Getreidepreise und Kriminalität in Deutschland seit 1882", p. 18.

life. This, then, is the first and most important cause of these crimes, a cause which is not individual, but entirely of a social nature.

In the second place, the opportunity to commit these offenses undetected is enormous (I refer especially to the adulteration of food). In general the consumer cannot judge whether the merchandise is pure or not, and in most cases there is no inspection by experts, or else it is worthless, since the experts are named by the producers themselves.

In the third place, we have to ask ourselves, in what way does the environment in which these persons live exercise an influence upon their social sentiments? We have already called attention to this point some pages above, and can be brief therefore. This environment tends to weaken the social sentiments which might act as a check upon very egoistic acts.

Considered from the point of view of the consumer the adulteration of food products is a grave crime, for it injures the health and may even endanger the life. But what *moral* impropriety will be seen in it by a producer who derives great profits from the exploitation of children, or who, by a corner in grain, causes a great increase in the price of bread? Is there, sociologically speaking, a difference between these two groups of acts? Certainly not; the one is as harmful as the other, nay, the last two probably more harmful than the first.

This kind of crime must be the despair of those who seek for some biological anomaly of the criminal as the primary cause of crime, for here the anomaly forms almost the rule. Dr. Puibaraud, in his "Malfaiteurs de profession", rightly says: "The adulteration of food is carried on under our eyes, at our very doors, and we are so used to it that we say nothing. They put fuchsine in our wine, margarine in our butter, chicory in our coffee, tallow in our chocolate, and we swallow it all in perfect good humor. What is the use of protesting? So things are, and 'business could not be carried on' if they gave us really pure food. So we swallow it all without gagging or moving a muscle. Provided we are not poisoned — too quickly — we profess ourselves satisfied." [1]

Everyone knows that the adulteration of food is enormous. If anyone has any doubts let him read the reports of the chemists upon a product whose adulteration is easy, milk, for example. His doubts will disappear rapidly; at least half of the milk is adulterated. It is only the adulteration of food products that constitutes a legal offense,

[1] Pp. 375, 376.

but the adulteration of other articles does not differ from this when considered from a sociological point of view, and it is unnecessary to say that there too the adulteration is enormous.

There are, to be sure, manufacturers and merchants who are not guilty of such acts; first, because certain articles cannot be adulterated; second, because in certain branches the oversight in the interests of the consumers is very rigorous; third, because certain producers find it more advantageous to be honest, knowing that thereby they will procure a large body of regular customers. These three reasons have nothing moral in them, though there is a fourth reason which affects certain producers, namely that they have scruples against such practices.[1]

Let us consider once more the curve of the individual differences. Those persons who should be placed between A and B are those who, if the conditions we have named are present, will commit without scruple misdeeds of the kind we are considering. The great average class, between B and C are those who, in general, are not guilty of acts prohibited by law, but who probably do things which in reality do not differ much from these, and, in any case, are not permissible by the moral code of the consumers (for commerce has a morality of its own). These are the persons who get rid of their merchandise by means of all sorts of tricks and dodges, are silent about the bad qualities of their wares and exaggerate the good ones; these are the dairymen who put water in their milk ("for absolutely pure milk is not wholesome", they say); the doctors who make visits when they are no longer necessary; these are those who . . . But let us stop; we could fill pages with the practices of those whose honesty is not proof against trial.[2]

In going from B to C the moral aversion to such acts, observed in individuals, becomes gradually greater, and the danger that they will commit such practices diminishes, and we finally approach those who should be placed between C and D, those who are in no way guilty of such acts.

As is always the case with economic crimes, it is, then, the environment that is the cause of these offenses, while individual differences explain in part *who* are the authors of them.

[1] Where capitalism is beginning to develop, adulteration, etc., is the order of the day (*e.g.* in Japan in our day. See "Zeitschr. f. socialwissenschaft", N. F. IV, p. 503); later a certain honesty, based upon interest, especially in the wholesale business, becomes the rule. (*Cf. Engels,* "Die Lage der arbeitenden Klassen in England", Preface pp. vii–viii.)

[2] See *Zerboglio,* "Les inconvénients de l'honnêteté" ("Ere nouvelle", 1894); also *Ferriani,* "Glückliche und schlaue Verbrecher", IV.

We come now to the last category of the criminals of this group, to the great criminals, to those who throw themselves into gigantic enterprises while knowing beforehand that these will certainly or probably fail, or those who make great purchases of stock, and afterward cause a rise in price through the dissemination of false news, etc.

If there is any kind of crime that is the consequence of the economic environment exclusively, this is the one. Such crimes can arise only in a time like ours, with its insatiable thirst for gold, with the unlimited opportunity to deceive the public, greedy for great profits. A superficial knowledge of economic history is enough to make it plain that the bourgeois crimes, and especially those which we are now discussing, can be committed only under an economic system of the kind that ours is.

This should make those anthropologists reflect who wish always to find the causes of crime in the man himself and not in his surroundings. Naturally the originators of such deeds are marked out by characteristic traits. But there is no reason to admit that persons with such dispositions could not have been born also under a different economic system. Yet such crimes do not appear under any other mode of production.

What is the kind of persons who commit these crimes which society has prepared for? We note first that chance must have prepared such individuals in the proper environment, for a crime of this kind. If they were in the class of agriculturists, for example, the idea of committing it would not have occurred to them; it is only in a special environment that such crimes can be committed.

These people are characterized, in the first place, by excessive cupidity. In this regard they come high in the curve. Their prodigality is without limits; once they have executed a great coup they buy splendid palaces, give costly fêtes, support several mistresses, etc. An individual of this type, Arton, had a mistress who cost him 300,000 francs in one year; he needed a million to cover his annual expenses.[1] This is why they are not content with the large incomes which they could obtain honestly; they wish to surpass others in wealth, being ordinarily very vain.[2]

We have said that such individuals would probably have succeeded in securing large incomes honestly, for all are of a high order of intelligence. In following their machinations we are astonished by their perspicacity and their cleverness. Plans like theirs could never

[1] *Laschi, op. cit.,* pp. 72, 73. [2] *Laschi, op. cit.,* p. 106.

have been conceived and still less executed by men of mediocre intelligence.[1]

"I believe," says Professor Morselli in his preface to Laschi's work which we have quoted, "in fact, that no common intelligence is needed to cover up malversations for a long time, to organize clever swindles, outrageous frauds and bankruptcies, exploitations of the credulous public. It needs no more talent, perhaps it needs less, to accomplish a great number of useful and honest things, to make a so-called discovery or invention. We have, as I have said elsewhere, a fetichism with regard to genius, talent, higher intelligence. The effort of mental energy which is required by the complex planning and execution of a financial crime does not differ, as far as cerebral dynamics are concerned, from the effort demanded by an action that is perfectly regular from a moral point of view." [2]

In the third place, this class consists of persons who, as to the intensity of their moral sentiments, take the lowest place. What an ordinary criminal does in a small way, they do on a gigantic scale; while the former injures a single person, or only a few, the latter bring misfortune to great numbers. And they do it with indifference, for the disapprobation of honest men does not touch them.

As I have already shown elsewhere, brought up in no matter what environment, such individuals would not excel in the strength of their social sentiments. But I have added that, nevertheless, the influence of the environment of these persons is very great. We do not know much of the circumstances under which they have passed their youth. At least Laschi makes no mention of them in "Le crime financier", the principal work upon this class of misdeeds. It is more than probable that their moral education is totally lacking, or has been only very superficial. Theresa Humbert, for example, had already been instructed by her father in the art of swindling on a large scale.

On the other hand we know the environment in which they have generally passed the rest of their lives. They belong to the world of speculation, an environment which has very special ideas upon economic morals. In most of the cases of this kind, facts are brought out which show that the moral ideas in these circles differ much from those of the rest of mankind. It is evident that those who commit these crimes go farther than the morality of their world permits.

[1] *Laschi*, *op. cit.*, pp. 97 *ff.*
[2] Pp. xx and xxi.
[NOTE TO THE AMERICAN EDITION: *Cf. B. Kritschewsky,* "Die Korruption in der französischen Demokratie" ("Neue Zeit", XXVIII[2]), pp. 12 *ff.*]

But it takes great moral perspicacity to distinguish in this field the demarcations between what is permitted and what is not, and it is just this perspicacity that some persons lack.   This is why most criminals of this kind, when they are brought into court, say with sincere conviction that they are innocent, that they have done nothing that is incompatible with morality.[1]

Then, speculation etc. is one of the infallible means for killing all social sentiments; it is egoism pure and simple.   Can we be astonished that some of these individuals [2] in such an environment enter into conflict with the penal law?   It seems to me not.   Nor is there any reason to grant that they are abnormal from a biological point of view.   So even the Italian school is forced to admit that the stigmata found elsewhere cannot be pointed out in these individuals.[3]   Furthermore, in this case we can hardly speak of atavism.   It may be that our ancestors were great offenders, but it is not probable that they ever were guilty of swindles of this kind.

It is not necessary to speak fully of the reasons which cause these acts to be classed as crimes.   They are harmful to the regular progress of capitalism and consequently are threatened with penalties. The punishment of the adulteration of food-stuffs, on the contrary, is a consequence of the opposition of the consumers to one of the harmful effects of this system.

In this connection it is interesting to note, first, that the penalties prescribed for these crimes are relatively light as compared with those for ordinary economic crimes, like theft, for example, especially when we reflect that the harm done by them is much greater; second, that the number of punishable acts is very limited as compared with those which really deserve punishment.   As Baccaro observes in his work, "Genesi e funzione delle leggi penali", it is these crimes which show clearly the class character of the penal law.[4]

[1] See *Laschi, op. cit.*, p. 107.
[NOTE TO THE AMERICAN EDITION: Upon the way in which great fortunes have been amassed, see *F. Kummer*, "Die Geschichte der grossen amerikenischen Vermögen" ("Neue Zeit", XXX[2]).]
[2] For descriptions of cases see *Zola*, "L'argent", and *Wulffen, op. cit.*, II, p. 334.
[3] *Laschi, op. cit.*, p. 180.
[4] Pp. 147, 148.

CHAPTER III.

SEXUAL CRIMES.

Most authors who treat of the correlation between criminality and economic conditions, have devoted their attention to economic crimes especially, and have had little or nothing to say about sexual crimes. Man's sexual instincts, they say, have nothing to do with the economic life, they are a factor apart, and accordingly there is no relation between criminal sexuality and economic conditions.

We flatter ourselves that we shall be able to show that their opinion is erroneous, that a relation between sexual criminality and economic conditions does exist, although it is by nature less direct than that between economic crimes and the mode of production.

Having already remarked that the social forms of the sexual life (marriage and prostitution) are, in the last analysis, determined by the mode of production, we will not return to this topic. And it does not fall within the province of this work to speak of the relation of the intensity of the sexual life in general to economic conditions. From history we see that the sexual life plays now a greater, now a smaller part. It would be hard to admit that the causes of these changes are within man and not outside of him, particularly when very evident causes are to be found in the environment. Who does not see that the intensity of the sexual life of the upper classes of Rome of the decadence is explained by the exaggerated luxury, the idle existence of this group, and the dependent position of a part of the women (slaves).

In our present society the relation between the sexual life and economic conditions is equally clear. Everyone knows that the sexuality which occupies a very great place in that part of the bourgeoisie which passes its life in idleness and prodigality, is the consequence of this manner of living. On the other hand the low intellectual condition of the proletariat is the cause of a sexual life much more intense than it would be if the environment permitted a harmonious development of the whole nature. Engels, in his "Condition of the Working-class in England", says of the English proletarians, what is applicable to the workers in other countries also. "Next to intemperance in the enjoyment of intoxicating liquors, one of the principal faults of English working-men is sexual license. But this, too, follows with relentless logic, with inevitable necessity out of the position of a class left to itself, with no means of making use of its freedom. The bourgeoisie has left the working-class only these two pleasures, while imposing upon it a multitude of labors and hardships, and the consequence is that the working-men, in order to get something our of life, concentrate their whole energy upon these two enjoyments, carry them to excess, surrender to them in the most unbridled manner." [1]

Further the dependent economic position of woman in our present society is also a factor of the increase of the intensity of the sexual life (especially prostitution).

However, it is not this question but sexual criminality upon which we must fix our attention. Here also we must divide the crimes into groups, as they differ too much among themselves to be treated of together. We shall take up in order, then: A. Adultery; B. Rape and indecent assault upon adults; C. Rape and indecent assault upon children.

A. ADULTERY.

It has been said, "the history of property is also that of theft." In the same way we may say that the history of monogamy is also that of adultery, or in other words, that there is no monogamy without adultery. There must be, therefore, powerful and constant causes occasioning this offense. As we have seen above when we were setting forth briefly the history of marriage, adultery by the man was a permitted act at different stages of the social development.[2] If we ask why men committed this permitted act, but one reason can be alleged; *they are not monogamous by nature.* On the part of the woman the same act constituted, on the other hand, most often a very serious offense, threatened with the most severe penalties, which did not, however, prevent adultery on her side also. The cause is not different for the two sexes; women, too, are not monogamous by nature, though perhaps more nearly so than men.

From what we have just said the etiology of this crime is fixed. The only difference between the present and the past is that adultery

---

[1] P. 128 (in the original, p. 131).
[2] *Cf. Post,* "Grundriss der ethnologischen Jurisprudenz", II, p. 359; *Letourneau,* "L'evolution du mariage et de la famille", p. 257; *Lafargue,* "Der Ehebruch in Gegenwart und Vergangenheit" ("Neue Zeit", VII); and *Ferrero,* "Le crime d'adultère — son passé, son avenir" ("Archives d'anthrop. crim.", IX).

by the man also is punished in our time — there is no change in the
etiology of the crime. It may be said that the fundamental cause
of adultery is to be found in the nature of man, then, and that it is
thus anthropological and not social. I cannot admit this view of the
matter any more than I can believe that the ultimate cause of theft
is the necessity of eating in order to live. If the fundamental cause
of the offense of which we are treating is to be found *in* man, it would
be present always and everywhere *without reference to the environment.*
Sociology shows however, that this is not so. Up to a certain degree
of social development men and women alike have been free in this
respect; in other cases it is only the woman who is forced to remain
true to her husband; and at times both have been compelled to
remain faithful. Consequently, for one who does not consider society
as an immovable body, but sees that everything is in motion, the
fundamental cause of this crime is to be found in the structure of
society itself, which in certain cases, prohibits a man from satisfying
his natural inclinations. When the polygamous tendencies are stronger
than the pressure of society a crime is committed.

If we consulted only the criminal statistics we should hardly ever
meet with adultery. It is unnecessary to add that the penal laws
dealing with this matter are so drawn up that a prosecution for adultery almost never takes place; it goes without saying, however, that
in reality the offense is very common.

In the first place we must look into the question of the classes of
society in which the offense occurs oftenest. Though there are no
statistics on the matter I believe that we shall not be far wrong in
saying that adultery takes place oftenest in that part of the bourgeoisie that lives in idleness, often also among the proletariat, and least
often among the intellectual bourgeoisie and the petty bourgeoisie.
In seeking for the causes of this fact we see clearly that they cannot
be found in the man himself, for the individuals forming these classes
do not differ as to their innate characteristics. Consequently, these
causes must be found in the environment; the following being the
principal ones.

First. The more marriage is contracted for convenience the greater
the danger of adultery. This is one reason why adultery is more
common among the "upper ten thousand", where marriage is often a
commercial affair, and why it is less frequent among the intellectual
bourgeoisie, in which there are more marriages of inclination.

Second. The more frivolous and trifling the life any class leads,
the more frequent will adultery be in it. This is another reason why

adultery is frequent among the idle rich, and less frequent in the intellectual class and the petty bourgeoisie.

Third. The more the social causes of marriage are felt in a certain class, the greater the moral aversion to adultery. This is one reason why this offense is found less often among the petty bourgeoisie than in the working class.

Fourth. The greater the number of marriages concluded for purely physical reasons without any intellectual reasons entering in, the more numerous will be the cases of adultery. This applies especially to the proletariat, among whom most of the marriages are contracted from affection, but where, because of lack of culture, there is often no possibility of intellectual communion. When this harmony is lacking it comes about that the difficulties of life, so great in this class, cause an estrangement from which infidelities frequently result.

Finally, let us consider briefly the question of which individuals in the different classes are guilty of adultery. The predisposition to polygamy is not the same for all. In the second place, the sexual instincts are much more intense in some cases than in others. In the third place the environment in which one has lived is not the same as that of another, and opportunities do not occur in the same way for each. The joint action of these causes explains sufficiently why one commits the offense in question and not another.

In setting forth the etiology of adultery we have been giving the reasons why it has been designated as a crime. Little by little the conception of marriage has been modified in consequence of the social changes that have taken place; there is a growing number of persons who consider the life in common permissible only when both parties desire it without being constrained by the law. The partisans of this opinion disapprove of adultery, but for different reasons from others, who consider it as the infraction of an acquired right. Professor Ferri formulates this new morality as follows. "What is vile about adultery is not that it is an assault upon individual property, it is the disloyalty of the act, the trickery and hypocrisy of it." [1]

While finding adultery immoral the adherents of this opinion believe that the law has no right to interfere. Even the persons who do not share their point of view believe that the penal code should cease to concern itself with this crime. Hence it comes, among other things, that the laws are so drawn that prosecutions are very rare. It is probable that adultery will disappear from the list of offenses.

---

[1] "Les criminels dans l'art et la littérature", p. 141. *Cf.* also *Letourneau,* "Évolution du mariage", pp. 282, 283.

B. Rape and Indecent Assualt upon Adults.

In his work, "Genèse normale du crime", Professor Manouvrier expresses himself as follows upon the crime of rape. "Every normally constituted man would be a born violator if the sexual appetite could find no other means of satisfaction than rape. The crime is rare, however, and we know why; there are women for the ugliest and the poorest. However, famine may come; there is also opportunity, and many devils capable of leading into temptation the brute that every man is at his birth. For the 'criminologists' must not delude themselves upon this point if they wish to make criminal anthropology truly scientific. If we were to take a well-born child of a distinguished European family, and isolate him from his birth from all the influences of environment except those strictly necessary for the preservation of his life, we do not know what strange beast he would turn into. On the other hand we do know that behind our acquired polish our natural brutality still persists." [1] Here in a few words is the environment theory applied to the origin of the most serious sexual crimes. Let us consult some facts to see whether the theory is correct.

First of all it must be remarked that this crime is not the act of a pervert but of a brute. It is important not to forget this since perversion does play a part in the crimes which we shall take up under C. Some authors do not make a distinction between these two kinds of crimes, which prevents their giving a really fundamental treatment of the etiology of them.

Let us see what the movement of this crime teaches. Its curve in the different months shows that it rises towards spring, to reach its maximum in summer, after which it regularly decreases, reaching its minimum in winter. An example of this is given in the following table, which includes also crimes committed against children.[2]

[1] Pp. 444, 445.
[2] *Aschaffenburg*, "Das Verbrechen und seine Bekämpfung", p. 13. Cf. *A. v. Oettingen*, "Moralstatistik", pp. 221, 222; *Prof. Tardieu*, "Étude medico-légale sur les attentats aux moeurs", pp. 22, 23; *Dr. P. Bernard*, "Des viols et attentats à la pudeur sur adultes", p. 562 ("Arch. d'anthr. crim." II); also the German criminal statistics.

France, 1827–1869.

MONTHS.	SEXUAL CRIMES COMMITTED UPON				DAYS OF CONCEPTION 1863–1871.	
	Adults.		Children.			
	Absolute Figures.	%	Absolute Figures.	%	Absolute Figures.	%
January	584	7.09	1,106	5.57	2,603	7.84
February	563	6.84	1,041	5.23	2,661	8.02
March	643	7.82	1,366	6.88	2,608	7.85
April	608	7.39	1,700	8.56	2,887	8.69
May	904	10.98	2,175	10.95	3,000	9.21
June	1,043	12.67	2,585	13.03	3,018	9.08
July	860	10.45	2,459	12.42	2,911	8.76
August	794	9.64	2,208	11.13	2,742	8.25
September	653	7.93	1,773	8.93	2,810	8.46
October	523	6.46	1,447	7.29	2,625	7.91
November	514	6.24	983	4.95	2,620	7.89
December	534	6.49	939	5.05	2,665	8.02

The movement of sexual crimes does not tell us much about their etiology. It is plain that the opportunity of committing them occurs much oftener in summer than in winter, and the chance of catching the criminal "in flagrante delicto" is also much greater during the hot months. Even without statistics we should know that the temptation to these acts is greater in warm weather, and further, the rise of temperature towards spring probably increases the sexual tendencies. But all this does not explain the origin of this class of crimes, for if it is true that the sexual tendencies in man are increased by the rise of the temperature toward spring, this affects the sexual life *in general*, and not the *sexual criminality* alone (as is shown by the column of the days of conception).

In the same way we learn little of the etiology of these crimes from their movement in the course of the years. In the first part of this work we have given some statistics on this question, which we recapitulate here with additional data.

England.

The author of the English criminal statistics of 1899 fixes attention upon the fact that the maximum of sexual crimes was reached in 1893 and 1894, when the price of wheat was very low, (p. 48).

France, 1825–1878.

As Professor Ferri shows in his study upon the influence of temperature,[1] the curve of rape committed upon adults presents some resemblance to that of economic events, the years that were economically bad coinciding with the minimum figures for the crime in question. Thus the unfavorable years of 1835–37, 1846–47, 1865–68 brought a diminution of rapes committed upon adults, and the favorable years of 1832–35, 1847–50, 1857–59 an increase. Although there are some exceptions, the influence of the economic situation is indubitable.

Italy, 1873–1890.

Dr. Fornasari di Verce says that indecent assaults increase with the improvement in economic conditions, and vice versa (p. 143). On the other hand, Dr. Colajanni proved for the different parts of Italy (1875–1880) that a greater consumption of meat did *not* lead in most cases (22 out of 35) to an increase in the number of indecent assaults (*op. cit.*, pp. 501–504).

New South Wales, 1882–1891.

As we have seen in Part One (p. 144) Dr. Fornasari di Verce has shown that in this country sexual crimes increase in prosperous years, and vice versa.

Prussia, 1854–1896.

As to this country, Professor von Oettingen gives, for the years 1854–1859 and 1862–1871, some figures which show a slight connection between the price of grain and sexual crimes (Part One, pp. 53, 54). Dr. Müller also shows (see the tables pp. 77, 78 and pp. 80, 81) that economic conditions exercise an influence upon sexual crimes; thus, for example, the years 1857–1859 were characterized by cheap grain and high figures for sexual crimes; the same was true of the years 1863–1866 and 1869. On the contrary the years 1854–1856 and 1861, show a high price for grain and low figures for the crimes in question. There were, however, some exceptions; during the crisis of 1873–74 the sexual crimes did not decrease, and in the following years the correspondence of the curve of these crimes with that of the economic situation is no longer to be noted.

The data upon the relation between the economic situation and

[1] "Das Verbrechen in seiner Abhängigheit von dem jährlichen Temperaturwechsel" ("Zeitschr. f. d. ges. strafrw.", II).

these crimes are not as numerous as those upon economic crimes, and there are also many exceptions. With some reservations, however, we can say that an improvement in economic conditions tends to increase the crimes in question. However, this does not teach us much with regard to the etiology of them; the statistics of births have long since shown us that the sexual life is more intense during the periods of economic prosperity, than during those of depression.[1] Better nourishment renders the sexual instincts stronger, without its being necessary that they should manifest themselves in a criminal manner. The proof of this is furnished by those who are sufficiently nourished both in good times and bad and are yet not guilty of these crimes. (For statistical proofs see the statistics given later.)

We must then try to discover the true crime-producing factors in other statistical data. First let us inquire whether married or unmarried persons are more often guilty? As we have seen above, German criminal statistics are the only ones which give us absolutely certain information on this point. These show (see p. 454) that at all ages bachelors, widowers, and divorced men are more often guilty of sexual crimes than married men, and at certain ages much more so. Unfortunately these statistics do not distinguish the rapes committed upon adults from those committed upon children. The data of Dr. J. Socquet give us some slight information.[2]

France, 1876–1880.

CIVIL STATUS.	To 1,000,000 of the Population in Each Group there were Charged with Rape upon Adults
Bachelors	8
Married men	3
Widowers	2

Marriage, then, tends to diminish the number of these crimes. The economic life having, in its turn an influence upon the number of marriages the relation between this life and the crimes in question is clear. If the economic situation of many persons did not prevent their contracting marriage at the period of life indicated by nature, these

---

[1] See *G. v. Mayr*, "Gesetzmässigkeit im Gesellschaftsleben", pp. 239 *ff.*, and "Statistik und Gesellschaftslehre", II, pp. 170, 171.

[2] "Contribution à l'étude statistique de la criminalité en France", p. 60. Dr. *A. Bournet*, in "De la criminalité en France et en Italie", p. 68, and *Ferri, op. cit.*, p. 39, and *Bernard, op. cit.*, p. 566, come to the same conclusion.

crimes would be much less frequent. As Dr. Augagneur says:
"Our laws and physiological exigencies do not harmonize."

A second question is, what is the class of the population that commits these crimes? As we have seen, the statistics of Italy and Austria show (see pp. 437, 438) that it is almost exclusively the poor
who are guilty of sexual crimes. In Italy 92.1% are indigent or have
only the strict necessaries of life; in Austria 91.2 % are without
fortune, and only 0.2% are well-to-do.

The statistics of the professions of convicts in Germany (see p. 441)
show also that those who are arraigned for these crimes are especially
working-men, and particularly unskilled laborers (among whom the
statistics include also white-slave traders, professional criminals,
etc., see p. 442). Unfortunately these statistics do not distinguish
between sexual crimes committed upon adults and those committed
upon children. The following table shows that the number is greater
for the first than for the second of these crimes.[1]

France, 1836–1880.

	1836–1840.		1876–1880.	
	PERCENTAGE OF TOTAL NUMBER ACCUSED OF RAPE AND INDECENT ASSAULT COMMITTED UPON			
	Adults.	Children.	Adults.	Children.
Engaged in the cultivation of the soil, laborers, farm servants, etc.	38	33	52	39
Workers engaged in handling the products of the soil, iron, wood, etc.	30	26	25	25
Bakers, butchers, cabinet-makers, etc.	5	4	4	4
Tailors, wigmakers, hat-makers	7	8	3	6
Merchants	3	5	3	5
Sailors, carters, porters	6	5	4	3
Domestic servants and keepers of inns, lodging houses and cafés	3	4	3	4
Liberal professions	5	11	4.5	10
Vagrants	3	4	1.5	4
	100	100	100	100

Although this table by itself has little value, since the comparative
figures for the population in general are lacking, it suffices to show,
by comparison with the preceding tables, that the crime with which
we are concerned is committed by working-people especially. The

[1] *Socquet, op. cit.*, pp. 61 and 69. See also *Ferri, op. cit.*, p. 43.

criminals in a large number of the cases are rural, as the last table proves to a certain extent, and as further appears from the following.[1]

France, 1846–1880.

RESIDENCE.	1846–1850.		1876–1880.	
	Absolute Numbers.	%	Absolute Numbers.	%
Rural population	804	74	412	67
Urban population	264	24	160	27
Residence unknown	16	2	38	6
Total	1,084	100	610	100

Even when we take account of the fact that the rural population in France is more numerous than the urban, we still see that the crime in question is committed in the country especially.[2]

We must further inquire what is the part of the proletariat that is guilty of rape upon adults? The answer must be that it is that which forms the lowest stratum of society. As preceding statistics have shown us (see pp. 427–430, 432), the number of illiterates or of those who know only how to read and write, is very great among the authors of sexual crimes. The following table gives us data more detailed and concerned only with rape upon adults.[3]

France, 1875–1884.

EDUCATION.	ABSOLUTE NUMBERS.	%	To 100 PERSONS UPON THE CONSCRIPTION LISTS (1880).
Unable to read or write . . .	319	28	13.8
Able to read and write . . .	802	71	—
With a higher education . . .	12	1	—

Upon the basis of this table we have the right to say, then, that this crime is almost never committed by persons having more than a primary education.

[1] *Socquet, op. cit.,* p. 60.
[2] *Cf. Bournet, op. cit.,* p. 68, and *Bernard, op. cit.,* p. 567.
[3] The first two columns are taken from *Bernard, op. cit.,* p. 569; the last is figured from the "Annuaire statistique de la France", VII, p. 526.
[NOTE TO THE AMERICAN EDITION: The same thing is shown by the criminal statistics of the Netherlands. *Cf. de Roos, op. cit.,* p. 114, and my own study already cited, " Misdaad en Socialisme ", pp. 34–35.]

This fact destroys the theory that the "human beast" exists
independent of environment; for if such were the case, this crime
would be relatively as frequent among more highly developed
persons as among those that are less so. This table proves what
is always forgotten by criminal anthropologists, that a man becomes a brute only under certain fixed circumstances, and commits
then acts that would be repugnant to him if he lived in a different
environment.

Those who commit these acts come from the strata of society in
which, in consequence of their living conditions, the sexual life is
considered from a purely animal point of view. What is the environment in which the children of the lowest classes grow up, and what is
the sexual morality that they derive from it? The simple truth is that
there is no sexual morality for them. In consequence of the detestable housing conditions (compare what was said upon this subject in
connection with prostitution) and of the bad society with which they
are thrown, the children are thoroughly conversant with the sexual
life in its most bestial manifestations. Their attention is fixed upon
the sexual life at an age at which it is still a closed book to children
brought up in a wholesome environment. As Dr. Lux says in his
excellent study upon sexual crimes, "Need, misery, and vice are the
natural surroundings of the children of the proletariat, and especially
of the lower proletariat; they form the environment out of which the
child draws his first and most lasting impressions; they are the school
from which they derive the lessons of a system of ethics which is in
marked contrast with the ethics of progressive humanity. Conceptions of moral restraints can hardly be awakened in the offspring
of the lowest ranks of the proletariat; on the contrary, so far as the
sexual sphere is concerned, they are suppressed by the undisguised
sexual intercourse of parents, other adults, and prostitutes, with whom
the children are continually coming into contact. . . ." [1]

One of the consequences of the lower position of woman in our
present society is that man considers women as destined to submit to
his sexual will. This is especially the case in the lower strata of the

---

[1] "Die Sittlichkeitsverbrechen in Deutschland in kriminalstatistischer
Beleuchtung", p. 266. Cf. Wittenberg and Wagner, "Die geschlechtlich
sittlichen Verhältnisse der evangelischen Landbewohner im Deutschen
Reiche", and Wagner, "Die Sittlichkeit auf dem Lande." See also Ferriani,
"Minderjährige Verbrecher", pp. 96 ff., and L. Braun, "Die Frauen frage",
pp. 385, 386.

[NOTE TO THE AMERICAN EDITION: Cf. Herz, op. cit., p. 35; Bonger, op.
cit., pp. 33, 34; Baernreither, op. cit. passim; and Geill, "Kriminal anthro-
pologische Untersuchungen dänischer Sittlichkeitsverbrecher", p. 358.]

population, where the woman is often only a means by which the man may satisfy his desires.

Finally, alcoholism is still to be added as a crimogenic factor. Above (pp. 509 *ff.*) we have seen that there are many chronic alcoholics among the authors of these crimes; in Germany 23.3 % and 20.5 %, in France 51.5 % and 55.7 %, in the Netherlands 10.84 %, and in Wurtemberg 36.3 %.

There is still another way in which alcoholism figures in the etiology of these crimes.   At a certain stage of intoxication the sexual instincts are stimulated, while the moral forces are weakened.[1] So in the cases where a sexual crime has been committed in a state of drunkenness we may be sure that alcohol has been one of the principal factors of it. The following figures give us some information on this point.

England.

In his report to the international penitentiary congress at Brussels, Dr. M. W. C. Sullivan shows, as the result of an investigation, that more than 50% of the sexual crimes were caused by alcoholism, and that acute alcoholism is especially active in the case of rape upon adults.[2]

Austria, 1896–1897.

Out of 179 cases of rape, etc., there were 46 (25.7%) committed in a state of drunkenness.[3]

France.

In his report at the Congress mentioned above, Marambat says that 6.6 % of the rapes and indecent assaults have been committed in a state of intoxication.[4]

Netherlands.

The criminal statistics show that 11.82% of those convicted of sexual crimes commit them under the influence of alcoholic drinks.[5]

Sweden.

Sigfrid Wieselgren, director general of the penitentiary establishments of Sweden, in his report to the Brussels Congress gives a table

---

[1] See among others *Grotjahn*, "Der Alkoholismus", pp. 53 and 86.
[2] "Actes du congrès pénitentiaire international de Bruxelles."
[3] *Loeffler*, "Alkohol und Verbrechen", pp. 518–521 ("Zeitschrift f. d. ges. Strafrw." XXIII).
[4] P. 113. See also *Bournet, op. cit.*, p. 69.
[5] "Crimineele Statistiek voor het jaar 1901", p. xxvii.

which shows that about 36% of those guilty of indecent assault were drunk at the time of the crime.[1]

Switzerland, 1892–1896.

According to the criminal statistics, 21.5 % of all the sexual crimes are due to alcoholism.[2]

To sum up, we see that the causes of these crimes are the economic condition which prevents some individuals from marrying at the natural age, the inferior social position of woman, alcoholism, and above all the sexual demoralization and lack of civilization in the lowest strata of society.

It is plain that not all the individuals who live in this environment are guilty of the crimes in question. The sexual instincts do not have equal force at all ages, nor with all individuals. There are individuals who have very pronounced sexual propensities, others who are almost indifferent in this respect, and between the two extremes lies the great majority. It is only for the first class that the danger of a crime against morals is great, for the others it is less so. If the opportunity (rape is almost always an "occasional" crime) presents itself to persons already predisposed, the moral check to restrain them is lacking. If they had lived in another environment, this act would be repugnant to them, as statistics prove; for this crime is not committed by persons of the other classes, although there are naturally proportionally more persons with strong sexual instincts among them. The opportunity to commit these crimes is happily not very frequent. As Voltaire has expressed it, "Rape is a crime as hard to prove as it is to commit."

We must add a few words upon the history of this crime and the causes that have led to its being classified as such. As Dr. Post (the principal authority upon this question) has shown, among many primitive peoples rape is only considered as a detriment to the property of the man.[3] It is only little by little as the position of woman

---

[1] "Actes etc.", p. 167.

[Note to the American Edition: Upon the influence of alcohol upon sexual crimes see further *Geill, op. cit.*, p. 362; *Aschaffenburg*, "Zur Psychologie der sittlichkeitsverbrechen", p. 408; *Bonhoeffer*, "Sittlichkeitsdelikt und Körperverletzung", p. 469.]

[2] "Die Ergebnisse der schweizerischen Kriminalstatistik während der Jahre 1892–1896."

[3] See "Der Ursprung des Rechts", p. 112; " Die Grundlagen des Rechts etc.", p. 377; and "Grundriss der ethnologischen Jurisprudenz", II, p. 382.

improves, and her individuality is recognized, that rape is considered as a grave encroachment upon the liberty of the woman, and that it is punished as such.

C. RAPE AND INDECENT ASSAULT UPON CHILDREN.

An examination of the etiology of these crimes shows that in great part the individuals who are guilty of them belong to the same category of criminals as those who commit sexual crimes upon adults. If they seduce or outrage a child and not a woman it is from accidental reasons (opportunity, lack of bodily strength, etc.); they are brutes who wish to satisfy their sexual instincts at any price; they are not, however, perverts. Although there is a quantitative difference between the man who violates an adult and one who commits this act upon a child (the latter being grosser and more egoistic than the former), there is no qualitative difference between the two so far as the majority of the criminals of whom we are speaking are concerned. We should only repeat ourselves if we treated of the etiology of these crimes more fully.

As with the crimes of which we were speaking above, there is with crimes against children also, a great increase toward spring, the maximum being reached in the month of June, after which there is a decrease, with the minimum in winter.[1] The statistics given for France show also that in this country the periods of economic prosperity bring an increase of these crimes, and the periods of depression a decrease.[2] And it is probably the same with other countries. As has been said also of the crimes against adults, all this shows us very little of the etiology of these crimes, since the intensity of the sexual life in general rises and falls in accordance with the economic situation.

Here also the married men play a smaller part than the unmarried and divorced; the poor classes show a larger number of crimes than those that have property (see p. 616); the illiterate, and persons who know how to read and write simply, show also proportionately higher figures than persons with a higher education,[3] and alcoholism again takes its place among the causes of this crime.[4]

[1] See among others *Garraud* and *Bernard*, "Des attentats à la pudeur et des viols sur les enfants", pp. 404–405 ("Arch. d'anthr. crim.", I).
[2] See *Lafargue*, p. 293; *Garraud* and *Bernard, op. cit.*, pp. 408–409.
[3] *Cf.* "Reports on the law relating to the protection of young girls", 1882, p. 37; *Dr. Ladame*, "De la prostitution dans ses rapports avec l'alcoolisme, le crime, et la folie", pp. 24–26; and *Amschl*, "Aberglauben als Heilmittel", pp. 397, 398 ("Archiv f. Krim-Anthr. und Kriminalstatistik", XV).
[4] *Cf. Tardieu, op. cit.*, pp. 21, 22; *Lavasseur*, "La population française", II, p. 448; *Starke, op. cit.*, pp. 172, 173.

A minute comparison of the statistics of sexual crimes committed upon adults and of those upon children shows that a part of the latter are of a character quite different from the former. By comparing, for example, the statistics of the civil status of persons arraigned, we see that the number of married men and widowers is proportionately much greater· in the case of crimes against children than against adults. The following table shows this : [1]

France, 1876–1880.

CIVIL STATUS.	To 1,000,000 of the Population of Each Group there were Arraigned for Rape Upon	
	Adults.	Children.
Bachelors	8	37
Married men	3	25
Widowers	3	50

A comparison of the statistics of the occupation of the two groups of these criminals (see p. 616) shows that in the crimes upon children, the liberal professions show twice as many as those committed upon adults. The same is true of merchants.[2]

The figures with regard to education show that the illiterate are about equally numerous in both groups of criminals, but that the percentage of those who have a higher education is 5 in the case of crimes upon children, and barely 1 for those upon adults.[3]

While, as we have seen, sexual crimes upon adults are chiefly committed in the country, the cities and manufacturing centers occupy a much more important place in the statistics of those upon children, as the following table proves.[4]

[1] *Socquet, op. cit.*, pp. 60 and 68.
[2] In his "Die Frau und der Sozialismus", *Bebel* gives almost the same proportion for Germany without indicating the source from which he takes his figures. As he remarks the percentage of the rich and well-to-do would be larger if those interested did not often succeed in hushing the matter up. We need only recall the revelations made by the "Pall Mall Gazette" (see "Les scandales de Londres").
[3] *Garraud* and *Bernard, op. cit.*, p. 432.
[4] *Socquet, op. cit.*, pp. 60 and 69.

France, 1876–1880.

RESIDENCE.	RAPE AND INDECENT ASSAULT UPON	
	Adults.	Children.
	%	%
Rural	67	53
Urban	27	43
Unknown	6	4

Contrary to what we find with regard to sexual crimes against adults it is also the departments with the great cities which, in comparison with the rural districts, give the highest figures.[1]

It appears from an examination of these data that sexual crimes upon children and those upon adults have, in part a different etiology. Many sexual crimes upon children are committed by persons who could also satisfy their desires with adults, but abuse children instead. These, then, are cases of sexual perverts.

A thorough examination of the causes of this perversion would be ill placed in the midst of our investigation of the social etiology of crime, for they are principally of a pathological nature. However prostitution should be mentioned as contributing more to sexual demoralization than any other cause. As Dr. Després says in his work "La prostitution en France", "Physicians think that rape [2] is an aberration of the genetic faculty and that this crime is more often the result of satiety than of deprivation of the natural exercise of the genital functions." [3]

Dr. Ladame expresses himself thus. "All the causes which divert the genetic faculty from its natural end may lead to crime, and among these causes prostitution plays, without doubt, the principal part." [4]

It is plainly difficult to show by figures the degree of importance of

---

[1] Cf. Bournet, op. cit., pp. 66–68; Socquet, op. cit., p. 73; Garraud and Bernard, op. cit., p. 435.

[2] The author makes the mistake of omitting here the words "of children." Statistics show that it is especially the country, where the sexual life is characterized rather by grossness than by perversion, that produces these crimes. Dr. Després has been led to this error through studying the geography of rape upon children and upon adults at the same time — by which method they are seen to be most numerous in the cities where prostitution exists exclusively. An examination of the two crimes separately gives different results.

[3] P. 43.

[4] Op. cit., p. 24. Cf. Tarde, "Penal Philosophy", p. 355, and Leuss, op. cit., p. 106.

prostitution in the etiology of sexual crimes. The Swiss statistics, which try, though very imperfectly, to record the causes of crimes, say that 5.3% of the sexual crimes are caused by prostitution.[1] It is unnecessary to say that this figure is too low.

We may add in conclusion that it is almost always upon the children of the poor that these crimes are committed. The children of well-to-do parents are so well guarded that crimes against them are the rare exceptions.[2]

[1] *Op. cit.*, p. 36.
[2] *Cf. Bérard des Glajeux*, "Les passions criminelles", pp. 121, 122.

[NOTE TO THE AMERICAN EDITION: Additional works that have appeared recently are: *R. Quanter*, "Die Sittlichkeitsverbrechen"; *F. Leppmann*, "Die Sittlichkeitsverbrecher" (very interesting!); *de Roos*, "De sexueele criminaliteit"; *L. Wachholz*, "Zur Lehre von den sexuallen Delikten"; *E. Wulffen*, "Der Sexualverbrecher"; *L. Ferrantem Capetti*, "Reati e psicopatie sessuali"; *J. Werthauer*, "Sittlichkeits-delikte der Gross-stadt"; *Kauffmann*, op. cit., pp. 133 ff.; *M. R. Senf*, "Geschlechtstrieb und Verbrechen."]

CHAPTER IV.

CRIMES FROM VENGEANCE AND OTHER MOTIVES.

BESIDES economic, sexual, and political criminality, there is still a fourth category of crimes, the motives of which are quite diverse. We shall treat, A. Crimes from vengeance, and B. Infanticide. The first group is important both quantitatively and qualitatively; the second, especially, qualitatively. The crimes committed from other motives are either very rare, or very insignificant, or may be explained by the same causes as those included under A, and hence may be passed over in silence.[1]

A. CRIMES COMMITTED FROM VENGEANCE.

In a sociological work like ours we need not consider the psychology of vengeance.[2] For our subject it is sufficient to show that the feeling is innate in everyone, although in different degrees. As soon as one person injures another, whether bodily, or in his interests, or his honor, the desire to retaliate in one way or another immediately appears. If this desire transforms itself into act, this act calls forth a stronger reaction on the part of the opposing party, etc. It is this that is called the instinct of vengeance.[3]

---

[1] For a complete enumeration of the motives of crime see: *Liszt*, "Die psychologischen Grundlagen der Kriminalpolitik", pp. 490–494 ("Zeitschr. f. d. ges. Strw.", XVI) and *Starke*, "Die éléments essentiels qui doivent figurer dans la statistique criminelle et des moyens de les rendre comparables", pp. 77, 78 ("Bulletin de l'inst. intern. de statistique", 1889).

[NOTE TO THE AMERICAN EDITION: See further the recent studies upon superstition and crime: *Löwenstimm*, "Aberglaube und Verbrechen", "Aberglaube und Gesetz"; *Wulffen*, "Psychologie des Verbrechens", II, pp. 219–229; *Helling*, "Verbrechen und Aberglaube."]

[2] Upon the psychology of vengeance see *Steinmetz*, "Ethnologische Studien zur ersten Entwicklung der Strafe", I, pp. 99 ff.

[3] Upon the instinct of vengeance see: *A. H. Post*, "Bausteine für eine allgemeine Rechtswissenschaft", I, pp. 140 ff.; *Colajanni*, "Sociologia criminale", II, p. 64; *Letourneau*, "L'évolution juridique", pp. 7 ff.; *Lafargue*, "Der Ursprung der Idee des Gerechten und Unrechten", p. 421 ("Neue Zeit", 1898–1899, II).

We must then begin by treating the causes calling forth feelings of revenge, and by fixing our attention upon the two principal categories of causes, those which spring from the economic life, and those which are due to the sexual life.

We shall speak first of the causes that are due to the economic life. The fundamental principle of the mode of production in which we live is competition, strife — in other words, doing injury to others. So there are innumerable cases in which the desire for revenge is excited by the economic life. Many sociologists extol the beauty of this struggle and pretend that its effect upon society is excellent. We shall refrain from examining the truth or falsity of this statement; for the matter in hand we need not concern ourselves with the fortunate victors, but simply with the vanquished. After the exposition of the present system of production it is superfluous to show all the opposing economic interests and the feelings resulting therefrom; we shall mention a few, and the others will be easily understood.

Imagine, for example, the state of mind of a small retailer who finds himself totally ruined by the competition of a large department store in the neighborhood; of that of workingmen suffering great privations during a strike, who see themselves supplanted by others, who think only of their immediate interest in acting as strike-breakers. Or imagine, again, the innumerable cases in which questions of inheritance awaken vengeful feelings. And side by side with all this, picture the economic life of village-communities where all the economic interests were parallel, and where consequently the economic life engendered neither envy nor jealousy. Anyone who grasps the enormous difference between these two modes of production, will understand also how the feelings of revenge are excited by the present economic system.[1]

In the second place, how far are vengeful feelings aroused by sexuality?[2] As Sutherland remarks in his "Origin and Growth of the Moral Instinct", there are no peoples who are not more or less jealous in sexual matters,[3] but great differences are to be observed in this respect. While Nansen, for example tells how the Eskimo women are almost ignorant of sexual jealousy,[4] there are other peoples among

---

[1] Cf. Prinzing, "Soziale Faktoren der Kriminalität", p. 558, and Aschaffenburg, "Das Verbrechen und seine Bekämpfung", p. 135.

[NOTE TO THE AMERICAN EDITION: Cf. especially: Müller-Lyer, "Phasen der Liebe", pp. 47 ff.]

[2] See Ferriani, "L'amore in tribunali", and L. Holtz, "Les crimes passionels", upon crimes of this class.

[3] II, p. 131.   [4] "Eskimo Life."

whom the woman is killed by her husband if another man evinces any regard for her.[1]

The facts show that the greater the power of the man over the woman, the greater also is the sexual jealousy of the man, a jealousy which, among other things, manifests itself in the very severe punishment of adultery.[2]   He who has a right to something wishes to keep it for himself and does not tolerate injury to it on the part of anyone else. When the man considers the woman as his chattel, or when he has great power over her, sexual jealousy is strengthened by the feelings connected with property.   These latter feelings were more predominant among the primitive peoples than true sexual jealousy, a proof of which is that fact that among many of these peoples the law of hospitality required putting the wife at the disposal of the guest.

From the present form of marriage (as among many primitive peoples) it follows that each party has a right with relation to the other.[3]   The violation of this right is considered as a serious injury and gives rise to a desire for revenge.   This phenomenon is not natural, but historical.   If the present state of society did not necessitate an artificial stability in sexual relationships, if the man and his wife were economically independent, they would not believe that they had rights over each other.[4]

Here is the first bond between sexual jealousy and the social environment, but there is also a second, though a more remote one, namely, that it is with those who have a gross conception of the relations of man and wife, that revengeful feelings arise after love disappears. Those who, because of the environment in which they live, have formed a different idea of the relation between man and wife, while feeling the most violent grief, remain strangers to the desire for revenge.   He who knows that neither love nor sympathy can be bidden, knows also that a right in this matter can bring no change in the feelings, and must remain only a nominal thing; he sees only the action of fate, where the brute sees an evil will.   This is one reason why the number of crimes of passion is smaller among civilized people than among the partly civilized.

We must notice, further, one kind of crime of passion, the revenge of a woman seduced and then abandoned.   Besides sexual jealousy

[1] See *Letourneau*, "L'évolution du mariage et de la famille", p. 275.
[2] See *Steimmetz*, *op. cit.*, II, p. 303, and *Sutherland*, *op. cit.*, I, chap. VIII.
[3] It is plain that this influences also those relationships that are not sanctioned by law.
[4] There is almost no mention of sexual jealousy where men and women both occupy an independent position. *Cf. Morgan*, "Ancient Society", p. 431.

there are, in these cases, other motives playing their part. Often the woman has not given herself for love alone, but also with the prospect of a marriage, or a betterment of her economic position. It is not sexual vengeance that is the sole motive here then, but also vengeance for economic reasons.[1] Further the prohibition of inquiring into the question of paternity may also enter in.[2]

After having pointed out the two principal categories of causes that awaken revengeful feelings we must now enquire why, with certain individuals, these feelings are translated into acts. Many criminologists prefer to find environment of small importance in these crimes and the individual factors the predominant ones. Let us see whether the facts will uphold this theory. To begin with let us ask what the movement of these crimes teaches us.

As statistics show, they increase towards spring, reach their maximum in summer, after which a decrease follows with the minimum in winter; as the following table proves.[3]

Germany, 1883–1892.

CRIMES.	ON THE BASIS OF A SUPPOSED AVERAGE OF 100 CRIMES A DAY THE DAILY AVERAGE FOR THE DIFFERENT MONTHS WOULD BE											
	January.	February.	March.	April.	May.	June.	July.	August.	September.	October.	November.	December.
Serious assaults .	75	78	78	84	102	116	119	116	110	106	93	80
Homicides . .	88	84	100	95	108	113	118	133	124	106	93	78

Some authors seek for a remote explanation, when there is one near at hand : in summer persons are more in contact with each other, a fact which gives opportunity for disputes, and an increased danger of consequent crimes.

We may sum up the principal data upon the movement of these crimes in relation to the economic situation (given in Part One of this work) as follows.

England, 1840–1890.

Fornasari di Verce draws attention to the fact that crimes against persons (represented in great part by crimes of vengenace) increase

---

[1] Cf. Holtz, op. cit., pp. 52–54.   [2] Cf. Holtz, op. cit., pp. 147–149.
[3] "Kriminalstatistik für das Jahr 1894", II, p. 52.

in times of economic prosperity and vice versa (see p. 144.   See also the data of Mayr, pp. 43 and 44).

Bavaria, 1835–1861.

Mayr shows for this period that crimes against persons increase when the price of grain falls and vice versa (see pp. 40–42).

Italy, 1873–1890.

According to Fornasari di Verce there is a diminution of homicides and assaults when economic conditions grow worse, and vice versa (see p. 143).

New South Wales, 1882–1891.

The same author says that homicides and assaults increase, while minor offenses against persons decrease, when economic conditions grow worse and vice versa (see p. 144).

Prussia, 1854–1896.

Dr. Starke and Dr. Müller show that the crimes we are considering increase when economic conditions improve, and decrease when they grow worse (see pp. 66 and 83).   However, they show at the same time that these phenomena did not take place at the beginning of the period observed by them.   Later they follow the regular course.[1]

Canton of Zurich, 1853–1892.

For the period mentioned Meyer proves that crimes against persons increase when economic conditions improve (see p. 69).

Examining these results we observe that the crimes in question increase in the priods of prosperity, and vice versa; but we see at the same time that there are also noteworthy exceptions (New South Wales and France), and that in Germany in the last 20 or 30 years, this tendency is no longer present.[2]   It is not difficult, it seems to me,

---

[1] In his "Getreidepreise und Kriminalität in Deutschland," *H. Berg* shows that crimes against persons in Germany were not influenced by economic occurrences during the years 1882–1898 (pp. 31 *ff.*).
[NOTE TO THE AMERICAN EDITION: I have proved the same for 1898–1908. (See my study, "Verbrechen und Socialismus", p. 808).]
[2] [NOTE TO THE AMERICAN EDITION: The same is true in the Netherlands. In Austria, Herz has shown a certain relation between the phenomena in question after 1863, but not in recent years.]

to explain why these crimes increase in periods of prosperity. Men are thrown then into contact more frequently, they live a little more for amusement, and consume (and this is certainly one of the principal reasons) more alcohol than usual. Some authors see in this movement of crimes against persons a natural law, according to which criminality would be a fixed quantity, manifesting itself in economic crimes in periods of depression, and in crimes against the person in periods of prosperity.

As I have already said more than once this theory is erroneous. If it were really true that an improvement of the economic situation *inevitably* brought about an increase of crimes against persons, the class of individuals who are always in fairly good circumstances would also be largely guilty of these crimes. Statistics show us the contrary.

Thus we arrive at the very important question, what are the classes of the population which are especially guilty of these crimes? As the statistics already given show they are the poorest classes (see pp. 437 *ff.*). In Italy, for example, 89.8% of those who commit homicide, and 91.1% of those guilty of assault, were indigent or had only the bare necessities of life, though these form but 60% of the population. The same is true of Austria, and the statistics of occupations gives a similar result for Germany (see pp. 441 and 442).

The statistics that give information upon the degree of education of these criminals are more interesting still. As we have seen above, only 0.1% of those guilty of assault had a higher education, while 40.5% of these criminals were illiterate, and 59.4% knew only how to read, or to read and write. In France from 1896 to 1900 the completely illiterate constituted 16% of those guilty of assault, and 15% of the assassins, while in the general population these were only 4.5% who did not know how to sign their names. In Italy only 1% of the assassins and only 0.6% of those guilty of assault had a higher education, 99% and 99.4% respectively were illiterate or knew only how to read and write. These are striking figures.

In this connection let us stop for a moment to consider the geography of these crimes, and place beside the figures on this point those of illiteracy. We will begin with a table of figures for homicide and assaults followed by death, for some of the countries of Europe.[1]

---

[1] The figures for homicide, etc., are taken from *Ferri*, "Atlante antropologico-statistico dell' Omicidio", pp. 246–248. The figures for illiteracy in Italy, Belgium, France, Germany, and Holland are taken from the official statistics, the others from the "Statesman's Year Book, 1902."

Country.[1]	Years.	Homicides and Assaults followed by Death to 100,000 Inhabitants.	Years.	Illiteracy %.
Italy	1880–84	70.0	1882	57.43
Spain	1883–84	64.9	1889	68.10
Hungary	1876–80	56.2	1880	59.70
Austria	1877–81	10.8	"	40.10
Belgium	1876–80	8.5	"	21.66
Ireland	1880–84	8.1	1882	30.00
France	"	6.4	"	13.10
Scotland	"	4.4	"	11.00
England	"	3.9	1883	14.00
Germany	1882–84	3.4	1881–82	1.54
Holland	1880–81	3.1	1880	11.50

No one will deny the striking parallelism between these columns, the highest figures for homicide being found where there are also the largest figures for illiteracy.   As we have seen already, however, international statistics have inherent defects.   The following figures are better in this regard : [2]

United States.

Birthplace.	Number of Homicides to 100,000 Inhabitants.	Illiteracy %.
Sweden, Norway, Denmark	5.8	0.42
Germany	9.7	0.57
England and Scotland	10.4	2.50
Austria	12.2	16.73
Ireland	17.5	41.65
France	27.4	43.60
Italy	58.1	51.77

We have here also, then, a striking parallelism.   We will now take up the geography of homicide, etc., in different parts of one country; some of the faults inherent in the geography of crime are thus eliminated.

[1] [Note to the American Edition: *Cf.* further: *Wadler, op. cit.*, pp. 176 *ff.*, upon the Balkan States, where the crimes in question are very frequent, and the degree of civilization is very low.   (In Servia, for example, in 1900 there was a percentage of illiteracy of about 79 !)]
[2] From *Colajanni,* "L'homicide en Italy", p. 49 ("Revue Socialiste", 1901).

Germany, 1893–1897.[1]

States and Provinces.	Number of Persons Convicted for Serious Assaults to 100,000 Inhabitants over 12 Years of Age.[2]	Percentage of Illiterates among the Recruits 1892–1893.	Percentage of Votes Given to the Socialist in the Election of 1898.[3]
Bavaria	391	0.03	18.0
West Prussia	334	4.01	4.9
Posen	326	1.72	1.7
East Prussia	265	0.98	18.3
Silesia	252	0.57	22.3
Baden (Grand Duchy)	250	0.02	19.1
Hesse	248	0.03	33.9
Alsace-Lorraine . . .	237	0.30	22.7
Pomerania	227	0.22	17.2
Westphalia	223	0.08	17.7
Germany	219	0.38	27.1
Prussia	211	0.59	24.1
Rhine Province . . .	201	0.08	15.0
Wurtemburg	197	0.04	20.3
Saxony (Province) . .	185	0.07	34.0
Brandenburg	184	0.15	35.6
Hesse-Nassau	161	0.14	30.9
Hanover	146	0.04	25.6
Sleswick-Holstein . .	106	0.10	38.9
Saxony (Kingdom) . .	82	0.01	49.4

The parallelism between the first two columns is undeniable; the states and provinces with low figures for illiteracy show also a small number of assaults, and vice versa, with some exceptions — notably Bavaria. The reason why Bavaria is at the head of the list is undoubtedly because of the alcoholism that prevails there.

[1] The first column is taken from "Kriminalstatistik f. d. Jahr 1898". II, pp. 27–30; the second from "Statistisches Jahrbuch f. d. deutsche Reich, 1894", p. 151; the last is figured from "Statistik der Reichstagswahlen von 1898", p. 3.
[Note to the American Edition: In my study already quoted, "Verbrechen und Socialismus", I have given figures for 1903–1907, which show in general the same results.]
[2] I have chosen the crime of serious assault, because it is committed especially out of revenge, and because the figures for homicide are too small in Germany to answer for this table.
[3] Later I will explain why these figures are added.

United States, 1890–1900.[1]

States.	Number of Inhabitants in 1900 to Each Murder (Annual Average from 1890 to 1900).	Percentage of Illiteracy in Population Over 10 Years of Age (1900).	States.	Number of Inhabitants in 1900 to Each Murder (Annual Average from 1890 to 1900).	Percentage of Illiteracy in Population Over 10 Years of Age (1900).
Nevada	1,086	12.8	Nebraska	6,360	3.1
Colorado	2,141	5.2	N. Carolina	6,645	35.7
Montana	2,704	5.5	United States . . .	7,649	13.3
Texas	2,986	19.7	Rhode Island . . .	8,241	9.8
Mississippi	3,001	40.0	Missouri	8,582	9.1
Florida	3,367	27.8	S. Dakota	8,924	4.2
California	3,519	7.7	N. Dakota	11,005	6.0
Delaware	3,849	14.3	W. Virginia	11,021	14.4
Louisiana	3,859	45.8	Indiana	11,037	6.3
Alabama	3,966	41.0	Minnesota	11,105	6.0
Wyoming	4,206	3.4	Iowa	11,147	3.6
Maryland	4,250	15.7	Michigan	11,810	5.9
Arkansas	4,300	26.6	Connecticut	12,443	5.3
Utah	4,855	5.6	Ohio	12,523	5.2
Tennessee	4,957	26.6	Wisconsin	13,435	6.7
Washington	5,079	4.3	New York	14,195	5.5
Oregon	5,235	4.1	Illinois	15,306	5.2
Kentucky	5,394	21.6	New Jersey	15,697	6.5
Georgia	5,817	39.8	Pennsylvania . . .	20,169	6.8
Idaho	5,992	5.1	Massachusetts . . .	29,222	6.2
S. Carolina	6,064	45.0	Maine	38.581	3.3
Virginia	6,079	30.2	New Hampshire . .	45,732	6.8
Kansas	6,253	4.0	Vermont	57,274	6.7

Although less complete than in the preceding table, the parallelism here is nevertheless striking; all the states below the average for illiteracy, except one, rank low also in the number of murders. There are however some very remarkable exceptions to the general tendency, some states with small figures for illiteracy having nevertheless high figures for homicide. It is not possible for me to explain the cause of this, the details with regard to this country being lacking (it is very remarkable that the newest states are those that constitute the exceptions). The relation between these crimes and illiteracy is undeniable however.

[1] From *Boies*, "Science of Penology", Appendix B.

Italy, 1880–1883.[1]

Provinces.	Simple Homicides and Assaults Followed by Death to 100,000 Inhabitants.	Illiteracy among the Conscripts (1896). %[2]	Provinces.	Simple Homicides and Assaults Followed by Death to 100,000 Inhabitants.	Illiteracy among the Conscripts (1896). %
Girgenti . . .	36.5	65.15	Italy	7.0	36.65
Campobasso .	29.5	56.35	Lecce	6.9	58.57
Avellino . . .	29.5	56.07	Ascoli Piceno .	6.7	53.81
Caltanisetta . .	29.0	58.02	Pisa	6.0	35.86
Catanzaro . .	27.3	65.76	Treviso . . .	5.9	24.95
Trapani . . .	26.1	58.49	Cueno . . .	5.5	18.68
Cosenza . . .	25.7	44.17	Alessandria . .	5.2	9.86
Palermo . . .	22.3	45.21	Turin . . .	4.9	19.71
Naples . . .	22.2	45.15	Florence . . .	4.3	35.16
Potenza . . .	21.4	55.63	Genoa . . .	4.2	24.16
Caserte . . .	21.3	43.11	Mantua . . .	4.0	25.06
Aquila . . .	20.7	38.56	Udine . . .	4.0	11.08
Calabria . . .	19.5	43.95	Venice . . .	3.9	31.92
Rome	17.7	35.33	Bologna . . .	3.9	24.68
Salerno . . .	17.4	60.37	Sienna . . .	3.9	48.56
Catania . . .	16.7	64.04	Piacenza . . .	3.5	37.82
Chieti . . .	16.6	57.44	Padua . . .	3.0	34.32
Sassari . . .	16.1	53.09	Porto Maurizio	3.0	13.64
Leghorn . . .	14.0	15.68	Novara . . .	2.9	12.18
Teramo . . .	13.8	61.37	Bergama . .	2.8	27.00
Arezzo . . .	13.4	38.60	Vicenza . . .	2.5	31.41
Ancona . . .	13.1	36.24	Brescia . . .	2.5	20.72
Lucca . . .	11.9	18.49	Emilia . . .	2.4	33.08
Messina . . .	10.9	49.52	Como . . .	2.3	8.89
Forli	10.2	49.63	Pavia . . .	2.3	21.39
Grosseto . . .	10.2	61.42	Verona . . .	2.3	31.86
Bari	10.1	64.60	Ferrara . . .	2.2	36.97
Ravenna . . .	10.1	43.23	Modena . . .	1.8	35.41
Perugia . . .	10.0	48.99	Belluno . . .	1.7	25.62
Cagliari . . .	9.7	68.08	Cremona . .	1.6	12.71
Pesaro e Urbino	9.4	53.94	Milan . . .	1.4	18.85
Massa e Carrara	8.3	34.46	Parma . . .	1.1	31.68
Macerata . .	7.5	43.43			

In this country also the parallelism is undeniable; almost all the provinces with low figures for illiteracy have also low figures for criminality, and vice versa.

[1] From *Ferri*, "Atlante dell' omicidio", pp. 250, 251; the figures for illiteracy are from "Annuario statistico italiano, 1900", pp. 177, 178.

[2] To my regret I have been unable to procure the figures for 1880–1883; the differences between the provinces were, however, probably the same as for 1896.

To conclude, here are some figures with regard to

The Netherlands, 1901.[1]

PROVINCES.	ASSAULTS TO 100,000 INHAB-ITANTS.	ILLITERACY AMONG THE CONSCRIPTS. %
Drenthe	15.9	7.2
Limburg	13.7	3.6
North Brabant	12.9	4.1
Groningen	12.6	2.8
Zeeland	8.3	2.3
Overyssel	8.2	3.3
Gelderland	8.2	1.7
Netherlands	7.6	2.3
Friesland	7.3	2.3
Utrecht	6.9	1.1
South Holland	4.2	1.1
North Holland	3.8	1.2

We have here then a confirmation in a general way of the rule proved for other countries.

In view of all the preceding data we must conclude that it is the less civilized persons who commit crimes of this class. How is this to be explained? This is what we shall proceed to examine.

The first reason is that the more civilized a person is the less revengeful feelings arise when some one injures him. The more the motives of actions are appreciated, the less the desire for revenge springs up. A child wants to revenge himself even upon an inanimate object that has hurt him; it is almost the same with uncivilized peoples, who so rarely take account of the motives of human action. It is not so long ago that men took vengeance upon maniacs, a thing which could not happen today.

In the second place, when the idea of revenge arises in a civilized man he is more in a position to restrain himself than the uncivilized; he is less impulsive; he knows that later he will repent of his act, and that it may have disagreeable consequences for him.

In the third place civilization inspires a great aversion to acts of violence.

Thus we come to the correlation between these crimes and the

[1] The first column is from "De crimineele statistiek van 1901", the second from "Jaarcijfers voor het Koninkrijk der Nederlanden, 1901", p. 47.

[NOTE TO THE AMERICAN EDITION: In my study, "Misdaad en socialisme", I have given the figures for a longer period (1901–1905), which confirm in general the results given above (p. 35).]

education of the poor. The child is often moved to revenge, there is no inner check to restrain his passions. When his education has been neglected he runs, as his age advances, more danger than others of being guilty of these crimes. And then children are very imitative. If we had good statistics with regard to violent criminals we should see that they almost always spring from surroundings in which violence is common. All authors who are especially concerned with this matter are in agreement on this point.[1] The fact that parents among the lower classes use blows as a means of instruction has for its national consequence that when the children are grown they themselves have no fear of making use of violence.[2]

One further observation must be made here. Many persons think it quite natural that one should not have the right to avenge himself for an injury. Sociology, however, teaches us quite otherwise. Among primitive peoples revenge, instead of being a thing prohibited, is a sacred duty. Little by little vengeance, at first unlimited, became confined to "an eye for an eye, a tooth for a tooth"; this in turn was replaced by the so called "composition"; and this in its turn yielded to penalties inflicted by an authority superior to both parties.[3]

If we enquire which are the countries where homicides and assaults are committed most frequently we find that they are the most backward, and thus give a picture of time past. Here we have in mind especially Sicily (see the table with regard to Italy some pages higher) and Corsica (while between 1880 and 1884 there was an annual average of 6.4 homicides to the million inhabitants, the figure for homicides in Corsica was 110.2). Nothing is more mistaken than to believe that we have here a question of race. As Professor Tarde remarks (see the quotation on pp. 109–110), there have been times when the people of these countries were much less violent than the northern peoples, now so little given to this kind of crime. These two islands have so high a figure because the "vendetta" is still universal there, and because it is considered as a duty.[4]

Although in less degree, the case is almost the same with the lower classes of other countries as regards this type of crime. There are those who from their manner of life most resemble our distant ances-

[1] Cf. Moreau (of Tours), "L'homicide commis par les enfants", pp. 53 and 77; Ferriani, "Entartete Mütter", pp. 73 and 167, and "Minderjährige Verbrecher", pp. 134 ff.

[2] Cf. E. Key, "Das Jahrhundert des Kindes", p. 149.

[3] Steinmetz, "Ethnologischen Studien zur ersten Entwicklung der Strafe", I, pp. 299 ff.

[4] Cf. Colajanni, op. cit., p. 39.

tors. They are not, at least so much as other classes of society, instilled with the idea that they have no right to avenge themselves personally.   On the contrary it is often considered an act of cowardice to allow an insult or an injury to pass without taking revenge.   This is why the police are often resisted and their interference considered as an intrusive meddling with matters with which they have no concern.

Such, in my opinion, are the principal reasons why the less civilized classes are guilty of these crimes, and thus we are given an idea of their etiology.

In the first table upon the relation between illiteracy and serious assaults (Germany) we added also the percentage of votes given to the socialists.   As the table shows the percentage of these votes is in general smaller in the localities where the kind of crime of which we have been treating is most frequent; and vice versa.   It is, then, evident that there is a correlation between the two phenomena, and this is easily explained.   In the working circles in which socialism is beginning to make its way, there is growing little by little, an interest in things other than those which formerly occupied the working-men in their leisure hours.   They begin to beome civilized and to have an aversion to the coarser amusements.   At the same time the feeling of solidarity is awakened in them, and thus a powerful moral check is created.

It was especially the figures for the crimes of vengeance that we placed beside those the votes given to the socialists, since the relation between the two phenomena stands out very distinctly. This correlation, however, holds for criminality in general, for almost all the countries with a large number of socialist voters show also fairly low figures for criminality, and vice versa.   Nevertheless this correlation is not as great for other crimes as for those which we are at present considering, which is explained by the fact that most of the criminals who are guilty of them are not much like other criminals, especially those who have no respect for property (criminals from poverty excepted).   These last, greedy of pleasure, and always looking out for their own interests, are those who, as regards the intensity of their social instincts, occupy the last place.   All this is inapplicable to criminals by violence; they are not always really wicked, and after their crime they often show a sincere repentance.   Socialism exercises no influence upon the category of individuals from whom the economic criminals (from cupidity) are recruited, persons, that is to say, who think only of their own interest, and show themselves insensible to a movement for the well-being of the whole working class.

We have still to speak of one question which is sometimes put in treating of this subject. If it is true, says some one, that it is principally in consequence of their ignorance and their lack of civilization that the lower classes commit the crimes in question, these crimes must little by little present themselves less often, for the development of these classes is improving, even if only gradually. Now criminal statistics do show a gradual diminution in these crimes. Homicide, the gravest form, has continually decreased in England, Switzerland, France, and Sweden (where it has been reduced to a very small figure), and in Italy (where a considerable diminution has been shown).[1] If we had criminal statistics much more ancient than the existing ones it would be shown that this crime has decreased enormously compared with remote epochs. The progress of civilization in the lower strata of society is very slow, and criminal statistics are all of relatively recent date.

Germany is, as far as I know, the only country where there has been any considerable increase in these crimes (except those against life) in the last twenty years. This exception does not, in my opinion, invalidate the rule. The lack of civilization among the lower orders is not the sole cause of these crimes; the innumerable conflicts engendered by the present social system are also a cause. Besides, the impulse given by the economic development in Germany during this period has hardly been equalled in other countries; it has seen its population grow and become congested, and conflicts increase in like proportion,[2] a cause sufficient to neutralize the civilization which brings it about. Further there is the possibility that the police and the courts have been more efficient during this period, so as to make the increase of crime seem greater than it really is.[3] Finally, alcoholism is increasing, and may also neutralize the effect of civilization.[4]

---

[1] For Italy, in addition to the official statistics already cited, see *Colajanni*, "L'homicide en Italie", pp. 43, 44, 51–52. I have not been able to procure figures for the movement of these crimes in other countries.

[NOTE TO THE AMERICAN EDITION: Herz mentions, for Austria (1862–1899) a decrease of crimes in their most serious form and an increase in the less serious. For Scotland and Ireland the criminal statistics show a remarkable decrease; in England this decrease has been very considerable in recent years, and for all forms of these crimes. In Belgium there is a decrease for the more serious forms, the others remaining stationary. In the Netherlands there has been a decrease in recent years. In the United States the crimes in question seem to be increasing (*cf. J. W. Garner*, "Homicide in American Cities" ("Journal of Criminal Law and Criminology", III, p. 675).]

[2] *Cf. Starke*, "Verbrechen und Verbrecher in Preussen", p. 236, and *Berg*, "Getreidepreisen und Kriminalität in Deutschland seit 1882", pp. 34 *ff.*

[3] *Cf. Lux*, "Sozial-politisches Handbuch", p. 152.

[4] [NOTE TO THE AMERICAN EDITION: Later it has been shown that the last remark is perfectly correct. In recent years (about the beginning of

We come, then, to one of the most important causes of this kind of crime, namely alcoholism. Not only is chronic alcoholism demoralizing (as we have seen on pp. 509 *ff.*), but drunkenness at the acute stage makes a person more disposed to commit acts of violence, and at the same time less able to control his instincts and passions. Further, the degree of civilization reached by the individual has a great influence upon his conduct when he is intoxicated; the civilized man is then much less dangerous than the man without education. Dr. Grotjahn puts it as follows: "The development of the moral consciousness is not without influence upon the harmlessness or danger of intoxication. Persons in whom the sense of responsibility for the consequences of their actions has been sharpened by education, whether they owe this to their teachers or their parents or to their own experience, in case they become intoxicated to the point of having their minds clouded, will still always keep a remnant of their power of judgment, which will hold them back from violent and disastrous actions. On the other hand, in the case of persons who lack all moral training, the scanty moral restraints which check their native impulses most quickly disappear."

An examination of the physiological process caused by large doses of alcohol not coming properly within the scope of a sociological work like this, it is sufficient to show that great quantities of alcohol undoubtedly do have this effect.[2] We shall accordingly pass on to the question of the correlation between violent crime and the acute stage of alcoholism.

There are different ways of attempting to settle this question. In Part One we have seen that some authors have tried the dynamic method, Fornasari di Verce, for example, showing that in Italy, Great Britain, Ireland, and New South Wales, these crimes increase and diminish with the consumption of alcohol. Professor Ferri shows that during the years 1849–1880 the increase and diminution of cases of assault in France coincide with the success and failure of the vintage.[3]

---

the century), the consumption of alcohol has decreased, and also the crimes in question: *cf.* my study "Verbrechen und Sozialismus", pp. 807 *ff.*]

[1] "Der Alkoholismus", p. 57. *Cf. O. Lang,* "Alkoholgenusz und Verbrechen", pp. 50, 51.

[2] See *A. Baer,* "Der Alkoholismus", pp. 30 *ff.; Grotjahn, op. cit.,* pp. 52 *ff.; Aschaffenburg,* "Alkoholgenusz und Verbrechen", pp. 73–77 ("Zeitschr. f. ges. Strafw.", XX. This is also to be found in "Das Verbrechen und seine Bekämpfung", pp. 69–72.)

[3] "Sociologie criminelle", p. 222.

[NOTE TO THE AMERICAN EDITION: *Cf.* for Germany *Bonger, op. cit.,* pp. 807 *ff.;* for Austria: *Herz, op. cit.,* pp. 57 *ff.;* for Belgium: *Jacquart, op. cit.,* pp. 98 *ff.;* and for the Netherlands: *Bonger, op. cit.,* p. 27.]

Another method consists in inquiring what day of the week assaults are most frequent. If the abuse of alcohol is really an important factor in the etiology of these crimes more of them must be committed upon Sunday, Saturday, and Monday, for the abuse of alcohol is greatest on these days. The following table throws some light on the matter.[1]

NUMBER OF ASSAULTS COMMITTED ON DIFFERENT DAYS.

	VIENNA (1896–97).	KORNEUBURG (1896–97).	CANTON OF ZURICH (1890).	DUSSELDORF.	WORMS (1896–98).
Sunday	68	72	60	121	142
Monday	49	12	22	32	57
Tuesday	27	11		9	34
Wednesday	19	14	41	9	34
Thursday	19	15		5	35
Friday	18	4		4	27
Saturday	28	11	18	35	37

The figures and the thesis agree, then, perfectly. It is plain, to be sure, that we cannot charge all the cases falling on Sunday to alcohol, since people come together more on that day, and hence the danger of a conflict is greater, but most of the Sunday cases are certainly due to alcohol.

Other authors compare the geography of these crimes with the consumption of alcohol. Professor Aschaffenburg, for example, in the study already quoted, points out the fact that in Germany the countries with the greatest number of assaults are also those where there is the largest consumption of alcohol.[2]

However, although these indirect methods are not without value, it seems to me that since they contain so many elements of uncertainty they yield to the direct method.[3] It is for this reason that I shall follow here especially the direct method and shall indicate the percentage of those who have committed these crimes when they were in a state of intoxication. Though making use of this direct method I do not think it infallible, but it is less liable to error than the others.

---

[1] The first two columns have been taken from *Löffler*, "Alkohol und Verbrechen", pp. 533, 534; the third from *Lang, op. cit.*, p. 43; and the two others from *Aschaffenburg, op. cit.*, pp. 86 and 88.

[NOTE TO THE AMERICAN EDITION: See also: *E. Kürz*, "Zur Prophylaxe der Roheitsdelikte", and *C. Hotter*, "Alkohol und Verbrechen in Niederbayrn."]

[2] P. 92: See also *Merens*, "Over het onderzoek narr den invloed der dronkenschap op de criminaliteit", pp. 170–200.

[3] See the criticism of these methods in *Merens, op. cit.*, pp. 128 *ff.*

The especial weakness of it is that the persons who are accused pretend in extenuation that they committed their crimes in a state of drunkenness.   Good statistics do not rely solely upon the statements of the prisoners, but also upon the facts brought out at the trial. And then, as Professor Löffler remarks, all those arraigned are not acute enough to simulate a state of drunkenness, and there are even those who, although addicted to overindulgence in alcohol, will deny that they were intoxicated, either from shame, or for fear of a more severe punishment.

Most criminal statistics do not concern themselves with this subject, and even those that do are less detailed than we might wish.   Nevertheless they are sufficient, I believe, to prove the correlation in question.

Austria, 1896–1897.[1]

CRIMES.	PERCENTAGE OF CONVICTS WHO COMMITTED THEIR CRIMES IN A STATE OF DRUNKENNESS.	
	Vienna.	Korneuburg.
Rebellion	77.7	70.0
Malicious mischief	63.4	43.5
Threats	56.8	46.7
Serious assaults	54.1	56.4

Baden (Grand Duchy), 1895.

In 1895 64% of the cases of rebellion and 46% of the assaults were committed in a state of inebriety.[2]

Belgium, 1872–1895.

Out of the 2,045 convicts who entered the central prison at Louvain from 1874 to 1895, 344 or 16.8% were drunk at the time of committing the crime; of the 130 sentenced to hard labor for life 53, or 40.7%; of the 88 condemned to death 38, or 43.1%.[3]   If we consider that a very great number of these criminals were guilty of economic crimes, and doubtless did not commit these in a state of intoxication, the percentage of those who must have committed crimes of vengeance in such a condition becomes very large.

[1] *Löffler, op. cit.*, pp. 518–521.   [2] *Aschaffenburg, op. cit.*, p. 85.
[3] *Masoin*, "L'alcoolisme dans ses rapports avec la criminalité", pp. 410–414 ("Bulletin de l'académie royale de médecine de Belgique", 1896).
[NOTE TO THE AMERICAN EDITION : For Austria see *Herz, op. cit.*, pp. 31 *ff.*, and for the Netherlands : *Bonger, op. cit.*, p. 35.]

France.

At the penitentiary congress at Brussels Marambat reported that out of a total of 787 convicted of homicide, assault, etc., studied by him, there were 260 or 33% who committed their crimes in a state of drunkenness.[1]

Hungary, 1897.

At the same congress Dr. J. Fekete stated that in 1897, 75% of the 25,000 street brawls, 66% of the 1,574 cases of resistance to the authorities, 50% of the 13,564 serious assaults, and most of the homicides were committed in a state of intoxication.[2]

Massachusetts, 1894–1895.[3]

CRIMES.	PERCENTAGE OF CRIMES COMMITTED IN A STATE OF INTOXICATION.
Malicious mischief	70.0
Homicide	64.7
Threats and violence	59.6
Murder	25.0
Resistance to officers	19.0

Norway, 1886–1889.[4]

CRIMES.	PERCENTAGE OF PRISONERS WHO HAD COMMITTED THEIR CRIMES IN A STATE OF INTOXICATION.
Resistance to officers	81.8
Homicide	66.6
Assault	55.0
Threats	40.0

Netherlands, 1901.

The criminal statistics of the Netherlands being among the few that give any information upon this point, the following table is of real importance : [5]

CRIMES.	PERCENTAGE OF CONVICTS WHO COMMITTED THEIR CRIMES IN A STATE OF INTOXICATION.
Serious assaults	51.88
Resistance to officers	58.04
Malicious mischief	41.69
Threats	39.77
Assaults	31.27

[1] "Actes etc.", p. 113.
[NOTE TO THE AMERICAN EDITION: For France see also *M. Yvernès*, "L'alcoolisme et la criminalité" ("Archives d'anthr. crim.", XXVII).]
[2] "Actes etc.", p. 58.
[3] *Merens, op. cit.*, p. 126.
[4] *Merens, op. cit.*, p. 107.
[5] "Crimineele Statistiek, 1901", pp. xxvi–xxvii.

Sweden, 1887–1897.

During this period, out of 2,020 convicted of crimes against the authorities, 1,648, or 81.5%, had committed their crimes in a state of intoxication, and 4,358, or 67.4% out of 6,464 convicted of murder, homicide, and other crimes of violence.[1]

Switzerland, 1892–1896.

The official statistics for these years tell us that 34.8% of the assaults and homicides were caused by alcohol.[2]

It cannot be claimed, of course, that none of these crimes would have been committed if their authors had not been drunk, but everyone will agree with me that these high percentages show that acute alcoholism is a very important cause.

We have now reached the end of our remarks upon the etiology of these crimes, and have shown that the principal causes are, first, the present structure of society, which brings about innumerable conflicts; second, the lack of civilization and education among the poorer classes; and third, alcoholism, which is in turn a consequence of the social environment.[3]

What part is played in these crimes by the so-called individual factors? It seems to me that it is like that which the individual factors play in other crimes — they explain in part which are the individuals that commit the crimes, but they do not explain why the crimes are committed.

This is totally contrary to what many criminologists claim, namely that it is especially the effect of individual factors that is seen in these crimes. Statistics prove the inaccuracy of this. If it were true these crimes ought to appear equally in all classes of society, which, as we have seen, is not the case. A choleric person naturally runs more danger of committing such a crime than one who is phlegmatic; but no one will deny that in all classes the proportion of the persons born with a choleric disposition is the same. However, the influence of environment brings it about that in the well-to-do classes even the

---

[1] *Wieselgren*, "Rapport sur l'influence de l'alcoolisme sur la criminalité" ("Actes du Congrès pénitent. de Bruxelles").

[2] P. 36.

[3] [NOTE TO THE AMERICAN EDITION: In his "Anthropologie der nicht-besitzenden Klassen", *Niceforo* defends the thesis that the crimes in question are caused by the physiological poverty of the poor classes, in its turn a consequence of environment (pp. 369 *ff.*).]

choleric run little danger of such a crime. Superficial civilization (for a veneer is all that a great part of the bourgeoisie possesses) is sufficient to limit these crimes to an insignificant minimum.

The obviousness of the reasons which have caused these acts to be classed as crimes is such that it is needless to speak of them. In a society like ours, with its numerous conflicts and its dense population, life would be impossible if the individual were not forbidden to avenge himself personally. Sociology teaches us that vengeance, at first permitted, and even obligatory, has become a prohibited act, because of the great harm it does to society.[1]

B. INFANTICIDE.

There are two chief motives for infanticide, which operate separately or together, namely, fear of dishonor, and poverty. We shall speak first of the former and put the question to begin with, what sort of persons are guilty of this crime? Criminal statistics answer that —

First, they are, almost without exception, women.

Second, they are unmarried women much oftener than married.

Third, the guilty are almost exclusively very poor. According to Italian statistics 88.1% of them are indigent; in Austria, 90.8%; and there are no rich or well-to-do women among them.

Fourth, the women of the working class are much more often guilty than those of the independent class, and the class of domestics furnishes especially a very high figure (Germany). These results are confirmed by the data of other countries. In Austria 80% of those convicted between 1880 and 1882 were domestics,[2] and in France the same was true of 35% of those convicted between 1876 and 1880.[3]

Fifth, the women working in the fields are especially likely to fall into this crime (Germany); the data of other countries also show that it is especially in the country that infanticide is committed. Dr. Socquet shows that in France between 1871 and 1875 there were, to the million inhabitants, 35 persons arraigned out of the rural population, and 22 to the urban.[4]

Sixth, illiteracy is very frequent among those convicted of infanticide. We have seen that in Austria 39.5%, in France 20.0%, and

[1] Cf. Steinmetz, op. cit., I, Pt. III.
[2] T. W. Teifen, "Das soziale Elend und die besitzenden Klassen in Oesterreich", p. 171.
[3] Socquet, "Contribution à l'étude statistique de la criminalité en France, 1876–1880", p. 41.
[4] Op. cit., p. 36.

in Italy 92.9% were illiterate. Women knowing more than how to read and write were not found among these criminals.

Most of the cases of infanticide are identical; it generally is, as Fournier says, "a girl who has allowed herself to have a child without the permission of the municipality", and who has been abandoned by her lover.

The ruling moral ideas place before her a frightful dilemma; if her pregnancy is known by those about her and the child remains alive, she is covered with ignominy, and a painful life awaits her. On the other hand if she makes the child disappear, the others ignore everything, and she avoids dishonor and its consequences. She therefore attempts to conceal her pregnancy as long as possible, in the hope of a miscarriage. But when she finds herself disappointed, when not only terrible physical pains, but also mental tortures are making her almost mad [1] — then it happens that she kills her child.

Statistics show that most of these crimes are committed by women of the lower classes. The number of unmarried mothers is here relatively great; infanticide is quite rare (though a little more frequent than one would suppose from the criminal statistics). There must be special circumstances, therefore, to lead some of these women to this crime. As we have seen in treating of marriage, the ideas of intimate relations between persons who are not married are much less severe in the proletariat, than in the bourgeoisie (a consequence of the fact that the social causes of marriage are much less strong in the latter than in the former), so that among the proletariat these relations are pretty common. If they have consequences, the father and mother generally marry. In this case the idea of killing the child does not come to the woman. The unmarried mothers (very often domestics), who are guilty of this crime are especially those who, seduced and then abandoned by men of a higher class, have no family that can receive them.

Besides women of the working class, there are also among the infanticides some of the petty bourgeoisie, where the moral disapproval of extra-matrimonial sexual commerce is very severe.

Not all women who find themselves in the situation described commit the crime in question, of course. One will reason more than another, and will prefer dishonor to the danger of a criminal trial; one woman has the maternal instinct more fully developed than another, etc. In relation to the social sentiments we see here a situa-

---

[1] Cf. Dr. Audriffent, "Quelques considérations sur l'infanticide", p. 5 ("Archives d'anthrop. crim.", XVII).

tion contrary to what occurs in the case of most crimes. Crime is an egoistic act, that is to say an act which injures the interests of others. This is true of infanticide, but this differs from most of the other crimes in being committed to escape moral disapproval, while they are committed only to obtain a personal profit or to satisfy the passions. This is why those guilty of infanticide are not generally those whose social sentiments have little intensity, as is mostly the case with those who are guilty of economic or sexual crimes. Infanticides are persons sensitive to the opinion of others, while those who have little social feeling easily bear shame.[1]

These individual differences explain in part which are the individuals who become guilty of the crime in question, but not the cause of its existence. There are only a few crimes whose social origin is as clear as that of infanticide. If the present structure of society did not make the present form of marriage necessary, and thus bring about moral disapprobation of extra-matrimonial sexual relations, there would be no infanticide caused by fear of dishonor.[2]

The repression of some of the strongest *natural* desires, required by our present *society*, is so great that these requirements are bound to be violated by some individuals in whom these desires are very pronounced. This is true not only in the sphere of the economic life, but also in that of the sexual life. As long as cupidity is awakened in many, while only a few can satisfy it, theft will exist; as long as the satisfaction of the sexual desires is permitted only after certain economic conditions have been complied with, the prohibition will be violated, and some persons will try to destroy the evidence of their acts.[3]

Besides the fear of shame, poverty also plays a part in the etiology of infanticide. Again, it is the two motives combined that are responsible. The great number of infanticides among domestics are not committed simply from fear of shame, but also because the mother, abandoned by everyone (especially in a country where inquiry into paternity is prohibited) does not know how to support her child. Besides these cases there are some committed from

---

[1] *Cf. Starke*, "Verbrechen und Verbrecher in Preussen", p. 156; *Loosjes*, "Bijdrage tot de studie van de criminaliteit der vrouw", pp. 164, 165; *Lombroso*, "La femme criminelle et la prostituée", p. 494; *Joly*, "Le crime", pp. 263, 264.

[2] In his "Evolution de la morale", *Letourneau* points out that in countries where public opinion is very indulgent to female frailty, infanticide is almost unknown (p. 73).

[3] *Cf. Brissot de Warville*, "Théorie des lois criminelles", I, p. 95. Of a literature that has long been copious may be named, especially, the interesting work of *Pestalozzi*, "Ueber Gesetzgebung und Kindermord."

poverty alone, for example when married women commit this crime (something, it should be added, which happens very rarely).

Some statistical data will show that poverty is a fairly important factor in the etiology of infanticide. Dr. Weiss shows that in *Belgium* infanticide increased greatly in the years that were bad economically (see p. 63 of Pt. I), and Dr. Starke does the same for *Prussia* (see p. 66).[1]

As we have pointed out above, infanticide for the cause of poverty was quite general among primitive peoples, since they were not in a position to support a large population. It was for this reason that the act was not considered immoral, and that it was even required in some cases. In consequence of the continually increasing productivity of labor, infanticide fell more and more into desuetude, and at the same time was considered more and more reprehensible.[2]

---

[1] *Cf. Sutherland*, "Origin and Growth of the Moral Instinct", I, pp. 113 *ff*.

[2] [NOTE TO THE AMERICAN EDITION: Of the recent literature upon infanticide I would call attention to: *W. Gleispach*, "Ueber Kindesmord", *A. Amschl*, "Das Verbrechen des Kindesmordes nach oesterreichischem Recht"; *G. van Dijck*, "Eenige beschowvingen over het misdrijf van kindermord"; *W. Kürbitz-Sonnenschein*, "Der Geisteszustand der Kindermörderinnen."]

CHAPTER V.

POLITICAL CRIMES.

FINALLY we have still to treat of political offenses, offenses which, in comparison with others, occur very rarely, and which by their nature are totally different.[1]

The origin of the state, and the possibility of political crimes, are bound up with a certain phase of the development of the economic life, that is to say with the origin of marked contrasts of fortune. Those who had monopolized the power in the state defended their position by laws whose infraction was threatened with severe penalties. Economic conditions, however, undergo considerable changes, and when these have reached a certain degree, the oppressed class, having become the more powerful, breaks the political power of the ruling class and seizes it for itself. If the dominant class does all that it can to maintain its position unimpaired to the last moment, it will necessarily happen that this development will lead to political crimes. This kind of political crime may be called great political criminality. In western Europe the last great struggle of this nature was that of the feudal classes and the bourgeoisie. The former, once necessary, had become superfluous and harmful; the bourgeoisie on the other hand, from an insignificant class had become the most important. It overturned the whole political system which embarrassed it, seized the power, and transformed the state according to the exigencies of the economic system. A repetition of the same process in eastern Europe we are now witnessing in the changes going on in Russia. The economic development no longer corresponds to the political system,

---

[1] It seems to me that *Lombroso* and *Laschi* extend the conception of political crime too much in making it any revolt against the authorities, as they do in their work, "Der politische Verbrecher und die Revolutionen." Very often these troubles are only more or less serious fights with the police and have no political character at all. Opinions may differ as to the value of Professor Lombroso's works, but I cannot imagine how any one can admire his work upon political crime. It is full of mistakes and superficial observations.

which sooner or later will inevitably be replaced by the modern system.

It would be a waste of time to insist upon the fact that those who commit these acts have nothing in common with ordinary criminals but the name. Most criminals are individuals whose social sentiments are reduced to a minimum, and who injure others purely for the satisfaction of their own desires. The political criminals of whom we are speaking, on the other hand, are the direct opposite; they risk their most sacred interests, their liberty and their life, for the benefit of society; they injure the ruling class only to aid the oppressed classes, and consequently all humanity. While the ordinary criminal is generally "l'homme canaille" (as van Benedikt phrases it in his "Biologie und Kriminalstatistik") the political criminal is "homo nobilis." History rights the matter, for the name of the ordinary great criminal is pronounced only with horror, and ends by falling into oblivion, while the political criminal survives in the memory of posterity as a hero.[1]

We must put in the same class the political criminals who aim to deliver a subjugated people from their oppressors. The authors of these crimes also have nothing in common with ordinary criminals.

Besides these two kinds of political crimes, which are plainly collective in their nature, there are cases of crimes committed by individuals which for the most part are attempts upon the life of the monarch or of one of his representatives. The more absolute a government, the more liberty is restricted, and the less chance there is, consequently, of seeing the situation changed by legal means, the greater will become the danger that one of those oppressed will kill the autocrat, either to better the situation or to take revenge for what he and his have suffered. Anyone who wants to follow the genesis of this kind of crime has only to turn to Russia. There all the factors meet which lead to political homicide; the repression of all freedom, a corrupt bureaucracy, and the impossibility of obtaining the least change by legal means.

These circumstances naturally excite the revengeful feelings which sooner or later show themselves in acts. Though we may have the conviction that these acts are almost always useless, though we may have a deep aversion to violence — this does not justify us in ranking those who do these things with ordinary criminals. It matters not

---

[1] [NOTE TO THE AMERICAN EDITION: Cf. *Vallon* and *Genil-Perrin*, "Crime et altruisme" ("Archives d'anthr. crim.", XXVIII).]

how we may abhor violence as such; every reasonable man will
justify it when it serves to defend oneself, and most of the acts of
political criminals in Russia are only acts of defense against the
unheard-of cruelty and violence of the government.[1]

Finally there remains a third kind of political crimes, analogous to
ordinary crime, the assassination of the monarch by individuals who
thus attempt to place themselves in power.   These are actuated by
the same vile motives that inspire the robber-murderer — cupidity,
desire to dominate, etc.

Now what are the political crimes committed in our days?   Leaving
aside the case of Russia, which is still living in an epoch that western
Europe has left behind, there are only the political crimes of socialists
and anarchists.   There is little to be said about those committed
by socialists.   The international social democracy attempts to
reach its end by legal means.   Since the fall of absolutism it has
been possible to exercise an influence on the state in this way, an
influence which varies with the country.   It is this possibility that
the social democracy makes use of.   In conformity with its fundamental principles it rejects all violence against the head of the state.
Accordingly its partisans have never committed such acts.   The
more democratic the constitution of a country, the less justification
the social democracy will have for political crimes, as in Switzerland,
for example, a country where the penal code, moreover, mentions but
few political crimes.   In other countries, where the democratic
institutions are weak, where the constitutional monarchy has still an
absolutist character, and where social democracy has become powerful, as in Germany, political crimes are inevitable.   Their number,
however, is insignificant in comparison with ordinary crimes.   From
a criminological point of view they have little importance, though
often punished severely, and they are generally limited to the crime
of leze majesty.   Social democrats are, then, sometimes guilty of
minor political offenses, and in some countries only.   Whether this
party will not in the future be guilty of crime of the great political
type, or, in other words, whether it will not come to political revolution, is another question and one that no one can answer with certainty.   Like all the bourgeoisie when the contest with the feudal
classes was still going on, the social democrats are a revolutionary
class; they wish to place society upon a basis different from the

---

[1] [NOTE TO THE AMERICAN EDITION: *Cf.* upon political crimes in Russia:
E. Tarnowsky, "Les crimes politiques en Russie" ("Archives d'anthr. crim."
XII), and *A. Wadler*, "Die politische Verbrechen in Russland" ("Zeitschr.
f. d. ges. Strafrw." XXIX).]

present one. It is possible that in democratic countries they will attain this by legal means, and consequently without there being any reason for political crime. However, it may also happen that at a given moment when the proletariat forms the majority of the legislative body, the ruling class may have recourse to a "coup d'état", to a political crime, in order to prevent the proletariat from governing. This possibility is even a probability in some countries, where the opposition of classes is very marked. In Germany, for example, where the social democracy is very powerful, it is very likely that the government will attempt some day to suppress universal suffrage by a "coup d'état." It is only in such a case that the social democracy will in its turn abandon the legal way and be forced to have recourse to other methods.

In the second place there are the political crimes of anarchists. Their number is not great enough for us to learn their etiology from statistics.[1] We must therefore analyze individual cases. What are the individuals that are guilty of these? The anarchists of the propaganda are most exclusively young men. Leauthier and Langs were 20 years old, Angelillo also, Henry 21, Caserio 21, Schwabe 23, Pallas 24, Lucheni 25, Vaillant and Bresci 31, and Salvador 33, at the time they committed their crimes, and as far as I know there were none of them who were over 33. In disposition they were very excitable. As soon as an idea took hold of them they thought of nothing else. Chance brought them into contact with anarchism which immediately made a conquest of them. Brought up in another environment they would have become, for example, religious devotees; in fact Caserio, Salvador, Vaillant, Cyvoct, and Henry were such before becoming anarchists.[2]

Extreme individualism is also a characteristic of theirs.[3] They abhor discipline, from which it follows that they nourish a fierce hatred of militarism. Even a mild form of discipline, such as that of a party of which one voluntarily becomes a member, is insupportable to them. Some of them have been socialists, but have soon left the party. Among these was Henry, who says in his defense: "For an instant I was attracted by socialism, but I did not delay in separating myself from this party. I had too much love for liberty, too much respect for individual initiative, too much repugnance to

---

[1] See *Dubois*, "Le péril anarchiste", pp. 25 *ff.*; *Aubry*, "La contagion du meurtre", pp. 256 *ff.*; and *Enthoven*, "Het anarchism van de daad", ch. II.

[2] *Cf. Lombroso*, "Les anarchistes", p. 116.

[3] *Cf. Hamon*, "Psychologie de l'anarchiste-socialiste", ch. IV.

incorporation, to take a number in the enlisted army of the fourth estate." [1]

Another characteristic of nearly all active anarchists, and one intimately connected with the preceding, is great vanity. Lucheni, for instance, in speaking of his crime said, "I wanted to kill a person of note, because that would get into print." Vaillant had himself photographed before making his attack, distributed his portraits right and left, and when arrested asked whether the journals had printed his picture, etc.

These traits of character, observed in the case of these individuals, are not rare; vain and excitable individualists are fairly numerous, yet almost none become active anarchists. We must therefore seek the explanation elsewhere, and ask ourselves the question, in what environment have they lived? When the president of the tribunal before which Lucheni appeared, asked him what was the motive that led him to commit his act, he replied, "It was poverty." This is applicable to almost all the active anarchists. See, for example, the life of Vaillant. An illegitimate child without any education, he had to earn his living at the age of 12; having escaped from his employer, with whom he was living, he implored his mother to take him in. Rebuffed he had himself arrested by the police, but when he was once more brought back to his parents they refused anew to receive him. He tried to make his own way, but failed in all that he undertook. It was when embittered by all the miseries he had experienced that he became acquainted with socialism, but finding this too theoretical he ranked himself on the side of the anarchists, and the last link in this chain of misery was his well-known crime.[2]

There are authors who claim that poverty is not to be considered as one of the principal causes of anarchy, and in support of their assertion cite the case of Henry and some others, who while not living in easy circumstances, yet did not know the blackest poverty. Those who reason thus have a false notion of the motives that impel anarchists. It is not only the poverty that they have themselves experienced that moves them, but also, and chiefly, the poverty of others. Those who remain insensible to the sufferings of their neighbors never become anarchists; for not being able to draw any personal profit from anarchism, they consider it madness. Placed in unfavorable conditions such persons become ordinary criminals, or commit suicide. They never sacrifice themselves for an ideal.

[1] *Lombroso*, "Les anarchistes", pp. 143, 144.
[2] *Cf. Seuffert*, "Anarchismus und Strafrecht", pp. 12 *ff*.

Thus we come to another psychological trait of the anarchists, namely that they are born with pronounced altruistic tendencies.[1] It is their altruism which separates them from the ordinary great criminal, whose social instincts are very weak.[2]

It seems paradoxical to say that persons who commit such acts are of an altruistic nature, but the paradox is only apparent. When two persons, an egoist and an altruist, see a child being maltreated, the former goes on his way saying that he would only get himself into trouble if he interfered; the latter, on the other hand, delivers the child from his tormentor, to whom he may give a good thrashing in addition. Here the violent person is the altruist, the other the egoist. Every comparison is imperfect, and this is the case with the one before us, but there is some analogy between the act cited and those of the anarchists. The crimes which they commit are egoistic towards certain persons, but altruistic with reference to others. As a consequence of their own poverty and of the irritation they feel when they see that of their fellows, they have been seized with a hatred of society and wish to avenge themselves. These sentiments are not tempered by much intellectual development. This is a very important factor in the development of active anarchism. Almost all these persons are either very ignorant or have only an elementary education, some know a little more, and persons of thorough education are not found at all among them. Further, most of them lack pronounced intellectual aptitudes, but are rather especially impulsive.[3]

These individuals, excitable, vain, with little intellectual capacity, and ignorant in addition, but oppressed by their own poverty and that of others, and filled with a hatred of society, come into contact with anarchism. It is unnecessary to give an exposition of this doctrine; [4] the active anarchists in their ignorance get no clear idea of

---

[1] *Cf. Hamon, op. cit.*, ch. V, and *Lombroso,* "Les anarchistes", pp. 131 *ff.*

[2] Some authors claim that active anarchists are ordinary criminals. But see *Hamon, op. cit.*, p. 15.

[3] With regard to Caserio see *Lacassagne,* "L'assassinat du président Carnot", pp. 535 and 539, and the unsigned article, "Caserio en prison", both in "Arch. d'anthr. crim.", LX and XVI respectively.

[NOTE TO THE AMERICAN EDITION: Upon Lucheni see further *Forel,* "Verbrechen und Konstitutionelle Seelenabnormalitäten" and *Ladame* and *Régis,* "Le regicide Lucheni." The books of *H. Varennes,* "De Ravachol à Caserio", and of *Hesse,* "Les criminels peints par eux-mêmes" III, "L'apostolat", contain interesting information upon the active anarchists.]

[4] An exposition of the anarchistic theories has been given by *Dr. Eltzbacher,* "Der Anarchismus", and a very just critique of this subject is that of *Plechanow,* "Anarchismus und Sozialismus."

[NOTE TO THE AMERICAN EDITION: Upon Anarchism in general see further: *H. Zoccoli,* "Die anarchie."]

any theory whatever, and certainly not of anything as vague and confused as anarchism. They have heard it said that it looks to the formation of a society of altruists where there will be no more poverty, and this appeals to their altruistic instincts; at the same time anarchism gives a preponderating part to the individual, and this draws their vanity. Thus their hate increases, and at the same time attaches itself to certain individuals, whom anarchism holds responsible for existing conditions. Further, the absurd opinion has been instilled into them that it is possible for society to be reorganized at a single stroke, and that to attain this end it will be necessary to use violence.

Is it astonishing that such individuals come to attempt homicide? No; to be sure all persons of this kind do not go so far; for that it would be necessary that other conditions should be complied with. It is plain that persons with a great aversion to violence would run little risk of attempting an assassination, with others it is courage that is lacking; others still attach too high a price to life and liberty to be willing to risk them; etc. We must note this last point especially. Generally active anarchists are persons who care nothing for a life in which they have nothing further to lose. Their conduct in court and their indifference in the face of death are proof of this; knowing beforehand that they will almost certainly not go unpunished their act is often an indirect suicide.

If we ask what the active anarchists wish to attain by their crimes the answer is principally that they wish to avenge upon society the misery experienced by others and by themselves,[1] they wish to terrorize the ruling classes, in order to force upon them social reforms; they wish to set an example to the working classes and finally, they wish to satisfy their vanity, by making themselves talked of. Once committed, the crime is often the commencement of a vicious circle, since society avenges itself upon the author, who, in turn, is avenged by his friends; imitation thus leading to new crimes.

As in the case of all other crimes, I find for anarchism only social causes, and in the last analysis, only economic causes. To be sure, the individuals who commit these crimes are already predisposed in that direction, but this is true of other crimes also. Only the predisposition in these latter is simple, while that which leads to anarchistic crimes is much more complex. However, this predisposition alone explains nothing. I would ask those who think that only individual factors play any part, whether fanatical persons with

---

[1] *Tarde*, "Les crimes de haine" ("Arch. d'anthr. crim.", IX, reproduced also in "Essais et mélanges sociologiques").

all the characteristics of the anarchists of our time have not been found in all ages and countries. Everyone, I think, will answer in the affirmative. Well then, anarchistic crimes have occurred only during a certain period and in certain countries. No one can deny that there are as many persons predisposed to anarchistic crimes in a country like Germany, as there are in Italy, for example. Yet anarchistic crimes do not occur in Germany, for the good reason that the material conditions of the proletariat there are so much better than in Italy, and the degree of intellectual development in the working people is so much higher; the German working-man derides the "naïveté" of the anarchists, and detests their futile crimes. It is in the environment alone then that we find the causes of active anarchism, the poverty and ignorance in which the lower classes live.

CHAPTER VI.

PATHOLOGICAL CRIMES.

So far we have been examining crime in its relation to the economic and social environment. We have not been able to discover the existence of individual factors; the celebrated formula, "crime = individual factor + social factor," has been shown to be incorrect if we are seeking for the causes of crime instead of asking why a certain individual has become a criminal. The conclusion obtained by sociology is the same as that arrived at in anthropology by authors like Manouvrier, Baer, and Näcke.

However, when one is trying to determine the cause of crime by sociology, certain cases are at times met with that cannot be explained in this way. For example, one person will steal useless objects which he is perfectly well able to buy; another will assault or kill without provocation, etc. These cases, it is true, are the exception, but they do exist and must not be neglected.[1] We have here, then, real individual factors, factors which are found in certain individuals only. Other crimes, forming the great majority, are committed from motives which form the basis of all human acts, but are stronger with some few than they are with the general body of mankind. It is these individuals who run more danger than most of committing a crime when they live in a certain environment. The great mass of criminals differ only quantitatively from persons who never get into the courts; the criminals we are about to consider on the other hand differ qualitatively also.

One thing more before we ask ourselves what this individual factor is. As many authors have remarked, it very often happens that, even in the cases we are about to treat, there is a social factor.[2]

---

[1] It is impossible to fix the percentage of these cases, the judges in general not being enough in touch with modern ideas etc.

[2] See *Benedikt*, "Biologie und Kriminalstatistik", p. 489 ("Zeitschr. f. d. ges. Strw.", VII): *Näcke*, "Verbrechen und Wahnsinn beim Weibe",

The proof of this is that individuals thus disposed to crime, but belonging to the well-to-do classes, seldom get to the point of committing them; because their education being better, the tendency is sooner noticed, they are better watched, and thus their committing a crime is often avoided. Born-criminals, in the sense of those who become criminals *whatever the circumstances may be* (the only meaning that can properly be given to the word "born" here), are doubtless very rare.[1]

What, then, is the nature of this individual factor? It is especially the Italian school that has busied itself with this problem, and in doing so has rendered a service to science, although it has given an undue importance to this individual factor, attempting to discover it in all crimes. The first hypothesis given by Professor Lombroso was that of atavism, according to which the criminal was an individual in whom reappeared the characteristics of his remote ancestors, the desire to steal, kill, etc. It will not be far from the truth if we assert that almost no reputable scientist now accepts this hypothesis as correct. It has been attacked both from the side of sociology and from that of anthropology. Sociologists have proved that the facts contradict Professor Lombroso's thesis, for primitive peoples are neither thieves nor murderers, and our ancestors, consequently, may be regarded as cleared of the same charge.[2]

Anthropologists also are strongly opposed to this hypothesis. In his article, "De geboren misdadiger" (the born-criminal) Professor Jelgersma says that most of the anomalies observed in certain criminals have no atavistic character, such as unsymmetrical eyes and ears, abnormal growth of hair, etc.[3] Dr. A. Baer makes the same remark in his "Der Verbrecher in anthropologischer Beziehung", and goes on as follows: "The number of such abnormalities, which betray a disordered and an apparently geniune atavistic condition, is . . . so small and so accidental, that no force can be recognized in them that

p. 175; "Die neuren Erscheinung auf kriminal-anthropologischem Gebiete und ihre Bedeutung", p. 340 ("Zeitschr. f. d. ges. Strw.", XIV).

[NOTE TO THE AMERICAN EDITION: Cf. *Th. Ziehen*, "Die Erkennung der psychopathischen Konstitutionen und die öffentliche Fürsorge für psychopathisch veranlagte Kinder", and *Stier, op. cit.*, p. 99.]

[1] [NOTE TO THE AMERICAN EDITION: Cf. *R. Gaupp*, "Ueber den heutigen Stand des Lehre vom 'geborenen' Verbrecher", and *J. Longard*, "Ueber 'Moral insanity.'" *De Lanessan* truly says that although these individual causes are found in equal proportions in the two sexes, women are much less criminal than men ("Le lutte contre le crime", p. 146).]

[2] See above, pp. 439 *ff.* Also *Patijn*, "Atavisme en Misdaad", ("Tijdschrift v. Strafr.", V).

[3] P. 106, "Tijdschrift v. Strafrecht", VI.

might serve for the explanation of criminality, or establish a causal connection with the criminal nature of an individual. Out of this mixture of stigmata of the most various origin and importance, to attempt to find the sole basis in their atavistic character is to do more than permissible violence to the facts.[1]

After this beginning the Italian school put forth another explanation, to which it attached the more importance as the hypothesis of atavism fell into discredit: the criminal is either an epileptic or morally insane. Although the correctness of this hypothesis has not been proved any more than the other,[2] the Italian school here found itself in a field recognized by criminal-anthropologists as its true one. At present one has even the right to say that the opinion in this regard is almost unanimous.[3] *The origin of the tendencies of part of the criminals is to be found in the pathological nature of the individuals themselves.*[4] These are disordered or degenerate, not, as some authors would have us believe, individuals differing more or less from the average, but persons who suffer from mental diseases, or whose nervous system is affected.[5]

Among those disordered and degenerate, some individuals [6] have tendencies not found in others (such as the desire to kill for the sake of killing), or their moral sentiments are excessively weak. It is to be noticed that we have met with degeneracy above, as it is to be named among the causes of alcoholism and prostitution also. In treating of economic crimes we saw that degenerates also run more danger than others of succumbing in the struggle for existence, and hence become criminals more easily. Thus we meet degeneracy both as a direct and as an indirect cause of crime.

---

[1] P. 339. In further refutation from the anthropological standpoint see *Ch. Féré*, "Dégénérescence et criminalité", ch. V; *Manouvrier*, "L'atavisme et le crime" ("L'ère nouvelle", 1894); *Dallemagne*, "Les théories de la criminalité", ch. I; and *Aschaffenburg*, "Das Verbrechen und seine Bekämpfung", pp. 170, 171.

[2] Upon the criminal as morally insane see: *Baer, op. cit.*, pp. 380 *ff.*; *Näcke, op. cit.*, p. 341; and *Dallemagne, op. cit.*, ch. III.

Upon the criminal as epileptic see: *Baer, op. cit.*, pp. 384 *ff.*; *Dallemagne, op. cit.*, ch. III; and *Aschaffenburg, op. cit.*, p. 172.

[3] *Cf. Lacassagne* and *E. Martin*, "Des résultats positifs et indiscutables que l'anthropologie criminelle peut fournir à l'élaboration ou l'application des lois" (Compte rendu du Ve Congres d'anthrop. crim.).

[4] *Kurella* is one of the rare authors who denies this (see "Naturgeschichte des Verbrechers", pp. 258 *ff.*):

[5] Upon page 107 of the article cited Professor *Jelgersma* shows that certain really atavistic stigmata found in some criminals are very well explained by degeneracy.

[6] [NOTE TO THE AMERICAN EDITION: *Cf.* further: *K. Bimbaum*, "Die psychopathischen Verbrecher", and *Stelzner, op. cit.*]

We might leave the matter here, for we have come to a field other than that of sociology. However, one more question presents itself. To what extent are the economic system and its consequences the cause of these maladies? It is plain that this important question belongs in a work on sociology. We shall accordingly attempt to answer it briefly with the aid of competent authorities.

First of all, we note that heredity plays a great part in these maladies. The authors who have taken up the subject agree. It has been remarked that:

First, the inheritance of defects is not inevitable; degenerate parents may have sound children, though the chances are not very great.

Second, the disease of the parents is not always transmitted as such to the child, but the child may be predisposed to this same disease or one analogous. Dr. Féré expresses this as follows: "The diseases of the nervous system . . . make up a single family, indissolubly united by the laws of heredity . . . everyone (of those who have these diseases), if he is still fertile, can reproduce them all." [1]

In speaking of heredity we come to the first relation between the diseases in question and the social environment, since, in our present society, human reproduction is intimately bound up with the economic life. A person who is diseased but rich is often in a position to marry and procreate, while he would have had a smaller chance if sexual selection alone had been effective. On the other hand many well and strong individuals are prevented at present from establishing a family, since they lack the means to support it.

A second harmful kind of selection in our present society is found in the effect of militarism, which takes the strongest individuals, decimates them in time of war, or returns them to society weakened and diseased, while the weak have the greater chance to procreate.

In the third place, the ignorance of the harmful effects for humanity of the reproduction of degenerates is one of the principal reasons why degeneracy is so frequently present. This ignorance is great in the well-to-do classes, and naturally greater still among the poor. It is often repeated, and with truth, that man takes great care to improve his live stock by selection but takes none whatever in the matter of his own race; the weak and the diseased continue to reproduce themselves to the detriment of all society. The lack of all feeling of responsibility, natural to our intensely individualistic society, also

[1] "La famille nevropathique", p. 10.

contributes its share toward bringing to birth so many unhappy creatures for whom it would have been better if they had never existed.

If we ask how it happens that one individual or another is degenerate, we must answer that very often this degeneracy is due to heredity, either in part or altogether. But if we enquire into the causes of degeneracy in general heredity ceases to be a cause. As Professor Dallemagne says: "Heredity creates nothing; from heredity to heredity we must still go back to the cause." [1]

What are at present the principal characteristics of the relation between degeneracy and the present economic system with its consequences? Some authors in treating of the etiology of degeneracy express themselves only in general terms, and point out no other cause than "unfavorable circumstances." Professor Jelgersma, for example, says: "The simple psychoses, melancholia, mania, etc. are caused by unfavorable circumstances. The cause of the psychoses of degeneracy is deeper; the unfavorable circumstances have exercised their influence from generation to generation, and thus an individual is born who is abnormal from birth." [2]

These unfavorable circumstances must be more precisely defined, therefore. We shall divide them into four great groups. [3]

First. *The material condition of the poor classes.* "To be well," says Dr. Toulouse, "one must be sufficiently fed, must clothe himself according to the season, be clean, not work beyond one's strength, and be more or less exempt from care." [4] This is a simple truth of which all the world is convinced when it is a question of themselves or of their families, but which the physicians forget only too often when they are speaking of the social causes of diseases. [5]

In the first place the poor classes are badly and insufficiently fed, and as a consequence grow weak, and the children born to them are inferior physically and mentally. The insufficient nourishment of the mother during her pregnancy, and the insufficient nourishment of

---

[1] "Dégénérés et déséquilibrés", p. 168.

[2] *Op. cit.*, p. 102. See also *Kende*, "Die Entartung des Menschengeschlechts", p. 34.

[3] [NOTE TO THE AMERICAN EDITION: Upon the relation between disease and society see the fundamental work "Krankheit und soziale Lage", (edited by *M. Mosse* and *Tugendreich* with collaboration of several authorities).

It should also be mentioned here that the eugenists (*e.g. Schallmayer* in the book just cited, pp. 841 *ff.*) deny that the causes mentioned under first and second have any significance in heredity.]

[4] "Les causes de la folie", p. 34.

[5] *Stinca*, "Le milieu social comme facteur pathologique", p. 148 ("Ere nouvelle", 1894).

the child during the first years of his life, are especially fatal to him. Then those who are badly fed are predisposed to tuberculosis, scrofula, and rickets, which, in their turn, may be the causes of degeneracy.[1] Rickety women often have a contraction of the pelvis, which hinders child-birth, and may cause a lesion to the infant's brain. Note, for example, the opinion of Dr. Näcke, who says: "The social misery, bad hygiene and food . . . often enough beget a miserable generation and must already have injured the germ. The same causes, however, on the other hand easily produce feeble women with qualitatively and quantitatively insufficient milk, and most of all with a narrow pelvis, through which births take place with difficulty and to the detriment of the brain of the child. If now the above named factors come in later to affect the child, the derangement of nutrition will be further increased, and it is no wonder if all kinds of rickety and scrofulous symptoms appear in the body, and all kinds of children's ailments injure both body and mind." [2]

In the second place, unsanitary dwellings and insufficient clothing are the cause of all sorts of diseases, especially tuberculosis, which in their turn may lead to degeneracy.[3] The density of population in the great cities exercises its influence in the same direction.

In the third place, the long duration and intensity of the work forced upon the proletariat also contribute to degeneracy. For each individual there is a fixed measure of labor that he cannot pass without experiencing harmful consequences in body and mind. Dr. Lewy describes them as follows: "The consequences of immoderately long hours of labor are, a certain overexcitement of the nervous system which later gives place to a permanent debility, with which may be associated a dull headache as well as an inability to think clearly. If the overwork continues for a longer time, soon all the systems of the body are affected, the heart and larger arteries as well are injured in structure and function, disturbances of the regular circulation appear, manifested partly in swellings in various parts of the body, especially in the feet, and partly through hemorrhages. The brain ceases to function regularly, and so-called brain-symptoms appear, such as vertigo, ringing in the ears, deafness, defective vision, paralysis, and apoplexy. In the same way the liver, kidneys, and the digestive tract may be drawn into the general weakening process. The muscles become weak and slack, the body disposed to epidemic

---

[1] See *Féré*, "La famille névropathique", pp. 133 *ff*.
[2] "Verbrechen und Wahnsinn beim Weibe", p. 155.
[3] *Cf. Maudsley*, "The Physiology and Pathology of Mind", pp. 232, 233.

diseases, but especially prepared to vocational diseases, to which persons in a run-down condition most easily fall victim. If, then the end of the worker is not brought about prematurely by some intercurrent disease like typhus, under the immoderate strain he uses up his existing forces faster than he is in a position to replace them, and wastes away with tuberculosis of the lungs, so much the quicker, of course, the weaker he is constitutionally, and the younger he was when he had to submit to excessive labor." [1]

The harmful consequences of long working hours make themselves felt especially in the trades which are already dangerous to health, like those where there is a great deal of dust produced, or those which use poisons like lead, mercury, etc. [2] Monotony of work joined with long hours is also a cause of physical and intellectual deterioration. Professor Vogt says: "The less variety work presents, the more fatiguing is it, since it is only the same part of the muscles that are continually called upon, while the rest of the muscular system, in accordance with a well-known physiological law, degenerates from misuse and wastes away. To a still higher degree the uniformity of work has a deteriorating effect upon the mental powers; these become weakened much more quickly in the case of long continued fatigue than the muscles, while the unexercised mental faculties at the same time become stunted." [3]

The present economic system has also led to the work of women and children, and consequently to an important cause of the degeneration of the race. The number of women forced to take part in trades for which they are ill-fitted by nature is very great. The fear of being discharged, and the impossibility of doing without their wages make women with child continue to work up to the last moment of their pregnancy, and recommence shortly after childbirth, leading to very harmful results both for them and for their children. [4] Then child labor prevents the normal development of the children and ages them prematurely. [5]

Further, the cares and restlessness consequent upon the uncertainty of life may be causes of the weakening of the nervous system and the origin of a neurosis.

Finally, when an individual of this class falls sick his restoration to

---

[1] Quoted by *Lux*, "Sozialpolitisches Handbuch", pp. 71, 72.
[2] *Cf. Zadek*, "Die Achtstundentag eine gesundheitliche Forderung", pp. 12 *ff.*
[3] Quoted by *Lux*, p. 173. See also *Toulouse, op. cit.*, p. 68.
[4] See *Braun*, "Die Frauenfrage", pp. 312 *ff.*
[5] *Cf. Näcke*, "Verbrechen und Wahnsinn beim Weibe", p. 196.

health may be hindered by the lack of care and medical assistance and the necessity of recommencing work too soon.[1]

Second. *The condition of the well-to-do classes.* Most of the causes producing degeneracy in the poor classes do not appear among the well-to-do. With the latter there can be no question of insufficient food or clothing, or of bad housing. Yet in the well-to-do classes the idle, from their manner of living and this lack of regular exercise, are led to excesses of all kinds, which may make them too, in another way, subject to degeneracy.[2]

In the active part of the bourgeoisie, among the manufacturers, merchants, etc., the case is different. They are constantly absorbed in the question of how to increase their wealth, or, if they are unfortunate, they live in fear of losing the position gained. They are in a state of agitation, of permanent overexcitement. So there are numbers in the bourgeois class who overtax their minds, with the resulting chance of neurasthenia, even where the individual is not predisposed to it. All this applies also to the liberal professions, though in a smaller degree; there also the great competition has harmful consequences for the nerves. In "La famille névropathique" Dr. Féré thus describes the consequences of overdriving: " . . . excessive cerebral labor, intellectual and, still more, moral overwork, the continual preoccupations of the struggle for existence are conditions eminently fit to bring on functional troubles in the nervous system. Neurasthenia, like hysteria, may be considered as a chronic fatigue. The fatigue, to be sure, gives place to a number of troubles peculiar to neurasthenia. And these troubles, even if only temporary, cannot fail to have the most harmful effect upon children conceived under these conditions." [3]

The opinion of the celebrated alienist Maudsley is also very interesting; he says: "Perhaps one, and certainly not the least, of the ill effects which spring from some of the conditions of our present civilization, is seen in the general dread and disdain of poverty, in the eager passion to become rich. The practical gospel of the age, testified

---

[1] Upon the relation of the condition of the poorer classes to degeneracy, cf. Zerboglio, "La fin de la névrose" ("Devenir Social", I) and "Les bases économiques de la santé" ("Devenir Social", III); "Die Not des Vierten Standes" (anonymous); Fornasari di Verce, "La criminalità e le vicende economiche in Italia", pp. 5–10; Dallemagne, "Dégénérés et déséquilibrés", p. 142; and Aschaffenburg, "Das Verbrechen und seine Bekämpfung", p. 172.

[NOTE TO THE AMERICAN EDITION: Cf. Niceforo, op. cit., pp. 474 ff.]

[2] Cf. Toulouse, op. cit., p. 86, and Zerboglio, "La fin de la névrose", p. 630.

[3] Pp. 103, 104.

everywhere by faith and works, is that of money-getting; men are estimated mainly by the amount of their wealth, take social rank accordingly, and consequently bend all their energies to acquire that which gains them esteem and influence. The result is that in the higher departments of trade and commerce speculations of all sorts are eagerly entered on, and that many people are kept in a continued state of excitement and anxiety by the fluctuations of the money market. In the lower branches of trade there is the same eager desire for petty gains; and the continued absorption of the mind in these small acquisitions generates a littleness of mind and meanness of spirit, where it does not lead to actual dishonesty, which are nowhere displayed in a more pitiable form than by certain petty tradesmen. The occupation which a man is entirely engaged in does not fail to modify his character, and the reaction upon the individual's nature of a life which is being spent with the sole aim of becoming rich, is most baneful. It is not that the fluctuations of excitement unhinge the merchant's mind and lead to maniacal outbreaks, although that does sometimes happen; it is not that failure in the paroxysm of some crisis prostrates his energies and makes him melancholic, although that also is occasionally witnessed; but it is that exclusiveness of his life-aim and occupation too often saps the moral or altruistic element in his nature, makes him become egoistic, formal, and unsympathetic, and in his person deteriorates the nature of humanity. What is the consequence? If one conviction has been fixed in my mind more distinctly than another by observation of instances, it is that it is extremely unlikely such a man will beget healthy children; on the contrary, it is extremely likely that the deterioration of nature which he has acquired will be transmitted as an evil heritage to his children. In several instances in which the father has toiled upwards from poverty to vast wealth, with the aim and hope of founding a family, I have witnessed the results in a degeneracy, mental and physical, of his offspring, which has sometimes gone as far as extinction of the family in the third or fourth generation. When the evil is not so extreme as madness or ruinous vice, the savour of a mother's influence having been present, it may still be manifest in an instinctive cunning and duplicity, and an extreme selfishness of nature — a nature not having the capacity of a true moral conception or altruistic feeling. Whatever opinion other more experienced observers may hold, I cannot but think, after what I have seen, that the extreme passion for getting rich, absorbing the whole energies of life, does predispose to mental degeneration in the offspring — either to moral defect, or to moral and intellectual deficiency, or to outbreaks of positive insanity under the conditions of life." [1]

We could cite a number of other competent authorities to prove that the present economic system exacts from those who direct production also, intellectual efforts such as the nervous system cannot endure indefinitely.[2]

Third. *Syphilis.* Aside from the fact that this malady is very probably the cause of general paralysis,[3] it takes its place among the important factors of degeneracy to this extent, that the children of syphilitics are often degenerates. This fact being generally recognized we shall not dwell on it. The celebrated German specialist in syphilis, Blaschko, says of it: "Syphilis leads to the birth of children who are mentally and physically stunted, and often crippled and imbecile." [4]

This would not be the time to speak of syphilis as a cause of degeneracy, if the extension of this malady were not intimately bound up with prostitution, which is, in its turn, determined by the economic environment. Dr. Blaschko says of it: "The principal source of venereal infection of course is, and remains, sexual intercourse outside of wedlock, especially prostitution." [5]

As a social cause of the great extension of syphilis it is well to point out the profound ignorance of the extent and the danger of venereal diseases,[6] to which less attention is paid than to others (hospitals not receiving patients affected by them, relief funds not aiding those having syphilis, etc.). Like other diseases these have the most harmful consequences for those who live under bad conditions.[7]

Fourth. *Alcoholism.* Alcoholism undoubtedly belongs to the very important causes of degeneracy. There are few questions upon which competent authors are as unanimous as they are upon this. There is

[1] *Op. cit.*, pp. 233–235.

[2] *Cf. Battaglia*, "La dinamica del delitto", p. 412; *Näcke*, *op. cit.*, p. 156; *Zerboglio*, "La fin de la névrose", p. 629. *Toulouse*, *op. cit.*, p. 85; *Kraepelin*, "Psychiatrie", I, pp. 88, 89; *Hellpach*, "Soziale Ursachen und Wirkungen der Nervosität" ("Politisch-anthropologische Revue", I).

[3] *Cf. Toulouse*, *op. cit.*, pp. 224 *ff.*

[4] "Die Prostitution im XIX Jahrhundert", p. 33; see also by the same author, "Hygiene der Prostitution und venerischen Krankheiten", pp. 7 *ff.* *Cf.* also *Kende*, *op. cit.*, p. 90, and Dr. *M. Alsberg*, "Erbliche Entartung bedingt durch soziale Einflüsse", p. 20.

[5] "Hygiene der Prostitution etc." p. 35.
Above we have seen that prostitution increases and diminishes with the fluctuations of economic conditions. Dr. *Schoenlank* proves in his "Die Syphilis und die Sozialzustände" ("Neue Zeit", 1887) that syphilis also increases and diminishes in these periods, an added proof of the intimate connection of syphilis and prostitution.

[6] *Cf. Hellpach*, "Der Kampf gegen die Geschlechtskrankheiten", p. 197 ("Sozialistische Monatshefte", VII).

[7] *Blaschko*, "Die Prostitution etc.", p. 32.

a wealth of material for quotation but we will limit ourselves to the words of Professor Dallemagne, who, after quoting the opinion of such authorities as Morel, Magnan, and others concludes by saying : "Alcohol is an essential factor of degeneracy. It can by itself create all the degenerate and unbalanced states, and this question appears definitely decided." [1] Dr. Legrain gives the following figures upon the consequences of chronic alcoholism of the parents upon the children.[2] Out of 215 families of alcoholics in four generations (814 individuals) there were found : 42% of alcoholics, 60.9% of degenerates, 13.9% morally insane, 22.7% had had convulsions, 20% were hysterical or epileptic, and 19% were insane.[3] These are striking figures, and banish all doubt of the harmful influence of alcohol !

It must still further be observed, that the very frequent adulteration of alcohol leads to especially harmful consequences;[4] and that alcohol exerts an especially harmful effect upon the ill-nourished.[5]

We have come now to the end of our remarks upon the social and economic causes of degeneracy. Although they are plainly not the only ones, yet it is certain that their part in the etiology of degeneracy is very important, and even preponderating.

[1] "Dégénérés et déséquilibrés", p. 167.

[2] Some authorities are of the opinion that children conceived during a state of intoxication run the danger of being degenerates; others, however, doubt this. See *Grotjahn*, "Der Alkoholismus", p. 165.

[3] "Conséquences sociales de l'alcoolisme des ascendants au point de vue de la dégénérescence, de la morale et de la criminalité", pp. 160–165 ("Compte Rendu IV, Congr. d'anthr. crim."). For other figures see also : *de Vaucleroy*, "Influence de l'hérédité alcoolique sur la folie et la criminalité" ("Actes du III Congr. d'anthr. crim.") ; *Grotjahn*, *op. cit.*, pp. 166 *ff.* ; *Verhaeghe*, "De l'alcoolisation", pp. 112 *ff.*

[4] See *Toulouse*, *op. cit.*, pp. 163–167 ; and *Grotjahn*, *op. cit.*, p. 220.

[5] See *Toulouse*, *op. cit.*, p. 178.

CHAPTER VII.

CONCLUSIONS.

WHAT are the conclusions to be drawn from what has gone before? When we sum up the results that we have obtained it becomes plain that economic conditions occupy a much more important place in the etiology of crime than most authors have given them.

First we have seen that the present economic system and its consequences weaken the social feelings. The basis of the economic system of our day being exchange, the economic interests of men are necessarily found to be in opposition. This is a trait that capitalism has in common with other modes of production. But its principal characteristic is that the means of production are in the hands of a few, and most men are altogether deprived of them. Consequently, persons who do not possess the means of production are forced to sell their labor to those who do, and these, in consequence of their economic preponderance, force them to make the exchange for the mere necessaries of life, and to work as much as their strength permits.

This state of things especially stifles men's social instincts; it develops, on the part of those with power, the spirit of domination, and of insensibility to the ills of others, while it awakens jealousy and servility on the part of those who depend upon them. Further the contrary interests of those who have property, and the idle and luxurious life of some of them, also contribute to the weakening of the social instincts.

The material condition, and consequently the intellectual condition, of the proletariat are also a reason why the moral plane of that class is not high. The work of children brings them into contact with persons to associate with whom is fatal to their morals. Long working hours and monotonous labor brutalize those who are forced into them; bad housing conditions contribute also to debase the moral sense, as do the uncertainty of existence, and finally absolute poverty, the frequent consequence of sickness and unemployment. Ignorance and lack of training of any kind also contribute their quota. Most demoralizing of all is the status of the lower proletariat.

The economic position of woman contributes also to the weakening of the social instincts.

The present organization of the family has great importance as regards criminality. It charges the legitimate parents with the care of the education of the child; the community concerns itself with the matter very little. It follows that a great number of children are brought up by persons who are totally incapable of doing it properly. As regards the children of the proletariat, there can be no question of the education properly so-called, on account of the lack of means and the forced absence of one or both of the parents. The school tends to remedy this state of things, but the results do not go far enough. The harmful consequences of the present organization of the family make themselves felt especially in the case of the children of the lower proletariat, orphans, and illegitimate children. For these the community does but little, though their need of adequate help is the greatest.

Prostitution, alcoholism, and militarism, which result, in the last analysis, from the present social order, are phenomena that have demoralizing consequences.

As to the different kinds of crime, we have shown that the very important group of economic criminality finds its origin on the one side in the absolute poverty and the cupidity brought about by the present economic environment, and on the other in the moral abandonment and bad education of the children of the poorer classes. Then, professional criminals are principally recruited from the class of occasional criminals, who, finding themselves rejected everywhere after their liberation, fall lower and lower. The last group of economic crimes (fraudulent bankruptcy, etc.) is so intimately connected with our present mode of production, that it would not be possible to commit it under another.

The relation between sexual crimes and economic conditions is less direct; nevertheless these also give evidence of the decisive influence of these conditions. We have called attention to the four following points.

First, there is a direct connection between the crime of adultery and the present organization of society, which requires that the legal dissolution of a marriage should be impossible or very difficult.

Second, sexual crimes upon adults are committed especially by unmarried men; and since the number of marriages depends in its turn upon the economic situation, the connection is clear; and those who commit these crimes are further almost exclusively illiterate, coarse, raised in an environment almost without sexual morality, and regard the sexual life from the wholly animal side.

Third, the causes of sexual crime upon children are partly the same as those of which we have been speaking, with the addition of prostitution.

Fourth, alcoholism greatly encourages sexual assaults.

As to the relation between crimes of vengeance and the present constitution of society, we have noted that it produces conflicts without number; statistics have shown that those who commit them are almost without exception poor and uncivilized, and that alcoholism is among the most important causes of these crimes.

Infanticide is caused in part by poverty, and in part by the opprobrium incurred by the unmarried mother (an opprobrium resulting from the social utility of marriage).

Political criminality comes solely from the economic system and its consequences.

Finally, economic and social conditions are also important factors in the etiology of degeneracy, which is in its turn a cause of crime.

Upon the basis of what has gone before, we have a right to say that the part played by economic conditions in criminality is preponderant, even decisive.

This conclusion is of the highest importance for the prevention of crime. If it were principally the consequence of innate human qualities (atavism, for example), the pessimistic conclusion that crime is a phenomenon inseparably bound up with the social life would be well founded. But the facts show that it is rather the optimistic conclusion that we must draw, that where crime is the consequence of economic and social conditions, we can combat it by changing those conditions.

However important crime may be as a social phenomenon, however terrible may be the injuries and the evil that it brings upon humanity, the development of society will not depend upon the question as to what are the conditions which could restrain crime or make it disappear, if possible; the evolution of society will proceed independently of this question.

What is the direction that society will take under these continual modifications? This is not the place to treat fully of this subject. In my opinion the facts indicate quite clearly what the direction will be. The productivity of labor has increased to an unheard of degree, and will assuredly increase in the future. The concentration of the means of production into the hands of a few progresses continually; in many branches it has reached such a degree that the fundamental principle of the present economic system, competition, is excluded, and has been replaced by monopoly. On the other hand the working class is becoming more and more organized, and the opinion is very generally held among working-men that the causes of material and intellectual poverty can be eliminated only by having the means of production held in common.

Supposing that this were actually realized, what would be the consequences as regards criminality? Let us take up this question for a moment. Although we can give only personal opinions as to the details of such a society, the general outlines can be traced with certainty.

The chief difference between a society based upon the community of the means of production and our own is that material poverty would be no longer known. Thus one great part of economic criminality (as also one part of infanticide) would be rendered impossible, and one of the greatest demoralizing forces of our present society would be eliminated. And then, in this way those social phenomena so productive of crime, prostitution and alcoholism, would lose one of their principal factors. Child labor and overdriving would no longer take place, and bad housing, the source of much physical and moral evil, would no longer exist.

With material poverty there would disappear also that intellectual poverty which weighs so heavily upon the proletariat; culture would no longer be the privilege of some, but a possession common to all. The consequences of this upon criminality would be very important, for we have seen that even in our present society with its numerous conflicts, the members of the propertied classes, who have often but a veneer of civilization, are almost never guilty of crimes of vengeance. There is the more reason to admit that in a society where interests were not opposed, and where civilization was universal, these crimes would be no longer present, especially since alcoholism also proceeds in large part from the intellectual poverty of the poorer classes. And what is true of crimes of vengeance, is equally true of sexual crimes in so far as they have the same etiology.

A large part of the economic criminality (and also prostitution to a certain extent) has its origin in the cupidity excited by the present economic environment. In a society based upon the community of the means of production, great contrasts of fortune would, like commercial capital, be lacking, and thus cupidity would find no food. These crimes will not totally disappear so long as there has not been a redistribution of property according to the maxim, "to each according to his needs", something that will probably be realized, but not in the immediate future.

The changes in the position of woman which are taking place in our present society, will lead, under this future mode of production, to her economic independence, and consequently to her social independence as well. It is accordingly probable that the criminality of woman will increase in comparison with that of man during the transition period. But the final result will be the disappearance of the harmful effects of the economic and social preponderance of man.

As to the education of children under these new conditions it is difficult to be definite. However, it is certain that the community will concern itself seriously with their welfare. It will see to it that the children whose parents cannot or will not be responsible for them, are well cared for. By acting in this way it will remove one of the most important causes of crime. There is no doubt that the community will exercise also a strict control over the education of children; it cannot be affirmed, however, that the time will come when the children of a number of parents will be brought up together by capable persons; this will depend principally upon the intensity that the social sentiments may attain.

As soon as the interests of all are no longer opposed to each other, as they are in our present society, there will no longer be a question either of politics ("a fortiori" of political *crimes*) or of militarism.

Such a society will not only remove the causes which now make men egoistic, but will awaken, on the contrary, a strong feeling of altruism. We have seen that this was already the case with the primitive peoples, where their economic interests were not in opposition. In a larger measure this will be realized under a mode of production in common, the interests of all being the same.

In such a society there can be no question of crime properly so called. The eminent criminologist, Manouvrier, in treating of the prevention of crime expresses himself thus : "The maxim to apply is, act so that every man shall always have more interest in being useful to his fellows than in harming them." It is precisely in a society where the community of the means of production has been realized that this maxim will obtain its complete application. There will be crimes committed by pathological individuals, but this will come rather within the sphere of the physician than that of the judge. And then we may even reach a state where these cases will decrease in large measure, since the social causes of degeneracy will disappear, and procreation by degenerates be checked through the increased knowledge of the laws of heredity and the increasing sense of moral responsibility.

"It is society that prepares the crime", says the true adage of Quetelet. For all those who have reached this conclusion, and are not insensible to the sufferings of humanity, this statement is sad, but contains a ground of hope. It is sad, because society punishes severely those who commit the crime which she has herself prepared. It contains a ground of hope, since it promises to humanity the possibility of some day delivering itself from one of its most terrible scourges.

BIBLIOGRAPHY

OF WORKS CITED

ACTON, W. Prostitution, Considered in its Moral, Social and Sanitary Aspects. London, 1870.

ADAMS-LEHMANN, H. B. Das Weib und der Stier. Neue Zeit, 1900–1901, II.

ADMINISTRATION de la justice criminelle et civile de la Belgique 1881–1885. Bruxelles, 1888.

AGAHD, K. Die Erwerbsthätigkeit schulpflichtiger Kinder im Deutschen Reich. Archiv f. soz. Gesetzgeb. u. Statistik, XII.

AGUINALIEDO, J. M. L., and DE QUIROS, C. B. Verbrechertum und Prostitution in Madrid. Berlin, 1909.

ALBANEL, L. Le crime dans la famille. Paris, 1900.

ALBRECHT, P. La criminalité de l'homme au point de vue de l'anatomie comparée. Actes du I Congrès d'anthropologie crim. Turin, 1886–1887.

ALETRINO, A. Twee opstellen over crimineele anthropologie. Amsterdam, 1899.

—— Over ontoerekenbaarheid. Amsterdam, 1899.

—— La situation sociale de l'uraniste. Compte rendu du V Congr. d'anthr. crim. Amsterdam, 1901.

—— Over eenige oorzaken des prostitutie. Amsterdam, 1901.

—— Handleiding bij de studie der crimineele anthropologie. Amsterdam, I, II, 1903, 1904.

—— Is celstraf nog langer gevorloofd en gewenscht? Amsterdam, 1906.

ALIMENA, B. Naturalismo critico e diritto penale. Rivista di disciplina carceraria, 1891.

ALSBERG, M. Erbliche Entartung bedingt durch soziale Einflüsse. Cassel und Leipzig, 1903.

ALTERTHUM, P. Das Problem der Arbeitslosigkeit. Berlin, 1911.

AMMON, O. Ursprung der sozialen Triebe. Zeitschr. f. Soc. wissensch., IV.

AMSCHL, A. Aberglauben als Heilmittel. Archiv f. Krim. Anthr. u. Kriminalistik, XV.

—— Das Verbrechen des Kindesmordes nach österreichischem Recht. Archiv f. Krim. anthr. u. Krim., XXX.

ANNUAIRE statistique de la France, V, VII, IX, XVI, XX. Paris, 1882 sqq.

ANNUAL Report (1912–1913) of the National Society for the Prevention of Cruelty to Children. London, 1913.

ANNUARIO statistico italiano, 1900. Roma, 1900.

ARBEIDERSLEVEN in Nederland. (Anonymous.) Amsterdam, 1908.

ARENDT, H. Menschen die den Pfad verloren. Stuttgart, 1907.

—— Kleine Weisse Sklaven. Berlin-Charlottenburg, 1911.

ARÏENS, A. Criminaliteit en drankmisbruik. Leiden, 1905.

ASCHAFFENBURG, G. Alkoholgenuss u. Verbrechen. Zeitschr. f. d. ges. Strafr. w., XX.

—— Zur Psychologie d. Sittlichkeitsverbrecher. Monatschr. f. Krim. Psych. u. Strafr. ref., II.

—— Das Verbrechen und seine Bekämpfung. Heidelberg, 1906.

ASCHROTT. Critique on "Verbrechen u. Verbrecher in Preussen" of Starke. Jahrbücher f. Gesetzgebung etc., 1884.

AUBRY, P. De l'homicide commis par la femme. Archives d'anthropologie crim., VI.

—— La contagion du meurtre. Paris, 1894.

—— De l'influence contagieuse de la publicité des faits criminels. Archives d'anthr. crim., VIII.

—— et CORRE, A. Documents de criminologie rétrospective. Paris, 1895.

AUDIFFRENT. Quelques considérations sur l'infanticide. Arch. d'anthr. crim. XVIII.

AUER, F. Soziales Strafrecht. München, 1903.

AUGAGNEUR, V. Les vraies causes et les vrais remèdes de l'alcoolisme. Mouvement socialiste, 1900.

—— La prostitution des filles mineures. Arch. d'anthr. crim., II.

AULL. Alkohol und Verbrechen. Halle a/S, 1908.

AVÉ-LALLEMANT, F. C. B. Das deutsche Gaunerthum, II, III. Leipzig, 1858.

BAER, A. Der Alcoholismus. Berlin, 1878.

—— Der Verbrecher in anthropologischer Beziehung. Leipzig, 1893.

—— Der Selbstmord im kindlichen Lebensalter. Leipzig, 1901.

—— Ueber jugendliche Mörder und Todtschläger. Archiv. f. Krim. etc., XI.

BAERE, L. DEL. De invloed van oproeding en onderwijs op de criminaliteit. Amsterdam, 1891.

BAERNREITHER, J. M. Die Ursachen, Erscheinungsformen und die Ausbreitung der Verwahrlosung von Kindern und Jugendlichen in Oesterreich. Wien, 1906.

BAETS, M. DE. L'école d'anthropologie criminelle. Gand, 1893.

—— Les influences de la misère sur la criminalité. Gand, 1895.

BAKER, J. Rapport sur l'influence de l'alcoolisme sur la criminalité. Actes du congrès pénitentiaire intern. de Bruxelles 1900 IV. Bruxelles et Berne, 1901.

BATTAGLIA, B. La dinamica del delitto. Napoli, 1886.

BAUMGARTEN, A. Die Beziehungen der Prostitution zum Verbrechen. Archiv f. Krim. Anthr. etc., XI.

BEBEL, A. Die Frau und der Sozialismus. Stuttgart, 1899. "Woman in the Past, Present, and Future" (translation of above by Walther. New York, 1886).

BECCARIA, C. Des délits et des peines. Tr. Ad. Hélie. Paris, 1870.
BECHTEREW, W. v. Das Verbrechertum im Lichte der objektiven Psychologie. Wiesbaden, 1914.
BEER, M. Geschichte des Sozialismus in England. Stuttgart, 1913.
BELFORT BAX, E. Ethics of Socialism. London.
BENEDIKT, M. Biologie u. Kriminalistik. Zeitschr. f. d. ges. Strafr. w., VII.
———— Die Vagabondage u. ihre Behandlung. Zeitschr. f. d. g. etc., XI.
BENNECKE, H. Bemerkungen zur Kriminalstatistik des Grossherzogtums Hessen, besonders zur Statistik des Bettels u. Landstreicherei. Zeitschr. f. d. ges. etc., X.
BENTHAM, J. Traités de législation civile et pénale. Paris, 1802.
BERARD, A. Les hommes et les théories de l'anarchie. Archives d'anthr. crim., VII.
———— Le Vagabondage en France. Archives d'anthr. crim., XIII.
BÉRARD DES GLAJEUX, M. Les passions criminelles. Paris, 1893.
BERETNING om Rigets Strafarbeits-Anstalten, 1897–1898, 1898–1899. Kristiania, 1900, 1901.
BERG, H. Getreidepreise und Kriminalität in Deutschland seit 1882. Berlin, 1902.
BERKUSKY, H. Die Blutrache. Zeitschr. f. Soc. w., XII.
BERNARD. De la criminalité en France depuis 1826, etc. Journal des Economistes, 1856.
BERNARD, P. Des viols et attentats à la pudeur sur adultes. Arch. d'anthr. crim. II.
———— et R. GARRAUD. Des attentats à la pudeur et des viols sur les enfants. Archives etc., I.
BERTRAND, E. Essai sur la moralité comparative des diverses classes de la population et principalement des classes ouvrières. Journal de la soc. de stat. de Paris, 1871–1872.
BERTRIN, G. De la criminalité en France dans les congrégations, le clergé et les principales professions. Paris.
BERUFLICHE und soziale Gliederung des Deutschen Volkes nach der Berufszählung vom 14 Juni 1895. Stat. d. Deutschen Reiches N. F., III. Berlin, 1899.
BINNY, J., and MAYHEW. The Criminal Prisons of London. London, 1862.
BIRNBAUM, K. Die psychopathischen Verbrecher. Berlin, 1914.
BLANC, L. Organisation du travail. Bruxelles, 1845.
BLASCHKO, A. Die moderne Prostitution. Neue Zeit, 1891–92, II.
———— Hygiene der Prostitution und venerischen Krankheiten. Jena, 1900.
———— Die Prostitution im XIX Jahrhundert. Berlin, 1902.
———— Prostitution. (Handwörterbuch der Staatswissenschaften VI.) Jena, 1910.
BLATCHFORD, R. Merrie England. London, 1895.
———— Dismal England. London, 1901.
———— Not Guilty. London, 1906.
BLAU, B. Kriminalistische Untersuchung der Kreise Marienwerder und Thorn. Berlin, 1903.
BLEIBTREU, C. Der Militarismus im XIX Jahrhundert. Berlin, 1901.

BLOCH, J. Das Sexualleben unserer Zeit. Berlin, 1907.
—— Die Prostitution, I, 1912.
BOAS, K. W. F. Alkohol und Verbrechen nach neueren Statistiken. Archiv.
f. Krim. etc., XXIX.
BOHMERT, K. Die sächsische Kriminalstatistik mit besonderer Rücksicht
auf die Jahre 1882–1887. Zeitschr. d. K. sächs. Stat. Bureaus, XXXV.
BOIES, H. M. The Science of Penology. New York and London, 1901.
BONGER, W. A. Eene apologie van den oorlag. Nieuwe Tijd, XIII.
—— Misdaad en socialisme. Nieuwe Tijd, XVI.
—— Verbrechen und Sozialismus. Neue Zeit, XXX².
—— Over de maatschappelijke factoren van de misdaad en hunne be-
teekenis in vergelijking met de individueele oorzaken. Tijdschrift v.
Strafrecht, XXIII.
—— Geloof en misdaad. Leiden, 1913.
BONHAEFFER, K. Ein Beitrag zur Kenntnis des grossstädtischen Bettel-
and Vagabondentums. Zeitschr. f. d. ges. etc., XXI.
—— Zur Kenntnis des grossstädtischen Bettel- und Vagabondentums.
Zweiter Beitrag: Prostituirte. Zeitschr. f. d. ges. Strafr. w., XXIII.
—— Sittlichkeitsdelikt u. Körperverletzung. Monatschr. f. Krim. psych.
etc., II.
BOOTH, CH. Life and Labour of the People in London. London, 1892.
—— Pauperism. London, 1892.
BOSCO, A. Gli omicidii in alcuni stati d' Europa. Bulletin de l'inst. intern.
de stat., IV.
—— Della statistica dell' omicidio negli stati uniti d' America. Bulletin
etc., X.
BOURNET, A. De la criminalité en France et en Italie. Paris, 1884.
BRACE, CH. L. The Dangerous Classes of New York. New York, 1872.
BRAUN, A. Berliner Wohnungsverhältnisse. Berlin, 1893.
BRAUN, L. Die Frauenfrage. Leipzig, 1901.
BRISSOT DE WARVILLE, J. P. Théorie des loix criminelles. Utrecht, 1781.
—— Recherches philosophiques sur la propriété et le vol. (Bibliothèque
phil. du législateur, du politique, du jurisconsulte, VI.) Berlin, 1782.
BROMME, M. W. TH. Lebensgeschichte eines modernen Fabrikarbeiters.
Jena u. Leipzig, 1905.
BRUSSE, M. J. Boefje. Rotterdam, 1903.
—— Onder de menschen. N. Rotterd. Cousant, 1903–1904.
—— Het rosse leven en sterven van de Zandstraat. Rotterdam, 1912.
BÜCHER, K. Die Entstehung der Volkswirtschaft. Tübingen, 1904.

CABET, E. Voyage en Icarie. Paris, 1842.
CALWER, R. Die erbliche Belastung der Prostituirten. Neue Zeit, 1893–
1894, II.
CARLIER, F. Les deux prostitutions. Paris, 1887.
CARNEVALE, E. Una terza scuola di diritto penale. Rivista di disciplina
carceraria, 1891.
CARRARA, M. Les petits criminels de Cagliari. Compte rendu du V Congr.
d'anthr. crim. Amsterdam, 1901.
CASERIO en prison. (Anonymous.) Archives etc., XVI.

CATLIN, G. Illustrations of the Manners, Customs and Condition of the North American Indians. London, 1851.
CAVAGLIERI, G., and FLORIAN, E. I vagabondi I, II. Torino, 1897, 1900.
CHAILLON DES BARRES. L'influence du bien-être matériel sur la moralité d'un peuple. Journ. d. Econ., 1846.
CHARPENTIER, R., and LEY, A. Alcoolisme et criminalité. Bruxelles, 1910.
CHEINISSE, L. Die Rassenpathologie und der Alkoholismus bei den Juden. Zeitschr. f. Demogr. u. Statistik der Juden, VI.
CHIOZZA-MONEY, L. G. Riches and Poverty. London, 1911.
CLAY, J. On the Effects of Good or Bad Times on Committals to Prison. Journal of the Stat. Soc. of London, 1854, 1857.
COLAJANNI, N. La delinquenza della Sicilia e le sue cause. Palermo, 1885.
────── Oscillations thermométriques et délits contre les personnes. Arch. d'anthr. crim., I.
────── L'alcoolismo. Catania, 1887.
────── La sociologia criminale. Catania, 1887.
────── L'homicide en Italie. Revue Socialiste, 1901.
────── Le socialisme et sa propagande en rapport avec la criminalité. Compte Rendu V Congr. d'anthr. crim. Amsterdam, 1901.
────── Il socialismo. Palermo-Milano, 2e ed.
────── Socialismo e criminalità. Roma-Napoli, 1904.
COLLARD, W. L. A. De handel in blanke slavinnen. Amsterdam, 1900.
COMMENGE, O. La prostitution clandestine à Paris. Paris, 1897.
COMPTE général de l'administration de la justice criminelle en France 1900, 1907. Paris, 1902, 1909.
CONSIDÉRANT, V. Théorie du droit de propriété et du droit au travail. Paris, 1848.
CORNE, A. Essai sur la criminalité. Journ. d. Econ., 1868.
CORRE, A. Crime et suicide. Paris, 1891.
────── Aperçu général de la criminalité militaire en France. Archives d'anthr. crim., VI.
────── et AUBRY, P. Documents de criminologie rétrospective. Paris, 1895.
COUTAGNE, H. De l'influence des professions sur la criminalité. Actes du II Congr. d'anthr. crim. Paris.
────── De l'influence des professions sur la criminalité. Actes du III Congr. d'anthr. crim. Bruxelles, 1893.
CRIMINALITY Promoted by Distress. (Anonymous.) Economist, 1856.
CRIMINEELE statistiek 1899, 1900, 1901, 1904, 1905, 1910. ó Gravenhage, 1900 sqq.
CUENOUD, J. La criminalité à Genève au XIX siècle. Genève, 1891.
CUNOW, H. Die Verwandtschafts-organisationen der Australneger. Stuttgart, 1874.
────── Die ökonomischen Grundlagen der Mutterherrschaft. Neue Zeit, 1897–98, I.
────── Arbeitstheilung und Frauenrecht. Neue Zeit, 1900–1901, I.
────── Zur Urgeschichte der Ehe und Familie. Ergänzungsheft. Neue Zeit, 1912–1913.

DALHOFT, N. Rapport sur l'influence de l'alcoolisme sur la criminalité.

Actes du congr. pénit. intern. de Bruxelles, 1900, IV. Bruxelles et Berne, 1901.

DALLEMAGNE. Dégénérés et déséquilibrés. Bruxelles et Paris, 1895.

—— Théorie de la criminalité. Paris.

DAMME. Die Kriminalität und ihre Zusammenhänge in der Provinz Schleswig-Holstein. Zeitschr. f. d. ges. etc., XII.

DARGUN, L. v. Ursprung und Entwicklungs-Geschichte des Eigenthums. Zeitschr. f. vergl. Rechtswissensch., V.

—— Egoismus und Altruismus in der National-Oekonom. Leipzig, 1885.

—— Mutterrecht und Vaterrecht. Leipzig, 1892.

DARWIN, CH. The Descent of Man. Chicago and New York. Rand, McNally & Co.

DENIS, H. L'influence de la crise économique sur la criminalité et le penchant au crime de Quetelet. Bull. de la Soc. d'Anthr. de Bruxelles, 1885–1886.

—— La criminalité et la crise économique. Actes du III Congr. d'anthr. crim. Bruxelles, 1893.

—— Le socialisme et les causes économiques et sociales du crime. Compte rendu V Congr. d'anthr. crim. Amsterdam, 1901.

—— Les index numbers (nombres indices) des phénomènes moraux. Académie royale de Belgique. II serie, Tome IV, 1911.

DESPRÉS, A. La prostitution en France. Paris, 1883.

DIETZ, H. Die Militärstrafrechtspflege im Lichte der Kriminalstatistik. Oldenburg, i/Gr. 1908.

DIX, A. Sozial-Moral. Leipzig, 1898.

—— Alkoholismus und Arbeiterschaft. Zeitschr. f. Soc. w., N. F., II.

DOCHOW, F. Die Kriminalität im Amtsbezirk Heidelberg. Berlin, 1906.

DOEHN, B. Der Anarchismus und seine Bekämpfung. Zeitschrift f. d. ges. Strafr. w., XX.

DOSTOJEWSKY, F. M. Memoiren aus einem Totenhaus. Translated by Moses. Leipzig.

DOUGLAS, W. M. The Criminal : Some Social and Economic Aspects. Proceedings of the Royal Philosophical Society of Glasgow, XXXIII. Glasgow, 1902.

DRAHMS, A. The Criminal. New York, 1900.

DRILL, D. Des principes fondamentaux de l'école d'anthr. criminelles. Actes III Congr. d'anthr. crim. Bruxelles, 1893.

—— Les fondements et le but de la responsabilité pénale. Comptes rendus IV Congr. d'anthr. crim. Genève, 1896.

DUBOIS, F. Le péril anarchiste. Paris, 1894.

DUBUISSON, P. Les voleuses des grands magasins. Archives etc., XVI.

DU CAMP, M. Les plaies sociales. La prostitution à Paris. Journ. d. Econom., 1870.

DUCPETIAUX, ED. De la condition physique et morale des jeunes ouvriers I. Bruxelles, 1843.

—— Mémoire sur le paupérisme dans les Flandres. Bruxelles, 1850.

DUGDALE, R. L. The Jukes. New York and London, 1884.

DUPRAT, G. L. La criminalité dans l'adolescence. Paris, 1909.

DURKHEIM, E. Le suicide. Paris, 1897.
DIJCK, G. VAN. Eenige beschouwingen over het misdrijf van Kindermoord. Groningen, 1908.

EGGERT. Not und Verbrechen. Jahresbericht der Rheinisch. Westf. Gefängnis-Gesellschaft 1903/4. Düsseldorf.
EINIGES über die Prostitution in Gegenwart und Zukunft. (Anonymous.) Neue Zeit, 1891–1892, I.
ELLIOT, J. H. The Increase of Material Prosperity and of Moral Agents Compared with the State of Crime and Pauperism. Journ. of the Stat. Society of London, 1868.
ELLIS, H. The Criminal. London, 1907.
—— Verbrecher und verbrechen. Transl. Kurella. Leipzig, 1895.
—— Geschlecht und Gesellschaft II. Transl. Kurella. Würzburg, 1911.
ELTSBACHER, P. Der Anarchismus. Berlin, 1900.
EMBDEN, D. VAN. Darwinisme en demokratie. ó Gravenhage, 1901.
ENFANTIN, B. P. Œuvres. Paris, 1868.
ENGELS, F. Die Lage der arbeitenden Klasse in England. Stuttgart, 1892.
—— The Condition of the Working Class in England. Transl. Wischnewetzky. London, 1892.
—— Umrisse zu einer Kritik der Nationalökonomie. (Gesammelte Schriften v. K. Marx u. F. Engels, 1841–1850, I. Stuttgart, 1902.)
—— Sur la conception matérialiste de l'histoire. Devenir social, III.
—— Der Ursprung der Familie, des Privateigenthums und des Staats. Stuttgart, 1898.
—— und K. MARX. Die heilige Familie. (Gesammelte Schriften etc., II. Stuttgart, 1902.)
ENGLANDS industrielle Reserve Armie. (Anonymous.) Neue Zeit, 1884.
ENQUÊTE betreffende werking en uitbreiding der wet van 19 September 1874 en naar den toestand van fabrieken en werkplaatsen. ó Gravenhage, 1887.
ENQUÊTE gehouden door de staatscommissie benoemd volgens de wet van 19 Januari 1890. ó Gravenhage, 1890–1894.
ENTHOREN, F. Studie over het anarchisme von de daad. Amsterdam, 1901.
ERGEBNISSE der schweizerischen Kriminalstatistik während der Jahre 1892–1896. Bern, 1900.
ERGEBNISSE der Strafrechtspflege der im Reichsrate vertretenen Königreichen und Ländern im Jahre 1899 Œsterreichische Statistik. Wien, 1903.
ETTINGER, S. Das Verbrecherproblem. Bern, 1909.
EVEREST, R. On the Influence of Social Degradation in Producing Pauperism and Crime, etc. Journal of the Stat. Soc. of London, 1855.
EVERT, G. Zur Statistik rückfälliger Verbrecher in Preussen. Zeitschr. d. k. preussischen stat. Bureaus, XXXIX. 1899.

FAUCHER, L. Mémoire sur le caractère et sur le mouvement de la criminalité en Angleterre. Journ. des Econ., 1850.
—— Etudes sur l'Angleterre I. Paris, 1856.

FAURE, ABBÉ. Souvenir de la Roquette. Paris.

FEHLINGER, H. Erwerbsarbeit und Kriminalität von Kindern u. Frauen in den Ver. Staaten. Archiv f. Krim. Anthr. etc., XLIX.

FEITH, J. Misdadige Kinderen. Amsterdam, 1911.

FEKETE, J. Rapport sur l'influence de l'alcoolisme sur la criminalité. Actes du congr. pénit. intern. de Bruxelles. Bruxelles et Berne, 1901.

FELD, W. Die Kinder der in Fabriken arbeitenden Frauen und ihre Verpflegung. Dresden, 1906.

FENTON, F. The Influence of Newspaper Presentations upon the Growth of Crime and other Anti-social Activity. Chicago, 1911.

FÉRÉ, CH. Dégénérescence et criminalité. Paris, 1888.

—— La famille névropathique. Paris, 1894.

FERRANTE CAPETTI, L. Reati e psicopatie sessuali. Torino, 1910.

FERRERO, G. Le crime d'adultère. Archives etc., IX.

—— et C. LOMBROSO. La femme criminelle et la prostituée. Transl. Meille. Paris, 1896.

FERRERO DI CAVALLERLEONE, L., et C. PLACIDO. Essais de criminologie militaire. Compt. rendus du VI Congr. d'anthr. crim. Turin, 1908.

FERRI, E. Studi sulla criminalità in Francia 1826-1878. Annali di Statistica, 1881.

—— Socialismo e criminalità. Torino, 1883.

—— Variations thermométriques et criminalité. Archives d'anthr. crim., I.

—— La sociologie criminelle. Paris, 1893. Amer. ed. transl. Kelly and Lisle, Boston, 1916 (Modern Criminal Science Series).

—— L' omicidio. Torino, 1895.

—— Atlante anthropologico-statistico dell' omicidio. Torino, 1895.

—— La théorie sociologique de M. Tarde. Devenir social, 1895.

—— Kriminelle Anthropologie u. Sozialismus. Neue Zeit, 1895-1896, II.

—— Le crime comme phénomène social. Annales de l'institut intern. de sociologie, 1896.

—— Eine Verirrung des XIX Jahrhunderts. Neue Zeit, 1898-99, II.

—— Les criminels dans l'art et la littérature. Transl. Laurent. Paris.

FERRIANI, L. La infanticida. Milano, 1886.

—— L'amore in tribunale Bologna. 1889.

—— Minderjährige Verbrecher. Autorisirte Ausgabe. Berlin, 1896.

—— Entarte Mütter. Autor. Ausgabe. Berlin, 1897.

—— Schlaue und glückliche Verbrecher. Aut. Ausg. Berlin, 1899.

FIAUX, L. La prostitution en Russie. Progrès médicale. 1893.

FINKELNBURG, K. Die Bestraften in Deutschland. Berlin, 1912.

FISCHER, E. Laienbemerkungen zur Reform des Strafrechts. Sozialistische Monatshefte X[1].

—— K. Denkwürdigkeiten und Erinnerungen eines Arbeiters. Jena u. Leipzig, 1903-1904.

FLETCHER, J. Moral and Educational Statistics of England and Wales. Journ. of the Stat. Society of London, 1847, 1849.

FLORIAN, E., and G. CAVAGLIERI. I vagabondi I, II. Torino, 1897, 1900.

FLYNT, J. Tramping with Tramps. New York, 1899.

FOLDES, B. Einige Ergebnisse der neueren Kriminalstatistik. Zeitschr. f. d. ges. Strafr. w., XI.

FOREL, A. Die sexuelle Frage. München, 1913.
—— Verbrechen und Konstitutionnelle Seelenabnormitäten. München, 1907.
FORNASARI DI VERCE, E. La criminalità e le vicende economiche d' Italia 1873–1890. Torino, 1894.
FOURIER, CH. Œuvres complètes I et III. Paris, 1841.
FRANCKEN, C. J. WIJNAENDTS. De evolutie van het huwelijk. Leiden, 1894.
FRANK, F. Das Fürsorgeerziehungsgesetz in Preussen. Neue Zeit, XXVII[1].
FRANKENSTEIN, K. Die Lage des Arbeiterinnen in dem deutschen Grossstädten. Jahrbuch für gesetzgebung etc., XII[2].
FRASSATI, A. Die neue positive Schule in Russland. Zeitschr. f. d. ges. Strafr., X.
FRAUENSTÄDT, P. Kriminalistische Heimatkunde. Zeitschr. f. Soc. w., VI.
FRÉGIER, H. A. Les classes dangéreuses de la population dans les grandes villes I. Paris, 1840.
FRÖHLICH, R. Ergebnisse einer Umfrage über den Alcoholgenuss der Schulkinder in Niederösterreich. VIII Intern. Congress g. d. Alkoholismus. Wien, 1901.
FULD, L. Der Einfluss der Lebensmittelpreise auf die Bewegung der strafbaren Handlungen. Mainz, 1881.

GAEDEKEN, P. Contribution statistique à la réaction de l'organisme sous l'influence physico-chimique des agents météorologiques. Archives etc., XXIV.
GALLE, J. Untersuchungen über die Kriminalität in der Provinz Schlesien. Gerichtssaal, LXXI and LXXII.
—— Die Kriminalität in Stadt und Land in ihres Beziehung zur Berufsverteilung. Zeitschr. f. d. ges. etc., XXX.
GALTON, F. Inquiries into Human Faculty and its Development. London, 1883.
—— Hereditary Genius. London, 1892.
GARNER, J. W. Homicide in American Cities. Journal of Crim. Law and Criminology, III.
GARNIER, P. Rapport sur l'influence de l'alcoolisme sur la criminalité. Actes du congr. pénitentiaire à Bruxelles, IV. Bruxelles et Berne, 1901.
—— La criminalité juvénile. Compte rendu V congr. d'anthr. crim. Amsterdam, 1901.
GAROFALO, R. La criminologie. Paris, 1890. Amer. ed. transl. Millar, Boston, 1914 (Modern Criminal Science Series).
—— La superstition socialiste. Transl. A. Dietrich. Paris, 1895.
—— L'influence des prédispositions et du milieu dans la criminalité. Bericht über den VII Intern. Kongr. für Krim. Anthr. Heidelberg, 1912.
GARRAUD, R., et P. BERNARD. Des attentats à la pudeur et des viols sur les enfants. Archives etc., I.
GAUPP, R. Ueber den heutigen Stand der Lehre vom "geborenen" Verbrecher. Monatschr. etc., I.
GAUTIER, A. Le procès Lucheni. Schweizerische Zeitschr. f. Strafrecht, XI.

GAUTIER, E. Le monde des prisons. Archives etc., III.

GEILL. Kriminal-anthropologische Untersuchungen dänischer Sittlichkeits-verbrecher. Archiv. f. Krim. Anthr. etc., XX.

GENIL-PERRIN, G., et CH. VALLON. Crime et altruisme. Archives etc., XXVIII.

GERECHTELIJKE. Statistiek van het Koninkrijk der Nederlanden 1887–1899. ó Gravenhage, 1888–1901.

GIRGUET, M. Mémoires. Paris, 1840.

GIZYCKI, P. v. Wie urteilen Schulkinder über Funddiebstahl? Zeitschr. f. Kinderforschung, VIII.

GLEISPACH, W. Ueber Kindesmord. Archiv etc., XXVII.

GODWIN, W. Inquiry Concerning Political Justice. London, 1796.

GOES, F. v. D. Socialisme en feminisme. Tweemaandelijksch Tijdschrift, VI.

GÖHRE, P. Drie maanden fabrieksarbeider. Transl. H. Mercier. Amsterdam.

GOUZER, J. Psychologie de l'anarchiste. Archives etc., IX.

GRAAF, H. T. DE. Karakter en behandeling van vervordeelden wegens landlooperij en bedelarij. Groningen, 1914.

GRABE, E. v. Prostitution, Kriminalität und Psychopathie. Archiv etc., XLVIII.

GRADNAUER, G. Das Elend des Strafvollzugs. Berlin, 1905.

GRANIER, C. La femme criminelle. Paris, 1906.

GROSMOLARD, M. Criminalité juvénile. Archives etc. XVIII.

GROSSE, E. Die Formen der Familie und die Formen der Wirtschaft. Freiburg i/B u. Leipzig, 1896.

GROTJAHN, A. Der Alkoholismus. Leipzig, 1898.

GRUBER, G. B. Der Alkoholismus. Leipzig, 1911.

GRUHLE, H. W. Ursachen des jugendlichen Verwahrlosung und Kriminali-tät. Berlin, 1912.

GUERRY, A. M. Essai sur la statistique morale de la France. Paris, 1833.

GUMPLOWICZ, L. Das Verbrechen als soziale Erscheinung. (Soziologische Essays. Innsbrück, 1899.)

——— Grundriss der Soziologie. Wien, 1905.

GUYOT, J. La prostitution. Paris, 1882.

GYSTROW, E. (Pseudonym of W. Hellpach.) Sozialpathologische Pro-bleme der Gegenwart. Soz. Monatshefte V [1].

——— Liebe u. Liebesleben im XIX Jahrhundert. Berlin, 1902.

HAMEL, G. A. VAN. De tegenwoordige beweging op het gebied van het strafrecht. (Verspreide opstellen, I. Leiden, 1912.)

——— L'anarchisme et le combat contre l'anarchisme au point de vue de l'anthropologie criminelle. Actes du IV Congr. d'anthr. crim. Genève, 1896.

——— J. A. VAN. Strafrechtspolitiek van voor honderd jaâr. (Gids, 1909, II.)

HAMON, A. De la définition du crime. Archives etc., VIII.

——— Psychologie de l'anarchiste-socialiste. Paris, 1895.

——— Psychologie du militaire professionnel. Paris, 1904.

HATZIG, K. Der Mädchenhandel. Zeitschr. f. d. ges. Strafr. w., XX.

HAURY. La paresse pathologique. Archives etc., XXVIII.

HAUSSONVILLE, D'. Le combat contre le vice, II "La criminalité." Revue des deux mondes, 1887.

HEIM, H. Die jüngsten und die ältesten Verbrecher. Berlin, 1897.

HELIE, J. Le vagabondage des mineurs. Mayenne, 1899.

HELLPACH, W. Soziale Ursachen und Wirkungen des Nervosität. Politisch. Anthrop. Revue, I.

—— Der Kampf gegen die Geschlechtskrankheiten. Soz. Monatshefte, VII.

—— See also: GYSTROW.

HELLWIG, A. Verbrechen und Aberglaube. Leipzig, 1908.

—— Die Beziehungen zwischen Schundlitteratur, Schundfilms u. Verbrechen. Archiv etc., LIII.

HELVETIUS, C. A. De l'homme. (Œuvres. Paris, 1795.)

HENDERSON, CH. RICHMOND. Introduction to the Study of the Dependent, Defective and Delinquent Classes. Boston, 1909.

HERKNER, H. Die arbeiterfrage. Berlin, 1905.

HERRMANN, T. Die Prostitution und ihr Anhang. Leipzig, 1905.

HERZ, H. Die Kriminalität des Weibes nach den Ergebnissen der neueren oesterreichischen Statistik. Archiv etc., XVIII.

—— Verbrechen und Verbrechertum in Oesterreich. Tübingen, 1908.

HESSE, R. Les criminels peints par eux-mêmes. Paris, 1912.

HESSEN, R. Die Prostitution in Deutschland. München, 1910.

HIRSCH, P. Verbrechen und Prostitution. Berlin, 1897.

HIRSCHBERG. Soziale Lage der arbeitenden Klasse in Berlin. Berlin, 1897.

HIRSCHFELD, M. Ursachen und Wesen des Uranismus. Jahrbuch f. sexuelle Zwischenstufen V.

—— Die historische Entwicklung des Alkoholmissbrauchs. VIII Intern. Congr. g. d. Alkoholismus.

—— Die Homosexualität des Mannes und des Weibes. Berlin, 1914.

HOBHOUSE, L. T. Morals in Evolution. London, 1908.

HOEGEL, H. Die Straffälligkeit der Jugendlichen. Archiv etc., X.

—— Die Straffälligkeit der Weibes. Archiv etc., V.

—— Die Grenzen der Kriminalstatistik. Statistische Monatschrift. XXXIII.

—— Kriminalstatistik und Kriminalaetiologie. Monatschrift etc., VIII.

HOLBACH. Système social. Londres, 1773.

HOLMES, TH. Pictures and Problems from London Police Courts. London, 1902.

HOLTZ, L. Les crimes passionels. Paris, 1904.

HOLZENDORFF, FR. V. Die Psychologie des Mordes. (Sammlung gemeinverständliches Vorträge, X.)

HOMBURGER, M. Der Einfluss der Schundlitteratur auf jugendliche Verbrecher und Selbstmörder. Monatschr. etc., VI.

—— Ueber den Zusammenhang zwischen der Zahlen der in den Fabriken beschäftigten Personen unter 18 Jahren und den Zahl der Verbrechen solcher Personnen. Monatschrift etc., VII.

—— Lebensschicksale geisteskranker Strafgefangene. Berlin, 1912.

HOOFDSTUK. Een vergeten. (Anonymous.) Amsterdam, 1898.

HOPPE, A. Alkohol und Kriminalität. Wiesbaden, 1906.
HOTTER, C. Alkohol und verbrechen in Niederbayern. Monatschrift etc., VIII.
HÜBNER, A. H. Ueber Prostituirte and ihre strafrechtliche Behandlung. Monatschr. etc., III.
HÜGEL, FE. S. Zur Geschichte, Statistik, und Regelung der Prostitution. Wien, 1865.
HUGO, C. Kind and Gesellschaft. Neue Zeit, 1894–95, I.
HULZEN, G. v. Van de zelfkant der samenleving. Gids, 1903.
HUNTER, R. Das Elend der neuen Welt. Transl. Südekum. Berlin, 1908.

ILLING, J. Die Zahlen der Kriminalität in Preussen, 1854–1884. Zeitschr. d. k. preussischen stat. Bureaus, 1885.

JAARCIJFERS voor het Koninkrijk der Nederlanden. Rijk in Europa 1901. ó Gravenhage, 1902.
JACQUART, C. La criminalité belge 1868–1909. Louvain, 1912.
JACQUETTY, G. Etude statistique de la criminalité juvénile en France. Lyon-Paris, 1912.
JAEGER, J. Zunahme der Verbrechen und Abhilfe. Leipzig, 1898.
JEANNEL, J. De la prostitution dans les grandes villes au XIXᵉ siècle et de l'extinction des maladies vénériennes. Paris, 1874.
JELGERSMA, G. De geboren misdadiger. Tijdschrift v. Strafrecht, 1891.
JELLINEK, C. Kellnerinnenelend. Archiv f. Socialw. und Socialpolitik, XXIV.
JHERING, R. v. Der Zweck im Recht, I. Leipzig, 1884.
JOLY, H. Le crime. Paris, 1888.
—— La France criminelle, 1889.
—— L'enfance coupable. Paris, 1904.
—— La Belgique criminelle. Paris, 1907.
JÖRGER, J. La famille "Zéro." Archives etc., XXIII.
JUDICIAL Statistics, England and Wales. Part I, Criminal Statistics, 1894– 1900, 1905. London, 1896–1902, 1907.
JUDICIAL Statistics, Ireland. Part I, Criminal Statistics. Dublin, 1906.
JUGENDGESCHICHTE einer Arbeiterin. (Anonymous.) München, 1907.

KAMPFFMEYER, P. Geschichte der modernen Gesellschaftsklassen in Deutschland. Berlin, 1896.
—— Das Wohnungselend der Grossstädte und seine Beziehungen zur Verbreitung der Geschlechtskrankheiten und zur Prostitution. Verhandlungen d. 1ᵉⁿ Kongresses d. deutschen Gesellsch. z. Bekämpfung der Geschlechtskrankheiten. Leipzig, 1903.
—— Die Wohnungsmissstände im Prostitution — und im Schlafgängerwesen und ihre gesetzliche Reform. Zeitschr. z. Bekämpfung d. Geschlechtskrankheiten III.
—— Die Prostitution als soziale Klassenerscheinung und ihre sozialpolitische Bekämpfung. Berlin, 1905.
KAN, J. v. Les causes sociales de la criminalité. Compte rendu V Congr. d'anthr. crim. Amsterdam, 1901.

KAN, J. v. Les causes économiques de la criminalité. Paris-Lyon, 1903.

KAUFFMANN, M. Psychologie des Verbrechens. Berlin, 1912.

KAUTSKY, K. Die sozialen Triebe in der Tierwelt. Neue Zeit, 1883.
—— Die sozialen Triebe in der Menschenwelt. Neue Zeit, 1884.
—— Die Indianerfrage. Neue Zeit, 1885.
—— Die Entstehung des Christentums. Neue Zeit, 1885.
—— Thomas More und seine Utopie. Stuttgart, 1888.
—— Der Alcoholismus und sein Bekämpfung. Neue Zeit, 1890-1891, I.
—— Das Erfurter Programm. Stuttgart, 1892.
—— Eine Naturgeschichte des politischen Verbrechers. Neue Zeit, 1892-93, II.
—— Lombroso und seine Vertheidiger. Neue Zeit, 1893-94, II.
—— Die materialistische Geschichtsauffassung und des psychologische Antrieb. Neue Zeit, 1895-96, II.
—— Karl Marx, oekonomische Lehren. Stuttgart, 1898.
—— Geschichte des Socialismus in Einzeldarstellungen, Ersten Band, Zweiter Theil. Stuttgart, 1895.
—— Sozialreform und soziale Revolution. Berlin, 1902.
—— Ethik und materialistische Geschichtsauffassung. Stuttgart, 1906.

KELLEO-KRANZ, C. DE. Formes primitives de la famille. Revue internationale de sociologie, VIII.

KEMPF, R. Das Leben der jungen Fabrikmädchen in München. Leipzig, 1911.

KENDE, M. Die Entartung des Menschengeschlechts.

KEY, E. Das Jahrhundert des Kindes. Auth. transl. Berlin, 1902.

KINBERG, O. Alcool et criminalité. Archives etc., XXVIII.

KNOBLANCH, F. Bettel und Landstreicherei im Königreiche Bayern 1893-1899. München, 1910.

KOHLER, J. Shakespeare vor dem Forum der Jurisprudenz. Würzburg, 1883.

KOLB, G. F. Handbuch der vergleichenden Statistik. Leipzig, 1860.

KORN, A. Strafrechtsreform oder Sittenpolizei. Jahrbuch f. Gesetzgebung etc., XXI[3].

KORNER. Critic on "Verbrechen und Verbrecher in Preussen 1854-1878" of Starke. Jahrbücher f. Nat. oek. u. Stat., N. F., XIII.

KOVALEVSKY, M. Tableau des origines et de l'évolution de la famille et de la propriété. Stockholm, 1890.
—— Les origines du devoir. Revue intern. de sociologie, II.
—— P. La psychologie criminelle. Paris, 1903.

KRAFFT-EBING, R. v. Psychopathia sexualis. Stuttgart, 1898.

KRÄPELIN, E. Psychiatrie I.

KRAUSS, A. Die Psychologie des Verbrechens. Tübingen, 1884.

KRAUSS, F. A. K. Der Kampf gegen die Verbrechensursachen. Paderborn, 1905.

KRIMINALSTATISTIK für das Jahr 1888, 1894-1896, 1898-1900, 1908, 1911. Statistik des Deutschen Reichs, N. F., 1888, etc.

KRITSCHEWSKY, B. Die Korruption in der französischen Demokratie. Neue Zeit, XXVIII[2].

KROPOTKIN, P. Paroles d'un révolté. Paris.
—— Mutual Aid among Animals. Nineteenth Century, 1890.
—— Mutual Aid among Savages. Nineteenth Century, 1891.
—— Mutual Aid among the Barbarians. Nineteenth Century, 1892.
—— Mutual Aid. London, 1908.
KÜHN, J. Die Prostitution im XIX Jahrhundert. Leipzig, 1871.
KULISCHER. Der Dualismus der Ethik bei den primitiven Völkern. Zeitschr. f. Ethnologie, 1885.
KUMMER, F. Die Geschichte des grossen amerikanischen Vermögen. Neue Zeit, XXX [2].
KÜRBITZ-SONNENSCHEIN, W. Der Geisteszustand der Kindermörderinnen. Archiv f. Krim. Anthr. etc., LII.
KURELLA, H. Naturgeschichte des Verbrechers. Stuttgart, 1893.
—— Zurechnungsfähigkeit, Kriminalanthropologie. Halle a/S 1903.
—— Anthropologie und Strafrecht. Würzburg, 1912.
KÜRZ, E. Zur Prophylaxe der Roheitsdelikte. Monatschr. etc., II.

LACASSAGNE, A. Marche de la criminalité en France 1825–1880. Revue Scientifique, 1881.
—— Les vols à l'étalage et dans les grands magasins. Actes IV congr. d'anthr. crim. Genève, 1896.
—— L'assassinat du président Carnot. Archives etc., IX.
—— et E. MARTIN. Des résultats positifs et indiscutables que l'anthropologie criminelle peut fournir à l'élaboration ou l'application des lois. Compte rendu V Congr. d'anthr. crim. Amsterdam, 1901.
LACAZE, H. De la criminalité féminine en France. Lyon, 1910.
LADAME, P. De la prostitution dans ses rapports avec l'alcoolisme, le crime et la folie. Neuchâtel, 1884.
—— et E. RÉGIS. Le régicide Lucheni. Archives etc., XXII.
LAFARGUE, P. Der wirtschaftliche Materialismus. Höttingen-Zürich, 1886.
—— Der Ehebruch in Gegenwart und Vergangenheit. Neue Zeit, 1889.
—— Die Kriminalität in Frankreich 1840–1886. Neue Zeit, 1890.
—— Der Ursprung der Idee des Gerichten und Ungerechten. Neue Zeit, 1898–99, II.
LANESSAN, J. L. DE. La lutte contre le crime. Paris, 1910.
LANG, O. Alkoholgenuss und Verbrechen. Basel, 1895.
LASCHI, R. Le crime financier. Lyon-Paris, 1901.
—— und C. LOMBROSO. Der politische Verbrecher und die Revolutionen. Auth. transl. Kurella. Hamburg, 1892.
LASPEYRES, E. Der Einfluss der Wohnung auf die Sittlichkeit. Berlin, 1869.
LASSALLE, F. Die Feste, die Presse und der Frankfurter Abgeordnetentag. Reden und Schriften, II. Berlin, 1893.
—— Offenes Antwort-Schreiben. Reden etc., II.
LAURENT, E. Les habitués des prisons de Paris. Paris, 1890.
—— La criminalité infantile. Paris, 1908.
—— Le criminel. Paris, 1908.
LEALE, H. De la criminalité des sexes. Archives etc., XXV.
LECOUR, C. J. La prostitution à Paris et à Londres. Paris, 1870.
LEGRAIN. Conséquences sociales de l'alcoolisme des ascendants au point

de vue de dégénérescence, de la morale et de la criminalité. Actes
IV Congr. d'anthr. crim. Genève, 1896.

LENZ, A. Die Zwangserziehung in England. Stuttgart, 1894.

LEPEL, V. v. Prostitution beim Theater. Zürich.

LEPPMANN, F. Die Sittlichkeitsverbrecher. Vierteljahrschrift f. gerichtl.
Medizin etc., XXIX, XXX.

LETOURNEAU, CH. L'évolution de la morale. Paris, 1887.

—— L'évolution du mariage et de la famille. Paris, 1888.

—— L'évolution de la propriété. Paris, 1889.

—— L'évolution juridique. Paris, 1891.

LEUSS, H. Aus dem Zuchthause. Berlin, 1903.

LEVASSEUR, E. La population française II. Paris, 1891.

LEY, A., et R. CHARPENTIER. Alcoolisme et criminalité. Bruxelles, 1910.

LINDENAU, H. Beruf und Verbrechen. Zeitschr. f. d. ges. Strafr. w., XXIV.

LINDENBERG, G. Die Ergebnisse der deutschen Kriminalstatistik 1882–
1892. Jahrb. f. Nat. oek. etc., III. Folge, VIII.

LINGUET, S. N. H. Théorie des loix civiles. Londres, 1767.

LIPPERT, H. Die Prostitution in Hamburg. Hamburg, 1848.

LISZT, F. v. Die sozial-politische Auffassung des Verbrechens. Sozial-
politisches Centralblatt, 1892.

—— Die gesellschaftlichen Ursacher des Verbrechens. Sozial-politisches
Centralblatt, 1872.

—— Das Verbrechen als Social-pathologische Erscheinung. Dresden,
1899.

—— Das gewerbmässige Verbrechen. Zeitschr. f. d. ges. Strafr. w., XXI.

—— Die gesellschaftlichen Faktoren der Kriminalität. Zeitschr. etc.,
XXIII.

—— Die psychologischen Grundlagen der Kriminalpolitik. Zeitschr. etc.,
XVI.

—— Kriminal-politische Ausgaben. Zeitschr. etc., IX, X, XII.

LOGAN, W. The Great Social Evil. London, 1871.

LOMBROSO, C. Der Verbrecher. Transl. Fränkel. Hamburg, 1894.

—— Les palimpsestes des prisons. Lyon-Paris, 1894.

—— Le crime, causes et remèdes. Paris, 1899.

—— Crime, Its Causes and Remedies. Transl. Horton. Boston, 1910.

—— et G. FERRERO. La femme criminelle et la prostituée. Transl. L.
Meille. Paris, 1896.

—— und R. LASCHI. Der politische Verbrecher und die Revolutionen.
Autorisirte Uebersetzung von H. Kurella. Hamburg, 1892.

LONGARD, J. Ueber "moral insanity." Monatschr. etc., II.

LOOSJES, C. Bijdrage tot de studie van de criminaliteit der vrouw. Haarlem, 1894.

LÖWE, PH. Die Prostitution aller Zeiten und Völker mit besonderer Berück-
sichtigung von Berlin. Berlin, 1852.

LÖWENSTIMM, A. Aberglaube und Strafrecht. Berlin, 1897.

—— Fanatismus und Verbrechen. Berlin, 1901.

—— Aberglaube und Verbrechen. Zeitschr. f. Soc. w., VI.

—— Aberglaube und Gesetz. Archiv etc., XXV.

LUX, H. Die Prostitution. Berlin, 1892.

Lux, H. Socialpolitisches Handbuch. Berlin, 1892.
—— Die Sittlichkeitsverbrechen in Deutschland in kriminalstatistischer Beleuchtung. Archiv für sociale Gesetzgeb. u. Stat. V.

Mably. De la législation ou principes des loix. Paris, 1792.
Mackirdy, A., and W. N. Willis. The White Slave Market. London.
Magnan. De l'enfance des criminels dans ses rapports avec la prédisposition naturelle au crime. Actes du II Congr. d'anthr. crim. Paris.
Maine, H. S. Village Communities in the East and West. London, 1876.
Makarewicz, J. L'évolution de la peine. Archives etc., XIII.
——Einführung in die Philosophie des Strafrechts. Stuttgart, 1906.
Malarce, M. A. de. Moralité comparée des diverses parties de la France d'après la criminalité. Journal de la Société de statistique de Paris, 1860.
Malgat, J. Rapport sur l'influence de l'alcoolisme sur la criminalité. Actes du congr. pénitent. intern. de Bruxelles, 1900, IV. Bruxelles et Berne, 1901.
Mandl, H. Die Wiener Presskorruption. Neue Zeit, 1884.
Manes, C. Capitalismo e criminalità. Roma, 1912.
Manouvrier, L. Les crânes des suppliciés. Archives etc., I.
—— Les aptitudes et les actes. L'ère nouvelle, 1893.
—— La genèse normale du crime. Bulletin de la Société d'anthropologie de Paris, 1893.
—— L'atavisme et le crime. L'ère nouvelle, 1894.
—— Existe-t-il des caractères anatomiques propres aux criminels? Les criminels présentent-ils en moyenne certains caractères anatomiques particuliers? Comment doit-on interpréter ces caractères? Actes II Congr. d'anthr. crim. Paris.
—— Quelques cas de criminalité juvénile et commençante. Archives etc., XXVII.
Manzini, V. Le varie specie di furto nella storia e nella sociologia III. Torino, 1913.
Marambat, V. Rapport sur l'influence de l'alcoolisme sur la criminalité. Actes Congr. pénitent. intern. de Bruxelles, 1900, IV. Bruxelles et Berne, 1901.
Marat, J. P. Plan de la législation criminelle. Paris, 1790.
Marie, A., et R. Meunier. Les vagabonds. Paris, 1908.
Marro, A. I caratteri dei delinquenti. Torino, 1887.
Martin, E. Etudes sur l'enfance coupable. Archives etc., XXVIII.
—— et A. Lacassagne. Des résultats positifs et indiscutables que l'anthropologie criminelle peut fournir à l'élaboration ou l'application des lois. Compte rendu V congr. d'anthr. crim. Amsterdam, 1901.
Martineau, L. La prostitution clandestine. Paris, 1885.
Marx, K. Zur Kritik der politischen Oekonomie. Stuttgart, 1897.
—— Das Kapital I. Hamburg, 1900.
—— und F. Engels. Die heilige Familie. (Gesammelte Schriften etc., II. Stuttgart, 1902.)
Masoin, M. L'alcoolisme dans ses rapports avec la criminalité. Bull. de l'ac. royale de médecine de Belgique, 1896. Bruxelles, 1896.
Maudsley, H. The Physiology and Pathology of Mind. London, 1868.

MAXWELL, J. Le crime et la société. Paris, 1912.

MAYHEW, A., and J. BINNY. The Criminal Prisons of London. London, 1862.

MAYR, G. v. Statistik der gerichtlichen Polizei im Königreiche Bayern. München, 1867.

—— Die Gesetzmässigkeit im Gesellschaftsleben. München, 1877.

—— Statistik und Gesellschaftslehre II, III, Freiburg i/B, 1897. Tübingen, 1910.

—— Forschungsgebiet und Forschungsziele der Kriminalstatistik. Zeitschr. f. d. ges. etc., XXXII.

—— Kriminalstatistik und Kriminalaetiologie. Monatschr. etc., VIII.

—— Nochmals Kriminalstatistik und Kriminalaetiologie. Monatschr. etc., IX.

MERCIER, E. L'influence du bien-être matériel sur la criminalité. Paris, 1854.

MERENS, A. H. J. Over het onderzoek naar den invloed der dronkenschap op de criminaliteit. Haarlem, 1902.

MESDAG, S. V. Iets over landloopers en bedelaars. Tijdschrift v. Strafrecht, XV.

MESLIER, J. Le testament de. Amsterdam, 1864.

MEUNIER, R., et A. MARIE. Les vagabonds. Paris, 1908.

MEYER. Schundlitteratur und Schundfilms. Archiv etc., LIII.

—— A. Die Verbrechen in ihrem Zusammenhang mit den wirtschaftlichen und sozialen Verhältnissen in Kanton Zürich. Jena, 1895.

MINOVICI, M. Remarques sur la criminalité en Rumanie. Comptes rend. VI congr. d'anthr. crim. Turin, 1908.

MISCHLER. Hauptergebnisse in moralischer Hinricht. Handbuch d. Gefängnisswesens II. Hamburg, 1888.

MISDADIGE jeugd in het havenbedrijf. (Anonymous.) Rotterdam, 1904.

MITTELSTAEDT. Critic on Starke. Zeitschr. f. d. ges. etc., IV.

MOLL, A. Handbuch der Sexualwissenschaften. Leipzig, 1912.

MÖNKEMÖLLER, O. Korrektionsanstalt und Landarmenhaus. Leipzig, 1908.

—— Zur Kriminalität der Kindesalters. Archiv etc., XL.

—— Die Kriminalität der Korrigendin. Monatschr. etc., V.

MOQUETTE, J. J. R. Onderzoekingen over volksvoeding in de gemeente Utrecht. Utrecht, 1907.

MOREAU, G. Le monde des prisons. Paris, 1887.

—— Souvenirs de la petite et de la grande Roquette. Paris.

MOREAU (de Tours), P. L'homicide commis par les enfants. Paris, 1882.

MOREAU-CHRISTOPHE, L. M. Du problème de la misère, III. Paris, 1851.

—— Le monde des coquins. Paris, 1863.

MOREL, J. La prophylaxe et le traitement du criminel récidiviste. Compte rend. V congr. d'anthr. crim. Amsterdam, 1901.

MORELLY. Code de la nature. 1755.

MORGAN, L. H. Houses and House-life of the American Aborigines. Washington, 1881.

—— Ancient Society, N. Y. 1878. Transl. Eichhoff. Die Urgesellschaft. Stuttgart, 1891.

MORRISON, W. D.   Crime and Its Causes.   London, 1891.
────── Juvenile Offenders.   London, 1896.
────── The Interpretation of Criminal Statistics.   Journal of the Stat. Soc. of London, 1897.
MORE, TH.   Utopia.   Transl. Ralph Robynson.   Cambridge (Eng.), 1891.
MOSSE, M., und G. TUGENDREICH.   Krankheit und soziale Lage.   München, 1912–1913.
MOTET, M.   De l'éducation correctionnelle.   Actes II congr. d'anthr. crim. Paris.
MULLER, N.   Biografisch-aetiologisch onderzoek over recidive bij misdrijven tegen den eigendom.   Utrecht, 1908.
MÜLLER, FR. W.   De prostitutie.   Zutfen, 1870.
MÜLLER, H.   Untersuchungen über die Bewegung der Kriminalität in ihrem Zusammenhang mit dem wirtschaftlichen Verhältnissen.   Halle a. S., 1899.
MÜLLER-LYER, F.   Formen der Ehe.   München, 1911.
────── Die Familie.   München, 1912.
────── Phasen der Liebe.   München, 1913.

NÄCKE, P.   Verbrechen u. Wahnsinn beim Weibe.   Wien u. Leipzig, 1894.
────── Die neueren Erscheinungen auf kriminal-anthropologischen Gebiete und ihre Bedeutung.   Zeitschr. f. d. ges. Strafr. w., XIV.
────── Emile Zola.   In memoriam.   Seine Beziehungen zur Kriminalanthropologie und Soziologie.   Archiv etc., XI.
────── Ein Besuch bei den Homosexuellen in Berlin.   Archiv etc., XV.
────── Critic on "Criminalité et conditions économiques" of Bonger. Archiv etc., XXI.
────── Die Ueberbleibsel der Lombroseschen kriminal-anthropologischen Theorien.   Archiv etc., L.
NANSEN, F.   Eskimoleben.   Leipzig und Berlin, 1903.
────── Eskimo Life.   Transl. Archer.   London, 1894.
NEHER, A.   Die geheime und öffentliche Prostitution in Stuttgart, Karlsruhe und München.   Paderborn, 1912.
NEUMANN, H.   Die jugendlichen Berliner unehelicher Herkunft.   Jahrb. f. Nat. oek. u. Stat. III.   Folge, VIII.
NICEFORO, A.   Criminalità e condizioni economiche in Sicilia.   Rivista di scient. didiritto 1897.
────── Les transformations du crime et la civilisation moderne.   Scuola positiva, XI.
────── Anthropologie der nichtbesitzender Klassen.   Transl. Michels. Leipzig und Amsterdam, 1910.
NIEBAER, H. J.   Slavery as an Industrial System.   The Hague, 1910.
NIEUWENHUIS, F. DOMELA.   Zur Frage der Prostitution.   Neue Zeit, 1884.
NOORDUYN, J. P. F. A.   De observatie, na de invoering der Kinderwetten, in het Rijksopvoedingsgesticht te Alkmaar.   Tijdschrift v. Strafrecht, XXIII.
NORDAU, M.   Die conventionnellen Lügen der Kulturmenschheit.
NOT des vierten Standes, Die.   (Anonymous.)   Leipzig, 1894.
NOTIZIE complementari alle statistiche giudiziarie penali degli anni 1890–1895, 1896–1900.   Roma, 1899, 1909.

ODIN, A. Genèse des grands hommes. Paris, 1895.

OETTINGEN, A. v. Moralstatistik. Erlangen, 1882.

ONDERZOEK naar den fabrieksarbeid van gehuwde vrouwen in Nederland. ó Gravenhage, 1911.

ONDERZOEKINGEN naar de toestanden in de Nederlandsche huisindustrie. ó Gravenhage, 1911–1912.

ONMATIG lange arbeidstijd en misbruik van sterken drank. (Anonymous.) Utrecht, 1895.

OPPENHEIMER, F. Der Staat. Frankfurt a. M., 1907.

ORCHANSKI. Les criminels russes. Actes II congr. d'anthr. crim. Paris.

O. S. Die Verbrecherwelt von Berlin. Zeitschr. f. d. ges. etc., IV, V.

OSTWALD, H. Das Leben der Wanderarmen. Archiv etc., XIII.

———— Das Zuhältertum in Berlin. (Gross stadt-Dokumente.) Berlin-Leipzig.

OWEN, R. The Book of the New Moral World. London, 1849.

———— A New View on Society; or Essays on the Principle of the Formation of the Human Character. Life of Robert Owen. Appendix B. London, 1857.

———— Reports of the Proceedings at the several Public Meetings held in Dublin.

PAGNIER, A. Le vagabond. Paris, 1910.

PAPPRITZ, A. Die wirtschaftlichen Ursachen der Prostitution. Berlin, 1903.

———— Die Welt, von der man nicht spricht. Leipzig, 1907.

PARENT-DUCHATELET. De la prostitution dans la ville de Paris. Paris, 1857.

PASHITNOW, K. A. Die Lage der arbeitenden Klasse in Russland. Stuttgart, 1907.

PATYN, J. G. Misdaadenatavisme. Tijdschr. v. Strafr., 1891.

PECQUEUR, C. Des améliorations matérielles. Paris, 1841.

PELMAN, C. Psychische Grenzzustände. Bonn, 1912.

PESTALOZZI, H. Ueber Gesetzgebung und Kindermord. (Sämmtliche Schriften VII, VIII.) Stuttgart und Tübingen, 1821.

PETER, H. Zur Lage der Kellnerinnen im Grossherzogtum Baden. Archiv f. Socialw. u. Socialpol., XXIV.

PETERSELIE, E. Untersuchungen über die Kriminalität in den Provinz Sachsen. Beilageheft zur Band LXIV Gerichtssaal. Stuttgart, 1904.

PFEIFFER. Das Wohnungselend der grossen Städte und seine Beziehungen zur Prostitution und den Geschlechtskrankheiten. Verhandlungen d. 1^{en} Kongr. d. deutschen Gesellsch. z. Bekämpfung d. Geschlechtskrankheiten. Leipzig, 1903.

PHILIPPOVICH, E. v. Wiener Wohnungsverhältnisse. Archiv f. soz. Gesetzgeb. u. Stat., VII.

PIKE, L. O. History of Crime in England. London, 1873/1876.

PINSERO, N. Miseria e delitto. Scuola Positiva, 1898.

PISTOLESE, A. Alcoolismo e delinquenza. Torino, 1907.

PLACIDO, C., et L. FERRERO DI CAVALLERLEONE. Essais de criminologie militaire. Compte rendu VI congr. d'anthr. crim. Turin, 1908.

PLASZ, L. Fürsorgeerziehung. Woche N°. 51, V.

PLATON. La république ou l'état. Paris, 1873.

PLECHANOW, G. Anarchismus und Sozialismus. Berlin, 1894.

—— Beiträge zur Geschichte des Materialismus. Stuttgart, 1896.

PLÖTZ, A. Die Tüchtigkeit unsrer Rasse und der Schutz der Schwachen. Berlin, 1895.

POLLITZ, P. Psychologie der Verbrechers. Leipzig, 1909.

PORTER, G. R. The Influence of Education shown by Facts Recorded in the Criminal Tables for 1845 and 1846. Journal of the Stat. Soc. of London, 1847.

POST, A. H. Die Geschlechtsgenossenschaft der Urzeit und die Entstehung der Ehe. Oldenburg, 1875.

—— Der Ursprung des Rechts. Oldenburg, 1876.

—— Bausteine für eine allgemeine Rechtswissenschaft. Oldenburg, 1880.

—— Grundriss der ethnologischen Jurisprudenz. Oldenburg und Leipzig, 1895.

—— Die Grundlagen des Rechts.

PRINS, A. Criminalité et répression. Bruxelles, 1886.

PRINZING, FR. Soziale Faktoren der Kriminalität. Zeitschr. f. d. ges. etc., XXII.

—— Der Einfluss der Ehe auf die Kriminalität des Mannes. Zeitschr. f. Socialwissensch., II.

—— Die Erhöhung der Kriminalität des Weibes durch die Ehe. Zeitschr. f. Socialw., II.

—— Die soziale Lage der Witwe in Deutschland. Zeitschr. f. Socialw., III.

—— Ueber frühzeitige Heiraten, deren Vorzüge und Nachteile. Jahrb. f. Nat. oek. u. Stat. III. Folge, XV.

PROAL, L. Le crime et la peine. Paris, 1892.

PROCESS gegen den Anarchisten Hermann Stellmacher. (Anonymous.) Berlin, Wien, Leipzig.

PROSTITUTION in Berlin und ihre Opfer. (Anonymous.) 1846.

PROUDHON, J. P. De la justice dans la révolution et dans l'église. Paris, 1858.

PUILARAUD, L. Les malfaiteurs de profession. Paris.

QUACK, H. P. G. De socialisten. II and suppl. volume. Amsterdam, 1899, 1904.

QUANTER, R. Die Sittlichkeitsverbrechen. Berlin, 1911.

QUETELET, A. Physique sociale. St.-Pétersbourg, 1869.

QUIROS, C. B. DE, und J. M. L. AGUINALIEDO. Verbrechertum und Prostitution in Madrid. Berlin, 1909.

RAE, J. Der Achtstunden-Tag. Weimar, 1897.

RAPPORT der commissie belast met het onderzoek naar den toestand der kinderen in fabrieken arbeidende. ó Gravenhage, 1872.

RAPPORT sur l'administration de la justice criminelle de 1881 à 1900. (Compte général de l'administration de la justice criminelle pendant l'année 1900.)

RAUX, M. Nos jeunes détenus. Lyon-Paris, 1890.
—— Les actes, l'attitude et la correspondance de Caserio en prison. Archives etc., XVIII.
—— Etude psychologique sur Ravachol. Archives etc., XVIII.
REGIS, E. Les régicides. Lyon-Paris, 1890.
—— Le régicide Caserio. Archives etc., X.
—— et P. LADAME. Le régicide Lucheni. Archives etc., XXII.
REHBEIN, Fr. Das Leben eines Landarbeiters. Jena, 1911.
REICH, E. Criminalität und Altruismus. Arnsberg, 1900.
REIN, W. Jugendliches Verbrecherthum. Zeitschr. f. Soc. w., III.
REPORT of the Departmental Committee on the Employment of Children. Act 1903. London, 1909.
REPORT on the Judicial Statistics of Scotland for the year 1908, 1910. Edinburgh, 1909, London, 1911.
REPORTS from the Select Committee of the House of Lords on the law for the Protection of Young Girls. Sessions, 1881 and 1882.
RETTICH. Die Würtembergische Kriminalität. Würtembergische Jahrbücher f. Stat. u. Landeskunde. 1894.
REUSS, H. Noth und Verbrechen. Preussische Jahrbücher, 1901.
RICHARD, G. Les crises sociales et la criminalité. Année sociologique, III.
RICHELOT, G. La prostitution en Angleterre. (Tome II, "De la prostitution dans la ville de Paris" de A. J. B. Parent-Duchatelet.) Paris, 1857.
RIEBETH. Ueber den geistigen und körperlichen Zustand der Korrigendin. Monatschrift etc., V.
RIVIERE, L. Mendiants et vagabonds. Paris, 1902.
ROEST V. LIMBURG, TH. M. In den strijd tegen de ontucht. Rotterdam, 1910.
ROHDEN, G. v. Von den sozialen Motiven des Verbrechens. Zeitschr. f. Soc. w., VII.
—— Der Kampf gegen die Verbrechensursachen. Zeitschr. f. Soc. w., IX.
ROHRMANN, C. Der Sittliche Zustand von Berlin. Leipzig.
ROLAND HOEST, V. D. SCHALK, H. Kapitaal en arbeid in Nederland. Amsterdam, 1902.
—— Arbeiders en alkohol. Nieume Tijd., VII.
ROLLET, H., et G. TOMEL. Les enfants en prison. Paris, 1892.
ROOS, J. R. B. DE. De strafmiddelen in de nieuwere strafrechtswetenschap. Amsterdam, 1900.
—— Inleiding tot de beoefening der crimineele aetiologie. Haarlem, 1908.
—— Quelques recherches sur les causes de l'augmentation des vols pendant l'hiver et des coups et blessures pendant l'été. Compte rendu VI congr. d'anthr. crim. Turin, 1908.
—— De sexueele criminaliteit. ó Gravenhage, 1909.
—— Parallelismen tusschen alkoholisme en criminaliteit. Tijdschr. v. Strafrecht, XXIII.
ROSENFELD, E. Die dritte Schule. Mitteilungen der intern. krim. Vereinigung, IV.
ROSSI, V. Influence de la température et de l'alimentation sur la criminalité en Italie, 1875–1883. Actes I congr. d'anthr. crim. Turin, 1886–1887.

Rossi, V. Il fattore economico nei moti rivoluzionari. Archivio di prichiatria, sciensi penali ed anthropologia criminale, IX.

Rotering. Das Landstreichertum der Gegenwart. Monatschr. etc., III.

Rousseau, J. J. Discours sur l'origine et les fondements de l'inégalité parmi les hommes. Amsterdam, 1762.

Rowntree, B. B. Poverty. London, 1903.

Royen, J. A. van. Wetgeving en armoede beschouwd in betrekking tot het misdrijf. Zwolle, 1846.

Rühle, O. Das proletarische Kind. München, 1911.

Russel, W. Abstract of the Statistics of Crime in England and Wales from 1839 to 1843. Journ. of the Stat. Soc. of London, 1847.

Ryckère, R. de. La servante criminelle. Paris, 1908.

Rylands, L. Gordon. Crime, Its Causes and Remedy. London, 1889.

Sacker, J. Der Rückfall. Berlin, 1892.

Sauer, A. Frauenkriminalität im Ambtsbesirk Mannheim. Breslau, 1912.

Scandales de Londres, publiés par la Pall Mall Gazette. Paris, 1885.

Schäffle, A. C. Fr. Bau und Lebendes socialen Körpers I, IV. Tübingen, 1875, 1878.

Schaffroth, G. Rapport sur l'influence de l'alcoolisme sur la criminalité. Actes congr. pénit. intern. de Bruxelles, 1900, IV. Bruxelles et Berne, 1901.

Schallmayer, W. Soziale Massnahmen zur Besserung des Fortpflanzungsauslese. (Krankheit und soziale Lage. München, 1910.)

Scheel, H. v. Kriminalstatistik. (Handwörterbuch der Staatswissenschaften, VI. Jena, 1910.)

Schippel, M. Das moderne Elend und die moderne Ueberbevölkerung. Stuttgart, 1888.

Schlesinger-Eckstein, Th. Die Frau im XIX Jahrhundert. Berlin.

Schnapper-Arndt, G. Sozialstatistik. Leipzig, 1908.

Schneider, C. K. Die Prostituirte und die Gesellschaft. Leipzig, 1908.

Schonfeldt, G. Beiträge zur Geschichte des Pauperismus und der Prostitution in Hamburg. Zeitschr. f. Social- und Wistschaftsgeschichte, 1897.

—— Die heutige Arbeiterfamilie und die öffentliche Erziehung vorschulpflichtiger Kinder. Neue Zeit, 1898–99, I.

Schonlauk, B. Zur Lage der in der Wäschefabrikation und der Konfektionsbrauche Deutschlands beschäftigten Arbeiterinnen. Neue Zeit, 1885.

—— Die Syphilis und die Socialzustände. Neue Zeit, 1887.

—— Zur Psychologie des Kleinbürgerthums. Neue Zeit, 1890.

—— Zur Statistik der Prostitution in Berlin. Archiv f. soz. Gesetzgeb. u. Stat., VII.

Schröder, P. Das Fortlaufen der Kinder. Monatschrift etc., VIII.

Schurtz, H. Altersklassen und Männerbünde. Berlin, 1902.

Seuf, M. R. Geschlechtstrieb und Verbrechen. Archiv etc., XLVIII.

Seuffert, H. Anarchismus und Strafrecht. Berlin, 1899.

S. G. Die weibliche Lohnarbeit und ihr Einfluss auf die Sittlichkeit und Kriminalität. Neue Zeit, 1899–1900, II.

SICHART, G.   Ueber individuelle Faktoren der Verbrechens.   Zeitschr. f. d. ges. Str. w., X.

SIGHELE, S.   La foule criminelle.   Paris, 1892.

―――― Le crime à deux.   Lyon-Paris, 1893.

―――― Psychologie des sectes.   Paris, 1898.

―――― Littérature et criminalité.   Paris, 1908.

SMIDT, H. J.   Geschiedenis van het wetboek van strafrecht II.   Haarlem, 1881.

S(MIDT), J.   Zur Verwahrlosung der Kinder in der Kapitalistischen Gesellschaft.   Neue Zeit, 1893–94, II.

―――― Aus den Ergebnissen der sächsischen Armenstatistik.   Neue Zeit, 1894–95, II.

―――― Einfluss der Krisen und der Steigerung der Lebensmittelpreise auf das Gesellschaftsleben.   München, 1894.

SOCIAL Evil in Chicago.   (Report of the vice commission.)   Chicago, 1912.

SOCQUET, J.   Contribution à l'étude statistique de la criminalité en France de 1826 à 1880.   Paris, 1884.

SPANN, O.   Untersuchungen über die uneheliche Bevölkerung in Frankfurt a/M.   Dresden, 1912.

―――― Die unehelichen Mündel des Vormundschaftsgerichtes in Frankfurt a/M.   Dresden, 1909.

―――― Die geschlechtlich-sittlichen Verhältnisse- im Dienstboten- und Arbeiterinnerstande.   Zeitschr. f. Soc. w., VII.

SPENCER, H.   Principles of Sociology.   London-Edinburgh, 1877.

―――― Descriptive Sociology.   No. 6. American Races.   London-Edinburgh, 1878.

―――― Psychology.   London-Edinburgh, 1881.

STARCKE, C. N.   Die primitive Familie.   Leipzig, 1888.

STARKE, W.   Verbrechen und Verbrecher in Preussen 1854–1878.   Berlin, 1884.

―――― Des éléments essentiels qui doivent figurer dans la statistique criminelle et des moyens de les rendre comparables.   Bulletin de l'instit. intern. de statistique, 1889.

STATESMAN's Year Book for the years 1902, 1910.   London, 1902, 1910.

STATISTICA giudiziaria penale per l'anno 1881, 1889, 1894.   Roma, 1884, 1891, 1896.

STATISTIK der Reichstagwahlen von 1898.   Ergänzungsheft zu den Vierteljahrsheften z. Stat. d. Deutschen Reichs, 1898, II.

STATISTIQUE pénitentiaire (de la France), 1882–1898.   Melun, 1882–1901.

STATISTISCHE Uebersicht der Verhältnisse der Oesterreichischen Strafanstalten und der Gerichtsgefängnisse 1883, 1884.   Wien, 1886, 1888.

STATISTISCHES JAHRBUCH für das Deutsche Reich, V, X, XV, XVII, XVIII, XIX, XXII, XXIV.   Berlin, 1884 sqq.

STEINMETZ, S. R.   De "Fosterage."   Tijdschrift v. L. Kon. Ned. aardrijliskundig Genootschap, 1893.

―――― Ethnologische Studien zur ersten Entwicklung der Strafe I, II.   Leiden-Leipzig, 1894.

―――― Das Verhältniss zwischen Eltern und Kindern bei den Naturvölkern.   Zeitschr. f. Socialw., I.

STEINMETZ, S. R. Der Krieg als sociologisches Problem. Amsterdam, 1899.

—— Die neueren Forschungen zur Geschichte der menschlichen Familie. Zeitschr. f. Socialw., II.

—— De ziekten der maatschappij. Vragen des Tijds., 1900.

—— Classification des types sociaux et catalogue des peuples. Année sociologique, III.

—— L'ethnologie et l'anthropologie criminelle. Compte rendu V congr. d'anthr. crim. Amsterdam, 1901.

—— Die Philosophie des Krieges. Leipzig, 1907.

STELZNER, H. F. Die psychopathischen Konstitutionen und ihre sociologische Bedeutung. Berlin, 1911.

STERN, J. Einfluss der sozialen Zustände auf alle Zweige des Kulturlebens. Stuttgart, 1891.

—— Thesen über den Sozialismus. Stuttgart, 1911.

STEVENS, J. Les prisons cellulaires en Belgique. Bruxelles, 1878.

STIER, E. Wandertrieb und pathologisches Fortlaufen bei Kindern. Jena, 1913.

STINEA. Le milieu social comme facteur pathologique. L'ère nouvelle, 1894.

STIRNER, M. (Kaspar Schmidt.) Der Einzige und sein Eigenthum. Leipzig.

STÖWESAND, W. Die Kriminalität in der Provinz Posen und ihre Ursachen. Beilageheft zu Band LXXVII Gerichtssaal. Stuttgart, 1910.

STRUNZ, K. Die erwerbsmässige Kinderarbeit und die Schule. Neue Zeit, 1898–1899, I.

STURSBERG, H. Die Zunahme der Vergehen und Verbrechen und ihre Ursachen. Düsseldorf, 1878.

—— Die Prostitution in Deutschland and ihre Bekämpfung. Düsseldorf, 1887.

SULLIVAN, W. C. Rapport sur l'influence de l'alcoolisme sur la criminalité. Actes du congr. pénitent. intern. de Bruxelles, 1900, IV. Bruxelles et Berne, 1901.

SUTHERLAND, A. The Origin and Growth of Moral Instinct. London, 1898.

—— Résultats de la déportation en Australie. Compte rendu V congr. d'anthr. crim. Amsterdam, 1901.

TARDE, G. La criminalité comparée. Paris, 1890.

—— La philosophie pénale. Paris, 1890. Amer. ed. transl. Howell, Boston, 1913 (Modern Criminal Science Series).

—— Misère et criminalité. Revue philosophique, 1890, I.

—— Les crimes de haine. Essais et mélanges sociologiques. Lyon-Paris, 1895.

—— Les délits impoursuivis. Essais etc. Lyon-Paris, 1895.

—— Les transformations de l'impunité. (Lacassagne, vercher l'éventreur et les crimes sadiques.) Lyon-Paris, 1899.

—— La criminalité et les phénomènes économiques. Compte rendu V congr. d'anthr. crim. Amsterdam, 1901.

TARDIEU, A. Etude médico-légale sur les attentats aux mœurs. Paris, 1878.

TARNOWSKY. Prostitution und Abolitionismus. Hamburg und Leipzig, 1890.
—— E. La delinquenza e la vita sociale in Russia. Rivista italiana di sociologia, 1898.
—— Le mouvement de la criminalité en Russie. Archives d'anthr. etc., XIII.
—— Répartition géographique de la criminalité en Russie. Archives etc., XVI.
—— Les crimes politiques en Russie. Archives etc., XXII.
TAXIL, L. La corruption fin-de-siècle. Paris.
TEIFEN, T. W. Das sociale Elend und die besitzenden Klassen in Oester-reich. Wien, 1894.
TEX, C. J. A. DEN. De causis criminum. Amsterdam, 1847.
—— G. M. DEN. Verkorting van den arbeidsdag. Amsterdam, 1894.
THOMPSON, W. An Inquiry into the Principles of the Distribution of Wealth. London, 1850.
THOMSEN, A. Betrachtungen über ein Sammlen der verbrecherischen Motive. Zeitschr. f. d. ges. etc., XVII.
THÓT, L. V. Die positive Strafrechtsschule in einigen europäischen Ländern. Monatschr. etc., VIII.
TOMEL, G., et H. ROLLET. Les enfants en prison. Paris, 1892.
TÓNNIES, F. Jugendliche Kriminalität und Verwahrlosung in Grossbritan-nien. Zeitschr. f. d. ges. etc., XIII.
—— Das Verbrechen als soziale Erscheinung. Archiv f. soz. Gesetzgeb. u. Stat., VIII.
TOPINARD, P. L'anthropologie criminelle. Revue d'anthropologie, 1887, II.
TOULOUSE, E. Les causes de la folie.
TUGAN-BARANOWSKY, M. Die sozialen Wirkungen der Handelskrisen in England. Archiv f. soz. Gesetzgeb. etc., XV.
—— Studien zur Theorie und Geschichte der Handelskrisen in England. Jena, 1901.
TUGENDREICH, G., und M. MOSSE. Krankheit und soziale Lage. München, 1912–1913.
TURATI, F. Il delitto e la questione sociale. Milano, 1883.
TÚRKEL, S. Einfluss der Lektüre auf die Delikte phantastischer jugend-licher Psychopathen. Archiv f. Krim. anthr. etc., XLII.

UITKOMSTEN der 7ᵉ en 8ᵉ tienjaarlijksche volkstelling. ó Gravenhage, 1891 en 1901.
—— des beroepstelling in het koninkrijk der Nederlanden gehouden op 31 December 1899. ó Gravenhage, 1901.
—— des Woningstatistiek voor het koninkrijk der Nederlanden. Volks-telling 30 December 1899. ó Gravenhage, 1903.

VACCARO, M. A. Genesi e funzioni delle leggi penali. Roma, 1889.
VALENTINI, H. V. Das Verbrecherthum im preussischem Staat. Leipzig, 1869.
VALLON, CH., et G. GÉNIL-PERRIN. Crime et altruisme. Archives etc., XXVIII.

VANDERVELDE, E. Het alcoholisme en de arbeids voorwaarden in Belgie. Nieuwe Tijd., IV.
—— Die oekonomischen Faktoren des Alkoholismus. Neue Zeit, 1901–1902, I.
—— Le socialisme et l'alcool. (Essais socialistes.) Paris, 1906.
VAUCLERAY. Influence de l'hérédité alcoolique sur la folie et la criminalité. Actes III congr. d'anthr. crim. Bruxelles, 1893.
VARENNES, H. De Ravachol à Caserio. Paris.
VERHAEGHE, D. Le parti socialiste et la lutte contre l'alcool. Mouvement socialiste. 1900.
—— De l'alcoolisation. Paris, 1900.
VERRIJN STUART, C. A. Inleiding tot de beoefening der Statistiek II. Haarlem, 1913.
VERSLAGEN over de verrichtingen aangaan de het armbestuur over 1898 en 1899. Bijlage E. Handelingen 2e Kamer des Staten-Generaal 1899–1900, 1900–1901.
VIERKANDT, A. Das Problem der Familien- und Stammesorganisation der Naturvölker. Zeitschr. f. Soc. w., XI.
VRIES, H. DE. Eenheid in veranderlijkheid. Haarlem, 1898.

WACHHOLZ, L. Zur Lehre von den sexuellen Delikten. Vierteljahrschrift f. Gerichtl. Medizin etc., XXXVIII.
WADLER, A. Die Verbrechensbewegung im östlichen Europa I. Die Kriminalität der Balkanländer. München, 1908.
—— Die politische Verbrecher in Russland. Zeitschr. f. d. ges. etc., XXIX.
—— Erkenntnistheorie und Kriminalstatistik. Zeitschr. f. d. ges. etc., XXXI.
WAGENER, H. Der Mädchenhandel. Berlin-Lihterfelde, 1911.
WAGNER, C. Die Sittlichkeit aus den Lande. Leipzig, 1896.
—— und H. WITTENBERG. Die geschlechtlich-sittlichen Verhältnisse der evangelischen Landbewohner im Deutschen Reiche. Leipzig, 1897.
WAITZ, TH. Anthropologie der Naturvölker III. Leipzig, 1862.
WALLACE, A. R. The Malayo Archipelago. London, 1869.
—— Menschliche Auslese. Zukunft, 1894.
WALSH, R. H. A Deduction from the Statistics of Crime for the Last Ten Years. Journ. Stat. Soc. of London, 1857.
WAPPÄUS, J. E. Allgemeine Bevölkerungsstatistik II. Leipzig, 1861.
WASSERMANN, R. Beruf, Konfession und Verbrechen. München, 1907.
—— Begriff und Grenzen der Kriminalstatistik. Leipzig, 1909.
—— G. v. Mayr als Kriminalstatistiker und Kriminalsoziologe und die moderne Methodenlehre. Monatschrift etc., VII.
WEBER, M. Ehefrau und Mutter in der Rechtsentwicklung. Tübingen, 1907.
WEIDEMANN, W. Die Ursachen der Kriminalität im Herzogtum Sachsen-Meiningen. Berlin, 1903.
WEINBERG, S. Der werdende Verbrecher. Neue Zeit, 1902–1903, II.
WEISS, B. Ueber einige wirtschaftliche und moralische Wirkungen hoher Getreidepreise. Jahrb. f. Nat. oek. u. Stat., 1881.

WEITLING, W. Garantien der Harmonie und Freiheit. 1842.
—— Die Menschheit wie sie ist und wie sie sein sollte. München, 1895.
—— Das Evangelium eines armen Sünders. München, 1896.
WELLENBERGH, P. Contribution à l'étude de la question de l'influence de la vieillesse sur la criminalité. Compte rendu V congr. d'anthr. crim. Amsterdam, 1901.
WERTHAUER, J. Sittlichkeits-Delikte der Gross-Stadt. Berlin.
WESTERMARCK, E. The History of Human Marriage. London, 1891.
—— Der Ursprung der Strafe. Zeitschr. f. Soc. w., III.
—— Ursprung und Entwicklung der Moral begriffe. Transl. Katscher. Leipzig, 1907/1909.
WESTGARTH, W. Statistics of Crime in Australia. Journ. Stat. Soc. of London, 1864.
WETZKER, H. Die Zunahme der Verbrechen. Sozialist. Monatsch., 1902, II.
WIESELGREN, S. Rapport sur l'influence de l'alcoolisme sur la criminalité. Actes du congr. pénitent. intern. de Bruxelles, 1900, IV. Bruxelles et Berne, 1901.
WILLIS, W. N. The White Slaves of London. London, 1912.
—— and A. MACKIRDY. The White Slave Market. London.
WILMANNS, K. Zur Psychopathologie des Landstreichers. Leipzig, 1906.
—— Das Landstreichertum. Monatschr. etc. I.
WINKLER, C. Iets over crimineele anthropologie. Geneeskundige Bladen, 1895.
WINTER, A. The New York State Reformatory in Elmira. London, 1871.
WITTENBERG, H., und C. WAGNER. Die geschlechtlich-sittlichen Verhältnisse des evangelischen Landbewohner im Deutschen Reiche. Leipzig, 1897.
WOLF, J. Das Verhältnis von Eltern und Kindern bei dem Landvolk in Deutschland. Zeitschr. f. Soc. w., I.
WOLTMANN, L. Die Darwinsche Theorie und der Socialismus. Düsseldorf, 1899.
WRIGHT, CARROL D. The Relation of Economic Conditions to the Causes of Crime. Philadelphia, 1900.
WULFFEN, E. Psychologie der Verbrechers. Grosslichterfelde-Ost, 1908.
—— Gauner- und Verbrechertypen. Berlin-Grosslichterfelde, 1910.
—— Der Sexualverbrecher. Berlin-Grosslichterfelde, 1910.
WURM, E. Die Alkoholfrage. Protokoll über die Verhandlungen des Parteitags der Soz. dem. Partei Deutschlands zu Essen. Berlin, 1907.
WÜRZBURGER, E. Ueber die Vergleichbarkeit kriminalstatistische Daten. Jahrb. f. Nat. oek. u. Stat., 1887.

YEARBOOK of New York State Reformatory, 1881–1886, 1888–1897. Albany-Elmira.
YVERNÈS, M. L'alcoolisme et la criminalité. Archives etc., XXVII.

ZADEK, I. Der Achtstundentag eine gesundheitliche Forderung. Berlin, 1904.

ZERBOGLIO, A. Les inconvénients de l'honnêteté. L'ère nouvelle, 1894.
—— L'alcoolisme : causes et remèdes. Devenir social, I.
—— La fin de la névrose. Devenir social, I.
—— La lutte de classe dans la législation pénale. Devenir social, II.
—— Les bases économiques de la santé. Devenir social, III.
ZETHIN, C. Geistiges Proletariat, Frauenfrage und Sozialismus. Berlin, 1902.
—— Die Arbeiterinnen- und Frauenfrage der Gegenwort. Berlin.
ZETKIN, O. Die barfüssige Bande. Neue Zeit, 1884.
ZIEHEN, TH. Die Erkennung der psychopathischen Konstitutionen und die öffentliche Fürsorge für psychopathisch veranlagte Kinder. Berlin, 1912.
ŽIŽEK, F. Soziologie und Statistik. München und Leipzig, 1912.
ZOCCOLI, H. Die Anarchie. Transl. Nacht. Leipzig-Amsterdam, 1909.
ZOLA, E. Au bonheur des dames. Paris.
—— L'argent. Paris.

INDEX

INDEX

703